The
New International
Lesson Annual

2010-2011

September–August

Abingdon Press
Nashville

THE NEW INTERNATIONAL LESSON ANNUAL 2010–2011

Copyright © 2010 by Abingdon Press

This book is printed on acid-free paper.

ISBN 978-0-687-65318-8

ISSN 1084-872X

10 11 12 13 14 15 16 17 18 19—10 9 8 7 6 5 4 3 2 1

MANUFACTURED IN THE UNITED STATES OF AMERICA

PREFACE

Thank you for joining countless Bible students around the world who use resources based on the work of the Committee on the Uniform Series, known by many as the International Lesson Series. *The New International Lesson Annual*, though a guide for many students, is mainly designed for teachers who seek a solid biblical basis for each session and a teaching plan that will help them lead their classes, no matter which student curriculum resource the adult students may use.

During the 2010–2011 year, our writers will help us explore the Bible. We begin with Exodus and selected Psalms to learn more about "The Inescapable God." Isaiah, Matthew, and Mark form the basis for the winter quarter devoted to "Assuring Hope." Worship is the theme for the spring quarter, which will include lessons drawn from Matthew, Mark, 1 and 2 Timothy, Philippians, Jude, and Revelation. "God Instructs the People of God," the final study for the year, looks at the theme of community through the lens of the books of Joshua, Judges, and Ruth.

The following features are especially valuable for busy teachers who want to provide in-depth Bible study experiences for their students. Each lesson includes the following sections:

Previewing the Lesson highlights the background and lesson Scriptures, focus of the lesson, three goals for the learners, a pronunciation guide in lessons where you may find unfamiliar words or names, and supplies you will need.

Reading the Scripture includes the Scripture lesson printed in both the *New Revised Standard Version* and the *New International Version*. By printing these two highly respected translations in parallel columns, you can easily compare them for in-depth study. If your own Bible is another version, you will then have three translations to explore as you prepare each lesson.

Understanding the Scripture closely analyzes the background Scripture by looking at each verse. Here you will find help in understanding concepts, ideas, places, and people pertinent to each week's lesson. You may also find explanations of Greek or Hebrew words that are essential for understanding the text.

Interpreting the Scripture looks at the lesson Scripture, delves into its meaning, and relates it to contemporary life.

Sharing the Scripture provides you with a detailed teaching plan. Written by your editor, who is a very experienced educator, this feature is divided into two major sections: *Preparing to Teach* and *Leading the Class*.

In the *Preparing to Teach* section, you will find a devotional reading related to the lesson for your own spiritual enrichment and ideas to help you prepare for the session.

The *Leading the Class* portion begins with "Gather to Learn" activities designed to welcome the students and draw them into the lesson. Here, the students' stories and experiences or other contemporary stories are highlighted as preparation for the Bible story. The next three headings of *Leading the Class* are the three "Goals for the Learners." The first goal always focuses on the Bible story itself. The second goal relates the Bible story to the lives of the adults in your class. The third goal prompts the students to take action on what they have learned. You will find a variety of activities under each of these goals to help the learners fulfill them. The activities are diverse in nature and may include among other strategies: listening, reading, writing, speaking, singing, drawing, interacting with others, and meditating. The lesson ends with "Continue the Journey," where you will find closing activities, preparation for the following week, and ideas for students to commit themselves to action during the week, based on what they have learned.

In addition to these weekly features, each quarter begins with the following helps:

- **Introduction to the Quarter** provides you with a quick survey of each lesson to be studied during the quarter. You will find the title, background Scripture, date, and a brief summary of each week's basic thrust. This feature is the first page of each quarter.
- **Meet Our Writer,** which follows the quarterly introduction, provides biographical information about each writer, including education, pastoral and/or academic teaching experience, previous publications, and family information.
- **The Big Picture**, written by the same writer who authored the quarter's lessons, is designed to give you a broader scope of the materials to be covered than is possible in each weekly lesson. You will find this background article immediately following the writer's biography.
- **Close-up** gives you some focused information, such as a timeline, chart, overview, short article, map, or list that you may choose to use for a specific week or anytime during the quarter, perhaps even repeatedly.
- **Faith in Action** provides ideas related to the broad sweep of the quarter that the students can use individually or as a class to act on what they have been studying. These ideas are usually intended for use beyond the classroom.

Finally, two annual features are included:

- **List of Background Scriptures** is offered especially for those of you who keep back copies of *The New International Lesson Annual*. This feature, found immediately after the contents, will enable you to locate Bible background passages used during the current year at some future date.
- **Teacher enrichment article** is intended to be useful throughout the year, so we hope you will read it immediately and refer to it often. This year's article, "Journeying Through the Seasons of the Church Year," will familiarize you with the liturgical seasons and *The Revised Common Lectionary*. You will find this article following the List of Background Scriptures.

We are always striving to make *The New International Lesson Annual* as helpful to you as possible. We welcome your input. Please send your questions, comments, and suggestions to me. I invite you to include your e-mail address and phone number. I will respond as soon as your message reaches my home office in Maryland.

Dr. Nan Duerling
Abingdon Press
PO Box 801
Nashville, TN 37202

Your presence among *The New International Lesson Annual* community is a blessing. Our prayers are with you and those who study with you as you are guided by the Word of God and the Holy Spirit to be transformed and conformed to the image of Christ.

Nan Duerling, Ph.D.
Editor, *The New International Lesson Annual*

CONTENTS

FIRST QUARTER

The Inescapable God
September 5–November 28, 2010

UNIT 1: GOD REVEALS
(September 5-26)

UNIT 2: GOD SUSTAINS
(October 3-31)

UNIT 3: GOD PROTECTS
(November 7-28)

SECOND QUARTER

Assuring Hope
December 5, 2010–February 27, 2011

UNIT 1: COMFORT FOR GOD'S PEOPLE
(December 5–January 2)

UNIT 2: A FUTURE FOR GOD'S PEOPLE
(January 9-30)

UNIT 3: JESUS, THE PROMISED SERVANT-LEADER
(February 6-27)

THIRD QUARTER

We Worship God
March 6–May 29, 2011

UNIT 1: A GUIDE FOR WORSHIP LEADERS
(March 6-27)

UNIT 2: ANCIENT WORDS OF PRAISE
(April 3–May 1)

UNIT 3: JOHN'S VISION OF WORSHIP
(May 8-29)

FOURTH QUARTER

God Instructs the People of God
June 5–August 28, 2011

UNIT 1: GOD'S PEOPLE LEARN FROM PROSPERITY
(June 5–July 3)

UNIT 2: LISTENING FOR GOD IN CHANGING TIMES
(July 10–August 7)

UNIT 3: A CASE STUDY IN COMMUNITY
(August 14-28)

LIST OF BACKGROUND SCRIPTURES, 2010–2011

Old Testament

Exodus 3	September 5	Psalm 8	October 3
Exodus 20	September 12	Psalm 19	October 10
Exodus 32	September 19	Psalm 46	October 17
Exodus 34:1-10	September 26	Psalm 47	October 24
Leviticus 19:9-10	August 21	Psalm 63	October 31
Joshua 1	June 12	Psalm 66	November 7
Joshua 1:1-6	June 5	Psalm 90	November 14
Joshua 2	June 19	Psalm 91	November 21
Joshua 5:13–6:27	June 26	Psalm 139	November 28
Joshua 7–8	July 3	Isaiah 40	December 5
Joshua 11–12	June 5	Isaiah 41:1–42:9	December 12
Judges 2	July 10	Isaiah 9:1-7	December 19
Judges 3:7-31	July 17	Isaiah 11:1-9	December 19
Judges 6–8	July 24	Isaiah 43	December 26
Judges 10:6–11:33	July 31	Isaiah 44	January 2
Judges 13	August 7	Isaiah 45	January 9
Judges 21:25	July 10, 17, 24, 31, August 7	Isaiah 48	January 16
Ruth 1:1-18	August 14	Isaiah 49:1-6	January 23
Ruth 2–3	August 21	Isaiah 53	January 30
Ruth 4	August 28		

New Testament

Matthew 1:18-25	December 19	1 Timothy 3:14-16	March 6
Matthew 28:1-17	April 24	1 Timothy 4:6-16	March 20
Mark 8:27–9:1	February 6	1 Timothy 5:1-22	March 27
Mark 9:2-13	February 13	2 Timothy 2:8-15	April 3
Mark 10:35-45	February 20	Jude 17-25	April 10
Mark 11:1-11	April 17	Revelation 4	May 8
Mark 13	February 27	Revelation 7:9-17	May 15
Philippians 2:1-11	May 1	Revelation 21	May 22
1 Timothy 2:1-6	March 6	Revelation 22	May 29
1 Timothy 3:1-13	March 13		

TEACHER ENRICHMENT: JOURNEYING THROUGH THE SEASONS OF THE CHURCH YEAR

There is a rhythm to the church year that helps us know who we are and whose we are. Every year the church journeys through the awaited coming, birth, life, death, and resurrection of Jesus. We also mark the sending of the Holy Spirit. We hear again the old, old story that is ever new, ever fresh, and ever enlivening us. The church year, also known as the liturgical year, always begins on the first Sunday of Advent and ends on the last Sunday after Pentecost, which is known as Christ the King Sunday. Let's walk through the various seasons to see what their relationship to our own spiritual journeys might be.

Advent

Advent is celebrated during the four Sundays just prior to Christmas. Although the commercial world would have us think that Christmas begins at Halloween, the church knows differently. Traditionally, altars have been adorned with purple, which symbolizes both royalty and penitence. In more recent years, blue has replaced purple during the season of Advent because that color speaks to us of hope. Many churches and Sunday school classes light an Advent wreath to mark the passage of the weeks. Some may set up a Jesse tree, named for the father of King David, and add symbols each week that anticipate the coming of our Lord.

At the beginning of Advent we are reminded that Christ will come again. As we draw closer to Christmas we read stories and prophecies that point us toward the Messiah, who would come to us as a baby.

Advent is a season of patient, expectant waiting and preparation. Encouraging class members to contemplate the coming of Christ as they await the commemoration of his birth will enable them to grow in their faith. This season inspires awe as we ponder the priceless gift of God's Beloved Son to us.

Christmas

Christmas is not just one day, after which trees come down, sales are in full swing, and Valentine chocolates begin to replace candy canes on store shelves. Instead, this special time of the church year begins on Christmas Eve/Christmas Day as we celebrate the nativity of Jesus. The season continues for twelve days. During the Christmas season we focus on the amazing reality of the incarnation—God is with us. White and gold are the festive colors that adorn our altars. Trees, often decorated with chrismons—symbols that point us to Jesus—add to the festive atmosphere. Creches are set up in sanctuaries and classrooms to visually present the Baby Jesus, his parents, and the other characters associated with the Christmas story. Poinsettias, which have legendary significance related to Christmas, decorate many churches. The music of the Christmas season particularly stirs our emotions and connects us to traditions within both the church and our own families.

The Christmas season ends on Epiphany, which is celebrated on January 6. The word "epiphany" means "manifestation" or "appearance." This is the day on which the Magi were thought to have come to worship Jesus, who according to the only account we have, the story in Matthew 2, would have been about two years old. The Magi, believed to have been astrologers from Persia, represent all nations coming to worship Jesus.

The Season after Epiphany

The Season after Epiphany begins on January 7 and stretches to the day before Ash Wednesday. The first Sunday following the Epiphany marks the baptism of Jesus and ends with his transfiguration. On both of these Sundays white is used, since these are festive occasions. The season itself is considered Ordinary Time, which we will discuss more fully when we consider the Season after Pentecost. Symbolizing growth and spiritual renewal, the color green is used during Ordinary Time. The number of weeks during the Season after Epiphany varies from four to nine, depending upon when Lent begins. The start of the Lenten season is itself dependent upon the date of Easter.

Lent

Lent does not begin on a Sunday, but rather on Ash Wednesday. Services on this day focus on our mortality: We are dust and to dust we shall return. As a reminder of that mortality, ashes are placed on our foreheads in the shape of a cross. Lent is said to be forty days, and it is, but if you count from Ash Wednesday to Easter, you will find that there are actually forty-six days. Why the discrepancy? Those six "extra" days are Sundays. Since Sunday is always the day that commemorates Jesus' resurrection, Sundays are therefore not counted as part of the penitential season of Lent.

During this Lenten period Christians examine themselves, seeking repentance and perhaps fasting, either from food or from something else important to them, so as to have more time to devote to their relationship with Christ, more time to listen for God. Most believers view Lent as a somber time, but the word itself comes from *lencten*, a Germanic root word that means "long." This description seems very appropriate when we consider that the days are lengthening (at least in the Northern Hemisphere). Spring, with the new life and hope that it brings, reminds us that at the end of this "lengthening season" the joy and hope of Easter await us.

That joy is still to come, though. Lent officially ends not with hope but with Jesus' agonizing pain and the disciples' anguished bewilderment. The "hosannas" of Palm Sunday (also known as Passion Sunday) have turned to angry cries of "crucify him" in a few short days. During this Holy Week, we recall on Thursday Jesus' final meal with his disciples; his institution of Holy Communion, which we are commanded to partake of in remembrance of him; his betrayal by a close associate, the treasurer of his band of disciples, Judas Iscariot; his fervent prayer and arrest in the Garden of Gethsemane. A hasty trial culminates in his crucifixion on God's (Good) Friday, when our Lord suffered for three hours on the cross. Holy Saturday is a quiet time, commemorating Jesus' time in the tomb.

Easter

Easter, like Christmas, is often thought by many to be a single day, but it actually lasts for seven weeks. The Easter season begins in many churches with an Easter Vigil service on

Saturday evening or a sunrise service on Sunday morning, and extends through Pentecost Sunday. Churches continue to use the white paraments on the altar, pulpit, and lectern throughout the season until the day of Pentecost. Since Pentecost celebrates the coming of the Holy Spirit in wind and flames, the main color for that Sunday is red.

Unlike Christmas, which is always a fixed date (December 25), Easter varies from year to year. It can be as early as March 22 or as late as April 25. The date is related to the vernal equinox—the first day of spring in the Northern Hemisphere—which is when the length of both the day and the night are about equal. This idea of determining Easter based on a seasonal marker may seem odd to Christian readers until we remember that Jesus' death and resurrection took place at the time of the Passover. Like Easter, Passover does not begin on a fixed date, but rather is celebrated on the first full moon after the vernal equinox. The (Christian) Council of Nicea, held in 325, determined that Easter would be celebrated on the first Sunday following the first full moon that occurred on or after the spring equinox. If the first full moon occurs on a Sunday, Easter is celebrated the following Sunday. As you may be aware, some churches, particularly those in the Orthodox tradition, do not celebrate Easter on the same Sunday that those who are Roman Catholic and Protestant generally celebrate. The reason for this disparity is that the Orthodox churches still count time according to the earlier Julian calendar, whereas most other churches use the Gregorian calendar, adopted in 1582 and named for Pope Gregory XIII.

Although a new season begins on Easter Sunday, it is important to note that the Great Three Days, known also as the Paschal Triduum, run from sunset on Holy Thursday until sunset on Easter. (Recall that in the Jewish tradition, sunset marks the beginning of a new day.) These three days mark the high point of the Christian calendar, though they neither begin nor end the liturgical year.

The Season after Pentecost

The Season after Pentecost, also known as Ordinary Time, spans about half the year. If you are a United Methodist, you may know this season as Kingdomtide, a name given in 1937, though in more recent years referred to as Ordinary Time, the name used by many other denominations. Symbolized by green, as is fitting a season of growth, there are no major church festivals, such as Christmas, Easter, or Pentecost, during Ordinary Time, though we do recognize several special days. The first Sunday after Pentecost is referred to as Trinity Sunday because the focus is on the three persons of the Trinity. We also commemorate All Saints Day, which falls on November 1 but is usually celebrated on the first Sunday in November. The last Sunday of this season, which falls between November 20 and 26, is Christ the King Sunday. This week culminates the Christian year; on the following Sunday we begin a new church year with Advent.

"Ordinary" here does not mean "mundane." Rather, the name comes from the word "ordinal," which means "numbered," and was first used in the Roman Catholic Church to express in numerical terms the number of Sundays that are not included in the two major cycles of the year: the first cycle being Advent-Christmas-Epiphany, and the second being Lent-Easter-Pentecost. God's people are not simply "marking time" until Lent or Advent in these "ordinary" periods. Rather, during Ordinary Time the church considers the meaning of Jesus' teachings, particularly as they relate to the kingdom of God. This is a time for believers to discern God within the context of our daily lives. This is a time, as we consider Jesus' teachings, to reach outward and include others in the life of the church. This is a time to look inward and become more intentional about the practice of spiritual disciplines. This is a time to look around and see where we can be healers and reconcilers in a broken world where justice is often trampled. Ordinary Time is, in short, a time to draw closer to God as we encounter what it means to live under the reign of God.

The Revised Common Lectionary

As you reflect on these seasons, you may have noticed a pattern. The two major cycles, the high points of the church year, tell the story of Jesus' birth, death, resurrection, and sending of the Holy Spirit. During these cycles there is a time of preparation and a time of celebration, followed by a season of growth. These times are symbolized by purple (or blue), white, and green. The church has not only identified these seasons but also has structured its preaching, in many denominations, around the church year by following *The Revised Common Lectionary*. The Lectionary is a series of weekly readings—generally one from the Hebrew Scriptures, one from the Psalms, one from an Epistle, and one from the Gospels. The series runs in a three-year cycle, with Year A focusing the Gospel lections on Matthew, Year B on Mark, and Year C on Luke. The Gospel of John is interspersed at appropriate points.

While most churches do not insist that a pastor preach from the Lectionary, churches within denominations that participated in The Consultation on Common Texts to create this series of readings often do use the Lectionary for their Sunday worship Scriptures. These churches include The Episcopal Church, The Evangelical Lutheran Church in America, The Presbyterian Church (U.S.A.), the Reformed Church in America, Roman Catholic Church in the United States, The United Church of Christ, and The United Methodist Church, among many others.

The Revised Common Lectionary is most often used as a preaching lectionary, although some Sunday school curriculum resources and some short-term studies, such as the *Scriptures for the Church Seasons* series (Abingdon Press), are also based on the appointed readings. The lessons in the book you are now holding, which are based on the work of the Committee on the Uniform Series, sometimes referred to as the International Lesson Series, are not based on the Lectionary. However, like the Revised Common Lectionary, the International Lesson Series provides a plan for covering much of both the Old and New Testaments over a three-year period. You will often find that the International Lesson Series includes Scriptures that are not highlighted in the Revised Common Lectionary. Hence, if you are part of a congregation that uses the Lectionary and resources based on the International Lesson Series, you will be exposed to a wide variety of Bible readings. These readings afford opportunities for continuing, in-depth spiritual growth.

As we worship, study, and move through the seasons of the church year we are always challenged to grow closer to our Lord and Savior. We focus on his birth, death, life, resurrection, and teachings in a patterned series of readings designed to enable us each year to hear anew and be transformed by the good news.

FIRST QUARTER
The Inescapable God

SEPTEMBER 5, 2010–NOVEMBER 28, 2010

Our study for this fall quarter focuses on the nature of God as the first person of the Trinity. We will consider how God reveals Godself, sustains humanity and all creation, and protects. During this quarter we will investigate the Book of Exodus and selected Psalms.

Unit 1, "God Reveals," includes four lessons that trace God's emerging relationship with Israel, as recorded in Exodus. The unit begins on September 5 with "God's Revelation to Moses," where we witness God calling Moses in Exodus 3 and this future leader's initial reluctance to say yes to God. "God's Covenant with Israel," the lesson for September 12 from Exodus 20, examines the Ten Commandments, focusing particularly on the first and second commandments. The familiar story of the golden calf in Exodus 32 is the backdrop for the lesson on September 19, "God versus 'gods,'" in which the Israelites make and worship a graven image. On September 26 we turn to Exodus 34:1-10, where we read in a lesson entitled "God Promises an Awesome Thing" a statement of God's nature as One who is merciful, gracious, slow to anger, and loving.

Unit 2, "God Sustains," focuses on psalms that sing of God's majesty, sovereignty, steadfast love, and comfort. Bearing the distinction of being the only biblical text to reach the moon, Psalm 8, which we will read on October 3, is a hymn of praise to "God's Majesty and Human Dignity." On October 10 we study Psalm 19, which marvels both at God's creation and God's law, in a lesson entitled "God's Law Sustains." Psalm 46:1-7, the Scripture for October 17, teaches that when we are in need and seek help in times of trouble, "God Provides Refuge." "God Is in Charge" is praised in Psalm 47, which we will delve into on October 24. We conclude this unit on October 31 with an exploration of Psalm 63, which promises that "God's Presence Comforts and Assures," particularly for those who seek God to fill their emptiness.

Unit 3, "God Protects," continues our survey of selected psalms by extolling the attributes of God who is good, everlasting, secure, and always present. On November 7 we turn to Psalm 66 to affirm with the psalmist that "God Is Awesome" and totally dependable. Although our lives are short, the lesson from Psalm 90 on November 14 reminds us that "God Is Forever," or, as the psalmist puts it, "from everlasting to everlasting." Psalm 91, which we will study on November 21, assures us that "God Delivers and Protects." The fall quarter ends on November 28 with a study of Psalm 139, which proclaims that "God Is All-knowing," intimately involved with us, and inescapably present with each person.

Meet Our Writer

DR. JEROME F. D. CREACH

Jerome F. D. Creach is the Robert C. Holland Professor of Old Testament at Pittsburgh Theological Seminary (PTS), where he has taught since 2000. Before accepting his current post he taught at Barton College in Wilson, N.C. (1994–2000), The College of William & Mary (1993–94), and the Baptist Theological Seminary at Richmond (1991-92). In addition to his work at PTS, Dr. Creach preaches and teaches frequently in churches in the Pittsburgh area. He has also taught and lectured at many retreat centers, churches, and other academic institutions.

Dr. Creach earned his Ph.D. at Union Theological Seminary and the Presbyterian School of Christian Education (Union-PSCE) in 1994. His work there focused on the book of Psalms. He has published three books on the Psalter: *Yahweh as Refuge and the Editing of the Hebrew Psalter* (Sheffield: Sheffield Academic Press, 1996); *Psalms* (Interpretation Bible Studies; Louisville: Geneva Press, 1998); *The Destiny of the Righteous in the Psalms* (St. Louis: Chalice Press, 2008). He has also written a commentary on the book of Joshua in the series *Interpretation: A Commentary for Teaching and Preaching* (Louisville: Westminster John Knox Press, 2003). He is active in the Society of Biblical Literature and the American Academy of Religion.

Dr. Creach is a Minister of the Word and Sacrament in the Presbyterian Church (U.S.A.). He is married to Page L. D. Creach, who is pastor of the Community Presbyterian Church of Ben Avon, a church in the north hills of Pittsburgh. They have two children. In his spare time Dr. Creach enjoys hiking, camping, and fishing. He is an avid fan of the Pittsburgh Steelers. He is also an authority on *The Andy Griffith Show*, with an ability to recite from memory the lines of every black-and-white episode.

THE BIG PICTURE: EXPLORING THE NATURE OF GOD

The theme of this unit is "The Inescapable God." Students may expect the lessons to explore various aspects of God's nature and God's interaction with humankind. This introduction will outline some of the main features of God's character and action that will be encountered in the texts. But it is important to recognize also that biblical texts communicate the nature of God in various ways, depending on the type of writing they represent. So, the introduction begins with a sketch of the kinds of passages the units will cover and the way these passages speak to and describe God.

Passages in This Lesson

This unit includes four lessons from the Book of Exodus and nine lessons from the Psalms. In the Christian canon Exodus is part of the primary history, the story of God's people that begins with creation (Genesis 1) and ends with Israel in exile (Ezra-Nehemiah; Esther). Exodus is set after the account of Jacob and his family (Genesis 25–50), which culminated in their move to Egypt. Jacob's son Joseph had become a high official there, and their move was a sign that God's hand had been upon them through difficult times (Genesis 37, 39–50). The family would live under Joseph's protective care. Exodus begins, however, with the note that "a new king arose over Egypt, who did not know Joseph" (Exodus 1:8). Soon Jacob's descendants were slaves and they cried out to God for deliverance. The Exodus texts in this lesson are part of the story of how God answered the pleas of these people. The story of Israel's slavery in Egypt is also related to the end of the primary history in one important way: Israel's captivity in Egypt becomes a paradigm for Israel's exile in Babylon, and God's deliverance of Israel from Egypt provides hope that God will once again restore God's people.

The Book of Exodus has a slightly different importance in the Jewish canon. Exodus is the second book of the Torah or the "Law." Torah consists of the first five books in the Old Testament (Genesis–Deuteronomy). Reading Exodus as part of this canonical division draws our attention primarily to the law codes in Exodus 20–23. We learn that the commandments were given to shape the life of a community, to help the community align itself with God's will.

Both of these ways of thinking about Exodus's place in the canon are needed to understand the importance of the Book of Exodus. Christians are typically more attuned to the narrative of Israel's release from slavery. The story is about liberation. It rightly inspires us and helps us understand important things about God. God does not want people to suffer. God frees people from what binds them. But it is important to remember the law codes at the center of the story as well. These laws (which include the Ten Commandments) do not constitute a legalistic system by which the Israelites could be right with God. Nor do they present such a system for us. But they do offer some important guidelines for how to respond to God's grace. Hence, when Exodus is read as both salvation story and as the Torah (Law) we have the complete picture: God's salvation for us and our response to God's goodness.

The Exodus passages in this unit will cover both of these dimensions of the book. Exodus 3 reports the call of Moses. God's appointment of Moses is God's first step toward delivering the Israelites. Hence, in this passage we see that God responds to suffering, and that God uses human agents to accomplish divine purposes. Exodus 20:1-17 records the Ten Commandments. Here we meet for the first time the full impact of the Book of Exodus—God's salvation and human response.

Exodus 32 and 34 tell the story of Israel's failure and restoration. This too is an important part of the Exodus story. Israel's worship of the golden calf (Exodus 32) illustrates the fact that humans cannot fully respond to God's grace properly. Nevertheless, God remains gracious and initiates restoration (Exodus 34).

The Psalms are very different from Exodus. They are poetry that speaks *to* God and less often *about* God. Most of the psalms originated in the worship of ancient Israel. So, they might well be understood as human response to the story of salvation, even to the story Exodus tells. This understanding will be important as we encounter psalms that are prayers. But the Book of Psalms is also a book of theology that has a purposeful order. The book has an introduction (Psalms 1 and 2), five main divisions or "Books" (Psalms 3–41; 42–72; 73–89; 90–106; 107–145), and a conclusion (Psalms 146–150). Book Four (Psalms 90–106) is particularly important theologically. This section of psalms seems to address the trauma of the Babylonian exile. It follows a psalm that laments the fall of the Davidic empire (Psalm 89) and "responds" with the assurance, as the NIV has it, "the LORD reigns" (or "the LORD is king," NRSV; see Psalm 93:1). Two psalms in this unit come from Book Four of the Psalter (Psalms 90 and 91), so this information will be very important in our interpretation.

Scholars often classify psalms according to the patterns of language they contain. Such patterns tell us something about what circumstances produced a particular psalm. That, in turn, may help us know how to pray a psalm or use a psalm in worship. The psalms in this unit belong to several types. Psalm 8, for example, is a hymn, a psalm that mainly praises God. The main subject is God's work as Creator. But the psalm also highlights the unique role of humans in God's kingdom. Humans have an office. They are in charge of the earth, the psalm seems to say. Psalm 66 is also a hymn. Like Psalm 8, it praises God for God's creative work. The whole earth offers praise, as verse 4 says. But Psalm 66 also praises God for delivering God's people from bondage in Egypt. It speaks of the same events as does the Book of Exodus. The references to these events, however, are subtle and poetic. The psalm does not mention Egypt or the exodus specifically, but when it declares, "he turned the sea into dry land" (66:6), it is clear that Egyptian slavery is in the background. But God's deliverance is not just a rescue from Pharaoh. Indeed, this psalm speaks of the exodus event as an extension of God's work in creation. Nature and history are intermingled here in a way they are not typically combined in narrative (though see Exodus 15, a hymn embedded in narrative, which makes this same combination).

Psalms 46 and 47 are also hymns, but they belong in special categories. Psalm 46 celebrates God's majesty just as Psalms 8 and 66. This psalm focuses its attention, however, on how God is known on Mount Zion. The beauty and stability of Zion, the psalm seems to say, give evidence of God's rule over the world. The psalm presents Zion as the center of the world and from that central point God reigns. Psalm 47 does not mention Zion, but it focuses on the universal reign of God like Psalm 46. The psalm calls for praise specifically because "God is the king of all the earth" (47:7).

Psalm 19 praises God as Psalms 8, 46, 47, and 66 do. Like these psalms, Psalm 19 highlights the creative power of God, or better, the way the creation pours forth praise for God's creative work. But Psalm 19 has one very unique feature: It presents the Torah (Law) as a primary sign of the world's order. Torah is like the sun that moves regularly through the sky, giving evidence of God's control of the universe. Hence, in a broad way Psalm 19 picks up the theme of Exodus 20.

The Nature of God

The biblical texts in this unit will present God in a wide variety of actions and will paint God with many different images. Here we will highlight some of the main features of the nature of God that will appear in these texts: the engaging God, the jealous God, the ruler of the universe.

One of the most important features of God is that *God engages* the world to bring about the peace that was intended in creation. In the beginning God put everything in order and pronounced it "very good" (Genesis 1:31). As the story progresses, however, the creation rebels against God's intentions; violence spreads throughout the world God made (Genesis 6:11). The rest of the Bible may be read as a story of God entering into the world to make things right. Indeed, the biblical narrative is really a series of interventions! This understanding of God is important for two reasons. First, it is important because many people in the modern Western world have a view of God that is influenced more by Greek philosophy than by the Bible. The God of the philosophers is detached from creation; this is the infamous clockmaker God, one who created the universe and left it, like a clock now wound up, to run on the natural laws built into the system. But the Bible portrays God as one who constantly enters the system to make repairs. Second, this understanding of God is important because some Christian traditions hold to such a strict view of God's sovereignty that it leaves little room for God to empathize with the creation. But the texts we will examine in this unit show that God feels deeply. In fact, God's empathy seems to be an indispensable part of God's rule of the world.

In this unit the passages from Exodus perhaps present most overtly the notion that God engages God's creation. In Exodus 3:7-8 God tells Moses, "I have observed the misery of my people who are in Egypt; I have heard their cry on account of their taskmasters. Indeed, I know their suffering, and I have come down to deliver them from the Egyptians." This is indeed no clockmaker God. God hears, sees, and has compassion. God enters the human world to bring justice. Exodus 32 and 34 show another dimension of God's engagement with God's people. God becomes angry at Israel's disobedience and comes down to destroy them (Exodus 32:10). God has expectations and acts against the people when they fail to meet them. But God is also moved by Moses and decides not to destroy Israel (32:11-14). Ultimately God restores the covenant (Exodus 34). This shows that God's engagement with God's people is so personal that the people affect God directly with their actions as well as with their prayers.

The psalms in this unit also testify to God's engaging nature. Psalm 46 declares that "the LORD of hosts is with us" (Psalm 46:7, 11). This claim says that God does not stay removed. God cares and God comes near. Psalm 66 refers indirectly to the exodus event (Psalm 66:6). It thus praises God for acting against the oppression of the Egyptians, just as the Book of Exodus does. Psalm 139 describes God as one who knows the psalmist intimately. In fact, God's personal knowledge of the one who prays the psalm is the psalm's main subject. This shows again that God is not a dispassionate observer. God formed the psalmist in the womb (Psalm 139:13) and watches over him or her at all times. Based on this understanding of God, the psalmist can therefore cry out to God, seek God's help, and ask for God's protection. Psalms 63, 90, 91, and 139 are all founded on the idea that God is one who engages God's people. The psalmist prays because he or she believes God hears, sees, and cares.

An important part of God's engaging character is the notion that God is *jealous*. Exodus 20:5 says this directly as part of the explanation of the Second Commandment ("You shall not make for yourself an idol"). But several other texts in this unit share the idea. Exodus 32 tells the story of how Israel failed to live up to God's relational expectations. God's jealousy then produces divine anger. Psalm 66:10-12 also illustrates what happens to Israel when Israel fails in its relationship with the Lord.

Jealousy is usually thought to be a negative human trait. But jealousy for God in the Old Testament is not the same as human jealousy. The term refers to God's passionate commitment to God's relationship with the people God chose as a special possession. This characteristic, perhaps more than any other, set Israel's God apart from the other gods of the ancient Near East. Israel's God is unique in the insistence on absolute devotion. The notion that God is jealous speaks to God's concern for God's relationship with God's people. Therefore, the word "zealous" may be a more apt translation. That is, God is not just jealous when Israel follows after other gods; God is also zealous about the quality and depth of the relationship. This is particularly true in Exodus 20:5 since the passage is likely concerned about the nature of Israel's relationship with God, not with Israel worshiping other gods. Moreover, this description of God makes clear that God is not simply concerned about Israel's obedience to the letter of the law. Rather, God desires Israel to love God with their entire being.

Perhaps the most overarching image of God in this unit is that of *sovereign ruler of the universe*. Psalm 66:1 calls "all the earth" to praise God. Similarly, Psalm 47:1 calls all people to clap and shout in celebration of God's reign. Most of the psalms here speak at least indirectly of God as creator; that is a primary motivation for the creation to offer praise. Psalm 8 invites us to look at the universe as God's handiwork. In Psalm 19 the primary sign of God's creative power is Torah. Torah gives evidence of the regularity of the creation, evidence that God maintains a check on chaos. Likewise, Psalm 46 portrays Mount Zion as the place God's people know and experience God's reign. Psalm 139 declares that no part of the world is outside God's reach or view. God rules over all.

Some of the passages in this unit might seem to say that God is God of Israel only, or that God favors Israel to the detriment of other peoples. But a close reading of these texts makes clear that God is seeking peace for all people. Psalm 47:9 makes the remarkable claim that the "princes of the peoples gather as the people of the God of Abraham." Clearly God cares about other peoples because God has created them. Even the statement that God has placed all people "under our feet" (Psalm 47:3) is probably a statement about Israel's responsibility for others rather than its authority over them (see the same language in Psalm 8:6, which describes humankind's responsibility for the rest of the creation). Therefore, God seeks equity for all people and places greatest responsibility on the people God brought out of slavery in Egypt.

CLOSE-UP:
A STATEMENT OF FAITH

In Exodus 34, we find Moses making two new stone tablets, having destroyed the original set when he came down from Mount Sinai and discovered Aaron and the people with a golden calf. Exodus 34:5-7 reports that God "descended in the cloud," appeared to Moses, and made this remarkable statement about God's own character:

⁶ The LORD passed before him [Moses], and proclaimed,
   "The LORD, the LORD,
   a God merciful and gracious,
   slow to anger,
   and abounding in steadfast love and faithfulness,
⁷ keeping steadfast love for the thousandth generation,
   forgiving iniquity and transgression and sin,
   yet by no means clearing the guilty,
   but visiting the iniquity of the parents
   upon the children
   and the children's children,
   to the third and the fourth generation."

Note that the first things on the list concern God's mercy, grace, slowness to anger, love, and willingness to forgive sin. Only then do we see the judgmental side of God. Even there, God's "visits" upon the guilty last only to the third or fourth generation, whereas God's love continues on to the "thousandth generation."

Although these words describing God's nature first appear in Exodus, at least portions of this description echo in Numbers 14:18; 2 Chronicles 30:9; Nehemiah 9:17, 31; Psalm 103:8; Joel 2:13; Jonah 4:2; and Nahum 1:2-3. Take a few moments to read each of these statements and compare them to the one found in Exodus 34:6-7.

- The first statement in Exodus 34 was spoken by God to Moses. After the Hebrew people rebelled and God was ready to "strike them with pestilence and disinherit them" (Numbers 14:12), the statement in verse 18 was spoken by Moses to God as a reminder of God's promise.
- In 2 Chronicles we read a letter King Hezekiah sent to the people calling for repentance and inviting everyone to celebrate Passover. In this letter he refers to God as "gracious and merciful" (30:9).
- In Nehemiah 9:17 we find much of Exodus 34:6 quoted in the context of a national prayer that Ezra offered as a confession that recalled their relationship with God.
- Psalm 103 also quotes much of Exodus 34:6 in a song of thanksgiving attributed to David. In this psalm we see how mercifully God deals with sinners.
- The prophet Joel uses the Exodus quotation to call people to return to God, pointing out the gracious nature of God.
- After Nineveh repented, Jonah uses the statement from Exodus 34:6 to explain to God why he ran away to Tarshish. He claimed he knew all along that God would relent from punishing the Ninevites.
- Nahum focuses more on the judgmental and avenging side of God, noting though that the Lord is slow to anger.

Israel returned repeatedly to the disclosure of God's nature initially made in the wilderness. It is a statement of faith that we would do well to integrate into our own portrait of God. A well-balanced image of the God Jesus called "Father" includes the judgment that Christians often attribute to the "God of the Old Testament" and the love, mercy, and grace that we see in Jesus.

FAITH IN ACTION: CONNECTING WITH THE INESCAPABLE GOD

During this quarter we are discovering through the Psalms and the Book of Exodus that God the creator and sustainer is always present and intimately involved with us. Too often, though, we live as if we do not even notice God. Challenge the students to participate in these activities, which you may want to assign over time rather than all at once. Post whichever activity you want to present on newsprint so that the adults can work on it at home.

Activity 1: The ecumenical monastic community of Taizé (ti zay') in France offers opportunities for drawing closer to God through prayer, meditation, and song. Silence is an important part of Taizé worship, as are candles and repetitive chants that have psalm-like qualities. Look up www.taize.fr/en_rubrique12.html on the Internet. Check out "Learning the Songs," which provides words and music. Spend some time in prayer and meditation, using selected songs to aid you as you draw near to God.

Activity 2: Enter into a meditative prayer through the Scriptures. Select a passage, for example Exodus 3:1-14, and allow that Scripture to speak to you. Focus on Moses' willingness to be drawn from his ordinary work to attend to that "still small voice" that called to him from the burning bush—a voice that the noisiness of our lives often overpowers. Be attentive to God. Surrender yourself to God in prayer.

Activity 3: Keep a small notebook and pencil near your bed in order to record dreams as you awaken. The Bible records communications from God through dreams, such as the ones Joseph (of Genesis) and Joseph (of Matthew) had. Review your dreams to see if they hold any messages to you from God. Recall that God is always present with us, even when we sleep.

Activity 4: During this quarter we encounter several psalms of praise. Encourage the students to contemplate reasons they have to praise God and then write their own psalm of praise. Emphasize that writing talent is not important; the voice from their hearts offering praise to God is what counts.

Activity 5: Fast from something that is important to you. That might be food, but it could be time spent in front of the television or computer screen, time devoted to sports or another hobby, or something else that you know exercises control over your time. The point here is not so much giving up something as it is spending time with God, focused on your relationship with God. Use the time you would have spent eating or watching or playing or whatever to enter into a serious conversation with God.

Activity 6: Praying with icons is a longstanding practice in the church, particularly in the Orthodox communities. Find a picture that speaks to you about God, perhaps a picture of Jesus or of the created world. Observe the details of this picture. Let it speak to you as though God is speaking. What is this picture telling you about yourself and what you need to do?

UNIT 1: GOD REVEALS
GOD'S REVELATION TO MOSES

PREVIEWING THE LESSON

Lesson Scripture: Exodus 3:1-6, 13-15
Background Scripture: Exodus 3
Key Verse: Exodus 3:6

Focus of the Lesson:
We all have experienced the surprise of someone calling our name whose voice we do not recognize. What happens to us when we hear this unfamiliar voice? When Moses heard God's voice, he responded by saying, "Here I am"; then he hid his face because he was afraid.

Goals for the Learners:
(1) to review how God's identity is revealed in the story of God's call to Moses in the burning bush.
(2) to feel thankful for God's willingness to speak to us and call us today.
(3) to develop and commit to a plan for learning how to recognize and obey God's voice.

Pronunciation Guide:
Adonai (ad oh ni')   Midian (mid' ee uhn)
Hobab (hoh' bab)   Reuel (roo' uhl)
Horeb (hor'eb)   theophany (thee of' uh nee)
Jethro (jeth' roh)

Supplies:
Bibles, newsprint and marker, paper and pencils, hymnals, optional picture of Moses and burning bush

---

READING THE SCRIPTURE

NRSV
Exodus 3:1-6, 13-15

¹Moses was keeping the flock of his father-in-law Jethro, the priest of Midian; he led his

NIV
Exodus 3:1-6, 13-15

¹Now Moses was tending the flock of Jethro his father-in-law, the priest of Midian,

flock beyond the wilderness, and came to Horeb, the mountain of God. ²There the angel of the LORD appeared to him in a flame of fire out of a bush; he looked, and the bush was blazing, yet it was not consumed. ³Then Moses said, "I must turn aside and look at this great sight, and see why the bush is not burned up." ⁴When the LORD saw that he had turned aside to see, God called to him out of the bush, "Moses, Moses!" And he said, "Here I am." ⁵Then he said, "Come no closer! Remove the sandals from your feet, for the place on which you are standing is holy ground." ⁶He said further, **"I am the God of your father, the God of Abraham, the God of Isaac, and the God of Jacob." And Moses hid his face, for he was afraid to look at God.**

¹³But Moses said to God, "If I come to the Israelites and say to them, 'The God of your ancestors has sent me to you,' and they ask me, 'What is his name?' what shall I say to them?" ¹⁴God said to Moses, "I AM WHO I AM." He said further, "Thus you shall say to the Israelites, 'I AM has sent me to you.'" ¹⁵God also said to Moses, "Thus you shall say to the Israelites, 'The LORD, the God of your ancestors, the God of Abraham, the God of Isaac, and the God of Jacob, has sent me to you':
This is my name forever,
and this my title for all generations."

and he led the flock to the far side of the desert and came to Horeb, the mountain of God. ²There the angel of the LORD appeared to him in flames of fire from within a bush. Moses saw that though the bush was on fire it did not burn up. ³So Moses thought, "I will go over and see this strange sight—why the bush does not burn up."

⁴When the LORD saw that he had gone over to look, God called to him from within the bush, "Moses! Moses!"

And Moses said, "Here I am."

⁵"Do not come any closer," God said. "Take off your sandals, for the place where you are standing is holy ground." ⁶Then he said, **"I am the God of your father, the God of Abraham, the God of Isaac and the God of Jacob." At this, Moses hid his face, because he was afraid to look at God.**

¹³Moses said to God, "Suppose I go to the Israelites and say to them, 'The God of your fathers has sent me to you,' and they ask me, 'What is his name?' Then what shall I tell them?"

¹⁴God said to Moses, "I AM WHO I AM. This is what you are to say to the Israelites: 'I AM has sent me to you.'"

¹⁵God also said to Moses, "Say to the Israelites, 'The LORD, the God of your fathers—the God of Abraham, the God of Isaac and the God of Jacob—has sent me to you.' This is my name forever, the name by which I am to be remembered from generation to generation."

UNDERSTANDING THE SCRIPTURE

Introduction. Exodus 3 tells the story of Moses' call to lead his people out of slavery and into the land God promised their ancestors. Exodus 6:2–7:7 basically repeats the call of Moses before God brings the plagues on Egypt.

The account in Exodus 3 follows a pattern found in many other call stories in the Bible. In such stories (1) the person being called meets God or an angel (3:2); (2) God commissions the person to a special task (3:10); (3) the person being commissioned expresses doubt or questions the task (3:11, 13; 4:1, 10); (4) God gives a sign of assurance that the task will be successful (3:12, 14-15; 4:2-9, 15-16). Exodus 3 emphasizes Moses' doubts about the commissioning.

Exodus 3:1-6. The story is set when Moses is shepherding the flocks of his father-in-law near the mountain of God. Here the holy mountain is called Horeb. In other texts, however, the same location is known as Sinai (Exodus 19:1). Moses' father-in-law is here named Jethro, though elsewhere he is called Reuel (Exodus 2:18) or Hobab (Numbers 10:29). The memory of these different place names and personal names may indicate the work of different authors and thus of different written sources used to create the Book of Exodus.

Moses is drawn to the location of his meeting with God when he sees a bush that is burning but not consumed. God's appearance from the midst of fire, storm, or wind is a common motif in the Old Testament (1 Kings 19:11-18; Psalms 29:3-9; Ezekiel 1). The event is often called a theophany, the revelation of God through natural phenomenon.

According to Exodus 3:2, "the angel of the LORD appeared" to Moses in the burning bush. But verse 4 indicates that God spoke directly to Moses from the bush, not through a mediator or divine messenger (the role of angels). This type of interplay between God and the angel shows the reluctance of the biblical writer to say matter-of-factly that God appeared and spoke (see Judges 6:12, 14; Ezekiel 1). God's instruction for Moses to remove his shoes (3:5) indicates the seriousness and holiness of the place because of God's presence (see Joshua 5:15). Moses shows awareness of God's holiness by hiding his face (3:6). Looking directly at the divine countenance was thought to be fatal (Isaiah 6:5).

In Exodus 3:6 God expresses the divine identity by saying, "I am the God of your father." "Father" here could be translated generically as "ancestor." The culture of the Old Testament, however, traced lineage through male forebears. Property was passed from father to son unless there were no male heirs (see the inheritance of daughters, for example in Joshua 17:4-6 and

remarkably in Job 42:15). Therefore, God's introduction to Moses with this language reminds Moses and the Israelites they are heirs to the promises made long before to Abraham, Isaac, and Jacob.

Exodus 3:7-12. God introduces the call to Moses by first expressing concern for the Israelites' condition in Egypt (3:7). God is not the detached deity described by philosophers. Instead, God is passionate about people and about justice.

The mission will be to deliver the Israelites from bondage and to take them to the land of Canaan. Moses raises objections to the commission God has given him. In verse 11 Moses raises the first and most general objection to God's call: "Who am I that I should go to Pharaoh?" The other objections are really an expansion of this one ("They will never believe me" [4:1]; "I am slow of speech" [4:10]). Ironically, the sign of assurance God gives Moses can only be seen after Moses answers the call (3:12)!

Exodus 3:13-15. One of the most difficult portions of the story is the exchange between God and Moses in verses 13-15. It is not certain why Moses asks God to reveal God's name. As Moses indicates in verse 13, the Hebrews had known this God previously as the God of their ancestors. So, perhaps it would have been necessary for Moses to tell this generation—the descendants of Abraham, Isaac, and Jacob—what this God will be to them. The name of God would help them understand since the name would indicate something of God's character. Although this is possible, Moses' inquiry about the divine name appears in a string of objections to Moses' call.

It is also not certain what God's response to Moses means. The sentence, "I AM WHO I AM" could be translated several other ways. In Hebrew the sentence consists of three words, two instances of the verb "to be" ("I am") connected by a relative particle ("who"). But verbs in Hebrew have no built-in tense as verbs in English. So, the sentence could also be translated, "I will be who I will be," or "I am who I will be," among other possibilities. The meaning of the answer God gives for the meaning of the divine name can only be surmised. Some have proposed that the answer is essentially evasive. A better explanation may be that Moses and the people will know who God is by seeing what God does.

In Exodus 3:15 God's statement "I AM WHO I AM" is linked to the name of God frequently used in the Old Testament. It is translated "the LORD." But the Hebrew word that stands behind the translation is actually a third-person form of the verb, "to be." Christians sometimes translate this name as it perhaps sounded, Yahweh. The name is formally translated "LORD," however, because Jews in the ancient world held it to be so sacred that it was not pronounced. And the scribes who passed on the Old Testament put signals in the text that instructed readers to say another, common word, Adonai, which refers simply to one who has authority over another (hence,

a "lord"). Since this name appears in verse 15 as God instructs Moses on how to address the Israelites, it seems that God's answer to Moses in verses 13-14 is meant to explain the divine name (Yahweh). Here "the LORD" is identified as the God of Israel's ancestors.

Exodus 3:16-22. After revealing the divine name, God does promise to strike Egypt and rescue the Israelites from slavery (3:17-22). Moses is to request that the Israelites be allowed to go "a three days' journey" into the wilderness to make a sacrifice (3:18). This is intended as a ruse to fool Pharaoh. God knows from the start, however, that it will not work (3:19). Rather, God will defeat Pharaoh in order to free the Israelites. In an interesting conclusion to Moses' commissioning, God states that the Israelites will not leave Egypt empty-handed (3:21-22). This becomes for the Israelites a model for how they will release their own debt slaves (Deuteronomy 15:13).

INTERPRETING THE SCRIPTURE

God's Elusive Presence

One of the most important implications of the story of Moses' call is the realization that we experience God always as one who is elusive, whose presence we cannot predict or control. This is extremely important in an age when some popular religious figures regularly speak of God speaking to them, giving them clear signs of God's plans for the world and for their lives. To be sure, God gives Moses clear instructions. But God appears to Moses in an unexpected and unique way. Moses saw a bush that was burning but not consumed and turned aside to see what it might mean. From the bush Moses heard God's voice. Moses had no control over God's appearance to him. It was due completely to God's initiative. So it

is with God's claim upon us and God's call for us to take on a particular task.

The Nature of God's Call

While God's presence is elusive, we can be sure that God has not abandoned us. But how do we judge God's presence and how do we discern if God has really called us to perform a particular task or to take on a certain role or identity? Although we cannot answer the question easily, it may be helpful to ask the question: Is the call we think we are hearing something easy and simple that makes us more comfortable? Or is it something hard that requires preparation and sacrifice? The story of Moses' call in Exodus 3, like most commissioning stories in the Bible, presents God's instruction to Moses to do something very hard. To answer the call Moses must travel from a place of comfort to a place of danger; he must risk his reputation, not to mention his life. Moreover, God asked Moses to stretch himself—to do things he did not think he had the resources to do—for the sake of God's people. This is not to say that God's call upon our lives always requires us to risk life and limb, as it did for Moses. Our own call to act with and for God will likely be less dramatic. Nevertheless, when God speaks to us with a commission to act it typically involves sacrifice. This is undoubtedly so because the nature of God is to sacrifice Godself for us, as God did most profoundly in Jesus' death. Hence, since God calls us to participate in God's own activity in the world, it should not be a surprise that our task will have the same character. But God's claim upon us is also likely to require sacrifice and self-giving because God calls those who have the capacity so to give and sacrifice, even if they do not immediately recognize it.

God Works Through Frail Creatures

Moses risked his life in answering God's call. But perhaps the greatest risk in this story is the one God took in calling Moses in the first place. Such is the nature of God's work in our world. God works through frail creatures to accomplish the divine purpose, and God's work through Moses is a good example of this fact.

To many readers, Moses may not seem weak and ineffective. They may have in mind an image of Moses like Charlton Heston in *The Ten Commandments*: rugged, handsome, powerful, charismatic. But the story itself suggests a different picture. The exchange between God and Moses, particularly the persistent doubts Moses expresses about his ability to carry out the mission, shows that Moses had some very real limitations. To be sure, Moses used his many inadequacies as excuses to avoid accepting

the task God had for him. Nevertheless, his objections apparently indicate God could have chosen someone with more potential for success: Moses was unknown to the Israelites, thus he legitimately worried they would not listen to him (3:11; 4:1); he may have had a speech impediment (4:10), or at best he was not trained in the art of persuasion and so he wondered if he could make a convincing case to Pharaoh. These limitations of Moses seem significant, not to mention the fact that he was a convicted murderer being asked to return to the scene of the crime to deliver God's people! In other words, God's call of Moses is yet another example in Scripture of what the apostle Paul said about how God works: "God chose what is weak in the world to shame the strong" (1 Corinthians 1:27).

This dimension of the story reminds us that God is the main actor in the story of the exodus and in our story. The point is not so much that we are weak and inadequate. Rather, our abilities are never enough to deliver us. God knows already that our efforts alone will fail (3:19). Ultimately only God can save us. So, while Exodus 3 focuses on Moses as God's agent, it also reminds us that Moses is an ordinary human being (thus, the generic quality of his commissioning) chosen by God to show God's extraordinary deeds.

Experiencing the God Who Acts

Exodus 3 reveals an essential feature of the character of God: God is moved by human suffering; God acts within human history and enters human experience to alleviate the suffering God sees. God is not an inanimate spirit. God is not the sum of all the good and just actions in the world. God is not just the prime mover who set the world in motion. To be sure, God may be understood in all these ways. But the biblical God is much more. The account of Moses' call depicts God as one who seeks a relationship with individuals God identifies as servants who carry out the divine mission. It also portrays God as one who has a relationship with a particular people, Israel. God works for them and through them to bring justice to the world. God's work is not always seen and identified clearly when events take place, but the Bible testifies to God's intimate involvement with humankind. This feature of God's character appears in the very first part of God's address to Moses, "I have observed the misery of my people. . . I have heard their cry . . . I have come down to deliver them" (3:7-8). In other words, the story of Moses' call encourages us to look for suffering in our world and to discern how and where God is acting to deliver those in pain.

SHARING THE SCRIPTURE

Preparing Our Hearts

Explore this week's devotional reading, found in Luke 20:34-40. When asked about the resurrection by Sadducees, who do not believe in resurrection, Jesus cited the story of Moses and the burning bush, which figures prominently in today's lesson. Jesus' point was that God is the God of the living, not the dead, and so for Moses to refer to Abraham, Isaac, and Jacob indicates that "to him all of them are alive" (20:38). What do you believe about the resurrection? How does your belief shape the way you live?

Pray that you and the adult learners will be open to the many ways God reveals God's own self to humanity.

Preparing Our Minds

Study the background Scripture from Exodus 3 and the lesson Scripture from Exodus 3:1-6, 13-15. Consider your response when you hear an unfamiliar voice.

Plan a lecture on Understanding the Scripture for "Review How God's Identity Is Revealed in the Story of God's Call to Moses in the Burning Bush."

Read the "Introduction to the First Quarter," "The Big Picture," "Close-up," and "Faith in Action." Decide how you will incorporate that material into this quarter's lessons.

Option: Locate online or in a book a picture of Moses and the burning bush.

LEADING THE CLASS

(1) Gather to Learn

❖ Welcome the class members and introduce any guests.

❖ Pray that the students will recognize God's identity as it is revealed in the story of Moses and the burning bush.

❖ Invite the adults to tell stories of times when someone they thought was a stranger phoned them or called their name, perhaps in some public place. How did the students react when the caller revealed his or her identity? [The caller may be someone known in the past, or may be a person who knew the learner by reputation but had not yet met.]

❖ Read aloud today's focus statement: **We all have experienced the surprise of someone calling our name whose voice we do not recognize. What happens to us when we hear this unfamiliar voice? When Moses heard God's voice, he responded by saying, "Here I am"; then he hid his face because he was afraid.**

(2) Review How God's Identity Is Revealed in the Story of God's Call to Moses in the Burning Bush

❖ Choose volunteers to play the parts of a narrator, God, and Moses. Have them read Exodus 3:1-6, 13-15 as a drama.

❖ Read "Introduction" in Understanding the Scripture so that the students will become familiar with the pattern of call stories.

❖ Give the brief lecture you have prepared from Understanding the Scripture to help the students become aware of more details of the story.

❖ Discuss these questions with the class:

(1) What do you learn about God from this passage?

(2) What do you learn about Moses?

(3) What do you learn about the nature of God's call? (Use "The Nature of God's Call" in Interpreting the Scripture to add to this discussion.)

(4) What would you have done or said had you been Moses?

❖ **Option:** Show a picture of Moses and the burning bush. Invite the students to comment on the emotions this picture evokes, such as fear, amazement, or confusion. Ask them to discuss how the picture is similar to and different from the way they envision the scene.

(3) Feel Thankful for God's Willingness to Speak to Us and Call Us Today

Write on newsprint:

❑ information for next week's lesson, found under "Continue the Journey."

❑ activities for further spiritual growth in "Continue the Journey."

❖ Point out that a burning bush experience has, to our knowledge, only happened to Moses. But God does speak to us in other ways. Theologians refer to "general revelation," which is available to anyone at any time, and "special revelation," which is given to a specific people at a certain time in history. List the following means of revelation on newsprint:

General Revelation:

■ Nature

■ Conscience

■ Providence (for example, God providing rain, sun, and harvest)

Special Revelation:

■ Lots

■ Visions

■ Dreams

■ Prophets

■ Voices

■ Angels

■ Miracles

■ Jesus Christ

■ The Bible

❖ Divide the class into teams and give each team a sheet of newsprint and marker. Assign each team at least one example of a type of revelation. Ask each group to provide several examples of each type of revelation.

❖ Encourage the groups to post their newsprint and report back.

❖ Wrap up this portion of the session by asking the students to give examples from their own lives of how God is speaking to them today. They may classify the revelation according to one of the categories discussed in their teams.

(4) Develop and Commit to a Plan for Learning How to Recognize and Obey God's Voice

❖ Distribute paper and pencils. Read the following questions aloud, pausing for the students to write responses.

(1) Which types of revelation have you experienced personally? Write all that apply on your paper. (pause)

(2) By what means did God last speak to you? (pause)

(3) What convinced you that it was God who spoke? (pause)

(4) How did you respond? (pause)

(5) If you ignored God, what will you plan to do now? (pause)

(6) If you listened to and obeyed God, what has that experience been like for you? (pause)

❖ Suggest that students armed with this information now have an opportunity to create a plan to improve their reception of God's word.

❖ Brainstorm ideas with the class concerning ways they can be more aware of God speaking to them. Recommend that they again look at the list of ways God reveals Godself and try to generate some questions about each one. Here are some examples:

■ Where in the natural world do I feel closest to God: on a beach, mountaintop, woods, at home with a dog on my lap?

■ When have I had dreams that I believe were messages from God? Do I keep paper and pencil handy to record my dreams and their messages?

■ Do I read the Bible simply for information, or do I use techniques that allow God to speak to me through it?

❖ Conclude by challenging the students to identify those places or techniques that are the most helpful to them in hearing God. Suggest that they pay careful attention to these in an attempt to listen for God.

(5) Continue the Journey

❖ Pray that those who have participated today will be better able to recognize and obey God's voice.

❖ Read aloud this preparation for next week's lesson. You may also want to post it on newsprint for the students to copy.

■ **Title: God's Covenant with Israel**
■ **Background Scripture: Exodus 20**

■ **Lesson Scripture: Exodus 20:1-11**
■ **Focus of the Lesson: People look for guidance from someone, or something, they can trust. Where can we find a trustworthy guide for our lives? In the Ten Commandments, God laid out unimpeachable instructions for building a trusting relationship with God.**

❖ Challenge the students to complete one or more of these activities for further spiritual growth related to this week's session. Post this information on newsprint for the students to copy.

(1) **Think about times when you have been asked to take on a task for God. If you said no, what reasons did you give? Were these reasons valid, or were they excuses? Did you ever change your mind about the no?**

(2) **List as many names for God as you can think of. What does each one reveal to you about the nature of God?**

(3) **Help someone who is struggling to discern a word from God about an important decision. Support this person as he or she tests whether the voice is from God.**

❖ Sing or read aloud "The God of Abraham Praise."

❖ Conclude today's session by leading the class in this commission: **We go forth to worship and serve the Lord our God. Thanks be to our merciful and gracious God.**

UNIT 1: GOD REVEALS

GOD'S COVENANT WITH ISRAEL

PREVIEWING THE LESSON

Lesson Scripture: Exodus 20:1-11
Background Scripture: Exodus 20
Key Verses: Exodus 20:2-3

Focus of the Lesson:
People look for guidance from someone, or something, they can trust. Where can we find a trustworthy guide for our lives? In the Ten Commandments, God laid out unimpeachable instructions for building a trusting relationship with God.

Goals for the Learners:
(1) to identify through the Ten Commandments ways we can build a trusting relationship with God and others.
(2) to become aware of their relationship with the one holy God.
(3) to develop ways of worshiping that reflect wholehearted devotion to God.

Pronunciation Guide:
shabbat (sha bat')

Supplies:
Bibles, newsprint and marker, paper and pencils, hymnals

READING THE SCRIPTURE

NRSV
Exodus 20:1-11
   ¹Then God spoke all these words:
   ²I am the LORD your God, who brought you out of the land of Egypt, out of the house of slavery; ³you shall have no other gods before me.
   ⁴You shall not make for yourself an idol,

NIV
Exodus 20:1-11
   ¹And God spoke all these words:
   ²"I am the LORD your God, who brought you out of Egypt, out of the land of slavery.
   ³"You shall have no other gods before me.
   ⁴"You shall not make for yourself an idol

whether in the form of anything that is in heaven above, or that is on the earth beneath, or that is in the water under the earth. [5]You shall not bow down to them or worship them; for I the LORD your God am a jealous God, punishing children for the iniquity of parents, to the third and the fourth generation of those who reject me, [6]but showing steadfast love to the thousandth generation of those who love me and keep my commandments.

[7]You shall not make wrongful use of the name of the LORD your God, for the LORD will not acquit anyone who misuses his name.

[8]Remember the sabbath day, and keep it holy. [9]Six days you shall labor and do all your work. [10]But the seventh day is a sabbath to the LORD your God; you shall not do any work—you, your son or your daughter, your male or female slave, your livestock, or the alien resident in your towns. [11]For in six days the LORD made heaven and earth, the sea, and all that is in them, but rested the seventh day; therefore the LORD blessed the sabbath day and consecrated it.

in the form of anything in heaven above or on the earth beneath or in the waters below. [5]You shall not bow down to them or worship them; for I, the LORD your God, am a jealous God, punishing the children for the sin of the fathers to the third and fourth generation of those who hate me, [6]but showing love to a thousand generations of those who love me and keep my commandments.

[7]"You shall not misuse the name of the LORD your God, for the LORD will not hold anyone guiltless who misuses his name.

[8]"Remember the Sabbath day by keeping it holy. [9]Six days you shall labor and do all your work, [10]but the seventh day is a Sabbath to the LORD your God. On it you shall not do any work, neither you, nor your son or daughter, nor your manservant or maidservant, nor your animals, nor the alien within your gates. [11]For in six days the LORD made the heavens and the earth, the sea, and all that is in them, but he rested on the seventh day. Therefore the LORD blessed the Sabbath day and made it holy.

UNDERSTANDING THE SCRIPTURE

Introduction. Exodus 20 reports the first words from God to the Israelites when the Israelites reached Mount Sinai. Verses 1-17 contain the Ten Commandments. The expression, "Ten Commandments," however, does not appear here. Later, in Exodus 34:28, God commands Moses to write the commandments on two tablets and identifies them as "ten words" (the exact expression "Ten Commandments" does not appear anywhere). These commands are also recorded in Deuteronomy 5 in slightly different form.

The Ten Commandments are simple imperatives, most of which are prohibitions. Eight of the commandments are formed by a second-person verb that is negated ("You shall not). The other two commandments are

simple imperatives ("remember" and "honor"). They may be distinguished from many other Old Testament laws that have stipulations or that state the consequences of disobedience. This more common case law is thought to come from actual legal proceedings in ancient Israel. The Ten Commandments, on the other hand, are more instructional in character. They reflect the teaching of elders and family leaders who attempted by such laws to shape relationships between members of the extended family (as in Exodus 20:12-17) and between all the people and God (as in Exodus 20:1-11).

Exodus 20:1-2. The first two verses are a prologue to the commandments. Verse 2 gives important context for the stipulations.

It identifies God as the one who rescued Israel from slavery, and Israel as the people dependent on God who delivered them. In essence verse 2 introduces the commandments as Israel's response to God's grace.

Exodus 20:3. The first commandment is the most general and thus serves as a summary of all the rest. There is some debate about the meaning of "before me." The expression in Hebrew literally means "in my presence." Does that mean the first commandment is a prohibition against putting the image of another deity in the Lord's sanctuary? Or does it mean more generally that Israel is to express devotion to no other god? The larger Old Testament context suggests the latter.

Exodus 20:4-6. The second commandment prohibits the making of idols. The jealousy of God described in Exodus 20:5 has led some scholars to think this commandment is a prohibition against worshiping other gods. But the issue here seems to be making an image to facilitate the worship of Yahweh. This point is made clear by several other texts that speak to the issue with language similar to Exodus 20:4-6. Exodus 32 tells the story of Aaron and the Israelites making a golden calf while Moses was on the mountain with God. The problem the story narrates is not that the Israelites wanted another god. Rather, they wanted their God to be one they could see and touch. They desired an object that looked familiar, like something from the created realm (as Exodus 20:4 outlines the various parts of the universe). Deuteronomy 4:9-20 elaborates on this issue. In that text Moses tells the Israelites that while at the holy mountain they heard God's voice, but they saw no form (4:15). Hence, Moses warns the people not to corrupt themselves by making an idol (4:16). Note that the words "form" and "idol" are the same words that appear in Exodus 20:4. Hence, the jealousy of God in Exodus 20:5 is jealousy over his character as one who cannot be manipulated and controlled by those God created.

Exodus 20:7. "Wrongful use" refers to using God's name in oaths and/or curses. In the ancient world certain speech forms were thought to be powerful, almost magical. And certain persons were thought to have special ability in using them (see the story of Balaam in Numbers 22–24). Using God's name in oaths or curses would invoke God's power and take advantage of it for one's own personal gain.

Exodus 20:8-11. The fourth commandment orders the Israelites to set aside the seventh day as a day of ceasing all labor (the meaning of the verb *shabbat* is "to cease"). The purpose is not rest for the human body in and of itself (though 20:10 includes a humanitarian concern). Rather, the sabbath is to be recognized as a sign of God's sovereignty over creation. Verse 11 ties sabbath to God's work in creation, as recorded in Genesis 2:2-3.

Exodus 20:12-17. The second tablet of commandments consists of instructions on how to treat other human beings. Verse 12 begins with the most immediate family relations. "Honoring" father and mother may mean taking care of them in their old age (see Matthew 15:1-9). Murder, adultery, and stealing (which perhaps refers to kidnapping; see Exodus 21:16) are all actions that disrupt the well-being of the community. Community health is based on the idea that each person only takes what he or she needs and is entitled to by God. Taking another's life or spouse, for example, are prime examples of crossing this line. Verse 17 remarkably takes verses 12-16 to an internal level, to the level of intentions and motives.

Exodus 20:18-21. Exodus 20:18-21 describes the scene on and beneath Mount Sinai when God spoke to the people. These verses remind us that the Ten Commandments were given in that setting.

Exodus 20:22-26. Chapter 20 ends with a section that elaborates on the second commandment. Exodus 20:22-26 is really the beginning of a new section that stretches to Exodus 23:33. This new section deals more specifically with stipulations of Israel's covenant with God. It is important to notice, however, that the law code in Exodus 20:22–23:33 begins here with instructions on proper worship. The whole law code should be read as a way for Israel to show obedience to God in gratitude for God's goodness.

INTERPRETING THE SCRIPTURE

The Ten Commandments and Salvation by Grace

The Ten Commandments are part of a larger body of legal material in the Old Testament. This material is sometimes read by Christians as a means of salvation that the New Testament rejects. Indeed, many Christians believe the Old Testament presents the legal statutes as something to follow in order to be saved. But the Ten Commandments (and the rest of the law) themselves argue against such an idea. The commandments begin with a statement about who God is and what God has done. Exodus 20:2 reminds Israel that the Lord brought them out of slavery in Egypt. The first commandment (20:3) then presents the action that should follow this recognition of God's actions: "You shall have no other gods before me" (20:3). The order of these statements is extremely important. God's action for Israel comes before Israel is asked to do anything. That means, therefore, that Israel's obedience to the commandments is always a response to God's grace. It is never a means to salvation in and of itself.

The first commandment (20:3) also puts the other commands in perspective. It is not just one in a list of requirements for faithfulness. Rather, the command to "have no other gods before me" is an overarching command that sets the stage for the rest. The other commandments are all illustrations of how Israel seeks to have no God except the Lord who brought them out of bondage. This seems to be the point Jesus made when he cited a different version of this command as the greatest commandment on which all others hang. He quoted Deuteronomy 6:5: "You shall love the Lord your God with all your heart, with all your soul, and with all your mind" (Matthew 22:37). As this expression of the first commandment's ideal indicates, it is really about faithfulness in relationship, not adherence to a legal code.

The Jealous God

The relational character of the first commandment, and of the commandments in general, is expressed well in Exodus 20:5, in the midst of the second commandment. As noted already, the second commandment is a prohibition against Israel making idols to represent God. The reason Israel is told not to create images of God is that God is jealous. Jealousy is usually thought to be a negative human trait. But jealousy for God in the Old Testament is not the same as human jealousy. The term refers to God's passionate commitment to God's relationship with the people God chose as a special possession. This characteristic, perhaps more than any other, set Israel's God apart from the other gods of the ancient Near East. Israel's God is unique in the insistence on absolute devotion. The notion that God is jealous speaks to God's concern for God's relationship with God's people. Therefore, the word "zealous" may be a more apt translation of the Hebrew word. That is, God is not just jealous when Israel follows after other gods; God is also zealous about the quality and depth of the relationship. This is particularly true in Exodus 20:5 since the passage is likely concerned about the nature of Israel's relationship with God, not with Israel worshiping other gods. Moreover, this description of God makes clear that God is not simply concerned about Israel's obedience to the letter of the law. Rather, God desires Israel to love God with their entire being. The Westminster Catechism (a creed in the Reformed Tradition) appropriately says that to rightly observe the commandments God's people are also to be zealous for God.

An illustration from the contemporary world might illuminate the zealousness of God as described in Exodus 20:4. Imagine a married couple very much devoted to each other. The marriage relationship carries certain "requirements," mainly obedience to the seventh commandment ("Do not commit adultery;" 20:14). But imagine the absurdity of one spouse greeting the other at the end of the day and declaring, "I have not committed adultery today, so my obligation to you is complete." Indeed, lovers who are zealous for each other can never fulfill the expectations of the relationship with mechanical compliance with such a stipulation. So it is with God's jealousy. God expects us to know God as the jealous/zealous one and, in return, to be zealous for God.

Right Worship and Right Actions

It has already been noted that the Ten Commandments are divided into two parts or two tablets. The first (20:1-11) lays out what is required for proper relations with God; the second (20:12-17) gives expectations for relations with other people. This division may give the impression that the first five commandments teach theology (right thinking about and worship of God) while the rest have to do with ethics (right actions). But the shape of the commandments themselves will not allow such a division. Although Exodus 20:1-11 is certainly about how to relate to God and to worship God properly, it also has important implications for how we treat others. This is

particularly evident in the third (20:7) and fourth commandments (20:8-11).

The prohibition against making "wrongful use of the name of the LORD your God" is not given just to avoid insulting God or speaking of God in a way that would make God unhappy. It is mainly aimed at people who would use God's name for their own advantage. This commandment is often associated with swearing, with using words that are offensive or profane. But Exodus 20:7 applies more directly to the practice of talking about God to gain favor or to convince others of one's piety. To say too lightly things like "God told me," "I believe this is God's will," or "I just love the Lord" might fall into this category. Such language can be used to manipulate others, to convince them we are right, to get them on our side.

The sabbath command is another important example, though very different from the previous one. Exodus 20:10 commands the Israelites to cease their labor on the seventh day. It also instructs them to relieve their servants and even their animals from work on the sabbath. This is surely an important ethical component of the sabbath law. But there is a more overarching ethical implication of this commandment that is more subtle. Sabbath observance is not just to relieve humans of their labors for a day each week. More importantly, it shapes the human heart by reminding the human of who created and who rules the world. To observe the sabbath is to remember God's work in creation and to align with the order God put in place at the beginning of time.

Throughout the Old Testament this openness to God and awareness of God's sovereignty is presented as perhaps the most important starting point for right relationships with others. Psalm 100, for example, reminds those who stand humbly before God that "It is he that made us, and we are his" (100:3). But the psalms often speak of another group, called "the wicked," who deny God's sovereignty (see Psalms 14:1 and 73:11-12 as examples). Their denial of

God's sovereignty in turn leads them to act violently towards others (Psalm 14:4). Exodus 20:8-11 presents sabbath observance as one important means of confessing God's sovereignty and of aligning oneself with God's good intentions towards others.

SHARING THE SCRIPTURE

Preparing Our Hearts

Explore this week's devotional reading, found in John 1:14-18. In this portion of the prologue of John's Gospel, Moses is presented as the one through whom the law was given; Jesus is seen as the one through whom grace and truth come. As you read today's lesson, you will see that the law and grace go hand in hand. Where do you find God's grace in the law?

Pray that you and the adult learners will experience a revelation from God as you study this week's Scriptures.

Preparing Our Minds

Study the background Scripture from Exodus 20 and the lesson Scripture from Exodus 20:1-11. Think about where you can find a trustworthy guide for your life.

Write on newsprint:
❑ questions for "Become Aware of the Learners' Relationship with the One Holy God."
❑ information for next week's lesson, found under "Continue the Journey."
❑ activities for further spiritual growth in "Continue the Journey."

Plan a lecture as suggested for "Identify Through the Ten Commandments Ways We Can Build a Trusting Relationship with God and Others."

LEADING THE CLASS

(1) Gather to Learn

❖ Welcome the class members and introduce any guests.
❖ Pray that those who have come today will find in the Ten Commandments ways to build a trusting relationship with God and neighbor.

❖ Point out that for many people television provides a guide for living. Noted television newscaster Ted Koppel gave a commencement address at Duke University in which he lauded the Ten Commandments as our guide for living (www.media research.org/mediawatch/1989/watch1989 0401.asp#analysis): **"The sheer brilliance of the Ten Commandments is that they codify . . . acceptable human behavior. Not just for then or now but for all time. . . . There have always been imperfect role models; false gods of material success and shallow fame; but now their influence is magnified by television. . . . [S]et your sights beyond what you can see. There is true majesty in the concept of an unseen power which can neither be measured nor weighed. There is harmony and inner peace to be found in following a moral compass that points in the same direction, regardless of fashion or trend."**

❖ Invite the students to comment on Koppel's view.
❖ Read aloud today's focus statement: **People look for guidance from someone, or something, they can trust. Where can we find a trustworthy guide for our lives? In the Ten Commandments, God laid out unimpeachable instructions for building a trusting relationship with God.**

(2) Identify Through the Ten Commandments Ways We Can Build a Trusting Relationship With God and Others

❖ Distribute paper and pencils. Ask the students to write as many of the commandments as they can recall.

❖ Encourage the students to open their Bibles and check their recall by reading silently Exodus 20:1-11. (Note that according to research done by Kelton Research and the 10 Commandments Commission in 2007, only 14 percent can accurately name all Ten Commandments. *USA Today* reported in March, 2007, that 60 percent of Americans can't name five commandments.)

❖ Present a lecture from the segments in Understanding the Scripture labeled Exodus 20:1-2, 3, 4-6, 7, 8-11, and 12-17. Your purpose is to help the adults understand the intent and implications of each of these commandments.

❖ Wrap up this segment of the lesson by asking: **If all of the members of our congregation were to keep these commandments perfectly, how would our community of faith have a better relationship with God and with other people?**

(3) Become Aware of the Learners' Relationship With the One Holy God

❖ Read aloud "The Jealous God" in Interpreting the Scripture to help the students understand God's passionate commitment to a relationship with us.

❖ Divide the class into four groups and give each group a sheet of newsprint and a marker. Assign one group verse 3 (no other gods), another group verses 4-6 (no handcrafted images of God), a third group verse 7 (wrongful use of God's name), and the final group verses 8-11 (keeping the sabbath). Invite the adults to look again at Exodus 20:1-11 and recall your lecture. Ask each group to list ways they perceive that their assigned commandment is violated.

❖ Invite the groups to post their results and report back to the class.

❖ Provide time for the learners to walk around (if possible) and silently reflect on the violations each group has listed. Encourage the adults to think about times when they have violated any of these com-

mandments. Suggest that they silently reflect on these questions, which you will read aloud and post on newsprint:
   (1) Why did you commit this violation?
   (2) How did the violation affect your relationship with God?
   (3) How did the violation affect your relationship with other people?

❖ Suggest that the adults return to their seats for a time of meditation as they ask themselves: **What changes in action and attitude do I need to make in order to draw closer to God?**

(4) Develop Ways of Worshiping that Reflect Wholehearted Devotion to God

❖ Point out that the word "worship" means to ascribe worth to something.

❖ Read aloud these words from "Worship as a Lifestyle" by Ron Carlson (www.gracecentered.com/worship_as_life style.htm): **"Authentic worship displays a life-style consistent with the discipleship demands of Jesus' Sermon on the Mount. Worship is more, much more, than the Sunday morning designated hour when saints and pseudo-saints gather together to do church. Though the assembly time is of critical import, it is only a component of a life-style characterized by service (note the worship definition of Romans 12:1-2). Our Sunday morning worship is only as good as our Monday morning life sacrifice."**

❖ Brainstorm with the class answers to this question: **How can we as individuals and as a class (or congregation) create a lifestyle of worship that incorporates the Ten Commandments and the Sermon on the Mount and clearly demonstrates our wholehearted devotion to God?** List ideas on newsprint.

❖ Challenge the class to suggest concrete ways to implement their ideas. For example, if their lifestyle of worship includes giving thanks to God, some students may choose to create a notebook of blessings in which they write a daily entry of things and people who have blessed them and for which they give thanks.

❖ Wrap up this portion of the lesson by reading or retelling "The Ten Commandments and Salvation by Grace" from Interpreting the Scripture to illustrate the importance of a faithful relationship with God, who Jesus called "Abba, Father."

(5) Continue the Journey

❖ Pray that the adults will worship God with wholehearted devotion.

❖ Read aloud this preparation for next week's lesson. You may also want to post it on newsprint for the students to copy.

■ **Title: God Versus "gods"**
■ **Background Scripture: Exodus 32**
■ **Lesson Scripture: Exodus 32:1-10**
■ **Focus of the Lesson: The commitments of our time and energy demonstrate where our devotion lies. What is worthy of our complete devotion and loyalty? The story of the golden calf illustrates that God, and God alone, deserves our complete devotion and loyalty.**

❖ Challenge the students to complete one or more of these activities for further spiritual growth related to this week's session. Post this information on newsprint for the students to copy.

(1) **Try to memorize all ten of the commandments. Use the key words suggested on www.epic storiesofthebible.com/challenge. php to help you remember.**

(2) **Think about the Ten Commandments in light of the devastation experienced on September 11, 2001 in the United States. What commands were broken—before, during, and after—the attacks? By whom? Why?**

(3) **Write in your spiritual journal an answer to this question: How do the Ten Commandments guide my interactions with God and neighbors?**

❖ Sing or read aloud "If Thou But Suffer God to Guide Thee."

❖ Conclude today's session by leading the class in this commission: **We go forth to worship and serve the Lord our God. Thanks be to our merciful and gracious God.**

UNIT 1: GOD REVEALS
GOD VERSUS "GODS"

PREVIEWING THE LESSON

Lesson Scripture: Exodus 32:1-10
Background Scripture: Exodus 32
Key Verse: Exodus 32:8

Focus of the Lesson:
The commitments of our time and energy demonstrate where our devotion lies. What is worthy of our complete devotion and loyalty? The story of the golden calf illustrates that God, and God alone, deserves our complete devotion and loyalty.

Goals for the Learners:
(1) to explore the story of the golden calf as an illustration of Israel's inability to show complete devotion and loyalty to God.
(2) to connect God's anger because of Israel's idol worship with consequences for their personal and corporate idolatry.
(3) to confess their idolatry and reaffirm devotion and loyalty to God.

Pronunciation Guide:
Jeroboam (jer uh boh' uhm)   Levite (lee' vite)

Supplies:
Bibles, newsprint and marker, paper and pencils, hymnals, optional picture of the golden calf being worshiped

READING THE SCRIPTURE

NRSV
Exodus 32:1-10

¹When the people saw that Moses delayed to come down from the mountain, the people gathered around Aaron, and said to him, "Come, make gods for us, who shall go before us; as for this Moses, the man who brought us up out of the land of Egypt, we do not know what has become of him." ²Aaron said to them, "Take off the gold

NIV
Exodus 32:1-10

¹When the people saw that Moses was so long in coming down from the mountain, they gathered around Aaron and said, "Come, make us gods who will go before us. As for this fellow Moses who brought us up out of Egypt, we don't know what has happened to him." ²Aaron answered them, "Take off the

rings that are on the ears of your wives, your sons, and your daughters, and bring them to me." ³So all the people took off the gold rings from their ears, and brought them to Aaron. ⁴He took the gold from them, formed it in a mold, and cast an image of a calf; and they said, "These are your gods, O Israel, who brought you up out of the land of Egypt!" ⁵When Aaron saw this, he built an altar before it; and Aaron made proclamation and said, "Tomorrow shall be a festival to the LORD" ⁶They rose early the next day, and offered burnt offerings and brought sacrifices of well-being; and the people sat down to eat and drink, and rose up to revel.

⁷The LORD said to Moses, "Go down at once! Your people, whom you brought up out of the land of Egypt, have acted perversely; **⁸they have been quick to turn aside from the way that I commanded them; they have cast for themselves an image of a calf, and have worshiped it and sacrificed to it,** and said, 'These are your gods, O Israel, who brought you up out of the land of Egypt!'" ⁹The LORD said to Moses, "I have seen this people, how stiff-necked they are. ¹⁰Now let me alone, so that my wrath may burn hot against them and I may consume them; and of you I will make a great nation."

gold earrings that your wives, your sons and your daughters are wearing, and bring them to me." ³So all the people took off their earrings and brought them to Aaron. ⁴He took what they handed him and made it into an idol cast in the shape of a calf, fashioning it with a tool. Then they said, "These are your gods, O Israel, who brought you up out of Egypt."

⁵When Aaron saw this, he built an altar in front of the calf and announced, "Tomorrow there will be a festival to the LORD." ⁶So the next day the people rose early and sacrificed burnt offerings and presented fellowship offerings. Afterward they sat down to eat and drink and got up to indulge in revelry.

⁷Then the LORD said to Moses, "Go down, because your people, whom you brought up out of Egypt, have become corrupt. **⁸They have been quick to turn away from what I commanded them and have made themselves an idol cast in the shape of a calf. They have bowed down to it and sacrificed to it** and have said, 'These are your gods, O Israel, who brought you up out of Egypt.'

⁹"I have seen these people," the LORD said to Moses, "and they are a stiff-necked people. ¹⁰Now leave me alone so that my anger may burn against them and that I may destroy them. Then I will make you into a great nation."

UNDERSTANDING THE SCRIPTURE

Introduction. Exodus 32 tells the story of the Israelites making a golden calf while Moses was on the mountain receiving the Ten Commandments. The issue in the story is not Israel's worship of foreign gods. Rather, the concern is that Israel crafted an image that represents Israel's God. Thus, Exodus 32 illustrates the issue the second commandment attempts to regulate: "You shall not make for yourself an idol" (Exodus 20:4). The problem essentially is that making gods the people may see and touch consti-

tutes a lack of faith. They were not able to believe God was with them simply because of the promise that God would be present and the evidence of God's deeds in history. This story is very similar to the story of Jeroboam setting up calves to represent Yahweh in Bethel and Dan (1 Kings 12:25-33; see the criticism of Jeroboam's image in Hosea 8:5). The Jeroboam account reminds us that Israel was always tempted to make and worship idols, and so are we. For Israel, and for us, the temptation to control our own destiny (or to attempt to do so) by shaping and defining God in tangible ways is perhaps the greatest temptation. It is very similar to the temptation of Adam and Eve in Genesis 3, who believed they could become "like God" themselves (Genesis 3:5).

Exodus 32:1-6. Verses 1-6 present two substitutions. First, the people replace Moses with Aaron. Moses is absent and the people declare, "we do not know what has become of him" (32:1). So they turn to Aaron. Then Aaron replaces the mysterious and invisible God with a golden calf. There is also another substitution that seems to be at work. Namely, the people identify Moses as "the man who brought us up out of the land of Egypt" (32:1). Other texts identify God as the one who brought the Israelites out of bondage (Exodus 20:2). Hence, the request in verse 1 seems to put Moses in the place of God.

The gold Aaron receives to make the image is probably the gold the Israelites took from Egypt (Exodus 3:22). It is a sign of their liberation from bondage. Therefore, when the people give it over for the making of an idol they further show they have forgotten how their liberation from Egypt occurred.

Aaron's statement in verse 4 is rather confusing. He made one image ("cast *an* image of *a* calf"), but he says, "*These* are your *gods*." The plural reference may be explained, however, by recognizing that Aaron's statement is nearly identical to that of Jeroboam in 1 Kings 12:28 (Jeroboam made two calves). When Exodus reached its final form the sin of Jeroboam was of great concern and Exodus 32 helped the Israelites identify the roots of their current theological crisis.

Exodus 32:7-14. God tells Moses what the Israelites are doing with a statement that seems to be sarcastic. He identifies the Israelites as "your people, whom you brought up out of the land of Egypt" (32:7). In other words, God speaks about Moses' leadership just as the Israelites did in verse 1. But God's condemnation of the golden calf in verse 8 makes clear that God will

have no part of this thinking. Because of their refusal to acknowledge God as their savior God calls them "stiff-necked" (32:9). They are like draft animals that refuse to be led by the farmer. Therefore, God is prepared to destroy them all and start over with Moses (32:10). God seems to identify the Israelites as Moses' people in order to deny them as God's people any longer.

Moses then intercedes for the Israelites and attempts to avert God's anger. He does so in part by identifying the Israelites with traditional language: "your people, whom you brought out of the land of Egypt" (32:11). Hence, Moses tries to restore the Israelites to fellowship with God with subtle, almost manipulative language. But in verse 12 Moses makes a direct plea: "Turn from your fierce wrath; change your mind and do not bring disaster on your people." The word "turn" could also be translated "repent!" What a bold petition Moses makes (Amos is the only other person in the Bible to ask God to change God's plan in this way; see Amos 7:2, 5). He makes the request based on two arguments as to why God should not destroy the Israelites. In verse 12 Moses essentially asks God, "What will the neighbors think?" Will the Egyptians not say that God took the Israelites out of bondage just to kill them? Then in verse 13 Moses asks, "What about your promises?" Will God be faithful to promises made to Abraham, Isaac, and Jacob? Verse 14 seems to say that Moses' arguments worked. God indeed changed course and did not destroy the Israelites.

Exodus 32:15-29. When Moses descends the mountain with the "two tablets of the covenant" (32:15) and he sees for himself what the Israelites are doing, "Moses' anger burned hot" (32:19), just as God's anger burned earlier. He addresses Aaron first since he is the leader in Moses' stead. But Aaron proves as weak before Moses as he was before the people. In verse 24 he humorously denies his direct responsibility. Then Moses calls for the people to take a stand for the Lord. The Levites alone respond (32:26). The slaughter that comes next is hard for most modern Western readers to fathom, or to square with their Christian ideals. It is a case, however, of extreme circumstances in which the survival of the community hangs in the balance (see Acts 5:1-11 for a story with similar consequences). The slaughter could have been averted if the people had responded positively to Moses' call.

Exodus 32:30-35. The story concludes with Moses' continued leadership. This time, however, he offers to sacrifice himself for the sake of the people (32:32, "blot me out of the book that you have written"). God again listens to Moses and does not destroy the Israelites, but he does punish them for their sins (32:34-35).

INTERPRETING THE SCRIPTURE

"Leave Me Alone"

As previously noted, the central problem in Exodus 32 is that the Israelites broke the second commandment (Exodus 20:4). The real issue, however, is not the breaking of a command, but what the command signifies. The prohibition against making images of Yahweh is probably intended to preserve the character of Israel's God as one who enters relationship with Israel and the world. Yahweh communicates, feels sorrow and joy, and is capable of being moved, angered, or pleased by God's people and the world God created. Exodus 32 illustrates quite well all of these aspects of God's relationship to Israel. When the Israelites make the golden calf to represent God they try to fix God in time and space and to deny that God is active and relational. Psalm 115:3-8 expresses the differences very well. It declares, "Our God is in the heavens; he does whatever he pleases" (115:3). In other words, God is boundless and cannot be captured in an image; God also has freedom and acts as God chooses. This means that God sometimes surprises us by offering grace when we have been disobedient or by averting punishment we know we deserve (Exodus 32:14, for example). Idols, by contrast, are static and predictable.

The relational character of God is apparent in Exodus 32 especially in God's interaction with Moses. Exodus 32:10 is an important verse. When God explains to Moses what has happened, how the Israelites have created and are now worshiping the golden calf, God then says, "Now let me alone, so that my wrath may burn hot against them and I may consume them." "Let me alone" is a remarkable statement for God to make to Moses. It seems to imply that God can only go through with the impulse to destroy the Israelites if Moses does not intervene. God is clearly affected by Moses' prayer. So, as the story goes, Moses does not leave God alone. Instead, Moses pleads for God to preserve the Israelites. This interchange illustrates just how essential relationships are to God. The creation of a stale, static image is the ultimate denial of this divine characteristic.

The prohibition against making images of Yahweh ensures that we understand God as relational. It also urges us to act in particular ways. If we think of God as inherently relational, for example, we will be more likely to pray, to intercede on behalf of others. In other words, we are encouraged to act like Moses, not to "leave God alone."

Exodus 32 and Genesis 3

The story of Israel making a golden calf is very similar to the story of the fall in the Garden of Eden in the nature of the sin it describes. God provided for Adam and Eve all they needed. God also gave Godself as a companion. But the first couple in the garden caved in to the temptation to "be like God" (Genesis 3:5). They exchanged what God gave them for what their own knowledge could provide. The result was a diminished relationship with the Creator and increased hardships in life and in relationship with each other. The golden calf story is very much the same story.

The rebellion of Adam and Eve is often referred to as "original sin." That language is appropriate in that their desire to be like God was for them the first and basic act against God. Exodus 32 may be fairly labeled the story of Israel's original sin. Israel with its golden calf did essentially what Adam and Eve did in the garden. They exchanged the good gifts of God (bringing them out of Egypt) and the promises of God for the future for what they could conjure up themselves—a lifeless and non-relational god. The temptation to do this to God remained their main temptation, and it remains ours as well. All other temptations are really expressions of this one temptation to reduce God or push God out of the way in order to gain control of our own destiny.

Carlisle Marney was a Baptist preacher in the middle of the twentieth century in Charlotte, North Carolina. Someone once asked him, "Where is the Garden of Eden?" Marney supposedly replied, "The Garden of Eden is at 227 Maple Street." According to the story, when Marney was a young boy growing up at 227 Maple Street, he stole some cookies from the cookie jar and ate them in secret. He was so ashamed that he hid in the closet, where his mother found him and asked why he was hiding and what he'd done. At that moment, Marney said, he knew he was just like Adam and Eve. He was also just like the Israelites at the base of Mount Sinai.

Idolizing the Messenger

In addition to the Israelites breaking the second commandment in Exodus 32, they also engage in idolatry of a more subtle form. In verse 1 the people come to Aaron with the request to make an idol and the comment, "as for this Moses, the man who brought us up out of the land of Egypt, we do not know what has become of him." The sequence of the Israelites' comments is fascinating. Clearly, the people are asking for an idol to represent God. God seems absent. But they also seem to imply that Moses would serve the purpose if he were present! They identify Moses as the one who brought them up from Egypt. Hence, it seems their idolatry is deeper than often recognized. They had been seeing Moses as their deliverer, or at least as the tangible sign of their deliverance all along.

It should be noted that Old Testament faith is incarnational (and thus anticipates *the* Incarnation, Jesus Christ). It always includes concrete expressions of God's presence. Hence, Israel's king is called God's son (Psalm 2:7) and is sometimes presented as God's representative on earth (Psalm 89:25-29). But in Exodus 32 the Israelites cross the line: They move from seeing Moses as a representative of God to seeing him as the power that actually delivered them. They fail to recognize that their leader is simply one of them. He represents them before God and he leads them into God's presence. He is not, however, God's presence in their midst. With such confused thinking, the people idolize Moses.

The temptation to create an idol in this way is always with us as well. Whether the temptation is to set up a leader as our idol or to worship some object or ideal, the effect is the same. It reduces God to something we can manage. For the Israelites it was easier to look to Moses or a cast image than to the mysterious God on the mountain. The former they could see, touch, and manipulate. The latter was beyond them. A healthy faith always experiences God's nearness indeed, but not at the expense of knowing God is ultimately beyond us. The God on the mountain is One who calls us to be more than we are.

SHARING THE SCRIPTURE

Preparing Our Hearts

Explore this week's devotional reading, found in John 5:39-47. In this passage, Jesus refers to Moses as the people's accuser. We will see a different view of Moses as the people's advocate in the background Scripture for today's session. An advocate is needed when we fail to honor our commitments to God. Where have you fallen short recently? Pray about this situation and ask for help in remaining loyal to the commitments you have made to God.

Pray that you and the adult learners will center your lives on the God who led the Israelites out of the wilderness and was called "Father" by Jesus.

Preparing Our Minds

Study the background Scripture from Exodus 32 and the lesson Scripture from Exodus 32:1-10. Consider this question as you read: What is worthy of our complete devotion and loyalty?

Write on newsprint:
- ❏ information for next week's lesson, found under "Continue the Journey."
- ❏ activities for further spiritual growth in "Continue the Journey."

Option: Locate a picture of the golden calf, preferably depicting people worshiping the idol.

LEADING THE CLASS

(1) Gather to Learn

❖ Welcome the class members and introduce any guests.

❖ Pray that those who have come today will recognize that good intentions do not always lead to the complete commitment that God requires of us.

❖ Post a sheet of newsprint. Go around the room (or call on volunteers if the class is large) and ask each person to complete this sentence: **I've been meaning to** . . . Students may note craft projects, home remodeling projects, personal plans, plans for study or spiritual disciplines, or anything else they have been meaning to do but haven't gotten around to completing.

❖ Ask: **What does our list of unfinished business say about our level of commitment to things that we apparently thought were important?**

❖ Read aloud today's focus statement: **The commitments of our time and energy demonstrate where our devotion lies. What is worthy of our complete devotion and loyalty? The story of the golden calf illustrates that God, and God alone, deserves our complete devotion and loyalty.**

(2) Explore the Story of the Golden Calf as an Illustration of Israel's Inability to Show Complete Devotion and Loyalty to God

❖ Introduce today's study by reading "Introduction" from Understanding the Scripture.

❖ Choose five volunteers to read the parts of the narrator, the people (two people), Aaron, and the Lord. Invite them to read Exodus 32:1-10 as a drama.

❖ Ask these questions, using information from Understanding the Scripture to augment the discussion:

    (1) **On a scale of one to ten, how would you rate Aaron as a leader of God's people? Why would you give him such a rating?**

    (2) **On a scale of one to ten, how would you rate the loyalty of the Israelites to God? What facets of their behavior prompt you to assign this number?**

(3) What, if anything, surprises you about God's response to the golden calf?

❖ Read or retell "Leave Me Alone" from Interpreting the Scripture to help the adults understand the implications of broken commandments.

❖ **Option:** Show the picture of the golden calf you have located. Encourage the students to comment on how this picture enriches the story for them or challenges their vision of what happened.

(3) Connect God's Anger Because of Israel's Idol Worship With Consequences for Personal and Corporate Idolatry

❖ Note that the Bible records instances of God's anger, due to the sin and disobedience of the Israelites, their worship of idols, intermarriage, ignoring the sabbath, and other reasons. Assign partners to read at least one of these references to God's anger in relation to idol worship and report to the class why God was angry and what action was taken or threatened.

- Numbers 25:3-5
- Deuteronomy 7:3-5
- Deuteronomy 29:16-28
- Judges 2:11-15
- 2 Kings 22:13-20
- 2 Chronicles 24:18-22

❖ Summarize the reports by noting that there are consequences for our failure to give our total allegiance to God.

❖ Brainstorm answers to this question, listing the participants' ideas on newsprint: **What are some of the "idols" that we may put in the place of God?** (Answers may include: *personal status, wealth, owning a certain brand of vehicle, living in an affluent neighborhood, wearing designer clothing, holding powerful positions in the workplace or community or church, earning a degree from a prestigious university, being a citizen of a particular country, belonging to a particular congregation or denomination, having powerful friends.*)

❖ Suggest that the adults meditate on these questions, which you will read aloud:

(1) What are the idols that I have put in the place of God? (pause)

(2) How has this skewing of my priorities affected my relationship with God? (pause)

(4) Confess Idolatry and Reaffirm Devotion and Loyalty to God

❖ Bring the students back together as you distribute paper and pencils. Challenge the adults to write a confession, for their eyes only, based on idols they have identified in their lives and the brokenness these gods have caused in their relationship with God and the Beloved Son, Jesus.

❖ Reiterate the importance of devotion to God by reading these words from 2 Chronicles 16:9: **For the eyes of the LORD range throughout the entire earth, to strengthen those whose heart is true to him.**

❖ Work with the class to write a loyalty oath to God that expresses their love and devotion to the One who desires to be in relationship with them. Here is an example, which is the oath that soldiers entering the United States military pledge: **I do solemnly swear (or affirm) that I will support and defend the Constitution of the United States against all enemies, foreign and domestic; that I will bear true faith and allegiance to the same; and that I will obey the orders of the President of the United States and the orders of the officers appointed over me, according to regulations and the Uniform Code of Military Justice. So help me God.** Point out that if soldiers are expected to give this unreserved allegiance, imagine how much more allegiance God's people should give to the Creator and Lord of the universe.

❖ Write the class's oath on newsprint.

❖ Wrap up this part of the session by reading in unison the oath that the class has drafted.

(5) Continue the Journey

❖ Pray that today's participants will set aside any idols in their lives and affirm their loyalty to God.

❖ Read aloud this preparation for next week's lesson. You may also want to post it on newsprint for the students to copy.

■ **Title: God Promises an Awesome Thing**
■ **Background Scripture: Exodus 34:1-10**
■ **Lesson Scripture: Exodus 34:1, 4-10**
■ **Focus of the Lesson: People have different ideas about how their behavior affects relationships. To whom are we accountable for our actions, and what do we expect when we err? In the face of Israel's unfaithfulness, God revealed to Moses that God is steadfast, forgiving, and faithful.**

❖ Challenge the students to complete one or more of these activities for further spiritual growth related to this week's session. Post this information on newsprint for the students to copy.

(1) **Recall that the image of the idol in this story is a calf, reminiscent of the bull worshiped by other religions of the Near East. What shape do your own idols take? Why are they so important to you? How do they stand in the place of God?**

(2) **Think about Aaron's response to the people's demand to "make gods" for them. What strategies do you have for overcoming peer pressure? Use them as needed this week to act responsibly according to your own beliefs and values.**

(3) **Encourage someone whose life is filled with idols to turn away from them and turn toward God.**

❖ Sing or read aloud "Praise, My Soul, the King of Heaven."

❖ Conclude today's session by leading the class in this commission: **We go forth to worship and serve the Lord our God. Thanks be to our merciful and gracious God.**

UNIT 1: GOD REVEALS

GOD PROMISES AN AWESOME THING

PREVIEWING THE LESSON

Lesson Scripture: Exodus 34:1, 4-10
Background Scripture: Exodus 34:1-10
Key Verse: Exodus 34:6

Focus of the Lesson:
People have different ideas about how their behavior affects relationships. To whom are we accountable for our actions, and what do we expect when we err? In the face of Israel's unfaithfulness, God revealed to Moses that God is steadfast, forgiving, and faithful.

Goals for the Learners:
(1) to discover God's attributes as revealed to Moses.
(2) to increase their sense of awe for the nature of God.
(3) to identify, and give thanks for, God's faithfulness and forgiveness in their lives.

Pronunciation Guide:
hesed (kheh' sed)   Jephthah (jef' thuh)
Yom Kippur (yom kip' uhr)

Supplies:
Bibles, newsprint and marker, paper and pencils, hymnals, optional Bible dictionaries or other word books

---

READING THE SCRIPTURE

NRSV
Exodus 34:1, 4-10
   [1]The LORD said to Moses, "Cut two tablets of stone like the former ones, and I will write on the tablets the words that were on the former tablets, which you broke. . . . [4]So Moses

NIV
Exodus 34:1, 4-10
   [1]The LORD said to Moses, "Chisel out two stone tablets like the first ones, and I will write on them the words that were on the first tablets, which you broke. . . ."

---

cut two tablets of stone like the former ones; and he rose early in the morning and went up on Mount Sinai, as the LORD had commanded him, and took in his hand the two tablets of stone. ⁵The LORD descended in the cloud and stood with him there, and proclaimed the name, "The LORD." ⁶The LORD passed before him, and proclaimed,

> "The LORD, the LORD,
> a God merciful and gracious,
> slow to anger,
> and abounding in steadfast love and
> faithfulness,

7 keeping steadfast love for the thousandth
      generation,
   forgiving iniquity and transgression
      and sin,
   yet by no means clearing the guilty,
   but visiting the iniquity of the parents
   upon the children
   and the children's children,
   to the third and the fourth generation."

⁸And Moses quickly bowed his head toward the earth, and worshiped. ⁹He said, "If now I have found favor in your sight, O Lord, I pray, let the Lord go with us. Although this is a stiff-necked people, pardon our iniquity and our sin, and take us for your inheritance."

¹⁰He said: I hereby make a covenant. Before all your people I will perform marvels, such as have not been performed in all the earth or in any nation; and all the people among whom you live shall see the work of the LORD; for it is an awesome thing that I will do with you.

⁴So Moses chiseled out two stone tablets like the first ones and went up Mount Sinai early in the morning, as the LORD had commanded him; and he carried the two stone tablets in his hands. ⁵Then the LORD came down in the cloud and stood there with him and proclaimed his name, the LORD. ⁶And he passed in front of Moses, proclaiming, **"The LORD, the LORD, the compassionate and gracious God, slow to anger, abounding in love and faithfulness,** ⁷maintaining love to thousands, and forgiving wickedness, rebellion and sin. Yet he does not leave the guilty unpunished; he punishes the children and their children for the sin of the fathers to the third and fourth generation."

⁸Moses bowed to the ground at once and worshiped. ⁹"O Lord, if I have found favor in your eyes," he said, "then let the Lord go with us. Although this is a stiff-necked people, forgive our wickedness and our sin, and take us as your inheritance."

¹⁰Then the LORD said: "I am making a covenant with you. Before all your people I will do wonders never before done in any nation in all the world. The people you live among will see how awesome is the work that I, the LORD, will do for you.

UNDERSTANDING THE SCRIPTURE

Introduction. Exodus 34 comes after two chapters dealing with Israel's apostasy. In Exodus 32 Israel disobeyed God by worshiping the golden calf and God nearly wiped them out. The key to Israel's preservation was Moses. Moses interceded for Israel by

pleading with God not to destroy them (Exodus 32:11-14). Exodus 33 reports more of the same. In Exodus 33:12-23 Moses prays for Israel again. He asks God to give him assurance that God will indeed help him "bring up this people" to the land God promised them (33:12). God responded, "I will do the very thing that you have asked" (33:17). Perhaps most important, in Exodus 33:19 God promises to proclaim "the name," that is God's name, before Moses. The name is a sign of God's presence with the leader God has chosen. It also is a way of limiting Moses' knowledge—God's presence cannot be known in full, only through God's name—but it is still a remarkable sign of God's grace. In Exodus 34 this revelation of God through God's name comes to fruition. God passes before Moses and tells Moses what the name means and, thus, what God is like.

Exodus 34:1-8. At the beginning of chapter 34 God takes the initiative to restore Israel after its apostasy. God tells Moses to cut two tablets like the ones Moses carried down the mountain and smashed in Exodus 32:15-19 (see earlier Exodus 31:18). God also instructs Moses to prepare to ascend Mount Sinai. The instructions here recall the first revelation at Sinai recorded in Exodus 19:9-24. The repetition of events and Moses' return to Sinai mark the restoration of the covenant God first established there with the people of Israel.

When Moses reaches the top of the mountain the scene recalls Exodus 19. Smoke and clouds cover the top of the mountain to signify God's mysterious presence. Verse 6 says, "the LORD passed before him," a line much like Exodus 33:22 ("my glory passes by"). In that passage God promised to pass by Moses in order to reveal Godself. God told Moses, however, that Moses would only be able to see God's backside because he could not stand to see God's face (33:20). Now in this next scene God reveals Godself to Moses again. This time when God passes by, however, God reveals the significance of the divine character in the name of God. The word "LORD" in verse 6 represents the name. "LORD" translates a Hebrew word that was perhaps pronounced "Yahweh" originally (see Exodus 3:14-15).

The remainder of verse 6 and verse 7 describe who "the LORD" is. The words that appear here also appear with only slight variations in Numbers 14:18; Nehemiah 9:17; Psalms 86:15; 103:8; 145:8; Jeremiah 32:18; Joel 2:13; Jonah 4:2; and Nahum 1:3. Therefore, it seems obvious that these words are a very important part of the Old Testament's understanding of who God is. The first part of this confessional statement emphasizes God's graciousness: God is "merciful and gracious, slow to anger, and abounding in steadfast love and faithfulness" (Exodus 34:6). The second part of the confession balances the first part by assuring that God is also a God of justice ("by no means clearing the guilty," 34:7).

Exodus 34:9. Moses appeals to God's goodness and mercy that were described in verses 6-7. He describes Israel as "a stiffnecked people." This description compares the Israelites to a draft animal that refuses to go the way the one plowing wants it to go. It resists the pull of harness and yoke by stiffening its neck against them. This is the character of Israel. So, Moses essentially just asks God to be patient with God's people.

The request for God to take Israel as an inheritance is quite remarkable. In the ancient Near East the inheritance was the wealth of a father passed on to his sons. It was in that world the greatest key to economic success and family identity. The oldest son received the largest portion and the rest was divided among other sons. (Daughters typically did not receive an inheritance except in rare circumstances; see Joshua 17:3-6 and especially Job 42:15). Numerous Old Testament texts show the importance of inheritance. Jacob and Esau are estranged because Jacob tricks Esau out of his inheritance rights (Genesis 25:29-34); Jephthah's brothers pushed him out of the inheritance of their father (Judges 11:1-3); Deuteronomy 21:15-17 stipulates that the son of an unfavored wife cannot be passed over in the inheritance. All of this attention to the inheritance shows its importance. Without an inheritance a man would perhaps sign on as a soldier or join a group of bandits to survive. Exodus 34:9 thus asks God to take Israel as his guarantee for the future. This is not much of a deal for God at all! The prayer really asks for God to appraise Israel at a much higher price than it is worth.

Exodus 34:10. After Moses' prayer God declares, "I hereby make a covenant." The expression "make a covenant" is literally "cut a covenant." This is the common way the Old Testament says two parties have made an agreement or tendered a contract. The word "cut" seems to be used because covenants (another translation is "treaty") in the ancient Near East were typically sealed by a sacred meal in which an animal was prepared ("cut" in pieces), cooked, and eaten. The irony here is that the only "agreement" seems to be that God will act on behalf of Israel. The Israelites are simply to "see" that God drives out the people of Canaan and gives the land to them (34:11). To be sure, there are stipulations for Israel later in Exodus 34. But these mainly elaborate on the instruction not to make covenants with the inhabitants of the land (34:12). In other words, the main feature of the covenant God makes with Israel is for God to have exclusive rights to protect and care for God's people.

INTERPRETING THE SCRIPTURE

Merciful and Gracious

The central feature of Exodus 34:1-10 is the poetic characterization of God in verses 6-7. The particular words used to describe God in these verses are important for understanding who "the LORD" is.

The first two words that characterize Israel's God are "merciful and gracious." These words may be understood as the general portrait of God that is filled out by the words that follow. The first word could also be translated "showing compassion." A form of this same term is used in Hosea 2:1 as a symbolic name for God's people (see also Hosea 1:6). God is "merciful" and those in relationship with God are known by their receipt of mercy. In Exodus 34 Israel benefits from God's mercy; Israel has nothing in and of itself to bring it favor. The second word, "gracious," is like the first. It denotes giving something that is not deserved or earned (see Genesis 33:11).

Slow to Anger

The Lord does become angry. In fact, God is frequently angry with his people. An expression such as, "the anger of the Lord burned hot against Israel," appears many times, including in some prominent passages in Exodus (Exodus 32:10). In fact, the Lord's anger is a main feature in Exodus 32, which provides the immediate context for this claim in Exodus 34:6 that God is "slow to anger." The word "anger" is the same word in Hebrew for "nose." The picture of God's anger, therefore, is of a person (or beast) whose nose gets red or whose nostrils flare when provoked. God is passionate and can become like an enraged beast when God's people are disobedient. But Exodus 34:6 proclaims that God is extremely patient and does not easily become angry. This too is a characteristic of God that is essential for the disobedient Israelites. They deserve God's wrath, but God offers grace instead.

Steadfast Love and Faithfulness

The next statement that defines the name of God is that God is "abounding in steadfast love and faithfulness" (34:6). "Steadfast love" translates the Hebrew term pronounced *hesed*, the first letter being a guttural; imagine imitating the sound of a camel spitting and you have it! This word is so rich in meaning that it cannot really be translated adequately. For that reason it might be good practice simply to use this word.

Hesed is sometimes translated "kindness" or even "loyalty." But neither of these English words captures fully its meaning. *Hesed* connotes the faithfulness of God in covenant. God makes promises to God's people and God always keeps these promises. This is what Israel relies on for its future. When in trouble they cry out for God's steadfast love to be made evident (Psalms 89:49; 90:14). A common refrain in the Psalms is "O give thanks to the LORD, for he is good; for his steadfast love endures forever" (Psalms 107:1; 118:1). *Hesed* is that feature of God's character that ensures Israel's future. "Faithfulness" is often paired with "steadfast love." This word reinforces *hesed*. It says God is reliable and steady, always to be trusted.

Moses' Prayer for Forgiveness

Moses' prayer in verse 9 is based on the character of God portrayed in verses 6-7. Moses intercedes for the Israelites by asking God to "go with us," "pardon our iniquity," and "take us for your inheritance." But Moses says nothing about Israel repenting, seeking to be faithful, or obeying God's commands. In fact, he seems to say Israel will likely not be faithful. But he asks God to forgive the people anyway. What a remarkable prayer! It appeals to God solely on the basis of God's goodness and confesses that Israel is a stiff-necked people who will in all likelihood fall short of God's expectations.

With its recognition of God's character, this prayer has important parallels to the portrait of God in Genesis 6-9, the story of the flood. The flood story begins with God's observation that "the wickedness of humankind was great in the earth, and that every inclination of the thoughts of their hearts was only evil continually" (Genesis 6:5). The events that follow are quite well known: The animals enter the ark (though rather less familiar is the note that of the clean animals Noah took seven pairs; Genesis 7:2-3); the flood came (7:11-24); the ark came to rest on the mountains of Ararat (8:1-5); Noah sent out a raven and then a dove to discover dry ground (8:6-12); finally Noah, his family and the animals came off the ark (8:13-19). Much less familiar, however, is what comes next, the real conclusion to the story. Genesis 8:20-22 reports that Noah made a sacrifice and God declared he would never again destroy the earth. Most importantly, verse 21 states that God made this decision despite the fact that humankind had not changed.

Genesis 8:21 reports God's decision about the future of the creation and God's relationship to it: "I will never again curse the ground because of humankind, for the inclination of the human heart is evil from youth; nor will I ever again destroy every living creature as I have done." This portion of the verse states God's decision to preserve the creation despite the fact that humans continue their inclination toward evil.

The statement in Genesis 8:21 includes a Hebrew particle that NRSV translates "for." This word often does have a causative meaning. In this case, however, it makes more sense to take it as concessive, "even though." Indeed, what God's statement indicates is that God decided not to destroy the earth again, despite the fact ("even though") that humankind had not become any more obedient. God simply chose to become more patient. In other words, the flood did not change humankind. But it did change God. God decided simply to approach the creation with unlimited patience and forbearance. This is exactly what Moses assumes, and what Moses prays for in Exodus 34:9.

At first glance this picture of God may seem at odds with the notion that God is sovereign and immutable. On the one hand this is true; Genesis 8:21 depicts God being changed by God's creatures. But on the other hand, it shows God's ultimate freedom. God is not bound by our conceptions of God. Instead, God is free to change, to alter the divine practice. This verse, and Moses' prayer in Exodus 34:9, show that God exhibits more grace than is expected or warranted because humankind can survive by no other means.

When Moses prays for Israel in Exodus 34:9 he seems to assume not only the graciousness of God described in Exodus 34:6-7 but also the rottenness of Israel (and indeed all humankind) portrayed in Exodus 32. Moses does not place confidence in Israel's turning to God. Rather, he trusts only in God's character. Particularly, he believes that the Lord is "a God merciful and gracious, slow to anger, and abounding in steadfast love and faithfulness" (Exodus 34:6). In Exodus 34:10 God responds to Moses' prayer with a one-sided covenant. God gives and Israel receives. God's action for Israel is typical of the biblical portrait of God's relationship with humankind.

SHARING THE SCRIPTURE

Preparing Our Hearts

Explore this week's devotional reading, found in Acts 3:19-26. From Solomon's Portico at the Temple, Peter preaches, calling the people to "Repent . . . and turn to God so that your sins may be wiped out" (3:19). This restoration with God is possible because God sent Jesus, the Messiah. Spend time examining your own life. What sins need to be confessed so that you may repent? Speak with God about these sins, knowing that God is "merciful and gracious, slow to anger, and abounding in steadfast love and faithfulness" (Exodus 34:6).

Pray that you and the adult learners will come to God with a contrite heart to be forgiven.

Preparing Our Minds

Study the background Scripture from Exodus 34:1-10 and the lesson Scripture from Exodus 34:1, 4-10. Think about to whom we are accountable for actions and what we expect to happen when we err.

Write on newsprint:
❑ information for next week's lesson, found under "Continue the Journey."

❑ activities for further spiritual growth in "Continue the Journey."

Plan the lecture as suggested in "Discover God's Attributes as Revealed to Moses."

LEADING THE CLASS

(1) Gather to Learn ·

❖ Welcome the class members and introduce any guests.

❖ Pray that today's participants will be ready to discover traits of God as revealed to Moses.

❖ Read: **Michael Phelps, winner of an astonishing eight gold medals at the 2008 Summer Olympics in China, was pictured in a British newspaper in 2009 apparently smoking from a bong. Although he did not confess to smoking marijuana, the picture certainly damaged his reputation. Some have suggested that he could lose endorsements, and huge sums of money, because sponsors would not want to be connected to someone who gives the appearance of abusing drugs. Phelps apologized for his "regrettable" behavior. But only time will tell how his relationships with these companies that are paying him big bucks to endorse their products—and with his fans,** who have viewed him as a "squeaky clean" athlete—will be affected.

❖ Ask: **How do you perceive that Michael Phelps's behavior affected his relationship with his fans and with those companies whose products he endorses?**

❖ Read aloud today's focus statement: **People have different ideas about how their behavior affects relationships. To whom are we accountable for our actions, and what do we expect when we err? In the face of Israel's unfaithfulness, God revealed to Moses that God is steadfast, forgiving, and faithful.**

(2) Discover God's Attributes as Revealed to Moses

❖ Recall that as a result of the people's worship of the golden calf, Moses became so angry that he broke the tablets of stone (Exodus 32:19) and commanded that apostates be killed. Three thousand died that day (32:28). God punished the people, but also gave them a second chance, because of God's own nature, which we will become familiar with today.

❖ Choose a volunteer to read Exodus 34:1, 4-10, in which God again appears to Moses.

❖ Note that God proclaimed God's own nature in verses 6-7. These characteristics have come to be known as the Thirteen Attributes, and they are used in prayers leading up to the Jewish Day of Atonement, Yom Kippur. (Refer to www.uscj.org/Koach/documents/Selihot-2004.pdf if you would like more information about these attributes as they are understood in the Jewish community.)

❖ Use information in Exodus 34:1-8 from Understanding the Scripture and portions of Interpreting the Scripture headed "Merciful and Gracious," "Slow to Anger," and "Steadfast Love and Faithfulness" to present a lecture on these important aspects of God's character. List key words on newsprint as you speak.

❖ **Option:** Divide the class into groups of three or four. Distribute Bible dictionaries or other reference books that supply meanings of biblical words. Assign each group one of the following words: *mercy, gracious, anger, steadfast love, faithfulness, forgiveness.* Ask the group to research their assigned word and then provide time for them to report back to the class.

(3) Increase a Sense of Awe for the Nature of God

❖ List on newsprint these references, which reiterate the attributes of God's nature, perhaps with slight variations when compared to Exodus 34:6-7. Allow two or three minutes for the students to read whichever of these passages they choose.
- ■ Numbers 14:18
- ■ Nehemiah 9:17
- ■ Psalms 86:15; 103:8; 145:8
- ■ Jeremiah 32:18
- ■ Joel 2:13
- ■ Jonah 4:2
- ■ Nahum 1:3

❖ Distribute paper and pencils. Provide quiet time for the students to focus on one or two of these attributes that they connect with at this moment in their lives, possibly because of a need or concern they have. Perhaps they long to experience God's steadfast love or mercy or faithfulness in a new and powerful way. Encourage them to write a confidential letter to God about a situation in their lives that cries out for some aspect of God's nature to minister to them.

❖ Allow additional time for the students to just listen for God and be open to any word from the Lord that may come to them. Tell the adults that they will not be asked to share their letter.

(4) Identify and Give Thanks for God's Faithfulness and Forgiveness in the Learners' Lives

❖ Invite the learners to recall instances of God's faithfulness and forgiveness in the

Bible. They need not remember exact chapter and verse but should be able to give a brief summary of the circumstances. After each biblical story is summarized, ask: **Have you as an individual or we as a church ever experienced something similar?** Encourage the students to tell such stories, and then focus on another biblical example.

❖ Wrap up this section of the session by inviting students to give thanks for a specific instance of God's faithfulness or forgiveness. You may go around the room, or simply ask students to call out their words of thanksgiving.

(5) Continue the Journey

❖ Pray this traditional prayer from Mongolia, taken from *The United Methodist Book of Worship*, which echoes themes of God's nature that we have encountered in today's lesson: **O God, that we may receive your blessing, touch our brows, touch our heads, and do not look upon us in anger. In a hard year, offer us mercy; in a year of affliction, offer us kindness; dark spirits banish from us; bright spirits bring close to us; gray spirits put away from us, good spirits draw near to us. When we are afraid, offer us courage; when we are ashamed, be our true face: be over us like a blanket, be under us like a bed of furs. Amen.**

❖ Read aloud this preparation for next week's lesson. You may also want to post it on newsprint for the students to copy.

■ **Title: God's Majesty and Human Dignity**

■ **Background Scripture: Psalm 8**
■ **Lesson Scripture: Psalm 8**
■ **Focus of the Lesson: The wonder, beauty, and majesty of the world amaze us. How can we respond to such grandeur? Psalm 8 declares that Sovereign God sustains creation, but God expects humans to share responsibility for the care of all living things.**

❖ Challenge the students to complete one or more of these activities for further spiritual growth related to this week's session. Post this information on newsprint for the students to copy.

(1) **Offer a word of thanks and praise to God in the midst of a difficult situation this week.**

(2) **Share Exodus 34:6-7 in your own words as a statement to others of who God is. Continue sharing by giving examples of how you have experienced God's nature in your own life.**

(3) **Recall that Moses had a very personal interaction with God. When have you clearly felt God's presence? Give thanks for the love that God has shown to you.**

❖ Sing or read aloud "There's a Wideness in God's Mercy."

❖ Conclude today's session by leading the class in this commission: **We go forth to worship and serve the Lord our God. Thanks be to our merciful and gracious God.**

UNIT 2: GOD SUSTAINS

GOD'S MAJESTY AND HUMAN DIGNITY

PREVIEWING THE LESSON

Lesson Scripture: Psalm 8
Background Scripture: Psalm 8
Key Verse: Psalm 8:6

Focus of the Lesson:
The wonder, beauty, and majesty of the world amaze us. How can we respond to such grandeur? Psalm 8 declares that Sovereign God sustains creation, but God expects humans to share responsibility for the care of all living things.

Goals for the Learners:
(1) to introduce the concept that human dignity finds its meaning in God's majesty.
(2) to recognize and appreciate God's sustaining role as sovereign.
(3) to identify and act on their roles as participants in God's creation.

Pronunciation Guide:
adamah (ad aw maw')   *ben adam* (bane aw dawm')
elohim (el o heem')

Supplies:
Bibles, newsprint and marker, paper and pencils, hymnals, pictures from space

---

READING THE SCRIPTURE

NRSV
Psalm 8
1 O LORD, our Sovereign,
    how majestic is your name in
      all the earth!
  You have set your glory above
    the heavens.
2   Out of the mouths of babes and infants
you have founded a bulwark

NIV
Psalm 8
1O LORD, our Lord,
    how majestic is your name in all the
      earth!
  You have set your glory
    above the heavens.
2From the lips of children and infants
    you have ordained praise

because of your foes,
    to silence the enemy and the avenger.
3 When I look at your heavens,
        the work of your fingers,
    the moon and the stars that
        you have established;
4 what are human beings that you
        are mindful of them,
    mortals that you care for them?
5 Yet you have made them a little
        lower than God,
    and crowned them with glory and
        honor.
6 **You have given them dominion
        over the works of your hands;
    you have put all things under
        their feet,**
7 all sheep and oxen,
        and also the beasts of the field,
8 the birds of the air, and the fish
        of the sea,
    whatever passes along the
        paths of the seas.
9 O LORD, our Sovereign,
        how majestic is your name in
        all the earth!

because of your enemies,
    to silence the foe and the avenger.
3When I consider your heavens,
        the work of your fingers,
    the moon and the stars,
        which you have set in place,
4what is man that you are mindful of him,
    the son of man that you care for him?
5You made him a little lower than the
        heavenly beings
    and crowned him with glory and honor.
6**You made him ruler over the works of
        your hands;
    you put everything under his feet:**
7all flocks and herds,
        and the beasts of the field,
8the birds of the air,
    and the fish of the sea,
    all that swim the paths of the seas.
9O LORD, our Lord,
        how majestic is your name in all
        the earth!

UNDERSTANDING THE SCRIPTURE

Introduction. Psalm 8 is a hymn of praise. There are many examples of this type of psalm in the Book of Psalms (for example, Psalms 67, 100, 145–150). But Psalm 8 is unique in at least two ways. First, it is the first hymn of praise one encounters when reading the Psalms straight through. The psalms that immediately precede it are prayers spoken by people who are suffering or who are persecuted (Psalms 3–7). Psalm 8 reveals that those suffering at the hands of evil forces are those made in the image of God and valued highly by their Creator. Indeed, the psalm proclaims that humans are God's agents on earth. Second, this psalm is the only hymn in the Psalter spoken entirely to God. It emphasizes God's sovereignty (8:1,

9) and proclaims that humans exercise their legitimate authority within the rule of God.

Psalm 8:1a. The first half of verse 1 and verse 9 are identical. They give structure to the psalm and draw attention to the majesty and sovereignty of God. The opening of the psalm seems to express what was promised at the end of Psalm 7, "I will . . . sing praise to the name of the LORD" (7:17). "Name" refers to God's essence and character. Psalm 8:1a and 9 declare that the whole created order gives evidence of God's sovereignty. It is not that the psalmist admires elements of creation as though God is *in* them. Rather, the psalmist wonders at the natural world because of the majesty of God who stands over them and has put them in place.

Psalm 8:1b-2. Perhaps the greatest difficulty in interpreting Psalm 8 is the question of how verse 1b relates to verse 2. This second section of the psalm seems to expound on verse 1a, but what exactly does it intend to say? The expression, "You have set your glory above the heavens" (8:1b), probably indicates that God is sovereign and thus sits as king over the creation. From above God subdued chaos and made the world with order and regularity. Verse 2 is an exaggerated statement that further makes the point. Even the weakest creatures ("babes and infants") give voice to the power of God that overcomes all forces that would thwart God's will. The "enemy" and "avenger" here most likely refer to the chaotic forces God overcame when creating the world (see Genesis 1:1–2:4). Psalm 24:1-2, which also affirms the sovereignty of God, contains another description of God's defeat of chaos that may help understand what is being said here.

Psalm 8:3-4. This section begins to focus on human beings and their place within the created order. But as it does the psalmist presents the high place of humans in creation as a marvel in the face of the magnificence of the rest of God's work. The question, "What are human beings?" has two important features that are keys to the meaning of the psalm. First, the word "human" translates the Hebrew expression *ben adam* ("son of man"). *Adam* is closely related to the word for earth or soil (*adamah*; "dust of the ground," Genesis 2:7). "Son of man" therefore connotes humanity's finitude and fallibility. The human is from the earth, not from the heavens. Second, it is important to note that the question ("What are human beings?") is not an abstract query about the nature and identity of humankind. Rather, the question puts the human in relation to God's greatness: "What are humans . . . that you would pay attention to them?" Hence, although the answer to the question is quite positive in

Psalm 8, the same question appears in Psalm 144:3-4 and Job 7:17; 15:14 in a way that casts negative light on humanity.

Psalm 8:5-8. Despite the lowliness of humans before God, verse 5 declares God made humans "a little lower than God." The word for God, however, is a general word (*elohim*) that may be translated "angels" or "gods." Only context can determine if the word refers to the one God, to the attendants around God's throne, or to the gods of the nations. In Psalm 8 it is impossible to tell the exact intention. The point, however, is not so much the identity of *elohim*, but the difference between the heavenly and earthly realms. God put humans in charge of the earth. The dominion of humans extends to all living creatures. Here they are classified as domestic and wild, birds and fish.

The portrait of humans in this section is much like the one in Genesis 1:1–2:4. The image of God bestowed on humans in Genesis 1:26-28 is defined by human dominion. So also Psalm 8 describes the unique place of humans in terms of the human place over other creatures.

The language of Psalm 8:5-8 suggests humans are royal creatures. In Egypt pharaoh was described as the "son of God," as one who represented the deity on earth. In other parts of the Old Testament the Israelite king is described in similar ways. Second Samuel 7 calls David God's son when God appoints him to his office (7:14). Psalm 89:26 presents David as the earthly representative of God's reign from heaven. Psalm 8, like Genesis 1:1–2:4, seems to present all humans in the royal office. This may be due in part to the fact that kingship came to an end in Israel in 587 B.C. When that occurred the royal office once reserved for the king was transferred to humankind as a whole. "Glory and honor" are words used to describe monarchs, but here they describe all human beings.

Psalm 8:9. The final verse contains the same words as the first line of the psalm (8:1a). But the repetition of these words adds emphasis and says something that the first occurrence of these words alone does not say. By repeating the words at the end the whole psalm is given a structure that calls attention to God's sovereignty. Just as God's majesty begins and ends the psalm, so also it creates the context for human glory.

INTERPRETING THE SCRIPTURE

God as Lord Over Creation

In light of Psalm 8, how should we view and experience the natural world? What should the sight of a beautiful landscape do for us spiritually? A casual reading of Psalm 8 might give the impression that the psalmist here glorifies nature and encourages us to do the same. The psalm seems to present the elements of the natural world as embodiments of God's presence. But this is not what the psalm says. Rather, the psalm declares that God is "above" (8:1b) the creation that God "established" (8:3). The distinction is important theologically. The point of the psalm's focus on the natural world is that the magnificence of the creation gives evidence of the might of the Creator. Creation provides such a testimony mainly because its vast dimensions give perspective on the power of God.

We should be aware that the features of the universe that so inspired the psalmist may not strike us the same way. The psalmist assumes God is literally enthroned in the heavens, above the vault that was thought to separate heaven and earth (God's "glory" is above the heavens; 8:1). For us the heavens are not as mysterious because we have adopted a scientific worldview. The majesty of God has not diminished. But we may have to struggle to appreciate mystery. One of our inherent failings is precisely that we have lost the capacity to wonder at creation. To regain it does not mean we must close our eyes to scientific knowledge. Rather, it requires us to imagine the God who transcends all that can be known through scientific inquiry. Moreover, we may be tempted to assume humankind's privileged place in the world rather than to marvel at it as the psalmist did. Psalm 8 should prod us to seek humility, to remember how small we are in the scheme of things.

Human Dominion and Stewardship of the Earth

Psalm 8 has the distinction of being the only biblical text to reach the moon! When the Apollo 11 mission began, numerous countries including the Vatican conversed about making a theological statement on the occasion. They selected this passage to be placed in a cylinder that would go with the astronauts and be placed on the moon's surface. But what statement does this psalm make about the space mission?

Certainly the placement of Psalm 8 on the moon made an appropriate statement about the place of humans in the created order. That God endowed us with a unique place is seen in human capability and creativity that produced such a technological feat. But the message is not wholly positive. Psalm 8 does not highlight the human's place in creation just to make a statement about human dominion. Instead, it mainly says something about human responsibility. This is implicit in the royal language used to describe the human race in the psalm. As those made "a little lower than God" and given dominion in the earthly realm, humans are to be God's agents. Their task is to care for and oversee the good creation. In other words, human dominion is to be a project of stewardship. But humans have turned dominion into domination. The many ecological challenges we have created for ourselves certainly illustrate that fact.

It is important to recognize that Psalm 8 has been misused when read mainly as a statement of human power and capability. Some environmentalists have criticized the Christian faith and the Bible for promoting the kind of arrogance toward the natural world that led to the current ecological crisis. They charge that the very notion of human dominion has led to abuse. But a more helpful picture is that texts like Psalm 8 intend to help us see our responsibility for the creation. Part of our fallen state is that we tend to take the good that God has given us (human dominion) and use it as though it is inherent to humanity. Human sovereignty is derived from God and is set within the limits of God's sovereignty. We often treat human dominion, however, as though it has no bounds. When that occurs, human dominion is turned into human autonomy. In this case, we would do well to remember that our dominion is set within God's overarching care for the creation (8:1, 9). Psalm 8 makes this abundantly clear. It does not present humankind as inherently superior to other creatures. Rather, it describes the high place of humans as a marvel in light of God's majesty. In other words, the psalm should call all people to humility, to recognize their place as caretakers of the earth as a sign of God's grace.

The Image of God and Human Suffering

As noted in Understanding the Scripture, Psalm 8:5-8 presents humankind just as Genesis 1:26-28 did, as those created in the image of God. This may seem to enhance the idea that humans are sovereign creatures. In one sense it does communicate that idea. Humans rule over a portion of the world just as God rules over all. But the image of God also entails suffering. Scripture frequently portrays God suffering for and with God's creation. It should not be a surprise that humans suffer also as they partner with God and take on responsibility for the earth.

Job especially wrestles with the idea that humans suffer in their royal office. In Job 7:17 Job quotes Psalm 8:4-5 when he questions the place of humankind in the created order. How can it be that humans are appointed guardians of the earth when they suffer so miserably? Job seems to deny the truth of Psalm 8 concerning humanity's royal status. But by the end of the book Job seems to reclaim this truth. He says, "I despise myself, and repent in dust and ashes" (Job 42:6). "Dust and ashes" refers to human weakness and vulnerability. Job seems to realize that human beings in their role as God's agents experience both glory and suffering, just as God does. In the end Job embraces the view of humankind in Psalm 8.

Human Dominion and Jesus Christ

The New Testament interprets Psalm 8 in light of the experience of God in Jesus Christ. Specifically, Hebrews says we know what human dominion is intended to be by looking at the ministry of Jesus. Hebrews 2:6-8 quotes the Greek version of Psalm 8:4-6 (our translations of the Psalms are based on the Hebrew so the quote in Hebrews 2:6-8 reads differently than the passage in the Book of Psalms). The Greek version reads "lower than the angels" rather than the ambiguous "lower than *elohim* ("God," "gods," or "angels")" in Hebrew. Hence, the writer of Hebrews uses the language in the Greek version to continue an argument begun in Hebrews 1: Jesus is greater than the angels. In making this point, however, the writer emphasizes that Jesus is one of us. Concerning human dominion ("subjecting all things under their feet;" Hebrews

2:8), Hebrews says "we do not yet see everything in subjection to them, but we do see Jesus" (2:9). Here Hebrews draws out the true meaning of humanity's royal office. Jesus sets the example for us for what it means to have dominion over the earth. Jesus rules as a suffering servant (Philippians 2:5-11). Hence, human dominion is defined as service and inevitably leads to pain and suffering.

SHARING THE SCRIPTURE

Preparing Our Hearts

Explore this week's devotional reading, found in Genesis 1:26-31. In this familiar passage we read about God's decision to make humankind in God's own image and entrust them with "dominion" over the rest of the creatures of the earth. How do you understand "dominion"? What does it mean to be a steward or caregiver of the earth? Plan to do something this week to protect and care for God's good earth.

Pray that you and the adult learners will be willing to assume greater responsibility for God's creation.

Preparing Our Minds

Study the background Scripture and the lesson Scripture, both from Psalm 8. Consider how we can respond to the wonder, beauty, and majesty of the world.

Write on newsprint:
- ❏ prayer of Saint Francis for "Continue the Journey," if you choose to have the class read in unison.
- ❏ information for next week's lesson, found under "Continue the Journey."
- ❏ activities for further spiritual growth in "Continue the Journey."

Go to http://hubblesite.org/gallery/album to download and print (preferably in color) several pictures taken by the Hubble telescope, or one of the PowerPoint presentations of selected Hubble pictures. You may wish to contact a computer savvy student to do this task. As an alternative, find pictures from space in books, or use pictures depicting nature here on earth.

Prepare to read aloud Psalm 8.

LEADING THE CLASS

(1) Gather to Learn

❖ Welcome the class members and introduce any guests.

❖ Pray that all who have come today will recognize the dignity of each human being.

❖ Show whatever pictures from space that you have been able to locate. Hold up or pass around the pictures. Invite the students to call out words to describe their emotional response to these pictures.

❖ Read aloud today's focus statement: **The wonder, beauty, and majesty of the world amaze us. How can we respond to such grandeur? Psalm 8 declares that Sovereign God sustains creation, but God expects humans to share responsibility for the care of all living things.**

(2) Introduce the Concept that Human Dignity Finds Its Meaning in God's Majesty

❖ Read aloud Psalm 8 expressively. If possible, post several pictures from the Gather to Learn segment where they may be seen as you read.

❖ Discuss these questions:
(1) What does the psalmist believe about God, to whom this psalm is addressed?

(2) What does the psalmist believe about the worth of human beings? (Psalm 8:3-4 and 5-8 in Understanding the Scripture will be helpful in explaining the relationship between humans and God.)

(3) What does the psalmist understand the role of humans to be? (Psalm 8:5-8 in Understanding the Scripture considers God's intention for humanity. "Human Dominion and Jesus Christ" in Interpreting the Scripture includes information that you may wish to bring into the discussion.)

❖ Read this sentence from "God as Lord Over Creation" in Interpreting the Scripture: **The point of the psalm's focus on the natural world is that the magnificence of the creation gives evidence of the might of the Creator.**

❖ Ask these questions:

(1) Where in the natural world do you find evidence of the Creator?

(2) What does this evidence suggest to you about the Creator?

(3) What response will you make to the Creator?

(3) Recognize and Appreciate God's Sustaining Role as Sovereign

❖ Note that Psalm 8 sings praise to our God as Sovereign and Creator.

❖ Enlist several volunteers to debate this statement: **Given that humans have trampled the dignity of other humans and made such a mess of the earth that a sustainable future is being called into question, we have to wonder whether God is still in charge.**

❖ Conclude this portion by asking:

(1) What steps might we as individual Christians and as a congregation take to help others recognize that God is Creator and Sovereign?

(2) What difference would it make if all people acknowledged God as the Creator and Sovereign who is capable of sustaining the earth and all who dwell within?

(4) Identify and Act on the Learners' Roles as Participants in God's Creation

❖ Read "Human Dominion and Stewardship of the Earth."

❖ Encourage students to report on criticisms they have heard leveled against Christians in regard to abuses of the earth. Such abusive behavior has roots in a serious misinterpretation of what it means for humans to have dominion.

❖ Lead the students in making a list of ways that they practice environmental stewardship, both as a church and as individuals, particularly by decreasing waste, preventing contamination, and helping the earth to become cleaner. The possibilities are endless, but here are a few to add to the list that you will write on newsprint: *recycling, buying locally, combining trips so as to save gas, using mass transit or walking, eating lower on the food chain, sharing tools/garden implements, avoiding paper plates and cups, using eco-friendly building materials such as bamboo, composting.*

❖ Form groups of three or four. Ask each group to identify an ecological challenge and develop a plan for working to alleviate the problem in their homes and/or at the church. They will want to use ideas they have listed, but may add others. Here are a few ideas for a sample plan to make the class refreshment table more eco-friendly:

■ Ask each class member to bring a reusable beverage cup and small plate. Have a few on hand for visitors.

■ Buy coffee, powdered cream, sugar, and so on in jars rather than individual packets to eliminate waste. Recycle the jars.

■ Use a tablecloth that can be washed or wiped, rather than paper.

■ Bring fruits in season that require no packaging.

■ Buy locally grown or baked food items.

❖ Call the groups together and ask each one to share several ideas.

❖ Challenge the participants to be mindful of how they treat God's good earth. Suggest that they become more conscious about decisions they make as they shop, drive, garden, and deal with waste. Encourage them to share ideas with others.

(5) Continue the Journey

❖ Close with this excerpt from "Prayer of Saint Francis of Assisi for All Created Things." You may wish to read it aloud, or post it on newsprint and ask the class to read in unison.

O most high, omnipotent,
   good Lord God,
to you belong praise, glory, honor,
   and all blessing.
For our brother the sun, who is our day
   and who brings us light,
who is fair, and radiant with a very great
   splendor;
Praised be our Lord.
For our sister the moon and for the stars,
   which you have set clear and lovely in
   heaven. . .
Praise and bless the Lord,
   and give thanks unto God,
   and serve God with great humility
   Amen.

❖ Read aloud this preparation for next week's lesson. You may also want to post it on newsprint for the students to copy.

■ **Title: God's Law Sustains**

■ **Background Scripture: Psalm 19**
■ **Lesson Scripture: Psalm 19:7-14**
■ **Focus of the Lesson: People search for evidence of meaning in the universe. What evidence can satisfy their search? Psalm 19 affirms that God's perfect law protects and sustains creation.**

❖ Challenge the students to complete one or more of these activities for further spiritual growth related to this week's session. Post this information on newsprint for the students to copy.

(1) **Research an environmental issue in your community, such as polluted streams or poor air quality. Let elected officials know what you think needs to be done about the problem. Contact a group that works to alleviate the problem (for example, Clean Water Action) and see what you can do to assist them.**

(2) **Help someone who lacks self-esteem to see himself through the eyes of God, as one created "a little lower than God" (Psalm 8:5).**

(3) **Take a walk this week. Note the wonders of nature. Give thanks to God for the gift of creation.**

❖ Sing or read aloud "For the Beauty of the Earth."

❖ Conclude today's session by leading the class in this commission: **We go forth to worship and serve the Lord our God. Thanks be to our merciful and gracious God.**

UNIT 2: GOD SUSTAINS
GOD'S LAW SUSTAINS

PREVIEWING THE LESSON

Lesson Scripture: Psalm 19:7-14
Background Scripture: Psalm 19
Key Verses: Psalm 19:7-8

Focus of the Lesson:
People search for evidence of meaning in the universe. What evidence can satisfy their search? Psalm 19 affirms that God's perfect law protects and sustains creation.

Goals for the Learners:
(1) to explore how God's law sustains God's creation.
(2) to make a connection between God's law and their place in God's created order.
(3) to show appreciation for God's creation by committing to keep God's laws.

Pronunciation Guide:
Amenhotep (ah muhn hoh' tep)   *torah* (toh' ruh)

Supplies:
Bibles, newsprint and marker, paper and pencils, hymnals

READING THE SCRIPTURE

NRSV
Psalm 19:7-14

7 The law of the LORD is perfect,
   reviving the soul;
the decrees of the LORD are sure,
   making wise the simple;
8 the precepts of the LORD are right,
   rejoicing the heart;
the commandment of the LORD is clear,
   enlightening the eyes;
9 the fear of the LORD is pure,
   enduring forever;
the ordinances of the LORD are true

NIV
Psalm 19:7-14

7 The law of the LORD is perfect,
   reviving the soul.
The statutes of the LORD are trustworthy,
   making wise the simple.
8 The precepts of the LORD are right,
   giving joy to the heart.
The commands of the LORD are radiant,
   giving light to the eyes.
9 The fear of the LORD is pure,
   enduring forever.
The ordinances of the LORD are sure

and righteous altogether.
¹⁰ More to be desired are they than gold,
    even much fine gold;
sweeter also than honey,
    and drippings of the honeycomb.
¹¹ Moreover by them is your
    servant warned;
    in keeping them there is great reward.
¹² But who can detect their errors?
    Clear me from hidden faults.
¹³ Keep back your servant also
    from the insolent;
    do not let them have dominion over me.
Then I shall be blameless,
    and innocent of great transgression.
¹⁴ Let the words of my mouth and
    the meditation of my heart
be acceptable to you,
    O LORD, my rock and my redeemer.

and altogether righteous.
¹⁰They are more precious than gold,
    than much pure gold;
they are sweeter than honey,
    than honey from the comb.
¹¹By them is your servant warned;
    in keeping them there is great reward.
¹²Who can discern his errors?
    Forgive my hidden faults.
¹³Keep your servant also from willful sins;
    may they not rule over me.
Then will I be blameless,
    innocent of great transgression.
¹⁴May the words of my mouth and the
    meditation of my heart
be pleasing in your sight,
    O LORD, my Rock and my Redeemer.

UNDERSTANDING THE SCRIPTURE

Introduction. Psalm 19 is one of three psalms in the Psalter that celebrate God's law (Psalms 1 and 119 are the others). "Law" here translates the Hebrew word *torah* which essentially means "instruction" (see 19:7). Therefore, the psalm is not about adherence to a legal system. Rather, it presents divine law as God's gift and as a sign of God's grace. In fact, torah in this psalm seems to be what orders the world. The regularity of the law is closely linked to the regularity of the sun in its course through the heavens.

The psalm has three main sections: verses 1-6 describe how the glory of God is proclaimed by the elements of the universe. The second section of the psalm (19:7-10) highlights the benefits of torah. This portion of the poem has often been treated as separate from the first, with the two parts supposedly put together artificially. It is certainly possible that the two sections did not originate from the same author, but they have been placed together here to highlight an important feature of God's law. Namely,

torah has power like that of the sun and it gives witness to God's sovereignty just as the elements of creation do. The final section of the psalm (19:11-14) is essentially a plea for forgiveness. The psalmist recognizes it is impossible to abide by God's law (19:11-13) and thus he or she prays that the words of the psalm that express trust in God will be acceptable (19:14).

Psalm 19:1-6. This section presents the elements of the created world giving witness to the greatness of God. The natural features of the creation do not speak. They nevertheless give testimony to God's creative power by means of their regularity and order.

Psalm 19:1-6 assumes an understanding of the universe that is quite different from our own in some respects. It gives special attention to four elements of the creation. The "heavens" refers generally to the area above the earth. This is where God sits enthroned over the world (see Psalm 115:3, 16). The dividing point between heaven and earth is the "firmament." This word refers to the vault or dome that ancient Near Eastern people imagined to be set above the earth. Genesis 1:6-8 portrays God's creation of the firmament and the purpose for which it was made. Namely, the vault of heaven was to separate the waters on earth from the waters "above the dome" (1:7). This reflects the ancient belief that a water source existed in the heavens that supplied rain. The specific notion of a heavenly sea held back by the firmament may derive from the appearance of the sky. On a clear day it is blue and seems dome-like. Psalm 104:3 describes God anchoring the heavenly temple in this sea above the firmament ("you set the beams of your chambers on the waters").

The divisions of time (day and night) mentioned in Psalm 19:2 are also part of creation that give witness to God's power. The mention of the separation of day and night begins to clarify how and why the creation testifies to the Creator's might. Namely, it shows an order and regularity that reveals God's control.

The sun is highlighted as the special manifestation of God's greatness (19:4-6). The sun's circuit over the earth probably represents the perfect justice of God. The expression "nothing is hid from its heat" (19:6) may communicate the idea that God's justice sees all things and, eventually, will correct all things.

The sun is presented as a bridegroom who leaves his tent anticipating his marriage. Such is the joy of the sun running its course. Note that Psalm 104:2 compares the heavens to a tent stretched out over the earth. In Psalm 19 the image is different. The tent refers to the place on the horizon from which the sun emerges to cross the sky.

Psalm 19:7-10. The second section focuses on the benefits of torah. Four synonyms for torah appear here that also occur in Psalm 119: decrees, precepts, commandment, ordinances. The fact that these terms appear alongside the expression, "fear of the LORD," indicates that the words are not primarily legal terms. Rather, they are signs of God's goodness and aid the believer in faith (the meaning of "fear of the LORD").

The repetition of the synonyms for "torah" communicate the idea that God's law is all-encompassing. It affects everything and pertains to everything. Most importantly, torah is the essential necessity of life. It enlightens (19:8) and gives life anew (19:7). The descriptions of torah's benefits in this section in fact seem to compare torah to the tree of the knowledge of good and evil that was located in the garden of Eden (Genesis 3:2-7). Furthermore, the moral benefits of torah are described with language reminiscent of the sun's regularity that appeared in verses 1-6 ("perfect" in 19:7; "true" or better "reliable" in 19:9). This parallel between the sun and torah is the key to the unity of Psalm 19.

Psalm 19:11-14. The final section of Psalm 19 turns attention away from the praise of torah and toward the human inability to abide by it. As verse 12a indicates, humans will always have errors they cannot even see themselves. Therefore, verse 12b pleads to God for forgiveness of "hidden faults." The plea to be free from the "insolent" could mean free from proud thoughts or "willful sins" (as the New International Version translates). Or, this verse could be a prayer to be free of the influence of those who would lead the psalmist to disobedience (as the New Revised Standard Version takes it). Either way, the whole section is a call for God's protection from the sins that would govern the psalmist's life.

The final verse of the psalm reinforces the request for God's grace. God is called "rock," a term that expresses dependence on God (see the appearance of this term with words like "refuge" and "fortress" in Psalm 18:2). God is also called "redeemer." A redeemer in Israelite society was one who rescued weak and impoverished members of his family (Ruth 4:1, 3). By God's grace the psalmist's words are brought into harmony with the elements of the universe that declare God's glory (19:1-6).

INTERPRETING THE SCRIPTURE

How Is Torah "Perfect"?

What does Psalm 19:7 mean when it says that "the law of the LORD is perfect?" Perfection is not something most Christians have learned to associate with the law. But we must keep in mind that Psalm 19 does not say humans can be perfect or that torah can lead to perfection. Rather, torah itself is perfect. Since torah is God's instruction and not simply legal stipulations, this makes sense. But to understand torah's perfection we must read Psalm 19:7-10 together with Psalm 19:1-6.

The first part of Psalm 19 celebrates what we might call the natural world. It seems to suggest that the natural world reveals something about God. Indeed, as verse 1 says, "The heavens are telling the glory of God; and the firmament proclaims his handiwork." What the creation reveals mainly is that God is in control. The order and regularity of the elements of the universe indicate that God has authority over chaos. Thus, these elements proclaim God's sovereignty. Psalm 19:7-10 then suggests, by comparison, that torah is similarly reliable. But it does more than simply "proclaim his handiwork." Torah presents specifically the way humans should go, the way they should live, the way they should order life in relation to God and each other. The fact that we cannot respond perfectly does not diminish the truth that God has given us a gift in torah. It should be the object of our meditation, the source of truth in our lives. Such attention to God's instruction does not mean we seek perfection. Rather, we express our faith in God's forgiveness by meditating on it.

Torah as Source of Life and Justice

Torah in verses 7-10 is related specifically to truth and justice. Here too the message about torah must be understood through the relationship between these verses and the first part of the psalm. Verses 4-6 highlight the sun's regularity. The reason the sun receives attention here as an analogy to torah is probably that the sun in the ancient Near East was associated with justice.

This association between the sun and justice is particularly apparent in sources from ancient Egypt. Some Egyptian artwork during the fourteenth century B.C. (during the reign of Amenhotep IV, 1353–1336 B.C.) depicts the rays of the sun each ending in a hand that drops ankh signs (symbols of life) onto the royal family. The implication of this picture seems to be that the rulers were sources of life and justice for their people. They received such power from the sun. Of course, ancient Egyptians thought the sun was a deity. It was the direct source of truth and thus helped Pharaoh to rule justly. Psalm 19 does not believe any such thing. Rather, it uses the well-known idea about the sun to create a message about torah. The commonly held notions about the sun are transferred in Psalm 19:7-10 to God's instruction.

Torah and Human Rule

Given the idea that torah promotes justice, it is not surprising that torah in the Psalms is closely associated with the king. As just noted, ancient Egyptians imagined their rulers to be especially blessed and directed by the rays of the sun. In the Psalter the king is directed by torah.

It is probably not accidental that all three psalms that focus on torah (Psalms 1, 19, and 119) appear next to a psalm about kingship (Psalms 2, 18, and 118). This pairing seems to communicate the idea that the human ruler (the Israelite king, or a king to come in the future) stands under the authority of God's law and that God's law will be known in the coming of God's future king. The pairing of Psalms 18 and 19 shows this relationship particularly well. Psalm 18 is presented as a psalm of David just as he became king (see the title which set the psalm "when the LORD delivered him from the hand of all his enemies, and from the hand of Saul"). At two points in Psalm 18 the psalmist makes statements much like those in Psalm 19:7-14. In Psalm 18:22-23 he says, "For all his ordinances were before me, and his statutes I did not put away from me. I was blameless before him, and I kept myself from guilt." In other words, the king here professes that he has meditated on torah and through such dependence on God has been found "blameless" (see Psalm 19:13). In Psalm 18:30 the king says, "This God—his way is perfect; the promise of the LORD proves true; he is a shield for all who take refuge in him." Here the king speaks of God with language that describes God's torah in Psalm 19:7-10 ("perfect" and "true"). The point of these verses in Psalm 18 and of the pairing of Psalms 18 and 19 seems to be that the Israelite king is to be guided by and stand under the authority of divine instruction.

Deuteronomy 17:14-20 makes explicit the association of the king with torah. It declares that the king is to have a copy of the law of Moses always before him. Moreover, he is to read it always "that he may learn to fear the LORD" (Deuteronomy 17:19). This is a remarkable passage for people ruled by a king. It says essentially that the king is not the highest authority. Torah is. Psalm 19, by its pairing with Psalm 18, seems to proclaim a similar message. But this message does not just apply to rulers. Indeed, it should say to us that we also are to be guided by God's instruction. We do not rule our own lives. We must be ruled by God.

Law, Faith, and the Forgiveness of Sins

The concluding verses of Psalm 19 should dispel any notion that the Old Testament advocates works righteousness. Indeed, some Christians may think this psalm contradicts Paul's argument for righteousness through grace, apart from the law (Romans 3). But a closer reading of Psalm 19:11-14 reveals something quite different. In fact, Psalm 19:11-14 argues for salvation by faith as profoundly as any passage in the New Testament. Verse 11 says torah "warns" the believer and that there is great reward in obeying it. The word for "warn" appears in Ezekiel 3:15-21 when the prophet is commissioned as a watchman to alert Israel to its sinfulness. It is also much like Paul's characterization of the law as a disciplinarian that makes us aware of our sin (Galatians 3:23-24). But Psalm 19 makes clear that complete obedience to God's commands is impossible. The psalmist prays for God's help and forgiveness (19:12-13) and declares "*then* I shall be blameless" (19:13, italics added). The psalmist's assurance that he or she can be "blameless" and "innocent" (19:13) can only be because of God's grace. The word for "innocent" in fact comes from the same root as the word "forgive" (NIV) in verse 12. The psalmist is only innocent because God declares the psalmist innocent.

The final verse of Psalm 19 reinforces the idea that salvation comes through faith. The psalmist asks for his or her words and meditations to be "acceptable." This term in other texts refers to sacrifices that are properly offered for the forgiveness of sins (see for example Leviticus 1:4). The psalmist's prayer, therefore, is presented as such an offering. This characterization of the psalm's prayer does not deny the importance of sacrifices. It affirms, however, that animal sacrifices are external expressions of the desire for reconciliation with God. The psalmist in Psalm 19:14 puts forward his or her prayer for forgiveness like a sacrifice.

SHARING THE SCRIPTURE

Preparing Our Hearts

Explore this week's devotional reading, found in 1 Chronicles 22:7-13. In speaking with his son Solomon about building a house for the Lord, David says, "may the LORD grant you discretion and understanding, so that when he gives you charge over Israel you may keep the law of the LORD your God" (22:12). In the next verse David links prosperity to obedience of the law. Christians often view the law in a negative light, but that is clearly not how the people of Israel viewed it. What light does David's admonition shed on the importance of the law? What role does the law play in your life?

Pray that you and the adult learners will recognize God's laws as a sustaining force in your lives.

Preparing Our Minds

Study the background Scripture from Psalm 19 and the lesson Scripture from Psalm 19:7-14. Consider the question: What evidence can satisfy people's search for meaning in the universe?

Write on newsprint:

❏ information for next week's lesson, found under "Continue the Journey."

❏ activities for further spiritual growth in "Continue the Journey."

LEADING THE CLASS

(1) Gather to Learn

❖ Welcome the class members and introduce any guests.

❖ Pray that all who have come will open their hearts and minds to the Scripture we will study today.

❖ Divide the class and assign one of these questions to each group:

(1) **What laws protect the people of our community, state, and nation?**

(2) **What laws are designed to protect creation?**

❖ Bring the groups together to hear several laws that each group identified. (Note that some students will take issue, and possibly rightly so, with certain laws, but do not let the discussion become mired in disputes about the helpfulness of these laws.)

❖ Read aloud today's focus statement: **People search for evidence of meaning in the universe. What evidence can satisfy their search? Psalm 19 affirms that God's perfect law protects and sustains creation.**

(2) Explore How God's Law Sustains God's Creation

❖ Read information from the Introduction and Psalm 19:1-6 in Understanding the Scripture to set the stage for today's study.

❖ Choose three readers: one to read Psalm 19:7-10; another, Psalm 19:11-13; and a third, Psalm 19:14.

❖ Ask: **How are we to understand the claim in verse 7 that "the law of the LORD is perfect"?** Allow the class some time to discuss this question and then read or retell "How Is Torah 'Perfect'?" from Interpreting the Scripture.

❖ Read again these words: **Torah presents specifically the way humans should go, the way they should live, the way they should order life in relation to God and each other.**

❖ Point out that although torah is often denigrated by Christians as "legalistic," torah is actually a gift of grace that teaches us as to how we are to live, according to God's instructions. Invite the students to call out some of God's laws that they believe sustain them.

❖ Read the last paragraph of "Torah and Human Rule" in Interpreting the Scripture. Raise these questions:

(1) How can we, who live in a secular society that includes people of many cultures and religions, promote laws for the common good that might be accepted by a wide spectrum of people?

(2) Specifically, which of God's laws might be applied and accepted by most people? Make a list of these laws on newsprint. (Note that many people would likely accept the Ten Commandments, though these are regularly broken. Most people would not, however, accept dietary laws and laws about offering sacrifices, as discussed in Leviticus.)

(3) Make a Connection Between God's Law and the Learners' Place in God's Created Order

❖ Distribute paper and pencils. Ask the students to put a dot in the center of their paper to represent themselves. Next, have them place four to six dots in a circle around the center dot. From the center dot, draw a line to each of the dots on the outer ring. On each line write a connection between the learner and God's law. For example, on one line they may write about what Jesus identified as the second great commandment: "Loving my neighbor enables me to be connected to another child of God." On another line they may write: "Keeping the sabbath allows me time to rest and recharge my batteries."

❖ Invite volunteers to read some of their ideas. Take note of how many different laws they included.

❖ Wrap up this portion of the session by asking: **If people begin to recognize that God's law sustains them, do you think they would be more likely to meditate on and learn these laws? Explain your answer.**

(4) Show Appreciation for God's Creation by Committing to Keep God's Laws

❖ Read or retell "Law, Faith, and the Forgiveness of Sin" in Interpreting the

Scripture to help the adults understand the relationship between God's laws, their obedience, and opportunities for forgiveness when we err.

❖ Provide quiet time for the students to meditate on Psalm 19:11-14 and ponder these questions:

(1) What are the "hidden faults" that I need to ask God to "clear" in my life?

(2) What changes do I need to make to live more faithfully by God's laws?

❖ Conclude this section by inviting those adults who wish to commit themselves to living more faithfully by God's laws to read in unison Psalm 19:14.

(5) Continue the Journey

❖ Offer this excerpt from a Jewish blessing for the learning of Torah: **Blessed art Thou, LORD our God, King of the universe, who has sanctified us with His commandments and commanded us to engross ourselves with the words of Torah. . . . May the LORD bless you and keep watch over you; May the LORD make His Presence enlighten you, and may He be kind to you; May the LORD bestow favor on you, and grant you peace.**

❖ Read aloud this preparation for next week's lesson. You may also want to post it on newsprint for the students to copy.

■ **Title: God Provides Refuge**

■ **Background Scripture: Psalm 46**

■ **Lesson Scripture: Psalm 46:1-7**

■ **Focus of the Lesson: Troubles that sometimes beset us demand abilities and resources beyond what we possess. Where can we turn for deliverance? The psalmist tells us that God is our refuge and strength, a tested help in times of trouble.**

❖ Challenge the students to complete one or more of these activities for further spiritual growth related to this week's session. Post this information on newsprint for the students to copy.

(1) Research local and state laws designed to protect the environment. Are there gaps? What can you do to help give greater protection to God's creation?

(2) Support the repeal of laws that you believe are not fairly enforced and/or are unjust. Contact legislators and groups working on the issue you have identified to make a difference.

(3) Read Psalm 19 aloud several times this week. As you read, ask God to make you aware of those "hidden faults" so that you may repent and receive forgiveness.

❖ Sing or read aloud "Cantemos al Señor (Let's Sing unto the Lord)," which is based on Psalm 19.

❖ Conclude today's session by leading the class in this commission: **We go forth to worship and serve the Lord our God. Thanks be to our merciful and gracious God.**

UNIT 2: GOD SUSTAINS

GOD PROVIDES REFUGE

PREVIEWING THE LESSON

Lesson Scripture: Psalm 46:1-7
Background Scripture: Psalm 46
Key Verse: Psalm 46:1

Focus of the Lesson:
Troubles that sometimes beset us demand abilities and resources beyond what we possess. Where can we turn for deliverance? The psalmist tells us that God is our refuge and strength, a tested help in times of trouble.

Goals for the Learners:
(1) to study God's acts of comfort and protection.
(2) to reflect on personal gratitude to God for being a refuge in times of trouble.
(3) to develop habits and practices that acknowledge God's presence and reaffirm their reliance on God.

Pronunciation Guide:
Ahaz (ay' haz)   *Selah* (see' luh)
Tyre (tire)

Supplies:
Bibles, newsprint and marker, paper and pencils, hymnals

READING THE SCRIPTURE

NRSV
Psalm 46:1-7

¹ **God is our refuge and strength,**
  a very present help in trouble.
² Therefore we will not fear,
    though the earth should change,
    though the mountains shake in
    the heart of the sea;
³ though its waters roar and foam,
    though the mountains tremble
    with its tumult.   *Selah*

NIV
Psalm 46:1-7

¹**God is our refuge and strength,**
  an ever-present help in trouble.
²Therefore we will not fear, though the
    earth give way
    and the mountains fall into the heart of
    the sea,
³though its waters roar and foam
    and the mountains quake with their
    surging.   *Selah*

4 There is a river whose streams
    make glad the city of God,
      the holy habitation of the Most High.
5 God is in the midst of the city;
    it shall not be moved;
    God will help it when the
      morning dawns.
6 The nations are in an uproar, the
    kingdoms totter;
    he utters his voice, the earth melts.
7 The LORD of hosts is with us;
    the God of Jacob is our refuge.   *Selah*

4There is a river whose streams make glad
    the city of God,
    the holy place where the Most High
      dwells.
5God is within her, she will not fall;
    God will help her at break of day.
6Nations are in uproar, kingdoms fall;
    he lifts his voice, the earth melts.
7The LORD Almighty is with us;
    the God of Jacob is our fortress.   *Selah*

UNDERSTANDING THE SCRIPTURE

Introduction. Psalm 46 is a hymn that praises God. It focuses its praise, however, on the knowledge of God gained on Mount Zion. This attention to Zion puts Psalm 46 in a category with several other psalms (particularly Psalms 48, 76, 84, 121, 127, 132) that have a similar interest in this locale.

Psalm 46:1-3. Psalm 46 opens with a confession of faith that contains language common in the Book of Psalms: "God is our refuge and strength" (46:1). A similar line appears in verses 7 and 11, thus framing the entire psalm with this language ("the God of Jacob is our refuge").

After the declaration of God's refuge in verse 1, the psalm confesses trust in God ("we will not fear") and describes a worst-case scenario in which that trust will remain. Verses 2-3 seem to describe an earthquake or similar natural catastrophe. Although these verses may have been inspired by such an event, what the psalmist depicts here is even worse. Ancient Near Eastern people believed the earth was a flat disc with water below it, around, and above it. The water above was held back by a firmament or dome in the heavens (see Genesis 1:6-8). The water around and below the earth had boundaries it would not cross, or so the people hoped. The key to the security of the earth was the mountains.

Mountains were thought to anchor the earth in the primeval sea (the water below). They were also thought to hold up the sky above. So, the prospect of the mountains shaking "in the heart of the sea" was a scary thought indeed. If the mountains failed to hold their position the chaotic waters would overwhelm the earth and human life would end. It is this threat of the reversal of creation, not unlike that described in the flood narrative in Genesis 6-9, that Psalm 46:2-3 has in view. But the psalm declares that God will be "with us" even if the order of the world collapses.

Psalm 46:4-6. Psalm 46:4-6 describes Mount Zion as a paradise in which water now becomes a source of life, not destruction. Recall that Genesis 2:10-14 portrays the garden of Eden as a source of water, with a stream that has four branches. It is no accident that Ezekiel 47:1-12 uses this same image and identifies paradise with God's holy mountain.

Verse 5 declares, "God is in the midst of the city; it shall not be moved." Zion is the symbol of God's creative work, of God's establishment of order at the beginning of time, and of God's continued maintenance of God's promise to keep the earth secure for humankind (Genesis 9:15). Verse 6 puts the fears of God's people in historical terms:

"the nations are in an uproar." But just as God pushed back chaos at the beginning of time, so also God subdues the nations and causes them to yield to the divine will.

Psalm 46:7, 11. Verses 7 and 11 include another expression that in Hebrew sounds like the words of verse 1: "the LORD of hosts is with us." "With us" in Hebrew (*immanu*) sounds like the word translated "our" (a word that literally reads, "for us;" Hebrew *lanu*). The structure provided by verses 1, 7, and 11 suggests that the overarching message of Psalm 46 is the presence of God with God's people. It is important to note, further, that the expression "the God of Jacob is with us" reads much like the name of the child the prophet Isaiah promised king Ahaz as a sign of God's presence: Emmanuel, "God with us" (Isaiah 7:14; *immanuel*). The psalm declares that this presence is known through the beauty and order of Mount Zion.

Psalm 46:8-10. Verse 8 invites us to "see" what God has done and continues to do. Verse 9 then seems to define what God's "works" are: God destroys the implements of war and brings wars to an end. This portrait is obviously future-oriented. The vision is closely tied to the recognition of God as king. Although God is king, God's kingdom is not present in fullness. Psalm 46:8-10 therefore anticipates the kingdom of peace, even as Jesus spoke of it. It is appropriate as a vision that comes to those who worship God on Mount Zion. Zion is the place where God sits enthroned as king.

In light of verse 9, verse 8 is hard to take at face value. What "desolations" does the psalmist have in mind? Since the next verse declares that God "makes wars cease to the end of the earth" the reference to desolations may be an ironic (humorous or sarcastic, perhaps) way of saying that God's might is used for bringing peace, not devastation.

Psalm 46:10 is one of the best-known lines in the Bible: "Be still and know that I am God." But the translation is really not very good. "Be still" might be better rendered, "stop what you are doing," or even "drop your weapons" or "cease fighting." The point seems to be that warfare is a sign of humans denying God's sovereignty. Hence, the command to "stop" is accompanied by a declaration of God's reign over the universe, "I am exalted among the nations, I am exalted in the earth" (46:10).

The imperative "be still" denotes reliance on God in much the same way the expressions "trust" and "seek refuge" express dependence on the Lord elsewhere in the Psalms. The idea underlying all these expressions is the same expressed by the apostle Paul, "the one who is righteous will live by faith" (Romans 1:17; Paul of course here quotes Habakkuk 2:4!). That is, no one can find a way out of the grip of evil on his or her own. Everyone must rely on God. "Be still" essentially means "give up your efforts to save yourself and allow God to be God."

INTERPRETING THE SCRIPTURE

God Alone Is Our Refuge

Psalm 46:1 includes one of the most frequent and important descriptions of God in the Book of Psalms and in the Bible: "refuge." This verse inspired Martin Luther's famous hymn, "A Mighty Fortress Is Our God." Indeed, the word "refuge" is a metaphor that speaks of God as a shelter, hiding place, or fortress in which one devoted to God may find protection. The exact experience that motivated this way of talking about God is not certain. When enemies attacked the Israelites they often fled to fortified cities or to rocky hilltops for protection. Perhaps such experiences led to this language for God.

What is clear is that when God is called "refuge" it implies the believer has made a choice of trusting in God rather than his or her own resources. Psalm 11 illustrates this point. The psalmist declares "In the LORD I take refuge," and then asks his or her advisors, "How can you say to me, 'Flee like a bird to the mountains'?" (11:1). The psalmist has clearly decided that the only real protection is in the care of God. In a similar way Psalm 46 declares that God is the only shelter and protection.

This choice of God as refuge, however, raises an important practical question. The psalmist declares God "refuge" when beset by enemies (see again Psalm 11:2, "the wicked bend the bow") or when the chaos of life threatens to overwhelm. Is there no self-preservation necessary, no efforts to ensure one's own safety? The answer in some situations, of course, is yes. But Psalm 46 has in mind a threat against which the psalmist is helpless. Often this threat is called "the wicked" (as in Psalm 11); here it is described as a chaos that threatens life itself. In other words, the threat that stands behind the claim of God as refuge is a force of evil that humans cannot overcome alone. Luther expresses this in his hymn when he declares, "Did we in our own strength confide, our striving would be losing."

God Orders the World From Zion

Psalm 46 clearly portrays Mount Zion as the location of God's presence. The psalmist has other important assumptions about Zion that are more subtly presented. All of the psalmist's ideas about Zion, however, relate to the notion that Zion is the center of the universe and, as such, is the place of orientation for the rest of the world.

One idea that lies behind Psalm 46 is that Zion is the location of Eden, the paradise of God. Ezekiel 28:13-14 makes this connection explicit. In an indictment of a figure referred to as the king of Tyre (perhaps the patron deity of that city), God states that he was in the beginning in Eden (Ezekiel 28:13) and later in the same address he identifies his origins "on the holy mountain" (Ezekiel 28:14). No other text, and none of the psalms make the connection this directly, but they portray Zion with features of the garden paradise that make the association almost unmistakable. Psalm 46 suggests this connection by describing the water on Zion: "There is a river whose streams make glad the city of God, the holy habitation of the Most High" (46:4). The river with its divisions is reminiscent of the river that divides in Eden: "A river flows out of Eden to water the garden, and from there it divides and becomes four branches" (Genesis 2:10). For the poet of Psalm 46, who lived with both the primordial dread of chaotic water and the reality of the scarcity of water necessary for life, Zion was a place where life-giving water flowed in abundance. The river and streams of the city symbolized the blessings of God known to those who worshipped there. This image of Zion was a reminder to the righteous people that God had created an orderly world. In such a world the wicked forces of the world would perish as surely as God had subdued chaos in the beginning.

Psalm 46 also presents Zion as the center of the world, the place from which God rules everything. This meant that God dwelled in Zion in a way God lived nowhere else on earth. Thus, anyone who came to worship on Zion could experience the presence of God with humankind. It also meant that Zion was a safe place for such worshipers because God had made it secure (46:5). For those who gathered there it was a reminder that God still reigned and that the threats of wickedness (symbolized by chaos) could not prevail.

These ideas about Mount Zion may seem quite strange to modern Christians. We do not have the same ideas about the structure of the universe and we do not look to one location as the center of the world. Nevertheless, the ideas about Zion in Psalm 46 remain extremely important for our faith. Many of the statements about Zion in this psalm apply now to the church. The church proclaims and embodies the idea that "God is with us" (46:7, 11). Moreover, the church provides for worshipers a place to experience security and safety in the midst of a chaotic world ("God is in the midst of the city;" 46:5). Perhaps most important, the church offers to those who gather for worship a vision of peace that God will ultimately establish (46:8-9). In these ways the church has inherited the role Zion once had.

God With Us

Finally, Psalm 46 illustrates what is perhaps the central truth of the Bible: God is with us! This message is expressed strongly, of course, in Matthew 1:23. Matthew 1:23 quotes Isaiah 7:14. As previously noted, the Isaiah passage records God's sign to king Ahaz that God is with the people of Judah and sees them through their hardship. Jesus is the clearest sign that God is in our midst. The Gospel of John also begins with this idea, though with slightly different language. John says "the Word became flesh and lived among us" (John 1:14). Literally, it says God "pitched his tent" with humankind. It is important to recognize, however, that these New Testament expressions of what God did in Jesus are borrowing Old Testament ideas of how God made Godself known to Israel. When Matthew quotes Isaiah 7:14, he is not just citing Isaiah's prophecy to claim that Jesus fulfills that specific promise of a child who will be born. He is really drawing on a larger Old Testament theme of the nearness of God. Psalm 46 is a perfect illustration of the point. This passage indicates that God "with us" is known by those who locate themselves on Mount Zion.

The declaration that God is with us is extremely important for our theology. It means that our God is not a clock-maker God who created the world but now remains distant from it. Our God is not just the prime mover, the one who set the universe in motion. Rather, our God is characterized by relationship with us. Just as God walked with the first man and woman in the garden (Genesis 3), so God constantly seeks ways to reveal Godself, to show divine goodness, and to make us aware of God's love for us.

SHARING THE SCRIPTURE

Preparing Our Hearts

Explore this week's devotional reading, found in Hebrews 6:13-20. Here the author focuses on the dependability of God's promises. We have hope because we can trust in God. We have hope because Jesus is our high priest. He is uniquely able to help us. What problems threaten to overwhelm you right now? Offer prayer in which you turn these problems over to God. Do whatever you feel God is calling you to do, but trust God to solve your problem.

Pray that you and the adult learners will seek God in times of trouble.

Preparing Our Minds

Study the background Scripture from Psalm 46 and the lesson Scripture, from Psalm 46:1-7. Discern where you can turn for strength and deliverance during times of trouble.

Write on newsprint:
❏ "A New Creed" of the United Church of Canada for "Develop Habits and

Practices that Acknowledge God's Presence and Reaffirm the Reliance on God."
- ❑ information for next week's lesson, found under "Continue the Journey."
- ❑ activities for further spiritual growth in "Continue the Journey."

Plan the lecture suggested under "Study God's Acts of Comfort and Protection."

LEADING THE CLASS

(1) Gather to Learn

❖ Welcome the class members and introduce any guests.

❖ Pray that all who have come today will experience God as One who comforts and protects.

❖ Read aloud this information gleaned from an article by Lillian Kwon (www.christianpost.com/article/20081001/churches-step-out-in-faith-amid-economic-challenges-01/index.html): **As this lesson is being written, the United States, and much of the world, is plunging deeper and deeper into an economic recession. The Church at South Las Vegas in Nevada, led by Pastor Benny Perez, is in a community hard hit by housing foreclosures. Giving has decreased by 10 to 12 percent, but attendance has increased. And the church is moving forward in faith with a 12.5 million dollar building project designed to help reach people for Christ. Despite the faltering economy, the church is holding fast to its vision, trusting that God is able to provide.**

❖ Ask: **What prompts people to stay focused on their vision and trust that God will come through for them in times of trouble?**

❖ Read aloud today's focus statement: **Troubles that sometimes beset us demand abilities and resources beyond what we possess. Where can we turn for deliverance? The psalmist tells us that God is our refuge and strength, a tested help in times of trouble.**

(2) Study God's Acts of Comfort and Protection

❖ Read Psalm 46:1-7 as a chorus. Invite the class to read verse 1, today's key verse, in unison. Choose readers for verses 2-3, 4, 5, 6, and 7.

❖ **Option:** If you have a hymnal with the Psalter, read responsively Psalm 46 in its entirety. (If you have *The United Methodist Hymnal,* use sung Response 1.)

❖ Present a lecture based on Understanding the Scripture (Introduction through Psalm 46:7, 11) in which you explain the view of the world that the people of the psalmist's day would have had, Zion and its meaning and importance, and the notion of the presence of God.

❖ Form groups of three or four each, and distribute paper and pencils. Challenge the groups to rewrite this psalm using contemporary examples to demonstrate confidence in God in difficult situations that turn the world upside down. Here are some examples the group may consider: *terrorist attack, failing economy, natural catastrophes, problems related to global warming.*

❖ Encourage one person from each group to read the psalm they have written.

❖ Point out that although our specific concerns may have changed, Psalm 46 is as timely today as it was when the psalmist penned it.

(3) Reflect on Personal Gratitude to God for Being a Refuge in Times of Trouble

❖ Read aloud this story of Vera Crowl, a University of Dayton student who majored in Community Counseling (www-ig.udayton.edu/Stories/Story/?contentId=22644). **Vera Crowl had spent the better part of 30 years addicted to drugs and alcohol. During five of those years she was homeless. Alone in her church sanctuary, an unmistakable call from God to become a substance abuse counselor was the beginning of her turnaround. As the daughter of a Roman Catholic deacon, Vera learned** that she was eligible for a scholarship. Her mother had made known to her a letter about the scholarship before Vera had disclosed God's call to her family. Amazingly, within two years of enrolling at the University of Dayton she earned her bachelor's degree in psychology. She went on toward her master's degree and was serving as a substance abuse counselor at the church where she heard God's call.

❖ Invite the class to comment on how Vera found God as a refuge in her times of trouble.

❖ Read aloud the second paragraph of "God Alone Is Our Refuge" from Interpreting the Scripture.

❖ Encourage the students to reflect silently on situations in their own lives when God has been a refuge for them—situations in which they have chosen to trust God rather than their own resources. Suggest that they think about what had happened and how God met their needs.

❖ Conclude this silent time by offering a prayer of thanksgiving for the way God has worked and continues to work in our lives.

❖ **Option:** Provide time for students to share their experiences—positive and negative—of God as a refuge. Be prepared to listen to and acknowledge students who feel that God has not been a refuge or source of strength at some critical point in their lives. Even if they have had positive personal experiences, some students may raise issues about faithful families who trusted God who, for example, have lost their livelihood or homes. Or they may ask where God was when entire societies, such as Darfur, have been unrelentingly oppressed.

(4) Develop Habits and Practices that Acknowledge God's Presence and Reaffirm the Reliance on God

❖ Read "God with Us" from Interpreting the Scripture.

❖ Ask: **In what ways or under what circumstances have you experienced the loving presence of God?** Suggest that the students talk with a partner to answer this question so that everyone will have a chance to share a brief story.

❖ Point out that many people are so busy that they fail to recognize God's presence. Ask: **What spiritual habits can you cultivate to help you become more aware of God?** List ideas on newsprint. Some possibilities include: *interacting with God directly through prayer and meditation; contemplating God's handiwork in the midst of creation; hearing God's voice in the Scriptures; participating in praise by singing hymns; worshiping with the faith community.*

❖ Wrap up this portion of the lesson by leading the class or doing a solo reading of "A New Creed" of the United Church of Canada, which emphasizes God's presence and our trust. If you want the class to join you, write the creed on newsprint prior to the session. Or, if you have access to *The United Methodist Hymnal*, invite the students to turn to page 883.

We are not alone,
we live in God's world.
We believe in God:
who has created and is creating,
who has come in Jesus,
the Word made flesh,
to reconcile and make new,
who works in us and others by
   the Spirit.
We trust in God.
We are called to be the church:
to celebrate God's presence,
to live with respect in Creation,
to love and serve others,
to seek justice and resist evil,
to proclaim Jesus, crucified and risen,
our judge and our hope.
In life, in death, in life beyond death,
God is with us.
We are not alone.
Thanks be to God. Amen.

(5) Continue the Journey

❖ Pray that all who have come today will seek to become more aware of God's presence and rely completely upon God.

❖ Read aloud this preparation for next week's lesson. You may also want to post it on newsprint for the students to copy.

■ Title: God Is in Charge

■ Background Scripture: Psalm 47

■ Lesson Scripture: Psalm 47

■ Focus of the Lesson: People look for good leaders whom they can honor. What style of leadership might we celebrate, and how might we celebrate it? The psalmist describes how people joyfully respond to God's sustaining leadership.

❖ Challenge the students to complete one or more of these activities for further spiritual growth related to this week's session. Post this information on newsprint for the students to copy.

(1) Think about times when your security has been challenged, perhaps by a job loss or other financial crisis, poor health, a failing relationship. Where did you turn for help? How did God act as your refuge?

(2) Research contemporary situations that prompt you to ask, "Where is God?" Examples may be found in situations such as Darfur, economic crises that are crushing families, and places where people live in fear of attack and death. What does Psalm 46 have to say in light of these situations?

(3) Offer support to someone who is experiencing a crisis and needs to know that God is present and able to help.

❖ Sing or read aloud "A Mighty Fortress Is Our God," which was inspired by Psalm 46.

❖ Conclude today's session by leading the class in this commission: **We go forth to worship and serve the Lord our God. Thanks be to our merciful and gracious God.**

UNIT 2: GOD SUSTAINS

GOD IS IN CHARGE

PREVIEWING THE LESSON

Lesson Scripture: Psalm 47
Background Scripture: Psalm 47
Key Verses: Psalm 47:6-7

Focus of the Lesson:

People look for good leaders whom they can honor. What style of leadership might we celebrate, and how might we celebrate it? The psalmist describes how people joyfully respond to God's sustaining leadership.

Goals for the Learners:

(1) to identify reasons to praise God's rule over all the nations.
(2) to appreciate that God's rule over all nations includes God's rule over their nation and their lives.
(3) to praise God with a joyous heart for God's sustaining leadership.

Pronunciation Guide:

Baal (bay' uhl) or (bah ahl')
Marduk (mar' dook)

eschatologically (es kat uh loj' i kuhl lee)
Selah (see' luh)

Supplies:

Bibles, newsprint and marker, paper and pencils, hymnals

READING THE SCRIPTURE

NRSV

Psalm 47

¹ Clap your hands, all you peoples;
shout to God with loud songs of joy.
² For the LORD, the Most High, is awesome,
a great king over all the earth.
³ He subdued peoples under us,

NIV

Psalm 47

¹Clap your hands, all you nations;
shout to God with cries of joy.
²How awesome is the LORD Most High,
the great King over all the earth!
³He subdued nations under us,

and nations under our feet.

4 He chose our heritage for us,
    the pride of Jacob whom he loves. *Selah*

5 God has gone up with a shout,
    the LORD with the sound of a trumpet.

6 Sing praises to God, sing praises;
    sing praises to our King, sing praises.

7 For God is the king of all the earth;
    sing praises with a psalm.

8 God is king over the nations;
    God sits on his holy throne.

9 The princes of the peoples gather
    as the people of the God of Abraham.
For the shields of the earth belong to God;
    he is highly exalted.

peoples under our feet.

4He chose our inheritance for us,
    the pride of Jacob, whom he loved. *Selah*

5God has ascended amid shouts of joy,
    the LORD amid the sounding of trumpets.

6Sing praises to God, sing praises;
    sing praises to our King, sing praises.

7For God is the King of all the earth;
    sing to him a psalm of praise.

8God reigns over the nations;
    God is seated on his holy throne.

9The nobles of the nations assemble
    as the people of the God of Abraham,
for the kings of the earth belong to God;
    he is greatly exalted.

UNDERSTANDING THE SCRIPTURE

Introduction. Psalm 47 is a hymn praising God as king. The language of the psalm indicates that it was used in a ritual procession in which God's kingship was celebrated. The psalm contains two summonses to praise (47:1 and 6). Following both summonses are sections that give the content of the praise called for (47:2-5 and 7-9). The particular focus of God's kingship and the reason for praise are God's control over the nations and God's special care for Israel. God's care for Israel, however, is for the purpose of including the nations in God's grace.

Psalm 47 is often discussed in relation to other psalms that speak of God as king or of God reigning over the world. Psalms 93 and 95–99 all contain similar language. Scholars sometimes refer to these psalms as "enthronement psalms" because they speak of God taking a throne or assuming the place as king over the universe (see the discussion of Psalm 47:5 that follows). Several points will help to clarify what these psalms are saying by this language. First, divine kingship has to do with God's sovereignty over both the created order (the natural realm) and the forces of history (nations,

peoples). Psalm 47 does not say explicitly that God controls the forces of nature. This idea, however, does stand behind statements about God's control of the nations. As king, God first put the forces of chaos in their place. The unruly waters produced fear for ancient people (see Genesis 1:6-10). The threat of enemies was in turn often described as agents of chaos (Exodus 15:8-9). Second, it is important to recognize that all people of the ancient Near East (the area from Egypt to Babylon, with Israel/ Palestine in the middle) spoke of their chief deity as a king. So, when Psalm 47 speaks of God this way it is saying indirectly that God reigns over the world, but Baal, Marduk, and other gods do not. Furthermore, Israel's neighbors all had stories about their deities *becoming* king through battles with other gods. The poetry of these other nations (like Israel's psalms) often depicted the god's enthronement, their becoming king. Psalm 47 and similar psalms in the Book of Psalms, however, rest on the assumption that Israel's God *always was* king.

Psalm 47:1-4. These opening verses declare God's sovereignty over all the earth by calling all "peoples" (NRSV) or "nations" (NIV) to praise God (47:1). The first word of verse 2 is "for," and verses 2-4 are often understood as the reason for praising God. The word in Hebrew, however, can serve essentially as quotation marks. That may be the intention here (as the translation in NIV indicates). In other words, verses 2-4 may not be so much the reason praise is offered (though it certainly does present reasons for praise) as much as they contain the content of the praise verse 1 urges.

Verses 3-4 speak particularly about how God acted on behalf of Israel. God "subdued peoples" under Israel. Here the special place of humankind is summed up in Israel. Just as God placed all living things "under [the] feet" of humans (Psalm 8:6), so God placed all nations under Israel's feet. In other words, God in God's sovereignty made Israel sovereign over other nations. The "pride of Jacob" seems to refer to the gift of the land (see Amos 6:8). God gave a special territory to Israel as its inheritance.

The point of Psalm 47:4, however, is not really that Israel is superior to other nations or that Israel has rights to the land of Canaan. Rather, the point is that Israel did nothing to earn its "heritage" or any of the blessings it enjoys. God gave these privileges to Israel. Therefore, Israel cannot boast of anything.

Psalm 47:5. The word *selah* comes between verses 4 and 5 and is not really part of either verse. No one knows exactly what this term means. It is not even certain which Hebrew root gives rise to the word. When the psalm was performed, *selah* may have signaled the people to bow down, shout, clap, or otherwise express joyful praise. Or the word may have been a cue to the musicians, meaning essentially "hit it!"

Whatever the word *selah* meant to those who first heard it, in Psalm 47 the term sets verse 5 off from the previous verses. It marks a transition and highlights verse 5 as the climax of the first section of the psalm. Verses 2-4 praise God as king and recall what God has done in the past. Verse 5 also speaks about God's kingship, but it highlights something that likely occurred at the time the verse was spoken in worship. "God has gone up" probably has in mind a ceremony in which the ark of the covenant was taken into the Temple or sanctuary (see the statement in 2 Chronicles 36:23 regarding the return of God and worshipers to Jerusalem, "let him go up"). Many other psalms likely have such a ceremony in mind. For example, Psalm 24 speaks of a procession into Zion and the Temple that was probably like the ceremony that stands behind Psalm 47.

Psalm 47:6-9. Verses 6 and 7 say five times "sing praise," with each occurrence using the same Hebrew word. The term used here is from same root as the word most commonly translated "psalm" (though the word at the end of Psalm 47:7, translated "psalm" is a different word in this case!). The reason for praise (and the content of praise; see previous discussion) is stated in the first half of verse 7: "God is the king of all the earth."

Those who belong to God include the foreign nations and their leaders. The "shields of the earth" essentially refers to the same people as the term "princes" (47:9). God is called "my shield" in some psalms (Psalm 18:2). The word refers to the role of the leader to protect his people.

INTERPRETING THE SCRIPTURE

How Big Is God?

There is always a temptation for us to make God too small. We fall into this temptation when we think of God as being on our side, whatever *our* may mean (American, Protestant, conservative, liberal, and so on). When God is reduced in size God becomes the deity of nationalism; or God becomes the one who supports a particular political party or political movement. To be sure, we may at times discern that God is at work in the life of a particular person, among some group of people, or in a political or social movement. But more often than not we must stretch ourselves to see that God is working beyond the bounds of our imagination, interests, and convictions.

Psalm 47 requires that kind of expanded thinking about who God is. Verses 3-4 seem to say that in fact God favors Israel over all other peoples. If that were true, then the fact that "God is king over the nations" (47:8) would seem to mean that God controls other nations for Israel's benefit. The psalm ends, however, with a statement that requires a different understanding. Psalm 47 concludes with the remarkable claim that all people "gather as the people of the God of Abraham" (47:9). Although verses 3-4 seem to present a biased picture of Israel's special place in the world, verse 9 will not allow Israel to be seen as being blessed at the expense of the nations. Rather, even the nations "under Israel's feet" belong to God.

Israel and the Nations

If we read verse 3 out of context we might conclude that God's people are meant to dominate the world and that all other people are to be subservient. But several features of Psalm 47 (and the rest of Scripture) will simply not permit us to think that way. The first, and perhaps most important, point is that all people are "God's people." Verse 9 makes this point as explicitly as any passage in the Bible. As noted previously, it states that the "princes of the peoples gather *as* the people of the God of Abraham" (47:9, italics added). The ancient Greek translation of this passage reads slightly differently. It translates the last part of the line, "with the people of the God of Abraham" (the Hebrew particle translated "with" has exactly the same consonants as the word for "people;" these ancient translators perhaps thought that one occurrence of these consonants was accidentally omitted). There is no other evidence for this reading. Even if it is the correct rendering, however, the statement is still remarkably inclusive. It means at least that Israel cannot war with other peoples without bringing pain to God because God identifies with all others as well.

Another important point concerns the statement that God has placed all people "under our feet" (47:3). This may sound like Israel has a place of superiority. The words, "under our feet," however, are the same words Psalm 8:6 uses to describe humankind's responsibility for the rest of the creation. So, although the expression does denote authority and privilege, it is authority and privilege for the sake of those "under the feet." Just as humankind as a whole is charged to care for the rest of God's creatures, Israel is given the role of ensuring the well-being of all other peoples. When understood this way, the idea that God has placed some people under the "authority" of Israel cannot be used to lord over others. Rather, Psalm 47:3 expresses the idea in Genesis 12:3, that all people are blessed because of and under the auspices of Abraham.

The role of Israel in relation to those "under their feet" should be read in light of the New Testament's insistence that all things have been placed under Jesus' feet. Ephesians 1:22-23 says: "And he [God] has put all things under his [Jesus'] feet and has made him the head over all things for the church, which is his body." The fact that the church is the body of Christ argues against any notion that Jesus lords over those under his feet. But the context of Ephesians 1–2 makes the point emphatic. Jesus sacrificed himself for us in order to reconcile us to God and to each other (Ephesians 2:11-22). Psalm 47 implies the same responsibility of Israel for the nations.

Liturgy and the Presence of God's Kingdom

It is important to recognize that Psalm 47 is a liturgy. The summons to praise in verses 1 and 6 make this clear. The psalm invites worshipers to speak what they believe about God. Specifically, Psalm 47 was composed for a celebration of God's kingship, a celebration that probably took place in the Jerusalem Temple.

What is striking about this fact is how untrue many of the statements in the psalm might have seemed to those who spoke them in the Jerusalem Temple. The people of Israel were constantly at the mercy of enemy nations all around them. Their history started, of course, with slavery in Egypt. After being delivered from bondage and entering the land God promised them, they struggled with the Philistines, the Edomites, Ammonites, and the Moabites. Eventually they would be destroyed and exiled by the likes of Assyria and Babylon. Even in the glory days of David and Solomon these people lived in a small and rather insignificant kingdom in comparison with the great empires of their day. In light of that fact, it

may seem rather silly to claim that Israel's God is "a great king over all the earth" (47:2) and "king over the nations" (47:8). It would seem even more ridiculous to claim that "he subdued peoples under us, and nations under our feet" (47:3). On what event or events did Israel base its claim to a unique place in the world order? How could Israel claim that its God was king over all the earth?

The answer to these questions is embedded in the fact that Israel, and later the church, understood their claims of God's kingship as a future reality. They understood God's reign eschatologically, as something to come, to be fulfilled when God brings creation to its fruition. The liturgical celebration of God's reign, therefore, celebrates something that is not fully evident right now. But that does not mean this psalm, or any other liturgy, presents a false hope or a naive view of the world. Rather, it gives us a way to state and restate what we believe about the world. Most importantly, what we say we believe about the world to come shapes the way we live and the world we live in right now. This is the power of liturgy, and the power of Psalm 47. The psalm invites us to proclaim: "God is the king of all the earth" (47:7). The proclamation only makes sense, however, when it is made in the company of other believers. Together we declare what we believe about the world. As we do, we create a community that not only believes in God's reign with the head but also responds to God's kingdom with the heart. To live as though we belong to the kingdom of God means that we work to bring justice and well-being as God also is working.

SHARING THE SCRIPTURE

Preparing Our Hearts

Explore this week's devotional reading, found in Jeremiah 10:6-10. In ringing language we are told that God is "King of the nations" (10:7). No other god can compare; they are all idols crafted of wood and precious metals. The One Israel calls God reigns supreme. Do you believe that? If so, what does it mean to you to worship this God? Offer praise and thanksgiving to God, for there is none like the Lord.

Pray that you and the adult learners will exalt God as Lord of all and in so doing recognize that everyone throughout the earth belongs to God.

Preparing Our Minds

Study the background Scripture and the lesson Scripture, both of which include all nine verses of Psalm 47.

Write on newsprint:

❑ list of leadership attributes for "Gather to Learn."

❑ information for next week's lesson, found under "Continue the Journey."

❑ activities for further spiritual growth in "Continue the Journey."

Study Understanding the Scripture to find reasons to praise God. You may want to highlight these points for quick reference during the session.

LEADING THE CLASS

(1) Gather to Learn

❖ Welcome the class members and introduce any guests.

❖ Pray that those who have gathered for class today will praise the God who rules over all the nations.

❖ Post this list of leadership attributes on newsprint prior to the session. Distribute paper and pencils. Give the students one to two minutes to jot down the letters of the four attributes they believe are most important.

(A) Courage that includes willingness to take risks.

(B) Empathy with one's followers.

(C) Competence both as a leader and in the technical aspects of one's job.

(D) Willingness to mentor others to become leaders.

(E) Ability to set goals.

(F) Commitment to seeing the project through to completion.

(G) Good people skills.

(H) Ability to control himself/herself.

(I) Cooperative spirit.

(J) Personality that is pleasing and garners respect.

❖ Tally the number of students that chose each letter by calling out the letters in turn and writing beside each letter the number who raise their hands. Any of the list above is an important leadership attribute, so there are no "wrong" answers.

❖ Read aloud today's focus statement: **People look for good leaders whom they can honor. What style of leadership might we celebrate, and how might we celebrate it? The psalmist describes how people joyfully respond to God's sustaining leadership.**

(2) Identify Reasons to Praise God's Rule Over All the Nations

❖ Read Psalm 47 as expressively as possible. For example, clap your hands as you read those words; increase volume as you read "shout"; add a lilt to your voice as you read "sing praises"; and so on.

❖ **Option:** If you have access to a hymnal with a Psalter, invite the class to read Psalm 47 responsively.

❖ Ask the students to turn over the papers they have already used for "Gather to Learn" and list as many reasons to praise God as they can find in this psalm.

❖ Invite the students to call out the reasons they have written. Remember that different translations will enrich the list, since words may be different. Add whatever reasons (or information about these reasons) you have gleaned from your study of Understanding the Scripture.

❖ Choose a volunteer to read Romans 13:1-7, which speaks in verse 1 about the importance of being "subject to the governing authorities."

❖ Challenge the students to compare the reign of rulers they have lived under (or know about from world politics) with what is said in praise of God the king in Psalm 47.

(3) Appreciate that God's Rule Over All Nations Includes God's Rule Over the Learners' Nation and Their Lives

❖ Read or retell "How Big Is God?" from Interpreting the Scripture.

❖ Invite the students to comment on ways that we often limit God's activity to "our corner of the world." Note that Psalm 47 pushes us to expand God's activity far beyond ourselves, indeed, possibly far beyond our comfort zone. Psalm 47 does not allow for "we/they" thinking, for all people are included in God's reign.

❖ Form groups of three or four. Provide paper or newsprint and a marker. Set a time limit of three to five minutes for them to discuss this question: **Where do you see evidence of God's reign in the way that your nation is ruled?**

❖ Allow time for the groups to report back.

❖ **Option:** Set a time limit for the groups to discuss this question: **Where do you see evidence that God's reign is ignored in the way that your nation is ruled?** Again allow time for the groups to report.

❖ Distribute paper (and pencils if you have not already done so). Ask the students to fold the sheet in half crosswise. Explain that what they will be doing is "for their eyes only," so they will not be asked to report back to the class. Invite them to draw symbols or write words on the top half to identify areas of their lives where they believe God is in charge. Also ask them to draw symbols or write words on the bottom half of areas in their lives where they have not allowed God to reign.

❖ Encourage the students to look at both halves of their paper and silently answer these questions, which you will need to read aloud: **What barriers prevent me from allowing God to be Lord of all areas of my life? How can I, with God's help, tear down these barriers?**

❖ Close this portion of the lesson by encouraging the participants to pray that God's rule will be acknowledged in all nations and in their lives. Provide a few moments of quiet time.

(4) Praise God With a Joyous Heart for God's Sustaining Leadership

❖ Post a sheet of newsprint. Encourage the adults to call out reasons why they would praise God as the sovereign who leads the world. What attributes of God's leadership do they want to highlight? List the ideas on newsprint. Draw a line after every third idea.

❖ Create a simple litany by reading each idea in unison, preceded by the words, **"We praise you God for . . ."** (as an example, your unfailing commitment to us). After the third idea (as noted by the line), use this refrain: **"You alone, O God, are the ruler of all nations."**

(5) Continue the Journey

❖ Pray that all of today's participants will go forth praising the God who reigns over all the earth.

❖ Read aloud this preparation for next week's lesson. You may also want to post it on newsprint for the students to copy.

■ **Title: God's Presence Comforts and Assures**

■ **Background Scripture: Psalm 63**

■ **Lesson Scripture: Psalm 63**

■ **Focus of the Lesson: People yearn for comfort to fill the emptiness in their lives. Who or what can fulfill this yearning? King David rejoices in the comfort and confidence he found in God's presence.**

❖ Challenge the students to complete one or more of these activities for further spiritual growth related to this week's session. Post this information on newsprint for the students to copy.

(1) **Study the media for news of ways in which the actions and policies of world leaders run counter to the rule of God. If these violations are taking place in your own community or country, write a letter to elected officials and boldly suggest what needs to be changed.**

(2) **Write your own litany or prayer expressing praise for God's rule over all the nations. Acknowledge that all people, whether** they are aware of it or not, are loved and overseen by God.

(3) **Practice putting God first when faced with hard choices between the actions and policies of your government and what you understand the reign of God to require.**

❖ Sing or read aloud "Praise to the Lord, the Almighty."

❖ Conclude today's session by leading the class in this commission: **We go forth to worship and serve the Lord our God. Thanks be to our merciful and gracious God.**

UNIT 2: GOD SUSTAINS

GOD'S PRESENCE COMFORTS AND ASSURES

PREVIEWING THE LESSON

Lesson Scripture: Psalm 63
Background Scripture: Psalm 63
Key Verse: Psalm 63:1

Focus of the Lesson:
People yearn for comfort to fill the emptiness in their lives. Who or what can fulfill this yearning? King David rejoices in the comfort and confidence he found in God's presence.

Goals for the Learners:
(1) to explore how God provided fulfillment in David's life.
(2) to desire to praise God from the heart.
(3) to find fulfillment and express joy in God's presence.

Pronunciation Guide:
hesed (kheh' sed)

Supplies:
Bibles, newsprint and marker, paper and pencils, hymnals

READING THE SCRIPTURE

NRSV

Psalm 63

1 O God, you are my God, I seek you,
   my soul thirsts for you;
 my flesh faints for you,
   as in a dry and weary land
   where there is no water.
2 So I have looked upon you in the

NIV

Psalm 63

1 O God, you are my God,
   earnestly I seek you;
 my soul thirsts for you,
   my body longs for you,
 in a dry and weary land
   where there is no water.

sanctuary,
  beholding your power and glory.
3 Because your steadfast love is
      better than life,
    my lips will praise you.
4 So I will bless you as long as I live;
    I will lift up my hands and call on
      your name.
5 My soul is satisfied as with a rich feast,
    and my mouth praises you with
      joyful lips
6 when I think of you on my bed,
    and meditate on you in the
      watches of the night;
7 for you have been my help,
    and in the shadow of your
      wings I sing for joy.
8 My soul clings to you;
    your right hand upholds me.
9 But those who seek to destroy my life
    shall go down into the depths
      of the earth;
10 they shall be given over to the
      power of the sword,
    they shall be prey for jackals.
11 But the king shall rejoice in God;
    all who swear by him shall exult,
    for the mouths of liars shall be stopped.

2I have seen you in the sanctuary
    and beheld your power and your glory.
3Because your love is better than life,
    my lips will glorify you.
4I will praise you as long as I live,
    and in your name I will lift up my hands.
5My soul will be satisfied as with the
      richest of foods;
    with singing lips my mouth will
      praise you.
6On my bed I remember you;
    I think of you through the watches of
      the night.
7Because you are my help,
    I sing in the shadow of your wings.
8My soul clings to you;
    your right hand upholds me.
9They who seek my life will be destroyed;
    they will go down to the depths of
      the earth.
10They will be given over to the sword
    and become food for jackals.
11But the king will rejoice in God;
    all who swear by God's name will
      praise him,
    while the mouths of liars will be silenced.

UNDERSTANDING THE SCRIPTURE

Introduction. The title of Psalm 63 indicates it is "A psalm of David, when he was in the Wilderness of Judah." The titles of psalms are important, yet often neglected elements of the poems to which they are attached. In fact, some translations, such as Today's English Version, do not include these elements of the psalms. But now it is apparent that the titles give us important information about how the psalms were interpreted by their earliest readers. The words "of David" probably did not signify Davidic authorship originally. The words could refer to a psalm in honor of, sponsored by, or in memory of David. Over time, however, the titles gave context to the words of the psalms. They came to be read as the words of David.

A learned scribe added the second part of the title of Psalm 63: "when he was in the Wilderness of Judah." The title connects the hardships of David to the trouble expressed in the psalm. Specifically, the dry wilderness of Judah in which David hid from his enemies became the "dry and weary land" in which the psalmist declares thirst for God. The title thus directs us as readers to look to David as an example. It suggests that when David suffered under the wrath of Saul or when he was pursued by his son Absalom, he relied on God for protection.

He called out to God as his refuge. We are invited then to read this psalm when we are in trouble and to remember that God is our hiding place, the one to whom we may turn when we are in dire straits.

Psalm 63:1-2. The psalm opens with a statement of longing for God, expressed as thirst. The same language appears in Psalm 42:2, "My soul thirsts for God, for the living God." In order to alleviate this thirst for God the psalmist goes to the place of worship (63:2). The term "sanctuary" probably refers to the Jerusalem Temple (see the same term in Psalm 73:17). The way the psalmist "looks upon" God or sees God is uncertain. This does not mean literally seeing God in fullness (see Ezekiel 1, for example, for the careful language the Old Testament uses about seeing God). But perhaps the psalmist stood before the Holy of Holies, which contained the ark of the covenant, the representation of God's throne. Or the psalmist may have seen the sunrise through the Temple entrance. In ancient artwork the sun often represents God's presence.

Psalm 63:3-8. The next section of the psalm recounts being in the Temple and describes the exuberance that results. Verses 3-8 are dominated by statements and acts of praise: "my lips will praise you" (63:3); "I will bless you/lift up my hands/call on your name" (63:4); "my mouth praises you" (63:5); "I sing for joy" (63:7). Verse 6 may refer to waiting in the Temple through the night for God's help. The psalmist may have come to the Temple seeking sanctuary from accusers and asking for a hearing from the priests. Hence, when a positive verdict is rendered the psalmist experiences God's help (63:7). The "right hand" in verse 8 describes the source of God's power and goodness (the left is thought to be sinister or dirty; Ecclesiastes 10:2).

Psalm 63:9-11. The final section of the psalm gives further evidence for the legal setting just described. "Those who seek to destroy my life" probably refers to false accusers. They are the "liars" mentioned in

verse 11. Although it is impossible to know exactly what situation these words have in mind, the reference to liars may suggest the kind of abuse of the court system that Exodus 23:1-3 instructs against (see also Exodus 20:16, "You shall not bear false witness against your neighbor"). Exodus 23:1 speaks of a "malicious witness" (or it could be translated "violent witness"). That seems to be what Psalm 63 has in mind.

Verses 9-10 may seem overly harsh, even if the verbs are merely statements of what will be in the future. Should the psalmist not ask for God's mercy on the enemy? How do these verses square with Jesus' command to "pray for those who persecute you" (Matthew 5:44)? The false accusers should probably be understood to be like those the prophet Amos says "sell the righteous for silver, and the needy for a pair of sandals" (Amos 2:6). Amos portrays such persons as those who abuse the legal system to enrich themselves. He says "they hate the one who reproves in the gate, and they abhor the one who speaks the truth" (Amos 5:10). The city gate was the place legal cases were heard and judgments were made. The accusers of Psalm 63:9-10 are likely the type of powerful and greedy citizens who took advantage of the poor in Amos' day. These verses therefore have in mind a judgment on persons such as Amos and Jesus spoke of (Matthew 25).

After declaring faithfulness and nearness to the heavenly King (Psalm 63:1-8), the psalmist then speaks of the earthly ruler (63:11). NRSV translates verse 11 as a declaration, but it could also be rendered as a petition: "let the king rejoice." Regardless of the correct translation, the psalmist here identifies with the ruler because he symbolizes God's justice given to the people. The king was thought to be the source of blessing for God's people. So the psalmist frequently prays for the king as in Psalm 61:6: "Prolong the life of the king; may his years endure to all generations" (see also Psalm 20). The king is identified, however, as the example of one who recognizes God's sovereignty.

The king "shall rejoice in God" and "exults" in the Lord, not in his own power and influence. Hence, the king is the direct opposite of the oppressors of verses 9-10.

INTERPRETING THE SCRIPTURE

Trouble, Hardship, and the People of God

If we take the title of Psalm 63 seriously, the psalm has something very important to say about suffering, especially as it is experienced by those who follow God and seek God's purpose in life. The psalm is presented as a prayer of David "when he was in the Wilderness of Judah." The exact occasion this reference has in mind is not certain. It likely refers, however, to the time David was fleeing from Saul (1 Samuel 23:14-15; 24:1) or from Absalom (2 Samuel 15:23, 28; 16:2). In other words, the psalm is set during a time when David was running for his life. If the setting is the trouble with Absalom, David's entire life and kingdom are on the verge of falling apart. He is in deep trouble and thus prays to God for deliverance.

The setting of Psalm 63 is essentially the same as that given for Psalm 3 (note Psalm 3's title, "A Psalm of David, when he fled from his son Absalom"). In fact, the psalm titles that give a setting in David's life are dominated by trouble and oppression (in the case of Psalm 51 the trouble is of David's own making). The implicit point made by these psalms is that devotion to God does not necessarily alleviate suffering; it helps us live through suffering and hardship by being connected to the source of life and goodness. This message is important for people who live in a world focused on comfort and success. Faith can become just another tool to bring about success. But Psalm 63 and other psalms like it suggest our faith does not take away our trouble or bring us success; rather, it gives us the resources to live in the midst of trouble by drawing near to God.

Your Steadfast Love Is Better Than Life

Psalm 63's statement of thirst for God reaches its high point in verse 3: "your steadfast love is better than life." This is a remarkable statement. The psalmist seems to say that God's steadfast love is more valuable than his or her own life. Psalm 63, therefore, may have been used in the early church to speak of the commitment of martyrs. They literally exchanged their lives for the cause of God, to be in God's presence. But this is not exactly what the psalm originally intended.

The expression "steadfast love" translates the Hebrew term *hesed*, a rich and important theological word that cannot accurately be put into English. The term refers to God's reliability, particularly as God relates to Israel as a covenant partner. But God's *hesed* is not something to trade for life; it represents the help of God that supports and restores life. Therefore, the psalms speak of *hesed* as something to be sought, desired, and cherished above all else. Psalm 63:3 makes essentially the same point as Psalm 27:4: "One thing I asked of the LORD, that will I seek after: to live in the house of the LORD all the days of my life." These and many other expressions of desire for God in the psalms speak of a singular devotion as though God is all that is needed (Psalm 23:1). Indeed, since God is the source of life, God is all that is needed. In our consumer-driven society such statements can help clear away the many voices that tell us we need so much and focus on what is really essential: to be near God, to feast on the riches of God's presence (Psalm 63:5).

God, Our Mother Hen

God is beyond our comprehension. Therefore, understanding God requires imagination. The way we imagine God to be and to relate to us is extremely important for our faith, and the psalms provide some of the best images to foster such imagination. In Psalm 63:7 the psalmist expresses trust in God by saying he or she rests "in the shadow of your wings." What image should these words conjure up for us? What does it mean to speak of God's "wings?" It is impossible to determine exactly what the psalmist had in mind in this reference. Nevertheless, at least three images may help us understand what this reference is saying about God and our relationship with God.

For the first image that may lie behind Psalm 63:7 we must go to ancient Egypt. In ancient Egyptian artwork Pharaoh is often depicted being sheltered under the wings of the falcon god, Horus. The picture helps express the special relationship Egyptians believed existed between their king and one of their chief deities. So, the language in Psalm 63 may invite us to understand ourselves with a similarly special relationship with God. Before God we occupy the place of royalty. Whether or not the image in Psalm 63:7 has this in mind, the general idea of each human being having a royal office is certainly good theology and it can be found in other psalms (especially Psalm 8).

Another possible image that lies behind Psalm 63:7 is the picture of the wings of the cherubim that stretched out from the ark of the covenant. The ark represented God's throne and therefore God's presence. The cherubim on the ark represented the heavenly attendants who were around God's throne (see Isaiah 6). The idea that this is the image the psalmist had in mind makes sense given that the rest of Psalm 63 speaks of experiencing God in the sanctuary where the ark was housed.

The two images just mentioned certainly have potential to help us reflect on God's presence with us and God's care for us. But a third image may be even more useful for this purpose. The most obvious implication of Psalm 63:7 is that God is like a mother bird brooding over her young. This image may not seem likely at first. After all, most of the language for God in the Old Testament is masculine and the Israelites certainly tried to distance themselves from some of the surrounding polytheistic religions—religions that included goddesses. Nevertheless, Jesus uses the image of a mother hen in Luke 13:34 to describe his desire to care for the people of Jerusalem: "How often have I desired to gather your children together as a hen gathers her brood under her wings." If we imagine this image when we read Psalm 63:7, we are encouraged to think of God's protective presence on the one hand and our dependence on God on the other hand. We, like the psalmist, find our help in God and experience joy as we rest beneath God's wings.

The possible images that lie behind Psalm 63:7 raise an important truth about the identity and character of God. God is beyond our ability to describe God with our language. While the Old Testament uses mostly masculine language for God (for some historical and social reasons, as noted), the authors of the Old Testament certainly did not think that God was actually male. Texts like Psalm 63:7 probably indicate some of the rich and imaginative ways they did think about God. They were willing to mix metaphors sometimes, undoubtedly because they knew God could not be captured in them. The language in Psalm 63 almost suggests the image of a "father hen." Such a mix of images is appropriate when speaking about God. God has more dimensions of care, concern, and protection for us than we can express.

SHARING THE SCRIPTURE

Preparing Our Hearts

Explore this week's devotional reading, found in Psalm 3:1-6. Psalm 3 and the Scripture for today, Psalm 63, share a common theme: the trust that David finds in God during very trying times. In Psalm 3, David was fleeing from his son Absalom, who wanted to kill his father. In Psalm 63, David was in the Judean wilderness, likely fearing for his life as he sought to escape either King Saul or Absalom. When have you needed assurance that God could sustain you even under the most challenging of circumstances? Offer up to God in prayer a situation that you need help resolving. Trust God for the answer.

Pray that you and the adult learners will experience God's comforting presence.

Preparing Our Minds

Study the background Scripture and the lesson Scripture, both of which are found in Psalm 63. Ask yourself: Who can fill the empty places in people's lives?

Write on newsprint:

❏ questions for "Desire to Praise God from the Heart."

❏ information for next week's lesson, found under "Continue the Journey."

❏ activities for further spiritual growth in "Continue the Journey."

Plan a lecture based on Understanding the Scripture for the section "Explore How God Provided Fulfillment in David's Life" to help the students delve into the meaning of the psalm.

LEADING THE CLASS

(1) Gather to Learn

❖ Welcome the class members and introduce any guests.

❖ Pray that all who have come today will recognize and give thanks for God's power to sustain them.

❖ Read aloud this story based on an edited extract of *Dewey* by Vicki Myron: **Vicki Myron, director of Spencer Public Library in Iowa, and the assistant director, Jean Hollis Clark, were startled on a January morning in 1988 to find a cold, starving kitten in their book drop. The staff kept him and nursed him back to health. Faced with serious economic woes, the town of Spencer was under great strain when this tiny kitten came into their lives. Residents began to see him as a metaphor for their own problems—and thought that if he could overcome adversity, so could they. People of all ages and life situations fell under Dewey's spell: the children eagerly awaiting story time with Dewey, the lonely widower, the man desperately seeking a job, a physically challenged girl, the librarian's teenage daughter. Soon, Dewey was a media star, receiving fan mail from around the world. When he died at age 19, 270 newspapers marked his passing and more than 1,000 e-mails poured into the library. Dewey, who had been shoved aside and left for dead, filled places in the lives of others who were struggling.**

❖ Read aloud today's focus statement: **People yearn for comfort to fill the emptiness in their lives. Who or what can fulfill this yearning? King David rejoices in the comfort and confidence he found in God's presence.**

(2) Explore How God Provided Fulfillment in David's Life

❖ Read aloud Psalm 63 as dramatically as possible. Invite the students to close their eyes as you read and imagine themselves as King David.

❖ Ask: **What words would you use to describe David's emotions during this wilderness experience in Judah?**

❖ Present the lecture you have prepared from Understanding the Scripture. Encourage the students to raise questions or add comments.

❖ Read these words from Interpreting the Scripture: **Since God is the source of life, God is all that is needed. In our consumer-driven society such statements can help clear away the many voices that tell us we need so much and focus on what is really essential: to be near God, to feast on the riches of God's presence (Psalm 63:5).**

❖ Ask: **David clearly discovered the key to joy even in the midst of hardship: total dependence on God. Why is that dependence so hard for most of us to accept?**

❖ Note: **David's psalm reflects an experience of physical and spiritual wilderness. While some people equate a spiritual drought with a lack of faith, saints through the ages have reported such times of spiritual aridness. These wilderness times, while challenging to endure, have generally enabled believers to grow closer to God and more faithfully serve in God's kingdom.**

❖ Read these quotations and invite the students to comment on any insights they gain from them. How do they think David might respond to these quotations?

■ **Take courage. We walk in the wilderness today and in the Promised Land tomorrow.** (Dwight Lyman Moody, 1837–1899)

■ **The Promised Land always lies on the other side of a wilderness.** (Havelock Ellis, 1859–1939)

■ **Thirst must be quenched! If our desires are not met by God, we will quickly find something else to alleviate our thirst.** (Erwin W. Lutzer, 1941–)

(3) Desire to Praise God From the Heart

❖ Read "Trouble, Hardship, and the People of God" from Interpreting the Scripture.

❖ Point out that in the midst of trouble and hardship we often find God most fully.

❖ Distribute paper and pencils. Invite the students to answer these questions, which you will post on newsprint:

(1) **When have you experienced great spiritual hunger and thirst for God?**

(2) **How did God comfort you in that situation?**

(3) **In what ways did you respond to this comfort?**

❖ Invite volunteers to tell their experiences briefly. (Even if no one chooses to speak, note the importance of praise and thanksgiving as a response.)

❖ Challenge the students to write their own psalms of praise for God's comforting presence in their lives. Read aloud these "starters" if the adults need help in beginning their psalms:

Your lovingkindness, O God, is the wellspring of my life. To you I sing praises.

I will praise you, gracious God, as long as I live.

Praise God all the earth, for our God is a very present help in times of deep distress.

❖ Call on volunteers to read aloud their songs of praise. Affirm what everyone has written.

(4) Find Fulfillment and Express Joy in God's Presence

❖ Read Psalm 63:1 as it appears in The Message by Eugene H. Peterson: **God—you're my God! I can't get enough of you!** Invite the students to repeat those words.

❖ Provide a few moments of quiet time for the adults to reflect on verse 1, today's key verse. Suggest that they think about these questions: Can they, along with the psalmist, say that they just cannot get enough of God? If so, invite them to bask in the light of God's presence. If not, suggest that they discern reasons why they cannot agree with the psalmist. What can they do to break down those barriers? End the silence with the words: **God—you're my God! I can't get enough of you!**

❖ Go around the room and offer the opportunity to each person to complete this sentence: **I experience joy in God when (or because).** . . . If someone chooses not to respond, he or she may say, "pass."

(5) Continue the Journey

❖ Pray that today's participants will go forth to praise God for the comfort and assurance they experience in God's presence.

❖ Read aloud this preparation for next week's lesson. You may also want to post it on newsprint for the students to copy.

■ **Title: God Is Awesome**
■ **Background Scripture: Psalm 66**
■ **Lesson Scripture: Psalm 66:1-12**
■ **Focus of the Lesson: Many people carry burdens that are too heavy to bear. What can ease our load? We can sing to the Lord because God's great power holds our lives in God's hand and keeps our feet from slipping.**

❖ Challenge the students to complete one or more of these activities for further spiritual growth related to this week's session. Post this information on newsprint for the students to copy.

(1) **Try to fast from sunrise until sunset, provided you are medically able to do so. How does the experience of hunger and thirst draw you closer to God?**

(2) **Locate pictures of a desert. Mentally try to put yourself into this landscape. How does this place affect your relationship with God?**

(3) **Recall that David thought of God during the night, while in bed. Should you awaken during the night, give thanks to God for who God is and how God has taken care of you. Meditate on who God is and how God has affected your life.**

❖ Sing or read aloud "God Will Take Care of You."

❖ Conclude today's session by leading the class in this commission: **We go forth to worship and serve the Lord our God. Thanks be to our merciful and gracious God.**

UNIT 3: GOD PROTECTS
GOD IS AWESOME

PREVIEWING THE LESSON

Lesson Scripture: Psalm 66:1-12
Background Scripture: Psalm 66
Key Verse: Psalm 66:5

Focus of the Lesson:
Many people carry burdens that are too heavy to bear. What can ease our load? We can sing to the Lord because God's great power holds our lives in God's hand and keeps our feet from slipping.

Goals for the Learners:
(1) to recount experiences of God's deliverance in Israel's history.
(2) to affirm an abiding conviction in God's power to save and deliver God's people.
(3) to develop their testimony of how God delivered them and use it to encourage others.

Supplies:
Bibles, newsprint and marker, paper and pencils, hymnals

READING THE SCRIPTURE

NRSV
Psalm 66:1-12
1 Make a joyful noise to God, all the earth;
2   sing the glory of his name;
        give to him glorious praise.
3 Say to God, "How awesome are
        your deeds!
    Because of your great power, your
        enemies cringe before you.
4 All the earth worships you;
        they sing praises to you,
    sing praises to your name."   *Selah*
5 **Come and see what God has done:**
    he is awesome in his deeds among
    mortals.

NIV
Psalm 66:1-12
1Shout with joy to God, all the earth!
2 Sing the glory of his name;
        make his praise glorious!
3Say to God, "How awesome are your
        deeds!
    So great is your power
        that your enemies cringe before you.
4All the earth bows down to you;
        they sing praise to you,
        they sing praise to your name."   *Selah*
5**Come and see what God has done,**
    how awesome his works in man's behalf!

⁶ He turned the sea into dry land;
  they passed through the river on foot.
There we rejoiced in him,
⁷ who rules by his might forever,
  whose eyes keep watch on the nations—
  let the rebellious not exalt themselves.
                                        Selah

⁸ Bless our God, O peoples,
  let the sound of his praise be heard,
⁹ who has kept us among the living,
  and has not let our feet slip.
¹⁰ For you, O God, have tested us;
  you have tried us as silver is tried.
¹¹ You brought us into the net;
  you laid burdens on our backs;
¹² you let people ride over our heads;
  we went through fire and
    through water;
yet you have brought us out to a
    spacious place.

⁶He turned the sea into dry land,
  they passed through the waters on foot—
  come, let us rejoice in him.
⁷He rules forever by his power,
  his eyes watch the nations—
  let not the rebellious rise up against
    him.   *Selah*

⁸Praise our God, O peoples,
  let the sound of his praise be heard;
⁹he has preserved our lives
  and kept our feet from slipping.
¹⁰For you, O God, tested us;
  you refined us like silver.
¹¹You brought us into prison
  and laid burdens on our backs.
¹²You let men ride over our heads;
  we went through fire and water,
  but you brought us to a place of
    abundance.

UNDERSTANDING THE SCRIPTURE

Introduction. Psalm 66 begins as a hymn of praise that extols God's mighty deeds on behalf of God's people (66:1-12). This portion of the psalm is oriented toward the community. It points particularly to the rescue of Israel at the Red Sea (66:6). But the psalm concludes with the testimony of an individual who thanks God for rescuing her or him out of trouble (66:13-20). The shift from communal to individual orientation has led some scholars to surmise that Psalm 66 is actually a combination of two psalms that were originally separate. The two sections of the psalm are connected, however, by the call to "come" and see/hear what God has done (66:5, 16). When Psalm 66 was performed in ancient Israel, the thanksgiving portion (66:13-20) likely featured sacrifices made by an individual who represented the community as a whole.

Psalm 66:1-4. The psalm opens with a series of imperatives that call for praise of God: "make a joyful noise" (66:1), "sing"

(66:2a), "give glorious praise" (66:2b), "say to God, 'How awesome are your deeds!'" (66:3). These calls to worship are appropriate to a psalm of praise. It is striking, however, that the imperatives are addressed to "all the earth" (66:1). Unlike a call to worship that invites praise from people who have gathered in a sanctuary, this call to "all the earth" cannot really reach its audience. From the place of worship it is not possible for all the people in the immediate vicinity to hear and answer the call, much less all people on earth. Nevertheless, this verse makes an important theological statement. The psalm calls all inhabitants of the earth to praise God because all people belong to God and are part of God's congregation. In other words, verses 1-4 make an important statement about the universal sovereignty of the Lord. Similar statements on God's sovereignty appear in other psalms such as Psalms 95, 96, and 98. Psalm 66:1 is nearly identical to Psalm 98:4.

The reference to enemies in verse 3 anticipates the allusion to the exodus event in verse 6 and the description of some nations as rebellious in verse 7. As verse 4 affirms, all the earth, in the end, sings praise to God and recognizes God's sovereignty.

Psalm 66:5-12. The second section of the psalm begins like the first, with a plural imperative. This is apparently another call for "all the earth" to "come and see what God has done" (66:5). The first divine act highlighted is the rescue of the Israelites at the Red Sea (66:6). Interestingly, though, Israel is not mentioned specifically. Verse 5 declares God did this "among mortals." NIV perhaps captures the sense of this line in the translation, "in man's behalf." In other words, the psalm claims that this central salvation event was not just for Israel; it was for all humankind. This understanding of the importance of the exodus is consistent with the call earlier for "all the earth" to praise God.

Verses 8-12 reinforce the idea that God's actions are for the sake of all humankind, not just for Israel. Verse 8 begins with another imperative addressed to all humankind ("O peoples"). Verse 9 states again that God saved Israel ("us") by "keeping us among the living." But then verses 10-12 recalls how God tested and punished Israel before bringing them "to a spacious place" (66:12). Hence, these verses reveal God's true character. The Lord who brought Israel out of Egypt is not just a God who is partial to this people to the detriment of others. Indeed, God shows concern about justice and equality not only by rescuing Israel from bondage but also by punishing Israel for unfaithfulness.

Psalm 66:13-15. In verse 13 the psalm shifts to first-person voice. It is no longer "all the peoples" who praise God. Now, an individual believer professes faith and makes promises to worship. Verses 13-15 are structured around the psalmist's promise to bring burnt offerings "into your house" (which probably refers to the Temple in Jerusalem). Verse 13 makes this promise initially and the promise appears again in greater detail in verse 15. In between is the explanation that such offerings will fulfill the vows the psalmist made when in trouble (66:13-14). The vows were not empty pledges or attempts to manipulate God. The offerings made give evidence to that fact. Rather, the vows are a sign of the faith of the psalmist who expressed in them gratitude for and dependence on God.

Psalm 66:16-20. This final section of the psalm again begins with a plural imperative. This time, however, the call is given by the individual who spoke in verses 13-15 to those "who fear God" to "hear" or "listen" (NIV) to testimony of God's acts for the psalmist (66:16). The main message is that the psalmist cried out to God and God heeded the prayer (66:19). This is general language. It is reminiscent, however, of language in Exodus. The Hebrew term for "listen" appears in Exodus 3:7, and "steadfast love" (Psalm 66:20) occurs in Exodus 15:13. So, it seems the exodus story has become the paradigm for the psalmist's personal experience. The account of God's rescuing the Israelites from slavery has given shape to the psalmist's own testimony of deliverance.

Verses 16-20 are addressed to "all you who fear God." This description refers to those who stand humbly before God and who worship God rightly as a result. The individual who gives testimony in these verses also speaks as one who "fears God." He or she praised God (66:17) after carefully examining his or her heart for evil thoughts ("cherished iniquity;" 66:18). This testimony does not claim moral purity. Rather, it claims right relationship with God, relationship characterized by reliance on God for forgiveness and salvation.

INTERPRETING THE SCRIPTURE

Psalm 66 in the Psalter

Some psalms seem to appear in their particular location in the Psalter because they share important ideas with the psalms around them. Psalm 66 certainly shares vocabulary and themes with Psalms 65 and 67; read together and read as a progression, these three psalms express the message of God's sovereignty more completely than any one of the psalms expresses alone.

Psalm 65, like Psalm 66, is a psalm of praise. It concludes with an extended celebration of God's rule over and blessings on the earth. Rivers, pastures, hills, meadows, and valleys are all decked out in signs of God's abundance (Psalm 65:9-13). Moreover, the psalm closes by saying that these elements of the natural world "shout and sing together for joy" (Psalm 65:13). Psalm 66 then begins with the same language that ends Psalm 65: "Make a joyful noise to God" (Psalm 66:1). Both psalms also speak of God's "awesome deeds" (Psalms 65:5; 66:3, 5). In Psalm 65 God's mighty acts consist of God ordering and blessing the world. Hence, all parts of the earth praise God. In Psalm 66 God's awesome deeds are God's saving actions for God's people. A representative of the people thus gives thanks and praise (along with sacrifices; 66:13-20). Hence, together Psalms 65 and 66 express a comprehensive understanding of God's sovereignty. God rules over and blesses the earth (Psalm 65), and God rules over all the peoples of the earth, as seen in God's acts for God's people (Psalm 66).

Psalm 67 follows these two psalms with a continuation of the themes in both. Like Psalm 66, Psalm 67 recognizes that God has control over and brings justice to the nations (Psalm 67:4; compare Psalm 66:7). All "the peoples" are called to praise God (Psalm 67:3, 5; compare Psalm 66:1, 4, and especially 8). Like Psalm 65, Psalm 67 rec-ognizes the earth's bounty as a sign of God's blessing (Psalm 67:6). Hence, Psalm 67 ties together the theological points of the previous two psalms. Together, Psalms 65, 66, and 67 give a complete picture of God's sovereign rule—over the earth, over God's people, over the nations—and the benefits of that rule for all the earth and all people.

Community and Individual

As noted above, one of the distinctive features of Psalm 66 is that it begins as a hymn that calls "all the earth" to praise God (66:1-12), but it ends with thanksgiving spoken by an individual (66:13-20). As also noted, when this psalm was performed or sung in worship the individual may have functioned as a representative of the whole congregation. The "I" voice was perhaps a personalized "We." However, the move from corporate to individual identity is also very important theologically for the individual's own faith. In Scripture, God never acts for an individual apart from God's action for the people as a whole and ultimately for all humankind. God first created humankind in God's image (Genesis 1:26-27) and blessed all people; only later did God narrow God's focus to Abraham and Sarah and their family. Or, in the New Testament God acted in Christ for all people (see John 1:1-18). Then, individuals responded to that action related to their own circumstances (John 1:35-51).

This pattern of corporate/individual faith that also appears in Psalm 66 is extremely important theologically for two reasons. First, it is important for understanding the nature of our faith in general. God acted for humankind and for Israel, and that action is then realized and personalized in the lives of individuals. Second, this pattern in Scripture is important for understanding how individuals should respond to God and imagine their relationship with God. Some expressions of the Christian faith seem to claim that relationship with God is so personal that God acts for individuals with no communal concerns. That is not to say that God does not care for individuals and know them intimately. But individuals should not imagine they have their own private God who does their bidding. Instead, we as individuals are invited to participate in what God has done and is doing for humankind. With that in mind, our response to God will be shaped in particular ways that are apparent in Psalm 66. For example, when we thank God for what God has done for us, we will do so as a person who is part of a community of faith, not as a lone soul who has private deals with God. Also, as we realize our place in the community of faith our praise and thanksgiving (and our prayers for help) will necessarily bring us into solidarity with other believers across time and space. We will realize we have something in common with Christians from centuries past and with believers in Africa and Asia, for example, even if we have never been there.

Ritual Sacrifice and Faith

Psalm 66:13-15 focuses on the fulfillment of a vow through sacrificial ritual. The importance of sacrifice in the psalm is made evident by the long list of what is sacrificed: "offerings of fatlings," "sacrifice of rams," "offering of bulls and goats" (66:15). The list is so long that it can hardly be taken literally as a description of what is sacrificed in one service. Rather, the psalmist seems to offer an exaggerated description as a way of saying he or she will give a complete and pure offering.

Many Christians read this portion of the psalm as irrelevant to their faith and life. Some may even read Psalm 66:13-15 as a portion of the Old Testament that the New Testament repudiated and has now moved

beyond (see John 2:13-22). This has often been true particularly of Protestant Christians who have downplayed the role of ritual in Christian worship and devotion. This part of the psalm, however, is very important for all people of faith. It should be recognized that the psalmist does not hold sacrifice to be so important because it somehow garners God's favor. Neither does the psalmist offer them to pay God back for God's mighty deeds in the past. Rather, sacrifice here is a ritual statement of gratitude. As such, the burnt offerings mentioned in verses 13-15 are part of a larger confession of dependence on God that dominates the Book of Psalms.

Perhaps most importantly, the sacrifices described in Psalm 66:13-15 provide a way to make faith live, to act. To be sure, ritual is in some ways not "real life." It is dramatic, rehearsed, and "staged" action. Nevertheless, ritual is essential for faith for at least two reasons. One, it reminds us that our faith is incarnational. It is always lived faith, public faith. It is never purely personal or internal. Two, ritual can remind us of how we ought to live when we don't feel like so living. In the case of Psalm 66:13-15, the psalmist's example sets before us the importance of formal expressions of gratitude in response to God's grace. This is particularly pertinent to the issue of financial stewardship. The reference to sacrifices in this psalm does not apply to us directly. We no longer make the kind of sacrifices described here. But the purpose of the sacrifice is captured in our tithes and offerings. When we take seriously that giving is a ritual, we remind ourselves that our offerings are thanksgiving for what God has done. They are not responses to a particular service of worship or to a church's program. By regular giving of our finances we are thus reminded that all of life is to be given in response to God.

The sacrifices described in Psalm 66:13-15—like our tithes and offerings—essentially give witness to and honor God's power and mighty works on our behalf (66:3). Such sacrifices are a tangible means of worship, like making "a joyful noise to God" (66:1). Indeed, although the origins of sacrifice are somewhat mysterious, it is clear that sacrifice was and is a response to God's holiness. God's "awesome deeds" (66:3) naturally call for our response.

SHARING THE SCRIPTURE

Preparing Our Hearts

Explore this week's devotional reading, found in Psalm 40:1-5. Here we see that the psalmist was in desperate straits—in a "desolate pit," also translated as "pit of tumult" (40:2). God not only rescued him from the pit but also gave him a new song of praise to sing. The psalmist recognizes God's incomparably "wondrous deeds" (40:5). What reasons do you have to give thanks to God? From what "miry bog" (40:2) has God rescued you?

Pray that you and the adult learners will be aware of and thankful for the greatness of God.

Preparing Our Minds

Study the background Scripture from Psalm 66 and the lesson Scripture from Psalm 66:1-12. Consider what can ease a burden that is too heavy to bear.

Write on newsprint:

❏ information for next week's lesson, found under "Continue the Journey."
❏ activities for further spiritual growth in "Continue the Journey."

LEADING THE CLASS

(1) Gather to Learn

❖ Welcome the class members and introduce any guests.

❖ Pray that all of today's students will recognize that our God is awesome and dependable.

❖ Play a game with the students. Distribute paper and pencils. Read these directions slowly, allowing time for the students to complete one step before moving on to the next.

■ **Step 1: You are going on a ten-day vacation with the rest of the class. You are allowed to bring one suitcase. List sixteen items that you would want to pack.**
■ **Step 2: Work with a partner, preferably one who is not related. Exchange the papers on which you have written your list.**
■ **Step 3: Tell your partner that he or she will be responsible for carrying your suitcases.**
■ **Step 4: Look over the list of items in the suitcase that you are assigned to carry. Hmm, you think. Way too heavy! Trim your partner's list down to eight items.**
■ **Step 5: Talk again with your partner to see what he or she deleted from your list and why. See if you can negotiate the return of an item you felt strongly about taking with you.**
■ **Step 6: Call the class together.**

❖ Read aloud today's focus statement: **Many people carry burdens that are too heavy to bear. What can ease our load? We can sing to the Lord because God's great power holds our lives in God's hand and keeps our feet from slipping.**

(2) Recount Experiences of God's Deliverance in Israel's History

❖ Set the stage for today's lesson by reading or retelling "Psalm 66 in the

Psalter" from Interpreting the Scripture. Refer the students to the Scriptures cited there as you feel appropriate.

❖ Choose readers for Psalm 66:1-4, 5-7, and 8-12.

❖ Discuss these questions:

(1) **Why is God being praised?** (Israel is praising God for "awesome deeds." Verse 6 alludes specifically to the Exodus.)

(2) **Who is being invited to sing God's praises?** (Note that verse 1 invites "all the earth" to praise God; God's deeds of grace and mercy are not limited to the chosen ones of Israel.)

(3) **What does this psalm reveal to you about God?** (Note the emphasis on God's great deeds, God's power over enemies, God's ability to deliver the people as evidenced by the exodus, God as One who tests but remains dependable and brings people out of difficult situations.)

(4) **Would you join the chorus in praise for this God? Why or why not?**

(5) **Read aloud in unison today's key verse, Psalm 66:5. If you were to invite people to "come and see" what God is doing in your church, what would people find?**

(3) Affirm an Abiding Conviction in God's Power to Save and Deliver God's People

❖ Read: **Recall from the game for Gather to Learn that we are all carrying heavy "suitcases" filled with many things we really don't need. Many of us are weighed down by guilt, worry, doubt, fear, and uncertainty about the future. The psalmist reminds us that we are to praise the God who has delivered us from burdens we cannot bear. And yet, burdens remain for many people. People lose jobs and homes; marriages disintegrate; loved ones die; we become estranged from friends and family. When torrents of grief**

and pain roll over us, can we really affirm that God is able to save us? Do we truly believe that our God is an awesome God? Think about that for a moment.

❖ Encourage the students to assess their conviction about God's power to deliver them by asking them to remember a situation in which they really needed God's help. Ask these questions, pausing after each one so that the adults may respond silently.

(1) **Have you ever been in a situation where it seemed that God was not answering your prayers or meeting your needs? If so, what was that situation? How did it challenge your faith?** (pause)

(2) **As time passed, were you able to see God's hand at work to save you from whatever problem or crisis overwhelmed you? How did you know God was present?** (pause)

(3) **How were you able to affirm that God is dependable and able to perform awesome deeds? Who did you tell about your experiences?**

❖ Offer volunteers the opportunity to complete this sentence: **I am convinced that God has the power to save and deliver me because. . . .** You are not looking for stories here; but rather, a few words summarizing why the student knows God is truly awesome.

(4) Develop Testimony of How God Delivered the Learners and Use It to Encourage Others

❖ Read aloud this story from www.he invites.org/fullStory.php3/0339.html: **Awaiting the arrival of her family for her wedding in India, a bride affirms the power of God's deliverance in the midst of a near tragedy. Traveling in a Jeep, nine people, most close family members of the bride, were plunged into a lake in a rural area when the driver fell asleep. Unable to swim, these Christians cried to God for help. Unaware of the accident, an elephant keeper whose animal was acting strangely freed the elephant, who went to the lake** and used his trunk to rescue all the stranded passengers.

❖ Point out that while most of us do not have stories as dramatic as this one to tell, most of us have experienced God's deliverance. Invite students to share such stories, either with the class as a whole or in a small group.

❖ Challenge each person to go forth to share a story of God's deliverance to encourage someone who is facing difficult circumstances.

(5) Continue the Journey

❖ Pray that those who have participated today will share the good news of God's awesome deeds.

❖ Read aloud this preparation for next week's lesson. You may also want to post it on newsprint for the students to copy.

- **Title: God Is Forever**
- **Background Scripture: Psalm 90**
- **Lesson Scripture: Psalm 90:1-12**
- **Focus of the Lesson: We want to live in such a way that at the end of our days we can say confidently, "My life was worthwhile." What help is available to make the most**

of our days regardless of their number? Psalm 90 reminds us that though life is fleeting, we can live wisely with God's eternal presence.

❖ Challenge the students to complete one or more of these activities for further spiritual growth related to this week's session. Post this information on newsprint for the students to copy.

(1) **Page through the Psalms looking for songs of praise. Find one that seems to fit your current life situation and reasons you may have to praise God. Read it each day this week.**

(2) **Share with others how God's awesome deeds have made a difference in your life.**

(3) **Give thanks to God for help in times of need.**

❖ Sing or read aloud "Come, Thou Almighty King."

❖ Conclude today's session by leading the class in this commission: **We go forth to worship and serve the Lord our God. Thanks be to our merciful and gracious God.**

UNIT 3: GOD PROTECTS
GOD IS FOREVER

PREVIEWING THE LESSON

Lesson Scripture: Psalm 90:1-12
Background Scripture: Psalm 90
Key Verse: Psalm 90:2

Focus of the Lesson:
We want to live in such a way that at the end of our days we can say confidently, "My life was worthwhile." What help is available to make the most of our days regardless of their number? Psalm 90 reminds us that though life is fleeting, we can live wisely with God's eternal presence.

Goals for the Learners:
(1) to examine Psalm 90 to contrast humanity's frailty and sinfulness with God's enduring power and goodness.
(2) to cultivate thankfulness that God cares about how they can get the most out of the gift of life.
(3) to declare how their relationship with God gives lasting meaning and significance to their lives.

Pronunciation Guide:
adamah (ad aw maw')   *hesed* (kheh' sed)

Supplies:
Bibles, newsprint and marker, paper and pencils, hymnals

READING THE SCRIPTURE

NRSV
Psalm 90:1-12
1 Lord, you have been our dwelling place
    in all generations.
2 **Before the mountains were**
    brought forth,
    or ever you had formed the earth and
    the world,

NIV
Psalm 90:1-12
1Lord, you have been our dwelling place
    throughout all generations.
2**Before the mountains were born**
    or you brought forth the earth and the
    world,

from everlasting to everlasting you are God.	from everlasting to everlasting you are God.

<table>
<tr><td>

3 You turn us back to dust,
   and say, "Turn back, you mortals."
4 For a thousand years in your sight
   are like yesterday when it is past,
   or like a watch in the night.
5 You sweep them away; they are
     like a dream,
   like grass that is renewed in
     the morning;
6 in the morning it flourishes and
     is renewed;
   in the evening it fades and withers.
7 For we are consumed by your anger;
   by your wrath we are overwhelmed.
8 You have set our iniquities before you,
   our secret sins in the light of your
     countenance.
9 For all our days pass away under
     your wrath;
   our years come to an end like a sigh.
10 The days of our life are seventy years,
   or perhaps eighty, if we are strong;
   even then their span is only toil and
     trouble;
   they are soon gone, and we fly away.
11 Who considers the power of your anger?
   Your wrath is as great as the fear that
     is due you.
12 So teach us to count our days
   that we may gain a wise heart.

</td><td>

3You turn men back to dust,
   saying, "Return to dust, O sons of men."
4For a thousand years in your sight
   are like a day that has just gone by,
   or like a watch in the night.
5You sweep men away in the sleep of death;
   they are like the new grass of the
     morning—
6though in the morning it springs up new,
   by evening it is dry and withered.
7We are consumed by your anger
   and terrified by your indignation.
8You have set our iniquities before you,
   our secret sins in the light of your
     presence.
9All our days pass away under your wrath;
   we finish our years with a moan.
10The length of our days is seventy years—
   or eighty, if we have the strength;
   yet their span is but trouble and sorrow,
   for they quickly pass, and we fly away.
11Who knows the power of your anger?
   For your wrath is as great as the fear
     that is due you.
12Teach us to number our days aright,
   that we may gain a heart of wisdom.

</td></tr>
</table>

UNDERSTANDING THE SCRIPTURE

Introduction. The central subject of Psalm 90 is time. It deals with the brevity of human life—there is too little time. But most importantly, the psalm asks how to live life in light of the certainty of death and the fleeting nature of human existence. Part of the answer is to focus first on the eternality of God, the one who gives life (90:1) and makes life purposeful (90:17).

Psalm 90 has an important location in the Book of Psalms. It is the first psalm in Book Four of the Psalter (the Psalms are divided into five "books" or divisions: Book I: Psalms 1–41; Book II: Psalms 42–72; Book III: Psalms 73–89; Book IV: Psalms 90–106; Book V: Psalms 107–150). Book III was dominated by psalms that complained to God about Israel's suffering. This ended with Psalm 89, a psalm that complained about the failure of the Davidic monarchy. Psalm 90 now begins a book of psalms that seems to answer that complaint with the assurance that "the LORD reigns" (Psalm 93:1 NIV).

Psalm 90 speaks about the brevity of human life in order to address a particular trauma Israel suffered, namely the Babylonian exile (587–539 B.C.). The brevity of life, the wrath of God (90:7, 9, 11), and humanity's "toil and trouble" (90:10) are ciphers for Israel's suffering. Isaiah 40 uses similar language and images to speak about this event.

Psalm 90 is the only psalm in the book of Psalms attributed to Moses (see the title of Psalm 90, "A Prayer of Moses, the man of God"). The titles of psalms were added later in order to provide context for reading them, either by associating them with a person (mostly with David) or with an event. The scribes who preserved the psalm understood it as a prayer for Israel when it was in distress and they imagined the prayer as the words of Moses. Who better to voice a prayer for God's people in such a situation than Moses? Moses had prayed for Israel when God became angry with them in the wilderness (Exodus 32). Now in Psalm 90 Moses prays across the ages for Israel in exile.

Psalm 90:1-2. The first verse expresses confidence in God as the source of protection and care. "Dwelling place" is closely related to the term "refuge" which appears frequently in the Psalms (2:12; 34:8; 71:3). The claim about God here is very personal—the Lord is *our* dwelling place (italics added). The concern for time is also apparent from the start. The Lord has been our dwelling place "in all generations." Verse 2, however, declares God's greatness by pointing to God's time. Before the world was put in order God was God.

Psalm 90:3-6. The second section of the psalm contrasts God's eternality with humanity's weakness. While God is eternal, we are made from dust and to dust we return. The word "mortals" (NRSV) reads woodenly "sons of men" in Hebrew (as NIV translates). "Men" (or better "humanity") renders the word *adam* which is related to the word for earth or soil (*adamah*). There is

nothing permanent about us. In fact, verses 5-6 compare human life to the herbage that sprouts with the morning dew and then fades away as soon as the sun strikes it (see similar images in Psalm 103:15-16 and Isaiah 40:6-8).

Psalm 90:7-12. Verses 7-11 continue to speak of humanity's fleeting existence. But here the psalmist links the brevity of life with God's wrath. Normally the Old Testament mentions God's wrath as a way of saying God punishes people for their sins. In Psalm 90, however, the connection is different (though see the discussion of sinfulness under "The Reality of Death"). Death is a sign of God's wrath in that it is God's ultimate "no" to human pretensions to autonomy. This is a way of saying that eternity belongs to God alone. Verse 12 asks for help to respond properly to the knowledge that life is brief: "teach us to count our days." "Count our days" does not mean to help us focus on the limited nature of life; rather, it means to cherish each day as a gift from God.

Psalm 90:13-17. The final portion of Psalm 90 shifts its language from reflection on the human condition to petitions for God to act concerning that condition. This section also takes on a distinctly "Mosaic" tone. Verse 13 recalls the prayer of Moses in Exodus 32 when he interceded for Israel when God was about to destroy the people because they had made the golden calf. The word, "turn" is exactly the word Moses used in Exodus 32:12. The word could also be translated "change your mind" or even "repent!" Only Moses and the prophet Amos (Amos 7:2, 5) make such a request of God.

Moses refers to Israel as "your servants" in verses 13 and 16. This label identifies Israel as subjects of God who identify with God as their king or "lord." It is also important that the previous psalm (Psalm 89) gave this title to David (89:3, 20, 39, 50). Psalm 89 complained that God had rejected God's servant by allowing his enemies to defeat him by defeating his line. The Babylonian exile brought an end to Israel's monarchy and called into question the covenant with David (Psalm 89:39). One way Israel dealt with this trauma and the uncertain future for the Davidic monarchy was to speak of the whole people as God's "servants," as heirs to the promises to David.

Psalm 89 complained that God removed God's "steadfast love" from David (89:49). Now Psalm 90:14 petitions God to "satisfy us in the morning with your steadfast love." Steadfast love translates a Hebrew word, *hesed*, that cannot adequately be translated. It refers to the covenant faithfulness God shows to God's people. Hence, NIV renders the term "unfailing love" in verse 14.

INTERPRETING THE SCRIPTURE

O God, Our Dwelling Place

Although Psalm 90 may seem to be mainly about time, notably the lack of time humans have, the first two verses emphasize space as well and they focus on God rather than humans. Psalm 90:1 declares God has been "our dwelling place" (an emphasis on space) "in all generations" (an emphasis on time). Verse 2 begins with space (mountains, earth, and world) and ends with time ("from everlasting to everlasting") as they relate to God.

These two verses therefore seem to have a structure that says something very important about God. Namely, the way verse 1 begins and verse 2 ends, with references to God's identity, communicates the idea that God is all-encompassing. Both time and space are in God's control. Hence, the limits of humans portrayed in verses 3-10 must be understood in relation to God's unlimited power.

The Reality of Death

One of the most important and pervasive messages of Psalm 90:1-12 is that life is short. Death is near at hand. The psalm goes to great lengths to express that truth: our lives are like grass that "fades and withers" (90:6); "our years come to an end like a sigh" (90:9); our days "are soon gone, and we fly away" (90:10). That message may at first seem negative. It may seem even more depressing that our human limits are a sign of God's wrath. Indeed, Psalm 90:1-12 may seem to run counter to the New Testament's hopeful word that in Christ death has lost its sting (1 Corinthians 15:55). But in fact this psalm is entirely consistent with the message of resurrection. What it really says is that life and eternity belong to God, not to us. The emphasis on death is also closely tied to the awareness that we are sinful creatures. As verse 8 says, our sins are set before God. They are a sure sign of our limitations, our finitude. Therefore, our lives—and our resurrection—come from the Creator and giver of life. Psalm 90's focus on death reins us in and reminds us that we live because God holds us in life.

This message of death's certainty and of human limits may seem so obvious that it does not need to be stated. The Book of Psalms elsewhere, however, indicates that in fact many do not face this truth. For example, Psalm 36:2 speaks of those who "flatter themselves" and who believe their sinful deeds will not be noticed. They live as though they have total control of the world, as though they are not ultimately under God's "wrath" (as Psalm 90:7-8 indicate). Although Psalm 90 does not use the term, other psalms call such people "wicked." This label does not refer to persons who are morally deficient. After all, as Psalm 143:2 acknowledges, all people fail to meet God's expectations. Rather, the word is used for those who do not admit their deficiencies. Those the Psalms call "righteous" are those who confess their sins and live in repentance (and are not self-righteous).

This ironic portrayal of the righteous and the wicked in the Psalms—which is implied in Psalm 90—has important implications for how we live. As the Psalms testify, those who refuse to admit their human limits (and refuse to confess their sins) inevitably act violently towards others. They take advantage of others because they believe they are entitled to more of the world than they really are (see again Psalm 36:3-4). But those who acknowledge that they live within the sovereignty of God are more willing to promote the well-being of others, as God intends. In other words, the perspective on human limitation Psalm 90 gives is not intended just to "put us in our place" in relation to God. It also helps us to live rightly towards other human beings.

The Gift of Life

If the main message of Psalm 90 is that God is eternal and we are not, then the wisdom of the psalm is in knowing how to react to that reality. The psalm's main "advice" comes in verse 12: "teach us to count our days." This line certainly does not mean to focus on how few days we have. Such a negative focus would rob us of the joy available to us in our days, however brief they may be. The context of the psalm also argues against the notion that we can count on longevity. Verse 10 declares that human life is short even for those who are physically sound. The wisdom of "counting our days" seems rather to be in recognizing that each day is a gift.

The message of Psalm 90:12 is captured well in the music of Christian folk musician David Bailey. At age 30 Bailey had a brain tumor that doctors said would end his life within six months. But he became one of the rare people who recover from such a tumor. Bailey returned to his music, which he had left for a corporate career, and now sings about hope and life, as a gift from God. One of the most important things he says he learned from his illness—even before he knew he would be cured—was not to ask "Why me?" but to ask "What now?" instead. That is really the message of Psalm 90:12. Instead of asking, "Why is my (and our) life so short," it is better to ask, "What can I do with the life I have?" David Bailey expresses this in a song called "Love the Time." The song emphasizes loving and cherishing each moment. We should love "the time it takes to watch the sunrise" and even the time it takes waiting in line, driving a child to school, any time we have we should find in it an opportunity to cherish the gifts of God. Our time, our lives, are surely such gifts.

If Psalm 90 is taken seriously as a prayer of Moses, it might lead us to think of and relate to Israel's existence in the wilderness. Relying on God to provide manna, they had to live by faith each day. With this in mind, Psalm 90:12 might be translated "teach us to live day by day." The point of this advice, and the point of Israel's living on manna in the desert, is that life with God must be lived by faith. Living by faith means we recognize that God, who is eternal, watches over us and holds our future. Living by any other view of the world will lead us either to squander our days because we think they are unlimited or to fret over the brevity of life as though we could change it.

Understood this way, Psalm 90:1-12 gives very much the same perspective Jesus gave his disciples when he told them not to worry about tomorrow (Matthew 6:25-34). His point, of course, was not that we should avoid planning for the future nor that we should shirk our responsibilities. Rather, we must recognize that none of our preparation for or worry about the future will add a day to our lives. Instead of fretting over such things, Jesus insisted that with the time we have we strive for the kingdom of God (Matthew 6:33). Such striving shows that we know what to do with our lives. We know truly how to "count our days."

SHARING THE SCRIPTURE

Preparing Our Hearts

Explore this week's devotional reading, found in 1 Timothy 1:12-17. Paul recalls the negative aspects of his prior life, but is grateful that through the mercy of Christ Jesus he has become a believer. He recognizes that "Jesus came into the world to save sinners" (1:15). With that salvation comes eternal life. What about you? Do you recognize that while this earthly life is short, God exists for all eternity and that through Christ you can experience the joy of life in God's presence forever? Offer a prayer of thanks for this amazingly good news.

Pray that you and the adult learners will recognize that you are children of the Creator of the universe.

Preparing Our Minds

Study the background Scripture from Psalm 90 and the lesson Scripture from Psalm 90:1-12. Think about where you can seek help to make the most of your life, however long it may be.

Write on newsprint:
- ❑ partial sentences for Gather to Learn.
- ❑ information for next week's lesson, found under "Continue the Journey."
- ❑ activities for further spiritual growth in "Continue the Journey."

LEADING THE CLASS

(1) Gather to Learn

❖ Welcome the class members and introduce any guests.

❖ Pray that all who have come will open their hearts and minds to the message God has for them today.

❖ Distribute paper and pencils. Invite the students to complete one or both of these two partial sentences, which you will write on newsprint:

I will be able to say my life has been worthwhile if . . .

I want people to remember me as . . .

❖ Provide time for volunteers to read what they have written. If you do this in small groups, more people will be able to share their ideas.

❖ Read aloud today's focus statement: **We want to live in such a way that at the end of our days we can say confidently, "My life was worthwhile." What help is available to make the most of our days regardless of their number? Psalm 90 reminds us that though life is fleeting, we can live wisely with God's eternal presence.**

(2) Examine Psalm 90 to Contrast Humanity's Frailty and Sinfulness With God's Enduring Power and Goodness

❖ Prepare the students to encounter Psalm 90 by reading or retelling the Introduction from Understanding the Scripture.

❖ Invite the students to read Psalm 90:1-12 responsively if you have access to a hymnal with a Psalter that includes these verses. If not, read these verses yourself as the students follow along in their Bibles.

❖ **Option:** Solicit volunteers who have different translations of the Bible to read these verses, or a portion of these verses, after the twelve verses have been read once. Talk with the students about how different words enable them to find new meanings.

❖ Post a sheet of newsprint. Draw a vertical line down the center of the page. Create a chart by heading the left side "God" and the right side "Humanity." Under each heading write something about what Psalm 90 teaches us about God and about people. For example, God exists "from everlasting to everlasting," whereas individual human beings live for 70-80 years.

❖ Encourage the adults to discuss the differences they see as they review the chart they had made. Use any information from the lesson to help clarify meanings of certain phrases. For example, "teach us to count our days" is not really about focusing on the few days that we have but rather living each day purposefully as a gift from God.

(3) Cultivate Thankfulness that God Cares About How the Learners Can Get the Most Out of the Gift of Life

❖ Read "The Gift of Life" from Interpreting the Scripture. Music by David M. Bailey is mentioned as embodying ideas in Psalm 90. Encourage the adults to name other songs, perhaps citing a specific line or two, that also relate to getting the most out of the life God has given us.

❖ Distribute hymnals and ask the class to turn to "Now Thank We All Our God." (If your hymnal does not include this hymn, check the Internet for the words, which were penned in the seventeenth century and are in the public domain.) Encourage the students to read the words silently, pausing at any that may especially speak to them. Or, read the words aloud yourself if the students do not have the words before them. Ask them to consider these questions, which you will read aloud.

(1) What are the "gifts of love" with which "this bounteous God" has blessed you?

(2) How do these gifts help you to get the most out of the life God has given you?

❖ Encourage volunteers to name at least one gift for which they are thankful. What difference has this gift made in their lives?

(4) Declare How the Learners' Relationship With God Gives Lasting Meaning and Significance to Their Lives

❖ Read these words that appeared in an Internet article entitled "Does God Matter: Questioning the Importance of God" (http://atheism.about.com/od/does godexist/a/doesgodmatter.htm): **Austin Cline argues from the perspective of an unbeliever when he writes, "It can be argued that even if a god did exist, that existence would not provide either meaning or purpose to a person's life. Christians seem to maintain that serving their god's will is what gives them purpose, but I hardly think that this is admirable. Mindless obedience might be praiseworthy in dogs and other domesticated animals, but it certainly isn't of much value in mature adult humans. Moreover, it is debatable whether or not a god which desires such uncritical obedience is worthy of any obedience in the first place."**

❖ Form groups of three to four students. Challenge the students to discuss how they would respond to Mr. Cline. Encourage them to give specific examples from their own lives as to how they believe a relationship with God gives their lives meaning and significance.

❖ Call the groups together. Allow each group a brief period to summarize their discussion and, if time permits, retell an example or two cited within their group.

(5) Continue the Journey

❖ Pray that the participants will go forth to share with others how their relationship with God gives meaning to their lives.

❖ Read aloud this preparation for next week's lesson. You may also want to post it on newsprint for the students to copy.

■ **Title: God Delivers and Protects**

■ **Background Scripture: Psalm 91**

■ **Lesson Scripture: Psalm 91:1-6, 9-16**

■ **Focus of the Lesson: Because we live in a fearful time, we look for peace and safety. Where can we find shelter in the midst of our fears? Psalm 91 tells us that if we trust in God, God will rescue and honor us.**

❖ Challenge the students to complete one or more of these activities for further spiritual growth related to this week's session. Post this information on newsprint for the students to copy.

(1) **Read Matthew 6:25-34, which is part of the Sermon on the Mount. Note that verse 30 expresses an idea that is similar to Psalm 90:6. Think about what it means to you to rely solely on God. Are there facets of your life that you need** to put completely in God's hands? If so, turn them over to God now.

(2) **Recall that Psalm 90 is often used during funerals because it is a source of comfort. Is there someone you know who is grieving who would be comforted by this psalm? If so, share this prayer of Moses with that person.**

(3) **Notice that Psalm 90 encompasses not only God's love but also God's wrath and indignation. Use a concordance to search your Bible for instances of God's love and God's wrath. How do you reconcile the inclusion of both love and wrath in the nature of God?**

❖ Sing or read aloud "O God, Our Help in Ages Past."

❖ Conclude today's session by leading the class in this commission: **We go forth to worship and serve the Lord our God. Thanks be to our merciful and gracious God.**

UNIT 3: GOD PROTECTS

GOD DELIVERS AND PROTECTS

PREVIEWING THE LESSON

Lesson Scripture: Psalm 91:1-6, 9-16
Background Scripture: Psalm 91
Key Verse: Psalm 91:14

Focus of the Lesson:
Because we live in a fearful time, we look for peace and safety. Where can we find shelter in the midst of our fears? Psalm 91 tells us that if we trust in God, God will rescue and honor us.

Goals for the Learners:
(1) to examine the rich imagery of God's promise of protection and safety in Psalm 91.
(2) to consider what it means to live in faith, trusting in God's protection.
(3) to work as agents of God's protection in their community.

Supplies:
Bibles, newsprint and marker, paper and pencils, hymnals

READING THE SCRIPTURE

NRSV
Psalm 91:1-6, 9-16

1 You who live in the shelter of the Most
     High,
    who abide in the shadow of the
      Almighty,
2 will say to the LORD, "My refuge and
    my fortress;
    my God, in whom I trust."
3 For he will deliver you from the snare
      of the fowler
    and from the deadly pestilence;

NIV
Psalm 91:1-6, 9-16

1He who dwells in the shelter of the
      Most High
    will rest in the shadow of the Almighty.
2I will say of the LORD, "He is my refuge
    and my fortress,
    my God, in whom I trust."
3Surely he will save you from the
      fowler's snare
    and from the deadly pestilence.
4He will cover you with his feathers,

4 he will cover you with his pinions,
   and under his wings you will find
     refuge;
   his faithfulness is a shield and buckler.

5 You will not fear the terror of the night,
   or the arrow that flies by day,

6 or the pestilence that stalks in darkness,
   or the destruction that wastes at
     noonday.

9 Because you have made the LORD
     your refuge,
   the Most High your dwelling place,

10 no evil shall befall you,
   no scourge come near your tent.

11 For he will command his angels
     concerning you
   to guard you in all your ways.

12 On their hands they will bear you up,
   so that you will not dash your foot
     against a stone.

13 You will tread on the lion and the adder,
   the young lion and the serpent you
     will trample under foot.

14 Those who love me, I will deliver;
   I will protect those who know my
     name.

15 When they call to me, I will answer them;
   I will be with them in trouble,
   I will rescue them and honor them.

16 With long life I will satisfy them,
   and show them my salvation.

and under his wings you will find refuge;
   his faithfulness will be your shield
     and rampart.

5 You will not fear the terror of night,
   nor the arrow that flies by day,

6 nor the pestilence that stalks in the
     darkness,
   nor the plague that destroys at midday.

9 If you make the Most High
     your dwelling—
   even the LORD, who is my refuge—

10 then no harm will befall you,
   no disaster will come near your tent.

11 For he will command his angels
     concerning you
   to guard you in all your ways;

12 they will lift you up in their hands,
   so that you will not strike your
     foot against a stone.

13 You will tread upon the lion and the cobra;
   you will trample the great lion and
     the serpent.

14 "Because he loves me," says the LORD,
   "I will rescue him;
   I will protect him, for he acknowledges
     my name.

15 He will call upon me, and I will answer
     him;
   I will be with him in trouble,
   I will deliver him and honor him.

16 With long life will I satisfy him
   and show him my salvation."

UNDERSTANDING THE SCRIPTURE

Introduction. Psalm 91 expresses confidence in God as one who defends those who trust in the Lord. The psalm consists of a confident declaration of faith in God's protection (91:1-13) followed by a divine speech that confirms the protection offered to the one who depends on God (91:14-16).

The key word in Psalm 91 is "refuge." The word itself appears three times (91:2, 4, 9). Numerous related words occur alongside this one: "shelter" (91:1), "shadow" (91:1), "fortress" (91:2), "dwelling place" (91:9). Each of these terms is a metaphor for God's protective power and each draws upon the idea that God provides shelter (from storm), shade (from the sun), and safety (from enemies). Given the abundance of this vocabulary, it is not surprising that many scholars have proposed Psalm 91 grew out of an experience in which the psalmist was rescued from trouble. The sheltering language further suggests that the words have the Temple in mind. That was likely the place the psalmist experienced God's provision of safety. Theories abound as to the exact circumstances; perhaps the psalmist came to the Temple seeking a fair trial after being accused of a crime and, after being vindicated, Psalm 91 was spoken. Regardless of the exact situation that helped created Psalm 91, it should be read in the context of hardship, suffering, and persecution.

Although the words of Psalm 91 might suggest a setting in the Jerusalem Temple, the place of this psalm in the Book of Psalms offers a slightly different way to read it. It is part of Book IV of the Psalter (Psalms 90–106). This section of the book follows a psalm that speaks despairingly of the end of Israel's monarchy (Psalm 89), a traumatic event caused by the Babylonian destruction of Jerusalem. Psalms 90–106 seem to "answer" the complaints of Psalm 89. These psalms in Book IV are dominated by claims that "the LORD is King" or (as some translations render it) "the LORD reigns" (see Psalms 93–99). This claim that God is still in control of the world was meant to be a comfort for those who had experienced defeat and exile. Psalm 91, with its promises of divine protection, is an important part of the assurance that "the LORD reigns."

Psalm 91:1-2. The first two verses of Psalm 91 are loaded with language and imagery that relate the psalmist's dependence on God. Verse 1 characterizes the one who trusts in God as one who "lives" and "abides" in the shelter or shadow of God. The language suggests permanent residence in the presence of the Divine. It is possible such terminology was influenced by the Temple personnel who literally lived in the Temple precincts (at least for the time they were on duty; see Deuteronomy 18:6-8). The description of the psalmist abiding in God's shelter could have come from the experience of seeking refuge from enemies in the

holy place. Or, this language may simply be a description of the person's security found among believers in the Temple's worship. Regardless of the explanation, these two verses contain an extended claim of faith and trust. Such faith characterizes the one whom God watches over and protects.

Psalm 91:3-13. This section of the psalm affirms the benefits of trusting in the Lord. It contains an extended description of how God keeps from harm the one who trusts. The list of dangers include attack of an enemy (91:5, 7), disease (91:3, 6), and demonic power (91:5-6). The time of God's protection is comprehensive: night, day, noontime (91:5-6). Such protection will be complete, as the famous statement in verses 11-12 suggests. Verse 13 also suggests this divine care will mark a turning back of natural forces; the psalmist will have charge over serpents and lions. Particularly this verse indicates the description of protection is illustrative and hyperbolic, not to be taken literally (see "The Hope of God's Protection" that follows). This is important especially as we apply Psalm 91 to the Christian life. It cannot be used as a literal promise never to suffer harm (91:11-12).

Psalm 91:14-16. Psalm 91 concludes with a divine affirmation of the benefits of trusting God, made earlier by the psalmist. Verse 14 includes two sentences that at first seem to present a cause and effect: "Those who love me, I will deliver; I will protect those who know my name." The first part of verse 15 speaks in a similar way: "When they call to me, I will answer them." These sentences should not be read, however, as an affirmation of works righteousness. To the contrary, what the psalm affirms about those whom God delivers is simply that they trust God. This is evident in the expression "call to me" in verse 15. But the characterizations of them as those who "love me" and "know my name" in verse 14 imply they understand and identify with God's character. The word for "love" moreover has the connotation of "cling to" or "desire" (see

Genesis 34:8). This section emphasizes God's action for the psalmist and the accent should be placed there: "I will be with them;" "I will rescue them" (Psalm 91:15); "I will satisfy them, and show them my salvation" (91:16).

The promise of long life in verse 16 connects this psalm to Psalms 90 and 92. Psalm 90:7-8 and 11 lament that the brevity of life is an expression of God's wrath and pleas

for God to bring purpose and fulfillment to the days God's people have (90:12, 15-17). Psalm 92:12-15 affirms that the righteous flourish into old age as they are planted in the courts of God's Temple. Between these two psalms, Psalm 91:16 seems like God's comforting answer to the complaint and pleading in Psalm 90 and the basis for joy and celebration in Psalm 92.

INTERPRETING THE SCRIPTURE

The Hope of God's Protection

Psalm 91:11-12 appears famously in the Gospels, quoted by the devil! (Matthew 4:6; Luke 4:10-11). The use of Psalm 91 in the story of the temptation of Jesus is important for understanding how the psalm was interpreted by Jews and Christians in the first century and for understanding how we should apply the psalm today. It seems to indicate first that the psalm was read as a messianic psalm by Jews and Christians in the first century. This makes sense since Psalm 91 speaks of God's unique protection of one who lives "in the shelter of the Most High" (91:1). The psalm uses military imagery that would fit a royal figure ("the arrow that flies by day," 91:5; "a thousand may fall at your side," 91:7). So, the tempter's use of the psalm's assurance of God's protection for Jesus should not be surprising.

Second, and most important, Jesus in his temptation gives an important lesson on how to apply the promises of Psalm 91 to one's life. The inclination to read verses like those the devil quotes as promises to be claimed must have been great. Ancient Jewish rabbis labeled this psalm "a song for evil encounters" (Babylonian Talmud, tractate *Shevuot* 15b). In line with this understanding of the psalm, portions of Psalm 91 were placed on amulets thought to offer

magical protection from evil. On one hand, the invocation of biblical words like those in Psalm 91 for protection is appropriate. In the ancient world there was great fear of magical power used for evil. Powerful words like those in Psalm 91 could be used to ward off such evil. Even though we may not believe in magical forces as ancient people did, we too can benefit from committing Scripture to memory or having a written record of key texts like this one to strengthen us in difficult or trying times. Such use seems to be suggested by the psalm itself.

On the other hand, Jesus insists this use of the psalm is not appropriate if used in an uncritical way. What the devil tempts Jesus to do is to act as though the words of Psalm 91 bind God and "require" God to act in certain ways. This is a subtle form of idolatry. The temptation is to replace God with the words of Psalm 91. The words become the source of power rather than a resource that points to God. In other words, the devil tempts Jesus to cease trusting in God and to place trust instead in this text. God, in this order of things, becomes nothing more than a genie in a magic lamp. We call on God by citing the text ("rubbing the lamp"), not by giving ourselves to God in faith. This is a misuse of the text in part because it is the opposite of what the text itself encourages and models. Indeed, we hope and believe God is with us and will protect us from evil, but Psalm 91 does not give us power over God to make God come to our aid.

Because the Lord Is Your Refuge

Psalm 91:10 makes the amazing claim that "no evil shall befall you" "because you have made the LORD your refuge" (91:9). It is striking that the psalm claims the psalmist will be safe and secure simply because she or he depends on God. This message may seem quite strange to Americans who are taught to think in terms of action and personal responsibility. Psalm 91 seems to suggest that the believer is to do absolutely nothing, and that such inaction will be all that is needed. The image of God as refuge in the Psalms does seem to promote passivity. Two points are important, however, to put the use of this language in the Psalms in perspective. First, the declaration of seeking refuge in the Psalms assumes that the psalmist is in distress and threatened by powers more powerful than she or he (either a human enemy or the power of evil in general). In the face of such evil the only proper response is to call on God for protection. Thus, to seek refuge in God is the greatest statement of faith in God in the Psalms.

The significance of the psalmist's seeking refuge in God is expressed well in Psalm 11. That psalm begins with a declaration of seeking refuge in God in the midst of an enemy's threat ("In the LORD I take refuge," Psalm 11:1a). But then the psalmist responds to those around him who obviously advised him to act differently: "How can you say to me, 'Flee like a bird to the mountains'" (Psalm 11:1b). The psalmist had a choice between trusting in God and trusting in his or her own resources. The next verse gives the reason it was essential to take refuge in God: "the wicked bend the bow, they have fitted their arrow to the string, to shoot in the dark at the upright in heart" (Psalm 11:2). What this indicates is

that "the wicked" represent a force too strong for the psalmist. The enemy being described is not personal or petty (and may represent evil on a cosmic scale). Moreover, the psalmist cannot ward off their threats by his or her own efforts. It is only possible by trusting in the Lord. Psalm 91's emphasis on and profession of dependence on God models this kind of trust.

Second, although the language of seeking refuge seems passive, other parts of the Christian canon speak in more active terms for those who pray such words. The prophet Amos rails against unjust members of society who "sell the righteous for silver, and the needy for a pair of sandals" (Amos 2:6). Isaiah and Micah add to this prophetic critique. So, although those who are helpless in the face of injustice may only be able to pray and take refuge in God, these other parts of the canon ensure that is not the only word on their behalf.

Psalm 91 and the Church Year

Psalm 91 is traditionally used at the beginning of the season of Lent. This is appropriate in that it appears in the Gospel story of Jesus' temptation, as previously discussed. But the psalm is a helpful Lenten resource apart from its use in the New Testament. With its extensive expression of trust in God it reminds us what Lent is all about. Indeed, the disciplines of the season—sacrifices of things we hold dear—are for the purpose of pointing us to God and reminding us that we depend on God for everything. Too often Lenten practices become almost like self-help exercises; giving up certain foods enhances our dieting efforts; praying every morning clears our mind and helps us concentrate at work; fasting one day per week gives us more time to work. Psalm 91, however, points us to the real purpose of the season: to remember the source of our security and salvation. It also gives us words to say to express this dependence on God.

SHARING THE SCRIPTURE

Preparing Our Hearts

Explore this week's devotional reading, found in Isaiah 52:7-12. These words may sound very familiar to you, for verse 7, along with Romans 10:15, is the basis for one of the soprano solos in Handel's beloved oratorio: "How beautiful are the feet of them that preach the gospel of peace, and bring glad tidings of good things" (*Messiah*, Number 38). Listen to this inspiring music, if possible. Look again at your Bible. What does the passage in verses 7-12 say to you about God? Do you find this message to be "good news"? If so, give thanks for it.

Pray that you and the adult learners will be able to affirm that the God of our salvation truly reigns.

Preparing Our Minds

Study the background Scripture from Psalm 91 and the lesson Scripture from Psalm 91:1-6, 9-16. Ask: Where can we find shelter in the midst of our fears?

Write on newsprint:
- ❏ information for next week's lesson, found under "Continue the Journey."
- ❏ activities for further spiritual growth in "Continue the Journey."

Plan a lecture based on Understanding the Scripture to unpack the meaning of Psalm 91 during the portion of the session entitled "Examine the Rich Imagery of God's Promise of Protection and Safety in Psalm 91."

Familiarize yourself with the information about Psalm 11 found in "Because the Lord Is Your Refuge" in Interpreting the Scripture.

LEADING THE CLASS

(1) Gather to Learn

❖ Welcome the class members and introduce any guests.

❖ Pray that all of the participants will allow the Holy Spirit to work in their lives as they encounter the lesson for today.

❖ Read aloud this information taken from a Lenten (2006) letter written by Nuhad Tomeh, the regional liaison for Syria, Lebanon, Iraq, and the Gulf for the Presbyterian Church (USA): **From Amman, Jordan, Ms. Tomeh refers to an article about "Iraqi Christians who came to Jordan as refugees, seeking security and a safe place, leaving behind their families, friends, and homes, hoping for a better future." Not only Christians came but so too did Muslims. Jordan accepted some, particularly those who had financial resources. Those who were poor, however, were stranded at the border between Iraq and Jordan. They depended upon The Middle East Council of Churches and ACT International— Action by Churches Together—to provide food and other necessities, but these agencies' resources dwindled. Some Amman churches are attempting to meet the needs of these poor refugees, but their resources are also limited. Ms. Tomeh has been deeply touched by their faith and zeal for the Lord. She writes: "I learned as I talked to some of them that their faith and belief is stronger than despair, and their hope is stronger than depression."**

❖ Ask: **Suppose you lived in a country ravaged by war and were in the minority in terms of your religious beliefs. Where would you turn for help and safety?**

❖ Read aloud today's focus statement: **Because we live in a fearful time, we look for peace and safety. Where can we find shelter in the midst of our fears? Psalm 91 tells us that if we trust in God, God will rescue and honor us.**

(2) Examine the Rich Imagery of God's Promise of Protection and Safety in Psalm 91

❖ Ask for two volunteers, one to read Psalm 91:1-6 and the other, Psalm 91:9-16.

❖ Distribute paper and pencils and invite the students to sketch the "refuge" or "fortress" or "dwelling place" that they imagine when they think of God. We cannot, of course, know what these metaphorical places look like, but the adults may have some mental picture.

❖ Encourage volunteers to either show their work or talk about the image they have drawn.

 ❖ Discuss these questions:

  (1) When you think about these images, do you feel that God is truly able to deliver and protect you?

  (2) Is God a "safe harbor," so to speak, when things in your world seem to be falling apart? Explain your answer.

❖ Present the lecture that you have prepared from the Understanding the Scripture portion. Try to point out connections between the images the students have drawn or talked about and the information you are imparting.

❖ Encourage the students to raise questions or comment on the meaning of the portion of Psalm 91 that we are studying today.

(3) Consider What It Means to Live in Faith, Trusting in God's Protection

❖ Read or retell the first paragraph of "Because the Lord Is Your Refuge" in Interpreting the Scripture. Be sure to read the final sentence of this paragraph: **"Thus, to seek refuge in God is the greatest statement of faith in God in the Psalms."**

❖ Invite the students to discuss this question with a partner or small group: **Given that a tenet of the dominant culture in the United States is that everyone should be highly self-sufficient, what challenges do U.S. Christians face in appropriating this psalm for their own lives?**

❖ Bring the groups back together and provide time for them to report on one or two challenges they identified.

❖ Distribute paper and pencils if you have not already done so. Invite the students to reflect on this scenario: **Is there a situation in your life now where you need to rely on God's protection? Perhaps you are experiencing financial problems, job insecurity, concern about health for yourself or a loved one, difficulties with a child, or grief. Talk with God as if you are writing a letter to a friend. Tell God what your need is and how you envision yourself putting your trust in God to protect you and pull you through this challenging time.** Let the adults know as they begin that they will not be asked to tell anyone else what they have written. If they honestly have no issues in their own lives, perhaps they will write about a situation that concerns them in the life of a friend or the world.

❖ Break this meditative time by reading today's key verse, Psalm 91:14.

(4) Work as Agents of God's Protection in the Community

❖ Invite the students to call out groups of people (not names of individuals) in your community who need to experience God's protection. These will likely be vulnerable people who are powerless, such as children, older adults, and people who for whatever reasons live on the margins of society. List these groups on newsprint.

❖ Challenge the students to think about what they, together, could do to stand as protectors for at least one of these groups. Try to write ideas next to the appropriate group as listed on the newsprint. Ideas could range from hands-on assistance to financial aid to political advocacy to raising awareness among the community regarding the plight of these people.

❖ Invite students who are willing to commit themselves to this work to raise their hands. Try to organize small groups who are interested in a particular group of people. Encourage them to meet together in person or via phone or the Internet to determine what, when, and how they will act as agents of God's protection for these people who have no voice.

(5) Continue the Journey

❖ Pray as the class members go forth that they will trust in God's protection and commit themselves to protect others as an act of Christian discipleship.

❖ Read aloud this preparation for next week's lesson. You may also want to post it on newsprint for the students to copy.

- **Title: God Is All-knowing**
- **Background Scripture: Psalm 139**
- **Lesson Scripture: Psalm 139:1-6, 13-16, 23-24**
- **Focus of the Lesson: We all experience lonely times when we believe that no one knows our circumstances. Who knows us, cares about us, and searches us? The psalmist proclaims that God knows us better than we know ourselves.**

❖ Challenge the students to complete one or more of these activities for further spiritual growth related to this week's session. Post this information on newsprint for the students to copy.

(1) **Give a verbal account of how God protected you during a difficult time. You may talk with anyone, but try especially to speak with someone who needs to hear that God is able to protect and deliver.**

(2) **Look at how your government is trying to protect its citizens, especially those who are most vulnerable. How is the protection the government is offering similar to and different from what God can offer?**

(3) **Find the lyrics to "On Eagle's Wings" by Michael Joncas. (You can locate them online at lyrics playground.com/alpha/songs/o/on eagleswings.shtml). How does this song, based on Psalm 91, help you to feel the assurance of God's protection?**

❖ Sing or read aloud "Thy Holy Wings, O Savior."

❖ Conclude today's session by leading the class in this commission: **We go forth to worship and serve the Lord our God. Thanks be to our merciful and gracious God.**

UNIT 3: GOD PROTECTS
GOD IS ALL-KNOWING

PREVIEWING THE LESSON

Lesson Scripture: Psalm 139:1-6, 13-16, 23-24
Background Scripture: Psalm 139
Key Verse: Psalm 139:4

Focus of the Lesson:
We all experience lonely times when we believe that no one knows our circumstances. Who knows us, cares about us, and searches us? The psalmist proclaims that God knows us better than we know ourselves.

Goals for the Learners:
(1) to discover that God knows everything about us and has wonderfully made us.
(2) to experience God's unceasing presence.
(3) to invite the Holy Spirit's examination of their hearts and actions so that they might have everlasting life.

Pronunciation Guide:
Sheol (shee' ohl)

Supplies:
Bibles, newsprint and marker, paper and pencils, hymnals

READING THE SCRIPTURE

NRSV
Psalm 139:1-6, 13-16, 23-24
1 O LORD, you have searched me and
    known me.
2 You know when I sit down and when
    I rise up;
    you discern my thoughts from far
    away.
3 You search out my path and my
    lying down,

NIV
Psalm 139:1-6, 13-16, 23-24
1 O LORD, you have searched me
    and you know me.
2 You know when I sit and when I rise;
    you perceive my thoughts from afar.
3 You discern my going out and my
    lying down;
    you are familiar with all my ways.

and are acquainted with all my ways.
4 **Even before a word is on my tongue,**
O LORD, you know it completely.
5 You hem me in, behind and before,
and lay your hand upon me.
6 Such knowledge is too wonderful for me;
it is so high that I cannot attain it.
13 For it was you who formed my
inward parts;
you knit me together in my mother's
womb.
14 I praise you, for I am fearfully and
wonderfully made.
Wonderful are your works;
that I know very well.
15 My frame was not hidden from you,
when I was being made in secret,
intricately woven in the depths of
the earth.
16 Your eyes beheld my unformed substance.
In your book were written
all the days that were formed for me,
when none of them as yet existed.
23 Search me, O God, and know my heart;
test me and know my thoughts.
24 See if there is any wicked way in me,
and lead me in the way everlasting.

⁴Before a word is on my tongue
you know it completely, O LORD.
⁵You hem me in—behind and before;
you have laid your hand upon me.
⁶Such knowledge is too wonderful for me,
too lofty for me to attain.
¹³For you created my inmost being;
you knit me together in my
mother's womb.
¹⁴I praise you because I am fearfully and
wonderfully made;
your works are wonderful,
I know that full well.
¹⁵My frame was not hidden from you
when I was made in the secret place.
When I was woven together in
the depths of the earth,
16   your eyes saw my unformed body.
All the days ordained for me
were written in your book
before one of them came to be.
²³Search me, O God, and know my heart;
test me and know my anxious thoughts.
²⁴See if there is any offensive way in me,
and lead me in the way everlasting.

UNDERSTANDING THE SCRIPTURE

Introduction. The main subject of Psalm 139 is God's complete and intimate knowledge of the psalmist. The psalm explores this subject in two main parts. Verses 1-18 focus on God's unlimited knowledge of and presence with the psalmist (this section may be divided further into three subsections, 139:1-6, 7-12, and 13-18). Verses 19-24 conclude the psalm with a prayer for the downfall of the wicked, those who are against the Lord and the Lord's vision for the world. This final section may seem out of step with the rest of the psalm. It is connected to the theme of God knowing the psalmist, however, by the concluding prayer for God to "search" and "know" the psalmist's heart

and thoughts (139:23). The final verse suggests that God's searching of the one who prays will find no evil intentions (139:24). Hence, the psalmist is the polar opposite of the wicked, against whom he or she prays in verses 19-21.

Psalm 139:1-6. The key term in the first six verses is "know." This word or the related word "knowledge" (139:6) occurs four times in this brief section. The psalmist says God "knows me" (139:1), my every move, my every thought (139:2). Furthermore, God "searches out my path," my direction in life, the way I live, everywhere I go (139:3). God's knowledge is so complete that God knows the psalmist's words before they are spoken

(139:4). At the end of this first portion of the psalm the psalmist declares that such unlimited knowledge is beyond his or her comprehension.

Psalm 139:7-12. This section of the psalm continues the focus on God's knowledge of the psalmist, but with an emphasis on God's inescapable presence. Verses 7 and 8 describe God's presence in somewhat ambiguous terms. The term "flee" in verse 7 could imply an attempt to escape God because of fear. Perhaps the psalmist is saying that such escape is not possible though it might be desired. Verse 8 continues the psalmist's reflection on God's nearness by imagining the farthest extent of the divine presence. The psalmist cannot escape the Lord in heaven (above the earth) or in Sheol, the abode of the dead (perhaps thought to be beneath the earth). As this section unfolds, however, it becomes clear that God's constant nearness is good news. Verse 10 includes comforting terms to describe the impact of God's presence: "your hand shall lead me" and "your right hand shall hold me fast." Verses 11-12 bring these claims about God's omnipresence to a remarkable crescendo. "Darkness" often symbolizes chaos, evil, and death (see Job 12:22; Psalm 88:6, 12, 18). But God is present in the darkness. Moreover, with God present, darkness is no longer darkness! Darkness is overcome by God's light.

Psalm 139:13-18. In this section the theme of God's knowledge of the psalmist is expressed by reference to God's care for the psalmist throughout life. God knew the psalmist at the beginning (139:13-16) and will be present at the end (139:18). Verses 13-16 clearly refer to God's watchfulness over the psalmist before birth. The servant in Isaiah 49:1 and the prophet Jeremiah in Jeremiah 1:5 speak in similar ways about the Lord shaping them in the womb, but their point is that God established them for a divine purpose. Psalm 139 simply emphasizes God's knowledge of and delight in the one being created. God knew him or her

from conception and, in fact, "knit" the psalmist together in the womb (139:13). Verse 16 states that God knew the days of the psalmist's life "when none of them as yet existed." This verse should not be read as a claim of divine determinism, that God somehow set forth every event in the psalmist's life before birth. Rather, this is a poetic way of saying again that God knows the psalmist intimately and cares deeply about his or her life.

Psalm 139:19-24. The last portion of Psalm 139 disturbs the beautiful description of God's knowledge of the psalmist that dominates verses 1-18. Lines like "O that you would kill the wicked, O God" (139:19) seem less than Christian. Statements like, "Do I not hate those who hate you, O LORD" seem to go against Jesus' command to love, bless, and pray for enemies (Matthew 5:43-48; Luke 9:51-56; compare Romans 12:14-21). Can we read this final portion of the psalm as Christian Scripture? The church through the centuries has consistently answered that question, "yes." To understand how this has been possible, two points are essential. First, the church has recognized that the enemies in this psalm and the wrongs the enemies perpetrate are not personal or petty. They represent wickedness on a grand scale. Indeed, the church has understood the wicked here as the powers and forces of evil that plague this world (Ephesians 6:12). In a similar way Paul spoke against those who oppose the way of God: "Let anyone be accursed who has no love for the Lord" (1 Corinthians 16:22).

Second, the church has recognized that this attack on the wicked is really a statement about justice for the oppressed. Victims of the wicked are often called "righteous" because they depend on God. The psalmist has faith in a God who will ultimately not tolerate the abuse of the righteous. He or she believes God is working to bring persecution to an end. This faith in God who desires and works for the end of the righteous' suffering in turn allows Christians to read Psalm 139:19-24 alongside Jesus' command to love enemies, not in opposition to it. To love enemies and pray for those who persecute the righteous is possible because of the belief that God alone has prerogative to mete out justice. Conversely, to pray for God to avenge the wrongs perpetrated by the wicked is to believe that there is a larger system of justice that, if the righteous trust in it, gives them space to love their enemies. By doing so, the righteous avert human violence because they do not take "vengeance" upon themselves. It is left to God.

INTERPRETING THE SCRIPTURE

An I-Thou Relationship

Jewish theologian Martin Buber famously described the relationship between the human being and God as an "I-Thou" relationship. This characterization of how humans stand before God is appropriate to describe Psalm 139:1-6. The psalmist professes an intimate, personal relationship with God. The psalmist dares speak in personal terms: "*you* have searched *me*" (139:1, italics added); "*you* know when *I* sit down and when *I* rise up" (139:2, italics added). Yet, the psalmist recognizes that God is God, God is "Thou." In other words, the psalmist does not profess a casual relationship with God as though God is a buddy or pal. God is God. Verse 5 particularly ("you hem me in") acknowledges that God is sovereign and the psalmist cannot but go where God wills. At the end of verse 6 the psalmist confesses that God's knowledge and power are beyond human comprehension. The language in verse 6 ("too wonderful for me") is reminiscent of Psalm 131:1 in which the psalmist stands in awe of God and expresses complete dependence on the Lord. The psalmist speaks with similar reliance on God in Psalm 139:1-6. The careful balance of intimacy and awe is important as a model for all human relationships with God. Too often people of faith have one without the other. Either God is thought to be so high, lofty, and sovereign that relationship with God seems nigh impossible. Or God is thought to be so familiar that all sense of God's power is lost. Psalm 139:1-6 shows beautifully that both concepts of God are necessary to understand who God really is.

He Descended Into Hell

To understand the intimacy and nearness of God these words from the Apostles' Creed have puzzled many worshipers who say the creed each Sunday. Some versions of the creed, in fact, omit this line. Nevertheless, Psalm 139:8 supports this line, at least indirectly. To be sure, the Creed is motivated by other texts, such as 1 Peter 3:18-20, not by Psalm 139. Still, this psalm is a beautiful expression of the claim that God is always present even in places and circumstances that seem God-forsaken.

Psalm 139:7-12 is often read as a statement about God's omnipotence: God is not limited by space and time; God is always everywhere. But these verses also say more. They refute some common ideas about the limits of God and the world God created. In fact, Psalm 139:7-12 seems to speak directly to the questions and claims of Psalm 88. Psalm 88 is one of the most depressing passages in the entire Bible. It expresses the depths of despair and loneliness. In this psalm the psalmist feels as though she or he is in Sheol, the abode of the dead. Sheol represents the opposite of life and health

(Psalm 88:3). It seems to be the polar opposite of Zion and its Temple. Psalm 88 thus assumes that in such a place God is absent. So the psalmist muses, "Are your wonders known in the darkness, or your saving help in the land of forgetfulness?" (Psalm 88:12) Psalm 139 seems to answer this question with a resounding "Yes!" Even in the abode of the dead God knows and therefore may be known by those God created.

The point Psalm 139 makes is not really about Sheol or what happens after death. Rather, it says in magnificent poetry that there is always hope because God is always near.

This section goes beyond a statement of God's omnipotence in verses 11-12. These verses, which conclude the second portion of the psalm, turn the assumed limits of God on their head. Even granting that God is all powerful, one might assume that God accepts the natural limits of the world God created. Darkness is darkness. But the psalmist here declares that such limits do not apply to God. All of this is the source of great hope for the psalmist, and the reason the argument is made in the first place.

You Formed Me in the Womb

Psalm 139:13-18 is one of the most well-known and much loved passages in the Psalms. As with any popular passage, however, there is great potential for it to be misused or misinterpreted just enough to distort its true intentions. Theologians often cite this section of Psalm 139 as an illustration of God's omniscience (all-knowing character) or in support of the doctrine of predestination. God knows the psalmist before birth (139:13, 15) and knows the psalmist's days before they take place (139:16). These features surely support such doctrinal propositions, they point out. Other Christians have used the passage to argue for the sanctity of life and sometimes to argue specifically against abortion. This application of the psalm also has some

validity, given the psalm's attention to God's care for the psalmist before birth. Nevertheless, both of these uses of Psalm 139:13-18 miss the true focus of the passage and therefore distort its message to some degree.

The psalmist in this passage does not articulate a doctrine of God so much as he or she describes a relationship with God. The real point of the whole psalm is that the mighty creator of the universe knows the psalmist intimately. We may observe that point in part by the way verse 13 begins. The English word "for" translates a Hebrew particle that connects this section to what went before it. The idea that God is present in the farthest limits of the earth (139:9) and in the darkness (139:12) is prelude to the claim that God formed the psalmist in the womb (139:13). Hence, the Hebrew particle might better be translated "Indeed!" The point is this: God was present when the psalmist was being formed in the womb just as God is present in every part of the created order. That God does not dismiss Sheol or darkness as outside God's realm leads to the psalmist's point that God also did not relegate his or her own formation to "natural causes." God was intimately involved. But once again the point is not that life begins at a certain point or that God values unborn children (though one might well affirm that God does), but that God knows and shapes the psalmist's life in every detail.

Two features of Psalm 139:13-18 reinforce the fact that the psalm emphasizes the psalmist's relationship with God. First, the verb in verse 18 that NRSV translates "I come to the end" really means "I awake" (as NIV translates). This may mean that the psalmist is speaking these words while seeking safety in a sanctuary or in the Jerusalem Temple. After a night of worry, the psalmist is assured of safety in the morning, a sign of God's presence. This scenario makes sense, given the psalm's emphasis on God's presence, even if the details of the psalmist's situation are uncertain. Second, the reference to a "book" that recorded the days of the psalmist also supports the focus on God's knowledge of the psalmist (139:16). In some other texts references like this one seem to refer to a heavenly record of the deeds of those who rely on God (Psalm 40:7-8). Thus, Psalm 139 affirms that the psalmist is always in God's care.

As the psalm closes in verses 23-24, we again hear the psalmist asking God to "search" his or her heart and thoughts. The psalmist wants to be led in "the way everlasting," and therefore does not want to be guilty of being among the wicked. The writer clearly is seeking self-knowledge so as to be completely in tune with the God who knows each individual.

SHARING THE SCRIPTURE

Preparing Our Hearts

Explore this week's devotional reading, found in 1 John 3:18-24. In this letter written to a congregation suffering because it is divided, John writes that God "knows everything" (3:20). That same idea is prominent in today's Scripture reading from Psalm 139. Ponder that idea for a few moments. Be honest: How do you react to the statement that God knows everything?

Pray that you and the adult learners will find it comforting to affirm that God knows each and every person intimately.

Preparing Our Minds

Study the background Scripture from Psalm 139 and the lesson Scripture from Psalm 139:1-6, 13-16, 23-24. Ponder who knows and cares about you, especially when you feel alone.

Write on newsprint:
❑ information for next week's lesson, found under "Continue the Journey."
❑ activities for further spiritual growth in "Continue the Journey."

Prepare a lecture from Understanding the Scripture for "Discover that God Knows Everything About Us and Has Wonderfully Made Us" to help the students unpack the meaning of the beloved Psalm 139.

Review the examen of conscience for "Invite the Holy Spirit's Examination of Hearts and Actions So that the Learners Might Have Everlasting Life." You may wish to try this activity yourself prior to the class session.

LEADING THE CLASS

(1) Gather to Learn

❖ Welcome the class members and introduce any guests.

❖ Pray that those who have gathered for today's session will find comfort among friends and in the presence of God.

❖ Post a sheet of newsprint and invite the students to list songs that focus on loneliness and rejection. Here are some possible additions to the list: "The Rose" (Bette Midler), "Yesterday" (The Beatles), "Bang, Bang" (Cher), "Like a Rolling Stone" (Bob Dylan), "American Pie" (Don McLean), "I Am a Rock" (Simon and Garfunkel), "St. Louis Blues" (W. C. Handy), and numerous other blues songs. Perhaps students can quote a line or two from a song they have suggested to demonstrate how the song speaks of loneliness.

❖ Ask: **Why do such songs resonate with so many people?**

❖ Read aloud today's focus statement: **We all experience lonely times when we believe that no one knows our circumstances. Who knows us, cares about us, and searches us? The psalmist proclaims**

that God knows us better than we know ourselves.

(2) Discover that God Knows Everything About Us and Has Wonderfully Made Us

❖ Choose volunteers to read Psalm 139:1-6, 139:13-16, and 139:23-24. Suggest that those who are listening close their eyes and imagine they are speaking to God themselves.

❖ Ask: **What does this psalm say to you about God?** List ideas on newsprint.

❖ Point out that one of the major ideas, that God is all-knowing and inescapably present in our lives, can be comforting to some and terrifying to others. Probe the class to find out why they believe such an understanding of God might be terrifying to some. (You may wish to list ideas on newsprint.) Then, solicit reasons as to why such an understanding might be comforting. (Again, you may wish to list ideas.)

❖ Ask the class these questions:

(1) **Why do you think people have such different responses to the nearness of our inescapable God?**

(2) **What can you do to help those who are terrified of God want to draw nearer to the Holy One who has created us and continues to sustain us?**

❖ Conclude this portion of the lesson by presenting the lecture you have prepared to unpack the meaning of Psalm 139.

(3) Experience God's Unceasing Presence

❖ Read or retell "An I-Thou Relationship" from Interpreting the Scripture.

❖ Reread these words: **The careful balance of intimacy and awe is important as a model for all human relationships with God. . . . Psalm 139:1-6 shows beautifully that both concepts of God are necessary to understand who God really is.**

❖ Form groups of three or four students and ask them to talk with one another about

their concept of an appropriate I-Thou (human to God) relationship.

❖ End this portion of the lesson by inviting the adults to share brief stories about ways in which they have experienced God's presence—and know with certainty that God is always with them. (Be aware that some adults may not experience this certainty. Be open to their questions. Hopefully the stories of some classmates will help those who are uncertain know that God can be experienced intimately.)

(4) Invite the Holy Spirit's Examination of Hearts and Actions So that the Learners Might Have Everlasting Life

❖ Invite the students to practice an examination of conscience, based on a method of spiritual discipline that Saint Ignatius of Loyola (1491–1556), founder of the Jesuits, believed had been given to him by God nearly 500 years ago. The examen is a prayer that people who practice it try to use at lunchtime and again at bedtime.

❖ Follow these steps to examine your day so far. (If it is very early, suggest the students review yesterday.) Distribute paper and pencil as an option for those who prefer to jot down their thoughts.

■ **Step 1: Be in an attitude of quiet receptiveness, recognizing that God is present. Look lovingly at all of God's people and creation that you see around you.** (Pause)

■ **Step 2: Review the gifts that you received today, even small things such as sunshine on your face or the laughter of a child. Thank God for being present in all facets of your life today.** (Pause)

■ **Step 3: With the help of the Holy Spirit, look honestly at your actions and attitudes today. Honestly consider your motives. Seek to draw closer to God.** (Pause)

■ **Step 4: Review your entire day, as if you were watching a video.**

Where was Christ present? Where did you need to include him but did not? Be aware the Christ is always with you. How was your relationship with God deepened today? (Pause)

■ **Step 5: Speak with Jesus about your day. Ask for forgiveness, give thanks for God's grace, offer praise for responses to situations that allowed you to grow closer to God.** (Pause)

❖ Encourage the students to talk with the class or small group about how this process worked for them. Did it flow well? Was it difficult? [Note that at home they will need more time to do this.] Make clear that you are not asking the adults to discuss the *content* of what they shared with God, but rather how the *process* worked.

❖ Conclude this portion of the session by challenging the students to try this method at home as a way of drawing closer to God.

(5) Continue the Journey

❖ Pray that as today's participants go forth they will enter into a deeper relationship with the God who is always present and wants to be in a close personal relationship with each person.

❖ Read aloud this preparation for next week's lesson. You may also want to post it on newsprint for the students to copy.

■ **Title: The Highway for God**

■ **Background Scripture: Isaiah 40**
■ **Lesson Scripture: Isaiah 40:1-5, 25-26, 29-31**
■ **Focus of the Lesson: In spite of weakness, trouble, and impediments, people search for a better life. Where do people look for hope? The prophet Isaiah promises the people that God, with whom none can compare, will fulfill their hopes.**

❖ Challenge the students to complete one or more of these activities for further spiritual growth related to this week's session. Post this information on newsprint for the students to copy.

(1) **Practice an examination of conscience on a regular basis this week. How does this exercise enable you to grow closer to God?**

(2) **Read Psalm 139 dramatically as your own prayer to God. Choose a verse or two to memorize.**

(3) **Read "Psalm 139," a poem by minister, educator, and writer Howard Thurman, which appears in his book** *For the Inward Journey.* **How does Thurman's work open up Psalm 139 for you?**

❖ Sing or read aloud "Immortal, Invisible, God Only Wise."

❖ Conclude today's session by leading the class in this commission: **We go forth to worship and serve the Lord our God. Thanks be to our merciful and gracious God.**

SECOND QUARTER
Assuring Hope

DECEMBER 5, 2010–FEBRUARY 27, 2011

During the winter quarter we will explore the promises of hope found in the message of the prophet Isaiah, as well as the hope found in Jesus, who Christians have long connected with Isaiah's Suffering Servant. In the first two units, both of which focus on Isaiah, we hear words of comfort and hope directed toward the Israelites in the midst of imminent destruction of Jerusalem and their captivity in Babylon. In the third unit, which examines texts from the Gospel of Mark, we see fulfillment of Isaiah's prophecy in the person of Jesus.

The five sessions of Unit 1, "Comfort for God's People," begin on December 5 with a study of Isaiah 40, entitled "The Highway for God," which considers how God provides comfort and strength to those in need. "I Am Your God," which we will look at on December 12, is based on the truth that God will not forsake us, as seen in Isaiah 41:1–42:9. On December 19, we consider background Scripture from Isaiah 9:1-7; 11:1-9; and Matthew 1:18-25 in a lesson focused on "The Mission of the Servant. "I Will Be With You" is the promise of God found in Isaiah 43 that we will encounter on December 26. The first unit ends on January 2 with an investigation of Isaiah 44 in which God announces, "I Am Your Redeemer."

Unit 2, "A Future for God's People," opens on January 9 with a lesson of hope for the captives—"Turn to Me and Be Saved"—as announced in Isaiah 45. On January 16, the second of these four lessons, "Reassurance for God's People," delves into Isaiah 48, where God's forgiveness and desire for reconciliation assure the captives that God is willing to put the past aside. "The Servant's Mission in the World," the session for January 23, looks at Isaiah 49:1-6, which is the second of the Servant Songs. Part of the fourth Servant Song, found in Isaiah 53, concludes this unit on January 30 where the prophet promises that we are "Healed by His Bruises."

Unit 3, "Jesus, the Promised Servant-Leader," includes four sessions that look at Jesus' teachings on the nature of his messiahship, his efforts to prepare the disciples for the suffering he will endure for the salvation of others, and his teaching that those who follow him will also endure suffering. "Jesus Is the Messiah," declares Peter in the session for February 6 from Mark 8:27–9:1. Mark 9:2-13 is the basis for "This Is My Beloved," the story of Jesus' transfiguration on the mountain, which we will explore on February 13. "Jesus Came to Serve" not to be served and to give his life for others is the message of Mark 10:35-45, which we will unpack on February 20. Our unit concludes on February 27 with a look at Mark 13, often referred to as the "Little Apocalypse" because it includes Jesus' teachings on the end-times and the "Coming of the Son of Man."

MEET OUR WRITER

THE REVEREND DR. KAY HUGGINS

As an ordained Presbyterian clergywoman, Kay Huggins devoted most of her three decades of ministry to congregational development. In the last few years, however, she has pursued two additional, but complementary, interests. Because she values adult education within the church and her side job in ministry is writing curriculum for mainline denominations, it seemed natural to accept a position on the board of the Ecumenical Institute for Ministry. There Kay became involved in teaching in the Master of Theological Studies program and eventually accepted a very part-time position as Associate Director for the Albuquerque program. Students in the MTS program are of all ages, various denominational backgrounds, and display a wide range of theological perspectives. It's a perfect challenge for a theologian who "loves God with her mind" and who cannot get enough of church development.

Kay's second but complementary interest in ministry is music and art. Weekly rehearsal (and twenty-two concerts a year) with the Albuquerque Concert Band and annual immersions in the Glen Workshop sharpen senses and deepen appreciation for God's gift of beauty given to ear and eye. The complements of playing the flute, making assemblages, and studying with eager students enhance pastoral ministry and create, for Kay, a unique calling of ministry in the name of Jesus. Kay lives in Albuquerque, New Mexico, with her husband, George; together they enjoy splashing in the pool, gardening, exploring their state, and welcoming friends and family into their home.

THE BIG PICTURE: EXPERIENCING HOPE

The quarter's title, "Assuring Hope," prompts us to consider the nature of hope. Does faith in Jesus supply hope (emphasis on the tangible gift of faith), or is our Christian faith a motivation for hopeful living (emphasis on the process of living a Christ-like life)? Gift or energy? Confidence or process? Something assured or something assuring? Is faith something we have or something we do? Such a subtle distinction opens up a productive conversation about the nature of faith and the benefits of believing. Most believers will grapple with this question as they grow toward maturity in faith. Indeed, finding the balance between a faith that one affirms and a faith that one lives evolves over a lifetime.

The adults who will gather for this study will be at various points along the have/do continuum of Christian faith. Scriptural resources to clarify and support their individual quests are abundant in this quarter. In these lessons, your class will be introduced to an exile community who had forgotten the essentials of their faith, as well as to a community of disciples who are striving to understand how to live according to Jesus' teachings. You might summarize the difference between the two communities in this way: When Israel was in exile, the assurance of hope was a necessary ingredient for their renewed relationship to God; without a confidence in God's mercy and power, the Israelites would never believe Isaiah's new word of redemption. The disciples, on the other hand, experienced the power of Jesus' life grounded in hope; for them hope provoked a new manner of living with God.

Before you begin this study, take the time to consider how you understand the unit's title, "Assuring Hope." Does your emphasis fall on the foundations of faith—those essential theological claims that assure your faith? Or does your emphasis fall on the less tangible, but more energetic and inspiring dynamic of hope? Words or deeds, affirmations or applications, gift or lifestyle: How are these two related in your personal faith? Are these perfectly balanced, intimately intertwined or distinctly valued? After your personal reflection, consider the learning curve of your students with regard to faith's affirmation or application. In these lessons both interpretations are considered. There is a time to state clearly the benefits of faith: Surely hope is a benefit assured by Jesus. There is also a time to challenge faithful living: Surely hope is a motivation assuring a bold Christian witness.

A Lengthy Context

The Book of Isaiah addressed the people of Israel over a lengthy and varied history. Although there are few definitive dates within the text, the contexts identified by scholars span more than two centuries. Such a timeline led many biblical interpreters to affirm the Book of Isaiah as a compilation of prophecy rather than the voice of a single individual.

Before we focus on the texts for our study, it is helpful to review Israel's history leading up to exile, while in exile, and during the return to and restoration of Jerusalem. Uzziah, the king of Judah, reigned from 783 to 742 B.C. Although his reign began in relative peace, by the time of his death, the power of Assyria was rising. It was both the blessing and the curse of Judah to have major trade routes through her land. By these routes the nation benefited from the goods and merchandise of the more sophisticated southern and northern empires;

however, the trade routes also became routes of domination. At times the power of Egypt was dominant and at other times, Assyria or Babylon took precedence. Lacking the resources, will, and expertise to counter these greater powers, the people of Israel and Judah often entered to risky alliances and frequently experienced betrayal or jeopardy from such treaties. When tensions were slight, the trade routes through Judah and Israel were buffer zones between benign powers. When one nation or another was on the move, the trade routes became battle lines and the rulers and people in the Promised Land suffered.

Soon after King Uzziah died, the land of Judah was "officially" a vassal of the dominant northern power of Assyria. Although that time was precarious for Judah, there were even darker days ahead for Israel. By 722 B.C. Israel fell to Assyria. This defeat precipitated a frantic response in Judah as King Hezekiah sought protection from Egypt to stem Assyria's aggression. Egypt failed to protect Jerusalem, however, and in 701 B.C. Hezekiah, having lost control over most of Judah, paid tribute to Assyria to save the holy city.

As was frequently the case along the volatile route between northern and southern powers, a new power arose: Babylon. With the decline of Assyria and the ascendancy of Babylon, Jerusalem was once again "caught in the middle" of the power struggle between north and south. In 605 B.C. Babylon defeated Egypt. Judah's King Zedekiah initiated a rebellion against Babylon that resulted in an invasion by King Nebuchadnezzar. In 587 B.C. Jerusalem, including the Temple, was destroyed and the majority of the people forcibly relocated to Babylon. There the people lived as exiles until a new power (Persia) arose in the north.

The Persian King Cyrus defeated the Babylonians in 539 B.C. and brought to an end the Israelite exile. Over the next several decades the Israelite returnees rebuilt the city and the Temple. The events mentioned in this overview are reported in the Book of Isaiah. The prophetic voice spoke of King Uzziah's death (Isaiah 6:1) and of Hezekiah's eventual surrender to Sennacherib (Isaiah 36–39). There are also numerous oracles against foreign powers (Isaiah 13–23). Finally, there is the deliverance of the people from exile by none other than King Cyrus of Persia, whom God had anointed (Isaiah 45:1).

Since the contexts are so rich and the timeline is so lengthy, scholars divide the Book of Isaiah into three sections. Chapters 1–39 refer to events from the eighth century B.C., the period of international turmoil that left Israel defeated and Judah vulnerable to Assyrian forces; the subtitle of this section is "First Isaiah." Chapters 40–55 spring from the sixth century, particularly the period of exile; these chapters are subtitled "Second Isaiah" or "Deutero-Isaiah." Although the concluding chapters of the book, 56–66, are less distinctive from Second Isaiah, they are assigned to the period after the Exile and return to Jerusalem; this section is known as "Third Isaiah" or "Trito-Isaiah." By theme and by theology, however, the voices of First, Second, and Third Isaiah offer a unified word of God. Individual speakers over two (or more) centuries conveyed to God's people two important themes. First, that the God of Israel reigns over all historical events and directs history toward unity and peace throughout creation. Second, that Jerusalem is not only the center of worship for Israel but will also one day draw all peoples and nations into the knowledge and praise of God.

A Message of Hope

All the passages for our study come from Second Isaiah, chapters 40–55. Therefore, the voice that spoke was a voice aware of the difficulties of exile, as well as a voice commissioned by God to announce the future. Because the experience of exile had worn down the very soul of the people, certain fundamentals were stressed. Second Isaiah spoke of God's order, power, mercy, comfort, justice, and healing. Each emphasis had to be renewed and old assumptions had to be challenged. Second Isaiah spoke to a hopeless people. Over the period of exile, they had slowly understood, confessed, and accepted their role in the devastation of Judah and Jerusalem. They had not, however, imagined the next step. That was the special mission of Second Isaiah. This prophet was commissioned by God to give hope to the hopeless. The task was nearly impossible; thus the prophet built up a case for the return of God's compassion by fitting the future into the broadest conceivable understanding of God's intentions. As each element was added, the whole inspired an assuring hope. With a determined repetition, the prophet announced the fundamentals:

- God was the creator of heaven and earth;
- God ordered creation toward unity and peace;
- God's mercy was greater than human frailty and sin;
- God's comfort was the offer of divine help;
- God's justice could be satisfied and would be effective;
- God was able to heal broken people and nations.

Each of these fundamentals needed to be freed from a faulty assumption. For example, Israel's faith had substituted the Temple in Jerusalem (the symbolic meeting place with God) for the sturdier belief in God's unbounded creative power. When the Temple fell, Israel mourned the defeat of God's power. Isaiah's first task was to remind the people that God was greater than any symbol—even the most powerful symbol, the Temple. Likewise, Isaiah taught that God's intentions were broader than the experience of Israel. By reminding Israel of her original commission—to be a light to the nations—Isaiah sought to rekindle the vision of all nations filled with the knowledge and blessing of God. A major obstacle for Isaiah was the broken condition of the people: Having confessed their sin, they could not imagine forgiveness; having understood their complicity, they did not expect divine mercy or help. The people were caught in a backward look that held no future.

Isaiah had to reorient the people to see through their current situation to God's new future. This was no small task. It was, rather, the creation of hope among a hopeless people. By innovation, fundamentals, repetition, and surprise Second Isaiah faithfully delivered God's word of assuring hope.

Jesus, the Promised Servant-Leader

Although the passages from Isaiah were studied within their historical context, those passages also include a trajectory of grace that rippled far beyond the time of the exiles. Indeed, as the early Christian community sought to understand the life, death, resurrection, and promised return of Jesus, they studied Isaiah. By these prophecies, early Christians plumbed the significance of a little appropriated symbol: the servant of God. As they read Isaiah's portrait of God's servant, especially the significance of suffering in the life of God's servant, they saw Jesus with clarity.

Although Isaiah spoke to his people about their concerns, his words carried a universal application that centuries later helped an early church confess their faith that "Jesus is Lord." As this quarter concludes, the focus on Jesus narrows from Messiah to Beloved of God, then from a leader who serves to the Son of Man returned as cosmic redeemer. The selections from the Gospel of Mark all have parallel accounts in Matthew and Luke. Since contemporary Christians tend to "harmonize" the Gospels, whether unconsciously or intentionally, it would be wise to read the Gospel parallels before each class session.

Mark is ordinarily assumed to be the first recorded Gospel. As a significant source both of content and structure for Matthew and Luke, it is informative to note Mark's sparser approach. With Mark you get the bare bones; Luke adds the craft of a storyteller, and Matthew "teaches" his Gospel. The last lesson, Mark's "Little Apocalypse," corresponds to Matthew 24:3-36 and Luke 21:7-36; the content is not the same, but each of these passages represents an end-time orientation shared by Jesus with his disciples shortly before his death.

In these four lessons you will touch on two aspects of the incarnation and of Jesus' redemption. Peter's confession of Jesus as the Messiah, in the lesson for February 6, represents the human understanding of Jesus as divine. Although the disciples had heard the reports of Jesus—as Elijah, John the Baptist, the prophet—they were beginning to recognize in Jesus a reality greater than human. Peter summarized their experience by offering the term Messiah. It became immediately clear that Peter failed to understand the breadth of his affirmation; Jesus warned him that he was still "setting (his) mind not on divine things but on human things" (Mark 8:33). There was, nevertheless, a qualitative shift occurring. Peter was gradually expanding his understanding of Jesus from mere human to marvelous God.

In the next passage the movement is from divine to human. Jesus was transfigured before his disciples: They saw him in heavenly glory, apparently quite at ease. Yet, when the divine voice spoke, the disciples were cautioned to pay attention not to the glory, but to the words Jesus uttered (see Mark 9:7). In each text Jesus' humanity and divinity are present; in neither text can his two aspects be finally—or even helpfully—separated.

The incarnation means that Jesus is human and divine. Likewise, Jesus' redemption is analyzed as a humanly current and a divinely cosmic event. First, Mark presented a very human analysis on quality of redeemed life: He contrasted Jesus' community with typical Gentile groups. Among the Gentiles, those in power used their power over others through inequality, abuse of power, and tyrannical posturing. Jesus clearly stated that in his community—a community redeemed by Jesus—there will be equality, service, and humility. Redemption, it is affirmed, begins with serving others.

Just as this lesson on Mark 10:35-45 provokes a very human approach to redemption, the final lesson, based on Mark 13, offers a divine aspect of redemption. In Jerusalem, Jesus' disciples begged for information about signs of the end time; Jesus satisfied their longing with a compassionate vision. Jesus described the return of the Son of Man (Jesus) and the gathering up of the faithful. Redemption, in this passage, displayed God's compassion reaching out for the redeemed from every corner of creation. Thus, redemption, as incarnation, has a very human and contemporary component (humble service to others) and a very divine and eternal component (the gathering of those who belong to God). Again, these dynamics cannot be separated.

The incarnation, as an illustration of assuring hope, includes God's identification with humans in Jesus, and Jesus' provisions of divine grace to humans. Likewise, redemption, as an illustration of assuring hope, includes the humble service offered by humans to one another and thereby to God, and the cosmic ingathering of God's people at the end of time.

This final unit from the Gospel of Mark coordinates well with the task of Isaiah. Both voices sought to present to a confused and somewhat frightened audience a new future provided by God. In each case, the people stretched to comprehend the new. We should count ourselves fortunate to have men and women as our spiritual ancestors who were able to see God's new deeds despite the testimony of the past and present. They looked to God's future and because they did so, we can claim a forward-looking faith, one that provides the assurance of hope.

CLOSE-UP:
THE INFLUENCE OF
THE BOOK OF ISAIAH

Isaiah's importance for Christians was eloquently expressed by the fourth-century commentator and translator, Saint Jerome, who wrote: "He [Isaiah] should be called an evangelist rather than a prophet because he describes all the mysteries of Christ and the Church so clearly that you would think he is composing a history of what has already happened rather than prophesying about what is to come." According to John F. A. Sawyer, author of *The Fifth Gospel: Isaiah in the History of Christianity*, Isaiah is cited or alluded to at least 46 times in the Gospels, 30 times in Paul's writings, and at least 30 times in Revelation. This means that, except possibly for the Psalms, Isaiah is the most frequently quoted or alluded to book of the Hebrew Bible in the New Testament. Here are some familiar examples: The image of the winepress as a symbol of God's wrath in Isaiah 63:3 appears also in Revelation 14:19 and 19:15. The angel in Joseph's dream quotes Isaiah 7:14 in Matthew 1:23 to assure Joseph that he is to wed Mary, who is with a child that is to be named Emmanuel. The voice of John the Baptist crying out reminds the reader immediately of the unnamed voice in the wilderness of Isaiah 40:3-5, which calls hopeless exiles to prepare to see the glory of the Lord. All four Gospel writers include this quotation from Isaiah to call people to prepare for God's Messiah (see Matthew 3:3; Mark 1:3; Luke 3:4-6; John 13). The four Songs of the Suffering Servant (Isaiah 42:1-4; 49:1-6; 50:4-9; 52:13–53:12) are linked in the New Testament with Jesus, the anointed one of God who suffers. Some images, such as the lamb led to the slaughter in Isaiah 53:7, create immediate connections with Jesus, such as seen in John 1:29.

Not only the New Testament but also Western art, music, and Christmas traditions have been greatly influenced by the Book of Isaiah. The ox and donkey of Isaiah 1:3 are familiar figures in a nativity crèche. The idea of a shoot coming out of Jesse (Isaiah 11:1) is the basis for the tradition of the Jesse tree at Christmas, which is generally decorated with symbols from the Old Testament that point toward Jesus. Many of the words of Handel's beloved *Messiah* are taken directly from Isaiah. Examples include: "And the Glory of the Lord" (40:5); "For Unto Us a Child Is Born" (9:6); and "All We Like Sheep Have Gone Astray" (53:6). Many hymns and carols, such as "Here I Am, Lord" (6:8); "O Day of Peace That Dimly Shines" (11:6-7); "Hallelujah! What a Savior" (chapter 53); and "Arise, Shine Out, Your Light Has Come" (60:1-3) are based on the words of Isaiah. Numerous artists, including Marc Chagall, Michelangelo, and Raphael have depicted scenes from Isaiah. One very well known series of paintings, based on Isaiah 11:6, is "The Peaceable Kingdom" by Edward Hicks (1780–1849).

Begun in 742 B.C., the Book of Isaiah continues even now to wield an enormous influence over our culture, our understanding of God, and relationship with Jesus.

FAITH IN ACTION: SHARING HOPE WITH OTHERS

During this quarter's study, "Assuring Hope," we have seen how the prophecy of Isaiah and his description of the Suffering Servant helped to raise the hopes and spirits of the Israelites who lived in exile. Similarly, through his life and teaching, Jesus demonstrated the importance of serving God by serving others. He called the Twelve—and us—to follow his example.

Who needs our help? The Bible identifies groups that need our help. In Matthew 25:35-36, Jesus talked about the importance of ministering to those in need of food, water, or clothing; or care because they were sick; or a visit because they were in prison. He reminded us, "you [will] always have the poor with you, and you can show kindness to them whenever you wish" (Mark 14:7). Likewise, James talked about how we show our faith by supplying the "bodily needs" of those who lack them (James 2:15-16). James included caring "for orphans and widows in their distress" in his description of "pure and undefiled" religion (James 1:27). Tragically, the groups that Jesus and James identified have expanded greatly over the centuries. We have the opportunity and responsibility to minister to them, to meet their needs, and to help them find hope and love in God.

In our sessions, there have been suggestions for hands-on ministry to meet urgent needs. Let's consider ways we can be advocates for those who lack power and know-how to bring about long-term, systemic change. Challenge the students to take action.

- *Identify a group in your community that has been pushed to the margins and discern how you can help.* Perhaps a senior center is being closed due to lack of funding. The adults it attracts may need the services offered, such as meals, basic medical care, help with taxes, and opportunities to meet with elected officials. How can your class act as advocates to find ways to continue providing these older adults with essential services, even if the senior center itself must be closed?
- *Open lines of communication.* The editorial page of your local newspaper is an excellent way to inform people of a problem. Depending on the issue, you may also be able to arrange for television or radio coverage. The Internet enables you to communicate rapidly and conduct research to see how others have handled similar situations. Within the congregation, use the bulletin, newsletter, or other means of communication the church already has in place.
- *Take political action.* Contact elected officials to make them aware of your concern. These contacts may be made via phone, letter, e-mail, or possibly in-person. Outline the problem and suggest ideas for resolution. Encourage the officials to enact legislation to aid those affected by the problem.
- *Act professionally.* Research information carefully and stick to the facts. Research includes talking with those who are affected by the problem, since you must know what their concerns and preferences for a solution are. As you dialogue with others who may see the situation quite differently, be willing to listen respectfully and express your ideas persuasively but with Christ-like humility.

UNIT 1: COMFORT FOR GOD'S PEOPLE
THE HIGHWAY FOR GOD

PREVIEWING THE LESSON

Lesson Scripture: Isaiah 40:1-5, 25-26, 29-31
Background Scripture: Isaiah 40
Key Verse: Isaiah 40:29

Focus of the Lesson:
In spite of weakness, trouble, and impediments, people search for a better life. Where do people look for hope? The prophet Isaiah promises the people that God, with whom none can compare, will fulfill their hopes.

Goals for the Learners:
(1) to explore the hopeful prophecy of Isaiah during the exile in Babylon.
(2) to recognize that God's promise of hope is for them.
(3) to change their lives to reflect the hopeful promise of Isaiah that God will care for them.

Supplies:
Bibles, newsprint and marker, paper and pencils, hymnals

READING THE SCRIPTURE

NRSV
Isaiah 40:1-5, 25-26, 29-31
1 Comfort, O comfort my people,
    says your God.
2 Speak tenderly to Jerusalem,
    and cry to her
that she has served her term,
    that her penalty is paid,
that she has received from the LORD's
    hand
    double for all her sins.
3 A voice cries out:

NIV
Isaiah 40:1-5, 25-26, 29-31
1Comfort, comfort my people,
    says your God.
2Speak tenderly to Jerusalem,
    and proclaim to her
that her hard service has been completed,
    that her sin has been paid for,
that she has received from the LORD's hand
    double for all her sins.
3 A voice of one calling:
    "In the desert prepare
        the way for the LORD;

"In the wilderness prepare the way of
the LORD,
make straight in the desert a highway
for our God.
4 Every valley shall be lifted up,
and every mountain and hill be made
low;
the uneven ground shall become level,
and the rough places a plain.
5 Then the glory of the LORD shall
be revealed,
and all people shall see it together,
for the mouth of the LORD has spoken."
25 To whom then will you compare me,
or who is my equal? says the Holy One.
26 Lift up your eyes on high and see:
Who created these?
He who brings out their host and
numbers them,
calling them all by name;
because he is great in strength,
mighty in power,
not one is missing.
**29 He gives power to the faint,
and strengthens the powerless.**
30 Even youths will faint and be weary,
and the young will fall exhausted;
31 but those who wait for the LORD shall
renew their strength,
they shall mount up with wings like
eagles,
they shall run and not be weary,
they shall walk and not faint.

make straight in the wilderness
a highway for our God.
4 Every valley shall be raised up,
every mountain and hill made low;
the rough ground shall become level,
the rugged places a plain.
5 And the glory of the LORD will be revealed,
and all mankind together will see it.
For the mouth of the LORD
has spoken."
25 "To whom will you compare me?
Or who is my equal?" says the Holy One.
26 Lift your eyes and look to the heavens:
Who created all these?
He who brings out the starry host one
by one,
and calls them each by name.
Because of his great power and
mighty strength,
not one of them is missing.
**29 He gives strength to the weary
and increases the power of the weak.**
30 Even youths grow tired and weary,
and young men stumble and fall;
31 but those who hope in the LORD
will renew their strength.
They will soar on wings like eagles;
they will run and not grow weary,
they will walk and not be faint.

UNDERSTANDING THE SCRIPTURE

Isaiah 40:1-12. For thirty-nine chapters, the Book of Isaiah presented the case against Israel. Then, suddenly, in the first word of chapter 40, a fresh message began. (See "The Big Picture: Experiencing Hope" for explanation of the shift in theme, content, and setting.) The core announcement was God's comfort to the people. God's word to the prophet included the full mes-

sage that Israel's time of judgment was completed and the nation was freed from the past. This was, however, a new word and, as with any truly new announcement, the prophet's challenge was to present this new information with authority, clarity, and conviction. Therefore, the prophet used an impressive literary form that was familiar to his audience (see for example 1 Kings 22:19-

24). Since the form is surprising to later generations, some background is required. Isaiah set the new word of God's comfort in the context of a heavenly assembly. According to the literary form, God assembled the heavenly host, made an announcement, and allowed the members to respond. This pattern structured our text. First, God spoke (Isaiah 40:1-2); then, various and unidentified voices responded (40:3-11). The first voice, in verses 3-5, described a great highway in the wilderness. The highway's design demanded dramatic shifts in creation: mountains lowered and valleys lifted up. The elegance of the highway provided travelers with an easy route through formerly difficult terrain. The most stunning attribute was the highway's universal revelation of God's glory. The second voice, beginning with verse 6, lamented the futility of human efforts. This voice, from the depths of human hopelessness, managed one positive comment: God's word endures forever. The final voice, verses 9-11, brimmed with good news. God will return to Jerusalem as a triumphant conqueror and as a shepherd carrying weak, lost lambs home.

Isaiah 40:12-17. In the remainder of chapter 40, Isaiah shifted from the metaphor of the heavenly council to engage another ancient literary form, a disputation. This literary form is also confusing since questions are assumed rather than stated. Woven through the remainder of the chapter are three responses to the exiles' opposition to God's new word of comfort. This section responded to the exiles' question regarding God's authority. Because of their defeat and exile, the captives doubted that God was the Lord of all creation. Isaiah's response to their doubts began with poetry reminiscent of the divine voice from the whirlwind that addressed Job (see Job 38). The verbs—measured, marked off, enclosed, and weighed—were ordinary ways of analyzing the world. Yet these tools of investigation were unable to calculate the distance of

heaven or establish the boundaries of the earth. Ancient measuring devices could neither weigh dust nor map a mountain. The greatness of creation eluded human capacity to satisfactorily analyze; only God understood creation as a whole. Thus, the wisdom of the Lord was higher and more comprehensive than the wisdom of humans. Moreover, just as humans failed to comprehend creation, they also were limited in their knowledge of God. Regardless of human inadequacies, God knew and measured all creation—including all nations and rulers. Since all wisdom belonged to the Creator, Isaiah encouraged the exiles to trust that God's new word of comfort was authentic. There was nothing that could oppose God's words—not even the fearsome strength of Babylon's royalty, army, and deities.

Isaiah 40:18-24. The second response addressed idolatry and was founded on the second commandment: "You shall not make for yourself an idol." (Exodus 20:4). Throughout their history, Israel understood both the prohibition and persistent temptation of idol worship. In the land of Judea, to ensure a good crop, the Israelites were tempted to establish field shrines to Baal, the Canaanite fertility god. Idolatry's temptation grew stronger in exile as the people of Israel lived under the domination of a polytheistic nation. In all likelihood, they were amused by the process of shaping wood or clay into the form of a deity, overlaying the image with gold or silver and, finally, bowing down before the idol to worship. Surely, as they observed the production of idols their minds returned to God's second commandment. However, their minds were confused by the obvious domination of the Babylonians and their tedious oppression. Could the God of Israel hear their prayers, respond to their distress, and end the Exile? Such questions were unavoidable while Israel was in exile. And, Isaiah's counter questions were also real rather than rhetorical: Have you not known . . . heard . . .

*footnote

understood the nature of God? Rather than a simple answer, Isaiah questioned the exiles to revive the songs of praise characteristic of the soul of Israel. Isaiah hoped the exiles would praise God as the Creator of every living being and the judge of every nation and ruler. By his response to the unspoken challenge of idol worship, Isaiah beckoned Israel to return to a confident faith in God. *read Measuring article*

Isaiah 40:25-31. Isaiah's last response disclosed the state of mind of Israel with unusual clarity. It began with a familiar invitation: look and see God. The Israelites were invited to "see" what they could not imagine: the strength of God. In order to begin to see, Isaiah challenged the people to remember that their God was not only a wonderful creator but also tireless, abounding in strength, and eager to share strength with the people.

The final resistance Isaiah addressed was the exiles' weariness and exhaustion. Thus the prophet concluded his message with images of God's power and willingness to share that power with the weak and the exhausted. The final affirmation, in verses 29-31, reminded Israel to wait for God's strengthening. Those who awaited God's empowerment would not be disappointed; rather by their single-hearted confidence in God they would experience God's future. That future began with the word comfort, but concluded with energy to "run and not be weary . . . walk and not faint."

INTERPRETING THE SCRIPTURE

The New Message

In our world there are more than 11 million refugees and displaced individuals; another 12 million people are stateless, living without citizenship in any nation. It is difficult to imagine the magnitude of their circumstances. We can, however, empathize with the hopelessness many feel everyday. Almost everyone knows a story of hopelessness—whether that story begins with physical illness, emotional breakdown, or material loss. Moreover, the pain of despair touches every culture through terrorism, war, natural disaster, civil strife, or economic collapse. Because we have seen, heard, and felt hopelessness, we have sympathy for those who dwell away from home and hope. Such sympathy paves the way into our text, Isaiah's new message from God to the exiles.

During the Exile, Israel was in a constant state of hopelessness. In hopelessness they submitted to the tyranny of Babylon's cruel power. With hopelessness they endured their bitter lives. Due to hopelessness they grew weary and despondent. For the exiles, days stretched into months, the months into years with no hope in sight; you can imagine this. Now imagine that God had a new message, a message of rescue, return, and renewal. Yet such a message, while ripe with good news, also posed problems. How would God's new message be communicated? What power would authenticate it? How could it be believed? Such challenging questions are integral to Isaiah 40. This passage requires two backdrops: the people's hopelessness and a creative new message from God.

In the Book of Isaiah, chapter 40 begins a new section (40–55) known as "Second Isaiah" or "Deutero-Isaiah." The first portion includes nine chapters (40–48) devoted to promise of release to the captive through the providential appointment of the Persian King Cyrus as the liberator. The first section is distinguished by a dramatic shift in style, content, and perspective. The accusatory tone of God's impending judgment, characteristic of the first 39 chapters of Isaiah, is replaced with comfort for the exiles. Rather than presenting another explanation for the deportation, the prophet offered what was most essential to the weary exiles: a divine plan and accessible images inspiring hope.

The divine plan began with an unexpected word: comfort. This divine word, wrapped with tenderness, became the announcement that Israel's punishment was completed. Those who endured the Exile had paid a double portion for their sins. By this dramatic announcement, God's word began to turn the people from their rebellious past and hopeless present to their amazing future.

The Highway Home

Isaiah's first word of comfort was complemented by an image of hope as a magnificent, royal highway home. This image transformed the deadly experience of deportation into a joyous journey back to Jerusalem. Although the route to and from exile covered the same terrain, there was no comparison between the two journeys. During the deportation, many struggled, fell, and died as the conquering army drove the Israelites from their homeland, marched them across the desert, fed them on prisoner's rations, and forced them to leave behind the old, the young, the ill, and the dying. The survivors' stories and songs etched the deportation on the hearts and minds of the whole exilic community, including the rising generation. Everyone understood the difficulty and despair of traveling across the wilderness.

Since despair characterized the wilderness deportation, Isaiah's image of God's highway home had to be wonderfully stunning. With words that literally sang, Isaiah described God's highway as a straight road, with neither mountain heights to ascend nor rough ground to traverse. On this amazing highway the people would return to their homeland in safety. Moreover, as the

people travel home something even more amazing happened. All humankind saw a mighty testimony to God's glory: Israel's God provided, in the wilderness, a highway home.

The One True God

You've probably had the uncomfortable experience of trying to offer hope to someone floundering in hopelessness. Finding the right words to say or the sustaining image to offer is always difficult, but if there is a close relationship the task is a little easier. Such a close relationship was Isaiah's secret resource as he presented the hope-filled image of the highway in the desert. Isaiah knew the experience of the exiles. He understood their anger and their apathy; he recognized their faithful ponderings and their fitful rebellions; he loved their tender care for each other, and he mourned their moral failures. Wisely, Isaiah was aware of the arguments the people might offer in contradiction to God's new message of comfort, hope, and a highway home. He knew they would complain that God may be great, but God had ceased to care about Israel. From his rich understanding of the spiritual and emotional impact of exile, the prophet addressed the people's anxieties.

As a fine theologian, Isaiah began with fear, the root cause of the exiles' anxieties. This fear was the palpable experience of feeling abandoned by God. Using poetic words—designed to stir the soul as well as the imagination—Isaiah called his audience to attention with a description of God's creative powers. Indeed, Isaiah affirmed that no person, power, or spiritual being was equal to the God of Israel.

To authenticate this point, Isaiah directed the people to ponder the heavens. There, displayed in the starry night, the people saw God's handiwork. Their God created each and every star one by one. This upward gaze at the heavens reminded the exiles of what they already knew about

God's creative power. Even from the exiles' perspective of hopelessness, Israel remembered that God's greatness overshadowed all physical and political realities. Thus, with grand words supported by an intimate relationship, Isaiah reminded the exiles of what they already knew and believed: Yahweh, their God, was powerful beyond every imaginable circumstance and reality. Isaiah's reminder carried subtle but effective subtext: The God who ordered the starry host, with intimacy (calling each star by name) and power, was surely able to provide a way out of exile to the beloved people, Israel.

Wait for God's Strength

With the exiles' fear—abandonment by God—hanging in the air, Isaiah's final section again sang; this song declared God's presence and help. First came the message: God "gives power to the faint, and strengthens the powerless" (40:29, key verse). Precisely at the point of Israel's collapse, there was God ready to bear them up and carry them on the journey ahead. If the exiles failed to fathom this declaration, Isaiah sang on. He painted a word picture of exhausted youth and falling young people. It was a risky image because it lay so near the existential exhaustion of the exiles. Nevertheless, Isaiah sang on. Next, he provided an image soaring with confidence: the weary rising up with powerful eagles' wings and the exhausted running with energy. In between these two images, Isaiah placed a challenge before Israel: wait.

The Exile would not end by personal or corporate effort; release came by waiting for the Lord's next deed of mercy. An extra push of religious commitment would not lead the people home; return came through waiting as the Lord's highway was prepared. The people would not escape by political conniving or conspiracy; only by waiting would God bring them into their future. It was, perhaps, not the word the exiles wanted to hear, but it was an essential word: Wait for the Lord to build the highway, initiate the rescue, and restore energy and strength to the hopeless. Wait for the Lord.

SHARING THE SCRIPTURE

Preparing Our Hearts

Explore this week's devotional reading, found in Ephesians 2:11-22. Here Paul speaks to the community of faith by reminding them of what was, how things are in the present, and what life will be like in the future. Read these words as if Paul were speaking to your church and to you. In Christ, we have peace with God and are no longer divided from one another. In Christ, we have "access in one Spirit to the Father" (2:18). In Christ, we have become "members of the household of God" (2:19). What does all of this mean to you in terms of how you live your life?

Pray that you and the adult learners will rejoice that you are among the family of God.

Preparing Our Minds

Study the background Scripture from Isaiah 40 and the lesson Scripture from Isaiah 40:1-5, 25-26, 29-31. Think about where people look for hope.

Write on newsprint:
❑ information for next week's lesson, found under "Continue the Journey."
❑ activities for further spiritual growth in "Continue the Journey."

Review the introduction to this quarter,

"The Big Picture," "Close-up," and "Faith in Action." Consider how you will use this additional information throughout the quarter. Prepare to use suggested portions of "The Big Picture" during this session.

LEADING THE CLASS

(1) Gather to Learn

❖ Welcome the class members and introduce any guests.

❖ Pray that all who have gathered today will be open to words of hope that God has for them.

❖ Read this story from CNN.com dated April 6, 2009: **Tens of thousands were forced from their homes in the wee hours of the morning when an earthquake measuring 6.3 in magnitude devastated L'Aquila, a college city in central Italy. Buildings dating back to the 13th century were destroyed. Narrow streets in this medieval town posed a challenge for rescuers. Survivor Maria Francesco told the press: "It was the apocalypse, our house collapsed. It's destroyed, and there's nothing left to recover." Residents and aid workers were digging through the rubble with their hands to find trapped victims.**

❖ Invite the adults to imagine themselves in such a dire situation. Ask: **Where would you find hope when all seems to be lost?**

❖ Read aloud today's focus statement: **In spite of weakness, trouble, and impediments, people search for a better life. Where do people look for hope? The prophet Isaiah promises the people that God, with whom none can compare, will fulfill their hopes.**

(2) Explore the Hopeful Prophecy of Isaiah During the Exile in Babylon

❖ Use "The Big Picture: Experiencing Hope" to introduce the texts from Isaiah. Read or retell this article from the beginning until you reach the section entitled "Jesus,

the Promised Servant-Leader." You may wish to write some of the dates on newsprint so that the students can visualize progression of this historical period.

❖ Choose three volunteers to read Isaiah 40:1-5, 25-26, 29-31.

❖ Consider Isaiah's message of comfort and forgiveness in verses 1-2. Ask: **Had you been one of the Israelite living in Babylon, how would you have heard this message after the bitter experience of judgment and exile?**

❖ Direct attention to the highway as described in verses 3-5.

❖ Read or retell "The Highway Home" from Interpreting the Scripture. Ask: **How might this highway have been a sign to you of God's comfort and strength?**

❖ Read the final paragraph of "The One True God" from Interpreting the Scripture. Look again at verses 25-26. Discuss the ways in which these two verses reveal who God is. (Note that the term "Holy One" is used in the writings of both First and Deutero Isaiah but is not generally found elsewhere. That term says something about Isaiah's understanding of God.)

❖ Read again Isaiah 40:29-31. Invite the students to describe the hope that this image of empowerment gives them.

(3) Recognize that God's Promise of Hope Is for the Learners

❖ Distribute paper and pencils. Encourage the adults to look once more at today's readings from Isaiah 40:1-5, 25-26, 29-31 and jot down any words or phrases that stand out for them.

❖ Bring the class together and call on volunteers to identify those words and phrases that "popped" for them. Ask them to state:

- what the words are.
- why they seem important.
- how this passage speaks to them about God and the hope they have in God.

❖ Point out that although these words of comfort and hope were first directed to those in exile, we read them as God's words to us as well.

❖ Conclude by posing this question for silent reflection: **How will you allow God's words of hope to affect your life and the lives of others you encounter?**

(4) Make Life Changes to Reflect the Hopeful Promise of Isaiah that God Will Care for the Learners

❖ Distribute additional paper. Reread the description in Isaiah 40:3-4 and invite the class members to state what they can assume the road was like before it is improved. Here are possibilities: *The road cuts through a barren land, is very bumpy and uneven, and includes mountains and valleys.* Encourage the students to draw a picture of this highway as they envision it.

❖ Ask the adults to look at this highway as if it represents their lives. What are the problem areas—the peaks, valleys, bumps, and arid land that is affecting them right now? Suggest that they write some labels on their picture. Assure them that no one else will see their work.

❖ Invite the learners to flip the paper over and draw the straight highway that will be built and on which the glory of the Lord will be revealed. Suggest that they label points along the road to indicate how they hope their lives will change as God continues to care for them.

(5) Continue the Journey

❖ Pray that all who have come today will believe in and give thanks for the promises God makes to care for the learners.

❖ Read aloud this preparation for next week's lesson. You may also want to post it on newsprint for the students to copy.

■ **Title: I Am Your God**
■ **Background Scripture:** Isaiah 41:1–42:9
■ **Lesson Scripture: Isaiah 41:8-10, 17-20**
■ **Focus of the Lesson: People take comfort in knowing that someone is capable of helping them in time of need. Who are people to trust for assistance? Isaiah declared that God alone creates, controls, and redeems.**

❖ Challenge the students to complete one or more of these activities for further spiritual growth related to this week's session. Post this information on newsprint for the students to copy.

   (1) **Offer hope to someone who is feeling hopeless. You may be able to give food, clothing, or shelter to someone in need. Or your presence in a hospital, prison, nursing home, or elsewhere may give hope.**

   (2) **Tell someone about how God has delivered you from an apparently hopeless situation. Perhaps you were healed against all odds, or overcame an addiction, or were able to rise above circumstances that seemed inescapable. Give glory to God.**

   (3) **Contact elected officials to encourage legislation that will care for those who feel hopeless, such as those who cannot seek medical treatment, even for death-dealing diseases such as cancer, because they have no means to pay.**

❖ Sing or read aloud "Prepare the Way of the Lord."

❖ Conclude today's session by leading the class in this benediction: **Let us go forth to worship and serve the Lord, in whom we have the blessed assurance of our salvation.**

UNIT 1: COMFORT FOR GOD'S PEOPLE
I AM YOUR GOD

PREVIEWING THE LESSON

Lesson Scripture: Isaiah 41:8-10, 17-20
Background Scripture: Isaiah 41:1–42:9
Key Verse: Isaiah 41:10

Focus of the Lesson:
People take comfort in knowing that someone is capable of helping them in time of need. Who are people to trust for assistance? Isaiah declared that God alone creates, controls, and redeems.

Goals for the Learners:
(1) to examine God's promise to restore Israel's abundance.
(2) to find encouragement through contemplating God's limitless capability and good wishes to help them.
(3) to claim the magnitude of God's promises.

Supplies:
Bibles, newsprint and marker, paper and pencils, hymnals, index cards

---

READING THE SCRIPTURE

NRSV

Isaiah 41:8-10, 17-20

8 But you, Israel, my servant,
    Jacob, whom I have chosen,
    the offspring of Abraham, my friend;
9 you whom I took from the ends of
    the earth,
    and called from its farthest corners,
    saying to you, "You are my servant,
    I have chosen you and not cast you off";
10 **do not fear, for I am with you,**
   do not be afraid, for I am your God;
   I will strengthen you, I will help you,

NIV

Isaiah 41:8-10, 17-20

8"But you, O Israel, my servant,
    Jacob, whom I have chosen,
    you descendants of Abraham my friend,
9I took you from the ends of the earth,
    from its farthest corners I called you.
I said, 'You are my servant';
    I have chosen you and have not
    rejected you.
10**So do not fear, for I am with you;**
   do not be dismayed, for I am your God.
   I will strengthen you and help you;

I will uphold you with my victorious
   right hand.
17 When the poor and needy seek water,
   and there is none,
   and their tongue is parched with thirst,
  I the LORD will answer them,
   I the God of Israel will not forsake
   them.
18 I will open rivers on the bare heights,
   and fountains in the midst of the
   valleys;
  I will make the wilderness a pool of
   water,
   and the dry land springs of water.
19 I will put in the wilderness the cedar,
   the acacia, the myrtle, and the olive;
  I will set in the desert the cypress,
   the plane and the pine together,
20 so that all may see and know,
   all may consider and understand,
  that the hand of the LORD has done this,
   the Holy One of Israel has created it.

I will uphold you with my righteous
   right hand.
17"The poor and needy search for water,
   but there is none;
   their tongues are parched with thirst.
  But I the LORD will answer them;
   I, the God of Israel, will not forsake them.
18I will make rivers flow on barren heights,
   and springs within the valleys.
I will turn the desert into pools of water,
   and the parched ground into springs.
19I will put in the desert
   the cedar and the acacia, the myrtle and
   the olive.
I will set pines in the wasteland,
   the fir and the cypress together,
20so that people may see and know,
   may consider and understand,
that the hand of the LORD has done this,
   that the Holy One of Israel has created it.

UNDERSTANDING THE SCRIPTURE

Isaiah 41:1-7. The setting established in chapter 40 of a heavenly council, composed of the representative gods and powers of all nations and moderated by the God of Israel, is also seen in chapter 41. In our text, the Holy One of Israel proposed a trial, called the witnesses, and established the rules of conduct. First there was silence as God's presentation unfolded; then the foreign nations and gods were allowed to testify. Finally, the court executed a judgment. References alluding to this trial are found in Isaiah 41:1, 21; 42:23; 43:9, 26; 44:7; 45:20, 21; 48:14. The literary setting of a royal trial, while not personally observed by common men and women, was the stuff of ancient stories, poetry, and songs. Wisely, Isaiah used the literary styles at hand to express his religious truth.

One aspect of his trial format requires definition for the modern reader; this trial was not a "criminal case." The issue was not crime and punishment. Rather, the trial was civil; the court was convened to authenticate or dismiss the Holy One of Israel's status as creator, guardian, and sustainer of all creation. The first set of evidence for God's sovereignty was presented through reference to the current and terror-provoking political situation. Cyrus II, king of Persia, had recently and swiftly conquered the regions of Media and Lydia, as well as several Greek-speaking cities on the western seaboard of Asia Minor. According to Isaiah, the God of Israel claimed responsibility for this military campaign. Isaiah offered the current political crises as an illustration of the nations' helplessness. The testimony also implied that the God of Israel ensured Cyrus' success (41:2). The first phase of the trial was over; the heavenly council sat in silence.

Isaiah 41:8-16. Isaiah's next argument on God's behalf shocked his audience. After demonstrating God's power through the military might of Cyrus, Isaiah envisioned God's introduction of Israel, the "least" among the powers assembled, to the heavenly host. Imagine the visual impression these words had on the exiles: the wealth, might, and power of foreign gods and kings contrasted sadly with the impoverished, broken, and exiled people of Israel. Nevertheless, Isaiah emphasized God's special relationship with Israel. Moreover, God explained that by divine decree Israel would be strengthened, helped, and upheld.

Israel was also called by a special title: servant. This title appropriately described God's covenant relationship with Abraham and Sarah. From the first account, God's covenant included the mission of blessing the nations (Genesis 12:1-2); thus Israel had always been a servant of God's purpose for all nations. Then, as if anticipating the response of humans and gods alike to the choice of Israel as God's servant, Isaiah described the self-esteem of the exiles as worm-like (41:14) and promised that by divine assistance the people of Israel would become as mighty as a great threshing machine able to crush mountains and hills (41:15-16). With a sweet reminder of the glorious yet-to-be-built highway to Jerusalem, the second phase of the trial concluded. Again there was silence.

Isaiah 41:17-29. Into the silence, God spoke. A persistent refrain, "I will . . ." repeated *six* times, marked out the length and height and depth of God's providence. Not only would God care for and comfort the poor and needy, God would also transform the wilderness from dry land to a verdant region. God's assertion of care for humans and nature's renewal was a declaration of sovereignty. It was also the final challenge to the heavenly host. Now was the time for rulers and gods of the nations to "set forth" (41:21) their case. God invited testimony and proofs from the past, present, or future. Silence, however, continued in the courtroom. The God of Israel appealed once more. The criteria for testimony were enlarged to permit witnesses for either the good or the harmful. Still, there was no response. Hearing no testimony, God declared the idols of the nations a mere "nothing" (41:24). The assembled nations and gods neither exerted power in the past nor did they intend to shape the future. Thus, the judgment was clear: The God of Israel, attested as "I, the LORD, am first, and will be with the last" (41:4c), was the rightful sovereign of all. All other claims to sovereign authority and power were dismissed as empty delusions (41:29); the Holy One of Israel's claim prevailed.

Isaiah 42:1-9. With uncontested authority, the sovereign God of Israel next made a formal presentation to the heavenly council. Much as military leaders or ruling kings ceremoniously presented their successors, so Israel's God announced the servant. The choice was intimate: God's servant was not only a delight to God but also shared God's spirit. The choice was also purposeful: God's servant was appointed to execute divine justice. This anonymous servant appears to be none other than Israel (see 41:8), though scholars debate the servant's identity.

Again, God's choice stunned the heavenly council, but even more stunning was the description of the manner by which the servant fulfilled the assigned task. Rather than mighty and dominating, God's servant Israel was diligent in doing justice in the mundane, seemingly insignificant corners of the world. There was nothing showy about the servant's dispensation of God's justice; there was simply the everyday practice of it. The servant was to enact God's purposes and teach God's ways, step by step and situation by situation, until God's justice filled the earth. Slow growth, rather than crushing domination, was to be the manner of God's servant. In this way God's original promise of blessing to all nations would be accomplished in every social system, family, and individual. Thus, transformed nations, living in justice, freedom, and truth, then joined Israel's praise of the sovereign God. All this was yet to come, but as God presented the servant Israel, the past was over and the new future was about to begin. Isaiah's literary form worked; by describing a heavenly council, Isaiah stretched the exiles' imagination of their relationship to God. The exiles no longer saw themselves as abandoned and judged; rather, by Isaiah's words, Israel was renewed as God's chosen servant.

INTERPRETING THE SCRIPTURE

God's Persistent Promise

Whenever we open the Bible, we have the opportunity to understand ourselves, our faith, and our God more fully. What could be more important! Thus, once again, we open the Bible, study an ancient writing, and expect a contemporary word from God. In chapter 41, the prophet Isaiah told the exiles a story to help them understand their recent past in a new way. The exiles had become a depressed and hopeless people— a people for whom superficial words were as useless as dust. Fortunately, Isaiah fed them the strong words of the God he was privileged to know. As Isaiah spoke, he rekindled the spirit of the exiles by reminding them that God's promises to Israel were persistent; these promises carried no expiration date.

During the Exile, the people of Israel entered a dark period of theological chastening, punishment, and spiritual separation. In exile, the people had recognized and repented of their arrogant rebellion toward God. During this time they accepted their servitude to the Babylonians as divine punishment. And as the months turned into years, theological confusion and doubt created a certain sense of distance from God. The obvious conclusion to this dark period was the end of the special relationship with God understood as the covenant. To this dreary conclusion, the prophet calmly declared that the relationship between God and Israel was still intact. Indeed as God once claimed Abraham to be the father of a great nation, so God continued to claim Abraham's offspring as God's very own. To substantiate his point, Isaiah described God's intention to gather the scattered Israelites from every corner of the known world as a sign of God's persistent promise. By declaration and by sign, Isaiah reaffirmed God's covenantal choice of Israel.

Then, Isaiah addressed the obvious question: Why would God do so? The answer did not lie in any supposed qualifications among the people. Rather God called the people together by choice: God loved Israel and had a purpose for Israel. Imagine the exiles' responses. Would they laugh or ask one another, "What did Isaiah say?" Would they lower their heads in disbelief or would one or two begin to smile? After years of discipline and distance, Isaiah announced that God was ready to make good on the promise made to Abraham's children. Although the relationship was tested by rebellion and exile, it was not ended. Israel was still God's chosen servant; Israel was still destined to be a light to the Gentiles.

God's Steady Support

Encouragement, however, is useless if fear persists. That is why the prophet moved directly from God's persistent promise to a brief saying designed to dispel the fears of the people. The key verse for this lesson is: "Do not fear, for I am with you, do not be afraid, for I am your God" (41:10). These words were a double dose against fear, the signature emotion of exile. Isaiah literally assured the exiles that God was present with them in their desperation and despair. Although they had assumed exile meant God deserted or abandoned them, Isaiah offered another interpretation. God had been beside them on every difficult day. Moreover, God was with them as God—as source and companion even in times of trouble.

This was a mysterious and engaging announcement intended to make the people rethink their exile and to reevaluate their circumstance. Had God really been a part of their misery? Was God's steadfast love so profound that God entered into their punishment, experienced their humiliations, and wept because of their sorrows? It was a shocking idea, but an idea that seemed believable as the prophet continued to speak.

In addition to the double dose against fear, the prophet announced the resources God was making available to the people. God was among them as strength, help, and support. Moreover, God was willing to use power and wonders to bless those who turned from fear to trust in the living God. With such an amazing announcement, Isaiah spoke on.

God Wills Wonders

There was joy accumulating in Isaiah's voice as his next speech painted a word picture of God's future. The images that make up this vision transformed the dry, thirsty experience of Israel's deportation and life in captivity. As Isaiah told the story, God answered the needy in a series of proclamations, each beginning with "I will." The first proclamation was the most necessary: I will answer them. By these words, God prom-

ised not only to hear but also to respond to Israel's plight. Perhaps you know the pain of God's silence; perhaps you also know the delight of God's response. If you recognize that pattern of silence followed by response, then you can imagine the situation of the exiled community. The people had lived for years in God's silence; then, through the voice of the prophet, God responded, "I will answer them."

The second proclamation promised that God's response to the people would not end after one or two gracious words or deeds. Although expressed by a negative phrase, I will not forsake them, the people heard a positive affirmation: God will continue to hear and respond to the needy. The next four proclamations describe a verdant valley where once was only desert wilderness. Rivers and fountains carry water from the heights to the desert valleys. In the wilderness, pools of water fed by fresh springs replace the illusionary mirages of the desert. There was sufficient water to maintain a forest of desert trees. Moreover, there was abundant water to ensure the growth of cypress, plane, and pine—trees that normally cannot survive the desert environment. These wonders in nature were the imaginative expression of God's great power to change Israel's circumstances from exile to renewal. Everything poor would prosper; everything destined for despair would become delight; everything that seemed impossible God would provide.

A Magnificent Promise for You

Tenderly, Isaiah concluded his speech. He had reminded the people of the persistence of God's promises. He had attempted to banish their fears. He had offered them a glorious word picture of God's intention to change their circumstances. Isaiah, however, had one final statement to make. His words were carefully selected; the pace of his message slowed down. Isaiah readied himself to uncover the mystery of God.

This mystery was greater than the rescue of Israel from exile in Babylon. This mystery vibrated throughout creation to every nation and people. God's great deed—a deed begun in covenant with Abraham, sealed in Israel's history of direction and correction, blossomed as a metaphorical watered desert, and shown in a glorious restoration—this great deed was meant for all. As the nations saw and considered God's grace toward Israel, they were able to know and understand God's nature. This was the mystery Isaiah intended to disclose: The Holy One of Israel was the sovereign God of all creation. By God's dramatic deeds it was possible for all to know God: the Babylonians and the Assyrians, the Egyptians and the Phoenicians, the despairing exiles and those Israelites left on the land, the living and the future generation, the needy throughout the centuries and even you, the current one who sees and considers what the Lord has done.

SHARING THE SCRIPTURE

Preparing Our Hearts

Explore this week's devotional reading, found in 1 John 4:13-19. Although 1 John is not a book that we often turn to, it contains several very familiar sayings that many of us learned as children: "God is love" (4:16); "Perfect love casts out fear" (4:18); "We love because he first loved us" (4:19). If you memorized these verses decades ago, try to read them with "fresh eyes." What do they mean to you now? What do they tell you about God? How do they set the tone for your relationship with God?

Pray that you and the adult learners will share God's love with others, especially during this season of Advent as we prepare again to celebrate the Savior's birth.

Preparing Our Minds

Study the background Scripture from Isaiah 41:1–42:9 and the lesson Scripture from Isaiah 41:8-10, 17-20. Think about who people are to trust when they need help.

Write on newsprint:
❏ information for next week's lesson, found under "Continue the Journey."
❏ activities for further spiritual growth in "Continue the Journey."

Plan to use portions of the Understanding the Scripture segment and the Interpreting the Scripture segment as suggested.

LEADING THE CLASS

(1) Gather to Learn

❖ Welcome the class members and introduce any guests.

❖ Pray that all who have come today will find encouragement as they consider God's ability and willingness to help them.

❖ Read this information aloud: **Service dogs are highly trained animals that are used to assist people with a variety of medical challenges. Guide Dogs, sometimes referred to as Seeing Eye Dogs, are trained to assist their owners as they navigate sidewalks and streets to avoid obstacles and traffic, to negotiate stairs, and to lead their owners at home and in public places. Another type of assistance dog works with those who are deaf and hearing impaired to alert their owners to sounds, such as fire alarms, microwave beeps, or crying babies. Other well-trained dogs assist owners who have mobility issues and need help, perhaps picking up** fallen objects, opening doors, or even pulling wheelchairs. Service dogs have also been found useful in aiding autistic children, alerting epileptic owners to oncoming seizures, and assisting people with severe mental illness.

❖ Ask: **How would you (or do you) feel knowing that a service dog could be available to assist you if you required such help?**

❖ Read aloud today's focus statement: **People take comfort in knowing that someone is capable of helping them in time of need. Who are people to trust for assistance? Isaiah declared that God alone creates, controls, and redeems.**

(2) Examine God's Promise to Restore Israel's Abundance

❖ Use information from Isaiah 41:1-7 in Understanding the Scripture to set the stage for today's reading.

❖ Choose a volunteer to read Isaiah 41:8-10.

- Invite the adults to imagine themselves as the Israelite exiles to answer these questions:
  - (1) **What do you believe about God's relationship with your people, the Israelites?** (See the second paragraph of "God's Persistent Promise" in Interpreting the Scripture.")
  - (2) **"After years of discipline and distance, Isaiah announced that God was ready to make good on the promise made to Abraham's children. Although the relationship was tested by rebellion and exile, it was not ended. Israel was still God's chosen servant; Israel was still destined to be a light to the Gentiles." Once you realized this truth, what would your response be?**

- Read or retell "God's Steady Support" from Interpreting the Scripture. Invite the students to tell brief stories of how God upheld them and quieted their fears during a difficult time in their lives.

❖ Select someone to read Isaiah 41:17-20.

- Talk with the class about what they envision in this land. (Note that in some ways it could be seen as a new Eden.) Contrast it to the Israelites' life as exiles in Babylon.
- Use information from "A Magnificent Promise for You" in Interpreting the Scripture to help the students see that the God of Israel is both the creator and the one who is able to sustain.

(3) Find Encouragement Through Contemplating God's Limitless Capability and Desire to Help the Learners

❖ Distribute paper and pencils. Suggest that the students identify problems that are besetting their community or nation and list these on their papers. Such problems may include *domestic violence, unaffordable housing, lack of medical care, gangs, drugs, crime, unemployment or underemployment, and economic instability.*

❖ Divide the learners into groups of three or four. Ask them to consider how they perceive that God is willing and able to help. Note that help from God may include help from the believers, either individually or as a body. In other words, the class needs to think about what the church might be able to do to overcome this problem.

❖ Invite the groups to report to the class.

❖ Solicit opinions as to whether the class could undertake any of the suggested solutions, recognizing that they are acting on behalf of God to assist other people.

(4) Claim the Magnitude of God's Promises

❖ Invite the students to review silently today's reading from Isaiah 41:8-10, 17-20.

❖ Encourage the learners to call out any promises of God that are stated or implied in this reading. List their ideas on newsprint.

❖ Distribute index cards. Challenge the students to claim at least one of the promises they have discerned and write that promise on their card. Suggest that they use the card as a Bible bookmark this week so that they will be reminded of God's promises whenever they open their Bibles.

(5) Continue the Journey

❖ Pray that those who have participated in today's session will claim God's promises for themselves, turn over to God their fears and anxieties, and help others to see God's activity in their lives.

❖ Read aloud this preparation for next week's lesson. You may also want to post it on newsprint for the students to copy.

- **Title: The Mission of the Servant**
- **Background Scripture: Isaiah 9:1-7; 11:1-9; Matthew 1:18-25**
- **Lesson Scripture: Isaiah 9:7; 11:1-8**
- **Focus of the Lesson: People need someone with authority who will take responsibility for leading them. Who can be the leader of the people? God will send a leader and give that leader complete authority. That leader is Jesus, conceived of the Holy Spirit and born from the line of Jesse and David.**

❖ Challenge the students to complete one or more of these activities for further spiritual growth related to this week's session. Post this information on newsprint for the students to copy.

(1) **Write some of your fears in your spiritual journal. Review each one. Copy Isaiah 41:10 into your journal. Memorize these words as a reminder that you have no need to fear because God is with you.**

(2) **Review Isaiah 41:17-20. Who do you know that is suffering from physical or spiritual thirst? What can you tell these people in order to reassure them that God hears and answers and is constantly present with them, even if the answer is not immediately forthcoming?**

(3) **List individuals and groups in your community that are in need of care. Pray daily for these people. Do all in your power to support them with your time, talent, and treasure.**

❖ Sing or read aloud "On Eagle's Wings."

❖ Conclude today's session by leading the class in this benediction: **Let us go forth to worship and serve the Lord, in whom we have the blessed assurance of our salvation.**

UNIT 1: COMFORT FOR GOD'S PEOPLE
THE MISSION OF THE SERVANT

PREVIEWING THE LESSON

Lesson Scripture: Isaiah 9:7; 11:1-8
Background Scripture: Isaiah 9:1-7; 11:1-9; Matthew 1:18-25
Key Verse: Isaiah 11:5

Focus of the Lesson:

People need someone with authority who will take responsibility for leading them. Who can be the leader of the people? God will send a leader and give that leader complete authority. That leader is Jesus, conceived of the Holy Spirit and born from the line of Jesse and David.

Goals for the Learners:

(1) to discover in Isaiah's prophesy for the ideal king a Savior to come from the house of David.
(2) to recognize that the coming of the Savior means the coming of peace.
(3) to praise God for the endless peace, justice, and righteousness that the Savior will bring.

Pronunciation Guide:

Tiglath-Pileser (tig lath pi lee' zuhr)

Supplies:

Bibles, newsprint and marker, paper and pencils, hymnals, picture of *Peaceable Kingdom* by Edward Hicks

---

READING THE SCRIPTURE

NRSV

Isaiah 9:7

⁷ His authority shall grow continually,
    and there shall be endless peace
  for the throne of David and his kingdom.
    He will establish and uphold it
  with justice and with righteousness

NIV

Isaiah 9:7

⁷Of the increase of his government
    and peace
  there will be no end.
  He will reign on David's throne
    and over his kingdom,

from this time onward and
  forevermore.
The zeal of the LORD of hosts will do this.

Isaiah 11:1-8
1 A shoot shall come out from the stump
    of Jesse,
    and a branch shall grow out of his roots.
2 The spirit of the LORD shall rest on him,
      the spirit of wisdom and
        understanding,
      the spirit of counsel and might,
      the spirit of knowledge and the fear of
        the LORD.
3 His delight shall be in the fear of the LORD.
      He shall not judge by what his eyes
        see,
      or decide by what his ears hear;
4 but with righteousness he shall judge
        the poor,
      and decide with equity for the meek of
        the earth;
    he shall strike the earth with the rod of
      his mouth,
      and with the breath of his lips he shall
        kill the wicked.
5 **Righteousness shall be the belt around**
      his waist,
    and faithfulness the belt around his
      loins.
6 The wolf shall live with the lamb,
      the leopard shall lie down with the kid,
    the calf and the lion and the fatling
      together,
      and a little child shall lead them.
7 The cow and the bear shall graze,
      their young shall lie down together;
      and the lion shall eat straw like the ox.
8 The nursing child shall play over the
      hole of the asp,
      and the weaned child shall put its
        hand on the adder's den.

establishing and upholding it
  with justice and righteousness
  from that time on and forever.
The zeal of the LORD Almighty
  will accomplish this.

Isaiah 11:1-8
1A shoot will come up from the stump
    of Jesse;
    from his roots a Branch will bear fruit.
2The Spirit of the LORD will rest on him—
      the Spirit of wisdom and of
        understanding,
      the Spirit of counsel and of power,
      the Spirit of knowledge and of the
        fear of the LORD—
3and he will delight in the fear of the LORD.
      He will not judge by what he sees
        with his eyes,
      or decide by what he hears with his ears;
4but with righteousness he will judge
        the needy,
      with justice he will give decisions for
        the poor of the earth.
He will strike the earth with the rod of
      his mouth;
      with the breath of his lips he will slay
        the wicked.
5**Righteousness will be his belt**
      and faithfulness the sash around
        his waist.
6The wolf will live with the lamb,
      the leopard will lie down with the goat,
    the calf and the lion and the
      yearling together;
      and a little child will lead them.
7The cow will feed with the bear,
      their young will lie down together,
      and the lion will eat straw like the ox.
8The infant will play near the hole of
      the cobra,
      and the young child put his hand into
        the viper's nest.

UNDERSTANDING THE SCRIPTURE

Isaiah 9:1-7. In this lesson, three passages combine to celebrate the gift of a child destined to be God's true and authoritative ruler. Although the fourth Sunday of Advent traditionally anticipates the birth of God's son, the three texts look beyond the birth to the qualities of leadership God's Son will exhibit. The first passage announces light, joy, and peace after a steady downward cycle of darkness, depression, and war. The setting, while not specified, bears the marks of two military campaigns by Tiglath-pileser III, king of Assyria, in the years 734 and 732 B.C. The result of these campaigns was the dismemberment of the nation Israel. First the coastal region, the way of the sea, fell, leaving Israel with no access to the Mediterranean. Next, two more regions were conquered: Gilead ("the land beyond the Jordan") to the east and the Plain of Megiddo ("the Galilee of the Nations") to the west of the Jordan River. These losses of lands, trade routes, and populations left Jerusalem isolated, insecure, and fearful of the future. One question dominated during this era: Would Israel ever be a unified nation again? By Isaiah's prophetic poem, this question received a positive and hopeful answer: Yes! The time of darkness was about to end; the people would soon rejoice. Their burdens were about to be lifted and the warriors who terrorized them would cease their campaigns. As the prophet sang of the new age about to begin, he offered a sign that all would recognize: a child born to rule in peace. By a series of titles, Isaiah described the child's future reign. First, as "Wonderful Counselor," this child would attain such wisdom that no outside counselors would be needed. As "Mighty God" and "Everlasting Father" the new king's plans would perfectly express God's intentions for the world. Finally, this child, as the "Prince of Peace," would initiate a season of God's peace. Isaiah lauds the growth and development of the newborn prince, finally acclaiming that the prince's reign would never end because the zeal of God was purposefully establishing a new future.

Isaiah 11:1-9. Whereas the first passage from Isaiah focused on the birth of a royal son, probably Hezekiah, and the manner in which this child would grow into his role as God's true ruler, the second passage from today's readings detailed the spiritual preparation of a promised godly ruler and the consequences of his reign for the people and, indeed, for all creation. There was no attribution of "the word of the Lord" as often found in prophecy, yet there was bold prophetic speech describing God's intentions. Two elements are stressed: the righteous king came from the lineage of David ("the stump of Jesse") and God graciously endowed the king with spiritual gifts. The gift of God's Spirit was described in three doublets. First comes the practical "wisdom and understanding" necessary to lead the people; such a gift enabled the king to reign with justice and to offer fair treatment to all. The second gift was "counsel and might," indicating diplomatic and military leadership. The king was not only a wise ruler within the bounds of the nation but this king also understood the dynamics of international politics and was aware of the strategies of war. Finally, the king was gifted with spiritual "knowledge of" and "fear" before God. This doublet presented the highest form of piety as the king's relationship with God. As this king ruled, his judgments were based on depth of perception rather than superficial reports and assumptions. He created peace, justice, and confidence in a manner that reminded all of the power of God's creative word. Finally, the king was adorned with a confident and obedient faith. By the rule of this king, peace spread throughout the land, and all creation shifted toward God's harmonious future. The enmity between the wildness of nature and humankind ended. In place of violence among humans, nonviolence became the norm. Indeed, the closing image painted a reconciled world, living near to God (on "my holy mountain," 11:9), and possessing a "full knowledge" of God.

Matthew 1:18-25. To set the story, it is helpful to understand the emphasis of Matthew in contrast to the Gospel of Luke. In Luke, the story of Jesus' conception and birth features his mother, Mary. But in Matthew, the leading character is Joseph, the man who will become Jesus' father. Although the stories are presented from different points of view, each parent expressed piety and great faithfulness. Both took great social risks to obey the word of God as it was presented to them. In his dream, an angel instructed Joseph to "name him Jesus" (1:21). Joseph fulfilled that command according to verse 25. To understand the significance of Joseph's naming/adoption of Jesus, Matthew employed a literary device known as a reflective quotation, meaning that the content points toward ways in which Jesus is the fulfillment of Old Testament Scripture. Ordinarily in Jewish interpretation the Scripture was stated first and followed by interpretation. Matthew's pattern was the opposite. Matthew described an event or occurrence in Jesus' story, then quoted a portion of Scripture. Our passage contains the first of these reflective quotations (see Matthew 1:23; 2:6, 15, 18, 23; 4:15-16; 8:17; 12:18-21; 13:35; 21:4-5; 27:9), which begin with words such as "to fulfill what had been spoken by the Lord through the prophet." The words from Isaiah in Matthew 1 are offered as an explanation of Jesus' identity and a fulfillment of prophetic intention. Isaiah's words perfectly matched Matthew's understanding of the miracle of Jesus' birth. When the Hebrew name Jesus (derived from Joshua, meaning "God helps" or "God saves") was related to the prophetic title, Emmanuel, the essence of Jesus' life became clear. One name, Emmanuel, interpreted another name, Joshua, to establish God's new trajectory of hope, comfort, and salvation. In Jesus, God was and is with the people in a new and profound way. Indeed, this is the reason Isaiah's prophecies of babies and kings continue to be dear to contemporary Christians. By Isaiah's words we understand our Lord and Savior, Jesus-Emmanuel.

INTERPRETING THE SCRIPTURE

God's Peaceable Mission

So often the word "prophecy" is assumed to mean prediction. Often, in everyday language, prophecy is further associated with dramatic changes. Scriptural prophecy, however, springs from God's patient and eternal yearning for creation. Nevertheless, when Isaiah spoke his prophetic words his audience sought to connect his symbols with events and people in their immediate experience. On the surface, there were appropriate points of connection; beneath the surface of Isaiah's words surged God's great mission for peace throughout creation.

Although the signs and symbols touched the actual experiences of the Israelites during the period of the Exile, Isaiah's message echoed far into history. Rather than merely predicting a particular political ruler to rescue the exiles, Isaiah understood his task as a contribution to God's long-range, universal redemption of creation.

In Isaiah 9:7, the prophet described attributes of reign of the one who would come as the "Wonderful Counselor, Mighty God, Everlasting Father, Prince of Peace" (9:6). This reign will be marked by peace, justice, and righteousness. These three are inseparable in God's mission. When righteousness abounds in the land and justice spreads to every individual, then peace permeates society and culture. God's reign embodies a community of women and men, children and youth able to reflect God's righteous nature, execute God's divine justice, and delight in God's peace with joyful, secure lives.

Isaiah was especially skilled in speaking about this mission with colorful words and symbols. By his gracious words, the people of his time saw sparks of God's mission in their leaders—particularly in Hezekiah, who was, indeed, a good king (see 2 Kings 18:3). Yet, Isaiah polished his dynamic words to reflect the passage of time and the eternal quality of God's mission. Speaking of the return of the throne of David's kingdom, Isaiah described a process of continual growth toward an endless peace "from this time onward and forevermore" (9:7).

A Peaceable Leader

In order to prepare the people for their role in God's gradual process of spreading peace throughout creation, Isaiah described the ideal king. This description set a standard for the type of leader the people should anticipate, support, and celebrate. More than a simple list of characteristics, Isaiah's words were filled with mystical insight and communicated in rich symbols.

The first image—a shoot coming out of Jesse's stump—was bold and shocking. Isaiah began in chapter 11 with Israel's history—especially that slice of history known as Israel's "golden age." The beloved royal line began when Samuel anointed David, the youngest son of Jesse, as king over Israel (see 1 Samuel 16:1-13). As a warrior king, David established the boundaries of the nation and brought a blessed relief from enemies throughout the nation. After David's death, Israel consistently looked back to his reign as the "golden age." Slowly, the people's hope for a renewal of a peaceful "golden age" diminished.

First came the division of the monarchy after King Solomon's death; there was never to be a unified nation again. Then invasions, alliances, and faithless kings further dampened the people's dream of a peaceful and peaceable kingdom. As the Exile began, only a faint hope for the renewal of the reign of David's house remained. It was to this faint hope that Isaiah spoke: From a seemingly dead stump of a family tree, God would bring forth a leader. Indeed, the future servant of God would come from the family of Jesse and, as was true with King David, so also the Spirit of the Lord would rest on him (1 Samuel 16:13). This was Isaiah's first indication of change; it was so unexpected, given Israel's history and current circumstances, that the people had to pay attention.

Isaiah said that the people were to recognize God's appointed leader by his spiritual qualities of intellect, insight, and inspiration. They would also recognize God's chosen leader by his actions: He would be glad in the Lord and his judgments would show respectful understanding for the poor and the meek. Moreover, this leader would guide the people by declaration rather than domination. By his wisdom, rather than brute force, all opposition would be dismissed. Finally, Isaiah spoke clearly: The one whom God selected displayed the essential characteristics of righteousness and faith. By a faithful, righteous, and spirit-led leader God's mission of peace would begin, once again, to flourish.

The role of the new leader was crucial, but just as crucial was Isaiah's preparation of the people to acknowledge God's chosen servant. The gradual change of God's mission required both a spiritual leader and an informed and wise people. With a people prepared by the prophet and leader gifted by God for spiritual and temporal leadership, God's mission of peace, justice, and righteousness gave creation another chance. Although Isaiah's words were full of God's universal mystery and purpose, he also spoke a practical message to his audience.

They were to prepare themselves to recognize and be ready to follow a peaceable leader.

A Peaceable Vision

What sustains you on difficult days? A hymn? A prayer? A familiar face? A memory? All these can contribute to our spiritual equilibrium. God's people use a myriad of such resources to endure hardship, injustice, sorrow, and pain. There is, however, one source of sustenance peculiar in God's gift of Scripture: visions. These visions are given to us as word pictures. Frequently, artists render them into visual forms. One such artist, Edward Hicks, devoted his life to representing Isaiah's vision of the peaceable kingdom.

In 1780, Hicks was born into a well-to-do Anglican family in Bucks County, Pennsylvania. Sadly, his mother died before he was two years old. He was cared for by a woman of strong Quaker beliefs and her influence on his early years established in Hicks a desire for a simple but useful life. He pursued his calling as a preacher and folk artist within the Quaker community. By meditating on and painting scriptural scenes Hicks provided sustaining images to his community and to subsequent generations. His most popular topic was Isaiah's peaceable kingdom; he produced 61 versions of Isaiah's visions.

Because Isaiah described God's reconciled creation so exquisitely, his visualization of Isaiah's vision is available to all. It is not necessary to be an artist to "see" these words. If you listen carefully you can hear the vision in Isaiah's words. Wild animals cease to attack domesticated animals; innocent children play unharmed among the animals; even the most vicious of carnivores, the bear, is content to graze; the nursing child explores a snake nest without provoking screams from a frightened parent. Can you see those words? Can you hear that vision?

Although Isaiah's words stem from his world—a world where nature posed ultimate dangers—we who live in a contemporary world—a world threatened by human-contrived dangers of politics, economics, and environment—still see his vision. It is a vision able to sustain hope for peace and brighten dark days. It is a vision glimpsed in a simple manger scene and sung in many a Christmas carol. Isaiah's hope connects with humanity's distress, regardless of generation, condition, or age. People throughout the ages have been looking for good leadership—a servant leader who comes bringing peace and justice.

SHARING THE SCRIPTURE

Preparing Our Hearts

Explore this week's devotional reading, found in John 4:19-26. This passage records an amazing conversation between a woman of Samaria and Jesus. A Jew would not normally speak with a Samaritan. Nor would a Jewish male speak with a woman. This conversation violates social norms so completely that when the disciples return, they were "astonished" (4:27). In the midst of this discussion, she refers to the coming Messiah and Jesus confirms his identity in verse 26 when he says to her: "I am he." This outsider can now go and witness to others about Jesus. What do you believe about Jesus? What are you proclaiming about him?

Pray that you and the adult learners will recognize the presence of Jesus in your lives and that you will witness to that presence so that others may come to know him too.

Preparing Our Minds

Study the background Scripture from Isaiah 9:1-7; 11:1-9; Matthew 1:18-25. The lesson Scripture is found in Isaiah 9:7; 11:1-8. Ask yourself: Who can lead God's people responsibly and with authority?

Write on newsprint:

❑ information for next week's lesson, found under "Continue the Journey."

❑ activities for further spiritual growth in "Continue the Journey."

Locate *Peaceable Kingdom* by Edward Hicks. Many churches have a picture from this famous series, but you can also find it on the Internet or in art books.

LEADING THE CLASS

(1) Gather to Learn

❖ Welcome the class members and introduce any guests.

❖ Pray that those who have gathered today may experience the peace that the Messiah offers.

❖ Invite the students to list on newsprint characteristics of an ideal leader.

❖ Encourage them also to list characteristics of an ideal servant.

❖ Review the two lists to see which traits overlap. Your purpose is to describe the ideal servant-leader.

❖ Read aloud today's focus statement: **People need someone with authority who will take responsibility for leading them. Who can be the leader of the people? God will send a leader and give that leader complete authority. That leader is Jesus, conceived of the Holy Spirit and born from the line of Jesse and David.**

(2) Discover in Isaiah's Prophecy for the Ideal King a Savior to Come From the House of David

❖ Choose a volunteer to read Isaiah 9:7.

• Encourage the students to discuss the kind of leader that is promised and the type of reign they can expect from this leader.

• Read or retell "God's Peaceable Mission" from Interpreting the Scripture for additional information about the traits of this leader.

❖ Select someone to read Isaiah 11:1-5.

• Read or retell "A Peaceable Leader" from Interpreting the Scripture.

❖ Select someone to read Isaiah 11:6-8.

• Show a picture from the "Peaceable Kingdom" series by Edward Hicks. Invite the students to comment on how the picture depicts the words of Isaiah. What other visions of peace does Hicks portray?

• **Option:** If you cannot locate a copy of a Hicks' picture, ask students to describe one. These are such famous scenes that at least one adult would have familiarity with it.

• Read or retell "A Peaceable Vision" from Interpreting the Scripture.

❖ Wrap up this portion of the session by talking together about how Christ's followers are called to embody this vision of peace.

(3) Recognize that the Coming of the Savior Means the Coming of Peace

❖ Look again at Isaiah 9:7. Notice the connection between "peace," "justice," and "righteousness," all of which will be prominent during the reign of the Coming King.

❖ Divide the class into groups of three or four and distribute newsprint and a marker to each group. Ask them to identify places in your community where peace and justice are not evident and list these ideas on newsprint. Here are some ideas if the class needs discussion-starters: *people cannot afford to buy food for every meal; people are living in the streets; people are victims of crime; schools are not meeting the needs of their students; safety nets for the elderly, ill, and unemployed are lacking.*

❖ Invite each group to report to the total class and post their newsprint.

❖ See if there is any consensus among the groups concerning the places in the community where peace and justice are in short supply.

❖ Encourage the class to work together to brainstorm ideas to address the problem areas they have identified. If the class is large, use the same groups to do this brainstorming. Have them write their ideas on newsprint, and then report to the whole class.

❖ Conclude by noting that although the world is still plagued by injustice, as Christ's followers we are called to do whatever we can to bring about his peaceable reign. Encourage the students to take whatever action they can to alleviate the situations they have identified.

❖ **Option:** If you have access to *The United Methodist Hymnal,* invite the class to read in unison "For Courage to Do Justice" (page 456). Note that Alan Paton, author of *Cry, the Beloved Country,* was a political activist and devout Christian in South Africa.

(4) Praise God for the Endless Peace, Justice, and Righteousness that the Savior Will Bring

❖ Call the students to turn in their hymnals to "For the Healing of the Nations." Invite them to sing or read this hymn.

❖ Discuss these questions:

(1) **What does this hymn suggest about how peace and justice might be achieved?**

(2) **What does this hymn suggest about actions you could take to help achieve peace and justice?**

(3) **What reasons do you have to praise God, despite recurrent threats to peace and safety?**

❖ **Option:** If this hymn is not available to you, use another concerning social holiness and ask the same three questions.

(5) Continue the Journey

❖ Pray that the students will go forth embodying both the mission and traits of the servant.

❖ Read aloud this preparation for next week's lesson. You may also want to post it on newsprint for the students to copy.

■ **Title: I Will Be With You**
■ **Background Scripture: Isaiah 43**
■ **Lesson Scripture: Isaiah 43:1-7, 11-12**
■ **Focus of the Lesson: Many people feel oppressed and look for a leader to deliver them. How are people to know whom to follow? In Isaiah 43, God promises deliverance even greater than the Exodus.**

❖ Challenge the students to complete one or more of these activities for further spiritual growth related to this week's session. Post this information on newsprint for the students to copy.

(1) **Research Isaiah 9:1-7 and 11:1-9, which form the Old Testament background Scripture for today's session. What implications do these verses have for you as you seek to understand Jesus' role and reign?**

(2) **Sketch your own vision of the peaceable kingdom. Where are the figures placed in relation to one another? What colors seem most appropriate? What story does your vision tell?**

(3) **Consider that the characteristics of the messianic figure may be found in anyone who is a servant of God. Review today's readings from Isaiah. Which traits describe you? Which do you see in other Christians? How do these traits bear witness to who you are and whose you are?**

❖ Sing or read aloud "Blessed Be the God of Israel."

❖ Conclude today's session by leading the class in this benediction: **Let us go forth to worship and serve the Lord, in whom we have the blessed assurance of our salvation.**

UNIT 1: COMFORT FOR GOD'S PEOPLE
I WILL BE WITH YOU

PREVIEWING THE LESSON

Lesson Scripture: Isaiah 43:1-7, 11-12
Background Scripture: Isaiah 43
Key Verse: Isaiah 43:2

Focus of the Lesson:
Many people feel oppressed and look for a leader to deliver them. How are people to know whom to follow? In Isaiah 43, God promises deliverance even greater than the Exodus.

Goals for the Learners:
(1) to identify the basis for Israel's hope of deliverance in God's past acts of deliverance and God's promise of God's presence.
(2) to feel confident in knowing God as their Savior.
(3) to share with others the assurance that God will care for them.

Pronunciation Guide:
Cush (koosh)   Seba (see' buh)

Supplies:
Bibles, newsprint and marker, paper and pencils, hymnals

READING THE SCRIPTURE

NRSV
Isaiah 43:1-7, 11-12
1 But now thus says the LORD,
 he who created you, O Jacob,
 he who formed you, O Israel:
Do not fear, for I have redeemed you;
 I have called you by name, you are mine.
2 **When you pass through the waters,**
 I will be with you;
 and through the rivers, they shall not
 overwhelm you;

NIV
Isaiah 43:1-7, 11-12
1But now, this is what the LORD says—
 he who created you, O Jacob,
 he who formed you, O Israel:
"Fear not, for I have redeemed you;
 I have summoned you by name; you
 are mine.
2**When you pass through the waters,**
 I will be with you;
 and when you pass through the rivers,

when you walk through fire you
    shall not be burned,
    and the flame shall not consume you.
3 For I am the LORD your God,
    the Holy One of Israel, your Savior.
I give Egypt as your ransom,
    Ethiopia and Seba in exchange for you.
4 Because you are precious in my sight,
    and honored, and I love you,
 I give people in return for you,
    nations in exchange for your life.
5 Do not fear, for I am with you;
    I will bring your offspring from
      the east,
    and from the west I will gather you;
6 I will say to the north, "Give them up,"
    and to the south, "Do not withhold;
 bring my sons from far away
    and my daughters from the end of
      the earth—
7 everyone who is called by my name,
    whom I created for my glory,
    whom I formed and made."
11 I, I am the LORD,
    and besides me there is no savior.
12 I declared and saved and proclaimed,
    when there was no strange god
      among you;
 and you are my witnesses,
    says the LORD.

they will not sweep over you.
When you walk through the fire,
    you will not be burned;
    the flames will not set you ablaze.
3For I am the LORD, your God,
    the Holy One of Israel, your Savior;
I give Egypt for your ransom,
    Cush and Seba in your stead.
4Since you are precious and honored in
    my sight,
    and because I love you,
I will give men in exchange for you,
    and people in exchange for your life.
5Do not be afraid, for I am with you;
    I will bring your children from the east
    and gather you from the west.
6I will say to the north, 'Give them up!'
    and to the south, 'Do not hold them back.'
Bring my sons from afar
    and my daughters from the ends of
      the earth—
7everyone who is called by my name,
    whom I created for my glory,
    whom I formed and made."
11"I, even I, am the LORD,
    and apart from me there is no savior.
12I have revealed and saved and
      proclaimed—
    I, and not some foreign god among you.
You are my witnesses," declares the LORD,
    "that I am God."

UNDERSTANDING THE SCRIPTURE

Isaiah 43:1-7. The opening section of this chapter is an oracle of salvation constructed as a meditation on "Do not fear. . . ." In the first verse, the people are instructed to resist fear because God has both redeemed and called them. The verbs connect with two foundational stories of Israel: God called Abram to be the father of a great nation and later, God rescued the people from enslavement in Egypt. The second verse offers two images: fire and water. The con- cept of being "tested by fire" was a familiar poetic expression (see Psalm 66:10-12); this image was tied to the liturgical life of Israel and functioned in the corporate imagina- tion of the nation Israel. The image of water, however, was a real danger faced as Israel fled from Egypt. Thus, these images announced God's protection from all real and imagined dangers. In verse 3, Isaiah lifts up the cur- rent political situation. The nations men- tioned—Egypt, Ethiopia, and Seba

(Arabia)—were challenged by Persia's military power; most assumed that once Cyrus conquered these nations, he would attack Babylon. Isaiah expected that such a military effort would bring release for the exiles; the current political situation provided hope. The fourth verse, the heart of the oracle, contains the justification for God's intervention in human affairs. Isaiah declares that God acted because Israel was precious, honored, and loved by God. From this intimacy, the oracle moves, with determination and terseness, to God's intention, to bring the exiles home (43:5), and God's commandments, "Give them up" and "Do not withhold" (43:6). In verses 5-7 the oracle returns to the opening affirmation: Since God created and formed Israel and was present with them, there was nothing to fear, even among the people who were now at "the end of the earth" (43:6).

Isaiah 43:8-15. The generation of exiles addressed by Isaiah was frequently referred to as a "blind and deaf" nation. Indeed, God disclosed such resistance in Isaiah's call to prophetic ministry (see Isaiah 6:9-10). Now, however, the season of resistance was concluded. This section opened with an invitation to assemble those who were "blind, yet have eyes" and "deaf, yet have ears," but in this case the blind and deaf refer to "the nations" (43:9). Once again, the stage was set for a trial. The nations and the peoples assembled and Israel was called as the one and only witness to God, the only Creator and Lord of all. Even though Israel failed in the past to acknowledge God's lordship over all, the people's history with God could not be denied. Israel was summoned to be God's witness because Israel knew God by word (the divine law) and by deed (God's rescue of the people from Egypt). Israel also had learned to trust God's providence by the constancy of God's mercy and by the persistence of God's righteous judgment. Finally, Israel, more than any other nation, understood a crucial divine truth: The people knew God's mercy was greater than God's judgment. As the trial progressed, God prompted Israel to remember the revelation entrusted to them (God alone is Creator), the singular power of God (judgment combined with mercy resulted in redemption) and the names of God (your Redeemer, the Holy One, and the Creator and King of Israel). Throughout the trial, the exiles, the original audience, experienced a new hope rising: The God of Israel had confidence in Israel.

Isaiah 43:16-21. This section departs from the direction set by the oracle of salvation (confidence based in creation, spiritual formation, and historical evidence) and prompted through the trial scene (God's confidence in Israel). Yet, instead of the witness of Israel the reader has been prepared to expect, Isaiah continued God's speech. The opening verses (43:16-17) were predictable: another recollection of God's mighty deeds, particularly related to the Exodus event. However, at verse 18, everything changes. God's word took a new course: Rather than encouraging Israel to remember, God instructed Israel to forget their historical lessons. The clarification followed in verse 19: God was about to do a new thing. If Israel's orientation was only backward, she would not grasp God's future. Likewise, if Israel's witness was limited to past deeds, she would be unable to testify to the present mighty deeds of God. God was about to reverse the course of history. Whereas the people once wandered aimlessly in the wilderness, they would walk purposefully to their homeland. Once they murmured for water and meat; in the future God would provide all that was necessary . . . and more. Indeed, God was about to "re-create" Israel as a people of present-tense praise for God's mighty deed of release from exile. Since the people could not comprehend the future by looking backward, God, through the words of Isaiah, opened their eyes and ears in a new way.

Isaiah 43:22-28. The final section begins with a sad note. Isaiah reminded the people of their spiritual deafness and blindness during the Exile. Although temple worship was impossible during the Exile, the people failed to provide any sort of worship to God. They did not glorify God; they did not sacrifice the first-born lambs; they did not present a portion of their resources to God. Rather, they burdened God with their sins. Isaiah's words described a hidden hurt in the human/divine relationship. In righteousness God judged the people, and in compassion God awaited their return. Faced with the failure of Israel to turn back to God, Isaiah announced God's new deed:

complete forgiveness reestablished God's bond with Israel. When the exiles were stuck in their past sin and present misery, God blotted out Israel's transgressions and forgot her sins. Thus the people were confronted with the purpose of God's judgment: Judgment was not the end; it was the prelude for the redemption of Israel's broken relationship with God. In former times, Israel refused to hear and see God's love for them; now, God wiped the slate clean. As forgiven people, God invited Israel into a new chapter in the human/divine relationship.

INTERPRETING THE SCRIPTURE

A Love Note

Chapter 43 is rich with specific announcements of God's salvation that touch the exiles' hearts and bring tears to contemporary readers. Yet, Isaiah wisely introduced the longer message of God's salvation (Isaiah 43) with a poetic affirmation of God's love (the verses selected for this lesson). Since the exiles understood that their former sins justified their current circumstances, this introduction of God's eternal relationship with the people was, indeed, good news. It is still good news for people who feel alienated from God, community, family, and/or friends. Just as Israel in exile grieved their broken relationship with God and needed Isaiah's beautiful words, so our world longs for a love note from God.

Every love note is shaped by the intimate knowledge of the beloved. Thus, Isaiah began with the exiles' agony over their broken relationship with God. The first verse lifts up a clear affirmation of God's love for Israel from the time of creation, call, and even into exile. However, one aspect of God's love especially touched the exiles: Israel's very existence was initiated by

God's creative word and deed. This emphasis on the initial relationship—in creation— resonated with people who were being treated as chattel or slaves. As Isaiah reminded them of their origin from God, the prophet addressed their experience of feeling less than human. It was just the right beginning.

Contemporary people may need a different approach. In our current world, the mystery of creation is entangled with debates between creationists and scientists. Moreover, the structure of individuality is traced to genes and cultural orientation rather than to God's loving formation. In our context, Isaiah's word "formed" rather than "created" resonates (43:1). Isaiah's affirmation, that God has formed humanity by call and relations, connects with a generation that has lost purpose and feels detached from God. The poetic principle of repetition allows Isaiah's words to address two very different audiences. To an ancient people who had lost touch with the mystery of God's creation and care, Isaiah announced that God created and redeemed them; to a contemporary people who have lost a sense of divine purpose and connection, Isaiah's words "formed you" and "you are mine" reconnect estranged humanity with God and God's intentions.

The restoration of the human/divine relationship had a powerful byproduct: the banishment of fear. Isaiah's words, "Do not fear," (43:1) prepared the people to face their future. As we study this love note from God, we have the opportunity to use Isaiah's approach as we cultivate a confidence in God's love and a fearless orientation toward the future. First comes love; by love fear is banished; without fear God's people face the future.

Remember the Relationship

Nothing nurtures a strong relationship like trust. Yet when a relationship is broken, trust is a dimly outlined reality. Broken relationships sap energy, imagination, and love. But God's word, spoken by Isaiah, was a perfect antidote to Israel's sense of the broken relationship with God. Once the foundation of that relationship was affirmed, Isaiah's words began the next stage of love's reconciliation. He offered memories of God's amazing care for Israel through poetry rather than narrative.

First was the memory of the Exodus. Although the narrative of Moses' call, preparation, interaction with Pharaoh, and God's mighty deeds culminating in a midnight escape is lengthy, Isaiah selected one image to convey the entire event. This image was actually the last difficulty the people faced as they fled from captivity: the waters of the sea. The narrative (see Exodus 14) describes the pursuit of the Egyptians, Moses holding up his staff, the waters walling up on either side, and God's gift of safe passage to the escaping slaves. Isaiah simply reminds the people that what was true in the past will be true in the present and the future: You will pass through waters and rivers protected and accompanied by God. This is the first memory.

The second memory is associated with the wilderness journey of Israel. Again, the narrative version in Exodus is lengthy. Again, Isaiah's compressed poetry evokes the whole story. In the wilderness, Israel's relationship with God was purified. The ancient symbol for such purification was that of metal refined by fire. In that process what is precious and valuable is not harmed, but that which is dross is consumed or melts away. In the wilderness, Israel's relationship with God was purified through the law, the leadership of Moses, and their physical dependence on God for food and water. The image of fire neither burning nor consuming reminded the exiles of God's mighty and benevolent deeds that purified the people of Israel as they wandered in the wilderness.

Recognize God's Current Redemption

As a transition from ancient memories to a recent memory, Isaiah stated the obvious: God was and is the Savior of Israel. The affirmation of Isaiah 43:3 is actually a series of names that express God's essence. "I am" is the name Yahweh, signifying God as the foundation of all things—the source of past, present, and future being is contained in this name. Next comes the personal identification "your God," reminding Israel of their covenantal relationship with Yahweh. The title "Holy One of Israel" identifies the glory of God experienced in worship. Finally comes the title of assurance, "your Savior." By these titles, the people remembered God's revelation to Moses, God's covenant with Abraham, God's presence in the Temple, and God's promise of saving power available to the exiles in their current despair.

The final affirmation dealt with the current political situation. The place names—Egypt, Ethiopia, and Seba (Arabia)—identified nations challenged by the rising power of Persia. The news reports that filtered down to the exiles caused great concern. Was this new political power a cause for fear or joy? Would Persia attack

Babylon? How would that alter the fate of the exiles? Isaiah's words made sense out of confusion. These nations were God's "ransom" payments for the exiles. God intended to use the international politics of power and military conflict to benefit Israel. As Isaiah placed current history alongside the great stories of the Exodus and the wilderness journey, he invited the exiles to remember and trust God's protection. Moreover, Isaiah disclosed the motivation of God's deeds. God was moving through history to save the people "because you are precious in my sight, and honored, and I love you" (43:4)—a fitting statement at the midpoint of this love note.

Closing Invitation

The love note concluded with two invitations. First the people were invited to enter into their future free from fear. In the future was the blessing of Israel's reunion. The broken, scattered remnants of Israel's nation were to be gathered and restored. This was assured because God's intentions never changed. Israel was beloved at creation, call, rescue, and forever. Moreover, Israel was formed to glorify God. By them—indeed, through their entire story—God revealed glory, purpose, and love. Thus, the people were invited to be God's witnesses. They were to know their story by narrative and symbol. They were to trust their God to accompany and protect them. They were to announce to all nations and people the mighty deeds of God. They were to be witnesses able to deliver, time after time, love notes from God to humanity. This was their purpose; this is also our purpose, especially on the day after Christmas!

SHARING THE SCRIPTURE

Preparing Our Hearts

Explore this week's devotional reading, found in Isaiah 63:7-14. As the prophet recalls "the gracious deeds of the LORD" (63:7) he bears witness to the saving power and presence of God. Despite God's love toward them, the Israelites rebelled. Their broken relationship with God prompted them to remember the pivotal point in their history: the Exodus from Egypt and all that God had done for them. What are the special moments in your life when God has been unmistakably present? How does that memory inform your current faith journey? Write your thoughts in your spiritual journal.

Pray that you and the adult learners will be aware of God's constant presence with them.

Preparing Our Minds

Study the background Scripture from Isaiah 43 and the lesson Scripture from Isaiah 43:1-7, 11-12. Ask yourself this question: How are people to know whom to follow?

Write on newsprint:
❑ information for next week's lesson, found under "Continue the Journey."
❑ activities for further spiritual growth in "Continue the Journey."

Post a large sheet of newsprint with the words "That Which Oppresses Us." Have markers available.

LEADING THE CLASS

(1) Gather to Learn

❖ Welcome the class members and introduce any guests.

❖ Pray that all who have come today will experience the presence of God.

❖ Invite all who are willing to come to the sheet of newsprint you have posted and write words that describe situations, events, or types of people who oppress others. Encourage the students to write randomly, as on a graffiti wall. (If the class is large, invite the students to call out ideas as you write, or post several sheets around the room.)

❖ Talk with the class about what they have written. Their ideas may have included *poverty, addictions, abuse, political oppression, or economic oppression, among others.* Ask: **When people feel oppressed, where do they turn to remedy the situation?**

❖ Read aloud today's focus statement: **Many people feel oppressed and look for a leader to deliver them. How are people to know whom to follow? In Isaiah 43, God promises deliverance even greater than the Exodus.**

(2) Identify the Basis for Israel's Hope of Deliverance in God's Past Acts of Deliverance and God's Promise of God's Presence

❖ Choose a volunteer to read Isaiah 43:1-7, 11-12.
  ❖ Discuss these questions:
    (1) What does this passage tell you about God?
    (2) What does this passage tell you about God's relationship with people, especially the Israelites?
    (3) How does this passage speak to you, as an individual or member of the congregation, about what you can expect from God?

❖ Select two or more volunteers to role-play a conversation among Israelites who heard Isaiah's words. Remember that these people are living in exile because God has allowed the Babylonians to overrun Jerusalem and cart them into captivity as punishment for their idolatry and sins. What questions do Isaiah's words pose for these people? What surprises? Encourage the roleplayers to express their opinions about God.

❖ Conclude this portion of the session with a thought question: **What hope and comfort do you receive from God's words to the Israelites?**

❖ Provide a few moments for volunteers to share their insights.

(3) Feel Confident in Knowing God as the Learners' Savior

❖ Point out that Isaiah offered hopeful words to the captives as he recalled their history with God during the Exodus from Egypt. All of us, similarly, have watershed experiences in our lives. Such experiences may build our confidence in God's willingness and ability to care for us.

❖ Write the numbers 1-5, vertically, on a sheet of newsprint. Explain that the group will be rating their confidence in God, with 1 being a vote of "no confidence" and 5 being a vote of total and complete confidence. Read each number and call for a show of hands for those who rate their confidence in God at that level. When you have finished the tally, encourage the participants to talk about why they feel—or do not feel—confident in God. (Recognize that some people have had experiences for which they blame God for an undesirable outcome. These people may have perfectly valid reasons for feeling the way they do, so encourage them to be forthright and honest. God can handle all of our emotions, as the psalms so poignantly reveal. Hearing other more positive experiences may help those who lack confidence to gain more confidence in God as their Savior.)

(4) Share With Others the Assurance that God Will Care for People

❖ Distribute paper and pencils. Encourage the learners to write several sentences about a difficult experience in their own lives in which God's saving grace buoyed them up.

❖ Provide time for volunteers to bear

witness to God's willingness and ability to care for them.

❖ Lead the class in writing a litany that expresses the assurance they have experienced. Try to include the experiences people have mentioned, using general terms. Here's an example: *We give thanks to you, O God, for your comforting presence in the pain and uncertainty of illness.* You will also need to craft a refrain, such as: *We trust and believe in your infinite wisdom and caring love.* Write this litany on newsprint and read it responsively.

❖ **Option:** See if someone can type and reproduce this litany so that class members may each receive a copy next week for their own use as they witness to others.

(5) Continue the Journey

❖ Pray that today's participants will go forth as witnesses to the continual presence of God in their lives.

❖ Read aloud this preparation for next week's lesson. You may also want to post it on newsprint for the students to copy.

■ **Title: I Am Your Redeemer**

■ **Background Scripture: Isaiah 44**

■ **Lesson Scripture: Isaiah 44:21-26**

■ **Focus of the Lesson: In the face of devastating circumstances, people want to know that there is hope for rebuilding their lives. How can we know that something can be rebuilt out of destruction? Isaiah 44 speaks comfort and hope that God will not forget Israel and will redeem all things.**

❖ Challenge the students to complete one or more of these activities for further spiritual growth related to this week's session. Post this information on newsprint for the students to copy.

(1) Reach out to someone who is fearful about something. Encourage this person to set aside this fear and trust that God will care for the one in need.

(2) Witness to someone about how God has been present with you during a time when you were afraid and anxious. The point here is not that your story necessarily had a "happily ever after" ending, but that God was present, no matter what.

(3) Spend time with God by asking this question: In what ways have I oppressed others? Be receptive to the answer, and ask God's forgiveness. If possible, ask forgiveness of anyone you have oppressed. Be sure to think of "hidden people," such as those who work in sweatshops to produce goods that you buy.

❖ Sing or read aloud "How Firm a Foundation," which is based in part on Isaiah 43:1-2. If you have access to *The Faith We Sing*, use the hymn "You Are Mine," which is based on Psalm 46:10, Isaiah 43:1, and 1 John 14:27.

❖ Conclude today's session by leading the class in this benediction: **Let us go forth to worship and serve the Lord, in whom we have the blessed assurance of our salvation.**

UNIT 1: COMFORT FOR GOD'S PEOPLE
I AM YOUR REDEEMER

PREVIEWING THE LESSON

Lesson Scripture: Isaiah 44:21-26
Background Scripture: Isaiah 44
Key Verse: Isaiah 44:22

Focus of the Lesson:
In the face of devastating circumstances, people want to know that there is hope for rebuilding their lives. How can we know that something can be rebuilt out of destruction? Isaiah 44 speaks comfort and hope that God will not forget Israel and will redeem all things.

Goals for the Learners:
(1) to examine God's redemption of Israel.
(2) to recognize that God remembers and regards them highly.
(3) to rebuild places of brokenness.

Supplies:
Bibles, newsprint and marker, paper and pencils, hymnals

READING THE SCRIPTURE

NRSV
Isaiah 44:21-26
21 Remember these things, O Jacob,
     and Israel, for you are my servant;
   I formed you, you are my servant;
     O Israel, you will not be forgotten by
     me.
22 **I have swept away your transgressions
     like a cloud,
    and your sins iike mist;
   return to me, for I have redeemed you.**
23 Sing, O heavens, for the LORD has done it;
     shout, O depths of the earth;

NIV
Isaiah 44:21-26
21"Remember these things, O Jacob,
     for you are my servant, O Israel.
   I have made you, you are my servant;
     O Israel, I will not forget you.
22**I have swept away your offenses like
     a cloud,
    your sins like the morning mist.**
   Return to me,
     for I have redeemed you."
23Sing for joy, O heavens, for the LORD
     has done this;

break forth into singing, O mountains,
    O forest, and every tree in it!
For the LORD has redeemed Jacob,
    and will be glorified in Israel.
24 Thus says the LORD, your Redeemer,
    who formed you in the womb:
I am the LORD, who made all things,
    who alone stretched out the heavens,
    who by myself spread out the earth;
25 who frustrates the omens of liars,
    and makes fools of diviners;
who turns back the wise,
    and makes their knowledge foolish;
26 who confirms the word of his servant,
    and fulfills the prediction of his
      messengers;
who says of Jerusalem, "It shall be
    inhabited,"
and of the cities of Judah, "They shall
    be rebuilt,
and I will raise up their ruins."

shout aloud, O earth beneath.
Burst into song, you mountains,
    you forests and all your trees,
for the LORD has redeemed Jacob,
    he displays his glory in Israel.
24"This is what the LORD says—
    your Redeemer, who formed you in
      the womb:
I am the LORD,
    who has made all things,
    who alone stretched out the heavens,
    who spread out the earth by myself,
25who foils the signs of false prophets
    and makes fools of diviners,
who overthrows the learning of the wise
    and turns it into nonsense,
26who carries out the words of his servants
    and fulfills the predictions of his
      messengers,
who says of Jerusalem, 'It shall be
    inhabited,'
of the towns of Judah, 'They shall
    be built,'
and of their ruins, 'I will restore them.' "

UNDERSTANDING THE SCRIPTURE

Isaiah 44:1-8. "But now" indicates a reversal of God's condemnation of Israel and points ahead to the salvation that God is ready to offer the people. God's forgiveness of all Israel's sins and transgressions was proclaimed in Isaiah 43:25. By this act of forgiveness, Israel's relationship shifted from the past, composed of mighty divine deeds, remarkable human sins, and the agony of exile, to the future, including release from exile, physical restoration of Jerusalem, and a new human/divine relationship. The structure of the final section of the oracle carried the content. First, Isaiah described the new relationship. Since God's forgiveness removed all fear, the people stood on the firm ground of God's loving, creative choice. Second, an image—water in the desert—promoted the idea of something greater than rescue; as water transformed desert land into verdant valleys, so God's spirit promoted growth among the nation of Israel. Interestingly, Israel's growth came through others joining Israel in the covenant relationship with God. Next came the declaration of God as the first and last, the only Redeemer. While the concept of monotheism is well known today, such a claim was truly revolutionary in the context of Isaiah's time. Israel's God was both the Creator of the natural world and the Lord of history. There is no God beside Yahweh. In verse 7, God calls forth witnesses who can testify on behalf of one who is like God. This declaration was stunning, for no other nations in the Near East received words of judgment and words of redemption. All the other nations worshiped gods who brought victory; if ever a nation was defeated, that nation's gods were also dethroned. Israel's relationship with God, however, endured a wide range of experiences with God—called, sheltered, rescued, guided by law and priesthood, judged, and exiled. Surprisingly, even in the defeat of exile, Israel's God still spoke through the prophets to the people.

Isaiah 44:9-20. In these verses Isaiah reviewed the case of idol worship. By an extended satire, Isaiah skillfully debunked idol worship. His literary technique was a form of compare and contrast crafted so that the audience drew comparisons and distinction from hints sprinkled throughout the satire. For example, the makers of idols were described as too terrified to present their case. They are unable to bear witness to their gods. Therefore, Isaiah offered a third-person description of those who make idols and occasionally inserted first-person exclamations from the idol artisans (see 44:16-17, 19-21). The audience recognized the humor of Isaiah's satire as petty exclamations from the idol workers contrasted with the greatness of God's creativity. The extended description of the artisans' labor encouraged the exiles' reflection on idolatry. Surrounded by the polytheism and power of Babylon, the exiles wondered about the strength of their God. In this satire, Isaiah reminded the people of the exhaustion of the idol makers and the failure of their fashioned wood, stone, or metal to provide rest and relief. They were, after all, only creating out of elements of creation. Isaiah thus reminded Israel that God was the source of creation, and therefore, the source of rest and relief—even to tired exiles and idol makers. A judgment against idolatry concluded the satire: Neither the workers nor the objects have power to redeem. Idolatry was a fraud—a trap for deluded minds, misspent energy, and weary laborers.

Isaiah 44:21-23. Isaiah's poetry returned for the trial's conclusion. Isaiah inspired the people of Israel to remember the whole sweep of God's covenant. Their status began with creation, was focused through call, stretched by servitude and hard labor in Egypt, redeemed by God's mighty deed of rescue, formed by law, leader, and worship in the wilderness, graced by the gift of land, corrupted by political alliances devoid of God's blessing, judged guilty by prophetic words, and driven to despair by exile. The people were charged to remember all these experiences. They were also expected to remember something greater: God's constancy and forgiveness. The signs of God's forgiveness were physical: clouds moving across the desert skies and mist clearing from Palestinian mornings. God's presence and forgiveness were as dependable as the forces of nature Israel knew. But, more than nature as a visual reminder of God's creative-redemptive power, creation herself offered a doxology of praise to God. In a compact verse with a mighty impact, Isaiah 44:23, God's praise began in the heavens and stretched to the depth of the earth. The mountains echoed this song; the forest joined in a rustling, leafy anthem; finally, every tree reflected God's greatness. From the widest arc of creation to the nearest intersection of humans and nature, God's intentions to redeem Israel turned the predictable cycles of change into a creation-wide hymn of constant praise.

Isaiah 44:24-28. The trial ended; the verdict confirmed God as the only creator and lord of creation. Still, the exiles awaited God's response to their unvoiced question: "How can this be?" The answer came in one long sentence, Isaiah 44:24-28, that conveyed a single, unified idea: The word of God will accomplish God's intention. Isaiah held the lengthy sentence together with the repetition of the word "who"; each "who" introduced another deed or attribute of God. The "who" pattern began as God formed humans in the womb. Before there

[handwritten in left margin: This was spoken of Jesus the ultimate of Jesus the Prophet]

was anything, there was God's love forming the beloved. God was the source of all creation. God was also the source of wisdom. In comparison to God's wisdom, humans exhibited folly and false understandings. Finally, the ~~greatness of God was known by~~ the gift of a servant ~~(unnamed, but previously introduced in Isaiah 42:1-4) and mes~~sengers of God's word (prophets such as Isaiah). Having affirmed the great deeds of God, Isaiah shifted the refrain from the God who acted to the God whose word created the future. Israel already knew the power of God's word through judgment and forgiveness. Now God's future was coming

through a flurry of divine words. First came the word of Jerusalem's restoration; next came the word that Judean towns would be raised up; then followed an odd word to "dry up your rivers"—a possible allusion to overcoming the fear of nature's chaos of floods. Finally, the word spoke the unimaginable: Cyrus, the Persian king conducting military raids throughout the Near East and into Egypt, was God's shepherd chosen to complete God's release, restoration, and rebuilding of Israel. The divine word could not have been more surprising, and yet, by that word the future of the exiles changed.

[handwritten: This is a recap of all we've read this morning]

[handwritten: ✷ Read footnote for Is.44:28]

INTERPRETING THE SCRIPTURE

Remember and Receive God's Mercies

I've said it, and perhaps you have as well: "I just want everything to be like it was before." It is, of course, an impossible wish; nothing ever goes back to the way it was before . . . before the accident, the suicide, the financial collapse, the baby's birth, the cancer scare, the recovery program, the teenage years, or the onset of dementia. In truth our current lives cannot "recapture" the past; rather, our greater hope is that the future will be as comprehensible and as dependable as the past.

In a similar way, Isaiah recognized the strong appeal of "the way things used to be" in the corporate consciousness of the exiles. Isaiah also knew the future for the nation would not be like the former days in Jerusalem and Judah. Aware that God was creating something new for the people of the covenant, Isaiah nevertheless challenged the people to remember the way things used to be. By the phrase, "remember these things" (44:21) Isaiah commanded the people to remember everything. Remember the love that called them into existence. Remember the patient nurturing by which

their faith was formed. Remember their rebellion. Remember divine mercy. Remember their responsibilities. The expansive command to remember was complemented by divine grace.

The exiles' remembrances were held together by God's mercy. In Isaiah 43:22, the prophet described the revelation that flowed from remembering. Not only did the people recognize God's past grace toward them but by remembering they also understood how God dealt with their sins. Returning to poetry, Isaiah described how sins dissolved as wispy clouds and evaporated as the morning dew. Although God's forgiveness cleared the way for the future, Isaiah led the people to forgiveness through remembering their past. As they remembered, they experienced God's forgiveness. All this was preparation for God's redemption.

Creation Sings in Celebration

Prophets employ a wide range of devices to emphasize their message. Some tell parables, others offer poetic images, still others employ dramatic speech. When Isaiah desired emphasis, his words sang. Isaiah

44:23 is a beautiful illustration of Isaiah's technique. With a lilting rhythm the prophet commanded the heavens, the depths of the earth, and every tree of every forest on every mountain to sing. Their celebrative song was a doxology of praise for God's redemption of Israel. The prophet inspired a beautiful chorus—and yet, it was an untimely song.

Quite likely, Isaiah's original audience was surprised by this command to sing. After all, they received Isaiah's words while still in captivity in Babylon. Their circumstances had yet to change. They were neither released nor redeemed. Yet the prophet's command that all creation sing sparked hope by its sheer audacity. Because the prophet boldly spoke of God's redemption of Israel as a completed fact, the people began to believe that God would indeed rescue them. Over the background of a song sung by the whole creation, the people listened attentively to the prophet.

God's Wide Wisdom

Isaiah's wide hope for the future began with remembrance, rested on expectation, and spread over all creation. In Isaiah 44:24-25, the prophet sketched the height and depth of God's creative power. This was not intended as an exercise in comprehension; rather, the focus on God as Creator was a prophetic move to establish the authority of the God who was about to act on behalf of the exiles. By remembering and reexperiencing forgiveness the people were primed for a new deed. By the song of creation, the people were prepared for the outcome of their redemption. Now, the prophet examined God's power to increase confidence among people as they greeted their future.

God not only created humanity, in general, at the dawn of creation; God formed each individual, in particular, in the darkness of a mother's womb. God's creativity came before the birth of each and every captive. Those who heard Isaiah's message were well known by God. Moreover, the God who made all things also ordered creation wisely.

The illustrations of God's creativity and providence are drawn from the wisdom vocabulary of the contemporary teachers, both among the exiles and within the dominant culture of Babylon. God's creative process was likened to that of a tentmaker measuring, stretching, and assembling fabric for the temporary dwelling. God, however, worked in the media of heaven and earth. God's completed project was permanent. Moreover, God's activity extended beyond the initial deeds of creation into the realm of human society. God's power tested the truth of the diviners and magicians; God's power frustrated and revealed the foolishness of these petty thinkers. As Isaiah spoke reverently of the height and depth of God's creative power and ability to direct the flow of history, the exiles understood that Isaiah's message came from the vast wisdom of God. This was a message they could trust.

A Sign for the Exiles

Isaiah's glimpse into the future probably stirred up questions among the exiles. As they thought new thoughts and considered new possibilities, they felt energy in Isaiah's words and wisdom from his message. But they could not stop themselves from wondering how these ideas and possibilities would come to pass. Their musings are similar to those of contemporary Christians.

Have you ever sat with a group of Christians trying to imagine their congregation as a new creation? Often the ideas begin slowly (We could begin a praise service . . .), then bubble up with remarkable speed (or a prison ministry, or an adult day care center, or a homeless shelter, or a Bible institute for immigrants, or, or, or). Finally, someone halts the process with a single word: "How?" Then the dreams go on the drawing board, the dreamers enumerate the resources required, and imagination bows to practicality. Surely someone whispered "How?" as the exiles attended to Isaiah's sweeping words of a new, bigger, more glorious future for Israel—and for creation.

This time, however, the prophet was ready with a response. While the people wondered about "how" the future would come, Isaiah offered a sign to the exiles. It was not a dramatic sign; rather, it was subtle and suitable. The people would know the answer to "how" when they saw God's word fulfilled. While the future entered the present, the signs of change were subtle. The exiles would not necessarily know all the political dynamics divinely directed on their behalf. Once the release created the opportunity for return, the passage would be gradual. Even as the first wave departed, the exiles would not understand the comprehensive shift that was taking place. As the people later labored to rebuild the walls of Jerusalem and replant the fields of Judah, the returnees might still miss the significance of God's mercy toward them.

One day in the future, however, hands would stop in the midst of labor, heads would turn toward the rising city and villages, and hearts would skip a beat in acknowledgement that this is the Lord's doing. Then those who had gone through the days from captivity to release to return to rebuilding would say: The Lord, who made all things, has done this. God was beside us throughout this long journey. No questions remain: God is our Redeemer.

SHARING THE SCRIPTURE

Preparing Our Hearts

Explore this week's devotional reading, found in Psalm 106:40-48. These verses within a communal confession of Israel's sins report on how God allowed the people's enemies to oppress them, and also how God remembered the covenant and showed compassion. In verse 47, the people cry out for salvation. What sins do you need to confess? How do you experience God's compassion even when you have turned away from God? Offer your own prayer of confession.

Pray that you and the adult learners will be aware of your current relationship with God and the relationship that God wants you to experience. Ask God to guide you if you need to move from where you are to where God wants you to be.

Preparing Our Minds

Study the background Scripture from Isaiah 44 and the lesson Scripture from Isaiah 44:21-26. Think about how we can know that when devastating circumstances strike us there is hope for rebuilding our lives.

Write on newsprint:
❏ information for next week's lesson, found under "Continue the Journey."
❏ activities for further spiritual growth in "Continue the Journey."

LEADING THE CLASS

(1) Gather to Learn

❖ Welcome the class members and introduce any guests.
❖ Pray that all who have gathered will experience God as their Redeemer.
❖ Read or retell this information: **On May 4, 2007, a huge tornado ripped through Greensburg, Kansas, totally destroying this rural town of 1,400 residents. By 2009, thanks to their vision and planning, Greensburg has emerged as an eco-friendly model for the nation and the**

world. Using wind, solar, and geothermal technologies, as well as other environmentally conscious building materials, Greensburg has become truly "green."

❖ Ask: **In the aftermath of such a disaster, how do you think the people of Greensburg found the strength and courage to pull together and reinvent their town?**

❖ Read aloud today's focus statement: **In the face of devastating circumstances, people want to know that there is hope for rebuilding their lives. How can we know that something can be rebuilt out of destruction? Isaiah 44 speaks comfort and hope that God will not forget Israel and will redeem all things.**

(2) Examine God's Redemption of Israel

❖ Set the stage for today's session by summarizing information in Understanding the Scripture from Isaiah 44:1 through verse 20.

❖ Call on a volunteer to read the lesson from Isaiah 44:21-26.

❖ Suggest that the adults imagine themselves as the Israelites who heard the prophet's words. Ask:

    (1) **What questions would you want to ask Isaiah about God's will for your future?**

    (2) **How might you respond emotionally to these words?**

    (3) **What actions might you take as a result of hearing these words?**

❖ Form two groups for an informal debate. Ask one group to champion the view that history is nothing more than the chronicling of events set in motion by natural, political, and human forces. Ask the second group to argue that God's redemptive action can be seen or sensed in history. Set a time limit, being sure that each group has equal time to make their case. Wrap up by allowing class observers to ask questions of both sides and make additional comments.

(3) Recognize that God Remembers and Regards the Learners Highly

❖ Read "Remember and Receive God's Mercies" from Interpreting the Scripture. Notice how God urged the Israelites to remember their past so as to be able to move into their future. The action of remembering is clearly important. Brainstorm answers to this question: **As a congregation, what collective memories do we have that will help shape us as we move forward in the future?** List ideas on newsprint.

❖ Continue the theme of remembrance by inviting the adults to remember ways in which God has moved in their individual lives. Distribute paper and pencils. Suggest that they draw a line on their papers and at one end write their birthdate and at the other end, today's date. Encourage them to mark off decades. Then ask them to try to remember one "God event" in at least two decades of their lives. Where did they encounter God? How did this encounter change them? How did this encounter illustrate to them that God loves them and highly regards them?

❖ Invite the students to work in pairs or groups of three. Each person is encouraged to share one of these encounters. Any who choose not to participate may just say "pass."

❖ Bring the groups together and ask:

    (1) **What similarities did you see in the way God has worked in your lives?**

    (2) **What similarities did you perceive between the way God works in lives today and lives in the days of Isaiah?**

(4) Rebuild Places of Brokenness

❖ Read aloud "A Sign for the Exiles."

❖ Ask this question for silent reflection: **Isaiah challenged the Israelites to look beyond their shattered lives to see new beginnings and a restored relationship with God. Surely this must have been difficult for those in exile. People may have** felt hopeful and yet also cynical that such a change could occur. They likely asked the question "how can this be?" How do you respond when challenged to see new possibilities in the midst of brokenness?

❖ Break the silence by asking the adults to think about places of brokenness in their community. Ask:

(1) **What needs to be rebuilt in our community?**

(2) **How can we mobilize people to see the need and work together to respond?**

(3) **What kind of help will we need to begin the process?**

❖ Conclude by asking those who will help with this rebuilding, using whatever talents they can bring, to raise their hands or stand as a sign of their commitment.

(5) Continue the Journey

❖ Pray that the participants will recognize God's redeeming presence in their lives and share that news in word and deed with others who seek a redeemer to rebuild their places of brokenness.

❖ Read aloud this preparation for next week's lesson. You may also want to post it on newsprint for the students to copy.

- ■ **Title: Turn to Me and Be Saved**
- ■ **Background Scripture: Isaiah 45**
- ■ **Lesson Scripture: Isaiah 45:18-24**
- ■ **Focus of the Lesson: Many people who seek to be leaders falsely claim knowledge, authority, and**

power. **How are the people to recognize false claims? God's mighty acts since the beginning of time present hope for the future while showing that none other can demonstrate such ability.**

❖ Challenge the students to complete one or more of these activities for further spiritual growth related to this week's session. Post this information on newsprint for the students to copy.

(1) **Read again today's key verse, Isaiah 44:22. Meditate on the images of cloud and mist as they relate to your transgressions. Give thanks to God the Redeemer that your sins have vanished as the mist.**

(2) **Reflect on the forgiveness that God offers to humanity. In the love and grace of God, offer forgiveness to someone who has wronged you.**

(3) **Help those who are in exile, perhaps political refugees, by sending money through church or responsible non-profit agencies. Volunteer to help displaced people in your own community.**

❖ Sing or read aloud "Great Is Thy Faithfulness."

❖ Conclude today's session by leading the class in this benediction: **Let us go forth to worship and serve the Lord, in whom we have the blessed assurance of our salvation.**

UNIT 2: A FUTURE FOR GOD'S PEOPLE

Turn to Me and Be Saved

PREVIEWING THE LESSON

Lesson Scripture: Isaiah 45:18-24
Background Scripture: Isaiah 45
Key Verse: Isaiah 45:22

Focus of the Lesson:

Many people who seek to be leaders falsely claim knowledge, authority, and power. How are the people to recognize false claims? God's mighty acts since the beginning of time present hope for the future while showing that none other can demonstrate such ability.

Goals for the Learners:

(1) to examine God's record of creation and rightful claims to power.
(2) to contemplate God's faithfulness to them.
(3) to identify any false gods they have followed and turn from them.

Supplies:

Bibles, newsprint and marker, paper and pencils, hymnals

READING THE SCRIPTURE

NRSV

Isaiah 45:18-24

18 For thus says the Lord,
   who created the heavens
     (he is God!),
   who formed the earth and made it
     (he established it;
   he did not create it a chaos,
     he formed it to be inhabited!):
I am the Lord, and there is no other.

NIV

Isaiah 45:18-24

18For this is what the Lord says—
   he who created the heavens,
     he is God;
   he who fashioned and made the earth,
     he founded it;
   he did not create it to be empty,
     but formed it to be inhabited—
he says:
"I am the Lord,

¹⁹ I did not speak in secret,
    in a land of darkness;
I did not say to the offspring of Jacob,
    "Seek me in chaos."
I the LORD speak the truth,
    I declare what is right.
²⁰ Assemble yourselves and come together,
    draw near, you survivors of the nations!
They have no knowledge—
    those who carry about their wooden
      idols,
and keep on praying to a god
    that cannot save.
²¹ Declare and present your case;
    let them take counsel together!
Who told this long ago?
    Who declared it of old?
Was it not I, the LORD?
    There is no other god besides me,
a righteous God and a Savior;
    there is no one besides me.
²² Turn to me and be saved,
    all the ends of the earth!
For I am God, and there is no other.
²³ By myself I have sworn,
    from my mouth has gone forth in
      righteousness
    a word that shall not return:
"To me every knee shall bow,
    every tongue shall swear."
²⁴ Only in the LORD, it shall be said of me,
    are righteousness and strength.

    and there is no other.
¹⁹I have not spoken in secret,
    from somewhere in a land of darkness;
I have not said to Jacob's descendants,
    'Seek me in vain.'
I, the LORD, speak the truth;
    I declare what is right.
²⁰"Gather together and come;
    assemble, you fugitives from the
      nations.
Ignorant are those who carry about idols
    of wood,
who pray to gods that cannot save.
²¹Declare what is to be, present it—
    let them take counsel together.
Who foretold this long ago,
    who declared it from the distant past?
Was it not I, the LORD?
    And there is no God apart from me,
a righteous God and a Savior;
    there is none but me.
²²"Turn to me and be saved,
    all you ends of the earth;
    for I am God, and there is no other.
²³By myself I have sworn,
    my mouth has uttered in all integrity
    a word that will not be revoked:
Before me every knee will bow;
    by me every tongue will swear.
²⁴They will say of me, 'In the LORD alone
    are righteousness and strength.' "

UNDERSTANDING THE SCRIPTURE

Isaiah 45:1-8. With the remarkable announcement of God's choice of the Persian Empire's King Cyrus (see Isaiah 44:28), the forty-fifth chapter added divine definition and determination to the future. Although Isaiah 45 presents material focused on a common theme, it is actually a collection of many short oracles fashioned into a whole piece. There are various literary styles and fragments included in the chapter: disputations, songs of praise, a trial scene, a series of woes (from the wisdom rather than the prophetic tradition), and commissioning announcements. Woven through these various literary types is Isaiah's central concern: to establish God's lordship over all history and creation. The opening oracle, verses 1-8, recounts God's calling of Cyrus. The text moves between past, present, and future to emphasize the continuity of God's purpose. Notice the progression: in the first verse God "grasped" Cyrus by the right hand, a sign of confirmation in royal office. In verse 3, comes the explanation that it was "the God of Israel" who calls Cyrus by his name, indicating the very present knowledge of God that is active in Cyrus' life. Verse 6 records the consequence of God's action, set in a future tense, "so that they may know" that there is no other god but God. The sweep of God's providence is timeless and the success of God's purposes sure. Isaiah selected strong images: mountains leveled and bronze doors smashed, hidden treasures, well-being and woe created by God alone, and even divine employment of a foreign king who does not know Yahweh, the God of Israel. Finally, Isaiah's words melt into a universal praise with a final song (45:8) that extols God's great yearning to cover the earth (and all nations and people) with salvation and righteousness.

Isaiah 45:9-13. In the next section, Isaiah addressed the resistance among the exiles to God's choice of Cyrus. Their concerns were not named. Isaiah borrowed a technique from the teachers of wisdom by using a repetition of woes intended to provoke a particular conclusion. The first woe was based on the analogy of a pot questioning the potter at work, and the second, on the absurdity of questioning human procreation. Because each woe contained a foregone conclusion, Isaiah easily shifted the conclusion back on the exiles as he confronted them through God's word, "Will you question me . . . or command me?" (45:11) This absurdity flowed directly into a proclamation of God as the creator of all and the commander over history. Isaiah intended to build a bridge over the exiles' discouragement into hope for the near future. The nature of God's intervention was specific: God, through Cyrus, will build up my city (Jerusalem) and set the exiles (the Israelites) free. This was a clear word, expressed without image, word-play, rhetorical innuendo,

or symbolism of any sort. However, if the exiles still objected, Isaiah added one more direct comment from God: Cyrus will accomplish God's intentions without thought of reward or payment, but solely because God was working through him.

Isaiah 45:14-17. The next section posed significant challenges for interpreters. This confusion may be abated by returning to Isaiah's central claim: One day all nations will recognize Yahweh, the God of Israel as the one true God. This recognition, stated in verses 14-15, was recorded in Isaiah 60:4-7, a description of the nations, with their various tributes of camels, flocks, gold, and silver, gathering at God's holy Temple in Jerusalem. These two verses represent a rarely voiced hope of Israel's ultimate recognition among the nations of the world. As a subtext, Isaiah offered the presentation of tribute to Israel to indicate the significance of the nations' confession of faith. However, the nations' confession of faith was of utmost significance. The broadest yearning of Yahweh was not the particular success (or failure) of Israel's political circumstances, but for the eventual fullness of the knowledge of God among all nations and peoples. This concept was difficult to grasp; it was also absolutely essential to the faith of Israel. If Israel's faith focused on mercy received from God during times of difficulty, there was the danger that she would never be moved to fulfill her divine calling: to be a light to the nations. To underscore the breadth of God's intentions for good toward all nations, Isaiah offered two theological ideas. First, the saving activity of God is hidden within the events of history. Second, the salvation of God, initiated through Israel, would never be confounded. In other words, Isaiah affirmed God's universal intention for the world's salvation.

Isaiah 45:18-25. In the first segment, verses 18-19, Isaiah offered the simple truth that God does not create chaos; rather, God created everything from chaos in such a way that creation flourishes. Because God imprinted the movement from chaos to order on every aspect of creation and because this was revealed to the people long, long ago, every Israelite should have known and affirmed this truth. Having stated the obvious—God is the creator—the next segment returned to the persistent theme of the futility of idol worship. This theme concluded with the familiar accusation: Idols made from created elements by human hands have no power to save. Only the creator, the God of Israel, saved the world. To emphasize the universal nature of this theme, Isaiah altered, slightly, a key phrase from the previous section. Thus, "There is no other god besides me" (45:21) became "For I am God, and there is no other" (45:22). This one and only God then declared the future of salvation. God's word set salvation in motion. Indeed, by God's word the time would come when every individual would bow in worship and every person would confess faith in God. Although all people are called to the one God, verse 25 makes clear that Israel has a special place in God's household.

INTERPRETING THE SCRIPTURE

Order Rather Than Chaos

Isaiah's message was greater than his words could hold. His was the awesome task of speaking God's truth to a despairing people who both needed and feared the renewal of the relationship with God. However, his message carried significance beyond the plight of the Israelites in exile; indeed, his message was directed to all humanity. Consider the scope of that message within its original setting. All humanity included both the oppressing Babylonian leaders and the impoverished peasant farmers who remained in Judah. All humanity included the Israelites who suffered because they remained true to their religious practices while in exile and those Israelites who formed alliances with the Babylonians especially through marriage. All humanity was a difficult concept for the exiles; perhaps it was as difficult in their day as it is in our contemporary experience.

The basis for Isaiah's inclusive message was creation. Creation, Isaiah affirmed, was not intended to be chaotic. Although most exiles saw only the chaos of their oppression and felt only the pain in their bodies, minds, and spirits, Isaiah calmly reminded them that God made the world to be inhabited. Every aspect of creation was shaped by God to provide sustenance and security for the human family. Although hot winds blew across the desert, God provided oases of water and shade. Although thunderstorms rumbled on the mountains, God provided seasonal rains at dependable times. Although humanity sought to dominate one another, God's intentions were quietly directing history toward peace. Isaiah, somehow, grasped these huge concepts. With simple phrases, Isaiah attempted to dispel the fears of the exiles and to rebuild their confidence in God's ordering of creation. Isaiah taught the people to see God's order within the chaotic events of their individual and corporate lives. His message rings as necessary today as centuries before.

Truth Rather Than Secrets

After painting the wide picture of God's gracious order in creation, Isaiah began to detail a small section. Because he understood the exiles' experience, Isaiah began where they were. Figuratively, they were in "a land of darkness" (45:19). This metaphor referred to the darkness of the land of Israel during the time of the Exile. After the depopulation, only the poorest of the poor scratched out a meager living. Commerce continued along the trade routes, but Israel no longer received the benefit. The shadow of the darkness reached the exiles in Babylon. They grieved over what had become of the land given to them by their God.

Isaiah addressed this sorrow with the image of darkness. But as Isaiah spoke of the darkness, his context was greater than the sorrow of the exiles. God's intentions, declared Isaiah, were not secrets; there was a path to God's truth. Israel, even in the despair of exile, could travel that path. In order to successfully seek the Lord, however, the exiles would need to reorient themselves. Instead of dwelling on the negative, Israel needed to seek God where God was. God was to be encountered in the midst of an orderly creation. Isaiah pressed this reorientation with a single affirmation: "I did not say to the offspring of Jacob, 'Seek me in chaos'" (45:19). Instead, God had given to the people abundant resources to enable them to know God.

Among these gifts, abundant in exile, were the tales of God's faithfulness to Israel throughout the generations from Abraham to the Exile, as well as the gifts of law, wisdom teachers, prophets, and worship practices. As Israel focused on these gifts wonderful blessings emerged. For example, the roots of synagogue worship, education, and support are traced to the exiles' gatherings outside the city gates at the river's edge (see Psalm 137). For example, the historical books of the Old Testament were written down and organized during this time, as were the words of the prophets. Even the prayers and songs of the Israel Temple worship, the Psalms, were collected and organized during the Exile. By these efforts the exiles sought God where God's light was brightest: in the truth of their experience and the righteousness of God's creative compassion.

Mysterious Salvation

In ancient Israel the prophetic word functioned much as the preached word functions in our contemporary world. The prophet prayed, consulted, listened for, and studied God's word; contemporary preachers pray, consult, listen for, and study God's word. Both have the same goal: to present God to the world in such a way the world will align itself to God's intention.

The work of prophets and preachers is similar in another, less obvious, aspect. They both live near the mysterious presence and the equally mysterious absence of God. Because both are acquainted with the mystery of God's ways, their testimony at times sets the absence of God beside the faithful confession of faith. For example, Isaiah testified, "Truly, you are a God who hides" (Isaiah 45:15) and then wrote, "There is no other god" (45:21). Contemporary preachers humbly admit the limits of human knowledge, and then affirm God's desire that every individual know, serve, and love God.

The key verse for this lesson makes the almost unbelievable assertion that God's salvation is for all. The path to this salvation is likewise mysterious. Isaiah describes the path with a simple "turn" (45:22); yet all who read that word must have been amazed. How could the exiles turn to God and be saved? How can we turn and be saved? Was this really within their power? Is it possible to turn and be saved today?

God's Oath, Humanity's Confidence

Isaiah skillfully wove hints to answer the above questions throughout today's passage. First, there was the hint that God created an ordered rather than a chaotic universe. Second, God's ways were evident rather than secret. Third, God said, "turn to me and be saved"—a message directed to humanity in every age and place. Finally, God's word confirmed Isaiah's message with an oath (45:23). A divine oath was the greatest testimony Isaiah could offer the exiles. By an oath God had entered into the covenant with Abraham, secured Moses as a leader, blessed the monarchy, and challenged the rebellious nature of Israel. By an oath God protected a remnant of the faithful during the Exile, and by an oath God pledged to spread divine knowledge and salvation throughout creation.

Were you surprised by Isaiah 45:23: "To me every knee shall bow,/every tongue shall swear"? Did you begin humming a familiar hymn—"He Is Lord" or "O For a Thousand Tongues to Sing"—as you read those words? I know I did. Deep within me is the conviction that God's Son Jesus is the way to salvation . . . but here, in Isaiah 45, I'm confronted by a set of words associated with Jesus the Christ, yet spoken as a bless-ing on the nation Israel. The jolt takes me back to the surprise of God's ways. God will accomplish each and every intention woven into creation: Humanity will learn to live in harmony with creation, one another, and with their creator.

Only when Isaiah's words were recognized by the exiles as containing the passion and purpose of God would they realize potential. What was true for the exiles of Israel became true for the first disciples of Jesus and continues to be true for the contemporary body of Christ. Salvation comes from the God who brought order out of chaos, the one who can be depended up to "speak the truth" (45:19); all other sources end in darkness, chaos, and confusion. Hope for the future is found in God and God alone.

SHARING THE SCRIPTURE

Preparing Our Hearts

Explore this week's devotional reading, found in Exodus 15:11-18. In this song that Moses sang to God after the people had safely escaped the dreaded Egyptians, God's power and prowess over the Hebrews' enemies are celebrated. This is the Redeemer who steadfastly loved the people and brought them to God's own holy mountain. How has God delivered you and given you new hope for the future? What songs of praise will you sing to God today?

Pray that you and the adult learners will acknowledge God as the one who brings salvation.

Preparing Our Minds

Study the background Scripture from Isaiah 45 and the lesson Scripture from Isaiah 45:18-24. Think about how people are able to recognize false claims.

Write on newsprint:

❏ information for next week's lesson, found under "Continue the Journey."
❏ activities for further spiritual growth in "Continue the Journey."

LEADING THE CLASS

(1) Gather to Learn

❖ Welcome the class members and introduce any guests.

❖ Pray that all who have come today will recognize God's faithfulness to them.

❖ Brainstorm answers to this question and write the group's answers on newsprint: **What are some traits of a cult leader?** Here are some possible responses: *claims to be the only authority and so rules with absolute power; expects total trust and loyalty from followers; claims to have direct contact with God that no one else has; often involved in unaudited fund-raising, which allows the leader to become wealthy while group members become poorer; may make extravagant promises; may* *engage in immoral sexual behavior; may lead followers to expect a cataclysmic event; usually has a charismatic personality that draws people to join the group.*

❖ Ask: **We know of cult leaders, such as David Koresh of the Branch Davidians in Waco, Texas, and Jim Jones of the Peoples Temple in Jonestown, Guyana, whose members died tragically. Why do you suppose people follow such leaders?**

❖ Read aloud today's focus statement: **Many people who seek to be leaders falsely claim knowledge, authority, and power. How are the people to recognize false claims? God's mighty acts since the beginning of time present hope for the future while showing that none other can demonstrate such ability.**

(2) Examine God's Record of Creation and Rightful Claims to Power

❖ Set the stage for today's Bible text by reading or retelling information from Understanding the Scripture for Isaiah 45:1-8, 9-13, and 14-17.

❖ Call on a volunteer to read Isaiah 45:18-24.

❖ Look at verse 18, which speaks about the Lord who created the heavens and formed the earth. Form three groups: one to look at Genesis 1:1–2:4, a second to review Genesis 2:4-25, and a third to consider Psalm 104. Provide newsprint and a marker for each group. Encourage them to list ways in which they see their assigned passages somehow reflected in Isaiah 45:18. Focus on God as the creator.

❖ Call the groups back together to report their findings.

❖ Invite the adults to silently scan Isaiah 45:20-24. Discuss these questions:

(1) What do these verses tell you about the nature of God?

(2) Given that God is the creator, the only One who has the power to tame chaos, why do you suppose people worshiped "wooden idols"?

(3) If you had been an idol worshiper, what response would you make to these words of the Lord?

❖ Read or retell "Order Rather Than Chaos" from Interpreting the Scripture.

❖ Conclude this portion of the lesson by suggesting that the participants again review the entire passage, verses 18-24, and then discuss this question: **How would you respond to someone who said, "What persuades you to believe that there is only one God who is both creator and savior"?**

(3) Contemplate God's Faithfulness to the Learners

❖ Distribute paper and pencils. Ask the students to think of at least one occasion on which God has shown faithfulness to them. Provide quiet time for them to write about this situation in whatever form they choose. As examples, they may write a psalm of thanksgiving, a letter of thanks to God, a journal entry about their experience, or a letter to a friend summarizing the experience.

❖ Call for volunteers to read or retell what they have written. Note themes that seem to run through the various situations. Help the class identify the changes that they experienced because of God's faithfulness. You might do this by using a very general paraphrase, such as "once you were extremely ill, but now you are healed;" or "once you encountered financial challenges, but now you are on a more stable footing."

❖ Provide a few moments of silent time to give thanks for God's faithful presence.

(4) Identify Any False Gods the Learners Have Followed and Turn From Them

❖ List on newsprint the adults' ideas about what constitutes a false god or idol in our day. Discuss the idea that while "wooden idols" are obviously meant to be gods, our contemporary idols—fame, power, wealth, certain possessions, perfect body, and so on—may not be as easy to identify. Consequently, many people are trying to worship both their idols *and* God.

❖ Ask: **According to Isaiah 45:20, idols cannot save. Why, then, do you think people continue to act as if their money, status, home, car, or whatever can give them lasting security and peace?**

❖ Encourage the students to read aloud today's key verse, Isaiah 45:22. If possible, ask the adults to stand facing one direction, and as they read the words "turn to me" turn to face the opposite direction. Ask them to be seated.

❖ Challenge the adults to identify silently one idol from which they will turn, and then make a commitment to worship only the Lord. Some may wish to write the name of the idol on the paper from the last activity. Suggest that they tuck the paper into their Bibles and refer to it each day in the coming week.

(5) Continue the Journey

❖ Pray that all who have gathered today will recognize idols in their own lives and turn to the one true God who alone offers salvation.

❖ Read aloud this preparation for next week's lesson. You may also want to post it on newsprint for the students to copy.

- ■ **Title: Reassurance for God's People**
- ■ **Background Scripture: Isaiah 48**
- ■ **Lesson Scripture: Isaiah 48:14-19, 21-22**

■ **Focus of the Lesson: People make mistakes, live incorrectly, and need to have the past put aside for right living in the future. How can past mistakes be corrected and replaced with right living? God promises to forgive sin and to redeem God's people.**

❖ Challenge the students to complete one or more of these activities for further spiritual growth related to this week's session. Post this information on newsprint for the students to copy.

(1) Recall that God's intention for the world was not chaos but form and order for inhabitants (Isaiah 45:18). Identify places where you see chaos. Ask God to show you specific actions you can take to help return order to these chaotic situations. Do whatever you can.

(2) Witness this week to someone who is worshiping modern idols. Invite this person to turn to God.

(3) Compare Isaiah 45:23 to Philippians 2:9-11 and Romans 14:11. What might these verses suggest to you about God, Jesus, and the relationship between the two?

❖ Sing or read aloud "How Great Thou Art."

❖ Conclude today's session by leading the class in this benediction: **Let us go forth to worship and serve the Lord, in whom we have the blessed assurance of our salvation.**

UNIT 2: A FUTURE FOR GOD'S PEOPLE
REASSURANCE FOR GOD'S PEOPLE

PREVIEWING THE LESSON

Lesson Scripture: Isaiah 48:14-19, 21-22
Background Scripture: Isaiah 48
Key Verse: Isaiah 48:20

Focus of the Lesson:
People make mistakes, live incorrectly, and need to have the past put aside for right living in the future. How can past mistakes be corrected and replaced with right living? God promises to forgive sin and to redeem God's people.

Goals for the Learners:
(1) to investigate God's claims on the people and God's promise to forgive sin and restore the people to righteousness.
(2) to consider their sins and the need for repentance and forgiveness.
(3) to ask God for forgiveness and to pledge to change sinful behavior.

Pronunciation Guide:
Chaldean (kal dee' uhn)

Supplies:
Bibles, newsprint and marker, paper and pencils, hymnals

READING THE SCRIPTURE

NRSV
Isaiah 48:14-22
¹⁴ Assemble, all of you, and hear!
  Who among them has declared these
    things?
  The LORD loves him;
    he shall perform his purpose on
    Babylon,

NIV
Isaiah 48:14-22
¹⁴"Come together, all of you, and listen:
  Which of the idols has foretold
    these things?
  The LORD's chosen ally
    will carry out his purpose against
    Babylon;

and his arm shall be against the
   Chaldeans.
¹⁵ I, even I, have spoken and called him,
   I have brought him, and he will
      prosper in his way.
¹⁶ Draw near to me, hear this!
   From the beginning I have not spoken
      in secret,
   from the time it came to be I have been
      there.
   And now the Lord GOD has sent me
      and his spirit.
¹⁷ Thus says the LORD,
   your Redeemer, the Holy One of
      Israel:
   I am the LORD your God,
      who teaches you for your own good,
      who leads you in the way you should
         go.
¹⁸ O that you had paid attention to my
      commandments!
   Then your prosperity would have
      been like a river,
   and your success like the waves of the
      sea;
¹⁹ your offspring would have been like
      the sand,
   and your descendants like its grains;
   their name would never be cut off
      or destroyed from before me.
²⁰ **Go out from Babylon, flee from Chaldea,**
   declare this with a shout of joy,
      proclaim it,
   send it forth to the end of the earth;
      say, "The LORD has redeemed his
         servant Jacob!"
²¹ They did not thirst when he led them
      through the deserts;
   he made water flow for them from
      the rock;
   he split open the rock and the water
      gushed out.
²² "There is no peace," says the LORD,
   "for the wicked."

his arm will be against the Babylonians.
¹⁵I, even I, have spoken;
   yes, I have called him.
 I will bring him,
and he will succeed in his mission.
¹⁶"Come near me and listen to this:
"From the first announcement I have
      not spoken in secret;
   at the time it happens, I am there."
And now the Sovereign LORD has sent me,
   with his Spirit.
¹⁷This is what the LORD says—
   your Redeemer, the Holy One of Israel:
 "I am the LORD your God,
   who teaches you what is best for you,
   who directs you in the way you
      should go.
¹⁸If only you had paid attention to my
      commands,
   your peace would have been like a river,
   your righteousness like the waves
      of the sea.
¹⁹Your descendants would have been like
      the sand,
   your children like its numberless grains;
 their name would never be cut off
   nor destroyed from before me."
²⁰**Leave Babylon,**
   flee from the Babylonians!
 Announce this with shouts of joy
   and proclaim it.
 Send it out to the ends of the earth;
   say, "The LORD has redeemed his
      servant Jacob."
²¹They did not thirst when he led them
      through the deserts;
   he made water flow for them from
      the rock;
 he split the rock
   and water gushed out.
²²"There is no peace," says the LORD, "
   for the wicked."

UNDERSTANDING THE SCRIPTURE

Isaiah 48:1-11. In this opening section of our text, the prophet used two references to remind the exiles of their sacred status with God. First, the prophet called the people "house of Jacob," recalling that their heritage began by God's choice of Abraham and continued as a familial covenant instigated and maintained by God. The second designation, "from the loins of Judah," evoked the Holy City of Jerusalem and the Temple. Without the glue of worship and oil of strong familial connections, the people's relationship with God fragmented and became dry. The people's connections to God were tenuous, but the prophet's words intended strengthening. In this section, the prophet extolled God's fidelity toward the people. He also cautioned the people about their rebellious history. Indeed, following every affirmation of God's nature (48:3, 5, 7) Isaiah placed a cautionary statement about Israel's faithlessness (48:4, 5, 7-8). This remarkably balanced presentation also included the reminder in verse 6 that Israel was called to be God's witness. Based on the past performance of Israel, the prophet was not hopeful. However, more than history informed the prophet's words. Isaiah was profoundly aware of the purposes of God toward Israel and creation. Thus, the section concluded with an explanation of God's judgment (described as deferred anger) as a refinement of Israel and God's intention to expand divine glory and knowledge throughout creation.

Isaiah 48:12-16. Next, the prophet appealed to the people to ponder deeply God's words and deeds. God was doing a new thing by commissioning Cyrus as a servant of divine purpose. Cyrus is unnamed here, but the pronouns "him" and "he" in verses 14 and 15 refer to Cyrus II of Persia. Israel never imagined God's assistance coming from an external agent; such an idea was unthinkable. Throughout Israel's history, help came from within the Israelite nation—

Joseph arrived in Egypt; Moses delivered the people from bondage; kings, prophets, and priests kept the nation together as God's chosen people. Now, however, Isaiah boldly declared that help was coming through the foreign king Cyrus. In this section, the prophet expressed the love of God for Cyrus and disclosed the specific deeds that Cyrus would accomplish. By military might and expertise, Cyrus would defeat Babylon and dismantle the power of the Chaldeans. Verse 14 (NIV) avers that Cyrus was "the LORD's chosen ally." Because Cyrus acted with God's blessing, he would complete his mission. This stunning announcement was a public declaration prior to any actions by Cyrus. Isaiah, an accredited prophet of God, put his own reputation on the line in order that the people would attend to this news. God was not dealing with Israel in secret; rather, Isaiah clearly announced God's intentions. All that was required of the people was to believe and bear witness to God's engagement on their behalf. The prophet concluded with a poignant affirmation: He, Isaiah, was sent with God's spirit. We can assume that the people would know God's creative word was effective, even in an exile of despair and humiliation.

Isaiah 48:17-19. By a litany of the names of God, "the LORD, your Redeemer, the Holy One of Israel," the prophet continued to describe the close relationship God desired to have with the exiles. The Lord had taught them what they needed to know, and had led them along the right path. They had had many experiences with God the teacher, which though not recorded in these verses surely were in their collective memory. God rescued the people from captivity in Egypt; formed them by the gift of the law during the wilderness period; and led them with prophets, kings, and priests in the time of the monarchy. Israel, however, had been a poor student of God. After the great rescue from Egypt, the people grumbled about the burdens of desert existence (see Exodus 16:3; 17:3). The law became a chore rather than a blessing, and Israel's leaders were more often disloyal than faithful to God. Indeed, the course of history, especially the recent history of exile, was a perilous path potholed with complaints, disobedience, and pursuit of other gods. If Israel only "had paid attention to" God's commandments, then history would have moved toward prosperity and success. The nation's rebellion from God brought judgment; exile was not a divine necessity, but a divine consequence of extended rebellion.

Isaiah 48:20-22. Despite their past failures, God was not finished with these exiles. Instead, God intended good for them and eagerly anticipated Israel's response of praise. Therefore, Isaiah concluded this chapter with an invitation to Israel to praise God with a hymn of thanksgiving. Although the painful circumstances of exile remained, Isaiah told the people how they should exit Babylon: Go out with joy and proclaim God's redemption to all who would listen. God's new deed of rescue demanded a spirited celebration. Indeed, only by the exiles' praise would the nations understand that the God of Israel was the sovereign Lord of creation and history. This celebration was not an optional activity; it was, rather, at the center of the future God was creating. Whereas once the people grumbled about the difficulties of a desert crossing, in the near future, God's providence would bring them safely home. The images in verse 21 recall the Exodus from Egypt. By using them here, Isaiah links the first Exodus with what will, in God's time, be a new exodus as the exiles return home from Babylon. When Israel sang praises to God, the world heard about the gracious purposes of God. Moreover, if Israel sang before the new reality appeared, then other nations might recognize the truth at the heart of history: God's intentions for all creation were gracious. Thus, before the divinely prompted deeds began, Isaiah coached the exiles. The people were to sing new songs bursting with confidence! Still, the shadow of rebellion persisted. Isaiah's last comment reminded the people that obedience, rather than rebellion, secured God's peace.

INTERPRETING THE SCRIPTURE

A Chosen Deliverer

The work of a prophet was to speak God's word, broadly. In these few verses from Isaiah 48, Isaiah spoke broadly—so broadly, it is difficult to identify to whom the pronouns in verses 14-16 refer. In verse 14, Isaiah seemed to address the foreign nations by offering them a preview of God's next deeds; in verse 15 he confronted the exiles' lack of confidence in God's plan; in verse 16, he seemed, almost, to address himself. Although the pronouns are somewhat ambiguous, the message to the assembly makes sense. This was an assembly to declare the chosen delivered, to draw the exiles' attention toward God's ways, to propose a new future, and to teach the audience a new song. As a skilled communicator, Isaiah offered this message simultaneously apparently to foreign nations, to dispirited exiles, and even to himself. It was a daunting task, but Isaiah was equal to it.

The contemporary church has the same task and faces a similarly varied audience. In our setting, many have not been raised within the circle of a loving congregation or learned faith as naturally as riding a bike or flying a kite. Some people come to God through the avenue of recovery from addiction, various paths of self-help, and a wide diversity of spiritual interests. As Isaiah stretched his message to include numerous audiences, so the contemporary church must declare God's truth in ways that can be heard by multiple audiences.

The task, however, remains singular: God's Word must be shared broadly with all. In today's passage, Isaiah continued the message begun in Isaiah 45:1; he explained God's choice of the Persian king, Cyrus, as the exiles' deliverer. He spoke with firmness, telling all that the Lord loved Cyrus and would ensure his endeavors. This announcement was so novel that for the exiles it was hard to receive and almost impossible to believe. Steadily, however, Isaiah shared with them God's Word. The deliverer was known; God would bring about the divine plan; the exiles would be freed from captivity. By these blunt statements, Isaiah captured the exiles' attention.

Now Hear This

Once Isaiah made his announcement, he began to cultivate the exiles' affection toward God. Once again, Isaiah's task and the task of the contemporary church intersect. Isaiah spoke to hopeless people who feared God's negative judgment would never end; the contemporary church speaks to uncertain people who assume God's presence is far from this world. In order to establish God's words in the "living" of the exiles, Isaiah sought to foster their relationship with God. In similar ways, the contemporary church looks backward at the mighty evidence of God's presence in the world to reestablish a relationship between God and ordinary people.

Taking a risky step, Isaiah used his reputation and credentials as a prophet to underwrite this surprising message. Persistently, he spoke a singular truth: God will redeem creation. Yet, as verse 17 affirms, Isaiah was speaking on behalf of God: "Thus says the LORD." Thoroughly, he accepted the risks and responsibility of his calling and offered his life as an example of living according to God's Word. By such persistent, consistent, and thorough commitment to God, Isaiah

provoked a desire among the exiles for a renewed relationship with God.

Such persistence and thoroughness continue to display the blessings and responsibilities of contemporary Christian living. As Isaiah humbly stated, "and now the LORD God has sent me and his spirit" (48:16), the contemporary church likewise offers its messages of recovery, redemption, and return to a close relationship with God. As Isaiah, we are God's invitations into full and abundant living. Such an invitation requires more than a verbal offer and response; living with God is a journey through life's difficulties, secured by confidence in God's intentions for good, and always obedient despite surrounding temptations.

If Only You Had Paid Attention

Have you ever lost your way while hiking in the woods or desert? I have. Moreover, I have a remarkably faulty sense of direction; in fact, I'm often confused by left and right while north, south, east, and west evade my consciousness. Fortunately, at an early age I was taught that moss grows on the north side of redwoods, and much later on, in the expanse of the Southwest, I learned to trace the arcs of summer and winter sun. Still, at times I become disoriented and need to clear my head before retracing my steps.

My experience of being temporarily disoriented bears a modest similarity to the situation of the exiles. Their guide was Isaiah, who reminded them that God had, indeed, established a way to freedom and the security of home. Isaiah gently reminded the exiles of the two cardinal directions necessary for their journey with God. First, they were to remember that God's instructions were designed for their safety and security. God's wisdom, contained in history and Torah law, was not frivolous. Rather, in the past and now with Isaiah's instruction, God taught the people to live as a godly community.

Second, Isaiah stressed that head knowledge was insufficient. The people needed to turn their hearts to God. Isaiah declared that the people were responsible for their current estrangement and exile. They had ignored God's law. They had turned deaf ears and blind eyes toward God's presence in the world. They had tried to live without God . . . and they had succeeded. Because they failed to pay attention to God, they had wandered away from God's way.

God had not, however, allowed the relationship to dissolve. Where sin abounded, God granted forgiveness. Where deaf ears and blind eyes diminished life, God restored hearing and sight. When the people thought God had forsaken them, there was God preparing a new chapter in their covenantal relationship.

Sing a New Song

Isaiah called the exiles to attention, drew them near to God, described (again) the way of God and, finally, led the people in a chorus of praise. The song Isaiah taught the people to sing was full of anticipatory praise. That means, they could not completely imagine the changes in their circumstances—they could only anticipate such changes. Still, as Isaiah took up a hymn of praise, the people learned the refrain. They sang with confidence, "The LORD has redeemed his servant Jacob!" (48:20). In that chorus they expressed their gratitude for God's great mercy toward them and their dedication to their calling as a servant to God. Their godly service began with singing—joyful singing.

The song Isaiah taught the exiles was unlike the old songs of Zion; this song was not based on God's former goodness in days long ago. Rather, this new song announced a triumph yet to happen and a release yet to be granted. The people sang their gratitude for what God was yet to accomplish. Isaiah's thoughtful coaching restored the peoples' confidence in God. Before Isaiah spoke, there was no future and no hope. After Isaiah declared God's patient providence, there was both future and hope.

Still, the prophet paused to offer one final caution: The way to future peace was present faithfulness. The shadow of earlier rebellions remained as a warning. As in the past, the willful choices of people who refused God's instruction and guidance continued to threaten. For the moment, however, there was only the joyful song and the happy hope of living in God's future as God's own people.

SHARING THE SCRIPTURE

Preparing Our Hearts

Explore this week's devotional reading, found in 1 Kings 8:33-40. These verses are found in a prayer offered by King Solomon at the dedication of the Temple in Jerusalem. Solomon's plea is that God will hear the people when they confess their sin, and offer forgiveness. Notice the different consequences of sin the king perceives. What sins do you need to confess to God today? What have been their consequences? Spend time in prayer before God's throne of grace.

Pray that you and the adult learners will be aware of their sins and seek God's forgiveness.

Preparing Our Minds

Study the background Scripture from Isaiah 48 and the lesson Scripture from Isaiah 48:14-22. Ponder how past mistakes can be corrected and replaced with right living.

Write on newsprint:
❑ questions for "Investigate God's Claims on the People and God's Promise to Forgive Sin and Restore the People to Righteousness."

❏ information for next week's lesson, found under "Continue the Journey."

❏ activities for further spiritual growth in "Continue the Journey."

LEADING THE CLASS

(1) Gather to Learn

❖ Welcome the class members and introduce any guests.

❖ Pray that those who have gathered today will recognize their need for repentance and forgiveness.

❖ Invite the class members to name biblical characters who made mistakes, including those who committed grievous sins. What did these people do? How did God redeem and use them despite their sin? Here are some examples: *Abraham had been called by God and given a covenant promise, but Abraham told people where he was living in Gerar that Sarah was his sister, after which the king almost committed adultery with her (Genesis 20); Moses was a murderer (Exodus 2:11-15), but God chose him to lead the Israelites out of slavery in Egypt; David had been anointed as Israel's king, but he abused his power with Bathsheba and had her husband Uriah killed in battle to cover up his sin (2 Samuel 11); Saul persecuted Christians until his experience on the road to Damascus transformed him into a faithful apostle (Acts 9:1-19).*

❖ Ask: **What do these stories of Bible figures reveal about how God deals with people who make serious mistakes?**

❖ Read aloud today's focus statement: **People make mistakes, live incorrectly, and need to have the past put aside for right living in the future. How can past mistakes be corrected and replaced with right living? God promises to forgive sin and to redeem God's people.**

(2) Investigate God's Claims on the People and God's Promise to Forgive Sin and Restore the People to Righteousness

❖ Read Isaiah 48:1-11 from Understanding the Scripture to introduce today's Bible study.

❖ Select a volunteer to read Isaiah 48:14-22 expressively.

❖ Form three groups. Assign one to work on Isaiah 48:14-16, another to review verses 17-19, and a third to consider verses 20-22. Post these questions on newsprint for each group to discuss. Note that all questions are not equally relevant for each passage.

> (1) **What is being said in this passage? By whom? To whom?**
>
> (2) **What do you learn about the nature and activity of God from this passage?**
>
> (3) **What do you hear about how the people have responded to God?**
>
> (4) **What does the passage say about what the people are to do now?**

❖ Call on a speaker to report for each group.

❖ Wrap up this section by encouraging the students to raise any questions they have about this passage. Work together to try to provide answers. Use information, as appropriate, from the Interpreting the Scripture portions.

(3) Consider the Learners' Sins and the Need for Repentance and Forgiveness

❖ Post three sheets of newsprint. Ask the students to call out definitions first for "sin," followed by definitions for "repentance," followed by definitions for "forgiveness." Use a different color marker for each set of definitions.

❖ Suggest that the adults talk with two or three other people about the reasons for, and importance of, repenting of one's sins and receiving forgiveness.

❖ Call the groups together. Try to synthesize the students' ideas by filling in the blanks with whatever seems appropriate to the group:

> *Given that sin . . ., believers are called to repent because . . .*
>
> *God honors that repentance by offering forgiveness, which enables the forgiven one to . . .*

(4) Ask God for Forgiveness and Pledge to Change Sinful Behavior

❖ Read "If Only You Had Paid Attention" from Interpreting the Scripture.

❖ Invite the participants to tell stories of times when they became disoriented and lost—and perhaps could reorient themselves because they relied on some markers they could interpret.

❖ Distribute paper and pencils. Suggest that the students sketch a forest by making some upright lines with a few branches on each. Ask them to label the "trees" with whatever helps them in their faith journeys to stay near to God, or to return to God when they have gotten lost in the thickets of sin. Examples of labels may include: *Scripture, worship, the community of faith, prayer, Bible study, meditation, hymns.* Ask volunteers to name a few of their labels.

❖ Continue with the sketch by asking the adults to sketch some dense thickets, perhaps by just making dark marks with their pencils. In these "thickets," for their eyes only, they are to write one or more sins that currently ensnare them.

❖ Challenge the students to write a sentence or two in which they ask God's forgiveness and commit themselves to pay attention to the markers ("trees") that God has provided for them. Encourage them to be as specific as possible: *"I will attend a support group to help me overcome my addiction to alcohol;"* or *"I will pray and meditate, seeking guidance from God as to how I can control my anger."*

❖ Suggest that the adults put their papers in their Bibles or other confidential place where they might refer to them.

❖ Conclude with these words of assurance by Saint Cyran (1581–1643): **He who has commanded us not to look back when we have put our hands to the plough does as he would have us do—he does not regard the past sins of a soul which seeks his kingdom.**

(5) Continue the Journey

❖ Pray that the participants will be able to seek God's forgiveness, assured that God wants them to set aside the past and move forward in faith.

❖ Read aloud this preparation for next week's lesson. You may also want to post it on newsprint for the students to copy.

- **Title: The Servant's Mission in the World**
- **Background Scripture: Isaiah 49:1-6**
- **Lesson Scripture: Isaiah 49:1-6**
- **Focus of the Lesson: People who are grateful for the benefits they receive like to reciprocate by serving others. How are people to respond to receiving abundance? God reminds Israel of the gifts they received from God and charges them to bring hope to the nations.**

❖ Challenge the students to complete one or more of these activities for further spiritual growth related to this week's session. Post this information on newsprint for the students to copy.

(1) **Think about how the themes of forgiveness and repentance may come to the forefront in the United States as we celebrate Martin Luther King Day.**

(2) **Write a prayer in which you repent of sin and seek God's forgiveness. Use this prayer daily throughout the week.**

(3) **Review the story of the Exodus, which Isaiah 48 clearly alludes to, by reading Exodus 15:1-21, the songs of Moses and Miriam. Think about how God has cared for you, especially during challenging times, and give thanks.**

❖ Sing or read aloud "Seek the Lord."

❖ Conclude today's session by leading the class in this benediction: **Let us go forth to worship and serve the Lord, in whom we have the blessed assurance of our salvation.**

UNIT 2: A FUTURE FOR GOD'S PEOPLE
THE SERVANT'S MISSION IN THE WORLD

PREVIEWING THE LESSON

Lesson Scripture: Isaiah 49:1-6
Background Scripture: Isaiah 49:1-6
Key Verse: Isaiah 49:6

Focus of the Lesson:
People who are grateful for the benefits they receive like to reciprocate by serving others. How are people to respond to receiving abundance? God reminds Israel of the gifts they received from God and charges them to bring hope to the nations.

Goals for the Learners:
(1) to study the proclamation of the gifts God gives to Israel and Israel's call to serve others.
(2) to identify ways that they can lead others to God.
(3) to make a commitment to serve others.

Supplies:
Bibles, newsprint and marker, paper and pencils, hymnals

READING THE SCRIPTURE

NRSV
Isaiah 49:1-6

1 Listen to me, O coastlands,
   pay attention, you peoples from far
      away!
   The LORD called me before I was born,
      while I was in my mother's womb he
      named me.
2 He made my mouth like a sharp sword,
      in the shadow of his hand he hid me;
   he made me a polished arrow,

NIV
Isaiah 49:1-6

1Listen to me, you islands;
      hear this, you distant nations:
   Before I was born the LORD called me;
      from my birth he has made mention
      of my name.
2He made my mouth like a sharpened
      sword,
      in the shadow of his hand he hid me;
   he made me into a polished arrow

in his quiver he hid me away.

3 And he said to me, "You are my servant,
    Israel, in whom I will be glorified."
4 But I said, "I have labored in vain,
    I have spent my strength for nothing
        and vanity;
    yet surely my cause is with the LORD,
        and my reward with my God."
5 And now the LORD says,
    who formed me in the womb to be
        his servant,
    to bring Jacob back to him,
        and that Israel might be gathered to
            him,
    for I am honored in the sight of the
        LORD,
    and my God has become my
        strength—
6 he says,
    "It is too light a thing that you should
        be my servant
    to raise up the tribes of Jacob
    and to restore the survivors of Israel;
    **I will give you as a light to the nations,
        that my salvation may reach to the
            end of the earth."**

and concealed me in his quiver.

3He said to me, "You are my servant,
    Israel, in whom I will display my
        splendor."
4But I said, "I have labored to no purpose;
    I have spent my strength in vain and
        for nothing.
Yet what is due me is in the LORD's hand,
    and my reward is with my God."
5And now the LORD says—
    he who formed me in the womb to be
        his servant
    to bring Jacob back to him
        and gather Israel to himself,
    for I am honored in the eyes of the LORD
        and my God has been my strength—
6he says:
    "It is too small a thing for you to be
        my servant
    to restore the tribes of Jacob
    and bring back those of Israel I have kept.
    **I will also make you a light for the
        Gentiles,
    that you may bring my salvation to the
        ends of the earth."**

UNDERSTANDING THE SCRIPTURE

Isaiah 49:1. A new section, complete with a new voice and a new direction, begins in chapter 49. In Isaiah 40–48, the prophetic voice clearly stated God's words to the people. God's word was presented with little personal commentary or individual reflection. Indeed, the personality of the prophet, the one delivering God's word, was hardly discerned. Rather, the booming voice of God filled the chapters with the announcement of God's great deeds of rescue and release to come. The message of chapters 40–48 concerned the conclusion of the "former times" and the initiation of God's new time of redemption. As chapter 49 opened, there was a new element in the very first verse. Surprisingly, an individual, with a distinct call and voice, was introduced as the servant. This is the type of subtle shift (from general announcement to particular voice) that thrills the careful reader of Scripture. The "something new" was someone who was called and known by God. At various points, beginning with the first Servant Song in Isaiah 42:1-4, the identity of "the servant" presents interpretive problems: Does the title "servant" apply to the nation of Israel, a foreign king, David's true successor, or a prophet? Such problems are not present in Isaiah 49:1. Here, the servant is clearly a particular human being . . . one who will speak not only of his labors but also of his future tasks. The scope of this servant's assignment is also suggested in the first verse. This servant will speak to the foreign nations and peoples surrounding Israel, both those who dwell along the coastline and those whose lands stretch far beyond Israel.

Isaiah 49:2-3. The servant's voice described both God's call and the providence of resources. As to calling, this servant experienced God's call as a persistent reality throughout his life. Indeed, the call was so woven into the servant's nature that it was best described as initiated prior to birth (49:1, 5). Such a sense of call is awesome by depth and conviction, but even the most passionately affirmed call requires the complement of gifts for leadership and the sustenance of God's graces. Notice that the servant quickly described two gifts and two graces received from God. The first mentioned was the gift of penetrating speech. Whereas a political leader of the ancient world relied on the might of metal swords, God's servant was equipped with a capacity of speech able to change world events. Although the image was poetic, the consequences of God making the servant's "mouth like a sharp sword" were practical. The world would change by the words of this servant. Moreover, the servant's words would reach far and wide. In the ancient world, distance was often calculated by an arrow's flight. Here, the servant's very being was polished in order to reach the widest possible audience (the coastlands and peoples far, far away). Gifted with powers of speech and endurance, the servant also acknowledged two graces bestowed by God. First, the grace of God's protection described with poetic images: the shadow of God's hand and God's quiver. Again, the images reveal a practical reality: Throughout the turmoil of exile, God protected the servant. Second, God's grace flowed over the servant as a blessing. This blessing, on the surface, reaffirmed God's call. Beneath the surface, however, was a wonderful mystery: God's intention to be glorified through a servant.

Isaiah 49:4. Not only was the servant confident of being called, gifted, and graced by God; this servant was also confident that God would hear and transform failure. In one compact verse a lifetime of failure was compressed. The sad facts of a servant's life did not add up to success. Failure flowed from the labors of this servant despite his exceptional trust in God's call and providence. In verse 4, the servant described his labors without success and personal exhaustion devoid of accomplishment. No poetic images softened his sadness. It takes great maturity of spirit to speak with such precision. The servant's words ached with all that was intended but unrealized. Still, the servant had confidence in God. His confession of failure was balanced by affirmation. The servant understood his cause was God's cause and, if there were to be success or reward, such would come from God. Since the servant's labor was undertaken for and with God, God (rather than the servant) comprehended the reasons for and the cost of the servant's vain efforts. Thus, a lament that began with a description of failure concluded with an affirmation of God's power to redeem, reward, and bless. Even through personal failure, this servant trusted God to accomplish great things.

Isaiah 49:5-6. With the conclusion of the compressed lament, the voice of the servant soared to new heights. Recalling again the mystery of a call instituted prior to birth, the servant acknowledged his original task. The assignment was to bring Israel back to God. It was a grand and glorious assignment; sadly, it was also a failed assignment. Nevertheless, the servant stated that failure did not cast him from God's grace. Indeed, the servant sang of being honored in God's sight and of receiving strength from God. The upswing of the fifth verse led to the surprise of the last verse in this song. Suddenly, God addressed the servant. The divine voice did not excuse the past or failure. The divine voice did not release the servant from his original call to reconcile the

Israelites with their God. The divine voice did not fast forward. Rather, by divine decree, God reminded the servant that the redemption of all creation was the goal. Israel would turn to God. By the light of the chosen people, all nations would see and know God. Without fail, God's salvation would cover creation. This task was reassigned to the servant: Restore Israel, bring light to those in darkness, and share salvation with all. Imagine, although the servant failed to accomplish the initial step (restoring the relationship between Israel and God), God trusted the servant to continue. Neither resistance nor ineptitude, rebellion nor exhaustion, ignorance nor wasted efforts stopped God's intentions for salvation for all people. Once again, the servant was commissioned. Once more God's intentions were carried into everyday human life by an individual servant bearing God's glory to all.

INTERPRETING THE SCRIPTURE

Listen to Me!

Have you even been called to teach a church school class or youth group? Did you wonder if you were prepared for the assignment? Did you ponder how you'd present the material, the themes, and even yourself? If you've ever taken a deep breath before entering the classroom (or living room or campfire circle) to face others and share your faith as a teacher, then you know how the servant felt as God brought him onto history's stage. The servant entered with a shout: "Listen to me!" Not exactly the approach you might adopt as a teacher welcoming the class for the first time. Since emotion and tone are absent from a written text, we don't know exactly how to take this: "Listen to me!" It could be a pleading appeal. It could be a demanding command. It could be intoned by a well-seasoned, well-respected elder. It could be a fresh, youthful voice.

We cannot determine the volume or meter or emotional content of the speaker. All we can agree upon is this: When Isaiah desired to shift the peoples' attention from God's coming future to the practical (and current) aspects of change, God through Isaiah set a servant before the people and put these words in the servant's mouth: "Listen to me!" And if we do that—if we listen as if everything depends on what comes next—surprise of all surprises, we catch God's mysterious and comprehensive yearnings. However, before we catch the mysterious and comprehensive yearnings of God, we must listen to a particular individual. He is identified as God's servant; he was called before his birth; he was named to service while in his mother's womb. He was, and is, someone to whom we should listen.

God's Call, Gifts, and Providence

The servant who commanded our attention turned out to be an individual especially endowed with gifts for ministry and graced with God's protection and blessing. This is not exceptional to the servant's particular call; it is, rather, a spiritual insight into the comprehensive nature of God's call. God draws individuals toward particular tasks or missions or relationships, and God equips those individuals with the necessary skills and insights. That's the spiritual balance within a call: God provokes passion and God provides resources. Indeed, if an individual feels unprepared to respond to a divine call, more time needs to be spent on discerning God's call. In an authentic call, task and resource are uniquely fitted together.

God intends those who respond to a call also to recognize and utilize the God-provided gifts accompanying that call. Since the servant was called to proclaim and to impact peoples far away, he affirmed two specific gifts empowering his call. First, God gave to him the gift of penetrating speech: His words cut to the heart of the matter. Second, God shaped his entire being as a delicate, yet sturdy being able to travel distances with ease and to hit a distant target. The servant was a gifted speaker and a man equal to the demands of a worldwide audience.

These gifts are not touted; rather, the servant simply acknowledged God as the true source of his speech and reach. Every call comes with gifts and all calls rely on God's grace. As the servant spoke, those who listened remembered his story. This was a person of promise and a person surrounded by God's protection. Although everyone in exile lived within an atmosphere of fear, the servant of God felt a blessed protection related to his call. He was hidden in the shadow of God's hand and he kept within the "quiver" of God's appointed. We might say that his life was charmed. A clearer interpretation, however, affirmed that he was prepared and protected for a specific time and task: The servant was to be a light to the nations so that God's salvation could reach all people.

I've Failed; Now What?

After such a stirring introduction, the next words from the servant are incomprehensible. After he described his call, his gifts, and his divine protection, everything pointed to success. However, in the verse 4, the servant confessed, "I have labored in vain." I wonder if there's a person encountering this passage right now who hasn't expressed that very thought. I know I have. I've been deeply discouraged by the seeming failure of my ministry. I've felt my words and my deeds were in vain. I've even experienced my body collapse in a huge sigh following a difficult but unsuccessful mission. I've also discovered that such experiences may become the prelude to a change in direction or sometimes, as with the servant of Isaiah 49, the response is a lament.

Without blaming others, seeking neither justification nor explanation, and devoid of self-centered over thinking, the servant tersely stated his failure. It was a failure of effort and strength; he did not accomplish the task for which he was called. He failed to bring God's people into a close and faithful relationship with God. Although the servant firmly believed in his call—and trusted God's purpose within his call—he failed personally. Despite his failure, the servant remained confident of God's intentions. The servant may have failed, but underneath his failure, he felt the pulse of God's yearnings. These yearnings would not fail. Thus the words of a lament transformed into an affirmation of faith in God's purposes. These sad words—I labored in vain, I spent myself for nothing—took on a holy quality by their attachment to God's cause. Surely, the high calling of the servant—to announce God's salvation to all people—would be accomplished regardless of the servant's failure.

The Mission Continues

God, of course, has the last word. After the commission, the gifts for service, and the failed mission, the voice of God responded to the servant. With a light touch, God questioned the servant. Was your task too small for you? Did you fail to understand its significance? Would you rather have a larger assignment? These are questions of a concerned parent. When the teenager is awash in the pointlessness of life, sometimes the only effective tactic is exaggeration and humor. In a similar, parental manner, God humored the servant—with an absolute seriousness. Then, God explained the work one more time:

Servant, you are to be a catalyst for reconciliation among my people. Servant, you are to be a light to the Gentiles. Servant, you are to spread my salvation throughout creation.

In an instant, the servant remembered. This has been God's intention since the original call of Abraham. God's clear direction was to use one people, Israel, in order to create a world-wide community of peace, justice, and compassion. If the nation failed in their witness, the servant picked up their failure. If the servant failed in his witness, God recommissioned him in order that God's cause would continue. There was always another opportunity. Corporately and individually, called and gifted, in season and out of season, God's desire for the salvation of all was not dulled. Even in a world characterized by religious animosity and blatant ignorance of the Holy One, God persistently calls, gifts, protects, and recommissions people like us to carry on the divine work of reconciliation, witness, and redemption. Isaiah's servant was unnamed—perhaps because that servant bears a contemporary name. Your name. Your neighbor's name. My name. My children's names. Especially in our world, God persistently calls, gifts, protects, and recommissions people like us to carry on the divine work of reconciliation, witness, and redemption.

SHARING THE SCRIPTURE

Preparing Our Hearts

Explore this week's devotional reading, found in Hebrews 10:19-25. In today's lesson, we see the servant, dejected by failure, called by God to persevere. Similarly, in Hebrews, believers are called to "hold fast" (10:23) to their faith and encourage others to do likewise. If there are aspects of your life where you feel the sting of failure, turn these over to God to sanctify and use for divine purposes. Try to motivate others who feel discouraged to turn their failures over to God as well.

Pray that you and the adult learners will continue to press forward in faith.

Preparing Our Minds

Study the background Scripture and the lesson Scripture, both of which are from Isaiah 49:1-6. Think about ways one can respond to receiving abundance.

Write on newsprint:
❏ commitment for "Making a Commitment to Serve Others."
❏ information for next week's lesson, found under "Continue the Journey."
❏ activities for further spiritual growth in "Continue the Journey."

LEADING THE CLASS

(1) Gather to Learn

❖ Welcome the class members and introduce any guests.

❖ Pray that those in attendance today will recognize the importance of being a servant to others.

❖ Brainstorm with the group a list of organizations in your community whose purpose is to serve others. Note, if possible, exactly who each group intends to serve. Here are some examples: *Boy Scouts, Girl Scouts, Lions Club, Rotary International, Big Brothers, Big Sisters, Delta Society (human-animal bond), volunteer rescue companies, 4-H, hospital auxiliaries, Sierra Club.*

❖ Invite adults who participate in any groups that serve others to state why their affiliation with such a group is important to them. What do they do for others? What rewards does this service offer them?

❖ Read aloud today's focus statement: **People who are grateful for the benefits they receive like to reciprocate by serving others. How are people to respond to receiving abundance? God reminds Israel of the gifts they received from God and charges them to bring hope to the nations.**

(2) Study the Proclamation of the Gifts God Gives to Israel and Israel's Call to Serve Others

❖ Invite a volunteer to read Isaiah 49:1-6.
   ❖ Ask these questions:
      (1) What has God called the servant to do?
      (2) How did God gift and equip the servant to accomplish his mission?
      (3) How would you describe the servant's emotional state?
      (4) Had you been the servant, what would have been your response to God's words in verse 6?

❖ Use information from Understanding the Scripture to help the class better understand this Bible passage.

❖ Remind the class that Isaiah 49:1-6 is the second of the four Servant Songs. Invite half the students to turn to Isaiah 42:1-4, which is the first Servant Song. The other half are to look at Isaiah 50:4-9, the third song. (We will be looking at part of the fourth song next week.) Encourage the students to create a composite picture of (1) the servant's relationship with God, (2) what the servant was expected to do, and (3) the message he was called to preach. Allow time for each group to state ideas, which you will list on newsprint. Be sure to include ideas from today's session, Isaiah 49:1-6.

(3) Identify Ways that the Learners Can Lead Others to God

❖ Read in unison today's key verse, Isaiah 49:6. Point out that on a smaller scale

God is calling each follower of Christ to be a candle that will light the way for others toward God.

❖ Read the following story from the Path2Prayer website, which appeared in *Alone with God* by Matilda Andross: **Among the contents of a "treasure box" belonging to a young man who had died was a list of forty boys. The young man had made the list, offered regular prayer for each one, given them each books, and showed them Bible texts. As a result of his witness, all forty made a decision to accept Christ.**

❖ Ask: **In addition to the ways the young man used to win others to Christ, what other ways can you suggest?** (For example, *you may invite someone to join a study group, attend worship and/or Sunday school, tell the person the story of your own faith journey, or assist someone in a way that demonstrates your love for Christ and him or her.*)

❖ Choose two volunteers to roleplay this encounter: **Avery has been bitter since his wife died of cancer. He never had use for Christ or his church, but now he is very lonely and adrift. He is obviously searching for "something" in his life that he cannot name. You try to talk with him about what your relationship with Christ has meant to you as you face life's challenges.**

(4) Make a Commitment to Serve Others

❖ Read "The Mission Continues" from Interpreting the Scripture.

❖ Recall that during the Gather to Learn segment you listed organizations within the community that serve others. Look again at this list. Add the church if it is not already listed. Cite specific examples of programs, such as *a food pantry, soup kitchen, mission teams that work locally or globally, daycare center for elders or children, parish nurse program, praying for others, or special projects to aid those in need at Thanksgiving or Christmas.*

❖ Distribute paper and pencils. Post these words on newsprint: **I, _____, commit myself to serve others in Jesus'**

name by _____. Encourage the adults to write their names and whatever action they propose to take. Note that they may just be able to take a first step, perhaps contacting an agency where they would like to volunteer. Or, they may be able to help someone immediately. The choice is theirs.

(5) Continue the Journey

❖ Pray that all who have made a commitment to serve will take action this week to fulfill their promise.

❖ Read aloud this preparation for next week's lesson. You may also want to post it on newsprint for the students to copy.

■ **Title: Healed by His Bruises**
■ **Background Scripture: Isaiah 53**
■ **Lesson Scripture: Isaiah 53:4-6, 10-12**
■ **Focus of the Lesson: People who are called to serve may sacrifice and suffer to help others. What is required of one who will serve others? Isaiah reveals that Israel's hope is secure in the Suffering Servant who will pay a terrible price for the sake of Israel—even death.**

❖ Challenge the students to complete one or more of these activities for further spiritual growth related to this week's session. Post this information on newsprint for the students to copy.

(1) **Perform a random act of kindness. Pay the toll of a driver behind you; help unload a grocery cart; take homemade goodies to a homebound neighbor; compliment a seatmate on the bus.**

(2) **Stretch your spirituality by reaching out to someone in need whose background or value system may be quite different from yours. Do whatever you can to help this person.**

(3) **Organize a work team for a local or global missions project.**

❖ Sing or read aloud "Forth in Thy Name, O Lord."

❖ Conclude today's session by leading the class in this benediction: **Let us go forth to worship and serve the Lord, in whom we have the blessed assurance of our salvation.**

UNIT 2: A FUTURE FOR GOD'S PEOPLE
HEALED BY HIS BRUISES

PREVIEWING THE LESSON

Lesson Scripture: Isaiah 53:4-6, 10-12
Background Scripture: Isaiah 53
Key Verse: Isaiah 53:5

Focus of the Lesson:
People who are called to serve may sacrifice and suffer to help others. What is required of one who will serve others? Isaiah reveals that Israel's hope is secure in the Suffering Servant who will pay a terrible price for the sake of Israel—even death.

Goals for the Learners:
(1) to discover what Isaiah said about the cost of servanthood.
(2) to appreciate that hope lies in the servant who takes on their sins and suffers in their place.
(3) to make a commitment to pay the cost of servanthood.

Supplies:
Bibles, newsprint and marker, paper and pencils, hymnals

READING THE SCRIPTURE

NRSV
Isaiah 53:4-6, 10-12
4 Surely he has borne our infirmities
      and carried our diseases;
   yet we accounted him stricken,
      struck down by God, and afflicted.
5 **But he was wounded for our**
      transgressions,
   crushed for our iniquities;
   upon him was the punishment that
      made us whole,
      and by his bruises we are healed.
6 All we like sheep have gone astray;
      we have all turned to our own way,

NIV
Isaiah 53:4-6, 10-12
4Surely he took up our infirmities
      and carried our sorrows,
   yet we considered him stricken by God,
      smitten by him, and afflicted.
5**But he was pierced for our transgressions,**
      he was crushed for our iniquities;
   the punishment that brought us peace
      was upon him,
      and by his wounds we are healed.
6We all, like sheep, have gone astray,
      each of us has turned to his own way;
   and the LORD has laid on him

(and the LORD has laid on him \
  the iniquity of us all.   )
10 Yet it was the will of the LORD to
      crush him with pain.
    When you make his life an offering for
        sin,
      he shall see his offspring, and shall
        prolong his days;
    through him the will of the LORD shall
        prosper.
11   Out of his anguish he shall see light;
    he shall find satisfaction through his
    knowledge.
        The righteous one, my servant, shall
          make many righteous,
        and he shall bear their iniquities.
12 Therefore I will allot him a portion
        with the great,
      and he shall divide the spoil with the
        strong;
    because he poured out himself to death,
      and was numbered with the
        transgressors;
    yet he bore the sin of many,
      and made intercession for the
        transgressors.

      the iniquity of us all.
10Yet it was the LORD's will to crush him
      and cause him to suffer,
    and though the LORD makes his life
        a guilt offering,
  he will see his offspring and prolong
      his days,
    and the will of the LORD will prosper
      in his hand.
11After the suffering of his soul,
    he will see the light of life and be
      satisfied;
  by his knowledge my righteous servant
      will justify many,
    and he will bear their iniquities.
12Therefore I will give him a portion
      among the great,
    and he will divide the spoils with
      the strong,
  because he poured out his life unto death,
    and was numbered with the
      transgressors.
For he bore the sin of many,
    and made intercession for the
      transgressors.

UNDERSTANDING THE SCRIPTURE

Isaiah 53:1. We arrive at the last lesson drawn from Isaiah in this quarter entitled "Assuring Hope." In the first unit we looked at Isaiah's message within the context of the Exile. In the second unit, the passages shifted toward "a new thing"—the exiles' situation was about to change, but the change would arrive in an unexpected manner. Indeed, the prophetic word that echoed through chapter 40 to 53 warned the people to expect something daring and revolutionary. God's future was not a repetition of the past. Our final selection is Isaiah 53. This text is known as the key interpretative text on the death of Jesus. Contemporary Christians usually see Jesus standing as a

shadow over Isaiah 53. Indeed, Jesus is seen as the servant in the fourth and final Servant Song, which extends from Isaiah 52:13 to 53:12. Difficult as it is to study Isaiah 53 without reference to Jesus, we discover an even deeper connection to him as we keep the text within its original context. Having said that, however, the difficulties begin. Scholars do not agree upon an exact date of composition or application. Additionally, there is no uniform voice; rather, the author shifts among a first person plural (group reflection), a third person singular (narration), and a first person singular (divine voice). Moreover, there is no agreement on the audience receiving Isaiah 53. Despite these unanswered questions, something remarkable emerges: an account of a community's struggle to receive and be led by God's word. This struggle was mysterious and, as the first verse implies, dependent upon God's revelation.

Isaiah 53:2-9. In these verses, a collective voice initiates the reflection (53:1-6). The "we" of this section may be the community of exiles, the prophet's friends or students, the leaders of the exiles, or the nation as a whole. Perhaps by employing the "we" voice the author invited the widest circle possible to reflect on the death of one known as "the servant." This group was in agreement on certain aspects of the servant's life. From his earliest days, he lacked the family support that would assist in his social and religious development. He was unattractive. As a youth and an adult he did not manifest any of the traditional indications of God's blessings. He was hated and abused. Nonetheless, there was something about this individual that affected others. In his difficulties, they saw their own; in his punishment, they recognized their rightful sentences; in his obedience to God, they sensed their disobedience. As the group pondered, another voice took up the servant's story. This voice (53:8-9) spoke with the detachment of a journalist to conclude: He died as a result of a " perversion of justice," and he was buried with the wicked. The servant's end was the grave.

Isaiah 53:10-11. After the facts of the servant's life have been made known, the community's reflection on his death began. Again, the problem of authorship is present. Do these words come from the prophetic legacy of Isaiah's students? Is this a community lament over the loss of a true prophet? Would such a reflection be restricted to the leaders, or would the whole nation take part? Whose words are these? Again, there is no definite answer to the questions; again, the lack of definition invites the broadest possible response. The widest response was theological: The ser-

vant's life and death was not a mere accident of circumstances. God did not forget to protect the servant; the servant's suffering and shame had divine significance. The servant—the one who announced God's future—was, indeed, part of the future God was creating. God's deep yearning for unity within creation began with Israel, but reached to every nation and people. Such a yearning did not fit smoothly into the politics of domination and violence. Israel caught a taste of God's rugged desire as she experienced the painful consequences of her engagement in politics as usual. Now, another illustration was offered through the life of the servant. The message was manifest in the servant: Those who steadfastly follow God's ways find themselves at risk in the world. Yet, because Israel survived exile with a renewed integrity and because the impact of the servant's message continued, the community voice declared: Life will continue and prosper until there is satisfaction for all.

Isaiah 53:12. The last word is God's word. The divine "I" speaking in verse 12 is the only "I" able to make such a pronouncement: The community's reflection was correct. They had pondered the servant's life and death. They had evaluated his teachings and his deed; they had compared his faithfulness with their own. They had plumbed the depths of despair and had reached for a new possibility. They had been open to correction and direction. Finally, after their words came God's word of confirmation. The servant was blessed with greatness; he had the right to share the bounty of his faithfulness with others. Because he had stood in the place of judgment, though he himself did not belong in that place, God received his petitions and prayers. All the abuse, violence, shame, and disregard heaped upon the servant were received with strength, compassion, and respect founded upon God's ways. Without bowing to the popular course, the practical path, or the politics of domination, the servant declared God's word. Through his steadfast declaration a new vision cleared away the confusion of exile. Israel, though broken and impoverished, was the beacon of God's light to the Gentiles. Although the actual circumstances of their lives in exile suggested the exact opposite, the servant's word was correct. Israel's role among the nations was revelatory light. God's confirmation was clear. Thus the hope, which first stirred as God's compassion for the Israelites in exile, expanded to fill the whole creation with hope for peace, justice, and unity. The path into the future was not disclosed; nor would it prove to be risk free. Yet, there was an example: the servant's life and death. Despite all indicators to the contrary, God's light shone through the servant's life as assuring hope for the exiles.

INTERPRETING THE SCRIPTURE

Let Us Declare

As Christians the foundation of our belief is a revelation—a personal and corporate revelation—about a particular person who draws us near to God. We know that Jesus is "the way, and the truth, and the life" (John 14:6) because, on a level beyond our rational minds, we have been converted to trust in him. Because Jesus has been revealed in our hearts, we use every means available to declare to those who do not know Jesus who he is and how we have experienced his presence. Our prayers brim with the expectation that God's Spirit will work in their lives as that same Spirit has worked in our lives. We know conversion to Jesus' way is beyond our individual and corporate efforts; conversion happens as the Spirit leads. We continue to declare Jesus so that all might come to him.

Knowing this helps us understand the situation of those who pondered the life and death of an unnamed "servant" of God who brought to exiled Israel a new, and a surprisingly full, hope. Although our times and circumstances differ; although our faith content and commitments are distinct; although our cultures are separated by thousands of years, as we study the account of the exiles struggling to declare God's new deed, we hear echoes of our most recent faith conversations with neighbors, kin, and strangers. Long ago and today, the declaration of what God has done continues.

At the heart of the exiles' declaration was the sorrowful end of the suffering servant's life. Yet, his suffering was purposeful in ways the exiles only slowly came to understand. Something about his steadfast love for God inspired the exiles. His tenacious grasp of God's intentions calmed them. His innocence revealed the outrageous tragedy of injustice. The end of his life healed the exiles' tendencies to doubt God, to fear their oppressors, and to mistrust any movement toward goodness, righteousness, and peace. This gradual revelation concerning the Suffering Servant formed a new declaration of faith in God. As we move through the text, we trace the dawning of God's light upon them. Gradually, that light also dawns upon us.

Let Us Remember

The most remarkable aspect of Isaiah 53 is the blending of voices; it is as if we are listening to a group discussion. The writer was privileged to share in the conversation about the purposes of God in, over, and through the servant's life. Perhaps you have been privileged to share in such conversations.

Often following a memorial or funeral

service, wherein the "official" remembering took place, comes a less formal time when individuals talk from their personal experience about the life of the deceased. Sometimes these stories are humorous; at other times they are poignant. When assembled together the richness of an individual life shines forth. In fact, as those stories often indicate, there was more to that life than anyone imagined.

If that experience sounds familiar to you, then you have the frame for the middle section of Isaiah 53. Those who knew the servant shared their insights. However, rather than a series of honorific tales, the stories remembered were a sad, ugly collection of disrespect, abuse, lack of standing, and violence. Moreover, this seemed to be the only type of stories shared. From birth to death, the servant had neither success nor respect. Indeed, the servant's life was devoid of the usual signs of God's grace: a happy home filled with children, physical beauty, wealth, and respect within the community.

Yet, even as the sad, ugly tales were exchanged, something else surfaced among those who considered the servant's life. By a strange (and spiritual) connection the lives of those who remembered the servant reconsidered their own lives. Gradually, they saw themselves through his experiences. What they saw shocked them. Could it be that the servant's life contained something meaningful—something transformative—for their lives? All assumptions and certainties were questioned as the stories circled around and surprisingly began to shed a glimmer of graceful light. People paused and saw themselves differently . . . as if their lives were somehow deeply connected to the servant's life. The climax of this connection is stated in verse 6: "the LORD has laid on him the iniquity of us all."

Let Us Consider

After group discussion, another voice held forth. This voice was devoid of the emotions of the mourners. Rather, this voice spoke with the weight of authority. Was this the senior member of the group? Was the speaker an elder or a prophet groomed to be Isaiah's successor? Was the speaker stating his own thoughts or reflecting, in summary form, the shared conclusion of the mourners? Again, it is impossible to identify the voice. However, the calm and straightforward tone rang with quiet conviction. This was a voice worthy of attention.

The central affirmation of verses 10-11 is that God was always a part of the servant's life. Evidently, as the mourners considered the many negative aspects, they came perilously close to a judgment that God rejected the servant. Intuitively they knew that the servant's life was consistently related to God. However, the circumstances of failure, abuse, ridicule, rejection, and unjust death were not compatible with the "old way" of thinking about God.

In the former theology, God's blessings were tangible. The man or woman who married and raised sons was blessed. The individual with charm and beauty was blessed. Property and possessions were blessings, as were long life and a peaceful death. Since the servant's life indicated none of the usual signs, the mourners' spiritual dilemma was deep. To their unease, an authoritative voice offered a new interpretation: God was always with the servant. The path of the servant, though unrecognized by society or by "the good old" theology of the monarchy, was a godly path. The servant lived a life deemed to be a failure by society; yet by his life a failed society learned a new way of righteous living.

And God Said . . .

Gracefully, the text shifted from human to divine words. Has that ever happened in your hearing? Listening to a sermon or a friend's story, have you ever felt (more than heard) God's Spirit testifying? These holy moments are frequently subtle. But to those attuned to the Spirit, these moments are true "mountain tops" of faith. From the perspective of God's voice, all troubles pass into beauty. By the impact of God's word, all worries dissolve into confidence. With the sound of God's love, confusion and doubt retreat, leaving space for clarity and faith.

The last verse of Isaiah 53 contains such a divine word. This verse confirmed God's love for the servant. The assurance was communicated in images easily grasped by the audience—both the intimate audience of mourning friends and the wider audience of the nation Israel. The first image was royal: a king dividing respect and wealth among the great and the strong. This image pictured the servant not as the shamed, defeated one, but as worthy of God's honor as a righteous one.

The second image was poetic: the servant's life and death "poured out" for many. This image allowed the meaning of the servant's life to transcend the boundary of human space and—a message delivered in word and deed—transmitted light to many. As God blessed the servant's life and death, a new trajectory of faith emerged. This trajectory continues in our final unit of study, "Jesus, the Promised Servant-Leader," which begins next week.

SHARING THE SCRIPTURE

Preparing Our Hearts

Explore this week's devotional reading, found in 2 Corinthians 5:16-21. Here we see Christ "who knew no sin" take on our iniquity "so that in him we might become the righteousness of God" (5:21). His suffering on our behalf has transformed us. We who are "in Christ" are healed, whole, new creations. We are also ambassadors for him. How are you serving Christ as a minister of reconciliation so that others might participate in the kind of relationship with Christ that you have in him?

Pray that you and the adult learners will serve as bridges of reconciliation for others.

Preparing Our Minds

Study the background Scripture from Isaiah 53 and the lesson Scripture from Isaiah 53:4-6, 10-12. Ask yourself: What is required of one who will serve others?

Write on newsprint:

❑ information for next week's lesson, found under "Continue the Journey."

❑ activities for further spiritual growth in "Continue the Journey."

LEADING THE CLASS

(1) Gather to Learn

❖ Welcome the class members and introduce any guests.

❖ Pray that those who have gathered will be open to the idea of redemptive suffering.

❖ Read this statement made by Martin Luther (1483–1546): **A Christian is the most free of all, and subject to none; a Christian is the most dutiful servant of all, subject to everyone.**

❖ Invite the students to comment on the truth of both parts of this seemingly paradoxical statement. In their experience, how is it possible to be completely free in Christ and yet, because of that freedom, a servant of all?

❖ Read aloud today's focus statement: **People who are called to serve may sacrifice and suffer to help others. What is required of one who will serve others?**

Isaiah reveals that Israel's hope is secure in the Suffering Servant who will pay a terrible price for the sake of Israel—even death.

(2) Discover What Isaiah Said About the Cost of Servanthood

❖ Note that today's passage is part of the fourth and final Servant Song found in Isaiah. That song begins at 52:13 and ends at 53:12. So that the class can hear the song in its entirety, read it aloud yourself.

❖ Invite the students to look closely at 53:4-6. Read or retell "Let Us Remember" from Interpreting the Scripture to see how the people recall this despised and rejected person.

❖ Read in unison today's key verse, Isaiah 53:5. Note that the servant does not suffer because of anything he has done but rather suffers for others.

❖ Direct the adults to verses 10-11. Use information from Understanding the Scripture to clarify meaning. Add that *The New Interpreter's Study Bible* links this vicarious suffering with Israel in exile: **"These verses offer them a revolutionary theology that explains the hardships of exile: The people had to endure the exile and the suffering it engendered because that suffering was done in service to God so that God, through their atoning sacrifice, could redeem the nations."**

❖ Close with verse 12 by reading or retelling "And God Said . . ." from Interpreting the Scripture.

(3) Appreciate that Hope Lies in the Servant Who Takes on the Learners' Sins and Suffers in Their Place

❖ Review with the class what the servant has endured for their sake. List the ideas from verses 4-6, 10-12 on newsprint.

❖ Discuss emotions that come to mind when the adults think about someone who is willing to endure this suffering for them.

❖ Discuss these questions:
(1) **In light of Isaiah 53, what would you say to someone who believes that all suffering is punishment?**
(2) **In light of Isaiah 53, what would you say to someone who believes that all suffering is to be avoided?**
(3) **What is the difference between seeking out suffering (perhaps beating oneself or otherwise causing physical pain) for the sake of suffering and a willingness to suffer for others?**

❖ State that since the early days of the church, Jesus has been viewed as the fulfillment of this prophecy of Isaiah (among many others). Ask:
(1) **Why do you think the early church made this connection between Jesus and the servant?**
(2) **What connections do you see?**
(3) **What might this passage say to the church as to its role as a suffering servant?**
(4) **In what ways do you think the church fulfills its role? Where do we fall short?**

❖ **Option:** Use information from "Close-up: The Influence of the Book of Isaiah" to add to the group's understanding of Isaiah's importance.

(4) Make a Commitment to Pay the Cost of Servanthood

❖ Create a list of services that people perform, either as paid workers or as volunteers. List ideas on newsprint. Paid jobs may vary widely in educational requirements and pay scale, in positions such as retail clerks to social workers to physicians to personnel in the armed forces to child care providers. Volunteer positions may be on behalf of the church, a non-profit or community agency, or informal arrangements to assist neighbors and family.

❖ Distribute paper and pencils. Challenge the adults to select a job that they do (perhaps from the list or something else) and list the sacrifices that this job entails for them. As an example, here are some ideas for a caregiver of aging parents: *on-call 24/7; parents' needs come first; frequent trips to medical appointments; reversing roles to act "in authority" is stressful; may need to scale back one's career or put it on hold completely; may need to forgo vacations.*

❖ Ask the adults to complete this sentence on their papers: **I am willing to commit myself to paying the cost of servanthood because . . .**

❖ Invite volunteers to read their sentences. Look for common themes.

(5) Continue the Journey

❖ Pray that as the students go forth they will be willing to make sacrifices and suffer for others if they are called to do so.

❖ Read aloud this preparation for next week's lesson. You may also want to post it on newsprint for the students to copy.

- **Title: Jesus Is the Messiah**
- **Background Scripture: Mark 8:27–9:1**
- **Lesson Scripture: Mark 8:27–9:1**
- **Focus of the Lesson: People may not understand their leader's identity and mission. How can people** know the truth of their leader's mission and goals? For people of faith, Jesus' words contain truth about his identity and mission to bring in the kingdom and about what he requires of his followers.

❖ Challenge the students to complete one or more of these activities for further spiritual growth related to this week's session. Post this information on newsprint for the students to copy.

(1) **Be aware of how you treat persons whose job it is to serve you. Are you respectful and appreciative of their work? Try to pay a compliment to each one.**

(2) **Engage in an act of service for someone in need as a means of honoring God.**

(3) **Think about how the suffering of a servant can be redemptive. Are you suffering on behalf of someone else? If so, how?**

❖ Sing or read aloud "Whom Shall I Send?"

❖ Conclude today's session by leading the class in this benediction: **Let us go forth to worship and serve the Lord, in whom we have the blessed assurance of our salvation.**

UNIT 3: JESUS, THE PROMISED SERVANT-LEADER
JESUS IS THE MESSIAH

PREVIEWING THE LESSON

Lesson Scripture: Mark 8:27–9:1
Background Scripture: Mark 8:27–9:1
Key Verse: Mark 8:29

Focus of the Lesson:
People may not understand their leader's identity and mission. How can people know the truth of their leader's mission and goals? For people of faith, Jesus' words contain truth about his identity and mission to bring in the kingdom and about what he requires of his followers.

Goals for the Learners:
(1) to learn what people believed about Jesus and how he challenged their beliefs.
(2) to evaluate their beliefs about Jesus and make a personal profession of faith.
(3) to affirm or change their behaviors in light of service to others.

Supplies:
Bibles, newsprint and marker, paper and pencils, hymnals

READING THE SCRIPTURE

NRSV
Mark 8:27–9:1

²⁷Jesus went on with his disciples to the villages of Caesarea Philippi; and on the way he asked his disciples, "Who do people say that I am?" ²⁸And they answered him, "John the Baptist; and others, Elijah; and still others, one of the prophets." **²⁹He asked them, "But who do you say that I am?" Peter answered him, "You are the Messiah."** ³⁰And he sternly ordered them not to tell anyone about him.

³¹Then he began to teach them that the

NIV
Mark 8:27–9:1

²⁷Jesus and his disciples went on to the villages around Caesarea Philippi. On the way he asked them, "Who do people say I am?"

²⁸They replied, "Some say John the Baptist; others say Elijah; and still others, one of the prophets."

²⁹"But what about you?" he asked. "Who do you say I am?"

Peter answered, "You are the Christ."

³⁰Jesus warned them not to tell anyone about him.

Son of Man must undergo great suffering, and be rejected by the elders, the chief priests, and the scribes, and be killed, and after three days rise again. [32]He said all this quite openly. And Peter took him aside and began to rebuke him. [33]But turning and looking at his disciples, he rebuked Peter and said, "Get behind me, Satan! For you are setting your mind not on divine things but on human things."

[34]He called the crowd with his disciples, and said to them, "If any want to become my followers, let them deny themselves and take up their cross and follow me. [35]For those who want to save their life will lose it, and those who lose their life for my sake, and for the sake of the gospel, will save it. [36]For what will it profit them to gain the whole world and forfeit their life? [37]Indeed, what can they give in return for their life? [38]Those who are ashamed of me and of my words in this adulterous and sinful generation, of them the Son of Man will also be ashamed when he comes in the glory of his Father with the holy angels." [9:1]And he said to them, "Truly I tell you, there are some standing here who will not taste death until they see that the kingdom of God has come with power."

[31]He then began to teach them that the Son of Man must suffer many things and be rejected by the elders, chief priests and teachers of the law, and that he must be killed and after three days rise again. [32]He spoke plainly about this, and Peter took him aside and began to rebuke him.

[33]But when Jesus turned and looked at his disciples, he rebuked Peter. "Get behind me, Satan!" he said. "You do not have in mind the things of God, but the things of men."

[34]Then he called the crowd to him along with his disciples and said: "If anyone would come after me, he must deny himself and take up his cross and follow me. [35]For whoever wants to save his life will lose it, but whoever loses his life for me and for the gospel will save it. [36]What good is it for a man to gain the whole world, yet forfeit his soul? [37]Or what can a man give in exchange for his soul? [38]If anyone is ashamed of me and my words in this adulterous and sinful generation, the Son of Man will be ashamed of him when he comes in his Father's glory with the holy angels."

[1]And he said to them, "I tell you the truth, some who are standing here will not taste death before they see the kingdom of God come with power."

UNDERSTANDING THE SCRIPTURE

Introduction. The Gospel of Mark opens with these words, "The beginning of the good news of Jesus Christ, the Son of God" (Mark 1:1). By this introduction Mark disclosed his faith in Jesus, his commitment to share the good news, and his sense that the beginning of Jesus' gospel moves toward a fulfillment. The story Mark told included travel narratives, accounts of miracles, direct and implied responses to Jesus, explanatory notes, and cautionary counsel for his audience. Throughout his account it was (and is) clear that Mark wrote from a sturdy faith in

Jesus in order to communicate and expand Christian faith. Also, it is clear that Mark had a plan as he composed his Gospel.

Mark 8:27. Our text is set at a transition point in Mark's Gospel. In the first eight chapters Mark emphasized Jesus' miracles and the various sorts of responses—from spirits as well as humans—to these miracles. Now, at the midpoint of the Gospel, Jesus led his disciples away from the crowds of Galilee and into the predominantly Gentile region of Caesarea Philippi. This land formerly belonged to Israel, but gradually, under Roman rule, it was more closely identified with the empire than with Jerusalem. From this physical location, in the foothills of Mount Hermon (now known as the Golan Heights), the disciples looked north to the dominance of Rome and south across Galilee toward Jerusalem. Standing at this boundary, Jesus posed the essential question, "Who do people say that I am?"

Mark 8:28-30. The disciples were likely more aware than Jesus of his reputation. The standard claims were easily announced: Jesus was John the Baptist (spiritually carrying forward his cousin's message and ministry), Elijah (the prophet promised to return before God restored Israel), or one of the prophets (again, signifying the continuation of God's prophetic guidance of the nation). Each of these titles suggested a particular future. John the Baptist challenged Rome and prepared the repentant to live godly lives awaiting God's judgment. Elijah's return announced that God's rescue had begun. The mention of prophets signified that God's spiritual power was once again active in Israel. For an oppressed people, these expectations were all life-giving; yet, from the disciples Jesus expected something more. Thus, the question was repeated and personalized: Who do you say I am? Contemporary readers fail to hear the radical nature of these questions. First, in Jesus' day, disciples asked and teachers answered questions. Second, in Jesus' day, public knowledge was subjected to Scripture. At this important point of transition, Jesus the teacher surprisingly posed a question. Moreover, he surprised the disciples again by asking for their personal opinion rather than scriptural evidence. Acting as the spokesperson for the Twelve, Peter answered Jesus, "You are the Messiah." He spoke a religious term with a fluid meaning indicating God's choice for prophet, priest, king. Jesus seemed to accept Peter's response. However, he "sternly ordered" the disciples not to make their insight public. (The actual verb is usually translated

"rebuked" and is used in Mark as Jesus' response to demons.) Jesus understood that the ambiguity of the term "Messiah" could create misunderstanding.

Mark 8:31-33. Mark structured the account of Peter's confession at Philippi with a careful hand. First, he offered insights into the appeal of Jesus' public persona. Next, he affirmed a significant, though ambiguous, religious title. Then, he provided an explanation of that title. At the point of transition between the power of Rome and Jerusalem, on a boundary line separating two human institutions, Jesus began to teach his disciples in an open way. He did not speak metaphorically; his speech was direct. He instructed his disciples that the "Son of Man" must suffer, be rejected, killed, and, after three days, rise again. Whereas Peter used the divinely empowered term, Messiah, Jesus chose "Son of Man," another fluid and ambiguous term that could mean a human being or the apocalyptic figure in Daniel 7:13 who saves the righteous. Jesus used this term because it began with common humanity—everyone suffers and understands suffering—then wrapped human experience with divine intention—some forms of suffering are redemptive. His message was clear: In his ministry, suffering was neither accidental nor avoidable. Suffering was common and divinely ordained. Such open speech was too direct for Peter, who privately rebuked Jesus and was immediately rebuked by Jesus. Mark's choice of words indicated the cosmic significance of this interaction. Rebuke was a term sufficiently strong to be used against evil spirits; the word Satan indicated that the forces against Jesus were more than human. Indeed, as the "quite open" teaching ended, the disciples were likely frightened and confused.

Mark 8:34–9:1. Again, Mark's hand is clear: five sayings about discipleship are assembled to clarify Jesus' teaching on ministry, suffering, death, and resurrection. Remember, all these topics were well known to Mark's original audience. Indeed, at this point, Mark's writing style seems to invite his audience into the narrative as members of the crowd by Jesus' side. To his audience, and to all future audiences, Mark offered one imperative and four illustrations of Jesus' explanation of discipleship. The imperative came first: Followers of Jesus must practice the self-denial of cross-bearing (a specific action) and following Jesus (a continuing endeavor). In order to explain the significance of self-denial, Mark compiled four illustrations. First came the reversal of the human impulse to save life at all costs. Christians encountered real life through releasing their grasp on personal life in order to live a Christ-centered, gospel-filled life (see Matthew 10:39; Luke 17:33; John 12:25). Next, two proverbial statements provoked reflections on what is real and valuable in life in verses 36 and 37. Finally, a warning, also found in Matthew 10:33 and Luke 12:9, emphasized the serious consequences of aligning life with the world's standards rather than with Christ's gospel. The choice was simple: Live with Christ by dying to self, or die to Christ by living for self. Wisely, Mark concluded this urgent message with comfort. Some who stood within the crowd would see (meaning to comprehend or mystically experience) God's kingdom before they died. This was not "pie in the sky" talk; rather, it was a sincere affirmation that glimpses of God's kingdom would come to those who were committed to following Jesus.

INTERPRETING THE SCRIPTURE

The Deciding Line

Since the last session, we've skipped over a few hundred years, many wonderful events, and a few devastations. The people were now resettled in Jerusalem and surrounding lands; however, slowly but surely the domination of Rome threatened their existence. In the new world of first-century Palestine, the Jewish people adapted, fought, resisted, complied, and wondered when they would taste freedom and dignity again. Then, onto the stage of human history stepped John the Baptist and after John came Jesus, the promised servant-leader.

In this session, we pick up Jesus' story midpoint. He and his disciples have traveled throughout Galilee. The highlights of their time were the many miraculous healings and mighty deeds. They also experienced resistance from demons and ordinary humans. Moreover, as Mark recounts the story, there was scarcely a moment for rest. In the middle of their ministry, Jesus led his disciples north—away from crowds, familiar settings, and everyday demands for healing and teaching. They paused on a border between two lands. To the north, the region of Caesarea Philippi was predominantly Gentile, with leanings toward Roman power and domination. To the south was the territory of Galilee, the homeland of Jesus and his disciples, an area known for zealous rebels. The setting implied a choice: say "goodbye" to Jerusalem (and take a chance on Rome) or throw in with the revolution (and attempt to topple the empire). Jesus ignored these predictable topics and posed another question: "Who do people say that I am?" On a boundary line the disciples were faced with the fundamental question of their decision to follow Jesus—and they were blessed with new insight into their teacher and leader.

Who Is Jesus?

Perhaps the most serious question you will ever be asked is: Who is Jesus? It is both a public and a personal question. The public has a right to know what the church believes about Jesus; likewise, every believer with a firm hold on faith has a personal account of Jesus to offer. As Mark told the story of Jesus and his disciples on the boundary between Caesarea Philippi and Galilee, he allowed the disciples to speak the public perceptions first. From these, we glean information on Jesus as a religious leader. He was an emboldened preacher, such as John the Baptist; he was charged with mystical significance, as Elijah ushering in God's reign; he was prophetic, a man who spoke God's word after a lengthy silence. His disciples did not offer secular titles such as king, warrior, or judge. In a similar manner, when contemporary believers are asked the Jesus-question, they express the church's basic truths about Jesus and refrain from secular titles such as doctor, therapist, guru, or commander-in-chief.

In the text, after the public declarations, Jesus asked his disciples for their personal responses: "But who do you say that I am?" (8:29). Peter spoke the one essential word: "Messiah," translated from the Hebrew to the Greek to the English as "Christ" and meaning the anointed one, God's special servant, and the one commissioned and gifted for a unique service. This title spoke volumes, for it captured Jesus' special relationship with God, his divinely ordained work, and his extraordinary gifts for service. Still, as the word left Peter's lips, Jesus forbade the disciples' discussion of the title "messiah."

What Does Christ Mean?

Jesus began to teach. Evidently, he was eager to prepare his disciples for the time when they would speak the word "Messiah" freely and openly. He wanted them to understand the term as naturally as he understood his relationship with God. In verse 32, Mark described this teaching as "quite open," meaning that Jesus spoke without metaphor or story. He did, how-

ever, use one phrase to amplify his teaching: Son of Man. This term can be traced back to Jesus' native language of Aramaic. In the simple form, Son of Man means a person—nothing more, nothing less. Thus, the term implied Jesus' humanity. But, the phrase was also used by Daniel to identify the one to rescue the faithful from terror and persecution (see Daniel 7:13). In this more complex usage, the phrase included an empowerment of divinity. Jesus frequently used "Son of Man" to indicate himself (see, for example, Mark 10:45). Still, he probably welcomed the image of a divine redeemer as well.

The oddity (and for Peter, the outrage) was that Jesus used suffering as the common denominator for both his humanity and his divinity. That Jesus suffered, as any other human, was an acceptable idea (yes, he experienced pain when he stubbed his toe). However, in the strict system of blessings and curses, suffering was understood as punishment for sin. Sin was thought to be behind illnesses, misfortunes, oddly dangerous circumstances. Such an understanding did not square with Jesus' statement to the disciples that he "must" suffer—especially since he obediently followed God's will! Even more outrageous was the notion that in Jesus God experienced suffering. Surely, thought Jesus' disciples, God was free from suffering and pain. Yet, Jesus affirmed that both his human life of obedience and his divine role as redeemer included suffering. No wonder Peter rebuked Jesus' words. These ideas were scandalous.

What Does Disciple Mean?

Of course, Jesus' disciples did not grasp what Jesus' cross entailed. The disciples, on the boundary line of Galilee and Caesarea Philippi, could not comprehend the role that suffering would play in Jesus' life and death. Neither could they imagine the relationship of suffering to the redemption of the world. Still, Jesus told them openly: suffering is a "must" on my path.

It would be a few more months and many more lessons before the disciples began to fathom this announcement of his passion. For our author, Mark, and his original audience, however, Jesus' passion was real. Thus, Mark added a collection of pithy statements on discipleship. These statements begin with the well-worn truth of Christianity: Jesus' followers must deny, pick up, and follow. To be Jesus' follower, a shift of orientation is necessary. No longer is self the center of the universe. Following Jesus requires putting the weak, the lowly, the needy, the impoverished, and the outcast at the center. Then, Jesus asks: What can you do for the least of these? Jesus expects an answer and action.

There is no way to follow Jesus abstractly; there is, rather, a life committed to serving those in need. Such a life begins with a decision, but it continues as a relationship. Following Jesus is not about finding footprints in the sand and faithfully walking behind Jesus; rather, following Jesus includes walking by his side, conversing at the beginning and ending of day, expecting a steady diet of delight and correction. The decision provokes action and the action seals an ongoing relationship. When the self is no longer the center of the universe, real life begins. This life cannot be purchased or demanded. This life is only available to those with open hands. This life is a glorious glimpse of God's coming realm.

Who do you say that Jesus is?

SHARING THE SCRIPTURE

Preparing Our Hearts

Explore this week's devotional reading, found in Luke 3:7-18. Here we meet John the Baptist, whose message inspired people to wonder whether he might be the promised Messiah. John was clear: He was not, but he pointed to the One who was—the One who would baptize "with the Holy Spirit and fire" (3:16). John knew the identity of the Messiah. As we will see in today's lesson, Peter, speaking on behalf of the disciples, also knew that Jesus was the Messiah. Who do you say the Messiah is? Are you willing, like John, to proclaim this message? If so, who will you tell today about Jesus the Messiah?

Pray that you and the adult learners will recognize and give thanks for the Messiah.

Preparing Our Minds

Study the background Scripture and the lesson Scripture, both of which are found in

Mark 8:27–9:1. Ask: How can we find the truth about a leader's mission and goals?

Write on newsprint:
- ❏ information for next week's lesson, found under "Continue the Journey."
- ❏ activities for further spiritual growth in "Continue the Journey."

LEADING THE CLASS

(1) Gather to Learn

❖ Welcome the class members and introduce any guests.

❖ Pray that all who gather this day will open their hearts and minds to explore what they believe about Jesus.

❖ Read this info: **After nearly fifty years of apparent success in the investment business, Wall Street manager Bernard (Bernie) Madoff was sentenced to 150 years in prison for "massive fraud" and operating a "multi-billion dollar *Ponzi* scheme." His clientele,** which included many famous, sophisticated investors, sustained serious financial losses. This scheme worked because those investors believed in their money manager and his investment philosophy, which netted annual returns of 10 percent or more. Madoff was well respected in the investment community, serving as the president of the board of directors of the NASDAQ stock exchange. Yet, neither Madoff himself nor his investment strategy was what it seemed to be. He swindled his clients out of nearly $50 billion.

❖ Discuss these questions:

(1) **What other examples can you think of where people trusted a leader whose true identity and goals were hidden from view?**

(2) **What affect did these leaders have on the lives of others?**

❖ Read aloud today's focus statement: **People may not understand their leader's identity and mission. How can people know the truth of their leader's mission and goals? For people of faith, Jesus' words contain truth about his identity and mission to bring in the kingdom and about what he requires of his followers.**

(2) Learn What People Believed About Jesus and How He Challenged Their Beliefs

❖ Choose two volunteers, one to read Mark 8:27-30 and the other to read Mark 8:31–9:1. Ask the other students to listen for words or phrases that catch their attention.

❖ Call on class members to report the words or phrases they noted. List these ideas on newsprint. Discuss these questions:

(1) **What do these words reveal about Jesus' identity?**

(2) **What do these words reveal about how those who claim his identity as Christians are to behave?**

(3) **How would such words challenge the beliefs of Jesus' followers in terms of what they were expecting from the Messiah?**

(4) **How seriously do you think most Christians take the words in 8:34-36? Give examples to support your answer.**

❖ Use information from "What Does Christ Mean?" in Interpreting the Scripture to provide additional ideas about Jesus' identity.

❖ Suggest that the students call out attributes of Jesus that, to their way of thinking, mark him as a genuine leader. List ideas on newsprint. Compare and contrast Jesus' attributes as a leader with those qualities that society values in a leader. Ask:

(1) **Where do you see similarities between Jesus and the attributes of society's revered leaders?**

(2) **Where do you see differences?**

(3) **What do these similarities and differences suggest about how we might be better served by leaders who are more Christ-like?**

(3) Evaluate the Learners' Beliefs About Jesus and Make a Personal Profession of Faith

❖ Read or retell "Who Is Jesus" from Interpreting the Scripture.

❖ Distribute paper and pencils. Form groups of three or four and encourage each group to make a list of beliefs they hold about Jesus. Provide time for each group to report. The class may want to add to the list. They may also want to question or clarify some of the beliefs that have been named. Such inquiry may be useful as long as it is done respectfully.

❖ Use these beliefs to create a creed that reflects the group's beliefs about Jesus. Write their ideas on newsprint. Start with words such as "I believe in Jesus." Add ideas from your list, such as *"Son of God and Son of Man," "the Messiah"* (or Christ), *"who was crucified, died, and was buried," "raised up by God on the third day."*

❖ Lead the class in reading this creed as

an expression of their personal faith in Jesus. Begin the reading by asking Jesus' question: "But who do you say that I am?" (Mark 8:29).

❖ **Option:** Suggest that the students write this creed on the back of the papers they used in their groups. Encourage the adults to "tweak" the creed so as to reflect personal beliefs that may not have been included. Challenge them to read their creed on a regular basis as an affirmation of faith.

(4) Affirm or Change Behaviors in Light of Service to Others

❖ Read or retell "What Does Disciple Mean" from Interpreting the Scripture.

❖ Invite the adults to meditate on these words from the reading, seeking to decide how they will answer Jesus: **"Jesus asks: What can you do for the least of these? Jesus expects an answer and action."**

❖ Prompt volunteers to state what they hope to do. In some cases, they will be affirming actions they already take. In other cases, the students will be looking toward new directions to serve the risen Christ by serving others.

(5) Continue the Journey

❖ Pray that the participants will go forth to bear witness to the Messiah, Jesus, and to serve others in his name.

❖ Read aloud this preparation for next week's lesson. You may also want to post it on newsprint for the students to copy.
■ **Title: This Is My Beloved**
■ **Background Scripture: Mark 9:2-13**

■ **Lesson Scripture: Mark 9:2-13**
■ **Focus of the Lesson: People need reassurance that they are listening to the right leader. How can we know who is right and who is wrong? A theophany (here, God's voice in the cloud) dramatically identified Jesus as God's chosen one, the one to whom they should listen.**

❖ Challenge the students to complete one or more of these activities for further spiritual growth related to this week's session. Post this information on newsprint for the students to copy.

(1) Scan newspapers, magazines, and online media for pictures of people who are leaders in their fields. Which ones can you identify? How well do you understand their mission and values? Which ones do you support? Why?

(2) Take some action this week to demonstrate self-denial and your willingness to take up the cross that Christ calls you to bear.

(3) Use a Bible dictionary or other resources to research the concept of "messiah." How did Jesus meet—or not meet—Israel's expectations of God's anointed one?

❖ Sing or read aloud "I Surrender All."

❖ Conclude today's session by leading the class in this benediction: **Let us go forth to worship and serve the Lord, in whom we have the blessed assurance of our salvation.**

UNIT 3: JESUS, THE PROMISED SERVANT-LEADER
THIS IS MY BELOVED

PREVIEWING THE LESSON

Lesson Scripture: Mark 9:2-13
Background Scripture: Mark 9:2-13
Key Verse: Mark 9:7

Focus of the Lesson:
People need reassurance that they are listening to the right leader. How can we know who is right and who is wrong? A theophany (here, God's voice in the cloud) dramatically identified Jesus as God's chosen one, the one to whom they should listen.

Goals for the Learners:
(1) to study the theophany at Jesus' transfiguration and the disciples' reaction to it.
(2) to reflect on the meaning of the transfiguration for their own lives.
(3) to identify and eliminate barriers to listening to Jesus.

Pronunciation Guide:
theophany (thee of' uh nee)

Supplies:
Bibles, newsprint and marker, paper and pencils, hymnals

READING THE SCRIPTURE

NRSV
Mark 9:2-13

²Six days later, Jesus took with him Peter and James and John, and led them up a high mountain apart, by themselves. And he was transfigured before them, ³and his clothes became dazzling white, such as no one on earth could bleach them. ⁴And there appeared to them Elijah with Moses, who were talking with Jesus. ⁵Then Peter said to Jesus, "Rabbi, it is good for us to be here; let

NIV
Mark 9:2-13

²After six days Jesus took Peter, James and John with him and led them up a high mountain, where they were all alone. There he was transfigured before them. ³His clothes became dazzling white, whiter than anyone in the world could bleach them. ⁴And there appeared before them Elijah and Moses, who were talking with Jesus.

⁵Peter said to Jesus, "Rabbi, it is good for

us make three dwellings, one for you, one for Moses, and one for Elijah." [6]He did not know what to say, for they were terrified. **[7]Then a cloud overshadowed them, and from the cloud there came a voice, "This is my Son, the Beloved; listen to him!"** [8]Suddenly when they looked around, they saw no one with them any more, but only Jesus.

[9]As they were coming down the mountain, he ordered them to tell no one about what they had seen, until after the Son of Man had risen from the dead. [10]So they kept the matter to themselves, questioning what this rising from the dead could mean. [11]Then they asked him, "Why do the scribes say that Elijah must come first?" [12]He said to them, "Elijah is indeed coming first to restore all things. How then is it written about the Son of Man, that he is to go through many sufferings and be treated with contempt? [13]But I tell you that Elijah has come, and they did to him whatever they pleased, as it is written about him."

us to be here. Let us put up three shelters— one for you, one for Moses and one for Elijah." [6](He did not know what to say, they were so frightened.)

[7]Then a cloud appeared and enveloped them, and a voice came from the cloud: "This is my Son, whom I love. Listen to him!"

[8]Suddenly, when they looked around, they no longer saw anyone with them except Jesus.

[9]As they were coming down the mountain, Jesus gave them orders not to tell anyone what they had seen until the Son of Man had risen from the dead. [10]They kept the matter to themselves, discussing what "rising from the dead" meant.

[11]And they asked him, "Why do the teachers of the law say that Elijah must come first?"

[12]Jesus replied, "To be sure, Elijah does come first, and restores all things. Why then is it written that the Son of Man must suffer much and be rejected? [13]But I tell you, Elijah has come, and they have done to him everything they wished, just as it is written about him."

UNDERSTANDING THE SCRIPTURE

Mark 9:2. The Gospel of Mark is a terse, crisp narrative that is unfortunately slim on details of date and geography. In this text, Mark begins with a unit of time: after six days. The intention may be to demonstrate the connection between this passage and the previous narrative of Peter's confession, including Jesus' first teaching on his suffering, death, and resurrection. Another possible reason for including the time frame was to alert Mark's audience to an imminent encounter with the divine. Some evidence, particularly Exodus 24:15-16, suggests that in the Jewish tradition six days was the period of preparation and purification necessary before a close encounter with God.

The reader is thus directed to continue the reflection of Jesus' identity while anticipating a deeper revelation. As the story unfolds, new light shines on Peter's confession and the divine voice affirms Jesus' identity and authority. Taking three disciples with him, Jesus hiked up a high, but unnamed, mountain, presumably in the same region of Caesarea Philippi (the setting for the previous encounter of Mark 8:27-91). A mountaintop setting is often the place of divine revelation, as it was for Moses. The disciples anticipated a time for prayer and perhaps an opportunity for individual instruction. Peter, for example, would have welcomed private time with

Jesus; his mind was probably exhausted with the teachings on suffering, death, and resurrection. Jesus' interactions with the disciples form a parenthesis around the events on the mountain. He took them up the mountain, an act of leadership, and while leading them down he ordered them to refrain from talking about the experience, an act of authority. Between these two actions, Jesus neither spoke, nor exhibited emotion, nor acted. He was passive throughout; the events on the mountain happened to Jesus, and the three disciples were privileged to be witnesses.

Mark 9:3-7. The actual transfiguration of Jesus was not described. Mark commented on Jesus' clothing but not on Jesus himself; this restraint heightened rather than subdued the mysteriously spiritual quality of the scene. After describing Jesus' clothing, two heroes of the Jewish faith appeared, Elijah and Moses. These two men, evidently recognized by symbolic attire or by inner revelation, were not only beloved spiritual leaders but they also represented the two modes of encountering God's creative word: through the prophets and in the law. Almost casually, Mark notes that the two men were talking with Jesus. Peter, of course, was the first to respond. He first noted how good it was to be there, alluding to the uniqueness of this experience. Peter's next words were directed toward his companions: "Let us make three dwellings" (literally, tents). Scholars are divided as to the interpretation of Peter's intention. Some believe that Peter desired to continue the blessed moment by providing a holy space for the three to linger. Others believe that he was simply interested in serving Jesus by attending to the physical needs of his guests. Mark, however, qualified Peter's words by noting his confusion and fear. Unexpectedly, the scene changed: A cloud, the traditional symbol of God's self-veiling and self-disclosure, obscured the three men and the surrounding glory. From the cloud—from God!—came the confirmation:

"This is my Son, the Beloved" (notice the change from "You are my Son, the Beloved" in the baptism of Mark 1:11) and the command, "listen, to him." Then, suddenly, Jesus stood alone. The glory, Elijah and Moses, the cloud and the voice were gone. Only Jesus remained.

Mark 9:8-10. Next, Mark's holy description gave way to an ordinary hike down the mountain. Once again, Jesus ordered the disciples to refrain from discussing the experience. This restraint, described as "the messianic secret," appeared first at Mark 1:23-25, as a demon declared Jesus' identity and was promptly silenced by Jesus. Secrecy was a form of protection; if Jesus' identity as God's servant and son were discussed too broadly before his death and resurrection, the possibilities for confusion and misrepresentation were great. Thus the demon was silenced and the three disciples were instructed to keep their experience a secret. However, the disciples were to keep their secret for only a defined period of time: until the Son of Man had risen from the dead. By this comment, Mark's audience recognized the fact that Jesus' suffering and glory belonged together. Any attempt to separate Jesus' obedience to God from his death was a corruption of the gospel. During his life, Jesus' identity was only partially disclosed; with his death and resurrection the whole of Jesus' identity was appreciated and praised. Even though James, John, and Peter had a glimpse of Jesus' glory, they would not fully understand him until they encountered the trauma of the cross and the glory of his resurrection.

Mark 9:11-13. Finally, the disciples raised a question Jesus would answer. Reeling from the holy experience on the mountain, they asked about Elijah and his return. In the religious expectation of first-century Judaism, Elijah and other major figures of the Old Testament were expected to return as an indicator that God's final restoration of creation was near. Jesus, however, opened his ministry with the announcement, "the kingdom of God has come near" (Mark 1:15). If Jesus' words were true—and the disciples surely believed his teachings—what about Elijah? Jesus agreed with the premise of the disciples' question; he affirmed that Elijah was a significant figure in God's restoration. However, Jesus heard within the disciples' question another question, the question of suffering. Responding to a topic the disciples refused to admit, Jesus inserted suffering into Elijah's return as he identified Elijah with John the Baptist ("Elijah has come"), the recently humiliated and beheaded forerunner of Jesus. The scriptural allusion was not specific; however, from this study, we clearly make the connection between Jesus' suffering and that of the servant in Isaiah 53. It was likely that the early church also heard that connection. However, as Jesus cautioned and taught his disciples, they had yet to understand the significance of suffering. For them, suffering was painful rejection by God. Although Jesus gently tried to point to the necessity of his passion, the words were beyond the disciples' comprehension. Neither the events of Jesus' life, nor the sad fate of John the Baptist/Elijah, nor the witness of Isaiah 53 could convince these disciples that Jesus' way led through suffering to death and beyond death to life with God. Such a theological insight awaited another time.

INTERPRETING THE SCRIPTURE

A Transforming Moment

The phrase "mountaintop experience" signifies different experiences within the Christian community. For some, a mountaintop experience happens at a place apart, such as a retreat center or church campsite. For others, a mountaintop experience refers to those high points of intimacy with God, when the mundane world slips away and the wonder of God is palpable. Still others find that mountaintop experiences evolve from mutual commitment to a Christian activity.

The event described in Mark 9:2-13 was a mountaintop experience for three of Jesus' disciples. They were lead "apart" by Jesus up a high mountain. Their eyes were treated to a glorious vision. They felt a common commitment and connection because of their experience. Still, this story offers more than the mountaintop experience of three disciples. By the phrase, "Six days later" (9:2) Mark linked this story to the preceding report of Peter's confession. The passages belong together: Peter's best word, "Messiah," is complemented by God's divine disclosure, "my Son."

With these two stories, Mark confronted the problem of religious language within the early church. Although early Christians had an inherited religious vocabulary from Scripture and tradition, these words were inadequate expressions of the truth of Jesus. Just as Peter formed the right answer, then received instruction and rebuke in order to allow a new meaning to expand the title Messiah, so the early Christians needed time to allow the impact of Jesus' suffering, death, and resurrection to fill their new faith vocabulary. Mark wisely gave them two stories.

As the early Christians pondered these two stories, they filled the traditional language with insights from their experiences as the body of Christ, from their individual lives in service and, especially, from the words of Jesus. All four elements united to define Jesus: his identity flowed from his Jewish heritage, his life revealed boundless love for all, his death transformed suffering into redemption, and his words communicated all that was necessary for abundant life. Not only did the disciples witness Jesus' transfiguration, but their story also became a transforming moment for future Christians.

A Direct Word

As a pastor there are some phrases I hear over and over again. One is, "Why doesn't God speak directly anymore?" The hunger to hear, really hear, God's voice is deep. Most people assume that if God spoke their lives would become immediately comprehensible. Not only would they know what to do, but they would understand why they should do so. In Scripture there are accounts of God's voice booming into human history. However, we must remember that these accounts were recorded long after the divine voice silenced—after hours or years of prayerful contemplation.

The truth of our faith is that God has spoken, does speak, and will continue to speak to humans. God's voice is sometimes a whisper or surprisingly similar to that of a loved one (spouse, parent, child, friend). God also uses visions, dreams, and emotional sensations as media of communication. In Mark's account of Jesus' transfiguration, several forms of divine communication are apparent. The disciples first beheld a radiant vision. Quite likely, the glory they saw frightened them. Indeed, the storyteller reported that Peter offered to build tabernacles, possibly because he was afraid and confused. I imagine the three disciples holding one another's shoulders as they peered into the brilliant light; then, I imagine their fingers tightening as a cloud blotted out the light, the three men, and the glory. Standing in awe and fear, the three heard words that echoed through the centuries to all generations of believers. First, the divine voice spoke—to the disciples— the confirmation announced at Jesus' baptism. Doubt receded as God declared: Jesus is my beloved child. Then, the voice emphatically commanded: "Listen to him!" The disciples, ancient and contemporary, got it. God's voice was (and is) heard in Jesus' words.

Quiet Confusion

Have you ever experienced your world turned upside down? Or as some people say, your personal history rewritten? It is the discovery that what you thought you knew just wasn't so. This was the way James, John, and Peter came down from the mountain. They were in a quiet confusion because their world was upside down and their history was being rewritten. They had gone up the hill thinking they were close to understanding Jesus; they came down the hill numbed by the glorious vision. They had gone up the hill expecting, with just a few more lessons, to understand Jesus; they came down the hill reeling from the wonder of God. They had gone up the hill with only a few questions left to ask; they came down with more questions than they dared asked.

On top of that mountain the disciples were blessed to receive an intense spiritual experience. As they descended, they longed for a clear, logical way to think about their experience. This was an ordinary pattern for dealing with an extraordinary experience: first the mystical, then the rational. Christian faith relies on the integration of these two diverse ways of knowing. Without the passion of mysticism, our thoughts are dry and brittle. Without the structure of rational thought, our passion disperses with the winds. There is a time to be stunned by God, a time to deeply contemplate and bring language to holy experience, and a time for quiet confusion. The disciples talked quietly among themselves. They were unable to form a question sufficiently large to encompass their mountaintop experience. Moreover, Jesus approved of—even demanded—their silence. He ordered them to speak with no one (including the nine other disciples) about what they had seen. They could not argue with this. With quiet confusion, and perhaps a little small talk, they came down from the mountain.

Explaining the Unexplainable

One of the disciples asked a question: "Why do the scribes say that Elijah must come first?" (9:11). It was a question about the end of time, a question that implied God's final judgment, and a question (according to James, John, and Peter) that might explain Jesus. Indeed, it was an ordinary question based on the ordinary assumptions that soon God would act to restore Israel. Moreover, it was a question that would sharpen the distinction between Jesus and the scribes, the most learned scriptural authorities. Apocalyptic intrigue combined with contemporary speculation regarding John the Baptist blended together in this question.

Jesus could have dismissed the inquiry with a simple "the scribes are right" or "they are wrong." However, Jesus used the question to probe his current teaching theme and the disciples' learning curve: the issue of suffering. With his answer Jesus forced the disciples back to their Scriptures. Indeed, he affirmed (1) the scriptural return of Elijah (easily located at Malachi 4:5-6), (2) a Scripture allusion to the Son of Man's suffering (in Daniel 7:13, which features the Son of Man, who rescued the righteous after their suffering, or perhaps Isaiah 52:13–53:12, the last of the suffering Servant Songs), and (3) his own declaration that Elijah has come and has suffered.

Once again, the disciples were forced to ponder Jesus' words. Although he attempted to explain the unexplainable, it would be much, much later, after the passion, the burial, and the empty tomb, until these disciples understood this lesson. In the meantime, three of the disciples likely probed the significance of Jesus, their leader, being announced as the Beloved of God.

SHARING THE SCRIPTURE

Preparing Our Hearts

Explore this week's devotional reading, found in Malachi 4:1-5. Here in verse 5, the prophet announces that Elijah will come before the "day of the LORD." On this day, those who have been faithful to God will be rewarded, while those who have turned from God will be destroyed. This passage connects with today's Scripture lesson, as Jesus declared that "Elijah has come" (Mark 9:13), referring to John the Baptist. What role do you envision for Elijah? Use a concordance to locate references to this prophet to learn what you can about him.

Pray that you and the adult learners will be prepared for the coming of the Lord.

Preparing Our Minds

Study the background Scripture and the lesson Scripture, both of which are found in Mark 9:2-13. Think about how you can know who is right and who is wrong.

Write on newsprint:

❏ information for next week's lesson, found under "Continue the Journey."

❏ activities for further spiritual growth in "Continue the Journey."

LEADING THE CLASS

(1) Gather to Learn

❖ Welcome the class members and introduce any guests.

❖ Pray that those who have gathered today will recognize Jesus as God's Beloved and commit themselves to following him.

❖ Invite the class to recall some campaign speeches they heard in a recent (or prior) election. Note that candidates vying for office, particularly those affiliated with the same party, may have similar ideas. Opposing parties may differ greatly. To present their ideas in the best light, politicians may "spin" their message. Some shade the truth or omit information or are flat out wrong in their assertions. These "muddy waters" make it difficult for voters to decide who is best able to lead them. Ask: **What are some criteria you use to decide who will be the best leader?**

❖ Read aloud today's focus statement: **People need reassurance that they are listening to the right leader. How can we know who is right and who is wrong? A theophany (here, God's voice in the cloud) dramatically identified Jesus as God's chosen one, the one to whom they should listen.**

(2) Study the Theophany at Jesus' Transfiguration and the Disciples' Reaction to It

❖ Choose volunteers to take the parts of the narrator, Peter, the voice from the cloud, at least one disciple, and Jesus. Ask them to read Mark 9:2-13 as a drama.

❖ Challenge the adults to enter into this scene by using all of their senses. Ask: **What did you see, hear, taste, touch, or smell?** List their ideas on newsprint. Ask: **How did this sensory perception make the scene come alive for you?**

❖ Consider how the scene affected the disciples by reading or retelling "Quiet Confusion" from Interpreting the Scripture. Invite the students to put themselves in the sandals of Peter, James, and John and ask questions that might have come to mind. Point out that the one question that is voiced in this passage, which concerns the prophet Elijah (see Mark 9:11), is raised after Jesus and the three disciples come off the mountain. Yet, perhaps the disciples had questions about the transfiguration event itself. If so, what might those questions have been?

❖ Use information from Understanding the Scripture to shed light on any questions that are raised about the text.

(3) Reflect on the Meaning of the Transfiguration for the Learners' Own Lives

❖ Suggest that the participants share stories, either with the class or in small groups, about mountaintop experiences they have had. Perhaps some will recall a time at camp, or on a youth retreat, or a Walk to Emmaus, or other opportunity for reflection and spiritual growth. Encourage the groups to discuss where they were, what happened, and the affect this event had on their spiritual journey with Jesus.

❖ **Option:** Talk with the group about planning a retreat to listen for Jesus in an uninterrupted setting. To keep costs low and increase participation, suggest that the class check with a neighboring church to see if you could use their facility for a Friday night and Saturday (even just a Saturday). Talk with your pastor to see if someone from your conference or diocese could lead this event. Set up a task force to plan this event, beginning with a mutually agreeable date and location.

(4) Identify and Eliminate Barriers to Listening to Jesus

❖ Read "A Direct Word" from Interpreting the Scripture.

❖ Brainstorm answers to this question, and list ideas on newsprint: **Why do people find it difficult to listen to Jesus?** Here are some ideas: *God no longer speaks to us; I don't have time to listen; I'm afraid that if I do listen, God will ask me to do something I don't want to do; if I listen, I may have to change my ways; I* *don't know how to discern that the voice I'm hearing is that of Jesus; listening is something clergy and church leaders need to do and then tell the rest of us what we need to know.*

❖ Look at the list. Ask: **How can any of these barriers be eliminated?** (for example, *studying the Bible, setting aside time to pray and meditate, learning to trust that God has our best interest at heart, recognizing that all followers of Christ are called to listen and respond*)

❖ Distribute paper and pencils. Invite the students to look at the list and select one or two barriers that inhibit them from listening to Jesus. (Remind the group that in both Greek and Hebrew the words for listen also include the idea that one is to heed and obey what has been said.) Challenge them to write a few words about what they will do, starting today, to listen to and heed the words of Christ.

(5) Continue the Journey

❖ Pray that those who have participated today will listen to and follow Jesus, God's Beloved Son.

❖ Read aloud this preparation for next week's lesson. You may also want to post it on newsprint for the students to copy.

- ■ **Title: Jesus Came to Serve**
- ■ **Background Scripture: Mark 10:35-45**
- ■ **Lesson Scripture: Mark 10:35-45**
- ■ **Focus of the Lesson: Great leaders make a gift of themselves and their work to those whom they would lead. What is the mark of great leadership? Jesus said that he came to serve, not to be served, and demonstrated that as an example to follow.**

❖ Challenge the students to complete one or more of these activities for further spiritual growth related to this week's session. Post this information on newsprint for the students to copy.

(1) **Spend time daily meditating. Listen for Jesus' words to you. Act on these words, if you can discern that they are in keeping with Jesus' teachings, example, and call on your life.**

(2) **Plan to go on a retreat, either alone or with others. A day or weekend away can often bring great spiritual clarity to a situation that otherwise seems muddled. Ask God to lead you where you need to go.**

(3) **Ponder Jesus' sufferings. How do you see those sufferings as redemptive? Are there experiences of suffering in your own life that you believe are for the sake of others? How does that understanding change your perspective on a difficult situation?**

❖ Sing or read aloud "Christ, Upon the Mountain Peak."

❖ Conclude today's session by leading the class in this benediction: **Let us go forth to worship and serve the Lord, in whom we have the blessed assurance of our salvation.**

UNIT 3: JESUS, THE PROMISED SERVANT-LEADER

JESUS CAME TO SERVE

PREVIEWING THE LESSON

Lesson Scripture: Mark 10:35-45
Background Scripture: Mark 10:35-45
Key Verse: Mark 10:45

Focus of the Lesson:

Great leaders make a gift of themselves and their work to those whom they would lead. What is the mark of great leadership? Jesus said that he came to serve, not to be served, and demonstrated that as an example to follow.

Goals for the Learners:

(1) to examine how Jesus corrected James and John's inappropriate request for special consideration.
(2) to articulate their understanding of service to others as demonstrated by Jesus.
(3) to develop and implement specific ways to serve others by following Jesus' example.

Pronunciation Guide:

Zebedee (zeb' uh dee)

Supplies:

Bibles, newsprint and marker, paper and pencils, hymnals; optional magazine pictures

READING THE SCRIPTURE

NRSV
Mark 10:35-45

35James and John, the sons of Zebedee, came forward to him and said to him, "Teacher, we want you to do for us whatever we ask of you." 36And he said to them, "What is it you want me to do for you?" 37And they said to him, "Grant us to sit, one at your right hand and one at your left, in your glory." 38But Jesus said to them, "You

NIV
Mark 10:35-45

35Then James and John, the sons of Zebedee, came to him. "Teacher," they said, "we want you to do for us whatever we ask." 36"What do you want me to do for you?" he asked. 37They replied, "Let one of us sit at your right and the other at your left in your glory."

do not know what you are asking. Are you able to drink the cup that I drink, or be baptized with the baptism that I am baptized with?" ³⁹They replied, "We are able." Then Jesus said to them, "The cup that I drink you will drink; and with the baptism with which I am baptized, you will be baptized; ⁴⁰but to sit at my right hand or at my left is not mine to grant, but it is for those for whom it has been prepared."

⁴¹When the ten heard this, they began to be angry with James and John. ⁴²So Jesus called them and said to them, "You know that among the Gentiles those whom they recognize as their rulers lord it over them, and their great ones are tyrants over them. ⁴³But it is not so among you; but whoever wishes to become great among you must be your servant, ⁴⁴and whoever wishes to be first among you must be slave of all. **⁴⁵For the Son of Man came not to be served but to serve, and to give his life a ransom for many."**

³⁸"You don't know what you are asking," Jesus said. "Can you drink the cup I drink or be baptized with the baptism I am baptized with?"

³⁹"We can," they answered.

Jesus said to them, "You will drink the cup I drink and be baptized with the baptism I am baptized with, ⁴⁰but to sit at my right or left is not for me to grant. These places belong to those for whom they have been prepared."

⁴¹When the ten heard about this, they became indignant with James and John. ⁴²Jesus called them together and said, "You know that those who are regarded as rulers of the Gentiles lord it over them, and their high officials exercise authority over them. ⁴³Not so with you. Instead, whoever wants to become great among you must be your servant, ⁴⁴and whoever wants to be first must be slave of all. **⁴⁵For even the Son of Man did not come to be served, but to serve, and to give his life as a ransom for many."**

UNDERSTANDING THE SCRIPTURE

Mark 10:35-36. In the Gospel of Mark, the disciples are not presented as individuals, but as necessary characters to clarify the call, teaching, expectations, and impact of Jesus on others. Throughout this Gospel, the disciples are portrayed as unaware of the significance of Jesus' ministry. Moreover, they seem to be preoccupied with their personal circumstances rather than their ministry with others. James and John, the fisherman sons of Zebedee who are the focus of today's Scripture, followed Jesus, apparently without a second thought (see Mark 1:16-20). Almost immediately they witnessed profound healings and exorcisms, as well as peculiar behavior on Jesus' part (see Mark 1:35-39). They were part of the Twelve commissioned by Jesus to proclaim the good news and cast out demons (Mark 3:13-15).

James and John had the additional privilege of being within the "inner circle" with Peter. From this intimate perspective they experienced things not shared with the others: the healing of a child assumed to be dead (5:35-42) and the transfiguration (9:2-8). They were also commanded by Jesus not to discuss these private experiences (5:43 and 9:9). Finally, at the conclusion of Jesus' ministry, only one city and one miracle shy of Jerusalem, James and John approached Jesus on a very personal matter. Although they had observed Jesus' miraculous powers, listened to his tales of the coming kingdom, and felt the surge of enthusiasm from crowds, they asked Jesus for a favor. They wanted something and Jesus, the compassionate teacher and leader, calmly welcomed their request. Indeed, Jesus encouraged them, asking, "What it is you want me to do for you?"—the same question Jesus would put to blind Bartimaeus in a story that immediately follows this encounter (see Mark 10:46-52). Thus, Jesus offered to James and John the same opportunity he offered to the blind man: State your heart's greatest longing.

Mark 10:37-40. James and John pitched their proposal. Using the seating order of royalty—a king flanked by his most trusted and worthy companions on either side—the two disciples claimed their due honor. They apparently thought God's realm recognized special status for Jesus' friends. Since they had followed Jesus from the very beginning, James and John boldly made their request. Jesus' response was firm. He declared that James and John neither knew nor understood the nature of God's coming kingdom. And then, he began to teach them. Jesus' teaching style usually began with an illustration, a parable, or a metaphor designed to help the inquirer enter into the depth of the lesson. In this private lesson, Jesus selected two specific, but complementary, metaphors: the cup and baptism. For contemporary believers it is difficult to hear these images without centuries of liturgical Christian overlay. Yet, as James and John heard Jesus' words, their minds filled with information drawn from the Old Testament. For example, in Isaiah 51:17, the cup is clearly identified as "the cup of (God's) wrath." (See also Jeremiah 25:15-16.) The waters, a traditional image for uncontrolled chaos, evoked fear; the image of being covered by water evoked horrifying thoughts of a watery death. The notion of being overwhelmed by water was described in the psalms of lament (see Psalm 42:7 and 69:1). To these scriptural images, the disciples added the Jewish custom of baptism, a washing ritual for welcoming converts into the Jewish community. Finally, the disciples knew about the significant ministry of John the Baptist at the River Jordan. John's baptism was practical (a symbolic confirmation

of a personal, religious vow) and future-oriented (received in anticipation of God's coming judgment). Considering the metaphors, James and John agreed they were ready and able to drink the same cup and to be baptized in the same manner as Jesus. Jesus concurred with their intentions, but he firmly stated that granting them "honors" in the kingdom was not his to do. Ironically, the ones we see on Jesus' right and left are the two who are crucified with him, the ones suffering as he does (see Mark 15:27-32).

Mark 10:41-45. The other disciples reacted with anger, or as the New International Version translates the Greek, "became indignant." Jesus identified this as a teachable moment and called the disciples together. Again, he began to teach by using an example: the leadership style of the oppressive Roman rulers and officials. Their way of lording power over people stood in complete opposition to the way Jesus acted and was teaching his followers to act in regard to other people—as servants. This term indicated the lowest form of status of a slave, an indentured servant, or someone incapable of providing for self or family. There was nothing honorable or attractive about the term or the life of a servant.

Still, in his final teaching before entering Jerusalem, Jesus described his leadership style as that of a servant. Moreover, he declared his purpose in service: to ransom many. The connection between the humility of the servant and the liberation of the many would have been heard as a profound and shocking statement, though the Gospel does not include the disciples' response. Possibly the Gospel author intended to confront his audience with this teachable moment and prompt them to make their own response. For a radical teaching to be received it is necessary, first, to prepare hearts and minds. Jesus did so by contrasting the power-hungry leadership style of the Roman officials with his own style of service. Both Jesus' disciples and Mark's readers were about to enter into Jesus' passion. That experience of his suffering, the suffering he prepared his disciples to encounter, and the suffering that all followers of Christ are subject to would be incomprehensible without a deep understanding of Jesus as the servant-leader. Such lessons are rarely communicated directly; rather, they depend upon a heart cultivated (or surprised) to be opened, emptied, and changed. Understanding that to follow Jesus requires one to live as a servant transforms the values, actions, and attitudes of all believers.

INTERPRETING THE SCRIPTURE

A Question of Wants

This passage displays the gentleness of Jesus in a manner that surely must have comforted the early Christian communities. While emotional content bounced from the disciples' high hopes to indignation, Jesus steadily responded with images and instructions that grounded his community. By carefully analyzing and applying these teachings, the ancient church became a potent Spirit-driven institution. As contemporary congregations lean into this passage, they too may be touched by potent spiritual truths.

Oddly, this core teaching began with an inappropriate request. Perhaps you—as a parent, friend, teacher, or counselor—have experienced such a moment. Perhaps someone approached you to request special consideration or privilege when that was neither yours to grant nor in line with the goals of the project or situation. If you recognize that situation, you can appreciate Jesus' kindly response to James and John.

Consider the setting: The disciples and Jesus were literally at the last stop before Jerusalem. Jesus was keenly aware of the consequences of his choice to go to the Holy City during Passover; he knew it would mean death. For the third time, Jesus had just explained to the disciples that he would be handed over, abused, killed, and would rise again on the third day (Mark 10:32-34).

Astoundingly, the response to this foretelling of his passion is a request by James and John for a favor. They were ready to fast-forward to the heavenly feasting table and eager to upgrade their reservations from the disciples' table to the head table with Jesus. He asked them: "What is it you want me to do for you?" (10:36). This question, when raised by Jesus, God's own son, trembled with potential. It was the type of question Jesus asked of the ill, the possessed, the destitute, and the friendless. His question was designed to reveal the content of the heart. It was a question that resonated through church history, and it is a question personally applicable to contemporary followers. Through his question, Jesus invited James and John to speak from the depth of their souls. If what they wanted were not so off-target, their response might have been amusing. Jesus was not amused, but neither did he rebuke them. Instead, he pressed them to explore their request and its consequences in depth.

An Able Answer

Using the metaphors of cup and baptism, which were Jewish scriptural images of God's judgment and punishment, Jesus began to teach James and John. Immediately, it becomes clear to the reader that the disciples failed to inventory their hearts; their minds remained set on rewards; they cannot fathom the metaphorical significance of cup and baptism. Still, Jesus did not criticize their request; rather, he gently received their bold affirmation of competence and pointed that affirmation in another direction. From all the readers knew of the disciples—slow to understand, floundering in faith, and actually frightened (see Mark 10:32)—their claim to be "able" contrasted with their inabilities as disciples. In the readers' minds a chuckle began: These two wouldn't last a minute if the going got tough. That James and John were more likely to cut and run was the obvious conclusion.

Jesus, however, accepted their affirmation. He acknowledged their lack of depth and their misunderstanding of his metaphors, but he did not chastise or correct them. Perhaps by seeing these two close followers not as faltering disciples but as growing believers, Jesus saw through their quick pledge to the capacities forming in their souls. Jesus' ability to see the whole individual was not unique. In every generation believers, teachers, preachers, and spiritual companions have responded to the "young in faith" by recognizing their amazing capacities yet to be manifest. When disciples see the whole person, rather than the incomplete, ignorant, wounded, or limited one standing before them, they bless as Jesus blessed. In such an encounter believers invite others to go further along the path of discipleship.

Jesus did deny James and John's request for seats of honor. Just as Jesus deferred to God the question, "When will the kingdom come?" so Jesus deferred to God in this issue of rank or honor within God's realm. His deference affirmed that God was behind every aspect of his ministry. Jesus left supernatural timelines and satisfactions to God's mysterious ways, even as he encouraged his disciples' intentions.

Anger Absorbed in Instruction

This story does not end sweetly, but with a flourish of anger among the disciples.

Anger makes teaching difficult because opinions are firmly formed and passionately supported. Anger also makes teaching potent because the stakes are high and if a new concept can be received, the learning is not quickly forgotten. Jesus' disciples were angry, indignant, and outraged by the presumption beneath the request from James and John. Even if these two cherished, as most humans cherish, a need for recognition, the others disciples were sufficiently mannered not to mention their desires for status. As the sparks began to fly, Jesus gathered his disciples. It was a passionate moment; Jesus drew upon an equally passionate illustration. Roman rule was not only demonized in everyday gossip but it was also brutal in everyday experience. To suggest that the way of Jesus ran a course diametrically opposed to the way of Rome drew immediate attention.

Yet, not everyone agreed on the specific direction of the "diametrically opposed" path. Was this a path of ritual purity as taught by the Pharisees? Was the new way characterized by the repentance and preparation heralded by John the Baptist? Was the way one of rebellion as recommended by the Zealots? Or could a new course be formed according to the Herodians' principles of accommodation? Was an escape to the desert, as practiced by the Essenes, the appropriate contradiction to Roman rule?

Although the disciples were trained by Jesus, they continued to be culturally conditioned. They knew the way of Rome was wrong, but they had yet to fully comprehend Jesus' way. Thus, Jesus instructed them clearly. His first point: You are not to lord greatness over each other. His second point: Service is the path to greatness. His third point: In God's great reversal, the slave is honored, the king is humbled. His fourth point: I did not come to be served, but to serve. His final point: My service will liberate many. This rapid-fire series of points was probably incomprehensible to the angry disciples. This was the type of core teaching the disciples would ponder and plumb after Jesus' death and resurrection.

As they remembered those words and searched their Scriptures for illumination and validation, they eventually came to Isaiah 52:13–53:12, the fourth Suffering Servant Song. By the words of the prophet, Jesus' instructions on servant leadership and a community of service became comprehensible. From Jesus' summary statements offered to angry disciples developed an internal standard for all followers of Jesus. The absence of hierarchy within the community of Jesus and the presence of mutual service was and is the new way. Forever, those who follow Jesus know: "Whoever wishes to be great among you must be your servant, and whoever wishes to be first among you must be slave of all" (10:43-44). The great reversal in understanding true leadership began . . . and continues.

SHARING THE SCRIPTURE

Preparing Our Hearts

Explore this week's devotional reading, found in John 13:3-16. In this familiar passage Jesus demonstrated the meaning of servanthood by washing the feet of the disciples. Jesus lovingly cared for his friends by taking the role of a servant as he and the disciples prepared for their last meal together. Afterward, Jesus explained to the disciples that "servants are not greater than their master" (13:16). Jesus had acted as a servant to them; they are to follow his example and act as servants to others. So are we. How have you acted as a servant within the last 24 hours? What else can you do now?

Pray that you and the adult learners will recognize that following Christ entails taking on the role of the servant.

Preparing Our Minds

Study the background Scripture and the lesson Scripture, both of which are found in Mark 10:35-45. What would you say are the marks of a great leader?

Write on newsprint:
❑ information for next week's lesson, found under "Continue the Journey."
❑ activities for further spiritual growth in "Continue the Journey."

Collect optional pictures from magazines or other sources that illustrate the "rat race" nature of our society. A picture showing people rushing by someone in need or people pushing and shoving would be excellent examples.

LEADING THE CLASS

(1) Gather to Learn

❖ Welcome the class members and introduce any guests.

❖ Pray that those who have come today will grow in their faith and understanding of what it means to follow Jesus.

❖ Read this information: **Robert K. Greenleaf, author of *Servant Leadership: A Journey into the Nature of Legitimate Power and Greatness*, explains at the opening of his book that the idea of *servant* leadership dawned on him as he read Hermann Hesse's *Journey to the East*. Greenleaf briefly retells this story of a group of men on a mythical journey: "The central figure of the story is Leo, who accompanies the party as the *servant* who does their menial chores, but who also sustains them with his spirit and his song. He is a person of extraordinary presence. All goes well until Leo disappears. Then the group falls into disarray and the journey is abandoned. They cannot make it without** the servant Leo. The narrator, one of the party, after some years of wandering finds Leo and is taken into the Order that sponsored the journey. There he discovers that Leo, whom he had first known as *servant*, was in fact the titular head of the Order, its guiding spirit, a great and noble *leader*."

❖ Ask: What does this story suggest to you about the relationship between the servant and the leader?

❖ Read aloud today's focus statement: **Great leaders make a gift of themselves and their work to those whom they would lead. What is the mark of great leadership? Jesus said that he came to serve, not to be served, and demonstrated that as an example to follow.**

(2) Examine How Jesus Corrected James and John's Inappropriate Request for Special Consideration

❖ Choose volunteers to read the parts of the narrator, James and John (who read in unison), and Jesus.

❖ Discuss these questions. Add information from Understanding the Scripture and Interpreting the Scripture as you find it appropriate.

    (1) **What do James and John think they are requesting when they ask Jesus to allow them to sit at his right and left hand in glory?**

    (2) **What associations would the disciples have had with the words "cup" and "baptism"?** (See Mark 10:37-40 in Understanding the Scripture.)

❖ Invite at least four volunteers to role-play a discussion among the disciples after they had heard the request of James and John. Try to include several perspectives: Perhaps some were truly angry with James and John because of their audacity in making such a request after Jesus has again announced his imminent suffering and death; perhaps some were angry because they wanted an equal share of the glory;

perhaps others were angry with themselves because they had not preempted James and John with their own requests.

❖ Help the observers react to the role-play by asking:

    (1) **In what ways do contemporary Christians act as James and John did?**

    (2) **What can we learn from James and John, from the response of the other disciples, and from Jesus?**

    (3) **In light of this story with its emphasis on suffering for the sake of others, what response can you make to people who proclaim a gospel of prosperity, that is, a teaching that belief in Christ brings material blessings and successful relationships?**

(3) Articulate an Understanding of Service to Others as Demonstrated by Jesus

❖ **Option:** Show any pictures you have collected. Invite the students to comment on the "rat race" they see illustrated. Ask:

    (1) **How do the people in the picture seem to relate to one another?**

    (2) **What would Jesus say about the way they treat (or ignore) each other?**

    (3) **How might this scene be different if a servant-leader were on hand?**

❖ Encourage the students to recall the summary you read of Hermann Hesse's book, *Journey to the East*, during the Gather to Learn activity. Ask:

    (1) **What similarities do you see between this story and Jesus' type of leadership?**

    (2) **If you were asked to define what Jesus means by the word "servant," what would you say?**

    (3) **Why do you think it is so difficult for many people to take on the role of the servant-leader?**

(4) Develop and Implement Specific Ways to Serve Others by Following Jesus' Example

❖ Brainstorm answers to this question and write ideas on newsprint: **What could we as a group do to live as Jesus' disciples by serving others?**

❖ Make plans to implement at least one of the group's ideas. Here's an example: Perhaps homeless people come to your church for food. The class could start a "Street Survival Kit" project by gathering items that most of us take for granted but that a homeless person may not be able to obtain easily. Create small cloth or canvas bags (available at places such as Walmart, grocery stores, and pharmacies) that include toiletries, non-perishable food, coupons for a local restaurant, pad and paper, socks, plastic eating utensils and cups, and a small New Testament. Ask people to contribute money to the project, or buy certain items, or fill a bag with supplies you have listed. Distribute these bags as people come seeking assistance.

(5) Continue the Journey

❖ Pray that all who have participated today will go forth to serve as Jesus taught his disciples to do.

❖ Read aloud this preparation for next week's lesson. You may also want to post it on newsprint for the students to copy.
- **Title: Coming of the Son of Man**
- **Background Scripture: Mark 13**
- **Lesson Scripture: Mark 13:14-27**

■ **Focus of the Lesson: People are curious about the end-times and wonder if there is hope for the world. What would satisfy their curiosity and give them hope? Jesus said that false messiahs and prophets would give signs, but that he would return with true power to call the people to himself.**

❖ Challenge the students to complete one or more of these activities for further spiritual growth related to this week's session. Post this information on newsprint for the students to copy.

(1) **Pray by name for the leaders in your church, asking God to empower them to lead by serving others.**

(2) **Take the role of a servant this week for someone who has no resources to repay you. If the recipient insists, suggest that he or she "pay" by performing an act of service for someone else.**

(3) **Be aware of stories you hear this week concerning how people are helping to meet the needs of others. Give thanks for those who are serving. Do whatever you can to serve others.**

❖ Sing or read aloud "Are Ye Able," which is based on Mark 10:35-45.

❖ Conclude today's session by leading the class in this benediction: **Let us go forth to worship and serve the Lord, in whom we have the blessed assurance of our salvation.**

UNIT 3: JESUS, THE PROMISED SERVANT-LEADER

COMING OF THE SON OF MAN

PREVIEWING THE LESSON

Lesson Scripture: Mark 13:14-27
Background Scripture: Mark 13
Key Verse: Mark 13:26

Focus of the Lesson:

People are curious about the end-times and wonder if there is hope for the world. What would satisfy their curiosity and give them hope? Jesus said that false messiahs and prophets would give signs, but that he would return with true power to call the people to himself.

Goals for the Learners:

(1) to explore what Jesus said about his coming in power as the Son of Man.
(2) to examine their own hopes and questions concerning the end-times.
(3) to reaffirm their belief in the one, true Messiah, Jesus of Nazareth as the hope for the world and to make a commitment not to be led astray.

Supplies:

Bibles, newsprint and marker, paper and pencils, hymnals

READING THE SCRIPTURE

NRSV
Mark 13:14-27

14"But when you see the desolating sacrilege set up where it ought not to be (let the reader understand), then those in Judea must flee to the mountains; 15the one on the housetop must not go down or enter the house to take anything away; 16the one in the field must not turn back to get a coat. 17Woe to those who are pregnant and to those who are nursing infants in those days! 18Pray

NIV
Mark 13:14-27

14"When you see 'the abomination that causes desolation' standing where it does not belong—let the reader understand—then let those who are in Judea flee to the mountains. 15Let no one on the roof of his house go down or enter the house to take anything out. 16Let no one in the field go back to get his cloak. 17How dreadful it will be in those days for pregnant women and that it may not be in winter. [19]For in those days there will be suffering, such as has not been from the beginning of the creation that God created until now, no, and never will be. [20]And if the Lord had not cut short those days, no one would be saved; but for the sake of the elect, whom he chose, he has cut short those days. [21]And if anyone says to you at that time, 'Look! Here is the Messiah!' or 'Look! There he is!'—do not believe it. [22]False messiahs and false prophets will appear and produce signs and omens, to lead astray, if possible, the elect. [23]But be alert; I have already told you everything.

[24]"But in those days, after that suffering,

the sun will be darkened,

and the moon will not give its light,

[25]and the stars will be falling from heaven,

and the powers in the heavens will be shaken.

[26]**Then they will see 'the Son of Man coming in clouds' with great power and glory.** [27]Then he will send out the angels, and gather his elect from the four winds, from the ends of the earth to the ends of heaven.

nursing mothers! [18]Pray that this will not take place in winter, [19]because those will be days of distress unequaled from the beginning, when God created the world, until now—and never to be equaled again. [20]If the Lord had not cut short those days, no one would survive. But for the sake of the elect, whom he has chosen, he has shortened them. [21]At that time if anyone says to you, 'Look, here is the Christ!' or, 'Look, there he is!' do not believe it. [22]For false Christs and false prophets will appear and perform signs and miracles to deceive the elect—if that were possible. [23]So be on your guard; I have told you everything ahead of time.

[24]"But in those days, following that distress,

" 'the sun will be darkened,

and the moon will not give its light;

[25]the stars will fall from the sky,

and the heavenly bodies will be shaken.'

[26]**"At that time men will see the Son of Man coming in clouds with great power and glory.** [27]And he will send his angels and gather his elect from the four winds, from the ends of the earth to the ends of the heavens.

UNDERSTANDING THE SCRIPTURE

Mark 13:1-13. We conclude this quarter's study with Mark's "Little Apocalypse." This is Mark's longest single discourse by Jesus and could be described as Jesus' farewell address to his disciples. The text is peppered with allusions to the social upheaval of the first century, as well as with prophetic allusions from the Hebrew Scriptures. Scholars are divided as to whether or not this apocalypse was set down in written form prior to or following the destruction of the Temple and the burning of Jerusalem in A.D. 70. Since convincing evidence is available for either point of view, it is best to acknowledge that this text comes from a period of extreme distress for the Jewish

population of Palestine. Some of the indicators of this distress in the chapter include war, natural disasters, flight from Jerusalem, desecration of the Temple, and destruction of the Temple. Indeed, the Temple served as a focal point. The disciples' comment on the Temple's large size led to the "Little Apocalypse." Jesus' response to the Temple was symbolic rather than practical. On a surface level, his words predicted the physical destruction of the Temple—an event that occurred. On a deeper level, however, Jesus alluded to the shift from the Temple sacrificial system to a new relationship with God available through his life, death, resurrection, and promised return. Sensing the deeper significance of his words, the disciples requested signs of the end-times. Jesus responded with various indicators of change. However, his emphasis was limited to signs, but expanded the necessity for courage and fidelity among the disciples. Although tempted by false prophets, caught up in wars, and shaken by earthquakes, the disciples were to remain calm; these were only indicators of changes yet to come. Even when traumatic times moved into the most intimate spheres—congregations and families—the disciples were to witness without fear.

Mark 13:14-23. Next, Jesus focused on the current events troubling the Jewish community. The sign he mentioned, the desolating sacrilege, was actually the final blow in a series of Rome's intrusions into Jewish faith and practice. Consider the accumulated impact of the intensification of Roman rule. Throughout the years of Jesus' ministry the display of Rome's military power annually strengthened during the Jerusalem festivals. Jesus, as any wise observer, knew it was only a matter of time before the emperor set his statue in the Gentile Court of the Temple. Such a statue broke the Jewish prohibition against image-making, as well as profaned the Temple with an idol of a self-declared Roman god. Jesus wisely warned: When the state went this far, it was a sign to run to the hills. Although acknowledging the great suffering caused by Rome, Jesus' words compelled a deeper-than-politics consideration. Whereas, most first-century apocalyptic writing included a blow-by-blow description of the destruction of the enemy, Jesus' apocalypse noticed what happened to the weakest members of the community: the pregnant women and the nursing mothers. He also alluded to the difficulty winter posed to the poor: flash floods in the wadis and limited provisions available to the poorest of the poor. The suffering was extreme, yet Jesus also called attention to God's mercy. Rather than pre-

dicting an exact number of days or years, Jesus affirmed that God measured the tribulation with mercy and compassionately stopped the tribulation to save the chosen ones. Once again, Jesus acknowledged the lure of false prophets and assured his disciples that his teachings sufficiently prepared them to discern right from wrong, good from evil.

Mark 13:24-27. In this section by subtle shifts and noteworthy omissions, Jesus' message of mercy encouraged his disciples. The cosmic images came from the prophets (see Isaiah 13:10; 34:4; and Ezekiel 32:7-8); however, in their original contexts such images introduced vivid scenes of judgment and destruction. Jesus, however, mentioned only the cosmic shifts, omitted the drama of judgment, and introduced Daniel's "Son of Man coming in the clouds" (Daniel 7:13-14). In Jesus' account, the Son of Man arrived after the suffering to dispatch angelic messengers to gather the elect. Just as the whole creation saw the Son of Man, so the redemption of the elect was universal in scope. Such a cosmic transformation broke the boundary of sight and words; thus, Jesus appealed to an ancient vision and to poetry to express God's mercy at the end of time.

Mark 13:28-37. The "Little Apocalypse" concludes with a collection of prosaic teaching woven together by key words: *near, pass away, know,* and *watch*. Since the disciples were curious about signs and timelines, Jesus reminded them of what they already knew: the growth of a fig tree, the endurance of God's word, and the situation of servants in the absence of a landowner. Around these simple illustrations, Jesus wove his most important teaching regarding the end time: Keep alert. The time of God's activity was, according to Jesus, always at hand. Therefore, the disciples were trained to look at the present time, see God's work, and join their efforts with God's. The nearness of God's reign did not release the disciples from their ministry; rather, it was an inspiration for their persistent witnesses. Regardless of the signs and the changes the disciples noticed, they were to be committed to the proclamation of the good news to all nations (Mark 13:10), rely on the Holy Spirit (13:11), and be alert for the arrival of God (the master of the house, 13:35). The "Little Apocalypse" ends as Jesus' ministry began: with an affirmation of the nearness of God's reign and a confidence in the gospel. "The time is fulfilled, the kingdom of God has come near; repent, and believe in the good news" (Mark 1:15).

INTERPRETING THE SCRIPTURE

Not Yet

What do you expect to hear from a spiritual leader facing death? Some desire a full rendering of wisdom and others look for supernatural knowledge. Some clamor for final instructions and others for a practical map of the future. In each Gospel, prior to his death, Jesus met the specific needs of his disciples. According to John, Jesus offers a new commandment, that you love one another, and enacts that commandment as a servant washing his disciples' feet (John 13:1-35). In Matthew, Jesus used the time in Jerusalem for intensive teaching in the Temple—a very practical approach to preparing his disciples for their future ministries (Matthew 21–25). Luke addressed the personal concerns of the disciples such as fear, betrayal, authority, self-reliance, and prayer (Luke 22:14-46). Mark's teaching prelude to the passion concluded with an apocalyptic discourse in response to the disciples' interest in the signs of the end-times.

In Mark, Jesus' response was practical and calm. Although the actual "signs of the times" indicated increased domination by Rome and, as a result, increased suffering for the Jewish people, Jesus first cautioned the disciples to remain within his path. He knew they would hear about Roman slaughters and terrorism, but these incidents were not to alarm them spiritually. Such social trauma indicated only that change was coming. Likewise, Jesus assured them that neither false prophets nor wars nor earthquakes signified the end time. Therefore, they were to persist in their ministries of proclamation, witness, and fidelity to Jesus' way.

Essentially, Jesus said, "not yet," and specifically Jesus meant: Hold fast to your faith and share in gospel ministry. While his words acknowledged the surrounding turmoil and personal suffering to be faced by the disciples, Jesus recommended patience instead of anxiety. Such calm continues to be needed in our contemporary world where voices still clamor to read the signs of the times and others rush to interpret a step-by-step arrival of God's realm.

Times of Turmoil

Jesus, however, also recognized that social unrest and Rome's domination would accelerate to a dangerous level. Thus, after calming the disciples, he gave them a sign: the emperor's statue in the Temple. This sign signaled the time to flee from Jerusalem and also provided an illustration of God's mercy. Whereas the apocalyptic literature of the Hebrew prophets and the first century was ripe with images of God's battles, destructions, and triumphs over enemies, Jesus' apocalyptic teachings were restrained. He did not speak of enemies or of their destruction. His restraint gave witness to a steadfast principle of Jesus' ministry: God was in charge.

Although Jesus claimed a spiritual relationship with God as a son, he never presumed to know God's mysterious ways. Jesus was content in his relationship to God:

It was sufficient to be God's child, to share in God's Spirit, and to do God's work in the world. His humility was evident as he announced the sign indicating a time to flee. His disciples were instructed to leave quickly without arrangements, to be confident in God's providence, and to be aware of the weak and the poor for whom fleeing would pose special problems. Although the sign indicated great danger, Jesus guided his disciples toward confidence in God and compassion toward those in need. Moreover, Jesus reminded his disciples that regardless of their circumstances, they were always within God's mercy. Indeed, after a time God would, by mercy, intervene. This was a very gospel-oriented apocalypse! Jesus' apocalyptic focus paralleled his teaching focus: Trust in God, show mercy to the needy, and wait for God's mercy. Jesus' apocalypse was without drama, dread, or destruction; it was the exact opposite from the ordinary emphasis of apocalyptic literature, then and now.

Vision and Poetry

Any piece of writing described as apocalyptic must include the basic element of unveiling the mysterious ways of God. Mark's "Little Apocalypse" includes such a glimpse into God's realm in verses 24 through 27. The language was scriptural and the images well-known to a first-century audience. The message, however, was clearly Christian, an obvious break from the traditional apocalyptic trajectory. After Jesus' description of God's restraint of suffering and God's merciful gift of an abbreviated tribulation, Jesus simply said, "after that suffering" (Mark 13:24) and described that which cannot be described: God's final act of intervention and redemption.

If taken literally, the images do not work. If the sun, moon, and stars are darkened, then nothing can be seen; how, then, will all see the Son of Man coming in clouds? If the powers in the heavens are shaken (and pre-sumably cast down with the stars), how will everyone witness the heavenly power and glory accompanying the arrival of the Son of Man? Literally, the images do not seem plausible, but as a vision of the arrival of God's glory on earth, these images announce transformation. Because the point of the images was the radiance of God's glory, all other signs of illumination receded. Because the purpose of the images was the presence of God's realm on earth, all creation was called to attention. Because the content of the end time was redemption, Jesus omitted the gory scenes of enemies suffering.

The disciples were directed to keep their attention on glory. Moreover, they were to notice how glory spread throughout creation as angelic messengers gathered God's elect. But what of evil? What of enemies? What of God-deniers? What of the wicked? Jesus was content to leave them in God's hands. Perhaps we should too.

Remember and Watch

Human curiosity is a blessing from God. By curiosity science, art, and human societies develop. With curiosity individuals explore their inner and spiritual lives. Through curiosity come countless inventions and advances that support the common good. Yet, as with all blessings, curiosity requires direction. Perhaps this need for direction motivated Jesus as he shared his apocalypse with his disciples.

The disciples arrived in Jerusalem in a state of amazement and fear (Mark 10:32). Their fear was provoked by Jesus' predictions of his death in Jerusalem; their amazement intensified as they saw the grandeur of Temple and religious pageantry. This mixture of fear and amazement inspired their curiosity. Jesus, however, felt their curiosity lacked direction. When the disciples expressed amazement over the monumental beauty of the Temple, Jesus calmly noted that every stone would be overturned.

When the disciples asked for signs, Jesus discussed the current situation and cautioned them to be faithful witnesses. When he recognized their interest in the end-times, Jesus lifted up God's mercy and refrained from mentioning God's judgment on evil.

In other words, throughout this text Jesus redirected curiosity to the spiritual realities of dependence on God, endurance in times of turmoil, and fidelity in the face of persecution. In keeping with this redirection of curiosity, Jesus' apocalypse ended with a litany weaving together the disciples' common wisdom and his teachings. Indeed, Jesus was assuring them that they had sufficient knowledge of God's ways from his teachings and from their own life experiences. Imagine that: Jesus trusted his disciples to rely on his words and to pay attention to their world. Imagine this: Jesus continues to trust the contemporary church. We are blessed with four Gospels, a grand collection of early writings, a history of profound theological reflection, a community of saints, and the ever-present direction of the Holy Spirit. Yet we, as the original disciples, are cautioned to remember what we have learned from Christian living and to watch for glimpses of God's grace every day. We are urged to live so as to be prepared for the day when the Son of Man will return.

SHARING THE SCRIPTURE

Preparing Our Hearts

Explore this week's devotional reading, found in Isaiah 2:5-12. Here the prophet announces the judgment that awaits the proud and arrogant in the Northern Kingdom (Israel). The sin of idolatry was particularly condemned. The Israelites did experience judgment, for they were later led into captivity in Babylon. Do you believe a day of judgment is coming? If so, how are you preparing for it? What changes do you need to make to live according to God's will?

Pray that you and the adult learners will repent and be prepared for the return of Christ.

Preparing Our Minds

Study the background Scripture from Mark 13 and the lesson Scripture from Mark 13:14-27. Think about what would give hope to those who are curious about the end-times.

Write on newsprint:

❑ partial sentence to be completed for "Reaffirm Belief in the One, True Messiah, Jesus of Nazareth, as the Hope for the World and Make a Commitment Not to Be Led Astray."

❑ information for next week's lesson, found under "Continue the Journey."

❑ activities for further spiritual growth in "Continue the Journey."

LEADING THE CLASS

(1) Gather to Learn

❖ Welcome the class members and introduce any guests.

❖ Pray that those who are participating today will be watchful and prepare for the return of Christ.

❖ Read: **Many cultures and religions have teachings about the end-times or times of major transition. Given the upheavals in the world, many people believe that we are living in the end-times and, therefore, are searching for information about what will happen and seeking hope about the future. As an example, perhaps you are familiar with the Mayan** belief that the end of the Great Cycle of the Mayan Long Count calendar will occur on December 21, 2012, the winter solstice. Cosmic events, such as the alignment of our solar system with the Milky Way galaxy of which we are a part, will occur. This winter solstice will not signal the end of the world but herald the start of a new era of light, truth, and peace.

❖ Ask: **How is your concept of the end-times similar to and different from that of the Mayan people?**

❖ Read aloud today's focus statement: **People are curious about the end-times and wonder if there is hope for the world. What would satisfy their curiosity and give them hope? Jesus said that false messiahs and prophets would give signs, but that he would return with true power to call the people to himself.**

(2) Explore What Jesus Said About His Coming in Power as the Son of Man

❖ Use information from Mark 13:1-13 in Understanding the Scripture to set the context for today's reading.

❖ Choose a volunteer to read Mark 13:14-27, in which Jesus speaks about the signs of the times and the return of the Son of Man.

❖ Explore with the class the images of confusion and suffering found in Mark 13:14-19. Use information from Understanding the Scripture to help the students to better understand these images. Point out that housetops (13:15) were flat. People used them to dry their vegetables, as sleeping quarters, and a place for prayer. An outdoor staircase led to the roof, so people would have hurried down the stairs without going into the house to pick up their belongings.

❖ Look at Mark 13:24-27. Ask:

    (1) How do these images make you feel? (Students may express a broad range of emotion, from joy that Christ has returned, to feelings of unpreparedness and uncertainty, to terror.)

    (2) How might these images prod Christians to make changes in their actions, attitudes, or beliefs? As you consider the actions, attitudes, and beliefs of the body of Christ today, what kinds of changes seem necessary?

(3) Examine the Learners' Own Hopes and Questions Concerning the End-times

❖ Invite the adults to a period of meditation in which they talk with God about what they really believe concerning Christ's return. Do they expect him to come again during their lifetime? Do they ever expect him to come? What drives their expectations—the Bible, teachings of their church, popular culture?

❖ Encourage volunteers to state their beliefs, hopes, and questions concerning the end-times. Be aware that some class members will readily accept the teachings in Mark 13, but there are other Christians who feel that because Jesus has not returned it is highly unlikely that he will. You may gently prod the class members to explain why they believe as they do, but do not try to force a change in their opinion. Leave that to the Holy Spirit.

❖ Close with this question: **What do you think the church needs to be doing now to help people prepare for Christ's return?**

(4) Reaffirm Belief in the One, True Messiah, Jesus of Nazareth, as the Hope for the World and Make a Commitment Not to Be Led Astray

❖ Read: **Jesus himself said, "Heaven and earth will pass away, but my words will not pass away. But about that day or hour no ones knows, neither the angels in heaven, nor the Son, but only the Father" (Mark 13:31-32). Yet, throughout history people have been led astray by false prophets who claimed that Jesus would return on a certain date. While writing this lesson, your editor googled the term** "failed prophecies for the end of the world"—and got 740,000 hits! Assuredly, many of these websites contain information on the same prophecies, and not all of these prophesies relate to the Christian church, but nearly three quarters of a million is an astounding number.

❖ Discuss this question: **Why do you think people are so easily led astray by false prophets, some of whom even urge their followers to sell all they have and gather together to be ready for Christ's return?**

❖ Distribute paper and pencils. Post this partial sentence on newsprint and invite the students to complete it: **I commit myself wholeheartedly to Jesus, the Messiah of God, because . . .**

❖ Suggest that the students refer to their commitment throughout the week.

(5) Continue the Journey

❖ Pray that all who have come today will remain fast in their commitment to Jesus, God's Messiah.

❖ Read aloud this preparation for next week's lesson. You may also want to post it on newsprint for the students to copy.

■ **Title: Instructions About Worship**
■ **Background Scripture: 1 Timothy 2:1-6; 3:14-16**
■ **Lesson Scripture: 1 Timothy 2:1-6; 3:14-16**
■ **Focus of the Lesson:** There is a renewed interest in ancient spiritual practices in today's society.

What gives our spiritual search meaning? Citing an ancient hymn, 1 Timothy affirms that Christ is the mediator of all truth about God.

❖ Challenge the students to complete one or more of these activities for further spiritual growth related to this week's session. Post this information on newsprint for the students to copy.

(1) Investigate theories of premillenialism and postmillennialism using the Internet, dictionary of religions, or other resource. Where do you stand on these ideas about the end-times and the return of the Son of Man?

(2) Locate examples of apocalyptic artwork. Which of these best capture the mood and types of events that Jesus referred to in Mark 13?

(3) Read a fictionalized version of the end-times, such as a book from the *Left Behind* series by Tim LaHaye and Jerry Jenkins. How does the portrait of the end-times painted here square with your understanding of the last days before Christ's return and his coming?

❖ Sing or read aloud "Lo, He Comes with Clouds Descending."

❖ Conclude today's session by leading the class in this benediction: **Let us go forth to worship and serve the Lord, in whom we have the blessed assurance of our salvation.**

THIRD QUARTER
We Worship God

MARCH 6, 2011–MAY 29, 2011

The spring quarter offers a New Testament survey of worship in the early church. We will be investigating hymns, prayers, apocalyptic visions, and letters of instruction that reveal the spiritual culture and the practices of the first Christians. The biblical texts we will explore include 1 Timothy, 2 Timothy, Jude, Mark, Matthew, Philippians, and Revelation.

During the four lessons of Unit 1, "A Guide for Worship Leaders," we will study the instructions given to Timothy regarding spiritual leadership of the church. This unit begins on March 6 with a lesson from 1 Timothy 2:1-6 and 3:14-16 that provides "Instructions about Worship" to help believers in their search for meaning. First Timothy 3:1-13 is the basis for the session on March 13, which examines the "Qualifications of Worship Leaders" to help the church choose good leaders. On March 20 we will learn how people "Prepare for Leadership," as explained in 1 Timothy 4:6-16. "Worship Inspires Service," a session rooted in 1 Timothy 5:1-22, concludes this unit on March 27 with a look at how we treat relatives and church members as family.

Unit 2, "Ancient Words of Praise," is a five-session series that takes us through the final weeks of Lent into Easter and to the week beyond. The unit begins on April 3 as we unpack 2 Timothy 2:8-15 to consider how we communicate our personal beliefs in a session entitled "Remembering Jesus Christ." A familiar benediction closes the reading on April 10 from Jude 17-25, reminding us that "Praise Builds Us Up." "Hosanna!" is the key word for this Palm Sunday lesson on April 17 from the Gospel of Mark, chapter 11, verses 1-11, where we hear those who lined the streets of Jerusalem lavishing praise upon Jesus as he entered the city. On April 24, we turn to the account of the first Easter morning found in Matthew 28:1-17 to hear the good news that "Christ Is Risen!" The second unit closes on May 1 with "The Christ Hymn," familiar words of praise among early believers, as recorded in Philippians 2:1-11.

Unit 3, "John's Vision of Worship," is drawn solely from The Revelation to John. The texts we will study focus on worship and praise that inspire hope in God's new heaven and earth. On May 8 we look at Revelation 4 in a session called "Heavenly Worship" to see how God communicates with us through symbols. "Thankful Worship," the lesson for May 15 that is based on Revelation 7:9-17, points us in the direction we need to look in times of trouble. Revelation 21, the text for May 22, promises new beginnings in a study entitled "All Things New." The spring quarter concludes on May 29 as we consider "Tree of Life," a lesson from Revelation 22 that helps us to appreciate the abundance with which God has blessed us.

MEET OUR WRITER

THE REVEREND JOHN INDERMARK

The Reverend John Indermark lives in southwest Washington state. John received his Master of Divinity degree from Eden Theological Seminary in St. Louis in 1976. Ordained in the United Church of Christ that year, John served as a parish pastor for sixteen years and now pursues a ministry of writing. He writes curricula for several series, including *Seasons of the Spirit*, *The Present Word*, and *The New International Lesson Annual*. By the time this material is published, John will have completed his eleventh book with Upper Room Books of Nashville. His most recent book is *Do Not Live Afraid: Faith in a Fearful World*.

John's wife of 35 years, Judy, is the lead dispatcher for Pacific County 911. John and Judy enjoy beachcombing, traveling in the Southwest and British Columbia, occasional flyfishing, and more than occasional gardening and landscaping.

THE BIG PICTURE: WORSHIPING GOD

This quarter offers an exploration of worship using a variety of texts from the New Testament Epistles, two of the Gospels, and finally the Book of Revelation. Some of the passages give guidance about worship and in particular to those who are entrusted with leadership for the worshiping community. Some of the passages consist of material it is believed were used in the liturgies of the early Christian church, and perhaps even originated in the community's worship before finding their way into these writings (for example, the poetic "Christ Hymn" in Philippians 2:5-11). The concluding passages all come from Revelation, traditionally attributed, as with the Fourth Gospel, to John. These passages reflect the author's visions of heaven and acts of worship encountered there.

This article includes two parts. The first will be an overview of the theme of worship from a more "wide-angle" view. Clearly, not everything that could be said about worship will be, but this portion will invite reflection on what we mean when talking about worship in our own experience. From there, the second half of the article will take a closer look at the specific outline of this study and provide some background material about the passages (and underlying books) that provide the focus.

An Overview of Worship

At several points during my pastoral sojourns, I have had the opportunity to serve in interim or transitional ministries in Presbyterian congregations. During my first such experience, I was introduced to a set of priorities set out by the denomination that were called "The Great Ends of the Church." Among those was: "the maintenance of divine worship."

"The maintenance of divine worship." The phrasing seems a little awkward for describing one of the overriding missions of the church. Maintenance sounds more suited to the janitorial care of a building, or filling potholes in a street. But maintenance of worship? Actually, I suppose the custodial understanding of maintenance has some bearing on our care and keeping of worship. Potholes appear and ceilings crack when we confuse worship with entertainment, or when we think that anything that revs up our emotions or stimulates our minds is automatically worshipful. Worship falls into disrepair when we forget why we engage in its actions, much less why we gather with friends and neighbors and sometimes strangers in large rooms with furniture we do not usually have at home. So maybe maintenance isn't such a bad word after all.

To begin, consider one emphasis in that phrase: maintenance of divine worship. A lot of things pass for worship these days. Folk masses and prayer meetings, youth rallies and follow-the-bulletin liturgies, seeker services and Quakered silences, hands-in-the-air revivals and carefully-staged television productions: There are a lot of choices of styles and forms out there. Besides that, a lot of places pass for sanctuaries. An ocean beach in early morning or a trout stream when mayflies take to flight describes two sanctuaries I infrequently but devoutly seek out. No doubt you have yours as well. And when we add them to all the high-steepled or low-ceilinged halls we traditionally call sanctuary, the settings for worship multiply.

But remember, the emphasis is on maintenance of *divine* worship. Neither the setting nor the form of worship guarantees that what we do in the sanctuaries will be *divine* in orientation. I once came across this description of worship's purpose: *The central aspect of worship is the feeling of being at one with God.* Worship that is divine brings us into encounter with God.

Sometimes that experience of oneness happens for me in the middle of the trout stream, but sometimes I'm too focused on keeping my backcast out of the brush. Sometimes that experience of oneness happens for me in the middle of stained-glass sanctuaries, but sometimes I'm too focused on what happened yesterday or what I have to do when I get home. Distractions occur no matter the setting. Most are personal—others are not. So for us who feel comfortable with ritual and written orders, if an element is left out or done out of order, wonderings about why that happened or whether someone will please correct the pastor or liturgist or communion server on the miscue may suddenly blot out the next three or five or more minutes.

The central aspect of worship is the feeling of being at one with God. The "maintenance of divine worship" has that as its priority, to keep encounter with God the primary consideration above all else. Forms and settings, styles and hours, all take second place to that concern. In one sense, worship as being at one with God stands at the heart of Jesus' exchange with the Samaritan woman in John 4:19-24. Their discussion initially involved misunderstanding over the place of worship: Samaritans worshiped on Mount Gerizim, Jews on Mount Zion, and never the twain shall meet. Or so it seemed. But Jesus urged that the particular location of worship was not the point. Place does not define worship: *Those who worship God must worship in spirit and truth.*

In spirit and truth. The worshipful encounter with God, whose aim is this experience of being at one with God, takes us into the realm of Spirit: our own, and that of God. Spirit asserts that worship is never only the sum of its liturgical parts. Spirit is the recognition that worship is always more than what meets the eye, or ear, or what's included in or omitted from the bulletin. Spirit enables us to consider that, in whatever place we gather in community for whatever form of liturgy we use, our companions are not only the folks with whom we share a common city or neighborhood or even theology. Spirit moves us to confess the very presence of God in our midst. Spirit moves us to worship that is experiential—worship that stirs the emotions, stimulates the mind, challenges the will, and engages our bodies and actions. The Greek and Hebrew words for "spirit" literally mean "breath." Worship in spirit is worship that breathes God's presence.

In spirit probably accounts for why music has always been a vital element of liturgy. When one sings, or even just listens, it is not individual notes and chords and words kept in precise order that capture our imaginations. A director once told my community's choir at a rehearsal that, in the climax to the song *Beautiful Savior*, if we hit our parts just right, notes would resonate that no one was singing. And he was right. We know it when some songs send chills down our spines. Music inspires because it aspires. It seeks something beyond the mechanical rendering of certain wavelengths vibrating eardrums. It seeks inspiration to touch the heart.

But as Jesus' words to the Samaritan woman reveal, worship that evokes encounter with God involves not only spirit but truth. We encounter God in worship when we encounter what is real and true: about ourselves, about the world, about the character of God. In the context of Jesus' words to the Samaritan woman, worship that is true brings us into encounter with the God revealed in Jesus Christ. And worship that is true, in those terms, is worship that inevitably leads to service. God's love for the world did not culminate in God's building a big cathedral so everybody could see God's sacred majesty. God's love for the world resulted in God's sending of Christ as a servant to reveal God's grace . . . and Christ's sending of us to do no less.

For some, the element of *truth* in worship is most identified with worship's forms, or the lack thereof. There are those who say worship would not be worship without bulletin or prayer book. Others declare worship must come from the heart, and therefore needs spontaneity unshackled by structure. Which is true? To stretch Jesus' encounter with the Samaritan woman a bit: The subordination of *place* of worship to spirit and truth also encourages the subordination of form of worship to spirit and truth. To ask which form of worship is right is to miss the point, and that point is: *the central aspect of worship is the feeling of being at one with God.* Whether you encounter God in spirit and in truth through the rhythm of liturgy, or through a spontaneous free-flow of praise and prayer, you are at worship.

That might seem like an innocent affirmation free of cost or consequences. But the crunch comes when we consider its practical consequences. Some recent literature on worship and the church argues that young adults tend to favor nonliturgical or at least noninstitutionally dominated forms of worship. Now we can argue whether that's a good thing or bad, whether it comes from watching too much MTV or other shows built on constantly changing images and sounds, until we're blue in the face. But from what those who work in young adults ministry say, that's just the way it is. That can present a problem—or, let's say more positively, a challenge—to the church that relies on three foundations for worship: tradition, tradition, and tradition. For congregations where the order of worship used locally is held on approximately the same level as the incarnation of Jesus: How will we touch and reach an entire generation that is far more informal? And, on the other side of the coin, how will churches where everything is new and different every week, where the only "tradition" is constant change, be able to meet the worship needs of those who value the rhythm of liturgy and lectionaries and a sense of continuity?

There are options. Blending both styles in one service is possible but difficult. Like rotating communion styles every other month, there will always be people unhappy with spontaneity and others disgruntled with liturgical elements. Offering a second service is ideal, but costly in terms of time and "footwork" needed not just to get it off the ground but to keep it in the air. For with two services, you need communication and fellowship programs that intentionally incorporate both sets of folks, so you don't end up with two congregations whose only common ground is this building and a pastor.

Like other maintenance work, to go back to our starting point in this conversation regarding liturgy, the maintenance of divine worship involves hard work and open lines of communication. It is maintenance that continually reminds us that the forms of worship we employ are secondary to our encounter with God. It is maintenance that continually calls us to worship in spirit, which is to say, worship that engages the whole of our being—mind and emotion, body and will—with the Spirit of God abroad among us. It is maintenance that continually calls us to worship in truth, which is to say, worship that engages the world as it is, and us as we are, in the presence of the God who in Jesus Christ calls us to gracious service.

When all is said and done, divine worship is at it always has been: the experience of standing on holy ground, realizing that the God who made all things and brought redemption in Christ is the God before whom we stand. Whenever and however we enable persons to experience the reality of God's presence, we maintain worship filled with spirit and with truth.

Looking at the Quarter—and Scriptures—Ahead

The first unit of this study considers the theme of "A Guide for Worship Leaders." All of its texts come from the First Letter of Paul to Timothy.

The first session engages a text that offers some counsel about the scope of prayers to be offered in worship, and the third session explores a text where one verse singles out the public reading of Scripture along with preaching and teaching. Beyond that, however, the vast majority of the verses taken up in all of these passages and sessions relate to qualifications for those who are entrusted with leadership in the community, including worship.

Does that seem overly puritanical to you? It would, if it leads to an obsession about leaders having somehow to be perfect—or at least perfect in the issues that most concern this faction or that in the church. Yet, in reacting to such attitudes that at times have characterized the church's approach, sometimes the pendulum has swung too far in another direction. For what 1 Timothy rightly stresses is that a concern for character is a right and good thing in assessing those who will lead the community, particularly worship.

Perhaps nowhere are the implications for that more clear than in cases where clergy become involved in ethical or sexual misconduct with parishioners. The victims of such behavior often report severe problems with their ensuing spiritual journey. The one they trusted to holy tasks of interpreting Scripture and presiding at the communion table betrayed that trust, and the abuse levies a heavy toll on that individual's faith.

The second unit of this study is entitled "Ancient Words of Praise." Each of the five session passages contain portions that are believed to have been part of the liturgy of that day's community. Second Timothy 2:11-13 includes what sounds like an early confession of faith, while the closing passage includes the very familiar words of Philippians 2:8-15, strongly believed to have been a hymn that either the writer composed for this epistle or, more likely, a hymn already in use by and known to this worshiping community that the author incorporates into the urging of this chapter. In between, a brief "benediction" is included from one of the shortest New Testament Epistles, Jude. Palm Sunday and Easter Sunday interrupt the use of epistles in this quarter with two Gospel passages that incorporate worship-oriented materials of thanksgiving and commissioning.

Finally, the quarter ends with four sessions based on passages from Revelation. Revelation is a work filled not only with extravagant visions but also with worship. That is not accidental. Many scholars believe that the persecutions and hardships that generated this apocalyptic ("end time") work centered around the refusal of some Christians to engage in emperor worship. It wasn't so much that Rome demanded people to stop believing in their gods. Worship was (and is!) a sign of allegiance, and Rome insisted at times on pain of death that veneration of the emperor was required of its subjects. Worship in Revelation is not an innocent activity. And its place in the visions of heaven serves as a coded challenge that worship belongs to God and God alone, and that Rome's power—presently so dominant—will be rendered impotent by God's coming realm. Those who take issue with bringing politics into worship miss the point of Revelation's underlying witness: that worship can be the most radical political statement of all. Namely, allegiance (worship) is owed only to One—and that One is God and the "Lamb," Revelation's predominant symbol of Christ, as one whose power comes not from inflicting death but overcoming it.

CLOSE-UP:
WORSHIP IN THE
EARLY CHRISTIAN CHURCH

Worship is the theme for this quarter's study, and so we turn to the Bible and to an ancient account written by a well-known spiritual leader to see how the church worshiped. Since all of the first Christians were Jewish, it is understandable that their worship was heavily influenced by the synagogue services.

Read the following information and invite the class to comment on how worship in the early church seems similar to and different from worship in your church. If time permits, encourage volunteers to read aloud some of the biblical references that follow and add others they can recall.

A look at the Bible reveals at least six elements of worship, though not an order for the service: *preaching* (Acts 20:7; 1 Corinthians 14:19, 29-36); *the reading of Scripture* (Colossians 4:16; 1 Thessalonians 5:27); *prayer* (Acts 2:42; 1 Corinthians 14:14, 16); *singing* (Ephesians 5:19; Colossians 3:16); *sacraments of baptism and the Lord's Supper* (Matthew 28:19; Acts 2:41; 1 Corinthians 11:18-34); *offering* (1 Corinthians 16:1-2).

In Chapter 67 of *The First Apology of Justin Martyr*, who was born about A.D. 100 and beheaded in A.D. 165 for his witness to Christ, we read about worship during the second century:

And on the day called Sunday, all who live in cities or in the country gather together to one place, and the memoirs of the apostles or the writings of the prophets are read, as long as time permits; then, when the reader has ceased, the president verbally instructs, and exhorts to the imitation of these good things. Then we all rise together and pray, and, as we before said, when our prayer is ended, bread and wine and water are brought, and the president in like manner offers prayers and thanksgivings, according to his ability, and the people assent, saying Amen; and there is a distribution to each, and a participation of that over which thanks have been given, and to those who are absent a portion is sent by the deacons. And they who are well to do, and willing, give what each thinks fit; and what is collected is deposited with the president, who succours the orphans and widows and those who, through sickness or any other cause, are in want, and those who are in bonds and the strangers sojourning among us, and in a word takes care of all who are in need. But Sunday is the day on which we all hold our common assembly, because it is the first day on which God, having wrought a change in the darkness and matter, made the world; and Jesus Christ our Saviour on the same day rose from the dead. For He was crucified on the day before that of Saturn (Saturday); and on the day after that of Saturn, which is the day of the Sun, having appeared to His apostles and disciples, He taught them these things, which we have submitted to you also for your consideration.

FAITH IN ACTION: EVALUATING WORSHIP EXPERIENCES

Over the last several decades worship in many of our churches has changed considerably. Much scholarly research has been done to determine how the ancient church worshiped. As a result, hymnals, books of worship, and prayer books of many denominations reflect this interest in returning to our roots, while at the same time drawing in the congregation with words and music that are more familiar to us. Many churches use a variety of worship styles—traditional, contemporary, emerging, seeker, blended—to reach people for Christ. While some church members are well satisfied with their worship, other congregations are engaged in what some have dubbed "worship wars" as each "side" contends for their preference.

Post the following questionnaire concerning worship on newsprint for the students to copy on paper you will distribute. Encourage them to complete the questionnaire themselves, poll three to five people this week, and compare the answers they hear. Set a time for the students to report to the class on what they learned.

(1) On a scale of 1–5, with one being the "not at all" and 5 being "essential," how would you rate the importance of church worship in your life?

(2) Name one or more things that "turn you off" about worship services you have attended.

(3) Name three activities (for example, singing, praying, preaching, taking Communion) that draw you close to God during worship.

(4) How would you describe the kind of service that ushers you into God's presence? Think here about the kind of music, sermon, level of formality, and so on that feels most spiritual to you?

(5) If you could add one element to your "regular" service to make it more meaningful for you, what would that be?

(6) What advice would you give to the person who selects the music?

(7) On a scale of 1–5, with one being "not at all" and 5 being "extremely," how would you rate the sermons in terms of helping you to grow in your knowledge of the Bible?

(8) On a scale of 1–5, with one being "not at all" and 5 being "extremely," how would you rate the sermons in terms of helping you to relate the Bible to your daily life?

(9) Think, for example, about seating, altar arrangement, being greeted at the door, flowers, banners, and friendliness of the people. How would you describe the emotional impact that the atmosphere of the church has on you?

(10) Think about the accessibility of your sanctuary. Are people who have mobility issues, hearing impairments, sight impairments, and other physical challenges welcomed by such things as handicapped parking spaces, elevators, ramps, large print bulletins and hymnals, wireless hearing devices, and a sign language interpreter? If not, what changes need to be made to include everyone in your worship space?

(11) How are children and teenagers welcomed into the worship service and encouraged to participate—or are they?

(12) What difference does attending worship seem to make in your life?

UNIT 1: A GUIDE FOR WORSHIP LEADERS
INSTRUCTIONS ABOUT WORSHIP

PREVIEWING THE LESSON

Lesson Scripture: 1 Timothy 2:1-6; 3:14-16
Background Scripture: 1 Timothy 2:1-6; 3:14-16
Key Verse: 1 Timothy 2:5

Focus of the Lesson:
There is a renewed interest in ancient spiritual practices in today's society. What gives our spiritual search meaning? Citing an ancient hymn, 1 Timothy affirms that Christ is the mediator of all truth about God.

Goals for the Learners:
(1) to uncover the literary and theological elements in the texts of this early creed and hymn (2:5-6).
(2) to define their understanding of the Christian faith.
(3) to create a personal statement of faith.

Pronunciation Guide:
Artemis (ahr' tuh mis)
chronos (khron'os)
diaspora (dee as' por ah)
ekklesia (ek klay see ah')
kairos (kahee ros')

poieo (poy eh' o)
proseuche (pros yoo khay')
Shema (Sheh' muh)
thelo (thel' o)

Supplies:
Bibles, newsprint and marker, paper and pencils, hymnals

READING THE SCRIPTURE

NRSV
1 Timothy 2:1-6

¹First of all, then, I urge that supplications, prayers, intercessions, and thanksgivings be made for everyone, ²for kings and all

NIV
1 Timothy 2:1-6

¹I urge, then, first of all, that requests, prayers, intercession and thanksgiving be made for everyone—²for kings and all those

who are in high positions, so that we may lead a quiet and peaceable life in all godliness and dignity. ³This is right and is acceptable in the sight of God our Savior, ⁴who desires everyone to be saved and to come to the knowledge of the truth. ⁵For

> there is one God;
> there is also one mediator between
>   God and humankind,
> Christ Jesus, himself human,

⁶   who gave himself a ransom for all —this was attested at the right time.

1 Timothy 3:14-16

¹⁴I hope to come to you soon, but I am writing these instructions to you so that, ¹⁵if I am delayed, you may know how one ought to behave in the household of God, which is the church of the living God, the pillar and bulwark of the truth. ¹⁶Without any doubt, the mystery of our religion is great:

> He was revealed in flesh,
>   vindicated in spirit,
> seen by angels,
>   proclaimed among Gentiles,
>   believed in throughout the world,
>   taken up in glory.

in authority, that we may live peaceful and quiet lives in all godliness and holiness. ³This is good, and pleases God our Savior, ⁴who wants all men to be saved and to come to a knowledge of the truth. **⁵For there is one God and one mediator between God and men, the man Christ Jesus,** ⁶who gave himself as a ransom for all men—the testimony given in its proper time.

1 Timothy 3:14-16

¹⁴Although I hope to come to you soon, I am writing you these instructions so that, ¹⁵if I am delayed, you will know how people ought to conduct themselves in God's household, which is the church of the living God, the pillar and foundation of the truth. ¹⁶Beyond all question, the mystery of godliness is great:

> He appeared in a body,
>   was vindicated by the Spirit,
> was seen by angels,
>   was preached among the nations,
> was believed on in the world,
>   was taken up in glory.

UNDERSTANDING THE SCRIPTURE

1 Timothy 2:1. Having used the initial chapter to provide Timothy with instructions on countering misleading teachers in this community, Paul moves on to instructions on worship practices. This verse offers a list of various forms of prayer that are to be made "for everyone" by the community. "Supplications" suggests prayers invoking God's providential care. "Intercessions" suggests prayers offered on behalf of individuals or groups in particular need. "Thanksgivings" express gratitude. Why the more generic term of "prayers" is used in the middle of this list of more specific forms of

prayer, or how it would be distinguished from the others, is unclear. The Greek verb attached to these forms of prayer is *poieo*, translated elsewhere as "to do." Prayer is not a passive activity. Prayer involves action. The verb subtly connects our prayers with the spirit of James 2:14, which questions offering words of blessing for another in need but taking no action on their behalf.

1 Timothy 2:2. The "everyone" for whom these prayers are to be made in verse 1 now takes on a narrower focus in verse 2 by singling out "kings and all who are in high positions." Other Pauline passages urge a respecting of civil authorities, most notably Romans 13:1-7. Here, a similar attitude is taken in regards to prayers on their behalf. One underlying reason comes in the second half of this verse: so that the community may experience a "quiet and peaceable life." Some commentators hear this counsel as growing out of the community's precarious situation within the empire, especially those who date its writing to the era near the end of the first century when hostility if not outright persecution had increased. This desire for stability and calm was driven by the community's desire for "godliness and dignity." Both of these terms are used extensively, and somewhat uniquely, by the Timothy correspondence to reflect a life of religious obligation and reverence that would, in turn, cause no offense to those outside the community.

1 Timothy 2:3-4. These verses continue the justification for prayers for those in authority by turning to theological reasons for doing so: It is "right and acceptable" to God. This verse attaches the title of "Savior" to God, as had been done in 1 Timothy 1:1 and would be again in 4:10. Most other instances of "Savior" in the New Testament are in reference to Jesus. Identifying God as Savior would have been a natural affirmation for Jewish Christians to make, as Judaism clearly regards God as Savior. Doing so here may seek to affirm for an increasingly Gentile church its Jewish moorings. "Everyone" is used once again, only now in reference to those whom God desires to save. The nature of salvation in this verse, in a way consistent with the Timothy correspondence, is joined to knowledge of the "truth." The Greek word translated as "truth" in the NRSV is used six times in 1 Timothy and six times in 2 Timothy. Some scholars see in this a shift in the emphasis upon faith from an act of trust in the earlier Pauline works now to a particular body of knowledge ("truth"). The previous concern in chapter 1 to address false teachers lends itself to that view.

1 Timothy 2:5-6. This is the first of two sets of verses in today's passage believed to have originated in an early Christian hymn. The opening affirmation of "one God" hearkens back to the Shema of Deuteronomy 6:4 ("Hear, O Israel: The LORD is our God, the LORD alone"), to be recited by pious Jews daily. These words, as with the affirmation of God as Savior, provide another hint at the Jewish moorings of this writer and the originating community of the hymn. The verses go on to identify Jesus as "mediator," a title also used in Hebrews 8:6, 9:15, and 12:24. There, Christ is mediator of a new covenant. Here in Timothy, Christ's mediation is between God and humankind, a mediation the author associates with Christ's humanity. The nature of the mediation in this passage comes in Christ being a "ransom." That assertion is also made by Matthew 20:28 and Mark 10:45—with one major difference. The Gospel writers indicate this ransom was "for many." First Timothy, however, asserts this ransom was "for all." The reference to "right time" is not specific to any one event. Rather, the meaning comes from the Greek word translated as time: *kairos*. *Kairos* is not time measured by calendars or watches (that would be *chronos*). The meaning of *kairos* is more of a fitting season that has come.

1 Timothy 3:14-15. As in other epistles, Paul indicates the epistle results from the possibility of his being delayed—whether by weather, travel issues, or imprisonment is not specified. The instructions here hearken back to the opening thirteen verses of chapter 3 that concern themselves with qualifications for service as bishop and deacon (more on that in the session on March 13). The practical import of those instructions is made clear by verse 15, indicating they are aimed at how folks are to "behave" in the household that is the church. The linking of household and church (*ekklesia*, the literal meaning of which is "called out") likely was the natural result of the Christian community still meeting in private homes.

Once again, we encounter the word "truth" as a synonym for the faith.

1 Timothy 3:16. Today's passage closes with what is considered by many yet another hymn fragment. The phrasing of "mystery" and "religion" so closely together may call to the hearer's (or singer's) mind the mystery religions that some followed in the ancient Mediterranean world. The hymn fragment itself consists of three couplets, where the nouns in each pair form a contrast (mystery?): flesh/spirit, angels/Gentiles, world/glory. Some also hear in the opening acclamation of "our religion is great" an echo or challenge to the Ephesian worship of Diana also called Artemis ("Great is Artemis of the Ephesians!") as in Acts 19:28. An intriguing detail in that vein is that 1 Timothy 1:3 places Timothy in Ephesus on Paul's urging.

INTERPRETING THE SCRIPTURE

Liturgy as Prayer and Confession

This quarter as a whole explores worship in the early church. In today's passages from 1 Timothy, we encounter not only instructions for worship but also two possible fragments of worship resources.

The instructions given regard the practices of prayer in the worship life of the "called out" (*ekklesia*) community that came to be known as church. The connections made in "Understanding the Scripture" with the church's moorings in Judaism are underscored by the importance ("first of all . . ." in 2:1) attached to the prayers of the early Christian community. One of the earlier designations for Jewish places of worship during the "diaspora" (period following exile, in reference to Jews who lived outside of Judah) was *proseuche*, a word that means "house of prayer." Worship in the synagogue combined readings from Torah and Prophets, a sermon or message, and a variety of prayers. That variety can be seen reflected in the list of prayers provided in 1 Timothy 2:1-6.

Prayer by definition brings us into communion with God and a recognition of Holy Presence among those of us inclined to hear and respond to the words and needs we offer. By this primary focus upon the practice of prayers, 1 Timothy reminds the church in all ages, including our own, that liturgy moves beyond social gathering into the realm of holy encounter. The offering of prayers further invites recognition and confession of a God who is engaged in our lives. How exactly that engagement takes shape as a result or through the act of prayer is a mystery (we will return to that theme later). But to urge prayers to God is, by necessity, to open ourselves to the possibility of God's responding to us—and, if the truth be told, through us.

Yet another element of liturgy implied in these instructions in 1 Timothy is that of sharing in a confession that is communal in nature. The prayers explicitly invite us to hold others before God. Implicitly, through the use of several hymn fragments in this passage, we are reminded that the faith we offer to God is not our own, nor did we come to it all on our own. Faith is a gift from God—and faith is also a gift passed on through community. We confess that every time we sing a hymn and feel moved by its words and/or sound. Why? That hymn has come to us from another. Personal devotion has a rightful and honorable place in the Christian life. But Christian community is where faith is nurtured and passed on, where we gather to pray for the needs of a far wider circle than those with whom we share pews or chairs. Prayer and confession combine in liturgy as we gather in

Holy Presence in company with others for the sake of the God-beloved world.

One for All

"One for all and all for one." Those words may recall for some the motto of the Three Musketeers and D'Artagnan. But surfacing in several places in the passage from 1 Timothy are other compelling affirmations of "one for all" that challenge us with a witness to Christian universalism.

Consider first the testimony of verses 3-4 that speak of "God our Savior, who desires everyone to be saved." That statement is made even stronger when it is understood that the Greek verb *thelo*, translated here as "desires," is also the chief word for "will." *God our Savior, who wills everyone to be saved.* How does that sound to your ears and to your theology?

To allow 1 Timothy to press this case even further, move on to verses 5-6. The faith witnessed there is to one God, and one mediator (Jesus), "who gave himself a ransom for all." As highlighted in *Understanding the Scripture*, the ransom is not "for many" but "for all." Also noted in that earlier section are the frequency of places in this passage where such radical inclusion is affirmed: Prayers are to be made "for everyone;" God desires/wills "everyone" to be saved; and now here, Christ's redeeming work is not for the chosen few or even the blessed many. No, it is "for all." This is the truth that the author of 1 Timothy brings to the community addressed, and through them, to us.

The warnings in the first chapter in this book against false teachers clearly reveal that this community faces divisions. It is quite likely that the opponents may even have called into question Paul's positions and views, perhaps to the point of considering him outside the faith or truth. That would not have been the first time in the Pauline literature. But the amazing thing is this: Even as strongly as the author pushes

back against those false teachers in chapter 1, here in chapter 2 the clear implication is that Christ's ransom was for them as well. As opposed as the author may have been to their activity, there is not exclusion of them from those God wills to save or for whom Christ gave himself as a ransom. "All," "everyone," states the scope of God's grace for the community of 1 Timothy.

Does "all," "everyone," state the scope of God's grace for our community of faith? Are all viewed (and received) as those whom God wills to save—and on God's terms, not ours?

Liturgy and Mystery

The passage closes with this intriguing declaration that "the mystery of our religion is great" (3:16). Maybe the author had the mystery religions of his day in mind, and this served as a sort of "if you think your mysteries are profound, check out these." Or maybe the author did want, as noted in the commentary on 3:16, to raise a rival cry to that raised by the Ephesians for their beloved goddess Diana or Artemis.

But for the moment, let us leave those matters aside, for in truth, we do not know exactly what the author had in mind then. Instead let us focus on what it might mean to say that the mystery of our faith is great. And let's be honest. While many of us enjoy reading mysteries or watching them on television, a great many more it seems like their religion wrapped up and packaged in neat answers and clear divisions between black and white. Mystery? No thanks. Tell me what to believe and what to do, plain and simple.

But faith, biblical faith, resists that. The faith of Jacob and Joseph involves the mystery of dreams and wrestlings with God. The faith of Mary wonders "how can this be?" while the faith of Jesus prays "if it is possible, take this cup from me." The faith of Paul confesses "now we see in a mirror dimly." To eliminate the mystery cuts out the core of biblical faith. To celebrate the mystery of holy encounter invites biblical faith. In the vision of 1 Timothy, it bids us consider how flesh and spirit form the dwelling and revealing place of God. It bids us consider how outsiders (Gentiles) and the most inside-of-insiders (angels) can both grasp and bear witness to the same faith. It bids us consider this world and what we call "glory" as trusting and receiving the One and Living God. Faith bids us rejoice in God's holy mystery who is Christ Jesus.

SHARING THE SCRIPTURE

Preparing Our Hearts

Explore this week's devotional reading, found in Hebrews 8:6-12. Most of this text is taken from Jeremiah 31:31-34 where the prophet speaks about a new covenant. The writer of Hebrews reports that Jesus is the mediator of this new ("better," 8:6) covenant. That same idea is found in the key verse of today's session, 1 Timothy 2:5, which reads: "There is also one mediator between God and humankind,/Christ Jesus, himself human." This verse, along with verse 5, seems to be a fragment from the liturgy of the early church. What does it mean to you to confess that Jesus is the mediator of a new covenant between God and the people?

Pray that you and the adult learners will prepare your hearts to worship God through your relationship with Christ Jesus.

Preparing Our Minds

Study the background Scripture and the lesson Scripture, both of which are from 1 Timothy 2:1-6; 3:14-16. Think about what gives your spiritual search meaning.

Write on newsprint:
❑ information for next week's lesson, found under "Continue the Journey."
❑ activities for further spiritual growth in "Continue the Journey."

Review the introduction to this quarter, "The Big Picture," "Close-up," and "Faith in Action." Consider how you will use this additional information throughout the quarter.

LEADING THE CLASS

(1) Gather to Learn

❖ Welcome the class members and introduce any guests.

❖ Pray that all who have come today will open their hearts and minds to find meaning in today's lesson that will help them walk more closely with the Lord.

❖ Point out that in many mainline Protestant churches and the Roman Catholic Church, there has been a liturgical renewal, which has long roots but truly flowered as a result of the Second Vatican Council (1962–1965). Hymn books, prayer books, and books of worship in many denominations reflect changes that came about as the church tried to recapture worship as it was practiced during the first several hundred years of our life together. Invite the students to recall changes they have seen in your church liturgy (for example, a different ritual for Holy Communion).

❖ Ask: **How have the changes in worship you have identified helped or hindered your spiritual journey?**

❖ Read aloud today's focus statement: **There is a renewed interest in ancient spiritual practices in today's society. What gives our spiritual search meaning? Citing an ancient hymn, 1 Timothy affirms that Christ is the mediator of all truth about God.**

(2) Uncover the Literary and Theological Elements in the Texts of This Early Creed and Hymn (2:5-6)

❖ Use whatever information you think your class would find helpful from "The Big Picture: Worshiping God" to introduce this quarter's focus on worship in the early church.

❖ Choose a volunteer to read 1 Timothy 2:1-4.

❖ Invite the class to read in unison the creed found in 1 Timothy 2:5-6.

❖ Use information from Understanding the Scriptures, as needed, to help the class answer these questions:

(1) **Why does the writer urge Timothy to pray for everyone?**

(2) **What do you think would happen if people took seriously the admonition to pray for everyone, including those who hold "high positions"?**

(3) **Look at elements of the creed fragment in verses 5-6: "one God," "one mediator between God and humankind," that mediator is Jesus, Jesus is human, Jesus gave himself, the purpose of his giving was to be "a ransom for all." To which of these elements can you give a hearty "amen"? Which elements, if any, challenge your beliefs? Why?** (Information from footnotes of *The New Interpreter's Study Bible* may help clarify the concept of "ransom." Redemption, which literally means "purchase with a price," referred to "ransom paid for release of prisoners of war or slaves." Paul used the word "ransom" "to describe Christ's deliverance of humanity from the consequence of sin.")

❖ Read "One for All" from Interpreting the Scripture. Discuss the questions in the final paragraph. Then ask: **How might our congregation be more welcoming to visi-tors and to people in the community who have no church home?**

❖ Call for a volunteer to read 1 Timothy 3:14-16.

❖ Use information in 1 Timothy 3:14-15, 16 in Understanding the Scripture to help the class unpack these verses, which in verse 16 include a fragment from an early hymn.

(3) Define the Learners' Understanding of the Christian Faith

❖ Brainstorm answers to this question: **If someone were to ask what you believe as a Christian, how would you respond?** Go around the room (perhaps more than once if the group is small) and invite each person to add one item to the list you are creating on newsprint.

❖ Engage the group in clarifying their understandings by asking questions such as:

(1) **Which items does everyone agree with?**

(2) **Which items are unclear to you? Why?**

(3) **Are there any items on the list that you disagree with? Why?**

❖ Distribute hymnals. Ask the students to turn to the section that includes the creeds and affirmations of faith. (If you are using *The United Methodist Hymnal*, look at pages 880–889). Invite the students to look at one or more creeds or affirmations and comment on points that are essential to their own beliefs. List these points on newsprint. Also encourage them to add to the class list anything they feel is important but has been omitted from the creed or affirmation.

(4) Create a Personal Statement of Faith

❖ Distribute paper and pencils. Invite the adults to work individually or with a partner to create a personal statement of faith. They may use any information the class listed, or ideas from the hymnal, or beliefs they hold dear that may not have been voiced.

❖ Encourage the volunteers to read their statements of faith to the class or to a small group.

(5) Continue the Journey

❖ Pray that all who have come today will recognize the importance of faith statements in their own spiritual journeys.

❖ Read aloud this preparation for next week's lesson. You may also want to post it on newsprint for the students to copy.

- ■ **Title: Qualifications of Worship Leaders**
- ■ **Background Scripture: 1 Timothy 3:1-13**
- ■ **Lesson Scripture: 1 Timothy 3:1-13**
- ■ **Focus of the Lesson: People are looking for trustworthy and sensible leadership. How shall we choose our leaders? This passage from 1 Timothy suggests that spiritual maturity is an important factor when choosing leaders.**

❖ Challenge the students to complete one or more of these activities for further spiritual growth related to this week's session. Post this information on newsprint for the students to copy.

(1) **Think about where you look for meaning in life. How do your worship experiences help you to find meaning?**

(2) **Offer intercessory prayers each day for governmental leaders.**

(3) **Take notice of all the things in your sanctuary that help you to worship God. Note cross, Bible, banners, flowers, stained glass windows, musical instruments, aromas, and tastes (particularly Communion elements). How do these things help to usher you more fully into God's presence?**

❖ Sing or read aloud "Holy God, We Praise Thy Name."

❖ Conclude today's session by leading the class in this benediction from Jude 24-25, which is the key verse for the lesson on April 10: **Now to him who is able to keep you from falling, and to make you stand without blemish in the presence of his glory with rejoicing, to the only God our Savior, through Jesus Christ our Lord, be glory, majesty, power, and authority, before all time and now and forever. Amen.**

UNIT 1: A GUIDE FOR WORSHIP LEADERS

QUALIFICATIONS OF WORSHIP LEADERS

PREVIEWING THE LESSON

Lesson Scripture: 1 Timothy 3:1-13
Background Scripture: 1 Timothy 3:1-13
Key Verse: 1 Timothy 3:9

Focus of the Lesson:

People are looking for trustworthy and sensible leadership. How shall we choose our leaders? This passage from 1 Timothy suggests that spiritual maturity is an important factor when choosing leaders.

Goals for the Learners:

(1) to describe the qualifications and responsibilities of spiritual leaders as set forth in 1 Timothy.
(2) to identify their qualifications for leadership roles.
(3) to evaluate current job descriptions for congregational leaders in light of the scriptural qualifications and recommend changes as appropriate.

Pronunciation Guide:

episkopos (ep is' kop os)
diakonos (dee ak' on os)

Supplies:

Bibles, newsprint and marker, paper and pencils, hymnals

READING THE SCRIPTURE

NRSV
1 Timothy 3:1-13

¹The saying is sure: whoever aspires to the office of bishop desires a noble task. ²Now a bishop must be above reproach, married only once, temperate, sensible, respectable, hospitable, an apt teacher, ³not a

NIV
1 Timothy 3:1-13

¹Here is a trustworthy saying: If anyone sets his heart on being an overseer, he desires a noble task. ²Now the overseer must be above reproach, the husband of but one wife, temperate, self-controlled, respectable,

drunkard, not violent but gentle, not quarrelsome, and not a lover of money. ⁴He must manage his own household well, keeping his children submissive and respectful in every way—⁵for if someone does not know how to manage his own household, how can he take care of God's church? ⁶He must not be a recent convert, or he may be puffed up with conceit and fall into the condemnation of the devil. ⁷Moreover, he must be well thought of by outsiders, so that he may not fall into disgrace and the snare of the devil.

⁸Deacons likewise must be serious, not double-tongued, not indulging in much wine, not greedy for money; ⁹**they must hold fast to the mystery of the faith with a clear conscience.** ¹⁰And let them first be tested; then, if they prove themselves blameless, let them serve as deacons. ¹¹Women likewise must be serious, not slanderers, but temperate, faithful in all things. ¹²Let deacons be married only once, and let them manage their children and their households well; ¹³for those who serve well as deacons gain a good standing for themselves and great boldness in the faith that is in Christ Jesus.

hospitable, able to teach, ³not given to drunkenness, not violent but gentle, not quarrelsome, not a lover of money. ⁴He must manage his own family well and see that his children obey him with proper respect. ⁵(If anyone does not know how to manage his own family, how can he take care of God's church?) ⁶He must not be a recent convert, or he may become conceited and fall under the same judgment as the devil. ⁷He must also have a good reputation with outsiders, so that he will not fall into disgrace and into the devil's trap.

⁸Deacons, likewise, are to be men worthy of respect, sincere, not indulging in much wine, and not pursuing dishonest gain. ⁹**They must keep hold of the deep truths of the faith with a clear conscience.** ¹⁰They must first be tested; and then if there is nothing against them, let them serve as deacons.

¹¹In the same way, their wives are to be women worthy of respect, not malicious talkers but temperate and trustworthy in everything.

¹²A deacon must be the husband of but one wife and must manage his children and his household well. ¹³Those who have served well gain an excellent standing and great assurance in their faith in Christ Jesus.

UNDERSTANDING THE SCRIPTURE

1 Timothy 3:1. The opening phrase about "the saying is sure" appears twice elsewhere in the epistle (1:15, 4:9). What is not so sure is whether it references the verses that follow about the qualifications for bishop or the preceding verses. Although aspirations can either be good or evil, depending upon what one aspires to, the verb translated here as "aspire" is positive. In this verse it infers a positive ambition for a "noble task." In 6:10, however, "love of money" asserts a negative meaning. The Greek word for bishop is *episkopos*. It is a

compound word whose literal meaning is "over-see." The name of the "episcopal" office follows then as one of oversight for the community.

1 Timothy 3:2-3. These verses list a variety of characteristics that address the qualifications of those who would aspire to the office of bishop. "Above reproach" finds parallel in verse 7's "well thought of by outsiders." Taken together, the list thus starts off with an assertion that the bishop be one who possesses a good reputation not only within the church community but outside of it as well. "Married only once" leans less in the direction of an implied possibility of polygamy and more in the way of an urging against remarriage after the death of a spouse, though why remarriage would be discouraged is left unspoken. "Respectable" once again draws upon the regard with which this individual is held by the community and those outside it. "Hospitable" reflects a key element of eastern Mediterranean customs regarding the reception of strangers. "Apt teacher" describes the one characteristic associated with particular skills exercised by the bishop for the community. The list of "nots" in verse 3—not a drunkard, not violent, not quarrelsome, not a lover of money—reveal the drawing of lines against behaviors that would bring the bishop and the community into public disrepute.

1 Timothy 3:4-5. The language and responsibilities of "household" dominate the next set of qualities expected of bishops. In an era when a church likely met most frequently in households (homes generally included far more people than what we today call "nuclear" families), the association of church life with household life is a natural one. A key term used twice in these verses, and appearing again in verse 12, is "manage." The word literally means "stand before," and brings the connotation of the leadership exercised by one in a position of authority. Here, the management is given specific example only in that day's cultural norm for raising children. The closing question in verse 5, which links care of the church with care of the household, gains greater force when understood in the context of the previous point made about churches meeting in households.

1 Timothy 3:6-7. The qualifications for bishop here connect to tenure within the faith community and, again, respectability in the wider community. The urging against recent converts is here expressed in concern for individual conceit that might result. The word for "devil" can also be translated as

"slanderer." Thus, the "condemnation" referred to here that is to be avoided may be that of wagging tongues who spread rumors about the individual—or perhaps the community. It is possible those whom the community might have wanted to elevate too rapidly to the office of bishop might have been persons of wealth or prestige, who might be seen as offering the community an easy shortcut to respectability versus the harder path that comes from the type of lifestyles urged before.

1 Timothy 3:8-10. "Deacon" translates the Greek word *diakonos*. Already in Acts 6 the office of deacon is affirmed, although at that point the office seemed to be primarily related to service ministries (the Greek word in non-church settings more typically means the table servant). However, the office of deacon likely had further evolved by the time of 1 Timothy. Deacons as evangelists can be inferred by Acts' using the term in relationship to Philip (see Acts 21:8). The initial qualifications for deacon here parallel those of bishop. Verses 9-10 introduce new ideas. "Mystery" was a loaded word in that era, as the "mysteries" could refer to a variety of religions popular in the eastern Mediterranean at that time and later. It is unclear what is suggested by "clear conscience," beyond perhaps not being disingenuous about the faith. "Hold fast"—making a wholehearted commitment to the faith despite its mystery—does not by itself specify a task reserved for deacons. Notice, too, that both deacons and bishops are not to be enamored with money. The concluding words about being tested and being found blameless point to some sort of probationary period. The passage sheds no light on what those tests were to be.

1 Timothy 3:11. This verse, above all others in the passage, raises major difficulties in interpretation. Do the "women" it addresses refer to the wives of deacons or to deacons who are women? To argue that it singles out women in the community as a whole makes no sense by its placement within a passage devoted to qualifications for these particular offices. Some urge for reference to wives of the deacons, sometimes on the grounds of opposing ministerial office to women (and deacon is, in other places of the New Testament, translated as "minister"). Yet Paul (in Romans 16) and other writers in the early church make clear reference to deacons who are women. This particular verse leaves room for either interpretation to be affirmed, but neither to be rejected. As further evidence, the NRSV footnote concerning translation reads, "Or *Their wives* or *Women deacons.*"

1 Timothy 3:12-13. The passage returns (if it ever left, depending on your view of the previous verse!) to qualifications to serve as deacon. "Management" of children and households once more comes to the fore, as well as a restatement of "only one marriage" seen regarding the bishops (3:2). The concluding verse may hint at one outcome of the "testing" suggested in verse 10. Here, those who serve well "gain a good standing." Is that a word about advancement in reputation alone, or perhaps some attainment in hierarchical standing? What is clear is that such service brings about boldness of the faith to which they had been called to "hold fast" in verse 9.

INTERPRETING THE SCRIPTURE

Discerning Leadership

OK. You are on the nominating committee of your church. It is late November, and the annual meeting or charge conference is coming up early in January. Your committee has a slate of officers to fill. How will you go about deciding who should be asked? What will help guide your determination of suitability for the offices now open?

To put the same question in another setting: You are on a committee that interviews ministerial candidates. What are the two things you look for most in someone to be entrusted with leadership in the community? How will you choose between those who say they are called of God to positions of leadership in the church?

First Timothy 3 is all about such questions. Admittedly, the modern church, whether in its wider denominational configuration or even in its local incarnation, may have far greater levels of organization. After all, 1 Timothy identifies only bishops and deacons—and we need to tread a little carefully before making them equivalent to offices that may carry those same names among us. But what this passage urges, whatever names be given to offices and whatever levels of institutional sophistication we may or may not display, is this: Leadership in the church bears careful consideration of qualifications. When authority is being vested in individuals to put a face upon who we are and what we believe and who we regard as leaders, then care is best taken in that investing of authority.

According to 1 Timothy the primary milieu for understanding those qualifications is that of the household. That connection arose out of the church's setting as, literally, house churches. The community met in folks' homes. The wider community could look at where the community met and draw conclusions about what kind of a group that was. So care was taken by 1 Timothy in looking for leadership that was respected for its household management.

We no longer live in a setting where the community chiefly meets in homes. How does that impact our translating of what 1 Timothy urges for leadership qualities in our day? What other metaphors can be drawn, and what other metaphors should be resisted, for taking our cues for the characteristics of leadership sought and needed in Christ's community today?

Through and beyond the language of household, 1 Timothy 3 points to a variety of ethical standards that still hold importance for our measures of church leadership today.

A Matter of Ethics

Running throughout the passage is a concern for leaders who will be respected beyond the community of faith. Does respectability mean an ethic of "going along to get along"? There are plenty of passages, in the prophets and the Gospels, that assert the importance of bearing witness to the faith and doing justice even when that brings risk. But 1 Timothy rightfully urges the community to a stance something like: Don't invite trouble for its own sake. Trouble will find the community all on its own. This is not an ethic of avoiding controversy. It is an ethic for leadership knowing which battles are worth fighting and which battles are mere diversions. Leaders who are respected by the wider community are not necessarily always agreed with by those outside (or inside!) the fellowship. Respect follows those whose words and lives have integrity.

There is an often overlooked ethic of power exercised responsibly in this passage. Listen again to these words: "not violent but gentle, not quarrelsome, and not a lover of money" (3: 3). Some leaders, inside and outside the church, are bullies with power. Violence does not necessarily come with a punch in the nose. An ignoring of a rightful concern is an act of violence in the community. An overly insistent seeking of self-interest (some might call that lobbying) that sets aside all other concerns is an act of violence. The contrasting quality of leadership lifted up by 1 Timothy is gentleness. Gentleness is not allowing oneself (or others) to be bulldozed. Gentleness simply, yet profoundly, suggests a spirit open to the pliancy of God's Spirit.

Adding "not quarrelsome" to the list after "not violent" is another expression of the same urging. What are quarrels but a group of two or more insisting their points of views must be preeminent? Forgotten by "quarrelsome," but remembered by the leadership sought in this passage, is the spirit that resolves to discover the preeminence of God's purposes for community, and an openness to whether those purposes conform or contradict one's own, and then to act appropriately.

The twice-asserted aversion to those greedy or lovers of money reminds the church and its leaders that, as much as things change, things stay the same. Money, like the aspiration noted in the commentary on verse 3:1, is neutral. Whether it turns to good or evil purposes depends entirely on the use. To love money, to be greedy, opens one to all manner of temptation, only a few of which need eventuate in outright theft. To be overly controlling in the use of money, to be obsessed with money's flow or lack thereof as a sign of faithfulness (of an individual or community)—these too are signs of the love of money. The potential for abuses by leaders is broad and destructive not just of the leaders but of those under their care. First Timothy 3 wisely reminds us that qualifications for leadership need to take into account the lure of money—and with it power—upon any and all who would be entrusted with authority in Christ's community.

Where Do We Go From Here?

It is possible to read such lists of qualities and characteristics for leaders as 1 Timothy 3 provides and wonder, is there anybody around who even comes close? There have been times in the church's life, and places in its current expression, where we have become extraordinarily legalistic about such things. Rarely, of course, have we slipped into the total denial of human nature and demanded of would-be leaders (and followers) absolute perfection in any and all such things. Those who have such views of others—or themselves—need to take a crash course in Paul's reminder that all have sinned and fallen short of the glory of God. And if we are pursuing the perfect Christian leader, we will have a very long wait for a very short list.

First Timothy 3 raises critical issues and characteristics for leadership. We would do well in seeking such qualities in our leaders—and in ourselves. Every generation has sought ways to best ensure such qualifications are met. For some, seminary education has been the baseline. For others, evaluations based on practical skills of ministry have become the focus. Systems of mentoring and accountability groups offer still other paths by which such qualifications might to be measured and instilled and developed.

First Timothy 3 testifies that the church has done well and will always do well to seek gifted and accountable leaders. But remember: Spiritual maturity is not only what we seek in leaders. Spiritual maturity is needed by those entrusted with ministries of nominations and ordination and pastoral search, so that our decisions on who to invest with such authority will not be a matter of who is most convenient or like us, but who God seeks to be a leader among us.

SHARING THE SCRIPTURE

Preparing Our Hearts

Explore this week's devotional reading, found in 1 Peter 5:1-5. As he concludes his first letter, Peter "exhorts the elders" to tend eagerly the flock of God and be an example to them. Note the use of the familiar metaphor for a leader of God's people: shepherd. When you think of an effective leader in the church, what characteristics come to mind? Which of these characteristics do you exhibit in the leadership positions you hold?

Pray that you and the adult learners will be aware of the traits that enable a layperson or ordained minister to lead God's people well.

Preparing Our Minds

Study the background Scripture and the lesson Scripture, both of which are from 1 Timothy 3:1-13. Think about how we choose trustworthy and sensible leaders.

Write on newsprint:
❏ information for next week's lesson, found under "Continue the Journey."
❏ activities for further spiritual growth in "Continue the Journey."

Check with your pastor if you choose the option for "Describe the Qualifications and Responsibilities of Spiritual Leaders as Set Forth in 1 Timothy" to locate qualifications for leaders that your denomination considers essential.

Contact the staff person responsible for volunteers in your church. This may be the pastor, program director, volunteer coordinator, or someone else. Obtain a copy of job descriptions that your congregation uses for various ministries. These descriptions may be produced by your denomination or created by your congregation.

LEADING THE CLASS

(1) Gather to Learn

❖ Welcome the class members and introduce any guests.

❖ Pray that those who have gathered for class today will be open and ready to hear the word that God has for them this day.

❖ Read the first two paragraphs from "Discerning Leadership" in Interpreting the Scripture. List on newsprint the students' answers to the questions about choosing leaders. Try to focus on traits that are necessary for both ordained and non-ordained leaders.

❖ Read aloud today's focus statement: **People are looking for trustworthy and sensible leadership. How shall we choose our leaders? This passage from 1 Timothy suggests that spiritual maturity is an important factor when choosing leaders.**

(2) Describe the Qualifications and Responsibilities of Spiritual Leaders as Set Forth in 1 Timothy

❖ Choose a volunteer to read 1 Timothy 3:1-13, noting that this passage describes the qualifications of two leadership positions in the early church: bishop and deacon.

❖ List qualifications on newsprint.

❖ Use information from Understanding the Scripture to help the class better understand the biblical passage.

❖ Read these excerpts from *The United Methodist Book of Worship*, which are taken from the "General Examination" of candidates for consecrated and ordained ministry. Invite the students to listen for qualifications for worship leaders that are stated or implied here. **"You are to lead the people of God in worship and prayer, and to nurture, teach, and encourage them from the riches of God's grace. You are to exemplify Christ's servanthood; to build up the people of God in their obedience to Christ's mission in the world, and to seek justice, peace, and salvation for all people."**

❖ **Option:** Read information from another denomination that is similar to the "General Examination." Use this information instead of or in addition to the information from The United Methodist Church.

❖ List on newsprint qualifications found in denominational resources.

❖ Compare the qualities listed in 1 Timothy with those you discerned from the denominational reading.

❖ Discuss these questions:
   (1) What other qualities do you think congregations expect their leaders to have?
   (2) Do these qualities seem reasonable in light of the biblical qualifications and those set forth by your denomination?

(3) Identify the Learners' Qualifications for Leadership Roles

❖ Distribute paper and pencils. Suggest that the learners review the lists of qualifications the class has already created. Invite them to select from these lists qualifications that seem to fit them and write them on their papers.

❖ Provide times for each adult to read aloud his or her list to the class (or a small group). Encourage listeners to add to each person's list, perhaps suggesting ministries that a certain person could undertake effectively.

❖ Conclude this activity by asking the students to consider what they have listed and what others have said to them. Suggest that on their papers they write (1) ministries that they feel led to continue; (2) ministries they feel led to investigate; and (3) ministries they are now working in that do not rely on their best qualifications for leadership, which they may need to make plans to step away from.

(4) Evaluate Current Job Descriptions for Congregational Leaders in Light of the Scriptural Qualifications and Recommend Changes as Appropriate

❖ Work with the entire class, small groups, or pairs to do this activity, depending on how many job descriptions you are able to obtain. Make several copies of each description, if possible. Encourage the students to go over these descriptions with an eye toward the scriptural and denominational qualifications they identified earlier in the session. Be sure the lists generated in previous activities are posted where they can be seen.

❖ Discuss these questions:

(1) **Where in the description do you see similar qualifications to those we identified earlier?**

(2) **Do there appear to be any qualifications that you question in light of the Scriptures? If so, what are they?**

(3) **What changes, if any, would you recommend to make the description more in line with Scriptures?**

(4) **Who can we contact about our ideas? Which person in our group will make that contact?**

❖ **Option:** If your congregation does not have written job descriptions, write one or two for specific jobs. For example, what qualities would you want to see in a Sunday school teacher, an usher, a choir member? Appoint someone in the class to share these ideas with the appropriate person on the church staff, perhaps the pastor.

(5) Continue the Journey

❖ Pray that today's participants will encourage all who are qualified for leadership to listen and respond to God's call on their lives.

❖ Read aloud this preparation for next week's lesson. You may also want to post it on newsprint for the students to copy.

■ **Title: Prepare for Leadership**
■ **Background Scripture: 1 Timothy 4:6-16**
■ **Lesson Scripture: 1 Timothy 4:6-16**
■ **Focus of the Lesson: People who are asked to serve in leadership positions may question their qualifications and preparedness. How**

should potential leaders respond to opportunities to serve? The writer of 1 Timothy encouraged leaders to give themselves to God's work without neglecting their personal spiritual quest.

❖ Challenge the students to complete one or more of these activities for further spiritual growth related to this week's session. Post this information on newsprint for the students to copy.

(1) **Think about pastors you know. List the leadership qualities of each one. Offer a prayer of thanksgiving for the different gifts that each one has brought to your congregation.**

(2) **Consider your own qualifications for church leadership. Are you using your gifts wisely? What tasks might you drop because they do not make the best use of your talents? What other ministries might you add?**

(3) **Measure yourself against the qualifications that are outlined in 1 Timothy 3. Assume that those outside of the faith are viewing you as the only Christian they know. Which of your traits would draw people to Christ? Which might push them away?**

❖ Sing or read aloud "A Charge to Keep I Have."

❖ Conclude today's session by leading the class in this benediction from Jude 24-25, which is the key verse for the lesson on April 10: **Now to him who is able to keep you from falling, and to make you stand without blemish in the presence of his glory with rejoicing, to the only God our Savior, through Jesus Christ our Lord, be glory, majesty, power, and authority, before all time and now and forever. Amen.**

UNIT 1: A GUIDE FOR WORSHIP LEADERS
PREPARE FOR LEADERSHIP

PREVIEWING THE LESSON

Lesson Scripture: 1 Timothy 4:6-16
Background Scripture: 1 Timothy 4:6-16
Key Verse: 1 Timothy 4:16

Focus of the Lesson:

People who are asked to serve in leadership positions may question their qualifications and preparedness. How should potential leaders respond to opportunities to serve? The writer of 1 Timothy encouraged leaders to give themselves to God's work without neglecting their personal spiritual quest.

Goals for the Learners:

(1) to study how a spiritual leader trains and prepares for service as identified in 1 Timothy 4.
(2) to reflect on their gifts for ministry and what it takes to nurture those gifts.
(3) to design a personal spiritual-fitness training program and make a commitment to implement it.

Pronunciation Guide:

agonizometha (ag o nid' o met ha)   *gumnasia* (goom nas eeh' ah)
diakonos (dee ak' on os)   *presbuteros* (pres boo' ter os)
eusebeia (yoo' seb' i ah)

Supplies:

Bibles, newsprint and marker, paper and pencils, hymnals

READING THE SCRIPTURE

NRSV
1 Timothy 4:6-16

⁶If you put these instructions before the brothers and sisters, you will be a good servant of Christ Jesus, nourished on the words of the faith and of the sound teaching that you have followed. ⁷Have nothing to do

NIV
1 Timothy 4:6-16

⁶If you point these things out to the brothers, you will be a good minister of Christ Jesus, brought up in the truths of the faith and of the good teaching that you have followed. ⁷Have nothing to do with godless

with profane myths and old wives' tales. Train yourself in godliness, [8]for, while physical training is of some value, godliness is valuable in every way, holding promise for both the present life and the life to come. [9]The saying is sure and worthy of full acceptance. [10]For to this end we toil and struggle, because we have our hope set on the living God, who is the Savior of all people, especially of those who believe.

[11]These are the things you must insist on and teach. [12]Let no one despise your youth, but set the believers an example in speech and conduct, in love, in faith, in purity. [13]Until I arrive, give attention to the public reading of scripture, to exhorting, to teaching. [14]Do not neglect the gift that is in you, which was given to you through prophecy with the laying on of hands by the council of elders. [15]Put these things into practice, devote yourself to them, so that all may see your progress. [16]**Pay close attention to yourself and to your teaching;** continue in these things, for in doing this you will save both yourself and your hearers.

myths and old wives' tales; rather, train yourself to be godly. [8]For physical training is of some value, but godliness has value for all things, holding promise for both the present life and the life to come.

[9]This is a trustworthy saying that deserves full acceptance [10](and for this we labor and strive), that we have put our hope in the living God, who is the Savior of all men, and especially of those who believe.

[11]Command and teach these things. [12]Don't let anyone look down on you because you are young, but set an example for the believers in speech, in life, in love, in faith and in purity. [13]Until I come, devote yourself to the public reading of Scripture, to preaching and to teaching. [14]Do not neglect your gift, which was given you through a prophetic message when the body of elders laid their hands on you.

[15]Be diligent in these matters; give yourself wholly to them, so that everyone may see your progress. [16]**Watch your life and doctrine closely.** Persevere in them, because if you do, you will save both yourself and your hearers.

UNDERSTANDING THE SCRIPTURE

1 Timothy 4:6. The "instructions" referred to here most likely encompass not only the verses that follow but also the first five verses of this chapter. In those earlier verses, the author weighed in against misleading and hypocritical teachings. Those teachings warned against abstinence from marriage and certain foods. A critical basis for the author's comments is laid open in verse 4: "everything created by God is good." So urged to offer these (and the following) instructions, the author suggests doing so will make Timothy a "good servant." "Servant" translates the Greek *diakonos*, translated earlier in chapter 3 as "deacon." Some take this verse, then, to

identify Timothy as one of the deacons in the community.

1 Timothy 4:7-8. What the author has specifically in mind with "profane myths" and "old wives' tales" is unclear. It may have to do with the teachings undercut in verses 1-5. First Timothy 1:4 links myths with "endless genealogies," a reference that may have something to do with speculations regarding angelic beings that was in vogue around that era. "Old wives' tales" was a phrase used outside of the biblical witness for matters that were without value. All in all, the author seems to be encouraging Timothy not to waste time or become entangled in speculative matters that serve no good purpose in or for the community. The positive aspect of the instruction in this verse centers on imagery drawn from athletics. "Train/training" comes from the Greek *gumnasia*, from which we get "gymnastics." Contrasted with physical training, that does have some value, is training in "godliness"—*eusebeia*—a word that occurs at least nine times in the Pastorals (1 and 2 Timothy and Titus) and carries the meaning of piety or devotion to God. Such "training," or what might be framed today as "spiritual discipline," is said in verse 8 to have short- and long-term benefits ("both the present life and the life to come").

1 Timothy 4:9-10. Verse 9 repeats "the saying is sure," used in 1 Timothy 3:1 (and commented on in last week's session). As in that earlier use, the "saying" in mind likely refers to statements that precede and follow it. Verse 10 carries on the thought of verse 8 in several ways. The word translated as "struggle" (*agonizometha*) is one used in athletic contests to depict the exertion necessary to achieve a goal or prize. The "end" to which such spiritual effort here is aimed comes in the second half of the verse: namely, our hope in God, who is "Savior." "Savior of all people" continues with a theme of universalism we have encountered earlier in 1 Timothy 2:4-6. The closing phrase of the verse presents some difficulty in precise understanding. What does it mean to be "the Savior of all," particularly when Timothy qualifies that phrase with "especially of those who believe"? Are we to understand that God is "more" a Savior for those in the community? Is God "less" a Savior for those who do not believe? Does the emphasis fall on how trusting God as Savior opens us to greater understanding, or simple awareness of that truth? The meaning is ambiguous and debated.

1 Timothy 4:11. Verse 10 seems to have taken the address of the epistle from Timothy back to the whole community: "we toil . . . we hope. . . ." Now in verse 11, however, the voice of the author is directed squarely at Timothy once more with instructions for his ministry. These are not options or possible paths for Timothy to consider: "you must insist on" brings the language of command and authority.

1 Timothy 4:12-14. "Let no one despise your youth" raises several points. The assertion of Timothy's youth is important in a culture and community where deference to age was a clear component. Indeed, the very name given to a significant office of leadership in the early church was *presbuteros*, which means "elder." Yet here, the author (Paul) asserts to Timothy—and to the community—that his youth is not to be a detriment to his exercise of authority. How that exercise occurs is given witness in the string of actions by which the author indicates Timothy's example is given best evidence: in speech and conduct; in love; in faith; in purity. What the epistle also makes clear is that such authority related to this is the opening line of verse 13: "until I arrive." Timothy, young as he is, does not only carry the weight of authority borne by his personal faith and example. Timothy is there as Paul's emissary, so the authority that Paul would bring is owed to Timothy his representative. To further undergird Timothy, the author goes on to assert Timothy's "gift." In the narrative that follows, the scene of something akin to an ordination service seems to be recalled. Besides Timothy as Paul's representative, there is the authority passed on by that "council of elders." The laying on of hands is a rite associated in biblical times and since with the gift of God's Spirit, the most important and effective source of authority in the church. So gifted, Timothy is then urged by the author to be an example to the community.

1 Timothy 4:15-16. The earlier listing of what that example consists of at the end of verse 12 now finds further summoning as the author urges Timothy to "put these things into practice."

If the early part of this passage used the language of athletics to frame the necessity of "spiritual training," the passage now concludes with concrete admonitions to do so. "Put into practice" translates a word that connotes cultivation. Care. Nurture. "Devote yourself" renders a phrase that suggests something like "to be in." Immersion would be another way of rendering its thought and encouragement. The closing verse identifies two matters of focus: on self, and on the teachings. Integrity in faith requires both. The verse closes with the intriguing declaration that such activity will be "saving" in its effect. There is not a contradiction of God as Savior here. Rather, the verse can be taken to suggest that we participate in God's saving activity by sharing in the life and work of God.

INTERPRETING THE SCRIPTURE

Training, Discipline, and the Spiritual Life

First Timothy 4:6-16 uses language from athletic preparation to encourage a regimen of spiritual discipline and exercise no less intentional—and no less beneficial—than discipline and exercise on behalf of improving our bodies. So what kinds of training does this passage call forth?

Foremost, we are to cultivate a life and a faith of integrity. First Timothy alludes to this by linking "words of faith" with "sound teachings you have followed" (4:6). Likewise, the example we provide is depicted to occur in both "speech and conduct" (4:12). The passage urges Timothy, and through him us, to pay attention to the ways in which our interior beliefs and attitudes find congruent expression in the exterior of our lives. "Do as I say and not as I do" does not cut it in spiritual life. As human beings created in the image of God, our calling is to lead lives that are whole and unified.

Why is such integrity encouraged? Sometimes folks are commended for their ability to compartmentalize their lives. That is, they can keep separate different aspects of their lives, sometimes practicing each with different attitudes and on occasion different ethics. Stories of ruthless business people who are tender-hearted toward family are not unheard of. The problem is that faith is not one compartment that we can turn off at will. God has created us for wholeness. Spiritual growth and maturity aim us toward that goal.

Religious disciplines and "spiritual regimens" form steps we can take to grow toward God. Surprisingly perhaps the author provides Timothy no specific prescriptions for how much time at prayer or what amount of biblical study and reflection are needed. But what is assumed in these instructions for Timothy—and for us—is that such disciplines and exercises are worth the time and attention they take. Such regimens require decision and commitment on our part to do and to keep.

We are witnessing a resurgence of interest in such disciplines in our time. Resources on spiritual formation are readily available for individuals and groups who have the desire to explore and engage in such practices. So consider 1 Timothy's urging to "train yourself in godliness" (4:7) in your own life. Where might "exercise" be needed for deepening your encounter with God? What practices have you found valuable that have perhaps slipped by the wayside? What practices of prayer or biblical encounter, service or hospitality, might you wish to learn more of and practice more of? Let 1 Timothy 4 serve as your invitation and encouragement to deepen your walk with God.

Let No One Despise You

Read those words aloud—and then say your name after them. You are someone not to be despised. What gives me the audacity to presume that is true of anyone who happens to read these words? Our creation is in the image of God. You are a child of God. Never forget that.

I remember a poster our denomination included in a mailing to churches years ago. It pictured a child, and the background as I recall it conveyed a sense of poverty. The caption to the picture was, "God made me, and God don't make junk."

For most of us, I think we can affirm that truth for ourselves. Maybe it's the affirmation of it for others we struggle with more. But not always. Sometimes, when all we hear from others are our shortcomings, or what we still need to do to be the perfect parent, or pastor, or church member, we may let ourselves fall into the trap of discounting who we are.

For the author of 1 Timothy to come right out and write verse 12 strongly infers that some folks were saying things about Timothy, namely about his short life experience, which undercut not just his sense of authority but also his sense of worth.

You're Too Young

Maybe it's been awhile since you've heard, "you're too young." But maybe, just maybe, you are nagged by comments like "you're just too . . ." and you fill in the blank. Sometimes parents say such things to children—and vice-versa. Sometimes husbands and wives say them to one another. Sometimes laypersons say them to pastors—and vice-versa.

If that is so in your life, and in particular if you are the one weighed down by those remarks, remember 1 Timothy's counsel: "Let no one despise your youth" (4:12). In other words, let no one despise you for your stage in life or who God made you to be.

That doesn't mean there aren't things we can and should change about how we are. Timothy would not remain forever young. It's just that if and when folks start to bludgeon you for being someone you're not, let no one despise you. You are a child of God. God made you, and God doesn't make junk. What God does make you for is—well, that's the theme of the next section.

Use Your Gifts

A preacher once told the story of a woman who was given a beautiful necklace by her husband. An occasion would come when the two would be going out, and the husband would notice she wasn't wearing it. He would ask, and her response was that she was saving it for the right time. This continued to happen until he stopped asking. Finally, the necklace was placed around her neck for the first time—for her funeral.

Not letting other people despise you is but half of the task. The other is not despising yourself, and in particular the gifts God has entrusted to you. In the case of 1 Timothy, when the author urges Timothy to "put these things into practice," "these things" (4:15) refers to the gift given to Timothy through the laying on of hands.

It may be that some of our gifts are of the "laying on of hands" variety—that is, gifts invested to us by others in some formal way. We are asked to serve on a church committee. We are approached to teach a class. It may be that some of our gifts are not of the "laying on of hands" variety but more of the "well, that's something I've always liked doing" type. Singing. Cooking. Building. Quilting. It didn't take a committee to invest those gifts to us. They belong to us.

But then, whether we actually use those gifts becomes the choice we must make—whether we put them into practice or tuck them safely into a drawer until some idealized time. Well, you get the picture.

Gifts are given to us. That is the clear message to Timothy. Romans 12:4-8,

1 Corinthians 12, and Ephesians 4:11-13 go into even greater detail about the gifts given each one for the good of the whole. But the exercise of gifts depends upon the decision of individuals. Beyond that, it depends upon the willingness of congregations to encourage and promote the gifts of all, rather than single out or lean on those of a few. The gifted are not the celebrities among us. The gifted are the whole people of God. Which is why the counsel to 1 Timothy is not aimed just toward ordained ministers or prominent laypersons: "put these things into practice," *put your gifts into practice*, is the word God speaks to each and every one of us.

SHARING THE SCRIPTURE

Preparing Our Hearts

Explore this week's devotional reading, found in Philippians 3:17–4:1. After using athletic imagery to encourage people to "press on toward the goal" (3:14), Paul calls people to observe the example that he has set and be a co-imitator of Christ with him. Concerned about those who live as enemies of Christ's cross, Paul urges his readers to "stand firm in the Lord" (4:1). How are you using your gifts to press ahead on behalf of Christ? What obstacles do you encounter? Under what circumstances must you "stand firm" on your beliefs?

Pray that you and the adult learners will stand firm so that you may be able to lead others to Christ and mentor them as they grow in their faith.

Preparing Our Minds

Study the background Scripture and the lesson Scripture, both of which are from 1 Timothy 4:6-16. Consider how potential leaders respond when given an opportunity to serve.

Write on newsprint:
❑ information for next week's lesson, found under "Continue the Journey."
❑ activities for further spiritual growth in "Continue the Journey."

LEADING THE CLASS

(1) Gather to Learn

❖ Welcome the class members and introduce any guests.

❖ Pray that those who have come today will be eager to prepare themselves to lead God's people.

❖ Invite the students to tell stories of times when they were nominated for an office in the church. How did they respond? If they accepted the challenge after an initial response of, "no, I'm not qualified," what happened to change their view of their potential for leadership? (If the students seem reluctant to tell their own stories, recall Moses' response in Exodus 3–4 and all the excuses he had for not wanting to assume the leadership position to which God had called him.)

❖ Read aloud today's focus statement: **People who are asked to serve in leadership positions may question their qualifications and preparedness. How should potential leaders respond to opportunities to serve? The writer of 1 Timothy encouraged leaders to give themselves to God's work without neglecting their personal spiritual quest.**

(2) Study How a Spiritual Leader Trains and Prepares for Service as Identified in 1 Timothy 4

❖ Enlist a volunteer to read 1 Timothy 4:6-16.

❖ Draw a vertical line on a sheet of newsprint and label one side "Things to Do" and the other "Things to Avoid." Fill in information the students identify, as described in this passage, to be a good minister on behalf of Jesus.

    ❖ Discuss these questions:

        (1) Which of these ideas continue to be viable in the twenty-first-century church?

        (2) How do you see the contemporary church implementing those ideas?

❖ Note verse 7: "Train yourself in godliness." Invite the learners to talk about how the church helps them to engage in such training. Worship and Sunday school are certainly two venues for such training. What other opportunities does the congregation offer? What opportunities can you find beyond the local church, perhaps in your district, conference, synod, or diocese? How do these opportunities relate to what Timothy is exhorted to do?

❖ Add to the list of opportunities by brainstorming ideas to complete this sentence: **I wish the church would offer opportunities, such as . . ., to help me become more closely conformed to Jesus.** Write ideas on newsprint.

❖ Conclude by inviting volunteers to take responsibility for sharing the ideas with leaders in the church who could implement their suggestions.

(3) Reflect on the Learners' Gifts for Ministry and What It Takes to Nurture Those Gifts

❖ Read "Use Your Gifts" from Interpreting the Scripture.

❖ Form three groups and give each one a sheet of newsprint and marker. Assign each group to read either Romans 12:4-8, 1 Corinthians 12:27-31, or Ephesians 4:11-13 and list on newsprint the gifts they find in their passage. Call everyone together and ask each group to read their lists and then post their newsprint.

❖ Distribute paper and pencils. Invite each participant to list gifts that he or she has that can be used within the church. These gifts may or may not be found on the lists. Encourage the group to think about interesting uses for the gifts they possess. For example, someone who can knit may make baby blankets to be presented at the time of baptism. A bread maker could have fresh loaves of bread available for visitors. An artist could create a mural for the children's Sunday school. A Certified Public Accountant (CPA) may take on responsibilities for finances of a group within the church.

❖ Affirm all of the gifts and encourage the students to help each other discern how they can use their gifts within the context of the church to build up the body of Christ. Let them know that new ministries can emerge if someone with the right gifts is willing to step to the plate.

(4) Design a Personal Spiritual-fitness Training Program and Make a Commitment to Implement It

❖ Ask students who engage in a regular physical fitness program to report briefly on how they set up their program and the discipline required to stick with it day after day. Their report could be something as simple as, "*I do cardio training by bicycling on Mondays and Fridays and running three miles on Wednesdays. On Tuesdays and Thursdays I do strength training using free weights and circuit machines. I stretch before and after each training session.*"

❖ Invite the students to turn again to the papers on which they wrote their gifts. Ask them to think about how they might cultivate at least one of these gifts. Suggest that they write whatever they will do on their paper. For example, if they are gifted with a good speaking voice and are asked to read Scripture during a worship service, how could they polish their gift? They could, for example, research commentaries each week to better understand the meaning of the Scripture so that they could read it with greater insight and better expression. Encourage the students to list as many ideas as they can and then silently pledge to God that they will implement ideas so as to be better trained to use their gift.

(5) Continue the Journey

❖ Pray that all who have participated will recognize their gifts and work hard to train themselves so as to be spiritually fit for ministry.

❖ Read aloud this preparation for next week's lesson. You may also want to post it on newsprint for the students to copy.

- ■ **Title: Worship Inspires Service**
- ■ **Background Scripture: 1 Timothy 5:1-22**
- ■ **Lesson Scripture: 1 Timothy 5:1-8, 17-22**
- ■ **Focus of the Lesson: When people lead good and admirable lives, others want to honor them. What service might we give to someone we honor? The writer of 1 Timothy says to serve well the widows who need help and the elders who have earned honor.**

❖ Challenge the students to complete one or more of these activities for further spiritual growth related to this week's session. Post this information on newsprint for the students to copy.

(1) **Encourage younger members of your congregation to prepare themselves for leadership positions. Do whatever you can to mentor them and help them identify and find appropriate places to use their gifts.**

(2) **Recall today's key verse: "Pay close attention to yourself and to your teaching" (4:16). What are your words and deeds teaching others about Jesus? Listen for feedback from others about how you "come across" and adjust your witness accordingly.**

(3) **Be alert for instances of ageism within your congregation. Help to ensure that people of all ages are invited to participate in and lead activities within your church.**

❖ Sing or read aloud "Here I Am, Lord."

❖ Conclude today's session by leading the class in this benediction from Jude 24-25, which is the key verse for the lesson on April 10: **Now to him who is able to keep you from falling, and to make you stand without blemish in the presence of his glory with rejoicing, to the only God our Savior, through Jesus Christ our Lord, be glory, majesty, power, and authority, before all time and now and forever. Amen.**

UNIT 1: A GUIDE FOR WORSHIP LEADERS
WORSHIP INSPIRES SERVICE

PREVIEWING THE LESSON

Lesson Scripture: 1 Timothy 5:1-8, 17-22
Background Scripture: 1 Timothy 5:1-22
Key Verse: 1 Timothy 5:8

Focus of the Lesson:
When people lead good and admirable lives, others want to honor them. What service might we give to someone we honor? The writer of 1 Timothy says to serve well the widows who need help and the elders who have earned honor.

Goals for the Learners:
(1) to examine what 1 Timothy says about honoring widows and elders.
(2) to recognize that when they serve those who are important to God, they serve, honor, and worship God.
(3) to serve and honor those who have faithfully served God.

Supplies:
Bibles, newsprint and marker, paper and pencils, hymnals

READING THE SCRIPTURE

NRSV

1 Timothy 5:1-8, 17-22

¹Do not speak harshly to an older man, but speak to him as to a father, to younger men as brothers, ²to older women as mothers, to younger women as sisters—with absolute purity.

³Honor widows who are really widows. ⁴If a widow has children or grandchildren, they should first learn their religious duty to their own family and make some repayment to their parents; for this is pleasing in God's sight. ⁵The real widow, left alone, has set her hope on God and continues in supplications

NIV

1 Timothy 5:1-8, 17-22

¹Do not rebuke an older man harshly, but exhort him as if he were your father. Treat younger men as brothers, ²older women as mothers, and younger women as sisters, with absolute purity.

³Give proper recognition to those widows who are really in need. ⁴But if a widow has children or grandchildren, these should learn first of all to put their religion into practice by caring for their own family and so repaying their parents and grandparents,

and prayers night and day; [6]but the widow who lives for pleasure is dead even while she lives. [7]Give these commands as well, so that they may be above reproach. **[8]And whoever does not provide for relatives, and especially for family members, has denied the faith and is worse than an unbeliever.**

[17]Let the elders who rule well be considered worthy of double honor, especially those who labor in preaching and teaching; [18]for the scripture says, "You shall not muzzle an ox while it is treading out the grain," and, "The laborer deserves to be paid." [19]Never accept any accusation against an elder except on the evidence of two or three witnesses. [20]As for those who persist in sin, rebuke them in the presence of all, so that the rest also may stand in fear. [21]In the presence of God and of Christ Jesus and of the elect angels, I warn you to keep these instructions without prejudice, doing nothing on the basis of partiality. [22]Do not ordain anyone hastily, and do not participate in the sins of others; keep yourself pure.

for this is pleasing to God. [5]The widow who is really in need and left all alone puts her hope in God and continues night and day to pray and to ask God for help. [6]But the widow who lives for pleasure is dead even while she lives. [7]Give the people these instructions, too, so that no one may be open to blame. **[8]If anyone does not provide for his relatives, and especially for his immediate family, he has denied the faith and is worse than an unbeliever.**

[17]The elders who direct the affairs of the church well are worthy of double honor, especially those whose work is preaching and teaching. [18]For the Scripture says, "Do not muzzle the ox while it is treading out the grain," and "The worker deserves his wages." [19]Do not entertain an accusation against an elder unless it is brought by two or three witnesses. [20]Those who sin are to be rebuked publicly, so that the others may take warning.

[21]I charge you, in the sight of God and Christ Jesus and the elect angels, to keep these instructions without partiality, and to do nothing out of favoritism.

[22]Do not be hasty in the laying on of hands, and do not share in the sins of others. Keep yourself pure.

UNDERSTANDING THE SCRIPTURE

1 Timothy 5:1-2. The instructions for Timothy now focus on relationships with particular groups within the faith community: age- and gender-related, widows, and church leaders identified as "elders." The passage as a whole uses a Greek word for "elder" three times, though in a way that might be confusing. Here in verse 1, "elder" has to do with its literal meaning of age. Hence, both the NRSV and NIV translate the Greek word as "older man." In verses 17 and 19, "elder" references those invested with particular authority or responsibility in the community. The whole of verses 1-2

offers counsel on how Timothy is to exercise his authority toward men and women of different ages. Timothy is to speak to older men as if they were *his* father. Given that culture's strong patriarchal presumptions, the words suggest a very tactful use of authority (one could not *tell* a father what to do in that era). Likewise, Timothy's exercise of authority in relationships with older women is to be as if each woman were his mother. The wisdom of age in both cases is to be respected—but even so, authority is not ceded. The use of family relationship to interpret Timothy's exercise of authority continues with those younger meriting treatment as brothers or sisters. Notably, the one "footnote" in all of these relationships comes in adding to the counsel regarding younger women as sisters: "with absolute purity."

1 Timothy 5:3-8. These verses provide the first of two extended instructions regarding widows in the community. Following the traditions of Judaism, the early church supported, financially and otherwise, the widows in their midst. In an era before pension funds and government support systems, a woman whose husband died could very easily have no means of support. That was not, however, universally the case—as indicated by these verses singling out not once but twice (5:3, 5) "real" widows. "Real" here sets apart those who have no other means of support. The primary means of support, beyond the synagogue or faith community, was the family (5:4). The expectation, defined in that verse as a "religious duty," was squarely placed upon immediate family and relatives. To ignore or deny that obligation, according to the author of 1 Timothy, was "worse than an unbeliever" (5:8). The word "honor" in verse 3 likely refers not simply to holding them in high regard but also to providing physical means of support (see also 5:17 where "honor" may also be translated as "compensation").

1 Timothy 5:9-16. The "list" spoken of here refers to some type of roster that would have been used by the community to identify those who would benefit from some sort of common fund and/or other means of special support. The definition of "real" widow becomes more specific in these verses in terms of age, married only once (Was the assumption that twice-married would have meant more opportunities for her provisioning by others?), and her good works in and beyond family. Equally intriguing, and sometimes baffling, are the comments that follow regarding young widows. Initially, there seems to be a negative attitude toward remarriage (5:11), yet later the counsel *is* for them to remarry, bear children, and "manage their households." The vices listed in verse 13 suggest the author has either heard of or personally experienced such behavior on the part of some younger widows. But does the broadbrush treatment of all seem fitting? The passage closes with urging the care of widows by "believing women." Are these widows, or single women, of means? Are these married women who perhaps have unbelieving spouses? The author leaves the matter of who precisely is meant unclear. But spelled out is his call for relatives to assist widows in their family, in part so that the church can help other "real" widows with no relatives to help.

1 Timothy 5:17-18. The passage now returns its focus to matters related to elders—although now, this is not elders as "elderly," but elders as particular leaders. "Rule" uses the same word translated in chapter 3 as "manage," in terms of the responsibilities there of bishops and deacons. Here, "elders" are giving a ruling or managing function in the community, though the author does not spell out exactly what that might be. Those who rule "well," however, are to be judged worthy of a "double honor." The presumption of the verse is that all elders were to be honored—the good ones were to receive double. Does "honor" here mean simply held in high regard? Or, as suggested with widows in verse 3, is "honor" an expression for some financial support? The latter interpretation is strongly if not irrefutably commended by two quotations that follow. The first, in verse 18, comes from Deuteronomy 25:4, used also by Paul in 1 Corinthians 9:9 to argue for support of those who labor in the gospel. The second quotation, intriguingly, is of Jesus (Luke 10:7, itself a reflection of the teaching in Leviticus 19:13) for the support to be given to the disciples sent out in mission. What makes the force of this argument even more powerful is that the Pastoral Epistles as a whole rarely quote the

Scriptures. To do so here, it can be argued, intends to emphasize the importance of the principle identified: namely, support of those who labor on behalf of the church.

1 Timothy 5:19-22. While not quoted outright, Deuteronomy 17:6 and 19:15 and the words of Jesus in Matthew 18:16 form the backdrop for considering accusations made against elders. The public nature of verse 20's procedure for "rebuke" implicitly understands how such behavior involves the whole of the community, not only in the damage done but also in providing a public witness that serves as a deterrent to such actions. The precise identity of the "elect" angels not only remains unclear but also raises the question: What exactly is a "non-elect" angel? Perhaps here it is best to recall the counsel given at the outset of the letter: "not to occupy themselves with myths and endless genealogies" (1:4). The closing admonition to "not ordain anyone hastily" recalls earlier instructions regarding bishops (3:6) and deacons (3:10). "Participate" translates the Greek word whose noun form translates as "community." Participation, whether in sin or in faith, entails community.

INTERPRETING THE SCRIPTURE

Adaptive Leadership

Much mention has been made in this and previous sessions about the way in which 1 Timothy has drawn upon the language and metaphor of household to describe life and duties within the Christian community. Clearly 1 Timothy 5:1-2 carries on in that same vein in its instructions to Timothy regarding his ministry. But these verses use the language of household to assert an even greater truth: the importance of adapting ministry to its audience.

In 1 Corinthians 9:19-22, Paul makes a similar point in reference to his own ministry. "To the Jews I became as a Jew . . . to those under the law I became as one under the law . . . to those outside the law I became as one outside the law . . . to the weak I became weak . . . I have become all things to all people." Such words are not about the abdication of identity and with it apostolic authority. Rather, they are a critical insight into how the gospel must be "translated" in ways that enhance receptivity on the part of those to whom it is offered.

The same is true in this passage from 1 Timothy. In this case, different ages and genders invite different approaches. Notice, too, that in the case of younger men and women, the counsel to Timothy is to speak as a peer—in this case, as a sibling, not as someone in a superior position. It is also worth noting, in these days of increased awareness of abuse of parishioners by clergy, Timothy's counsel toward young women carries a caveat of "absolute purity." That is, Timothy's needs for companionship and intimacy are no part of the pastoral office when it comes to those with whom he is in a position of authority. To carry the analogy one step further, to abuse that relationship, given the language of household here, would be an act of incest.

To return to the main thrust of this passage, the author counsels Timothy's ministry to be adaptive toward those with whom Timothy is in ministry. It is a point worth remembering not only in the exercise of ministry by pastors and laity today but perhaps especially for the church as a whole. Sometimes, we take the view as though our ministry is what it is, and folks outside can either like it or find something more fitting. The problem is that they often opt for the latter. First Timothy 5:1-2 encourages congregations to be diverse not only in what they do but even how they do it. Who are the ones who need us to relate to them as we might our parents or grandparents, for the sake of the gospel? Who are the ones who need us to relate as peers and siblings, for the sake of the gospel? And how can we do such things—when we freeze ourselves into offering only one style of worship, and one way of administrative structure or involvement? For whose sake, and for the gospel's sake, are we willing to adapt what and how we do things around here?

Caring for Vulnerable Ones

The treatment of widows, along with orphans and strangers, is explained extensively in the Scriptures of Judaism. These represented the most vulnerable ones in society, and care for them was linked decisively with God's purposes for justice and compassion. The early church clearly carried on those traditions. Early on, Acts 6:1 and following reflects practical matters associated with such ministry, and the designation of deacons to ensure its fair conduct. James 1:27 makes a sweeping affirmation of such ministry when it equates genuine religion with, first of all, "care for orphans and widows." So care for widows, to which an extensive part of today's passage is devoted, belongs at the core of Christian community and mission.

It might be asked: Why does 1 Timothy single out widows for so much attention? The answer likely comes in this being a pressing concern for this particular community. The frequency of marriages arranged between older men and younger women (sometimes in their teens) is often seen as a major factor for why communities in this day might have a large number of widows.

It might also explain why little is said about care for widowers, as their numbers would have likely been far fewer—and factors of access to work and inheritance made them less susceptible to being left without resources of their own.

So have such instructions for the care of widows taken a back seat in terms of priority in our day? After all, there are more safety nets in place to provide for support. Do sponsoring bingo games and social gatherings equate to the type of ministry 1 Timothy has in mind regarding "real" widows who are left alone and without resources?

The answer can be: yes, but. . . . The care of widows (and the increasing percentage of widowers) remains a vital ministry. To care for those who have lost the one with whom they have shared much of life, and perhaps much of their faith, is a good and faithful act. But remember: The care for widows (and orphans, and strangers) called forth in our Jewish and Christian traditions arose from a desire to be in ministry to the most vulnerable among us.

So perhaps the missional questions for the church today include: Who are the most vulnerable among us now? Who are the ones deprived of and separated from the most basic necessities and support for life? These are not questions that can be answered for each community with a single answer. Remember 1 Timothy: Among the variety of vulnerable ones possible, the plight of widows seemed most pressing—and thus took the most attention. Who is it, as individuals and groups, whose plight is most pressing in your community? Who are the ones most vulnerable, whose needs you are in a position to respond to with the gospel's call and compassion?

Leadership: Support and Accountability

First Timothy 5:17-22 raise two imperatives for the faith community.

First, those who labor in its leadership deserve and need to be fairly and justly recompensed. Navigating what that means in terms of volunteers in ministry is tricky enough. In these days of spiraling health care costs and comparative salary levels of other professionals in your community, it gets even more difficult. But difficulty is not an out to avoid paying pastors and educators and musicians what is right.

The second imperative is that ministry always and everywhere involves accountability. That is, the authority carried by whatever office is bestowed does not come without conditions of ethics. Leaders in churches, just the same as leaders in other institutions, are accountable. The failure or avoidance of accountability contributes to the erosion of authority for those positions of leadership.

Those who lobby for just and fair support of church leaders need to be equally adamant about matters of accountability. Those who lobby for accountable leaders need to be adamant about providing recompense that reflects their professional skills and gospel faithfulness. Leadership in the family of God requires both support and accountability. Without the first, we risk getting what we pay for—without the second, we risk getting what we did not bargain for.

SHARING THE SCRIPTURE

Preparing Our Hearts

Explore this week's devotional reading, found in John 12:20-26. In response to a request from some visitors, Jesus taught his disciples that following him and serving him were two sides of the same coin. God honors those who serve Jesus. In what ways are you serving Jesus today? What else might you do?

Pray that you and the adult learners will recognize that worshiping Jesus leads one to serve him by meeting the needs of others.

Preparing Our Minds

Study the background Scripture from 1 Timothy 5:1-22 and the lesson Scripture from 1 Timothy 5:1-8, 17-22. Identify the kind of service you might give to someone you want to honor.

Write on newsprint:

❑ questions found under "Recognize that When the Learners Serve Those Who Are Important to God, They Serve, Honor, and Worship God."

❑ information for next week's lesson, found under "Continue the Journey."

❑ activities for further spiritual growth in "Continue the Journey."

LEADING THE CLASS

(1) Gather to Learn

❖ Welcome the class members and introduce any guests.

❖ Pray that those participating in today's session will see the relationship between worshiping God and serving others.

❖ Invite the students to identify ways that we honor people who have performed some admirable service. List their ideas on newsprint. Encourage them to think about local awards (including within the church) as well as major awards, such as a Nobel Peace Prize. If your congregation seldom honors its members, brainstorm ways that they could do so. The ideas could include individual recognition, such as a certificate, pin, or other gift. The ideas may also include recognition of a group, such as holding a dinner to honor those who serve.

❖ Read aloud today's focus statement: **When people lead good and admirable lives, others want to honor them. What service might we give to someone we honor? The writer of 1 Timothy says to serve well the widows who need help and the elders who have earned honor.**

(2) Examine What 1 Timothy Says About Honoring Widows and Elders

❖ Invite a volunteer to read 1 Timothy 5:1-8, 17-22.

❖ Read or retell "Caring for Vulnerable Ones" from Interpreting the Scripture.

❖ Ask the students to identify examples from the Hebrew Scriptures that also speak about caring for those who are vulnerable. Here are some possibilities that you may wish to read or list on newsprint for others to read: Exodus 22:21-22; Psalm 146:9; Isaiah 1:17; 10:1-4; Jeremiah 7:5-7; 22:3; Zechariah 7:9-10; Malachi 3:5.

❖ Use 1 Timothy 5:3-8, 9-16 from Understanding the Scripture to provide additional information.

❖ Lead the group in reading in unison today's key verse, 1 Timothy 5:8. Point out that caring for vulnerable family members is an issue of faith. According to this verse, those who do not care for family are in the same category as those who deny the faith.

❖ Invite comment on this statement by discussing these questions:

    (1) In your experience, are most families caring for relatives who need help in caring for themselves? Give evidence to support your answer.

    (2) What situations in our society make it difficult for people to care for others, even family members?

    (3) What kinds of caregiving tasks may need to be done? (Answers here may include: *helping with bill paying, transporting to appointments, overseeing medical care, providing food and shelter, visiting, assisting with personal hygiene.*)

    (4) If relatives are not caring for vulnerable family members, what role is the church playing—or should it be playing?

❖ Read or retell "Leadership: Support and Accountability" from Interpreting the Scriptures. Ask:

    (1) Given the educational level of our pastor, the hours our pastor works, and our expectations of the pastor, are we following the admonition in Timothy to pay our leaders fairly? If not, why not? What changes do we need to make?

    (2) What standards of accountability do we expect of our pastor? Are our expectations fair? If he or she is not meeting those standards, what steps does the congregation need to take to help the pastor improve accountability?

(3) Recognize that When the Learners Serve Those Who Are Important to God, They Serve, Honor, and Worship God

❖ Talk together about the view in 1 Timothy that we each have a family but that we also are members of the family of God. As such, we are to treat each other as parents and siblings. In doing so, we serve, honor, and worship God.

❖ Distribute paper and pencils. Post these questions that you have written on newsprint prior to the session. Tell the students that they will not be asked to discuss their answers:

    (1) In what ways are you serving God by serving your own family?

    (2) In what ways are you serving God by serving your church family?

    (3) What would Jesus say to you about the way you treat members of your family?

    (4) What would Jesus say to you about the way you treat members of your church family?

    (5) What changes in attitude or actions do you need to make to bring your treatment of family and church family into line with the idea that when you serve them you are truly worshiping and serving God?

(4) Serve and Honor Those Who Have Faithfully Served God

❖ Challenge the class to do something to recognize the pastor(s) and other church leaders. They may want to plan a dinner or celebration for the entire congregation to recognize faithful leadership. Perhaps they would prefer to collect money to buy tickets for a favorite activity of the person/people they choose to honor. Or they may decide to purchase gift cards to a restaurant or store. Be sure to include low-cost options. For example, each class member could write a letter of appreciation and assemble them into a keepsake book. Or members could invite the pastor/leader to someone's home for a group dinner to which each person contributed a dish.

❖ Agree on an idea and then spend some time "fleshing out" a plan of action to implement the idea. You may need to form a task force to take care of details.

(5) Continue the Journey

❖ Pray that all who have come today will continue to serve God in whatever ways they can and uphold those who are called to lead the church.

❖ Read aloud this preparation for next week's lesson. You may also want to post it on newsprint for the students to copy.
- **Title: Remembering Jesus Christ**
- **Background Scripture: 2 Timothy 2:8-15**
- **Lesson Scripture: 2 Timothy 2:8-15**
- **Focus of the Lesson: People find it difficult to articulate their beliefs and values. What can help us articulate our beliefs and values? The experience of worship moves Christians to a deeper understanding of what they believe.**

❖ Challenge the students to complete one or more of these activities for further spiritual growth related to this week's session. Post this information on newsprint for the students to copy.
   1. **Think about those you consider to be family. Are there members who need financial assistance? Are there some who need help with chores or transportation or just someone to talk with or enjoy a meal or outing with? Do what you can to support these people.**
   2. **Volunteer for a hands-on project that serves vulnerable members in your community. Food pantries, soup kitchens, homeless shelters, tutoring programs, hospitals, and nursing homes generally need help. Take at least one step this week by identifying a project and finding out how you can become involved.**
   3. **Do something to honor a church leader who has made an impact on your life with Christ.**

❖ Sing or read aloud "Christ, from Whom All Blessings Flow."

❖ Conclude today's session by leading the class in this benediction from Jude 24-25, which is the key verse for the lesson on April 10: **Now to him who is able to keep you from falling, and to make you stand without blemish in the presence of his glory with rejoicing, to the only God our Savior, through Jesus Christ our Lord, be glory, majesty, power, and authority, before all time and now and forever. Amen.**

UNIT 2: ANCIENT WORDS OF PRAISE
REMEMBERING JESUS CHRIST

PREVIEWING THE LESSON

Lesson Scripture: 2 Timothy 2:8-15
Background Scripture: 2 Timothy 2:8-15
Key Verse: 2 Timothy 2:15

Focus of the Lesson:
People find it difficult to articulate their beliefs and values. What can help us articulate our beliefs and values? The experience of worship moves Christians to a deeper understanding of what they believe.

Goals for the Learners:
(1) to analyze the text as both poetry and theology.
(2) to identify language and images that encourage them in their faith.
(3) to communicate their beliefs to someone else.

Pronunciation Guide:
diamartyromai (dee am ar too' rom ahee)   *kakourgos* (kak oor' gos)
dokimos (dok'-ee-mos)

Supplies:
Bibles, newsprint and marker, paper and pencils, hymnals

READING THE SCRIPTURE

NRSV
2 Timothy 2:8-15
[8]Remember Jesus Christ, raised from the dead, a descendant of David—that is my gospel, [9]for which I suffer hardship, even to the point of being chained like a criminal. But the word of God is not chained. [10]Therefore I endure everything for the sake of the elect, so that they may also obtain the salvation that is in Christ Jesus, with eternal glory. [11]The saying is sure:

NIV
2 Timothy 2:8-15
[8]Remember Jesus Christ, raised from the dead, descended from David. This is my gospel, [9]for which I am suffering even to the point of being chained like a criminal. But God's word is not chained. [10]Therefore I endure everything for the sake of the elect, that they too may obtain the salvation that is in Christ Jesus, with eternal glory.

If we have died with him, we will also live with him;

¹² if we endure, we will also reign with him; if we deny him, he will also deny us;

¹³ if we are faithless, he remains faithful— for he cannot deny himself.

¹⁴Remind them of this, and warn them before God that they are to avoid wrangling over words, which does no good but only ruins those who are listening. **¹⁵Do your best to present yourself to God as one approved by him, a worker who has no need to be ashamed, rightly explaining the word of truth.**

¹¹Here is a trustworthy saying:
If we died with him,
  we will also live with him;
¹²if we endure,
  we will also reign with him.
If we disown him,
  he will also disown us;
¹³if we are faithless,
  he will remain faithful,
  for he cannot disown himself.

¹⁴Keep reminding them of these things. Warn them before God against quarreling about words; it is of no value, and only ruins those who listen. **¹⁵Do your best to present yourself to God as one approved, a workman who does not need to be ashamed and who correctly handles the word of truth.**

UNDERSTANDING THE SCRIPTURE

[handwritten margin note: Jewish leaders saw Christianity as something totally new. Peter + Paul are showing Jewish roots.]

2 Timothy 2:8. The call to "remember" is a common one in the biblical witness, especially in Deuteronomy and Psalms. Remembrance here is connected to "Jesus Christ" and in particular to two fundamental assertions made of him: "raised from the dead" and "a descendant of David." Many understand this as a primitive confession of the church, likely rooted in the church's liturgy. A similar liturgical grounding on this verse may be heard in "remember Jesus Christ" as sounding the invitation to the sacrament of communion, a meal of remembering Jesus. "Raised from the dead" in 2 Timothy's confession picks up the basic proclamation of the church that served as the gospel's "good news" for Jew and Gentile alike. The Davidic connection encouraged here would have been especially key to those in the church with Jewish backgrounds. The link asserts the viability of the church's confession of Jesus as "Christ"—the Greek equivalent of "messiah" or "anointed one." The sermon of Peter on Pentecost makes strong allusions to the Davidic traditions (Acts 2:25-36). Romans 1:3 provides an even

closer parallel to the confession of 2 Timothy 2:8. The final phrase of 2:8 is not a claim of the gospel being the author's (or Paul's) alone, but rather that this is the essence of Paul's proclamation shared by the church as a whole.

2 Timothy 2:9-10. In verse 3 of this chapter, the author had urged Timothy to "share in suffering." Verse 9 (as previously in 1:12) affirms that the author shares in that suffering. Even for those who question the Pauline authorship of the Timothy correspondence, this section like others seems to carry with it the voice of Paul writing in or after imprisonment. The twofold reference to chains makes clear that the suffering or hardship in mind is quite literally understood. An equally compelling image of captivity comes when the author speaks of being restrained "like a criminal." "Criminal" translates the Greek word *kakourgos*—and means literally, "evildoer." Even more powerful, kakourgos is the same word used in Luke to identify those who were crucified with Jesus. The author goes on to link his ability to endure such treatment not to extraordinary personal attributes but rather to his concern for the community ("for the sake of the elect").

2 Timothy 2:11-13. Already noted in these commentaries is the introductory phrase to various teachings in the epistle, "The saying is sure" (1 Timothy 1:15, 3:1). What follows here is a "saying" considered by most interpreters to be the fragment of an early hymn or other liturgical confession. The stylized form of what reads in English as "prose poetry" poses four pairs of statements to invite the readers and communities into reflection on faith and its sometimes paradoxical nature. Nowhere is that theme of paradox more clear than in the opening pair: death in Christ means life in Christ (8:11b). The thought closely parallels the baptismal imagery of dying and rising in Christ of Romans 6:4-5. The second pair includes the same verb for "endure" used in verse 10, so that the implied "suffering" that attaches to the original reference to endurance now is joined to our reigning with Christ (a paradox of seeming weakness that issues in power). The third and fourth pairs are, in themselves, somewhat paradoxical to one another (will Christ deny the deniers, or even in our faithlessness will he remain faithful?).

The nature of this hymn or confession fragment as belonging to the whole community and not simply a recitation of individual beliefs comes through in each of the four lines opening with "if we." The salvation in Christ affirmed in verse 10 gathers us and fashions us into community.

2 Timothy 2:14. Second Timothy 1:6 "reminded" Timothy of the calling of his faith. Here, the author passes on this ministry of calling to remembrance into Timothy's hands—for now Timothy is to be the one who is to remind the community of these teachings. The word translated as "warn" in this verse more closely means "to witness thoroughly" (*diamartyromai*). That

"martyr" became a synonym for those who died for the faith sometimes causes us to overlook that a martyr is first and foremost in the biblical materials one who bears witness. Timothy's witness is, in this verse, to be focused against using words in the community as wrecking balls. "Ruins" in this verse is, in Greek, *katastrophe*—the English derivative is clear, and with it what is being warned against in terms of negative outcomes. "Sticks + Stones" adage untrue

2 Timothy 2:15. The final verse offers an encouragement encountered elsewhere in the Timothy correspondence, for Timothy to serve in word and action as an example of the faith. "Approved" translates a word meaning to "test" or "prove," and carries echoes back to the teaching that deacons were to be so tested before entrusted with authority (1 Timothy 3:10). One of the more intriguing words in the whole passage, and helpful to its understanding, is translated here as "rightly explaining the word of truth." The literal meaning of the Greek, "keeping [on] a straight course the message," prompts the reader to envision cutting a straight path, as in taking a straight line between points a and b, rather than wandering off this way and that. The visual nature of this description helps further discern what was intended in the earlier warnings against "wrangling over words" in this passage and back even further to 1 Timothy 1:4's caution against being occupied with "myths and endless genealogies." The danger in such partisan conflicts or esoteric ruminations is that they deflect the community from its central aim and purpose: namely, witness to the gospel in word and deed and lifestyle. Such a focus entails work, as suggested by the encouragement to Timothy to "do your best" to be such a "worker," whose very life becomes what Timothy "presents to God" (to use other language connected to liturgy and worship).

INTERPRETING THE SCRIPTURE

Remember Jesus Christ

"Remember Jesus Christ." On first hearing, one might think the words would be redundant in the context of a Christian community. The very name (Christian) by which we claim (and are claimed by) our identity and vocation has Christ "built in," so to speak. So why the need to remember?

Because at times we do tend to forget. Consider this in the light of the two explicit calls to remembrance in this passage: "raised from the dead" and "a descendant of David."

We need to remember Jesus Christ, raised from the dead, when we fall into patterns of cynicism that leave us without hope. We need to remember Jesus Christ, raised from the dead, when we lean toward views (and their consequences) that life is only what is here and now and ethics is limited only by what I can get away with. Jesus Christ, raised from the dead, infuses this world and our lives with hope, even when all around us and sometimes within us seems unraveling. Jesus Christ, raised from the dead, summons us to act with faithfulness to God's power, even when the powers that be act as though they are the final word. Remember Jesus Christ, raised from the dead.

And remember Jesus Christ, a descendant of David. In the immediate context of this passage, that remembrance calls to mind the messianic hopes of Judaism that Jesus has come to fulfill. Remember Jesus Christ, a descendant of David, to trust all of God's promises will come to fulfillment. But Jesus Christ, a descendant of David, provides another powerful truth that the church has far too often neglected if not outright denied. Namely, Jesus Christ as descendant of David reminds us of our inextricable connection to Judaism and its followers. Jesus Christ, descendant of David, is a living refutation of the church's illicit dalliance with anti-Semitism. Jesus Christ, descendant of David, confirms that pogroms and holocaust are blasphemies against the very faith that far too often remained silent if not complicit in their face. "Remember Jesus Christ" is a call to our liturgies of word and sacrament in the church—but it is far more. It is a call to pattern our faith and lifestyles on the One who is the core of our faith.

Faith Sources and Resources

Imagine your life as a blank artist's canvas. Who, and what, has "painted" what you have come to know and trust as faith? Where have you been most influenced, not simply in what you think, but in what you feel and experience faith to be?

For some, experiences of Christian education and formation will rise to the surface. Sunday school classes and confirmation programs. Adult groups, conference speakers, retreats. Personal connections will likely play large roles. A teacher or companion who shed light on matters of the heart. The example of a friend or elder. The spontaneity and sense of wonder in children.

The experience of worship, corporate and private, can play a significant role in our coming to and growing in faith. Those who have long-term involvements in the church may not even be aware of how strongly liturgy has shaped beliefs. It is not simply the creeds we recite that connect us to the body of faith passed on to us. Consider how the hymns you have sung and learned over the years form your spirituality. The story of Paul's and Silas's imprisonment in Philippi in the Book of Acts tells of how they passed the night—singing hymns and offering prayers (16:25). Similar stories arise from others held hostage or prisoner. Words and songs remembered from childhood come to the surface as resources of faith in such critical times.

The liturgy and worship of the church, on conscious and unconscious levels, lead us back to our sources of faith—and in doing so, provide us resources for its living. As noted in the earlier commentary on this passage, verse 8 and verses 11-13 are both considered to have been drawn from the worship life of the early church. Their presence in this passage, as for example with Philippians 2:5-11, reminds us that the writers of the epistles drew upon an already-existing body of liturgical materials to frame their faith. As one interpreter noted, such insertions would have allowed the readers to suddenly find themselves "saying" or "singing along" with words already familiar. Have you ever found yourself doing that, when a preacher uses as an illustration the words of a familiar hymn or Scripture? They tie the proclaimed word into what is already our experience. We learn not only by introduction to the new, but by re-acquaintance with the old.

We stand and worship on holy ground not only in the grace that surprises and makes all things new but in the grace into which we feel ourselves returning to a familiar home.

Misleading and Leading Words

"In the beginning was the Word, and the Word was with God, and the Word was God" (John 1:1). To equate the presence and working of God in the world with the metaphor of "word" places a premium on the value and power of words in the faith community. For that very reason, however, the words we use in regard to faith are filled not only with great possibility but also great danger. Words are themselves neutral. How they are used will determine whether they are for good or for ill

Second Timothy 2:14 lays out the case against the negative potential for words in the community. The author warns against "wrangling over words," using a compound verb that literally means "word battles." The reason given has to do with the consequences, spelled out as serving no useful purpose but (mis)leading us into "ruin" (as noted in the commentary above, the word in Greek is *katastrophe*).

One does not need knowledge of Greek to be acquainted with word battles and catastrophes in the church. In such cases, words are not used to identify but to skewer. Words cease to name and instead defame. Words that once sought to clarify positions held become accusations and slurs. Fundamentalist. Liberal. Instead of being transformative of society, word battles pitch us into the same quagmire as those who hurl "babykillers" and "warmongers" in our "civil" disagreements on various issues in our day.

The author urges Timothy, and through him us, to be engaged in a different quality of word-work. The final phrase in this passage is for Timothy to "rightly explain" the word of truth. As noted in the commentary, "rightly explain" has to do with "cutting straight"—perhaps a modern phrasing would be, "cut to the chase." Rather than engaging in circular arguments and "word wrangling" that succeed only in distracting and alienating, go for the core and cut to the center of what (and who) is truly at stake. "Do your best" is what the author counsels Timothy—and us. Words do sometimes fail us, either in their speaking or hearing by us. But do not give up, or give in, to words as battle implements. Our words, as the Word whom we follow, intend to bear God's presence and grace, God's justice and compassion, into this world. Seek to speak that word. Seek to hear that word. Seek to live that word—in Jesus Christ.

SHARING THE SCRIPTURE

Preparing Our Hearts

Explore this week's devotional reading, found in Titus 3:1-7. Here the author, presumably Paul, calls Titus to "remind" the people to behave as those who follow Christ. He contrasts such behavior with the way people often act before they encounter Christ and are saved by grace. Reflect on this passage. Put yourself into it, asking questions related to the text: How do I relate to those in authority? How do I control my tongue? Do I still exhibit any of the negative behaviors that Paul lists? If so, what changes do I need to make in my spiritual life to expunge those behaviors? In sum, how are my words and deeds communicating my personal beliefs about Christ?

Pray that you and the adult learners will strive to be the people God calls you to be so that you may draw others to Christ.

Preparing Our Minds

Study the background Scripture and the lesson Scripture, both of which are from 2 Timothy 2:8-15. Consider what might be able to help you articulate your beliefs and values.

Write on newsprint:
- ❏ information for next week's lesson, found under "Continue the Journey."
- ❏ activities for further spiritual growth in "Continue the Journey."

LEADING THE CLASS

(1) Gather to Learn

❖ Welcome the class members and introduce any guests.

❖ Pray that those who participate in today's session will find words and images that help them convey their beliefs about Christ.

❖ Encourage the students to think about a local, national, or global issue that causes passions to run high. In the United States, issues such as immigration reform, health care reform, and this country's involvement in foreign wars are examples of such issues. Without debating the merits of any particular stance on these issues, invite the adults to give examples of behaviors that indicate people are having trouble articulating their beliefs in a positive way. (Ideas here include: *vilifying those who hold the opposing view, often by assigning labels or using inappropriate images; behaving uncivilly toward the opposition; being unwilling to listen to the other side.*)

❖ Read aloud today's focus statement: **People find it difficult to articulate their beliefs and values. What can help us articulate our beliefs and values? The experience of worship moves Christians to a deeper understanding of what they believe.**

(2) Analyze the Text as Both Poetry and Theology

❖ Choose a volunteer to read 2 Timothy 2:8-15.

❖ Use newsprint to list all the beliefs, stated and implied, that the learners can find in these verses.

❖ Follow up with information from Understanding the Scripture to help the adults better understand the text. (Verses 11-13 are paradoxical and, therefore, perhaps more difficult to understand.) "Remember Jesus Christ" in Interpreting the Scripture also includes information about specific beliefs.

❖ Point out that some of this material was apparently part of the worship liturgy of the early church. "Faith Sources and Resources" in Interpreting the Scripture will provide you with additional information on the topic of resources for liturgy.

❖ Ask the class to look again at verse 14 and then read or retell "Misleading and Leading Words" from Interpreting the Scripture. Ask: **What steps can you take to help the church avoid "wrangling over words"?** (Possibilities include: *being clear and concise when you want to make a point; staying true to your point without getting involved in an argument; encouraging each person to speak so that all are heard and no one person attempts to speak for everyone.*)

❖ Invite the class to read today's key verse, 2:15, in unison.

❖ Provide a few quiet moments for the participants to consider their work for Christ, what they are doing that he approves of, and how they can do better in presenting themselves before him.

(3) Identify Language and Images that Encourage the Learners in Their Faith

❖ Distribute hymnals, paper (two sheets per person), and pencils. Invite the students to locate hymns that express their beliefs about Jesus. Some hymnals have sections of hymns specifically related to Christ and various facets of his life and teaching. Suggest that these sections may be especially fruitful places to look.

❖ Invite the adults to jot down any phrases or images from a hymn that they find especially helpful in articulating their beliefs. Suggest that they write the title and page number as well.

❖ Encourage the students to use their second sheet of paper to write a paragraph or two entitled "This I Believe." They may want to write in their own words, but some adults may prefer to use words from the hymn(s) they have selected.

❖ End this portion of the lesson by soliciting volunteers to read their brief essays.

❖ **Option:** List on newsprint those ideas that everyone in the class seems to agree on. You will have a draft of a "This We Believe" statement that includes everyone.

(4) Communicate Beliefs to Someone Else

❖ Point out that one reason some people feel reluctant to talk with others about their faith is that religious beliefs are personal and therefore off limits for many as a discussion topic. Another reason is that many people do not know what to say that will allow them to communicate their beliefs in a winsome way that draws others to Christ. Perhaps several students in the class have had the uncomfortable experience of being "browbeaten" by a well-intended witness who had rigid views that he (or she) felt everyone should accept. Those adults may find it difficult to talk with others for fear of causing a negative response.

❖ Invite the students to suggest actions and attitudes that enable someone to make a witness that others find engaging. List these ideas on newsprint. Here are some possibilities: *listen respectfully to the other person's ideas and concerns; find a natural opening to discuss your faith; tell your own story; act as an equal, not as someone who is superior; use readily understandable language; read body language; know when it is time to end the conversation.*

❖ Form groups of three. Ask one person to roleplay as a witness, a second to be the one who hears the witness, and the third to be an observer. If time permits, allow each person to play all three roles.

❖ Bring the class together. Invite those who have been observers to comment on what they had seen. What kinds of comments or strategies seemed to work? Why were these so successful?

❖ Conclude by challenging the adults to use some of these positive strategies to share their faith with others.

(5) Continue the Journey

❖ Pray that the participants will go forth to share their beliefs with others.

❖ Read aloud this preparation for next week's lesson. You may also want to post it on newsprint for the students to copy.

■ Title: Praise Builds Us Up
■ Background Scripture: Jude 17-25
■ Lesson Scripture: Jude 17-25
■ Focus of the Lesson: People need frequent assurance for daily living. Where can we find words of assurance to sustain us? Jude's benediction expresses complete confidence in God's ability to sustain us.

❖ Challenge the students to complete one or more of these activities for further spiritual growth related to this week's session. Post this information on newsprint for the students to copy.

(1) Seek a natural opportunity to talk with someone about who you believe Jesus to be and the role that he plays in your life.

(2) Write at least five endings to this statement: "I believe that Jesus. . . ." How does your life reflect what you believe?

(3) Memorize the lyrics of a hymn that expresses beliefs you hold dear about Christ.

❖ Sing or read aloud "Freely, Freely."

❖ Conclude today's session by leading the class in this benediction from Jude 24-25, which is the key verse for the lesson on April 10: **Now to him who is able to keep you from falling, and to make you stand without blemish in the presence of his glory with rejoicing, to the only God our Savior, through Jesus Christ our Lord, be glory, majesty, power, and authority, before all time and now and forever. Amen.**

UNIT 2: ANCIENT WORDS OF PRAISE
PRAISE BUILDS US UP

PREVIEWING THE LESSON

Lesson Scripture: Jude 17-25
Background Scripture: Jude 17-25
Key Verses: Jude 24-25

Focus of the Lesson:
People need frequent assurance for daily living. Where can we find words of assurance to sustain us? Jude's benediction expresses complete confidence in God's ability to sustain us.

Goals for the Learners:
(1) to review Jude's benediction and its affirmations of Jesus as the Savior who builds us up and strengthens us.
(2) to appreciate the connection between assurance and praise.
(3) to praise God.

Pronunciation Guide:
parousia (puh roo' zhee uh)

Supplies:
Bibles, newsprint and marker, paper and pencils, hymnals

READING THE SCRIPTURE

NRSV
Jude 17-25

¹⁷But you, beloved, must remember the predictions of the apostles of our Lord Jesus Christ; ¹⁸for they said to you, "In the last time there will be scoffers, indulging their own ungodly lusts." ¹⁹It is these worldly people, devoid of the Spirit, who are causing divisions. ²⁰But you, beloved, build yourselves up on your most holy faith; pray in the Holy Spirit; ²¹keep yourselves in the love

NIV
Jude 17-25

¹⁷But, dear friends, remember what the apostles of our Lord Jesus Christ foretold. ¹⁸They said to you, "In the last times there will be scoffers who will follow their own ungodly desires." ¹⁹These are the men who divide you, who follow mere natural instincts and do not have the Spirit.

²⁰But you, dear friends, build yourselves up in your most holy faith and pray in the

of God; look forward to the mercy of our Lord Jesus Christ that leads to eternal life. ²²And have mercy on some who are wavering; ²³save others by snatching them out of the fire; and have mercy on still others with fear, hating even the tunic defiled by their bodies.

²⁴Now to him who is able to keep you from falling, and to make you stand without blemish in the presence of his glory with rejoicing, ²⁵to the only God our Savior, through Jesus Christ our Lord, be glory, majesty, power, and authority, before all time and now and forever. Amen.

Holy Spirit. ²¹Keep yourselves in God's love as you wait for the mercy of our Lord Jesus Christ to bring you to eternal life.

²²Be merciful to those who doubt; ²³snatch others from the fire and save them; to others show mercy, mixed with fear—hating even the clothing stained by corrupted flesh.

²⁴To him who is able to keep you from falling and to present you before his glorious presence without fault and with great joy—²⁵to the only God our Savior be glory, majesty, power and authority, through Jesus Christ our Lord, before all ages, now and forevermore! Amen.

UNDERSTANDING THE SCRIPTURE

Jude 17. The letter of Jude is primarily a warning to the community, addressed in this verse (as well as in verses 1, 3, and 20) as the "beloved", against false teachers that have arisen. This section (verses 17-25) comes at the conclusion of the exhortation, containing both further condemnations of these teachers as well as more positive instructions for the community and a concluding benediction. The call to remembrance in this verse appeals to "predictions" by the "apostles." The reference to the apostles is intriguing. The opening of the epistle identifies the author as Jude, the brother of James, which would also make him the brother of Jesus. If the traditional attribution to Jude is held, Acts 1:14 infers that the author may have been part of the Christian community prior to Pentecost. Thus, he would have had personal acquaintance with the apostles and is likely speaking firsthand about the prophecies delineated in the following verse. Many believe this to be a pseudonymous work (where an unnamed author claims the name of a known figure within the community).

Jude 18-19. The specifics of the predictions made in verse 17 now come into view with several key elements. "In the last time"

points to beliefs about the end of time, associated in the early Christian community with the imminent return or parousia of Christ. The reference to "last time" leads some scholars to adopt an early date for the letter's writing, as belief in the imminent return of Christ waned as the church entered its second and then third generation. Writing in *The New Interpreter's Bible*, Duane F. Watson characterizes "scoffers" as "a strong derogatory term denoting mockery of religion or of the righteous by attitude, word, or deed." Clearly, the author of Jude is not pointing to a situation merely involving differences in belief, but outright hostility to what is considered at the center of faith. Such hostility, according to the author, is identified not so much in theological terms but ethical ones ("indulging their own ungodly lusts"). Similar charges of immoral activity were levied earlier in the epistle against these teachers and those who follow their lead (verses 4, 7, 11). Verse 19 points to the result of their behavior that likely formed a large motive in the epistle's writing: division in the community. The added charge that the opponents are without God's Spirit forms a natural link to such division, since God's Spirit is elsewhere affirmed as the source of unity in the church (see, for example, 1 Corinthians 12:13).

Jude 20-21. The repetition of "beloved" (see verse 17) emphasizes the direct and pastoral address offered to the community as the focus now turns away from the false teachers toward the community itself and its calling to live faithfully.

"Build up" translates a Greek word that more literally means "build a home up." It is a word that is employed elsewhere to speak of the faith community and its members (1 Corinthians 3:10-12; 1 Peter 2:5). Such building is to be upon their "holy faith." "Holy" may be used not only in terms of the theology but also the ethics of the community, in contrast to the behavior of the opponents who have already been portrayed as anything but holy.

Three imperatives declare how such building up is to occur. "Pray in the Holy Spirit" points to the community's practice of prayer that maintains their relationship with God through the Spirit (in contrast to the opponents who are "devoid" of Spirit). Such prayer may also reflect what Paul alludes to in Romans 8:26 and 1 Corinthians 14:15. "Keep yourselves in the love of God" places the community's attention on God's love, as opposed to the opponent's "denial" of Christ (verse 4) and "dreamers" (verse 8) who engage in unspecified speculations that reject authority. "Look forward," the final of the three commands, directs the community's attention to the future where Christ's mercy leads to life. This future orientation connects to the previous reference to the apostles' predictions concerning the "last time."

Jude 22-23. The focus shifts in these verses to positive concern for and action toward those who have come under the influence of the false teachers. The core principle to be employed is the practice of "mercy," a word used twice in these verses to indicate how the community is to act toward those seen as erring or wandering. "Wavering" translates a Greek word that literally means "split mind" or "split judgment." Implied here are those who have been attracted to the teachings and practices of the opponents, but who still carry beliefs congruent with the community. Their minds are not made up—and the principle for addressing them is identified not as judgment or ultimatums, but rather mercy. The call to "save" such ones allies the work of the community with the vocation and identity of God as one who saves (verses 5 and 25). The sense of the second half of verse 23 (having mercy with fear) is unclear, though perhaps it might be akin to the adage of "loving the sinner while hating the sin." The notion of hatred comes in the closing phrase of the verse regarding their tunics. This verse may have baptism in the background—as at baptism, the newly initiated one is given a new tunic to wear. The immorality of the opponents defiles the promises made at baptism, of which the tunics would be symbols.

Jude 24-25. Most scholars take these verses as an ancient doxology or benediction used in the liturgy of the early Christian community. "Without blemish" stands in contrast to the defilement mentioned in the previous verse. The identification of God as Savior occurs in other New Testament epistles (1 Timothy 1:1; Titus 1:3) and would link to the early church's close ties with Judaism (for example, Jude 5). The fourfold attribution of glory, majesty, power, and authority to God sounds a note of praise or doxology similar to the heavenly liturgies in Revelation 19:1.

INTERPRETING THE SCRIPTURE

Building on Faith

Make a list of the reasons you participate in the study of this resource with others. Now listen to the words of Jude verse 20 as you reflect on those reasons: "build yourselves up on your most holy faith." Faith is not something we get, whole and intact, and then keep by doing nothing with or about it. We grow in faith. We nurture our relationship with God. Or, to use the more literal meaning of the verb noted in the commentary on verse 20, we "build our home" in faith by engaging in activities and studies that deepen our understanding and then encourage our practice of what it means to be a disciple of Jesus Christ.

The ways in which that may be done are diverse. But for the moment, let us explore more deeply the three things that Jude lifts up in regards to building ourselves up in faith.

First, "pray in the Holy Spirit" (verse 20). The Spirit is God's presence with us. To pray in the Spirit is not so much any one style of prayer as it is a deep and conscious awareness that prayer brings us into and reminds us of God's presence. Prayer is a spiritual practice that continually pulls us back into the recognition that we do not live for or unto ourselves alone. Prayer is a spiritual practice that also reminds us we do not live purely by our skill or cunning alone. Prayer engages us in awareness of and responsiveness to the presence of God in our lives and in this world. Prayer is not simply our conversation with God. More broadly, it is our opening of the totality of our lives and hopes and fears and needs to God. To pray in the Spirit builds upon the faith that God is among us.

The second emphasis of Jude for building ourselves up in faith is to "keep yourselves in the love of God." That is, never forget that you are someone—and your neighbor is someone—loved of God. The former delivers us from self-effacement that confuses humiliation with humility. The latter delivers us from pride that sees God as ours and ours alone. The love of God is for all creation (remember John 3:16: for God so loved *the whole world*), not just one people or one nation or one gender or one political philosophy. Keeping ourselves in the love of God saves us from falling prey to limiting God's love only to those persons and those attributes that we judge to be lovable by our standards.

Thirdly, Jude counsels: "look forward to the mercy of our Lord Jesus Christ that leads to eternal life." Look forward. Too much of life, and too much of religion, looks backward alone. History can be a great teacher, but nobody gets to live in the past. We are called to live in the present—and we find strength to do so, especially when the present becomes trying and difficult, by the promise that the future belongs to God. That promise is trustworthy for God is trustworthy—and the life that is eternal begins even now, and stretches beyond our understanding.

Opponents and Mercy

Some find it difficult to believe in Jonah being swallowed by a great fish. Some consider it ludicrous for a camel to pass through the eye of a needle. But these expressions pale in scandal and in challenge to one of the fundamental teachings of Jesus: Love your enemies.

The epistle of Jude uses some extraordinarily strong and confrontational language to speak of false teachers who engage in scurrilous behavior. Yet even Jude counsels that those who find themselves leaning in such perilous directions are to be treated with mercy. It is not the only place beyond the Gospels we encounter such counsel.

Writing to the church at Rome, to a community who faced precarious circumstances and dangerous (and powerful) opponents, Paul encouraged the community to bless those who persecuted them and to not repay evil for evil. Why? Vengeance belongs to God. And from that principle comes the ethic: "Do not be overcome by evil, but overcome evil with good" (Romans 12:14-21).

Overcome evil with good, says Paul. Show mercy to those who threaten to disrupt the community, says Jude.

What say you? Clearly, those strategies are not the common ways of doing things in the world around us—and sometimes not in the church. In our battles over who is the most patriotic or who is the "real" Christian, we tend to rely on anything but mercy. We lean toward fighting fire with fire, and calling a spade a spade, rather than taking the far more challenging way of overcoming evil with good. Perhaps it's because we really don't believe it. Do you? Is mercy the path to take with those with whom we are in conflict? Is Jesus' call to love one's enemies a naive sentiment of simpler times?

Or is such love, and such mercy, ultimately the only way we will find our way out of our partisan bickerings and belittlings into the community we can yet be in Christ?

Bene-diction: "The Good Word"

This particular unit of the quarter has for its overall focus "Ancient Words of Praise." The final two verses of our passage from Jude are a doxology (the literal meaning of which is "praise/glory word"). Speak these words aloud. They easily could serve, and often have served, as that element of the church liturgy we typically refer to as the *benediction*, from the Latin meaning "good word."

Benedictions close worship services because they provide us with a "good word" with which to carry us out of the sanctuary and into our daily living. And this word provided by Jude, likely derived from the worship experience of Jude's own worshiping community, is a good one indeed. It begins on the note that God is able to keep us from falling, and more than that makes it possible for us to stand. We need such assurance when we encounter trying times. We need such assurance even in smooth times, when we might be seduced into thinking we stand all by ourselves and by our own effort. We do not. God, the grace of God, the love of God, the power of God is that which makes it possible for us to stand and live.

Yet another good word Jude offers to our liturgies and to our living is that God is our Savior. God is not the one who is out to catch us red-handed so as to justify a long-intentioned punishment. God is the one who is out to help us, out to lift us up, out to bring us to life. Remember also that one of the words for "save" in Greek can also be translated as "heal" or "make whole." God is the one who would heal us, who would make us whole when and where we feel broken.

Such a God deserves our highest praise. The closing attributions of "glory, majesty, power, authority" to God affirm not only such praise of God—they encapsulate our hopes. For in spite of other claimants to glory and majesty and power and authority in our midst, we praise the God to whom these qualities truly belong. And so long as they do, we will now and always be in the good hands of the God who is Savior.

SHARING THE SCRIPTURE

Preparing Our Hearts

Explore this week's devotional reading, found in 2 Corinthians 4:1-12. Here Paul writes about ministry as he understands and practices it. Read Jude 17-25 and note how different Paul's way is from those referred to as "scoffers" in Jude. In that community, as well as the Corinthian community, there are those who create divisions within the church. Paul, however, focuses on "the glory of God in the face of Jesus Christ" (4:6). Similarly, readers are called on to give glory to God in verse 25 of Jude. What parallels do you see in this passage from 2 Corinthians and Jude 17-25?

Pray that you and the adult learners will give praise and honor and glory to God through Jesus Christ our Lord.

Preparing Our Minds

Study the background Scripture and the lesson Scripture, both of which are from Jude 17-25. Think about this question as you read: Where can we find the words of assurance that we need for daily living?

Write on newsprint:
❑ information for next week's lesson, found under "Continue the Journey."
❑ activities for further spiritual growth in "Continue the Journey."

LEADING THE CLASS

(1) Gather to Learn

❖ Welcome the class members and introduce any guests.

❖ Pray that all who have gathered today will find assurance for living their lives in the way of Christ as we study together God's Word.

❖ Brainstorm answers to this question with the class: **What kinds of problems beset people in your nation and community?** Keep the answers generic. For example, "unemployment," rather than "Sam Jones lost his job last week."

❖ Talk about where people look to find assurance so that they can continue to live even in the face of a job loss, home foreclosure, family break-up, natural catastrophe, and so on.

❖ Read aloud today's focus statement: **People need frequent assurance for daily living. Where can we find words of assurance to sustain us? Jude's benediction expresses complete confidence in God's ability to sustain us.**

(2) Review Jude's Benediction and Its Affirmations of Jesus as the Savior Who Builds Us Up and Strengthens Us

❖ Introduce today's Scripture by reading Jude 17 from Understanding the Scripture.

❖ Select a volunteer to read Jude 17-23.

❖ Make a list on the left side of a sheet of newsprint of the characteristics of "scoffers" identified in verses 17-19. Make a list on the right side of characteristics of the body of Christ from verses 20-23. Encourage the class to talk about the differences they see.

❖ Read again verses 20-21. Use "Building on Faith" in Interpreting the Scripture to discuss how God's "beloved" people are called to act. Ask:
  (1) In what ways do you think today's church members follow this teaching?
  (2) What examples can you give to support your answer?

❖ Invite the class to look again at verses 22-23. Read information for these verses from Understanding the Scripture. Encourage the adults to comment on how their own congregation treats others with mercy.

❖ Lead the class in reading in unison today's key verses from Jude 24-25. Note that we are using these verses as our session benediction throughout this quarter. Ask:

(1) What do these verses say to you about God?

(2) What do they suggest to you about the kind of response we are to make to God?

(3) Appreciate the Connection Between Assurance and Praise

❖ Note that in Jude's benediction we see a clear connection between the assurance of Christ's ability to save and care for us and the praise that we give to God.

❖ Read this May 24, 1738 entry from the journal of John Wesley, the Anglican priest who founded the Methodist movement: **In the evening I went very unwillingly to a society in Aldersgate Street, where one was reading Luther's preface to the Epistle to the Romans. About a quarter before nine, while the leader was describing the change which God works in the heart through faith in Christ, I felt my heart strangely warmed. I felt I did trust in Christ alone for salvation; and an assurance was given me that He had taken away my sins, even mine, and saved me from the law of sin and death.**

❖ Suggest to the students that they think about Wesley's moment of absolute assurance in Christ's salvation and the words of doxology (praise) that Jude writes. Ask: **What connections do you see between assurance and praise?**

❖ Invite the class members to report on times when they knew without question that God was with them. (Remind the students that their stories need not be as dramatic as Wesley's.) They may report to the entire class or to a partner.

❖ Count to three and ask everyone to speak a word of praise in unison to Christ for the assurance he has given and continues to give in all situations.

(4) Praise God

❖ Form groups of three or four students. Distribute paper and pencils and optional hymnals. Read "Bene-diction: 'The Good Word'" from Interpreting the Scripture. Invite the groups to respond in one of the following ways.

- **Option 1: Rewrite Jude 24-25 in your own words and then share your benediction with your group.**
- **Option 2: Write your own benediction of praise to God and then share your benediction with your group.**
- **Option 3: Locate a hymn, perhaps in a section entitled something such as "Closing of Worship" that for you serves as a benediction—a good word. Tell the group your choice and why you made that selection.**

❖ Call the groups together. Ask them for any new insights they have gleaned from their activities.

❖ Find out which closing hymns were selected and sing a verse or two of one to conclude this portion of the session.

(5) Continue the Journey

❖ Pray that today's participants will feel assurance in their hearts that God is with them at all times—and that their response to this mercy will be praise.

❖ Read aloud this preparation for next week's lesson. You may also want to post it on newsprint for the students to copy.

- **Title: Hosanna!**
- **Background Scripture: Mark 11:1-11**
- **Lesson Scripture: Mark 11:1-11**
- **Focus of the Lesson: People joyously and lavishly praise those whom they believe are worthy. Who merits extravagant praise? Mark's Gospel says that the people shouted hosanna to Jesus because they believed he was bringing the reign of God.**

❖ Challenge the students to complete one or more of these activities for further spiritual growth related to this week's session. Post this information on newsprint for the students to copy.

(1) Be alert for teachings that you feel are false and undermine the body of Christ. What are these teachings? Do some research to discern whether or not those who are "on the other side" have any biblical support for their beliefs. Search the Bible to strengthen your own understanding of its stance on the issue.

(2) Memorize the benediction in Jude 24-25. Recite it as often as you can and claim its promises.

(3) Offer praise to God through word, song, dance, or visual arts.

❖ Sing or read aloud "It Is Well with My Soul."

❖ Conclude today's session by leading the class in this benediction from Jude 24-25, which is also the key verse for this lesson: **Now to him who is able to keep you from falling, and to make you stand without blemish in the presence of his glory with rejoicing, to the only God our Savior, through Jesus Christ our Lord, be glory, majesty, power, and authority, before all time and now and forever. Amen.**

UNIT 2: ANCIENT WORDS OF PRAISE
HOSANNA!

PREVIEWING THE LESSON

Lesson Scripture: Mark 11:1-11
Background Scripture: Mark 11:1-11
Key Verse: Mark 11:9

Focus of the Lesson:
People joyously and lavishly praise those whom they believe are worthy. Who merits extravagant praise? Mark's Gospel says that the people shouted hosanna to Jesus because they believed he was bringing the reign of God.

Goals for the Learners:
(1) to recount the story of Jesus' entry into Jerusalem.
(2) to identify and respond to cries of hosanna.
(3) to participate in joyful and exuberant worship.

Pronunciation Guide:
apostello (ap os tel' lo)
Bethphage (beth' fuh jee)
Kiriath-jearim (kihr ee ath jee'uh rim)

Supplies:
Bibles, newsprint and marker, paper and pencils, hymnals

READING THE SCRIPTURE

NRSV
Mark 11:1-11

¹When they were approaching Jerusalem, at Bethphage and Bethany, near the Mount of Olives, he sent two of his disciples ²and said to them, "Go into the village ahead of you, and immediately as you enter it, you will find tied there a colt that has never been ridden; untie it and bring it. ³If anyone says to you, 'Why are you doing this?' just say

NIV
Mark 11:1-11

¹As they approached Jerusalem and came to Bethphage and Bethany at the Mount of Olives, Jesus sent two of his disciples, ²saying to them, "Go to the village ahead of you, and just as you enter it, you will find a colt tied there, which no one has ever ridden. Untie it and bring it here. ³If anyone asks you, 'Why are you doing this?' tell him, 'The

this, 'The Lord needs it and will send it back here immediately.'" [4]They went away and found a colt tied near a door, outside in the street. As they were untying it, [5]some of the bystanders said to them, "What are you doing, untying the colt?" [6]They told them what Jesus had said; and they allowed them to take it. [7]Then they brought the colt to Jesus and threw their cloaks on it; and he sat on it. [8]Many people spread their cloaks on the road, and others spread leafy branches that they had cut in the fields. [9]Then those who went ahead and those who followed were shouting,

> **"Hosanna!**
> **Blessed is the one who comes in the name of the Lord!**

[10] Blessed is the coming kingdom of our ancestor David!
Hosanna in the highest heaven!"

[11]Then he entered Jerusalem and went into the temple; and when he had looked around at everything, as it was already late, he went out to Bethany with the twelve.

Lord needs it and will send it back here shortly.'"

[4]They went and found a colt outside in the street, tied at a doorway. As they untied it, [5]some people standing there asked, "What are you doing, untying that colt?" [6]They answered as Jesus had told them to, and the people let them go. [7]When they brought the colt to Jesus and threw their cloaks over it, he sat on it. [8]Many people spread their cloaks on the road, while others spread branches they had cut in the fields. [9]Those who went ahead and those who followed shouted,

> **"Hosanna!"**
> **"Blessed is he who comes in the name of the Lord!"**

[10]"Blessed is the coming kingdom of our father David!"
"Hosanna in the highest!"

[11]Jesus entered Jerusalem and went to the temple. He looked around at everything, but since it was already late, he went out to Bethany with the Twelve.

UNDERSTANDING THE SCRIPTURE

Mark 11:1a. All four Gospels relate the story of Jesus' entry into Jerusalem, each with slightly different details and emphases. Listen to the perspective Mark offers in his narrative. "Approaching Jerusalem" recalls that the previous episode with Bartimeaus took place outside of Jericho. The road from Jericho to Jerusalem was a steep climb of approximately eighteen miles with an elevation gain of nearly 3,000 feet. Thievery on the road could prove hazardous to travelers (the parable of the good Samaritan is set in that location), so it is likely Jesus and the disciples made the journey in a single day. Bethphage and Bethany were small villages less than 2 miles from Jerusalem to the east. The Mount

of Olives is a ridge just to the east of Jerusalem that runs in a north-south direction.

Passages in Ezekiel 11:23 and particularly Zechariah 14:1-4 associate the Mount with messianic hopes of God's return and victory. While Mark does not specifically note it in this passage, Jesus' entry into Jerusalem coincides with the gathering of pilgrims for Passover. Mark has already revealed that Jesus understands the journey to Jerusalem brings with it suffering and death and rising for the "Son of Man" (Mark 10:33-34).

Mark 11:1b-3. These verses comprise the account of instructions Jesus gives to prepare for the entry and the disciples following through on them. Two disciples are mentioned, though Mark does not give us their names. "Immediately" (also translated as "at once") is a favorite expression of Mark, used some 35 times in this Gospel to underscore the immediacy and power of Jesus' teachings and actions. Mark does not clarify whether the "colt" is that of a horse or a donkey, though the latter would have been far more common in the region. The episode leaves it undisclosed whether Jesus has prearranged this loan of the colt without the disciples' knowledge, or whether this is a matter of Jesus "knowing" what will happen. In either case, the passage clearly depicts Jesus as the one who controls the action as it unfolds. That is a key theme in the events of Holy Week as well. Jesus is not passively caught up in events out of his control. Jesus acts with intention and obedience, even when matters turn violent. It is unclear in verse 3 whether "Lord" refers to Jesus, God, or perhaps even the owner of the colt. It is to be noted that nowhere in Mark does Jesus use "Lord" in reference to himself.

Mark 11:4-6. The "mission" of the disciples whom Jesus "sent" (the Greek verb is *apostello*, from which we get "apostle" as one who is sent) falls into place exactly as Jesus had indicated. Even the challenge by bystanders is met. The episode as a whole foreshadows what will happen when Jesus gives instructions to the disciples for preparations to observe the Passover (Mark 14:12-16). Jerusalem's entry and Jerusalem's table take place in accordance with Jesus' purposes.

Mark 11:7-8. Before the procession, final preparations are made. The placing of cloaks on the colt would have been a simple act of making the ride more cushioned. The details of spreading cloaks on the road and leafy branches cut in the fields bears far more attention. It may be that the spreading of garments on the road reflected an ancient enthronement custom, such as witnessed in 2 Kings 9:13. Notice Mark says "leafy branches." Only John's Gospel (12:13) iden-

tifies these as palms. The problem with palms is that they were not common in the Jerusalem region. They were, however, in Jericho—called the city of palm trees (see Deuteronomy 34:3). Would palms have been cut prior to their journey to Jerusalem? Palms were brought to Jerusalem for the festival of Tabernacles, which took place in the fall. The link with Tabernacles, and the possibility of palms on this day, may be significant. During the Maccabean revolution, palms were carried into the Temple for its rededication. In the time of Jesus, other revolutionists—Zealots—sought a "rededication" of the land from Roman rule. Some sources suggest that the Zealots used palms as symbols for their movement, to identify themselves as latter-day Maccabeans. If so we wonder what might the palms have suggested—or incited—in the crowd as Jesus entered into Jerusalem.

Mark 11:9-10. The cries of the crowd come from the Egyptian Hallel ("praise") psalms of 113–118, traditionally sung or recited during the three pilgrimage festivals of Passover, Pentecost, and Tabernacles, but particularly at the beginning and end of Passover. The initial and closing cry, "hosanna," translates to something like "save us, we pray" or "help us," or "save now." If the crowds are not merely quoting the lines of Scripture from Psalm 118:25-26 but associating the blessings of the psalm with Jesus, then two things become clear. First, there is some recognition that Jesus comes to Jerusalem in the name (and therefore purpose) of God. Second, the acclamation of the coming kingdom of David associates Jesus not only with that kingdom but, in some sense, with the Davidic hopes. What Mark leaves unclear, and what the events of Passion Week further complicate, is what exactly these acclamations mean for those who offer them. The cry of hosanna reflects a recognition of need—but, as with the misunderstandings of the disciples, the rest of the Passion narrative leaves unresolved whether the help or saving envisioned had anything to do with the help and saving Jesus intended.

Mark 11:11. Jesus goes to the Temple, but unlike Matthew and Luke, Mark does not narrate the cleansing of the Temple on Palm Sunday. Rather, "the hour is late." The journey from Jericho would have taken all day, and he leaves. But not without first "looking around." That verb has special meaning in Mark. It is the verb Jesus uses in 3:5 when viewing the hypocrisy of some religious leaders. It is the verb Jesus uses in 3:34 when viewing the crowd and perceiving them as family. It is the verb Jesus uses in 10:23 when he looks at the disciples after they wonder how anyone can be saved after his hard words to a rich young man. When Jesus "looks around," he sees beneath the surface. He sees the deeper things. And here, he sees Jerusalem.

INTERPRETING THE SCRIPTURE

Sacred Geography

It is part of human nature to attach special meaning to places where significant events have occurred—or, in some cases, where hopes are "placed." We carry memories and attachments, for good or ill, to the homes and neighborhoods where we grew up as children. For some of us, there may be places in this world that we go back to, figuratively or literally, to gain perspective or to recall some experience. In many communities, cemeteries function that way. Folks gather there to decorate graves or simply to observe in silence the "resting place" of one whom we have loved or befriended.

So it is understandable that the stories of faith come attached to particular places. "Holy Land" likely brings to mind a very specific geography. That connection is deepened by the way our moorings in Judaism have been tied so closely to the promise of land, of "place." It is not so that this particular terrain differs physically from other places on earth. I once drove a German minister to a conference meeting in central Washington, and as we descended down a mountain pass into the southern reaches of the Yakima valley, he noted how similar it seemed to places he had visited in Israel. Land and place and story weave together in powerful ways in the biblical narrative and in the hopes those narratives bring.

Consider the Palm Sunday narrative's reliance on "sacred geography" in telling its story. The story is, above all else, a narrative of journey or pilgrimage to Jerusalem. Jesus is not alone in making this journey at this season. He would have been part of crowds that poured into the city from practically every direction in order to observe the festival of Passover. Pilgrimage to Jerusalem on Passover was expected of all Jews who were able, physically and financially, to make the journey. It was not that the story of Passover could not be read in another place. It was that the place of Jerusalem brought to its observance special meaning in the gathering of community at the site of the Temple.

The other element of sacred geography in this narrative is the Mount of Olives. As noted in Understanding the Scripture, this mount was not simply a prominent physical feature. The Mount of Olives was associated with the story of God's return in victory. It was a place of messianic hope. It loomed to the east of Jerusalem as a reminder that God was not yet finished with the work of redemption. Ironically, as this particular story plays out, what separated the ridge on which Jerusalem was set and the Mount of Olives was a valley or ravine in which was a garden called Gethsemane. Sacred geography on Palm Sunday leads to sacred stories in the rest of this week.

Hosanna!

For a moment, separate the cry of "hosanna" and its literal meanings from the context of Palm Sunday. Say, for example, you were walking down the street and heard someone cry out from a nearby building or a dark alley: "Save us!" "Help us!" Would the first thought that comes to your mind be that this was an act of praise? Or might you think that the one who cries out stands in need of someone to intercede for them in the midst of a desperate situation?

Bring your thoughts back into the context of Palm Sunday. To be sure, "hosanna" is linked with a quotation from Psalm 118:25-26. Hosanna is part of that psalm's "liturgy" that gives thanks for God's deliverance. It is a psalm traditionally associated with the Feast of Tabernacles (see the comments on Tabernacles in Understanding the Scripture). It was also a psalm, however, that was read as part of the Passover seder meal. And Passover, you will recall, celebrated God's deliverance of Israel from the oppression of Egypt.

So consider all of those liturgical and narrative backgrounds that flow into the cry of "hosanna" on Palm Sunday. It is an act of praise—but it is far more than that. It is a plea for God to intervene, to take saving action. We cannot read the mind of the crowd, to know whether they simply shout "hosanna" as pilgrims might ordinarily sing or recite the words of Psalm 118 as they journeyed toward Jerusalem. But what we do know is this: Mark chose to include "hosanna" in his Palm Sunday narrative, while Luke 19:28-40, for example, omits it. "Hosanna" serves a purpose in Mark. And in this Gospel that is so thoroughly interested in the actions of Jesus, "hosanna" strikes the chord that yet another action of Jesus is forthcoming, one that is "helping" and "saving" in nature.

The question comes to mind: Is the action expected by those who cry "hosanna" the same as the action intended by the One who now comes and enters in the name of God?

Expectations, Exuberance, and the Rest of the Story

One way to view the story of Palm Sunday and its exuberant crowd shouting "hosanna" is as a critique of the cautious approach some Christians bring to this—or other—faith-based "parades." Shouldn't we be shouting the news of Christ's coming, and our delight in following? But it is entirely plausible, from the story of Palm Sunday and the ensuing events of Holy Week, that the attitude of caution implicitly critiqued is precisely what Mark and the other Gospels encourage us to do. In fact, what the Gospels caution against may be such self-forgetting exuberance that makes possible the seismic shift between shouts of "hosanna" on Sunday and shouts of "crucify" on Friday.

To return to the point made at the end of the previous section, it is not at all clear that the "hosannas" of the crowd reflect expectations of God's reign congruent with how Jesus understood the meaning of his Jerusalem entry. The disconnect between the shouted praise and the ensuing days takes shape in several ways. In Mark, the procession into Jerusalem abruptly ends with no action, except for Jesus "looking around" at everything. In Luke, the procession of welcome leads to tears over the city by Jesus and the cleansing of the Temple. In Matthew the shouts of "hosanna" quickly are stifled by the din of overturned tables in the Temple and the growing anger of religious leaders.

"Hosanna" in Mark is implicitly linked to Davidic hopes ("Blessed is the coming kingdom of our ancestor David"). There is much opinion abroad about what those hopes consisted of, particularly in how widespread were the Zealots' ambition to institute a land free of Roman rule, a revolt that would "force" God to intervene. To say that such militaristic and triumphalist hopes dominated the cries of "hosanna" would be overstatement, but to suggest the cries of "hosanna" reflected trust that suffering and crucifixion would be the initial means of that reign's establishment would be extraordinarily naive.

The people cry "hosanna," but their praise on Palm Sunday does not match the cries uttered during Holy Week. Our cries for "hosanna" need to steer clear of self-forgetting exuberance that separates itself from what is about to come. Our cries for "hosanna"—our praised confession of the need for God's saving and helping—are best offered when they open us to the works of God in Jesus Christ and do not dictate how God should be about the redemption business.

SHARING THE SCRIPTURE

Preparing Our Hearts

Explore this week's devotional reading, found in 1 Chronicles 16:8-15. The context of this psalm of thanksgiving is the movement of the ark from Kiriath-jearim to Jerusalem (1 Chronicles 13) and placing it in its tent. Once the ark is placed, public worship that includes offerings, food, and music is celebrated. Note the reasons that the people praise God in verses 8-15. Which of these reasons prompts us to sing praise? What other reasons do you have to rejoice in the Lord?

Pray that you and the adult learners will joyously offer praise and thanksgiving to God.

Preparing Our Minds

Study the background Scripture and the lesson Scripture, both of which are from Mark 11:1-11. Who do you believe merits extravagant praise?

Write on newsprint:
❏ information for next week's lesson, found under "Continue the Journey."
❏ activities for further spiritual growth in "Continue the Journey."

LEADING THE CLASS

(1) Gather to Learn

❖ Welcome the class members and introduce any guests.

❖ Pray that those who have gathered today will be ready to hear and respond to the word of the Lord.

❖ Suggest that the students recount stories of parades they have witnessed or participated in that were held to honor someone. Perhaps they recall such an event being held after a team won a championship. Encourage them to talk about how people honored those they felt were worthy of praise.

❖ Read aloud today's focus statement: **People joyously and lavishly praise those whom they believe are worthy. Who merits extravagant praise? Mark's Gospel says that the people shouted hosanna to Jesus because they believed he was bringing the reign of God.**

(2) Recount the Story of Jesus' Entry Into Jerusalem

❖ Read Mark 11:1-11 dramatically by choosing a narrator, someone to read Jesus' words, and two people to act as bystanders. Encourage the rest of the class to read verses 9b-10. Invite the class to imagine that they were in Jerusalem.

❖ **Option:** If you have palms available, distribute them and invite the students to wave them as the Scripture is read.

❖ Roleplay a discussion between two of the disciples. Set the stage with these words: **Assume you have heard and followed**

Jesus' directions regarding preparation for his arrival. You have done as you were told, and the scene is just as Jesus had said it would be. What kinds of questions would you be asking concerning who Jesus is?

❖ Discuss these questions with the class:

(1) Had you been present in Jerusalem for the Passover, what might you have been thinking as this scene unfolded?

(2) What expectations might you have had of Jesus? (Read or retell "Expectations, Exuberance, and the Rest of the Story" from Interpreting the Scripture and Mark 11:7-8 from Understanding the Scripture to help clarify the kinds of expectations people may have had.)

(3) Had you been a Roman official who witnessed this procession, what concerns might you have had? How would you have responded?

❖ Point out that in many churches today it is called Palm/Passion Sunday. In a few short days, the shouts of "hosanna" will become angry yells to "crucify him." Provide a few moments for the students to reflect on what their words say to—and about—Jesus.

(3) Identify and Respond to Cries of Hosanna

❖ Lead the class in a unison reading of today's key verse, Mark 11:9.

❖ Explain the meaning of a key word in this text by reading or retelling "Hosanna!" from Interpreting the Scripture.

❖ Form several small groups. Read this information and provide each student with paper and a pencil to record their ideas. **Imagine cries of "hosanna" today. As already noted, for some first-century witnesses to Jesus' entry into Jerusalem, the words "save us" or "help us" had political overtones in light of the oppression they** experienced under Roman rule. Who or what is crying "hosanna" today? What expectations do these people have for Jesus to save them from the challenges they face? (Encourage the class to think not only on an individual basis, such as a personal illness or financial crisis, but also on a larger scale. For example, voices are crying "hosanna" to save the earth in light of global warming. As another example, voices are crying for the poor around the world to be recognized, cared for, and given a hand up.)

❖ Provide time for each group to report on their ideas.

❖ Conclude this portion of the session by asking the students:

(1) What do you think Jesus is calling you to do in response to these cries of hosanna? (You may want to encourage them to think of a response they could make as a group.)

(2) How does your response not only alleviate suffering but also lavish praise upon Christ?

(4) Participate in Joyful and Exuberant Worship

❖ Invite the learners to turn in their hymnals to "Hosanna, Loud Hosanna" and read or sing this Palm Sunday hymn. Ask: **What does this hymn say to you about how and why people praise Jesus?**

❖ List on newsprint ways the adults can think of to praise Jesus. Remember that praise may come in many forms, such as music, dance, drama, service, witnessing, and prayer.

❖ Distribute paper and pencils. Encourage the students to jot down some elements in a worship service that they feel would enable them to lavish praise upon Christ. Suggest that they give an example of something they have selected, such as a kind of music, art work, or service that would bestow praise.

❖ Hear ideas from the adults. Talk about ways your congregation already includes their ideas—or could include such ideas—in worship.

(5) Continue the Journey

❖ Pray that all who have participated in today's class will lavish exuberant praise upon Christ.

❖ Read aloud this preparation for next week's lesson. You may also want to post it on newsprint for the students to copy.

■ **Title: Christ Is Risen!**
■ **Background Scripture: Matthew 28:1-17**
■ **Lesson Scripture: Matthew 28:1-17**
■ **Focus of the Lesson: We love some people so dearly that we remember them after they die. How does our love for others continue even after their death? When the angel reported that Jesus had risen from the dead, those who heard the news worshiped.**

❖ Challenge the students to complete one or more of these activities for further spiritual growth related to this week's session. Post this information on newsprint for the students to copy.

(1) **Do some research concerning religious pilgrimages. Perhaps you have been on such a journey** yourself. **Why do people make pilgrimages? What are they hoping to experience in the area they visit—and learn about themselves?**

(2) **Read the accounts of Jesus' entry into Jerusalem as found in Mark 11:1-11, Matthew 21:1-11, Luke 19:28-40, and John 12:12-19. What similarities and differences do you note? What do the differences suggest about the way each author is telling his story? Which story makes the greatest impression on you? Why?**

(3) **Listen for and respond to cries of "hosanna," "save us," from people around the globe.**

❖ Sing or read aloud "Mantos y Palmas (Filled with Excitement)," which is based, in part, on Mark 11:8-10.

❖ Conclude today's session by leading the class in this benediction from Jude 24-25, which was the key verse for the lesson on April 10: **Now to him who is able to keep you from falling, and to make you stand without blemish in the presence of his glory with rejoicing, to the only God our Savior, through Jesus Christ our Lord, be glory, majesty, power, and authority, before all time and now and forever. Amen.**

UNIT 2: ANCIENT WORDS OF PRAISE
CHRIST IS RISEN!

PREVIEWING THE LESSON

Lesson Scripture: Matthew 28:1-17
Background Scripture: Matthew 28:1-17
Key Verse: Matthew 28:9

Focus of the Lesson:
We love some people so dearly that we remember them after they die. How does our love for others continue even after their death? When the angel reported that Jesus had risen from the dead, those who heard the news worshiped.

Goals for the Learners:
(1) to retell the story of Jesus' resurrection from death and how followers worshiped the risen Christ.
(2) to connect Jesus' resurrection to their deceased loved ones' life after death.
(3) to discover and make use of rituals that worship and praise the risen Christ.

Pronunciation Guide:
theophany (thee of' uh nee)

Supplies:
Bibles, newsprint and marker, paper and pencils, hymnals

READING THE SCRIPTURE

NRSV
Matthew 28:1-17

¹After the sabbath, as the first day of the week was dawning, Mary Magdalene and the other Mary went to see the tomb. ²And suddenly there was a great earthquake; for an angel of the Lord, descending from heaven, came and rolled back the stone and sat on it. ³His appearance was like lightning, and his clothing white as snow. ⁴For fear of him the guards shook and became like dead

NIV
Matthew 28:1-17

¹After the Sabbath, at dawn on the first day of the week, Mary Magdalene and the other Mary went to look at the tomb.

²There was a violent earthquake, for an angel of the Lord came down from heaven and, going to the tomb, rolled back the stone and sat on it. ³His appearance was like lightning, and his clothes were white as snow. ⁴The guards were so afraid of him

men. ⁵But the angel said to the women, "Do not be afraid; I know that you are looking for Jesus who was crucified. ⁶He is not here; for he has been raised, as he said. Come, see the place where he lay. ⁷Then go quickly and tell his disciples, 'He has been raised from the dead, and indeed he is going ahead of you to Galilee; there you will see him.' This is my message for you." ⁸So they left the tomb quickly with fear and great joy, and ran to tell his disciples. **⁹Suddenly Jesus met them and said, "Greetings!" And they came to him, took hold of his feet, and worshiped him.** ¹⁰Then Jesus said to them, "Do not be afraid; go and tell my brothers to go to Galilee; there they will see me."

¹¹While they were going, some of the guard went into the city and told the chief priests everything that had happened. ¹²After the priests had assembled with the elders, they devised a plan to give a large sum of money to the soldiers, ¹³telling them, "You must say, 'His disciples came by night and stole him away while we were asleep.' ¹⁴If this comes to the governor's ears, we will satisfy him and keep you out of trouble." ¹⁵So they took the money and did as they were directed. And this story is still told among the Jews to this day.

¹⁶Now the eleven disciples went to Galilee, to the mountain to which Jesus had directed them. ¹⁷When they saw him, they worshiped him; but some doubted.

that they shook and became like dead men.

⁵The angel said to the women, "Do not be afraid, for I know that you are looking for Jesus, who was crucified. ⁶He is not here; he has risen, just as he said. Come and see the place where he lay. ⁷Then go quickly and tell his disciples: 'He has risen from the dead and is going ahead of you into Galilee. There you will see him.' Now I have told you."

⁸So the women hurried away from the tomb, afraid yet filled with joy, and ran to tell his disciples. **⁹Suddenly Jesus met them. "Greetings," he said. They came to him, clasped his feet and worshiped him.** ¹⁰Then Jesus said to them, "Do not be afraid. Go and tell my brothers to go to Galilee; there they will see me."

¹¹While the women were on their way, some of the guards went into the city and reported to the chief priests everything that had happened. ¹²When the chief priests had met with the elders and devised a plan, they gave the soldiers a large sum of money, ¹³telling them, "You are to say, 'His disciples came during the night and stole him away while we were asleep.' ¹⁴If this report gets to the governor, we will satisfy him and keep you out of trouble." ¹⁵So the soldiers took the money and did as they were instructed. And this story has been widely circulated among the Jews to this very day.

¹⁶Then the eleven disciples went to Galilee, to the mountain where Jesus had told them to go. ¹⁷When they saw him, they worshiped him; but some doubted.

UNDERSTANDING THE SCRIPTURE

Matthew 28:1. Matthew reported in 27:61 that Mary Magdalene and "the other Mary" had been present at Jesus' burial. It is not clear whether the "other Mary" in today's opening verse or this previous passage refers to the mother of Jesus. It would seem odd to refer to Jesus' mother in that way, however. Mark 16:1 and Luke 24:1 suggest the women come to anoint the body; but in Matthew, the body has already been sealed within the tomb, so no anointing would have been possible or at least anticipated.

The opening phrase of verse 1 can also mean "late on the Sabbath." Only the secondary phrase that follows makes it clear that early Sunday morning was the time in mind. Matthew gives no hint of what the women or others did on Saturday.

Matthew 28:2-4. The earthquake that occurs hearkens back to the earthquake on the afternoon of the crucifixion. Then the splitting of the earth was linked by Matthew to the appearance of "saints" who had died. Earthquakes are a feature of a theophany, that is, an appearance of God (see for example, 1 Kings 19:11-12). According to Matthew 27:62-66, the guards had been posted out of the desire of some religious leaders to avoid a theft of Jesus' body that would be promoted as a "raising." Their subsequent sealing of the tomb (27:66) only heightens the dramatic intervention represented by the appearance and action of the angel in 28:2. Matthew earlier told stories of angels in regards to Joseph's flight to Egypt, subsequent return, and Jesus' time in the wilderness (2:13, 19; 4:11). Some have noted that the appearance of the angel (lightning, white as snow) parallels descriptions of divine figures in Daniel 7:9 and 10:6, a book well-noted for its end-of-the-age visions.

Matthew 28:5-7. "Do not be afraid" is a phrase used frequently in biblical stories of encounters with God or angelic visitors. In Matthew's Gospel, the phrase offers assurance at several key junctures: an angel to Joseph as he considers whether to wed Mary (1:20); Jesus to Peter while he walks on the waters (14:27); Jesus to the disciples at the transfiguration (17:7); and now the angel to the women here (and Jesus to those same women in 28:10). The message of the angel is twofold: Jesus is not here; Jesus is risen. To assure them of at least the former, the angel invites them to view where Jesus lay. This parallels John 20:1-9, where Peter and the "disciple whom Jesus loved" peeked into the tomb to see he was gone. Having been told to "come and see," however, the next command is "go quickly and tell." As in Luke's Easter account, the women are the first witnesses to resurrection.

Matthew 28:8-10. Matthew reports the women left with fear and joy. In Mark's opening narrative of Easter (16:1-8), fear results in the women not telling anyone (16:8). The inclusion of joy in Matthew's accounts lends credence to the faithful outcome of what the angel described as the "message for you"—that is, the message that is now yours to give. Interrupting the journey, however, is an appearance of Jesus. "Greetings!" translates a rather ordinary and common greeting, much like the English "hello," though the context makes the ordinary greeting all the more extraordinary! Their initial response is one of respect (taking hold of his feet meant they bowed if not laid down before Jesus) and worship. Their response echoes the worship of Jesus by the disciples after he came into the boat with them after walking on the water (14:33). Jesus' words repeat almost verbatim the angel's words to the women with one important exception: "tell his disciples" in verse 7 now becomes "tell my brothers." Consider the import of the familial term "brothers." In Matthew, the recent history of the disciples was betrayal (26:47-49), flight (26:56), and denial (26:69-72). At the crucifixion scene in Matthew, only the women stand vigil at the cross (27:55). Yet here, the Resurrected One names as brothers those who were nowhere to be found in crisis. It is as much an act of forgiveness and restoration as Jesus words on the cross in Luke 23:34 and his scene by the lake with Peter in John 21:15-19.

Matthew 28:11-15. In verse 10, the women are charged to "go and tell" the news of Easter. Now, Matthew turns to the guards who "went and told" the problem of an emptied tomb. "Large sum" in verse 12 suggests that the cover-up is even more costly than the betrayal (limited to thirty pieces of silver). The religious officials' offer to "satisfy" the governor if he hears of the guards' falling asleep is somewhat unconvincing. Why would a Roman military governor accept the protestations of an occupied people when it came to a charge that rivaled deserting one's post? Perhaps the officials count on the fact, alluded to in Matthew 27:65, that Pilate originally wanted little if anything to do with the tomb's guarding in the first place. It was, if you will, a second time that Pilate "washes his hands" of accountability (see also Matthew 27:24). The closing line of Matthew 28:15 suggests Matthew's overriding motive for including this story in his Gospel: as explanation for a counternarrative in his and his community's day to the claim of resurrection.

Matthew 28:16-17. Matthew leaves unresolved the question of which mountain in Galilee Jesus directs the disciples to go. Earlier in Matthew, mountains served as the site of Jesus' temptation (4:8), teaching (5:1 and following), and transfiguration (17:1). Some suggest the mount of teaching makes theological sense, with Jesus preparing the disciples to receive the final "teaching" for their mission. But Matthew provides no geographical detail to assure that. "Worship" uses the same word here of the disciples as it did with the women in verse 9, and much earlier, of the disciples in the wake of Jesus' walking on the water (14:33). The Greek verb translated here as "doubted" appears in only two places in the entire New Testament: here, and in 14:31, when Jesus speaks to Peter after he attempted to walk toward Jesus on the water: "Why did you doubt?"

INTERPRETING THE SCRIPTURE

The Easter Stories

A careful reading of today's passage reveals not one but several Easter stories, including one that reaches well beyond the narrative.

There is, first of all, the story of an emptied tomb. As with all of the other Gospels, Matthew does not offer a report of the actual event of the resurrection itself, but rather a testimony to its results. The Gospel testifies to an earthquake, and to an angel who descends and rolls back the stone, but does not say a word about seeing Jesus walk out, much less any description of the exact moment death transforms into life. Matthew does not offer proof of a process. Matthew invites trust in a proclamation.

There is, secondly, the story of the women. The angel and then Jesus invite trust by first laying the groundwork with the words, "do not be afraid" (28:5, 10). The passage notes with striking irony that fear struck down the men of arms but not the women who followed Jesus. A dose of reality is that the initial "do not be afraid" to the women does not instantly and totally banish their fears. They leave the tomb "with fear and great joy" (28:8). Like the narrative itself, Easter faith is not necessarily instantaneous, removing all stumbling blocks to trust in the remarkable news and the even more remarkable future that has been opened.

The third story of Easter is that involving the guards and religious leaders. The fear that had shaken the guards at the tomb launches an alternative narrative to what has happened. There has been no resurrection, but the theft of the body. The decision to pose this alternative reflects a more contemporary expression in politics often referred to as "spin." Each side wants to present its version of the "truth." The religious leaders offer not only cover to the claims against resurrection but also cover to the guards by promising protection from any repercussions of their alleged "falling asleep on the job."

The fourth story of Easter is that of the disciples. The women apparently succeed in passing on the word not only of resurrection but also of the direction to go to Galilee. As with the women, the disciples see Jesus. But notice, again, how the narrative of Easter does not provide an instantaneous and incontrovertible transformation: "they worshiped him, *but some doubted*" (28:17, italics added). There is no grammatical construction here that demonstrates that those who doubted did *not* worship. Jesus' ensuing words in verses 18-20, sometimes called the Great Commission, likewise does not insert a caveat like *go therefore (except the doubters) and make disciples of all nations.* The Easter community and the commissioned community include the doubters. Easter's faith takes time to trust.

"Trust" leads us to the last Easter story, the one written between the lines of Matthew 28:1-17. And that story of Easter would be the one where the central characters are: us. you. me.

It is the Easter story that moves past whether or how we believe Easter "happened" to Jesus, and into how and why Easter matters to us. It is the Easter story that confronts us with its "do not be afraid" and "he is not here" every time, for example, we gather to mourn the death of a friend or loved one. It is the Easter story that confronts us when the mortality in question is our own. It is the Easter story that asks: What difference does it make in the way we conduct our lives day in and day out?

Liturgy as Evangelism as Liturgy

Christ is risen! The words shout the core of Easter's liturgy and worship, for we worship and praise the God who brings life out of death. Easter and liturgy are inseparably intertwined, as reflected in the narrative of Matthew. When the women encounter the risen Jesus, they worship him. When the disciples see the risen Christ, they worship him. Why? The One crucified is the One whom God raised. And not only that: The One whom God raised serves as the promise and guarantor that our own lives do not end in emptiness or utter non-existence. Christ's raising is our hope, and our motive for living now.

Christ is risen! But already, liturgy moves into the realm of evangelism—of proclaiming news unlike any other. Matthew's text is also clear on that. At the now-emptied tomb, the women are given a command: Go and tell. And even when the women encounter the risen Jesus and engage in worship, Jesus does not leave them in spiritual reveries to pass the time. The first Easter worship service ends when Jesus, like the angel before, commissions the women: "go and tell." The church has no right to engage in Easter worship if it does not overflow into Easter living, in word and deed. The news of Easter is the word we are given to challenge and comfort and transform the whole of life. Jesus' resurrection is not a private spiritual possession of the enlightened. Resurrection is the promised gift to creation. "Go and tell" reminds us that Easter worship is inevitably outward bound. Go and tell: Christ is risen!

And from worship to evangelism, Easter returns us to worship. A story worth telling is one worth celebrating. Easter's story, which moves us out of the pews and into the world to our present-day Galilees, is a story worthy of our best efforts at worship and liturgy. For the proclamation we bring and the celebration we raise is nothing less than that Christ is risen indeed—and the world, our lives, need never again be the same!

Galilee

The journey to Jerusalem dominates the Gospels' narratives of Jesus' life and ministry. When reached, the Sunday of Palms moves swiftly and inexorably toward Thursday's table and garden and betrayal, Friday's trials and killing, Saturday's holy quiet and stillness, and Sunday's incredible news. And yet, the story of the risen Jesus resumes the narrative of movement. And both the angel and then the risen One tell the women where that movement now aims: Galilee. That means, on a purely physical and geographical note, the journey is on again. Galilee is not a suburb of Jerusalem. Depending on where this "mount" is in Galilee, the literal journey could have been some distance and required several days. Easter brings significant movement again, but locating Galilee as the destination says even more about the "why" than the "how long" of Easter's trek. In *Parables and Passion*, I explain that

Galilee, for most of the disciples and the women, is home. Galilee is the place where people reared families, exercised vocations, and played out the ordinary rhythm of life and death. The news of Easter is not sounded primarily for the sake of sanctuaries adorned with lilies, where you might expect to hear such proclamation. The news of Easter is taken back to all the usual and familiar places of our living, where death's defeat is not a given. The possibility of new life and rebirth needs echoing in settings where we spend the vast majority of our time and energy, where our fears can be very real. We are Easter people: not because of where we spend Easter morning but because of how we bring Easter to our other days.

SHARING THE SCRIPTURE

Preparing Our Hearts

Explore this week's devotional reading, found in 1 Corinthians 15:1-8. Here Paul discusses Jesus' resurrection and, in verses 12-29, the resurrection of those who have died "in Christ." Paul reviews the events associated with Easter morning and with Jesus' post-resurrection appearances, even to Paul himself. As you approach this Easter, consider what you believe about Jesus' resurrection. What difference does it make in your life—and in the world—to believe that he has indeed been resurrected from the dead by God?

Pray that you and the adult learners will hear the news, "Jesus is risen," with glad and believing hearts and share that news with others.

Preparing Our Minds

Study the background Scripture and the lesson Scripture, both of which are from Matthew 28:1-17. Contemplate how our love for others continues even after their death.

Write on newsprint:
- ❑ Bible verses for "Connect Jesus' Resurrection to the Learners' Deceased Loved Ones' Life After Death."
- ❑ information for next week's lesson, found under "Continue the Journey."
- ❑ activities for further spiritual growth in "Continue the Journey."

LEADING THE CLASS

(1) Gather to Learn

❖ Welcome the class members and introduce any guests.

❖ Pray that those who have gathered today will find comfort and assurance as they consider Matthew's account of Jesus' resurrection.

❖ Read this information taken from Ed Newman's blog, "Ennyman's Territory":

Rebecca Bruley, whose passion is sewing, creates bears from a garment that someone has worn. Although Rebecca's Remembrance Bears, a home-based business in Duluth, Minnesota, offers these stuffed animals for anyone, they are often made of clothing of a deceased person. A Bible verse and a poem written by Rebecca's daughter are attached to each bear before sending it home to a family who will remember their loved one as they hold this bear.

❖ Ask: **How would a tangible object, such as one of these bears, help you to remember a loved one?**

❖ Read aloud today's focus statement: **We love some people so dearly that we remember them after they die. How does our love for others continue even after their death? When the angel reported that Jesus had risen from the dead, those who heard the news worshiped.**

(2) Retell the Story of Jesus' Resurrection From Death and How Followers Worshiped the Risen Christ

❖ Invite the students to read silently Matthew 28:1-10.

❖ Encourage each adult to state one detail of this story that stands out in their minds. To give everyone a chance, go around the room and limit each person to one detail. If the class is large, form groups to give each person a chance to speak.

❖ Ask these questions. Use information from Understanding the Scripture for verses 1, 2-4, 5-7, 8-10 to augment the discussion.

    (1) Why are the details that you have identified so important?

    (2) What would the story lose without a particular detail?

❖ Retell the story of the stationing of the guard at the tomb, found in Matthew 27:62-66. This part of the story is not in our reading but sets the stage for Matthew 28:11-15, which you or a volunteer will read next.

❖ Discuss how the religious leaders are

trying to put a different "spin" on the story of the resurrection.

❖ Invite someone to read Matthew 28:16-17. Discuss the idea of worshiping even in the midst of doubt. Do we do that? If so, how is worship affected by doubt? Conversely, how is doubt affected by worship?

❖ Pull all of the sections of this week's reading together by reading "The Easter Stories" from Interpreting the Scriptures.

(3) Connect Jesus' Resurrection to the Learners' Deceased Loved Ones' Life After Death

❖ Make note of the fact that in the early church some people questioned the relationship between Jesus' resurrection and the new life of their own loved ones. Some people still raise this question today.

❖ Post the following Bible verses on newsprint. Form small groups and assign a passage to each group to discuss and discern what this passage says about life after death. Provide time for the groups to report.

- Acts 4:1-2
- Romans 6:4-11
- 1 Corinthians 15:12-28
- Ephesians 5:14 (fragment of an early hymn)
- 1 Thessalonians 4:13-18

❖ Conclude this portion of the session by inviting volunteers to respond to this scenario, which you will read: **Molly Anderson is distraught over the death of her twin sister Marge, who was killed in an automobile accident. What words of comfort could you offer to Molly to assure her that because Christ lives so too does Marge?**

(4) Discover and Make Use of Rituals that Worship and Praise the Risen Christ

❖ Read "Liturgy as Evangelism as Liturgy" from Interpreting the Scripture.

❖ Suggest that the celebration of Christ's resurrection on Easter is, for most Christians, the high point of the Christian calendar. Ask: **What makes worship on Easter Sunday so special for you?** List ideas on newsprint. Perhaps the students will name hymns, flowers, instruments, art work, special liturgy, or the excitement of a large congregation, among other possibilities.

❖ Direct attention to Matthew 28:16-17, where those disciples who saw the risen Christ worshiped him, "but some doubted." Talk about the importance of being honest about doubts. Assure the students that all people have questions and doubts about their faith. Whereas some people will continue to worship, study, and trust, despite their doubts, others will give up and no longer believe. Invite the participants to talk about times when they doubted and what happened to enable them to worship and praise Christ again.

❖ Invite the class to repeat these ancient words of confession first uttered by the disciples: "The Lord has risen indeed" (Luke 24:34). Challenge them to go and tell this news to others.

(5) Continue the Journey

❖ Pray that all will go forth praising God for the resurrection of Jesus.

❖ Read aloud this preparation for next week's lesson. You may also want to post it on newsprint for the students to copy.

- **Title: The Christ Hymn**
- **Background Scripture: Philippians 2:1-11**
- **Lesson Scripture: Philippians 2:1-11**

■ **Focus of the Lesson: One way people honor others they revere is to imitate them. In what ways does our imitation mold our behavior? As a pattern for living and worship, we imitate Christ Jesus as we recall his life and sacrifice on our behalf.**

❖ Challenge the students to complete one or more of these activities for further spiritual growth related to this week's session. Post this information on newsprint for the students to copy.

(1) **Think about the role that your belief in Jesus' resurrection plays in terms of why you worship God. Put another way, if you did not believe that God resurrected Jesus from the dead, would you still be a Christian?**

(2) **Participate in Easter worship not only on Sunday but also by living as one whose life has been unalterably changed because of the resurrection of Christ.**

(3) **Go and tell the good news to others.**

❖ Sing or read aloud "Christ the Lord Is Risen Today."

❖ Conclude today's session by leading the class in this benediction from Jude 24-25, which is the key verse for the lesson on April 10: **Now to him who is able to keep you from falling, and to make you stand without blemish in the presence of his glory with rejoicing, to the only God our Savior, through Jesus Christ our Lord, be glory, majesty, power, and authority, before all time and now and forever. Amen.**

UNIT 2: ANCIENT WORDS OF PRAISE

THE CHRIST HYMN

PREVIEWING THE LESSON

Lesson Scripture: Philippians 2:1-11
Background Scripture: Philippians 2:1-11
Key Verse: Philippians 2:5

Focus of the Lesson:
One way people honor others they revere is to imitate them. In what ways does our imitation mold our behavior? As a pattern for living and worship, we imitate Christ Jesus as we recall his life and sacrifice on our behalf.

Goals for the Learners:
(1) to examine the Christ hymn as an affirmation of faith.
(2) to focus on who Jesus is and remember what he did for them.
(3) to create a contemporary affirmation of faith based on the themes of this early hymn.

Pronunciation Guide:
kenodoxia (ken od ox ee' ah)   *phroneo* (fron-eh'-o)
koinonia (koy-nohn-ee'-ah)   *schema* (skhay'-mah)
morphe (mor-fay')

Supplies:
Bibles, newsprint and marker, paper and pencils, hymnals, optional commentaries.

MAY 1

READING THE SCRIPTURE

NRSV

Philippians 2:1-11

[1]If then there is any encouragement in Christ, any consolation from love, any sharing in the Spirit, any compassion and sympathy, [2]make my joy complete: be of the same mind, having the same love, being in full accord and of one mind. [3]Do nothing from selfish ambition or conceit, but in

NIV

Philippians 2:1-11

[1]If you have any encouragement from being united with Christ, if any comfort from his love, if any fellowship with the Spirit, if any tenderness and compassion, [2]then make my joy complete by being like-minded, having the same love, being one in spirit and purpose. [3]Do nothing out of

humility regard others as better than your-selves. ⁴Let each of you look not to your own interests, but to the interests of others. **⁵Let the same mind be in you that was in Christ Jesus,**
6   who, though he was in the form of God,
    did not regard equality with God
    as something to be exploited,
7   but emptied himself,
    taking the form of a slave,
    being born in human likeness.
  And being found in human form,
8   he humbled himself
    and became obedient to the point
      of death—
    even death on a cross.
9   Therefore God also highly exalted him
    and gave him the name
    that is above every name,
10 so that at the name of Jesus
    every knee should bend,
    in heaven and on earth and under
      the earth,
11 and every tongue should confess
    that Jesus Christ is Lord,
    to the glory of God the Father.

selfish ambition or vain conceit, but in humility consider others better than your-selves. ⁴Each of you should look not only to your own interests, but also to the interests of others.
  ⁵Your attitude should be the same as that of Christ Jesus:
⁶Who, being in very nature God,
  did not consider equality with God
    something to be grasped,
⁷but made himself nothing,
  taking the very nature of a servant,
  being made in human likeness.
⁸And being found in appearance as a man,
  he humbled himself
  and became obedient to death—
    even death on a cross!
⁹Therefore God exalted him to the
    highest place
  and gave him the name that is
    above every name,
¹⁰that at the name of Jesus every knee
    should bow,
  in heaven and on earth and under
    the earth,
¹¹and every tongue confess that Jesus
    Christ is Lord,
  to the glory of God the Father.

UNDERSTANDING THE SCRIPTURE

Philippians 2:1. The verse begins with a rhetorical "if then there is." The following four characteristics—*encouragement, consolation, compassion, sympathy*—presume the existence of these things already present in the Philippian community. Linking the first (encouragement) with the qualifier "in Christ" asserts a key theme in this entire passage as well as the whole of Paul's writings. "In Christ" speaks of the mystery of life lived in relationship with God through Jesus Christ. To be "in Christ" is not only an expression of faith but also of community, with God and with one another. Another word to be noted for special attention in this opening verse is

"sharing:" the Greek *koinonia*, a word likewise referencing our community in Christ with God and with one another. Linking that sharing (community) with "Spirit" affirms the way the Spirit gives life to Christian community, a theme Paul develops extensively in 1 Corinthians 12:4-11. An important difference between the NRSV and the NIV in this verse relates to what love is specified: (NRSV: "any consolation from love"; NIV: "any comfort from *his* love" *italics added*). In the Greek, there is no reference to "his," and the passage leaves it open as to whether the love the author has in mind is that of Christ for us, or ours for Christ (or one another).

BUT ALL LOVE IS ~~FROM A~~ GOD.
THE SOURCE OF

Philippians 2:2-4. The intention for recalling the qualities listed in verse 1 is now made clear: to make Paul's joy complete. How that joy is to be made complete by the community is enjoined by: "be of the same mind, having the same love." "Mind" occurs twice in verse 2 (and it also occurs in verse 5). The Greek word *phroneo* goes beyond a reference to intellect. It encompasses "attitude" and viewpoint. "Same mind" is not thinking in lockstep, but rather having a common view and perspective. What brings that commonality is our life "in Christ." Verse 3 uses two words that will become crucial as this passage unfolds. The first is "humility." In this era, humility was not embraced as a virtue by the surrounding culture, but viewed with suspicion as implying servitude (not a quality in vogue in an empire built on military power and political dominance). The other word, translated as "conceit," is *kenodoxia*. It is a compound word that literally means "empty of glory." In the second half of this passage, "emptying" and "glory" both play pivotal roles.

Another difference between the NRSV and NIV in verse 4 has important consequences for meaning. The NIV reading suggests we not look "only" to our own interests but "also" to those of others. The NRSV omits both "only" and "also." In the Greek text of this verse, there is no word for "only" and some but not all manuscripts have "also." One possible solution is to translate "also" as "rather."

Philippians 2:5. Verse 5 introduces what many believe to have been an ancient hymn of the church. It is unclear whether Paul borrowed this from a preexisting source (for example, a hymn that the Philippians used in their liturgy) or whether Paul wrote this specifically for this occasion with an eye for it being used in worship. *Phroneo* ("mind") occurs again, only now the origin for this attitude or perspective has clearly to do with Christ. The lack of clarity in the grammar at the verse's end leaves open several possibilities. Is it that we have the same mind *as* Christ Jesus, suggesting a clear imitation of Christ? Or is it that we have the same mind *that you have* in Christ Jesus, slightly leaning the verse back toward verse 2 and the community's "same mind." The emphases need not be taken as contradictory, but rather complementary, understanding that the "imitation of Christ" always brings connection to the community that lives in Christ, and vice-versa.

Philippians 2:6-8. The "hymn" form proper begins with these verses that constitute its first half. The focus is upon the "humiliation" of Christ, not inflicted but freely taken on. "Form" occurs three times in these verses, although two Greek words are used. *Morphe* occurs in verses 6 and 7 ("form of God," "form of a slave"), and generally refers to an internal "essence," while *schema* in verse 7 ("human form") is more of an external "appearance." The most striking theological assertion is that of Christ choosing not to exploit "equality" with God but rather "emptying" (*keno*—see note on "conceit" in verse 3) himself of such prerogative and taking on the form of a servant or slave. Again, such humility would have cut against the grain of what the wider culture would have viewed as positive. "Being born in human likeness" is one of the few references Paul makes to Jesus' birth. In the hymn, humility is expressed in obedience, which is the essential virtue of a servant. Such obedience takes the particular form, in Jesus' life, of the cross. The movement of emptying self of privilege to fully assume the human condition leads ultimately to Christ sharing the inevitable experience of human mortality.

Philippians 2:9-11. "Therefore" in verse 9 is more than a bridge word between the previous section on Christ's humiliation with the second half of the hymn that celebrates Christ's exultation. Even more importantly, "therefore" asserts that it is *precisely* the path of obedience that leads to the experience of glorification. The unique character of

Christ's obedience and God's honoring of it is reflected in Paul's choice of language. The verb used for "highly exalted" occurs nowhere else in the entire New Testament. The celebration quickly moves into a repeated assertion of the "name" of Christ. The phrase that God "gave him the name" restates a point made in the first half of the hymn; that is, Jesus did not "make a name for himself." His *name*, which in Semitic cul-ture carried with it the idea of one's identity and renown, comes as a gift from God. The liturgical nature of this poem or hymn becomes more striking as it envisions the worship due to the One whom God has named. "Jesus Christ is Lord" is one of the earliest summaries of Christian faith. The hymn ends with the glorification of God, which itself is the most essential facet of all worship. *Which is This entire quarter's theme.*

INTERPRETING THE SCRIPTURE

Preaching From the Hymnal

John Calvin is credited with once saying, "the Nicene Creed was meant to be sung rather than spoken." In other words, the framing of our faith in creeds and statements of doctrine aims at leading the community to worship. Another way of looking at it would be this: The most profound statements of theological acumen may remain dry as dust unless they are joined to action of the heart (and exercise of the will) in leading us to union with God and with one another.

The previous commentary has already noted that many scholars have long associated this passage in Philippians with a hymn or liturgical poem. Clearly, Paul does not give us a "hymnal number" so that argument can be made without dispute. But the association of this passage, along with others considered in this unit, as arising out of the community's liturgical experiences and resources makes a very important point that links to John Calvin's remark. Namely, the exposition of faith and its celebration are not two separate movements. Or to put the matter another way, what we sing in church serves as a *primer* for what we hold to be true. *Webster's 2 meaning*

That has several implications. First among them is this: We ought to be paying attention to the messages of the hymns we use. Having a good old familiar tune does not necessarily mean the song "fits" the text being preached upon. Second, music is itself a medium that conveys faith. Part of the reason we feel comfortable with words that, if we were merely saying them aloud might give us pause (for example, framing the faith in martial terms), is that music itself has a power all of its own to convey the *experience* of faith. *like Onward Christian Soldiers*

Let me give an example. Two years ago, I helped officiate at an ecumenical service for our community's Finnish-American festival held at the local cemetery. A men's choir from Finland had been asked to sing, although we did not tell them what to sing. So at the end of this service of remembrance, they took their place and began to sing a cappella. I do not speak Finnish. But I got that feeling sometimes called "a chill up your spine" as the tune quickly came into recognition: "Abide With Me." It was, for me, the most moving element of that ceremony. To be sure, as they sang, the English words came to mind. But even more powerfully, the tune and harmonies unlocked deep remembrances of hearing that song as a child at my home church's Lenten services, where that hymn closed each evening service.

The hymnal, in its words and in its melodies, can be a powerful and evocative source of preaching. And one of the reasons, as Paul may have had in mind if he did indeed draw this passage from the Philippians' liturgical tradition, is that music touches deep places that words alone sometimes cannot go.

The Way of the Servant

The first half of Paul's hymn depicts the movement of humiliation in regards to Jesus' not grasping any prerogative that might have been claimed. In music, this half of the hymn would be set in a minor key. It begins on the note of equality with God, which is then yielded for the sake of being born in human likeness as a servant. From there, the way of the servant humbly descends through obedience to the intersection with crucifixion and death.

This is not the narrative of triumphalism. This is not the narrative of "my God is stronger than your God." This is the narrative of the not long-before journey through Passion Week. This is the narrative of the way of the servant.

Sometimes, the church is quite comfortable accepting this way to describe the life of Jesus. But let's not get carried away and bring these ideas into the council meeting or into our own lives. Wasn't Jesus doing this for us, so we wouldn't have to?

You could argue that, except for verse 5: "let the same mind be in you that was in Christ Jesus." In other words, as this lesson's focus reminds us: This is a call to live in imitation of Christ—to live in imitation of Christ's servanthood; to live in imitation of Christ's servanthood as individual disciples and, yes, as communities.

The "same mind" of the one who yielded prerogative of position is not an easy way, when what we often prefer is having things go our way and people like us and, heaven forbid, not making demands of others (or ourselves) that might drive them (or us) away. The narrative of the servant is not a narrative written on too many book leaf covers on how to succeed in life and busi-ness—and church. But there it is, in the "hymn" Philippians invites us to sing, and in the singing to ask ourselves: If we share in Jesus' servanthood, whose feet might we end up washing?

The Way of Glory

The first question of the Westminster Shorter Catechism asks: "What is the chief end of man?" The answer it gives is this: "Man's chief end is to glorify God and enjoy him forever."

The glorification of God is where the second half of Paul's hymn eventually ends. The "descent" narrated in theological minor keys in the first half of the "hymn" now is paired with the "ascent" narrated by the second half's major keys of exaltation, naming, confessing—all leading to the glory of God.

The second half of the hymn is not a rejection of the first half, a sort of "don't worry about all that humiliation because what life's *really* about is glory." In fact, "therefore" in verse 9 serves notice that Christ did not get to the glorification part without the first half. Therefore, out of the way of the servant comes the rejoicing, comes the celebration. It's like an age-old problem faced by the church. Easter is our victory, our celebration, but it doesn't make sense unless it comes with Passion Week and Good Friday and the tomb-death-silence of Holy Saturday. As it was with Jesus, so it is for us.

But the passage is clear: Humility does not end in death, but in God's uplifting to life and hope. The One against whom others conspired and spoke hatred to achieve his crucifixion is now the One whose name outshines and rises above all. That, too, is part of what "let the same mind be in you" is about: namely, that our hope and destiny are linked to the exaltation proclaimed in the second half of this hymn. And that this is all about, not *our* glory, but God's glory.

How do we glorify God? That is not something that awaits the end of history, but begins here and now. Our glorification of God is by no means limited to what we do as liturgy, but rather by what we actually do—the justice we seek, the compassion we exercise, the love we express—that gives glory to God in the whole of our lives.

Glory is not what God gives to us; it is what we offer to God in our worship, in our service, in our relationships. Where glorification leads is where the end of the Philippian hymn leads: to the fulfillment of God's purposes in Jesus Christ for all of creation. For that hope, we give glory to God.

SHARING THE SCRIPTURE

Preparing Our Hearts

Explore this week's devotional reading, found in 1 Peter 2:18-25. This is a difficult passage that needs to be read within the context of the slavery that existed during this period. While we find slavery abhorrent, the idea found in this passage of enduring injustice, as Christ did, is helpful to us. Jesus suffered for us. In doing so, he entrusted himself to God. How are you experiencing injustice? What do you need to entrust to God today?

Pray that you and the adult learners will praise Christ, who endured injustice and suffering for our sakes.

Preparing Our Minds

Study the background Scripture and the lesson Scripture, both of which are from Philippians 2:1-11. Think about how our behavior is molded as we imitate others.

Write on newsprint:

❑ list of names for "Focus on Who Jesus Is and Remember What He Did for the Learners."

❑ information for next week's lesson, found under "Continue the Journey."

❑ activities for further spiritual growth in "Continue the Journey."

Locate several commentaries that include Philippians and bring these to class.

LEADING THE CLASS

(1) Gather to Learn

❖ Welcome the class members and introduce any guests.

❖ Pray that those who have come today will seek to be like Christ.

❖ Encourage the students to describe someone who has served as a mentor or advisor to them by answering questions such as: How did this mentor help them? In what ways did they try to imitate the one who was guiding them? How did the mentor's behavior help shape their own behavior? How would they rate this mentor/mentee relationship?

❖ Read aloud today's focus statement: **One way people honor others they revere is to imitate them. In what ways does our imitation mold our behavior? As a pattern for living and worship, we imitate Christ Jesus as we recall his life and sacrifice on our behalf.**

(2) Examine the Christ Hymn as an Affirmation of Faith

❖ Read Philippians 2:1-4 as the students follow along in their Bibles.

❖ Unpack the meaning of these verses by using the commentary for them in Philippians 2:1, 2-4 of Understanding the Scripture.

❖ Invite the class to read in unison Philippians 2:5, which is today's key verse.

❖ Read this verse from several other translations, as listed here, and encourage the adults to discuss what this verse really means:

- "Your attitude should be the same as that of Christ Jesus." (New International Version)
- "Take to heart among yourselves what you find in Christ Jesus." (Revised English Bible)
- "Have among yourselves the same attitude that is also yours in Christ Jesus." (New American Bible)
- "Make your own mind the mind of Christ." (New Jerusalem Bible)

❖ Choose a volunteer to read Philippians 2:6-8.

❖ Read or retell "The Way of the Servant" to help clarify the meaning.

❖ Select someone to read Philippians 2:9-11.

❖ Read or retell "The Way of Glory" to help clarify the meaning.

❖ Ask the students to consider the hymn in its entirety to answer these questions:

(1) What do you learn about Jesus?

(2) What do you learn about God?

(3) What lessons for living as a Christian do you learn from this hymn, assuming you choose to let Christ's mind be in you?

(3) Focus on Who Jesus Is and Remember What He Did for the Learners

❖ Post these names/descriptions of Jesus on newsprint:

- Advocate: 1 John 2:1
- Alpha and Omega: Revelation 1:8
- Beloved Son: Luke 3:22
- Bread of Life: John 6:35
- Faithful Witness: Revelation 1:5
- Good Shepherd: John 10:11
- Great High Priest: Hebrews 4:14
- Head of the Church: Ephesians 1:22
- Image of God: 2 Corinthians 4:4

- Light of the World: John 8:12
- Messiah: Luke 2:11
- Pioneer and Perfecter of Our Faith: Hebrews 12:2
- Resurrection and Life: John 11:25
- Rock: 1 Corinthians 10:4
- Savior: Luke 2:11
- Son of David: Matthew 1:1
- True Vine: John 15:1
- Word: John 1:1

❖ Read aloud each name/descriptive word on this list and invite the students to state what this name says to them about who Jesus is and what he did on our behalf. If time permits, suggest that volunteers look up each verse and read them to the class.

❖ Wrap up this portion of the session by encouraging the students to draw relationships between these names/descriptions of Jesus and what they have learned about him in Philippians 2:1-11.

(4) Create a Contemporary Affirmation of Faith Based on the Themes of This Early Hymn

❖ Form several groups of two or three adults. Distribute paper and a pencil to each person. Direct half of the groups to write verses 6-8 in their own words and the other half of the groups to do the same for verses 9-11. Have commentaries available, if possible, for the groups to consult.

❖ Provide time for each group to read its paraphrase. Do this by asking a group that worked on verses 6-8 to read, followed by one that worked on verses 9-11. Repeat this pattern until all groups have had a chance to present their work. Thank the groups for creating a contemporary version of this historic hymn of the early church.

❖ **Option:** Read "Preaching from the Hymnal" from Interpreting the Scripture. Invite the students to name a hymn tune that seems to capture the mood of Philippians 2:5-11. Perhaps they will choose two tunes, a somber one for the portion concerning Christ's humiliation and a very upbeat one for God's exaltation of Christ.

(5) Continue the Journey

❖ Pray that all who have participated will continue to allow their minds to be molded after the mind of Jesus.

❖ Read aloud this preparation for next week's lesson. You may also want to post it on newsprint for the students to copy.

- ■ **Title: Heavenly Worship**
- ■ **Background Scripture: Revelation 4**
- ■ **Lesson Scripture: Revelation 4:1-2, 6-11**
- ■ **Focus of the Lesson: Symbols help people communicate. In what ways do symbols communicate concepts and ideas across time? The symbolism in the Revelation to John, patterned after Hebrew Scriptures, points to worship and praise of God.**

❖ Challenge the students to complete one or more of these activities for further spiritual growth related to this week's session. Post this information on newsprint for the students to copy.

(1) **Research the word "kenotic," which means to empty, as this word relates to Jesus emptying himself. What do you learn about Jesus from this word study?**

(2) **Make notes as you read your Bible on Jesus' attitudes and actions. Which of these can you imitate? How will your imitation of Christ help someone else? How will it help you?**

(3) **Memorize either the Apostles' Creed or the Nicene Creed. Repeat the creed at least once each day as an affirmation of faith.**

❖ Sing or read aloud "At the Name of Jesus," which is based on Philippians 2:5-11.

❖ Conclude today's session by leading the class in this benediction from Jude 24-25, which is the key verse for the lesson on April 10: **Now to him who is able to keep you from falling, and to make you stand without blemish in the presence of his glory with rejoicing, to the only God our Savior, through Jesus Christ our Lord, be glory, majesty, power, and authority, before all time and now and forever. Amen.**

UNIT 3: JOHN'S VISION OF WORSHIP
HEAVENLY WORSHIP

PREVIEWING THE LESSON

Lesson Scripture: Revelation 4:1-2, 6-11
Background Scripture: Revelation 4
Key Verse: Revelation 4:2

Focus of the Lesson:
Symbols help people communicate. In what ways do symbols communicate concepts and ideas across time? The symbolism in the Revelation to John, patterned after Hebrew Scriptures, points to worship and praise of God.

Goals for the Learners:
(1) to explore the origin of the symbols used in the text.
(2) to identify sections of the text that urge them to worship.
(3) to be alert for visual and written symbols used in worship.

Pronunciation Guide:
eucharistia (yoo khar is tee′ ah)
pantokrator (pan tok rat′ ore)

Supplies:
Bibles, newsprint and marker, paper and pencils, hymnals

READING THE SCRIPTURE

NRSV
Revelation 4:1-2, 6-11

¹After this I looked, and there in heaven a door stood open! And the first voice, which I had heard speaking to me like a trumpet, said, "Come up here, and I will show you what must take place after this." ²**At once I was in the spirit, and there in heaven stood a throne, with one seated on the throne!**

NIV
Revelation 4:1-2, 6-11

¹After this I looked, and there before me was a door standing open in heaven. And the voice I had first heard speaking to me like a trumpet said, "Come up here, and I will show you what must take place after this." ²**At once I was in the Spirit, and there before me was a throne in heaven with someone sitting on it.**

6bAround the throne, and on each side of the throne, are four living creatures, full of eyes in front and behind: 7the first living creature like a lion, the second living creature like an ox, the third living creature with a face like a human face, and the fourth living creature like a flying eagle. 8And the four living creatures, each of them with six wings, are full of eyes all around and inside. Day and night without ceasing they sing,

"Holy, holy, holy,
the Lord God the Almighty,
  who was and is and is to come."

9And whenever the living creatures give glory and honor and thanks to the one who is seated on the throne, who lives forever and ever, 10the twenty-four elders fall before the one who is seated on the throne and worship the one who lives forever and ever; they cast their crowns before the throne, singing,

11 "You are worthy, our Lord and God,
  to receive glory and honor and power,
  for you created all things,
    and by your will they existed and
      were created."

6bIn the center, around the throne, were four living creatures, and they were covered with eyes, in front and in back. 7The first living creature was like a lion, the second was like an ox, the third had a face like a man, the fourth was like a flying eagle. 8Each of the four living creatures had six wings and was covered with eyes all around, even under his wings. Day and night they never stop saying:

"Holy, holy, holy
is the Lord God Almighty,
  who was, and is, and is to come."

9Whenever the living creatures give glory, honor and thanks to him who sits on the throne and who lives for ever and ever, 10the twenty-four elders fall down before him who sits on the throne, and worship him who lives for ever and ever. They lay their crowns before the throne and say:

11"You are worthy, our Lord and God,
  to receive glory and honor and power,
  for you created all things,
    and by your will they were created
    and have their being."

UNDERSTANDING THE SCRIPTURE

Revelation 4:1-2. "I looked" repeats a refrain used frequently throughout Revelation that underscores the "visionary" nature of the testimony that follows. The door standing open recalls the image used in the previous chapter (3:20) of Christ standing outside the "door" of the Laodicean church. There, the hope is that the community being addressed will open the door to divine presence and fellowship. Here, the door is opened to provide a vision of heaven, where the divine presence dwells. "Voice" (4:1) occurs almost forty times in Revelation, stressing the auditory nature of those visions. John sees and hears, and out of that experience testifies. The phrase "in the Spirit" recalls the very opening to this book and indeed John's call to set his vision into writing (1:10). It is significant that this initial encounter "in the Spirit" occurs on the Lord's day—the day of worship. No other book in the entire New Testament revolves around worship as does Revelation. Finally, John indicates at the close of this portion of today's passage that there is a "throne" and One seated on it. The second section in "Interpreting the Scripture" will explore more thoroughly the significance of those details of throne and the One seated there. Suffice it to say here that the throne served as a dominant symbol of political power and authority, and more pointedly the imperial throne of Rome. For Revelation is not only about worship, it is also about who holds power.

Revelation 4:3-8a. The imagery and symbolism of these verses in Revelation draw deeply on visionary passages in the Hebrew Scriptures. As with some of the symbolism in Revelation, the author leaves unclear the precise meaning. Does, for example, the portrayal of God as looking like jasper and carnelian seek to communicate the preciousness of those minerals or their hardness, or even their brilliance in the light? Or the rainbow that surrounds the throne that appears like emerald: Is this an allusion to the covenant struck with Noah and the sign of the bow, where never again would the earth be destroyed by a flood (and is Rome that threatening "flood" in this day)? The presence of these valuable stones and minerals (along with gold and crystal) lends an image of exotic wealth. Could their purpose be to far surpass the riches Rome claimed from all her conquests? The other symbolic detail that rises to the surface is numbers. The ancient peoples had a variety of traditions regarding the meaning of numbers. "Twenty-four elders" represented the sum of 12 plus 12: a symbol of the twelve tribes and the twelve apostles, signifying the continuity of God's covenant in the heavenly court. Other numbers are also significant: seven, as in seven days; four, as in the four directions; six, as in the six days of creation. Perhaps Revelation used these numbers in ways that the symbolism might have been readily evident to its original audience. If that is so, especially in terms of the numerology in place here and elsewhere (for example, the age-old mystery of the identity of "666"), the precise meanings of these symbols do not usually come through to us in our time. The emphasis on the eyes of the "living creatures" may underscore to the original audience that nothing happens outside of God's sight, not even the deeds of the empire that seek to hide in violence their attempts to squelch the community. All is seen and will not be forgotten.

Revelation 4:8b. The "song" in 8b is prefaced with the descriptions that it is raised "day and night" and "without ceasing." There are no moments when God's praise as the enthroned One ceases, for there are no moments when God cedes that throne to any other. It is a liturgical act of defiance against any and all who would claim the mantle and authority of God. The fact that the later Caesars claimed the prerogative of divinity and demanded worship provide the context for Revelation's blending of images of worship and power. God and God alone is worthy. And that is at the core of this song. To repeat the acclamation of "holy" not twice but three times affirms that God's holiness is beyond all measure. In Semitic thought and speech, to repeat a term twice meant it had no peer: as in, "king of kings." Such a king was above all. And so the equivalent of "holy of holy of holy" went even beyond that. It is not just that God is holier than all other aspects of holiness. It is saying, and singing, and praising, that God and holy are one and indistinguishable—and unrivaled in any way. The designation of God as "Almighty" uses a term unusual in the New Testament outside of Revelation: *pantokrator*, literally "strong over all." It occurs only ten times, and nine of those are in Revelation. The closing affirmation of the song speaks of such holiness and power that stretches beyond time. "Who was and is and is to come" reflects the earlier teaching of Revelation 1:8, where those same words are prefaced by the image of God as Alpha and Omega—the names of the first and last letters of the Greek alphabet.

Revelation 4:9-11. The threefold acclamation in verse 9 of "glory and honor and thanks" will be repeated later in the sevenfold acclamation of the multitudes before the same throne (7:12). "Thanks" translates *eucharistia*, which also came to be used for the celebration of communion by the church (Eucharist). This connection to worship becomes even more explicit in the language of verse 10, where the verb for "worship" is used (one of 25 times in Revelation). Another song completes this passage, this one celebrating the worthiness of the One upon the throne. Here, "power" replaces "thanks" in the threefold acclamation. The affirmation of God's power serves as Revelation's counter-witness to the claims of the empire to hold all power. Power in this song derives from God's creation of all things. The empire may be able to momentarily afflict the power of death. But God, and God alone, has the power to call forth life. And that is the cause of Revelation's hope as well as the grounding of its worship.

INTERPRETING THE SCRIPTURE

Symbols: When Words Are Not Enough

You are traveling down a road in a car. You approach an intersection. Do you continue or do you stop? There is no billboard providing running commentary on your choices. All that stands there is a light with three colors. And that is all you need to know.

Symbols come into play in our lives as "shorthand" directions or reminders about the path before us—and sometimes behind us. Symbols also come into play in our lives when words themselves cannot fully express the reality to which that symbol points. On that same road, you may pass a small white cross. It may not tell you everything you want to know, but it serves as a reminder, and likely a caution.

Symbols in our religious journey play similar roles. You can read all the commentaries you want about the meaning of communion. But something verbally inexpressible happens when you see bread broken and wine poured into a cup, and then taken into your own hands. Sometimes music serves as a powerful symbol among us. Words may or may not be sung—but melodies and harmonies alone, when connected to experiences in our past, can summon feelings that run the gamut from joy to chills up our spines to tears running down our cheeks, and sometimes, all of the above.

The author of Revelation faced a hard situation. By tradition, he had been exiled by the Roman Empire to live out his last days on a lonely isolated island called Patmos. The beloved community was facing ever harsher repression. When it came time to frame the argument for hope and God's ultimate triumph, words in the form of logical arguments alone would not suffice. Drawing on resources from the Hebrew faith, the author of Revelation painted word pictures, splashed the colors of visions and voiced the sound of choruses far removed from our experience to make sure the community understood who truly held power, and who would at last stand healed and comforted and embraced. We do not always have clear understandings of all the symbols Revelation employs: numbers and creatures, visions and voices. But in those symbols we do catch a glimpse that faith is inevitably more than cut-and-dried knowledge. It is trust, radical trust, in a future not easily trusted in the midst of pressing and oppressing times. Symbols form codes that show the way forward, that direct our hope in ways that words alone cannot convey.

Faith as Counterculture

To paraphrase an old line, repetition is the mother of intention. So to get a clear idea about what the intention of Revelation 4 is, do this: count the number of times that "throne" or "thrones" occur. By my count, it is used 14 times. And just in case you think this might be a momentary diversion of the author of Revelation from the wider purpose of this book, know that "throne" occurs more than 40 times in this work. In the rest of all the other New Testament books, "throne" only appears 15 times.

To say that "throne" is a dominant symbol of this text, and indeed the whole book, is serious understatement. But just what does the symbol of "throne" mean to suggest? As noted in Understanding the Scripture, "throne" has everything to do with power and authority. And in this day, the only throne that mattered, at least in the mind of the imperial cult and spin-masters, was the throne upon which Caesar sat and from which he reigned. For the church, that was not a favorable situation. Scholars may diverge in terms of when specifically Revelation was written, or the particular persecutions that may have preceded or evoked it. But there is no difference in opinion over the fact that the empire—and its throne—exercised its power ruthlessly, and the church suffered for it.

So when Revelation keeps invoking the symbol of God's throne, and portrays it with language rich in metaphors of wealth and power and enduring through all time, make no mistake. Revelation is throwing down the gauntlet to political power and authority that considers itself a law unto itself with the vision of a throne—and therefore power and authority—that is without rival. The other fascinating way in which Revelation makes this counter-to-its-culture witness is in the saturation of this passage and the book as a whole with worship. The imperial cult had come to insist on veneration of the emperor. It did not matter, in some ways, which religion you claimed or which god you served. The emperor was to be paid his due in the form of worship or veneration. Revelation says "no." In today's passage, it insists God alone is "worthy" to receive glory and honor and power.

We sometimes get ourselves all tangled in knots by the exotic symbolism of Revelation, and much of it is mysterious. But its central assertion, to the church of its time and to our own, is clear: No power, no rule, no authority—political or otherwise—can claim the allegiance and devotion owed to God alone. And when powers begin to make such claims, the church needs to remember and bear witness to our radical trust in God.

Songs of Praises

OK, now we've done the imperial critique. So we can turn back to worship and just sing praises.

Well, yes—and no. Worship is at the core of Revelation, and songs are often the way God's praise gets expressed in this book. But it is not worship or praise that provides escape from unwanted political or social intrusions upon sacred ground. Rather, in Revelation, worship and praise form faith's intrusions against any and all who would usurp sacred ground for their own purposes and against God's life-giving purposes.

Look for a moment at the two songs lifted up in praise of God. The commentary has already identified how the thrice-repeated "holy, holy, holy" means to assert God as holy far above and even out of range of anything or anyone else claiming to be the "holy." The next two phrases in that hymn use the power terms of "Lord" and "Almighty" (*Pantokrator*) to underscore that the God to whom praise is due brooks no rivals (Revelation 4:8). And just in case it seems the Roman Empire had been on the throne for a very long time, the song sings of the God "who was and is and is to come"—that is, the God who was here long before Rome ascended to the top of the hill and long after it will have crumbled like all other pretenders.

In a similar way, the second song in this passage declares God, and God alone, to be "worthy"—a word of rebuke to those who lauded Caesar as worthy by virtue of brute power. God is worthy, however, for an even greater demonstration of power: creation. Rome can only kill. God alone can bring life. And that will be a critical piece of Revelation's faith and worship when it shortly turns to the symbol of the Lamb whom God restored to life.

We have fantastic songs to sing in praise of God and they are songs that aim us not out of this world, but back into it with the faith and confidence and trust that the God who raised Jesus is worthy of all praise. This God's reign will not topple in time like all other empires, but will indeed be forever.

SHARING THE SCRIPTURE

Preparing Our Hearts

Explore this week's devotional reading, found in Psalm 11. The writer of this psalm truly trusts in the God who is his refuge. Here in verse 4 we see, as will also be the case in our text from Revelation, that God is on a throne in heaven. God, who keeps a watchful eye on humankind, will punish the wicked and restore the righteous ones. What in your life right now prompts you to take refuge in God? What do you say to those who try to convince you to flee, to run from God?

Pray that you and the adult learners will put your faith and trust in the God who sits on the heavenly throne.

Preparing Our Minds

Study the background Scripture from Revelation 4 and the lesson Scripture from Revelation 4:1-2, 6-11. Ask yourself: In what ways do symbols communicate concepts and ideas across time?

Write on newsprint:
❑ information for next week's lesson, found under "Continue the Journey."
❑ activities for further spiritual growth in "Continue the Journey."

Become familiar with the symbols in both Understanding the Scripture and Interpreting the Scripture.

LEADING THE CLASS

(1) Gather to Learn

❖ Welcome the class members and introduce any guests.

❖ Pray that those who have assembled for today's session will come in an attitude of worship.

❖ Invite the class to discuss these questions:

(1) How do you define the word "symbol"? (A helpful definition differentiates between "sign" and symbols: A sign stands for something else and literally means what it says; a symbol may be a sign but adds layers of meaning that offer personal, cultural, and/or universal associations. For example, a red metal octagon that warns drivers to halt is a sign. A cross, however, is more than two pieces of wood with horizontal and vertical beams; it also calls to mind for Christians the sacrificial death of Jesus and all that entails.)

(2) Name or describe some well-known symbols.

(3) What value do symbols have for individuals and a society?

❖ Read aloud today's focus statement: **Symbols help people communicate. In what ways do symbols communicate concepts and ideas across time? The symbolism in the Revelation to John, patterned after Hebrew Scriptures, points to worship and praise of God.**

(2) Explore the Origin of the Symbols Used in the Text

❖ Choose a volunteer to read Revelation 4:1-2 and 6-11. Suggest that the entire class read in unison the two hymns found in 8 and 11.

❖ Encourage the students to generate a list of symbols found in these passages. List their ideas on newsprint.

❖ Use information from Understanding the Scripture and Interpreting the Scripture to augment the discussion.

❖ Invite the adults to turn to Isaiah 6:1-5, Ezekiel 1:1-14, and Ezekiel 10. Provide a few moments for them to scan these passages. Then ask:

(1) **What similarities do you see between the images in these prophetic Scriptures and the images in Revelation?**

(2) **What might those similarities suggest to you about the origin of the symbols used in Revelation?**

Challenge the adults to identify other biblical texts that have images similar to those found in Revelation 4.

(3) Identify Sections of the Text that Urge the Learners to Worship

❖ Encourage the adults to look again at today's text to identify images or words that encourage them to worship. Ask them to call out their ideas.

❖ Distribute hymnals and invite the adults to look at "Holy, Holy, Holy! Lord God Almighty," a hymn based on Revelation 4:8-11. Direct the students to read this hymn by forming four groups and asking each group to read one verse. (Since this is a very familiar hymn, you are being asked to read rather than sing it so that everyone will concentrate on the words.)

❖ Continue studying this hymn by distributing paper (preferably unlined) and pencils. Ask the students to choose an image that speaks to them about worshiping God and make a sketch of that image. Assure them that artistic ability is not important. When most have finished, suggest that they show their sketch to a partner and explain why the image they selected motivates them to worship.

(4) Be Alert for Visual and Written Symbols Used in Worship

❖ Take a "field trip" to your sanctuary or chapel. Walk around this sacred space, stopping at symbols that enhance worship. Pause not only at the altar, where you will likely find a cross, Bible, flowers, and perhaps offering plates, but also at stained glass windows, carvings, pictures, banners, musical instruments, and other symbols of worship. If you cannot literally go into these sacred spaces (either because they are in use during the Sunday school hour or because some class members have difficulty walking), encourage the students to take a mental trip by envisioning themselves in the space. At each physical (or mental) stop, ask the learners to comment on what this symbol means to them and how it helps them to worship.

❖ Wrap up this portion of the lesson by asking the students to read again in unison the hymn of praise found in Revelation 4:11.

(5) Continue the Journey

❖ Pray that all who have participated will be open to the messages that God sends to us through the symbols we find in the written word and in art.

❖ Read aloud this preparation for next week's lesson. You may also want to post it on newsprint for the students to copy.

- **Title: Thankful Worship**
- **Background Scripture: Revelation 7:9-17**
- **Lesson Scripture: Revelation 7:9-17**
- **Focus of the Lesson: In times of trouble, people may tend to focus on their problems. Where can we look to find inspiration to focus on God in times of trouble? John depicted a large group of excited worshipers who had come through a difficult ordeal.**

❖ Challenge the students to complete one or more of these activities for further spiritual growth related to this week's session. Post this information on newsprint for the students to copy.

(1) **Visit a church of a denomination different from your own. Perhaps you could attend a Saturday evening service at a Roman Catholic church. Be aware of symbols that help you to worship and symbols that may be unfamiliar. Try to find out what these unfamiliar symbols mean.**

(2) **Consult a book or website regarding symbols of the Christian church. As you page through it, linger over symbols you do not recognize. Read about their origin and meaning. Decide which of the symbols you encountered could help you to worship more intensely.**

(3) **Locate in a book or online Albrecht Dürer's (1471–1528)** *The Apocalypse of Saint John.* **Look especially at "St. John in the Clouds," a depiction of Revelation 4. Use this picture as a means to enter into worship.**

❖ Sing or read aloud "Hail, Thou Once Despised Jesus," which is based on Revelation 4:2-11.

❖ Conclude today's session by leading the class in this benediction from Jude 24-25, which is the key verse for the lesson on April 10: **Now to him who is able to keep you from falling, and to make you stand without blemish in the presence of his glory with rejoicing, to the only God our Savior, through Jesus Christ our Lord, be glory, majesty, power, and authority, before all time and now and forever. Amen.**

UNIT 3: JOHN'S VISION OF WORSHIP
Thankful Worship

PREVIEWING THE LESSON

Lesson Scripture: Revelation 7:9-17
Background Scripture: Revelation 7:9-17
Key Verse: Revelation 7:10

Focus of the Lesson:
In times of trouble, people may tend to focus on their problems. Where can we look to find inspiration to focus on God in times of trouble? John depicted a large group of excited worshipers who had come through a difficult ordeal.

Goals for the Learners:
(1) to discern the meaning of the visual images and symbols in the text.
(2) to explore reasons to praise God from both the text and personal experience.
(3) to incorporate the principles of worship described in the text into their daily lives.

Pronunciation Guide:
Antiochus Epiphanes (an ti' uh kuhs i pif' uh neez)

Supplies:
Bibles, newsprint and marker, paper and pencils, hymnals

READING THE SCRIPTURE

NRSV
Revelation 7:9-17

⁹After this I looked, and there was a great multitude that no one could count, from every nation, from all tribes and peoples and languages, standing before the throne and before the Lamb, robed in white, with palm branches in their hands. **¹⁰They cried out in a loud voice, saying,**

"Salvation belongs to our God who is seated on the throne, and to the Lamb!"

¹¹And all the angels stood around the

NIV
Revelation 7:9-17

⁹After this I looked and there before me was a great multitude that no one could count, from every nation, tribe, people and language, standing before the throne and in front of the Lamb. They were wearing white robes and were holding palm branches in their hands. **¹⁰And they cried out in a loud voice:**

"Salvation belongs to our God,
who sits on the throne,
and to the Lamb."

throne and around the elders and the four living creatures, and they fell on their faces before the throne and worshiped God, [12]singing,

> "Amen! Blessing and glory and wisdom
> and thanksgiving and honor
> and power and might
> be to our God forever and ever!
> Amen."

[13]Then one of the elders addressed me, saying, "Who are these, robed in white, and where have they come from?" [14]I said to him, "Sir, you are the one that knows." Then he said to me, "These are they who have come out of the great ordeal; they have washed their robes and made them white in the blood of the Lamb.

[15] For this reason they are before the throne of God,
> and worship him day and night within his temple,
> and the one who is seated on the throne will shelter them.

[16] They will hunger no more, and thirst no more;
> the sun will not strike them, nor any scorching heat;

[17] for the Lamb at the center of the throne will be their shepherd,
> and he will guide them to springs of the water of life,
> and God will wipe away every tear from their eyes."

[11]All the angels were standing around the throne and around the elders and the four living creatures. They fell down on their faces before the throne and worshiped God, [12]saying:

> "Amen!
> Praise and glory
> and wisdom and thanks and honor
> and power and strength
> be to our God for ever and ever.
> Amen!"

[13]Then one of the elders asked me, "These in white robes—who are they, and where did they come from?"

[14]I answered, "Sir, you know."

And he said, "These are they who have come out of the great tribulation; they have washed their robes and made them white in the blood of the Lamb. [15]Therefore,

> "they are before the throne of God
> and serve him day and night in his temple;
> and he who sits on the throne will spread his tent over them.

[16]Never again will they hunger;
> never again will they thirst.
> The sun will not beat upon them, nor any scorching heat.

[17]For the Lamb at the center of the throne will be their shepherd;
> he will lead them to springs of living water.
> And God will wipe away every tear from their eyes."

UNDERSTANDING THE SCRIPTURE

Revelation 7:9. The passage opens with the scene of a "great multitude." The radical inclusiveness of those from whom this crowd comes (every nation, all tribes and peoples and languages) likely aims at helping the isolated and persecuted community to whom this is addressed perceive themselves as part of such an all-encompassing community. Even the extraordinary reach of Rome's borders and power cannot compare. The throne, as noted in last week's comments, is a symbol of power that belongs to God. The new symbol, explored in more detail in Interpreting the Scripture is the "lamb." All sorts of symbolic possibilities are raised by the use of "lamb." It recalls the acclamation of John the Baptizer whom John's Gospel declares as crying out, as the

Baptizer sees Jesus for the first time: "Here is the Lamb of God" (John 1:29b). The lamb also carries with it the imagery of sacrifice, in particular the ritual sacrifice of the Passover lamb that recalled the story of God's deliverance in Exodus 12. That connection of sacrificial imagery with the lamb had already been made explicit in Revelation 5:6. The detail of "white robes" may be baptismal imagery, as new white robes were used or given to those to be baptized. Verse 14 will expand on the meaning of robes. The palm branches were a symbol of victory in the ancient world, and specifically part of the celebration associated with the Feast of Tabernacles, that celebrated the cleansing of the Temple after it had been misused by the Syrian king Antiochus Epiphanes. (Perhaps this was a veiled reference to the hope of overturning Rome's oppressive rule). The other symbolism brought to this passage by the palm branches is Christ's entry into Jerusalem at the outset of Passion Week.

Revelation 7:10. The earlier hint of the Palm Sunday story by the use of palms here finds another possible connection with the opening acclamation now sung to God and to the lamb: "Salvation belongs to our God . . . and to the lamb." All of the Gospels except Mark record the Palm Sunday crowd as welcoming Jesus into Jerusalem with "hosanna." The word means something like "please, save us." The coming of such saving that Palm Sunday anticipates, although perhaps in ways sorely misunderstood, now finds affirmation in the salvation that belongs to God. In Greek, there is no word that corresponds to "belong," so the language of the text is more accurately literally "Salvation to our God." Again, take note of the detail of the throne in this ascription of praise. Caesar's throne, which served as a symbol of power ruthlessly used, finds contrast in the power of salvation that rests upon God's throne. Not only does the empire's power differ from that of God by its limitation but also by its purposes and consequences.

Revelation 7:11-12. The scene now expands to include angels and elders and the "living creatures" (encountered in last session's passage) The detail of their falling on their faces reflects a traditional posture or gesture of worship. It is intriguing to note, at this point, that their subsequent act of worship is specified as directed to God. Is the Lamb then not worshiped? Is this an undercurrent of the humility of Christ taken up two weeks ago in the passage from Philippians, even though, at the end of that passage, "so that at the name of Jesus every knee should bend (another stance of worship)"? Revelation has a well-deserved reputation for raising questions regarding this and other symbolism. The song these figures bring to God is a sevenfold ascription of praise. It is almost identical to the ascription of praise in Revelation 5:12, with two differences. First, this chapter's song uses "thanksgiving" while chapter 5 uses "wealth" in the list. Second, the song in chapter 5 is addressed specifically to the Lamb. So perhaps, the author essentially repeats the song here and has it addressed to God as a way of balancing the praise between God and Lamb.

Revelation 7:13-14. The narrative now takes the form of a brief dialogue between the author/seer and one of the elders regarding the identity of the multitude robed in white as coming from the "great ordeal." The word translated by "ordeal" means something like "pressure" or "affliction." The narrative does not go on to speculate on the specific identity of these circumstances. The clear background is the suffering and persecution experienced by the community addressed by this work. The detail of robes washed white in the "blood" of the Lamb strongly suggests the suffering has gone far beyond mental anguish imposed by imperial authorities. But again, the linkage of blood with lamb brings deeper associations with the story of the Exodus as well as considerations of the meaning of Christ's death for deliverance.

Revelation 7:15-17. The narrative shifts from the identity of those robed in white to what they now do and experience. Their actions unfold in the language of religious service. The word translated in verse 15 as "worship" is a broader term that can mean not only ritual acts but also any service rendered in obedience to God. Two details of this passage play key roles in next week's passage, and will be more fully explored there: "shelter" and the closing line about God wiping away tears. Perhaps the most striking and distinctive element of this passage is its pairing of lamb and shepherd in the most unexpected of ways. For here, the Lamb will be the shepherd. Even as Lamb brings a host of preexisting symbolism to the passage, so does shepherd. Shepherd had been the vocation of Israel's most beloved king, David. Out of that came, especially in the time of the prophets, the use of shepherd as a symbol for leaders. And it was not always favorable. Ezekiel 34 opens with one of the Old Testament's most devastating critiques of Israel's kings and leaders. They have fed upon the flock rather than feeding it. (In Hebrew, the word "to shepherd" is identical for "to feed.") Ezekiel ends that chapter with the hope that God will be the good shepherd. Here in Revelation, that hope finds affirmation in the image of the Lamb who will be their (our) shepherd.

INTERPRETING THE SCRIPTURE

The Symbol of the Lamb

As noted in the last week's interpretive comments on "Symbols: When Words Are Not Enough," symbols provide recognizable reminders of some truth for which there may neither be the time nor perhaps the language to fully disclose. Today's Understanding the Scripture portion has already touched upon some of the "shorthand" that the symbol of a lamb conveyed to the audience of Revelation. Sacrifice mingled with deliverance, as in the rituals and narratives of the Passover. Jesus as the Lamb of God, as evoked by John the Baptizer's words and Jesus' death on the day of or after Passover (John's Gospel has Jesus die close to the time when the Passover lamb would have been sacrificed; the other Gospels have Jesus eat a meal that bears strong resemblance to the Passover meal). Other symbolism known to the community may underlie this passage's reference to the Lamb that is "at the center of the throne."

There is another element of symbolism that plays a role in the background of this passage. Back in Revelation 5:6, the author speaks of seeing a lamb "standing as if it had been slaughtered." "As if" suggests there is something that does not quite fit entirely; otherwise why not speak of a lamb that had been slaughtered? The key comes in the previous verse when the author hears one of the elders speak of the Lion of Judah who has conquered and is worthy to open the seals (a scene that will follow in chapter 6). But who actually opens the seals? The Lamb (6:1). The fierce power associated with the symbolism of a lion is supplanted by the sacrificial triumph of the lamb.

Recall those connections made in the opening commentary on this passage between elements of this passage and the Palm Sunday narrative. The predominant messianic expectations in this era centered around a conquering figure who would bring deliverance from Rome—a "Lion of Judah" who would bring deliverance to an oppressed people. Yet the "enthronement" that came to pass in Jerusalem was not that symbolized by a lion but a lamb. It is not that power was not exercised for the sake of

God's realm, but rather that power was exercised in a way that was not entirely expected.

I say "not entirely," because not every messianic tradition awaited militaristic fulfillment in a war between good and evil. In fact, one tradition regarding the symbolism of "lamb" as a redemptive figure is sometimes identified as a source for Revelation's use of this symbol. Isaiah 52:13–53:12 is the last of the so-called "Servant Songs." Nestled in that passage is this image of the servant "like a lamb that is led to the slaughter" (53:7). Isaiah's song of the servant—and lamb—does not end in death, nor in the annulment of God's realm. Rather, Isaiah and Revelation both depict a lamb through whose sacrifice comes life. Both employ language and theology that is full of symbols, for the mystery far exceeds the ability of words to fully express much less capture. Yet for both Isaiah and Revelation, the lamb becomes the symbol of God's triumph.

Worship in Context

Closely related to the symbol of lamb is the identity of community. The worship depicted in Revelation 7:9-17 is, on the one hand, a vision of pure worship rendered in the very presence of God. We may not always attain such purity of awareness of the presence of God, or sense of standing before the very throne of God, as in Revelation's portrayal. Yet, sometimes in word and sometimes in sacrament, sometimes in music and sometimes in silence, we do experience something of the sacred among us in our worship, where it seems little if anything comes between us and the presence of the Holy.

But worship is not only standing on holy ground. For as the second half of our passage makes clear, worship is also being acutely aware of and bringing with us into holy encounter the ground upon which we presently stand. In other words, the gift of worship is not only that it bears to us the gracious presence of God; it recognizes and

takes seriously the presence of those who come. When the elder asks a question of the author in this passage, it is not a question about his understanding of God or his knowledge of the ascriptions of praise offered to God. Instead he asks, "Who are these, robed in white, and where have they come from?" That is, do you know who's at worship with you today?

Perhaps it is a question that seems out of place, even in our time. After all, unless we are out visiting some other congregation we pretty much know who's at worship. We know them by name. We know them as neighbor, and friend, and sometimes as stranger or visitor. But the heavenly liturgy in Revelation reminds us we need to take the question far more seriously and to heart. Do we really know who's at worship, that is, are we aware of what may be pressing upon (the more literal meaning of "great ordeal" in verse 14) the lives of our companions in the pews? Do we know what experiences are leading them, or driving them, to seek out holy encounter?

Worship is always done in the context of the life of those who gather. If it is not, the sermon will never ring true, the prayers will always miss the mark. Not because our theology may be out of kilter, but because our sense of the Holy bids us to be in common life with those who gather. Mindfulness of God is fundamental to worship, but that by no means excludes mindfulness of others. God has created us for relationship with God and with one another.

Shepherded Praise

The praise of God in Revelation, and in our lives, affirms and celebrates how God has been experienced. That is certainly true of the first two ascriptions of praise in verses 10 and then 12. "Salvation belongs to our God" is not an abstract doctrine; it is the lived experience of this people, even in the midst of an oppressive situation that seemed to deny the hope of saving by its inflicting of violence and in some cases death. All of the attributes lifted up to God in verse 12 are assertions of where this community's hope lies. Hope does not reside on the throne in Rome, which is the conventional wisdom of that day. Hope resides upon the throne of God and the Lamb.

And the Lamb who has, like them, experienced the worst of what the thrones of this world can inflict is praised to be, for them, their shepherd—their "feeder." As this passage draws to a close, praise celebrates that shepherding care that will guide and lead, comfort and restore. That is a word the audience of Revelation desperately needed to hear, and then celebrate. That is a word we need to hear and then celebrate. We can hear all manner of things, but those that we celebrate are the ones we take to heart, ground our lives and hope upon, and then live accordingly. Worship of God is the celebration of God. Let the people say, Amen!

SHARING THE SCRIPTURE

Preparing Our Hearts

Explore this week's devotional reading, found in Psalm 23. Although you may know this beloved psalm well enough to recite it from memory, try to read it with "fresh eyes," perhaps from a translation you seldom use. What does this psalm reveal to you about the shepherd? Why do you believe that you can turn to this shepherd in times of trouble? Talk to the shepherd, calling upon him for guidance and help.

Pray that you and the adult learners will walk closely with the shepherd all the days of your life.

Preparing Our Minds

Study the background Scripture and the lesson Scripture, both of which are from Revelation 7:9-17. As you study, think about where you can look to find the inspiration you need to focus on God in times of trouble.

Write on newsprint:
❏ Bible verses for Gather to Learn.
❏ information for next week's lesson, found under "Continue the Journey."
❏ activities for further spiritual growth in "Continue the Journey."

LEADING THE CLASS

(1) Gather to Learn

❖ Welcome the class members and introduce any guests.

❖ Pray that today's students will become assured that even in the midst of crisis they can turn to and worship God.

❖ Post this list of Bible verses that can inspire people facing challenging situations. Call on individuals to read these verses as time allows. Talk with the class about how these verses help them to focus on God when the going gets tough. Invite them to add other verses.
- Psalm 23; 27:1; 34:7-9; 46:1
- Luke 12:22-34
- Philippians 4:6-7, 19

❖ Read aloud today's focus statement: **In times of trouble, people may tend to focus on their problems. Where can we look to find inspiration to focus on God in times of trouble? John depicted a large group of excited worshipers who had come through a difficult ordeal.**

(2) Discern the Meaning of the Visual Images and Symbols in the Text

❖ Read Revelation 7:9-17. Encourage the class to join you by reading in unison the words of praise in verses 10 and 12.

❖ Prompt the adults to identify what they hear and see in this passage. List their findings on newsprint.

❖ Look especially at several images: white robes, palm branches, the Lamb, and shepherd. Encourage the students to discuss what each of these means, not just literally, but as a symbol. What else is being revealed by the use of these images? If the class is large, form small groups and assign each group an image.

❖ Add to the discussion by reading or retelling "The Symbol of the Lamb" and "Shepherd-ed Praise," both from Interpreting the Scripture.

❖ Conclude this discussion by looking at the "great multitude." Ask:

(1) **Who is included in this white-robed group?**

(2) **What does the inclusiveness of the group suggest to you about the nature of God's kingdom?**

(3) **Sunday at 11:00 a.m. is the most segregated hour of the week in America, according to the late Dr. Martin Luther King, Jr. What might this diverse "great multitude" praising God in heaven suggest to us about how we are called and expected to worship here on earth?**

(3) Explore Reasons to Praise God From Both the Text and Personal Experience

❖ Invite the learners to turn again to Revelation 7:10 (today's key verse) and 7:12.

❖ Form groups of three or four students. Give each group a sheet of newsprint and a marker. Ask them to recall all that we have discussed today and to write an amplified version—an explanation—of either verse 10 or verse 12. Consider:

• **what is being said to God.**

• **what is being said or implied about God.**

• **who is doing the praising.** (Recall that these worshipers have all been through "a great ordeal.")

❖ Bring the groups together to present what they have written.

❖ Look as a class at the reasons the people worship, as stated in verse 15-17. **What reasons are given here?** List these on newsprint.

❖ Encourage the students to add to this list reasons that they worship and praise God. Review the list and ask:

(1) **Do you think that most people who attend worship on Sunday praise God for these reasons? Give evidence to support your answer.**

(2) **If we do not worship for these reasons and with this intensity, even for an hour, what might that suggest about our relationship with God?** (You may want to note that some folks say they "don't get much out of worship." Talk about why this inability to experience God's presence may be a problem for some. Are they participating fully? Or do such folks expect to be "entertained," or let the leaders do all the work while they sit passively? What can be done to help people put their entire selves into worship?)

(4) Incorporate the Principles of Worship Described in the Text Into the Learners' Daily Lives

❖ Distribute paper and pencils. Be sure the lists you have made throughout the session are posted where everyone can see them. Challenge the students to embrace some of these worship ideas and write on their papers how they will use them on a daily basis. For example, some may sing praises each day; others may give thanks to God for bringing them through trials; others may prostrate themselves before God in humility.

❖ Close this part of the lesson by asking volunteers to state how they hope to use what they have learned from today's Bible text to enhance their own worship.

(5) Continue the Journey

❖ Pray that today's participants will worship God with thankful hearts, even in the midst of a crisis.

❖ Read aloud this preparation for next week's lesson. You may also want to post it on newsprint for the students to copy.

- ■ Title: All Things New
- ■ Background Scripture: Revelation 21
- ■ Lesson Scripture: Revelation 21:1-8
- ■ Focus of the Lesson: Many people would like to have a new beginning that wipes away all that has been. What is it like to begin anew? The Revelation of John tells us that God, who is the beginning and the end, will make all things new.

❖ Challenge the students to complete one or more of these activities for further spiritual growth related to this week's session. Post this information on newsprint for the students to copy.

(1) Locate information about Christians who are currently undergoing an ordeal. Pray for them. What else can you do to support these persecuted ones?

(2) **Spend devotional time this week simply praising God. If you are able, try different positions for worship, such as sitting, standing, lifting your arms, kneeling, lying face down on the floor. What impact do these various positions have on your worship?**

(3) **Read again Revelation 7:9. What kinds of outreach is your congregation doing through missionaries and programs to help make this vision of "a great multitude," including people from all nations and tribes who speak many languages, become a reality?**

❖ Sing or read aloud "Ye Servants of God," which is based on Revelation 7:9-12.

❖ Conclude today's session by leading the class in this benediction from Jude 24-25, which is the key verse for the lesson on April 10: **Now to him who is able to keep you from falling, and to make you stand without blemish in the presence of his glory with rejoicing, to the only God our Savior, through Jesus Christ our Lord, be glory, majesty, power, and authority, before all time and now and forever. Amen.**

UNIT 3: JOHN'S VISION OF WORSHIP
ALL THINGS NEW

PREVIEWING THE LESSON

Lesson Scripture: Revelation 21:1-8
Background Scripture: Revelation 21
Key Verse: Revelation 21:5

God will dwell among us
BS

Focus of the Lesson:
Many people would like to have a new beginning that wipes away all that has been. What is it like to begin anew? The Revelation of John tells us that God, who is the beginning and the end, will make all things new.

Wilkerson

Goals for the Learners:
(1) to examine the new heaven and new earth described in the Revelation of John.
(2) to reflect on what it means to say that God dwells with us.
(3) to make a new beginning in some facet of their lives.

ISAIAH 65-17
66-22
25: v 5 7-8

Pronunciation Guide:
Alpha (al' fuh)
Omega (oh meg' uh)
skenoo (skay no' o)

Revelation
— new heaven
— new earth
— holy city

Ezekiels Temple vision
40: 1-43:11

Supplies:
Bibles, newsprint and marker, paper and pencils, hymnals

Micah 4: 1-4
hope — peace
Swords to plowshares

READING THE SCRIPTURE

NRSV
Revelation 21:1-8

¹Then I saw a new heaven and a new earth; for the first heaven and the first earth had passed away, and the sea was no more. ²And I saw the holy city, the new Jerusalem, coming down out of heaven from God, prepared as a bride adorned for her husband. ³And I heard a loud voice from the throne saying,

NIV
Revelation 21:1-8

¹Then I saw a new heaven and a new earth, for the first heaven and the first earth had passed away, and there was no longer any sea. ²I saw the Holy City, the new Jerusalem, coming down out of heaven from God, prepared as a bride beautifully dressed for her husband. ³And I heard a loud voice from the throne saying, "Now the dwelling

"See, the home of God is among mortals.
He will dwell with them;
they will be his peoples,
and God himself will be with them;

4 he will wipe every tear from their eyes.
Death will be no more;
mourning and crying and pain will
be no more,
for the first things have passed away."

5And the one who was seated on the throne said, "See, I am making all things new." Also he said, "Write this, for these words are trustworthy and true." 6Then he said to me, "It is done! I am the Alpha and the Omega, the beginning and the end. To the thirsty I will give water as a gift from the spring of the water of life. 7Those who conquer will inherit these things, and I will be their God and they will be my children. 8But as for the cowardly, the faithless, the polluted, the murderers, the fornicators, the sorcerers, the idolaters, and all liars, their place will be in the lake that burns with fire and sulfur, which is the second death."

of God is with men, and he will live with them. They will be his people, and God himself will be with them and be their God. 4He will wipe every tear from their eyes. There will be no more death or mourning or crying or pain, for the old order of things has passed away."

5He who was seated on the throne said, "I am making everything new!" Then he said, "Write this down, for these words are trustworthy and true."

6He said to me: "It is done. I am the Alpha and the Omega, the Beginning and the End. To him who is thirsty I will give to drink without cost from the spring of the water of life. 7He who overcomes will inherit all this, and I will be his God and he will be my son. 8But the cowardly, the unbelieving, the vile, the murderers, the sexually immoral, those who practice magic arts, the idolaters and all liars—their place will be in the fiery lake of burning sulfur. This is the second death."

UNDERSTANDING THE SCRIPTURE

Revelation 21:1-2. The vision of a "new heaven and a new earth" calls to mind two oracles in Isaiah 65:17 and 66:22. In Isaiah, such imagery offered an affirmation of God's power in creation, a subtle rejection of the Babylonian deities' and empire's claim of supremacy. Newness in Revelation (as in Isaiah 42:9) speaks prophetically and politically of God's ability to wrest new possibilities out of the hands of seemingly entrenched powers. The detail about the disappearance of the sea plays on several symbolic levels. In God's first act of creation in Genesis 1:1 and following, the sea stands as a symbol of chaos out of which God brings order and life. On another level, Rome came to call the Mediterranean Sea *Mare Nostrum*—"Our Sea." The imagery here in Revelation may blend a new act of God's creation with a coded depiction of the

disappearance of Rome's "chaos." The sight of the holy "city" reminds that "city" occurs some 30 times in Revelation, almost half of the references in its final two chapters. In the earlier chapters, its contrasting use is in reference to the "great city" of Babylon, yet another symbol for Rome and its empire.

Revelation 21:3-4. These two verses consist almost entirely of the words of the One seated on the throne. (Recall, from previous sessions, that throne serves as a symbol for power—here, the power of God). "Home" and "dwell" translate the noun and verb forms of the Greek word (*skenoo*) that literally means, "to tent or tabernacle." This is the same verb used in 7:15 to depict the God who will "shelter" the ones before God's throne. "Their God" and "his peoples" recalls Psalm 100:3, with its worshipful casting of this relationship in terms of God's shepherding of Israel. The line regarding the wiping away of all tears goes back almost verbatim to Revelation 7:17. The assertion about death ceasing to be reflects another eschatological vision: Isaiah 25:6-9, particularly verses 7-8. With death gone, its "companions" of mourning and crying and pain will likewise cease to be. "First things" does not mean first as in chief, but rather in order of appearance. Like Isaiah's word of "do not remember the former things," (43:18), the author of Revelation invites the readers and hearers to direct their attention elsewhere.

Revelation 21:5-8. That elsewhere is the "new." The proclamation that God is making all things new is noteworthy on two accounts. First it is preceded by "see." Revelation uses "see" six times in the NRSV translation in this way: a summons to attend to an announcement. Other translations, such as the KJV, frequently use the word "behold" rather than "see." "See" also suggests that the movement of faith involves turning our sight (be it vision or perspective) from something that may be distracting attention to that which needs to be seen in order to fully comprehend whatever call follows. The second noteworthy piece about this proclamation is the verb tense. It does not say God *will* make all things new. It is asserts God *is making* all things new. God is acting, even in the midst of what might seem to be a God-forsaken time where Rome's rule oppresses, to bring this new heaven and earth into being. To underscore that point, the direction to "write . . . these words" follows, where what has been declared is given the two-fold assessment of being "trustworthy and true." "Alpha and Omega," the first and last letters of the Greek alphabet, have been used earlier in Revelation 1 and will appear again in Revelation 22. They are a symbol of God's timeless and eternal character. "Those who conquer" translates an expression that occurs several times in Revelation, and has to do here and most of the other times as

encouragement for the audience to maintain faith in difficult times. The blessings for those who do, and the curses upon those who don't, take up the remainder of these verses.

Revelation 21:9-14. The author now shifts to a vision of the holy city made possible by a spiritual experience ("in the spirit [the angel] carried me away"). Both this introduction and the vision that follows resemble Ezekiel's Temple vision (Ezekiel 40:1–43:11). These opening verses in Revelation focus largely on views with numeric symbolism: 12 gates and angels and tribes, and likewise 12 foundations with the names of the apostles. Notice, too, the apostles are identified by saying they are "of the Lamb." While Christ is clearly intended, the author keeps the lamb imagery used earlier.

Revelation 21:15-21. The author indicates the angel has a measuring rod, which is then used to measure various aspects of the holy city. The overall description is that of a cube ("its length and width and height are equal"), with each of the dimensions measuring 1,500 miles. Almost the entire Temple vision of Ezekiel is permeated with measurements. The exacting detail over precise measurements in Ezekiel seems to relate to the desire to "get it right" in terms of the Temple's rebuilding and the ritual that will be offered there. In Revelation, the focus on measurements seems less on precision and more on the city's enormity. Enormity on another scale comes in all of the precious gems that serve to describe the materials with which the city is made. Perhaps the extravagance of wealth represented aims to shame the riches to which Rome laid claim.

Revelation 21:22-27. While earlier passages in Revelation speak of a heavenly temple (7:15, 16:1), the author of Revelation now speaks of no temple. The function of a temple could be said to "house" or at least symbolize the Holy Presence so that God may be found among us. Now, that will no longer be the case. God is to be so clearly among and within that place and its peoples (as in 21:3), that access to the Holy will make a temple unneeded. Drawing upon associations of God's presence and glory with light, as in Exodus 34:29 when Moses comes down from the mountain with his face still shining, Revelation offers that no light will be needed here because of the immanence of God (and the Lamb). The hope of nations walking by God's light recalls Micah 4:1-4's vision of hope and peace, where nations will not only walk in God's paths but also beat swords into ploughshares.

INTERPRETING THE SCRIPTURE

The Promise of the New

A new heaven and a new earth. I am making all things new. A time when death will be no more. . . It doesn't get more new than that. Who wouldn't want such all-encompassing newness?

Well, for one, those who are quite happy with the old. The Book of Revelation would have held little appeal—in fact, it would have greatly threatened—those ensconced in the power and privilege of Rome's empire. It would have the same effect for a host of others who, while not yet possessing such control or affluence, might have presumed them to be the aspirations they would do most anything to attain. Certainly some, in that day, would have willingly done whatever the empire desired so as to align themselves with its privileges.

While Revelation may at many points seem remote and mysterious to us in its thickly veiled symbolism and wild imagery, at this point of the new versus the old it touches one of the most common struggles for individuals and for institutions, including the church. The promise of the new always carries with it the implicit possibility that some of that which is old must be set aside. I believe we understand that and even accept that in general terms. But what happens when the old in need of being set aside falls into the category of "how we've always done things around here"? Or what happens when the new in need of accepting represents something, or someone, we would prefer to keep on the outside looking in?

It could be argued that Revelation's vision of the new is entirely related to the eventual establishment of God's reign, and that it is more than a stretch to inject its "old versus new" into present-day matters of life of individuals or institutions.

Yet how does the voice from the throne describe the work of God in regard to that still-distant reign: "I *am making* all things new." Revelation, and its promise of newness, is not limited to what happens at the end of history. Revelation, and its promise of newness, reaches into the days in which we live. God is at work *now* making all things new. That means, among other things, God's renewal may from time to time come to bear on the "old" in our lives, especially when that "old" represents actions or attitudes whose time is long gone.

"See, I am making all things new." Even you. Even me. Even the whole of creation. To some who prefer the way things are, that is a threat. To others, hopefully the community of Christ, "all things new" is promise and hope.

God With Us

Even though we have just recently observed the celebration of Easter, the passage from Revelation breaks open a very Christmas-like affirmation: God will be with us. God will dwell among us. God's home is among us. As noted in the Understanding the Scripture portion for verses 3-4, the root for the Greek words translated as "home" and "dwell" literally means "to tent" or, in an older style of phrasing, "to tabernacle" (a tabernacle is a tent).

That imagery is fascinating when it comes in reference to God's dwelling among us, promised and present. For a tent or tabernacle is, above all else, portable. It can be moved. God's presence and dwelling is not static, but dynamic. Consider that in terms of Revelation's later comment in verse 22 that there is no "temple." A temple is solid, permanent, fixed. One goes to a temple to seek out the Holy. To speak of God's dwelling as a tent, on the other hand, invokes an image of God able and willing to move about among us where needed.

To the audience originally addressed by Revelation, that character of dynamic mobility may have been critical. Communities under persecution did not always have the luxury of attending a central "sanctuary" where they might be easily found out. So even a church driven underground, into the catacombs as later came to be the literal truth, could hold onto the hope of God "tenting" among them, moving where they needed to be for the sake of safety and practicing their faith.

The earlier linkage of "God with us" with Christmas imagery is not only one of God coming among us in the person of Jesus. In the Gospel of John, there is no nativity story. Instead there is the prologue of "In the beginning was the Word" that lifts up the themes that Gospel will pursue in terms of Jesus' relationship to the One who sent him. At the climax of that text, John affirms: "And the Word became flesh and lived among us" (1:14). The word translated as "lived" is *skenoo*—"to tent." The Incarnation serves the beginning of John's Gospel as the promise of God's home and dwelling

among us does in Revelation 21. *God with us* forms the gospel's basis and hope.

Alpha, Omega, and the Life of Faith

Simply put, "Alpha and Omega" is the same as saying "from A to Z." They are the first and last letters of the Greek alphabet. So what is involved in the assertion of verse 6 that God is Alpha and Omega?

From the perspective of time, the title invokes God's timelessness. However far back we attempt to peer, however far ahead we seek to glimpse, there is no time absent of God. For the church addressed by this book, that means that God's presence is there even in the midst of persecution. Even the worst that Rome (and Rome's contemporaries) can do, and it can be and still is horrific, cannot eliminate God. In other words, that worst cannot eliminate hope.

From the perspective of power, and much of Revelation's language invokes throne imagery (and this affirmation of Alpha and Omega comes from the throne), Alpha and Omega asserts that the beginning and end of power resides in God's good hands. Without a doubt, there are claimants to power of all kind, especially the variety that draws its strength (and fear) from the power to inflict death. But in the end, as at the beginning, the only power that endures belongs to God. And that power has saving, not destroying, purposes.

From the perspective of worship—and recall that this scene as with other visions has worship as a dynamic component—worship in terms of Alpha and Omega brings us to devote ourselves to life's ultimate source and ultimate destiny. Worship belongs to God and God alone. Those were treasonous words in the days of emperor worship. And, in some senses, those still can be risky words in cultures that invoke patriotism or materialism or any other "-ism" as due the single-minded allegiance or devotion that Revelation proclaims belongs to God alone.

"I am Alpha and Omega." In the end, as in the beginning, God reigns. In the end, as in the beginning, God fashions creation and seeks humanity for life-giving purposes. In the end, as in the beginning, our dwelling place is with God, and God's with us. In the end, as in the beginning, God is good.

SHARING THE SCRIPTURE

Preparing Our Hearts

Explore this week's devotional reading, found in Isaiah 43:15-21. In this passage where God promises to protect and restore those who are exiles in Babylon, God announces, "I am about to do a new thing" (43:19). This same idea permeates today's lesson and is very similar to our key verse from Revelation 21:5. As you read the passage from Isaiah, think about what God has already done for the people. How does God's past performance assure you that God will be true to promises? Where in the world and in your life do you want to see God do a new thing?

Pray that you and the adult learners will be open to all things new.

Preparing Our Minds

Study the background Scripture from Revelation 21 and the lesson Scripture from Revelation 21:1-8. Recall what it is like to begin something anew.

Write on newsprint:
❏ statements for "Reflect on What It Means to Say that God Dwells With Us."
❏ information for next week's lesson, found under "Continue the Journey."
❏ activities for further spiritual growth in "Continue the Journey."

LEADING THE CLASS

(1) Gather to Learn

❖ Welcome the class members and introduce any guests.

❖ Pray that the class will be open to new insights that God may have for them today.

❖ Point out that especially during the economic upheavals of recent years many people have been required to reinvent themselves in terms of their career. Others have chosen to reinvent themselves because they found one career unfulfilling and decided to pursue a passion. Invite volunteers to talk about a career change they, or someone they know well, have experienced. Consider questions such as: What prompted you to begin anew? What was it like for you to start over? What did you have to do to make this change work? How do you feel this change has affected your life?

❖ Read aloud today's focus statement: **Many people would like to have a new beginning that wipes away all that has been. What is it like to begin anew? The Revelation of John tells us that God, who is the beginning and the end, will make all things new.**

(2) Examine the New Heaven and New Earth Described in the Revelation of John

❖ Select a volunteer to read Revelation 21:1-8.

❖ Use information from Understanding the Scripture for Revelation 21:1-2, 5-8, and "The Promise of the New" in Interpreting the Scripture to help the adults understand the symbolism and what it is that God intends to do. Be sure to point out that God is "making all things new," which is different from saying God will wipe out the current creation and "make all new things."

❖ Discuss these questions:

(1) **What differences would you expect when comparing the way things are now with the newness that God will bring about?**

(2) **Given that most people find any kind of change to be a challenge, often because they have a vested interest in the way things currently exist, do you think there are those who would not anticipate "a new heaven and a new earth"? Give evidence or examples to support your answer.**

(3) **What does this passage tell you about God?**

(4) **What does this passage tell you about humanity?**

(5) **What did this passage say about worship?**

(6) **What affect might this passage have on your own walk with Christ?**

(3) Reflect on What It Means to Say that God Dwells With Us

❖ Ask someone to read again Revelation 21:3-4.

❖ Use information from Understanding the Scripture for Revelation 21:3-4 and "God with Us" from Interpreting the Scripture to delve into these verses.

❖ Form several groups of three to four students. Encourage the groups to talk about what it means to them as individuals and as the church to know that God dwells with them. Post these statements to guide the group discussions:

(1) **Give an example or two to illustrate how God dwells with you personally.**

(2) **Give an example or two to illustrate how God dwells with your congregation.**

(3) **Comment on what you believe about God dwelling with you now—and in the future.**

❖ Call the groups together to comment on any insights they discerned.

(4) Make a New Beginning in Some Facet of Life

❖ Brainstorm with the class a list of new beginnings that people may make throughout their lifetimes. Record examples such as these on newsprint: *starting school; moving to a new community; entering a new school; starting a job; finding a mate and getting married; starting a family; welcoming a new member to the family; starting a new friendship; changing jobs or careers; retiring; starting life anew after losing a spouse; beginning again after a catastrophe.*

Distribute paper and pencils. Suggest that the students review the class list and think about new beginnings in their own lives. Perhaps they are in the midst of a transition or will be as they anticipate a move, retirement, or other new facet of life. Challenge them to write about this new beginning. What do they hope will happen? What surprises have they encountered during this transition? Where have they seen God in the midst of this new beginning? Where do they hope to go from here?

❖ Solicit volunteers to tell about their own new beginnings.

❖ Encourage the adults to support one another as they each make a new beginning in some facet of their lives.

(5) Continue the Journey

❖ Pray that all who have come today will give thanks for opportunities to begin anew.

❖ Read aloud this preparation for next week's lesson. You may also want to post it on newsprint for the students to copy.

■ **Title: Tree of Life**

■ **Background Scripture: Revelation 22**

■ **Lesson Scripture: Revelation 22:1-9**

■ Focus of the Lesson: Our lives are filled with abundance. What is our attitude toward receiving the bounty provided for us? The Revelation to John makes it clear that there is no more appropriate response to what God has done than to worship God.

❖ Challenge the students to complete one or more of these activities for further spiritual growth related to this week's session. Post this information on newsprint for the students to copy.

(1) **Ponder changes in the seasons. What physical signs of newness and renewal do you see in the spring? How would you like to see your own life renewed? Write your thoughts in a spiritual journal.**

(2) **Participate, if possible, in a celebration of renewal, such as a birthday party or anniversary. Or think about such an event. How is your life renewed by such events?**

(3) **Recall that God dwells with us. Create in your home a worship space, perhaps on a table, that becomes a special place for God to dwell with you. On the table place a Bible, cross, candles, or other symbol that reminds you of God's presence. Offer a word of praise whenever you are near this space.**

❖ Sing or read aloud "This Is a Day of New Beginnings," based on today's key verse, Revelation 21:5.

❖ Conclude today's session by leading the class in this benediction from Jude 24-25, which is the key verse for the lesson on April 10: **Now to him who is able to keep you from falling, and to make you stand without blemish in the presence of his glory with rejoicing, to the only God our Savior, through Jesus Christ our Lord, be glory, majesty, power, and authority, before all time and now and forever. Amen.**

UNIT 3: JOHN'S VISION OF WORSHIP
TREE OF LIFE

PREVIEWING THE LESSON

Lesson Scripture: Revelation 22:1-9
Background Scripture: Revelation 22
Key Verse: Revelation 22:2

Focus of the Lesson:

Our lives are filled with abundance. What is our attitude toward receiving the bounty provided for us? The Revelation to John makes it clear that there is no more appropriate response to what God has done than to worship God.

Goals for the Learners:

(1) to review all the images of nature in this text.
(2) to appreciate worship as an appropriate response to receiving God's abundance.
(3) to investigate the implications for our world to have access to a "tree of life" as described in Revelation.

Pronunciation Guide:

martureo (mar-too-reh'-o)
Parousia (puh roo' zhee uh)

pre- or postmillenialism
   (muh len' ee uhl iz uhm)

Supplies:

Bibles, newsprint and marker, paper and pencils, hymnals, basin of water, branch or leaves, elements for a worship table such as a cross and Bible, optional pictures of nature

READING THE SCRIPTURE

NRSV

Revelation 22:1-9

¹Then the angel showed me the river of the water of life, bright as crystal, flowing from the throne of God and of the Lamb ²through the middle of the street of the city.

NIV

Revelation 22:1-9

¹Then the angel showed me the river of the water of life, as clear as crystal, flowing from the throne of God and of the Lamb ²down the middle of the great street of the

On either side of the river is the tree of life with its twelve kinds of fruit, producing its fruit each month; and the leaves of the tree are for the healing of the nations. ³Nothing accursed will be found there any more. But the throne of God and of the Lamb will be in it, and his servants will worship him; ⁴they will see his face, and his name will be on their foreheads. ⁵And there will be no more night; they need no light of lamp or sun, for the Lord God will be their light, and they will reign forever and ever.

⁶And he said to me, "These words are trustworthy and true, for the Lord, the God of the spirits of the prophets, has sent his angel to show his servants what must soon take place."

⁷"See, I am coming soon! Blessed is the one who keeps the words of the prophecy of this book."

⁸I, John, am the one who heard and saw these things. And when I heard and saw them, I fell down to worship at the feet of the angel who showed them to me; ⁹but he said to me, "You must not do that! I am a fellow servant with you and your comrades the prophets, and with those who keep the words of this book. Worship God!"

city. **On each side of the river stood the tree of life, bearing twelve crops of fruit, yielding its fruit every month. And the leaves of the tree are for the healing of the nations.** ³No longer will there be any curse. The throne of God and of the Lamb will be in the city, and his servants will serve him. ⁴They will see his face, and his name will be on their foreheads. ⁵There will be no more night. They will not need the light of a lamp or the light of the sun, for the Lord God will give them light. And they will reign for ever and ever.

⁶The angel said to me, "These words are trustworthy and true. The Lord, the God of the spirits of the prophets, sent his angel to show his servants the things that must soon take place."

⁷"Behold, I am coming soon! Blessed is he who keeps the words of the prophecy in this book."

⁸I, John, am the one who heard and saw these things. And when I had heard and seen them, I fell down to worship at the feet of the angel who had been showing them to me. ⁹But he said to me, "Do not do it! I am a fellow servant with you and with your brothers the prophets and of all who keep the words of this book. Worship God!"

UNDERSTANDING THE SCRIPTURE

Revelation 22:1-2. In a variety of ways throughout this passage, the concluding chapter of Revelation hearkens back to its beginning. In verse 1, that connection comes in the verb "showed." The first verse of Revelation speaks of the revelation given to Jesus to "show" not simply the author of Revelation but "his servants"—the whole community—"what must soon take place." The river flowing from the throne of God in 22:1 contrasts with the vision of Daniel 7:9-10, where flames flow from the throne of God. "Rivers" stood as dominant symbols of life in the largely arid regions of the

Middle East. It is not surprising to find the image here at the end as at the beginning of all things (Genesis 2:10). It should not be overlooked, however, that this river flows not through a wilderness but a city. A city is a place of human habitation and community. In contrast to the symbolism of the city of Babylon (which is Rome) in the earlier chapters of Revelation, now the realm of God has for its dwelling place a holy city. One other subtle note on the tree symbolism in this verse: the Greek word for "tree" is not one used in, say, Jesus' parables about trees in general. Rather, the word in Luke

23:31 as well as several places in Acts and Galatians and 1 Peter has to do with crucifixion references. The tree of life, by the author's very choice of words, carries with it the imagery of the (life-giving) cross.

Revelation 22:3-5. The worship rendered to God uses the same word as in 7:15, which may include liturgy but also connotes other forms of religious service. "They will see his [God's] face" is a startling declaration of the intimacy of relationship to God. The law and traditions of Judaism clearly taught that one could not look upon the face of God. Yet in God's realm, that prohibition is lifted. The marking of God's names on the foreheads of the saints in verse 4 serves as a largely unexplored image in contrast to the overly exhausted speculations regarding the "mark of the beast" in 14:11. Everything from credit card numbers to barcodes have been trotted out to summon fear and engage in endless guesswork about matters that really would be better addressed by simply living trusting God, doing justice, loving mercy, and following the example of Christ. Verse 5 repeats chapter 21's imagery of a city without need of light because of the immanence of God (21:23-25). "Reign" (22:5) occurs repeatedly in Revelation. It asserts God's dominion over all others, including that day's present rival of Rome. The verse's noting *"they* will reign" suggests the saints have a share in that realm's rule, though the passage leaves unexplained what exactly is meant.

Revelation 22:6-7. The first half of verse 6 mirrors the affirmation of trustworthiness made in Revelation 21:5 regarding the promise of a new heaven and new earth. The second half of verse 6 hearkens back to Revelation 1:1, only here an angel rather than Jesus "shows" what must soon take place. That "soon" is repeated soon after in the declaration that "I am coming soon" (22:7). The question is this: What is meant by soon? This phrase becomes a key element of the second half of this book, and thus the ending message it leaves with its audience, then and now. "I am coming soon" appears twice more in later verses (12, 20). Clearly, the author intends to encourage the audience with imminent expectation for God's action on their behalf.

Revelation 22:8-9. "I, John" is like a personal signature on a letter to authenticate who is its source. It had been used in Revelation 1:9 and is again in this verse. The "signature" presumes this name would have carried weight in the community to which it is addressed. Otherwise, why bother using it? Not once but twice in this verse John affirms he "heard and saw" these things. That coincides with the way that John's oracles have involved both vision and hearing. Words interpret what has been seen. Vision gives texture and life to mere words. Both undergird one another. The verb for "worship" in verse 8 and again in verse 9 is different from the word for "worship" in verse 3. In these two verses, the Greek word is specifically an act of liturgical response to the Holy. The immediate objection by the one shown such devotion in verse 9 echoes an almost identical incident noted in 19:10. Such an act, the verse ends, can only be directed toward God.

Revelation 22:10-15. The call to "not seal" these prophetic words indicates this is to be an "open book." In other words, these are not words to be hidden away until some future time when they become relevant. They are relevant now for the community to whom John addresses them. That means, among other things, their relevance to us today is best served by not presuming they speak only to our day (or our future), but to begin by seeking to understand what they meant in those days past so we have clues and insights in terms of how to read and hear them now. "The time is near" is basically the same as "I am coming soon" in verse 12.

Revelation 22:16-21. Verse 16 offers a word from Jesus to the seer. The word for "testimony" is *martureo*, the root for "martyr." The irony is that it was likely close to the period of Revelation's writing that martyr, "witness," came to take on its added meaning of one who dies for the faith. In the worst of these times, being a faithful witness could bring just that. The warning against modifying any of these words in verse 19 parallels a warning in Deuteronomy 4:1-2. It is revealing that the final two messages of Revelation involve prayer for Jesus' return and benediction. The visions lead back into worship, which is a time and place of encounter with God. And it is God's grace that is invoked to carry the saints—to carry us—until that coming day arrives.

INTERPRETING THE SCRIPTURE

A River Runs Through It

This title of the movie based on the book by Norman Maclean arises from the closing lines of the book. There, the words offer the author's perspective of how "eventually, all things merge into one, and a river runs through it."

The son of a Presbyterian minister, Maclean may have found the inspiration for his words in Revelation's closing vision. In the merging of all things in the reign and presence of God, there is a river whose waters runs through the holy city. Waters formed the opening setting for God's act of creation in Genesis 1:1-2. So it is fitting that in the fulfillment of all things, as at the beginning, there are waters. There is a river.

The symbolism of water in the Scriptures is rich and deep. From the parting of the seas to the providing of water in the wilderness for Israel; from the storms at sea that brought Jonah and disciples into recognition of the Holy; from the baptism of Jesus in the river Jordan or Jesus' offer of living water to a Samaritan woman: waters form the backdrop and sometimes the means of God's gracious presence among us.

Little wonder why the care of creation, including its waters, is more than just a politically correct act required, if for no other reason, than enlightened self-interest. Care of the waters becomes a physical act that honors the gift of water bestowed by water's holy symbolism in our faith. "A river runs through it." "It" is not just the holy city of our longing and hope; "it" is the very faith we hold that has been commended to us in stories of rivers and waters as old as creation itself and as fresh as the life water still brings today.

Tree of Life, Leaves for Healing

The "nature" images in Revelation 22 continue, moving from a river to a tree of life whose leaves promise healing. This imagery parallels that of Genesis 2. As some scholars have noted, the biblical narrative begins and ends in a richly watered garden.

"Tree of life" invokes memories of the Genesis 2 narrative of creation, where the tree of life as well as the prohibited tree of knowledge stands within the garden called Eden (2:15-17). Curiously, after the story of the Fall, Genesis 3:24 describes measures to prevent access specifically to the tree of life. In the garden of Revelation 22, the tree has no guard or prohibition. Instead, its leaves serve as a healing balm for the nations. The tree symbolizes unfettered access to life in this realm.

The detail that the healing is for the "nations" is noteworthy. God's realm and reign is about community deliverance. To be sure, the beleaguered community, which is undergoing persecution in the days of Revelation, dominates this book's concern for God's deliverance. But that deliverance does not stop there. While verse 15 later invokes exclusionary language, to be expected in a community tormented by persecutors, here the term "nations" insists that God's realm and reign is not parochial but wide-embracing.

"Coming Soon"

The theme of Christ's return, sometimes called the *Parousia*, runs strong here in Revelation. "I am coming soon" occurs no less than three times in Revelation 22. Other New Testament materials likewise speak of this hope expressed in imminent terms. Paul sought to comfort the community at Thessalonica who grieved for members who had died prior to that return by saying "we who are alive, who are left until the coming of the Lord, will by no means precede those who have died" (1 Thessalonians 4:15).

To be sure, throughout history the expectation of Christ's imminent return has fueled a host of individuals and communities to predict or presume upon Christ's return in their lifetime. There are probably more bumper stickers per-capita based on the very limited number of verses that speak of rapture than any other biblical text, except John 3:16. *Left Behind* enthusiasts embrace novel upon novel with this same appeal to Christ's coming.

So what positive purpose does it serve to know that Christ is coming soon? For the community of Revelation, it likely offered a word of hope. Suffering would not be unending. Release would come. For communities today, it may speak similarly. But perhaps its strongest message is in terms not just of personal faith and readiness but issues of justice and compassion. Christ's return is a tenet that reminds powers that be, old and new, that the world is not theirs to do with as they please without consequences. There will be an accounting. More broadly, consider Jesus' teaching about the sheep and goats in Matthew 25:31-46. Christ's reign, the result of said return, in that parable focuses its gaze upon what has been done to the least among us. For in such individuals, the parable teaches, Christ is already among us. How have we treated the Christ there, beyond whatever lip service we give to this or that theory of rapture or pre- versus postmillenialism? Christ's return will not be concerned with such tangential matters. Christ's coming, and coming soon (and for all of us, the end of our life brings that coming at hand), seeks to know how we have trusted and lived the Christ-like life.

Worship: To Whom It Is and Is Not Due

It might seem simply an act of respect that the author of Revelation, in respect to the angel who has opened all of these sights and sounds to him, "fell down to worship at the feet of the angel." But while respect may be owed, worship is not. Worship (a word that has built into it, in English, the idea of worthiness) belongs only to One. "Worship God," the angel says (Revelation 22:9).

More is at stake here than the gesture of the author. The whole of Revelation, in one sense, is all about the declaration that One and One alone is to be worshiped. Part of the context for that is the crisis faced by the church and its members when confronted with the demands to worship the emperor. Rome cared little who else was worshiped, so long as veneration of the emperor was included. Revelation, however, stands firm in the worthiness of One alone—and that One's name does not include Caesar.

That stand made by Revelation, in hopes of the standing of the church in the face of Rome's demands, was not an invention of Revelation's author. In the temptation narrative of Jesus in the wilderness, the Accuser offers all the kingdoms of the world in exchange for a single act of worship. Jesus' response? "Worship the Lord your God, and serve only him" (Luke 4:8). And even the words Jesus evokes are not original to him. They derive from Israel's ancient narrative of life in the wilderness reflected in Deuteronomy 6:13 and elsewhere. God alone merits worship. All others—whether their appeal be based on fear and threat as with Rome, or as in the case of Revelation's author, on gratitude to one who has favored him—fall short.

When worship is seen not only in its liturgical expression but also as any extension of ultimate commitment or obedience, the message of Revelation becomes even more challenging and ever more pertinent. No one merits, for any reason, our ultimate commitment or loyalty, our worship, except God. Worship belongs to God alone, for God alone is Alpha and Omega, our source and destiny. Thanks be to God!

SHARING THE SCRIPTURE

Preparing Our Hearts

Explore this week's devotional reading, found in Ephesians 3:14-21. We hear Paul's prayer for the people, which some scholars believe was part of a baptismal liturgy of the early church. Notice the four petitions that Paul lifts up to God. What petitions are on your heart today? Do you need to be strengthened, or have Christ dwell more fully in your heart, or more fully comprehend God's work, or know Christ's love? Whatever your prayer this day, conclude it by adding the doxology from verses 20-21.

Pray that you and the adult learners will give thanks for the opportunity to worship God and lift prayers to the throne of grace.

Preparing Our Minds

Study the background Scripture from Revelation 22 and the lesson Scripture from Revelation 22:1-9. Think about how you receive the bounty that fills your life.

Write on newsprint:

❑ information for next week's lesson, found under "Continue the Journey."
❑ activities for further spiritual growth in "Continue the Journey."

Set up a worship table that includes whatever elements you prefer, such as a cross, Bible, and candle. Be sure to include a pitcher or basin of water to represent the river of life and several leaves or a small branch to represent the tree of life.

Locate pictures of nature. Large expanses, such as seen in Ansel Adams' photographs, will be especially helpful

LEADING THE CLASS

(1) Gather to Learn

❖ Welcome the class members and introduce any guests.

❖ Pray that those who have gathered for today's session will be aware of the abundance that God has poured out upon them.

❖ Distribute hymnals and read together the verses of "Mountains Are All Aglow." Invite the adults to talk about the bounty of God they perceive in this hymn. Look especially at the images of the natural world.

❖ Read aloud today's focus statement: **Our lives are filled with abundance. What is our attitude toward receiving the bounty provided for us? The Revelation to John made it clear that there is no more appropriate response to what God has done than to worship God.**

(2) Review All the Images of Nature in This Text

❖ Select a volunteer to read Revelation 22:1-9.

❖ List on newsprint the images of nature that the students find in this passage (river, tree of life, fruit, leaves, night, light).

❖ Discuss with the class what Revelation 22 reveals about each of these images. Use information from "A River Runs Through It" and "Tree of Life, Leaves for Healing," both found in Interpreting the Scripture, to add insight to the discussion.

❖ Draw attention to the worship table you have set up. Be sure the class understands the significance of the basin of water (river of life) and small branch or leaves (tree of life). Ask: **As you view these symbols, what observations can you make about God's abundant gifts to us in nature?**

❖ **Option:** Share pictures you have brought of nature. If you have some showing a panoramic view of a natural scene (perhaps the Grand Canyon or a swath of a national park), invite the students to comment on the kinds of emotions these pictures evoke.

(3) Appreciate Worship as an Appropriate Response to Receiving God's Abundance

❖ Note that worship is an appropriate response to the grandeur of God's world. Invite the adults to tell stories of times they were awed by nature and worshiped God there, either formally with a group or informally as they offered praise and thanks for this abundant creation.

❖ Point out that God's abundance is available to us no matter where we live, even in the midst of a busy city. All of us have been blessed by God in some way. Distribute paper and pencils. Encourage the adults to list blessings they have experienced in the last week or so.

❖ End this portion of the session by reading the following prayer and inviting the adults to fill in the pause by going around the room so that each person may add a blessing. If the class is large, encourage everyone to state one of their blessings

together as you pause. **Gracious God, our Creator, Redeemer, and Sustainer, we praise you and give you thanks for the blessings of (pause). May we be ever mindful of these abundant gifts and grateful for the love you have poured out upon us. In Jesus' name we pray. Amen.**

(4) Investigate the Implications for Our World to Have Access to a "Tree of Life" as Described in Revelation

❖ Lead the class in reading today's key verse, Revelation 22:2.

❖ Read "Tree of Life, Leaves for Healing" from Interpreting the Scripture if you have not done so already.

❖ Focus on the phrase: "the healing of the nations" and brainstorm with the class answers to this question, which you will write on newsprint: **What needs to be healed around the world today?** Answers are probably limitless, but here are some examples: *hatred, wars, poverty, exploitation of people, racial and ethnic tensions, inadequate medical care, degradation of the environment, lack of access to basic necessities of life.*

❖ Form groups of three or four students. Give each group a marker and a sheet of newsprint. Challenge the groups to create a vision of the world where the "tree of life" is actually "healing the nations." Some groups may choose to write their vision in words, whereas others may prefer to sketch a scene.

❖ Provide time for the groups to share what they have written or drawn.

❖ Talk with the class about what they can do, either as individuals or as a group, to address one of the issues they have raised that needs healing. Challenge them to go forth and take action. Remind them that each person has something to contribute and that small steps taken by many people can have a major impact.

(5) Continue the Journey

❖ Pray that the learners will continue to appreciate and give thanks for the abundance that God has showered upon them.

❖ Read aloud this preparation for next week's lesson. You may also want to post it on newsprint for the students to copy.

- ■ **Title: God's Promises Fulfilled**
- ■ **Background Scripture: Joshua 1:1-6; 11–12**
- ■ **Lesson Scripture: Joshua 1:1-6; 11:16-19, 21-23**
- ■ **Focus of the Lesson: People make promises in good faith, but they do not always fulfill them. Why is it so difficult to keep a promise? God makes promises that may seem to be unfilled, but in time, we can be confident that God stands behind the promises.**

❖ Challenge the students to complete one or more of these activities for further spiritual growth related to this week's session. Post this information on newsprint for the students to copy.

(1) **Keep a journal of your blessings. Record at least three blessings each day in your book. Give** thanks for what God is doing in your life.

(2) **Paint or draw your conception of Revelation 22:1-5. You will need to reread and ponder these verses in order to discern how this scene could look.**

(3) **Find a quiet space in a natural setting. Worship God there alone or with a friend. How does worship in such a setting feel different from worship in a sacred building?**

❖ Sing or read aloud "Shall We Gather at the River," based on Revelation 22:1-5.

❖ Conclude today's session by leading the class in this benediction from Jude 24-25, which is the key verse for the lesson on April 10: **Now to him who is able to keep you from falling, and to make you stand without blemish in the presence of his glory with rejoicing, to the only God our Savior, through Jesus Christ our Lord, be glory, majesty, power, and authority, before all time and now and forever. Amen.**

FOURTH QUARTER
God Instructs the People of God

JUNE 5, 2011–AUGUST 28, 2011

We will explore Joshua, Judges, and Ruth to discern what it means to live out God's love within a community. These three books are all part of the Deuteronomistic historian's record of God's dealings with the Israelite people as they settled into the Promised Land and became enmeshed in a cycle of disobedience, oppression, repentance, deliverance through a judge (leader) sent by God, and renewed faithfulness to God. The story of Ruth provides us with a concrete example of how people live lovingly in community.

Unit 1, "God's People Learn From Prosperity," focuses on texts from Joshua that highlight both God's blessings in response to the people's obedience and God's anger in response to their disobedience. The lesson from Joshua 1:1-6; 11–12 for June 5, demonstrates "God's Promises Fulfilled" through a faithful leader, Joshua, who obeys the Lord's commands. Joshua 1:7-16 is the basis for the session on June 12, "God Has Expectations," which considers the rules by which the Israelites are to live. We turn to Joshua 2 on June 19 to see how "God Protects" not only the Israelite spies but also Rahab. On June 26 we experience the thrill of victory with Joshua and the Israelites, as recorded in Joshua 5:13–6:27, where "God Is Victorious" over Jericho. The tables turn on the Israelites when Achan disobeys and "God Reacts to Disobedience," as recorded in Joshua 7:1–8:29, which we will study on July 3.

In Unit 2, "Listening for God in Changing Times," we witness the Israelites' repeated cycle of obeying, then turning away from God that leads to an enemy attack, God's raising up of a leader to deliver the people, and their return to obedience. Judges 21:25 is part of the background Scripture each week. The lesson for July 10 from Judges 2 reminds us that in the midst of their apostasy the Israelites were urged to "Listen to God's Judges." On July 17 we see the people get help from an unexpected source, Ehud, whom Judges 3:7-31 reports God raised up as a judge so that the people could "Use God's Strength." Judges 6–8 is the basis for "Let God Rule," the session for July 24 that focuses on Gideon. God compassionately calls the people to "Return to Obedience" in Judges 10:6–11:33, the background Scripture for July 31. To learn how to raise their unborn son, Samson's parents are challenged to "Walk in God's Path," according to Judges 13 in the session for August 7.

All three sessions from the Book of Ruth in Unit 3, "A Case Study in Community," help us to understand how Ruth's choice to be faithful to Naomi affected an entire community. On August 14, Ruth 1:1-18 reveals the importance of wisely "Choosing a Community." Ruth 2–3 and Leviticus 19:9-10 form the backdrop of "Empowering the Needy," where on August 21 we see Boaz's kindness to Ruth. This unit ends on August 28 with Ruth 4, in which by "Respecting Community Standards" Boaz accepts his familial responsibility.

MEET OUR WRITER

THE REVEREND DR. MICHAEL FINK

Michael Fink retired in 2003 and moved to the quaint east Tennessee town of Dandridge, named after Martha Dandridge Washington and designated as the second oldest town in Tennessee. Born 60 years earlier in Sylacauga, Alabama (also the birth place of "Gomer Pyle," Jim Nabors), Mike was reared in Homewood, Alabama, a Birmingham suburb.

While an honor-roll student at Georgia Tech, he felt called to vocational Christian ministry. He transferred to Samford University, a Baptist university in Alabama, where he graduated with a double major in math and English. The next decade was spent in Louisville, Kentucky, and southern Indiana, where he garnered three graduate seminary degrees, a wife, and three daughters while also serving on the staff of a church in Louisville and as pastor for five-and-a-half years at First Baptist Church, Crothersville, Indiana.

After teaching three years in the Department of Religion at Campbell University in North Carolina, Mike and his family settled for the next quarter century in Nashville, Tennessee, where Mike served in various editorial, management, and staff capacities with a major Christian publisher. During those years he led Christian education conferences, consulted on Christian publishing, and ministered in 23 states in the United States as well as in ten foreign countries. He also co-authored one book, contributed to five others, and published Bible studies, sermons, poetry, and articles in numerous publications.

Since retiring, Mike has taught as an adjunct professor at Carson-Newman College in Jefferson City, Tennessee, has worked part-time at a hardware store, has done contract work on the Uniform Lesson Series with the National Council of Churches, and has written Bible study lessons now for the third time in *The New International Lesson Annual*.

Mike's wife, Evelyn, is a preschool specialist who loves gardening, music, and shepherding their family of three daughters, two sons-in-law, and four grandchildren. Their oldest daughter does part-time accounting work for the Minnie Pearl Cancer Foundation; their middle child is an administrative specialist with Dell Computer; and their youngest daughter is a pilot with Southwest Airlines.

Together Mike and Evelyn enjoy entertaining friends and boating in their kayak and pontoon boat on Douglas Lake. They like to travel and almost always have a book on CD playing as they drive. Since retiring, they have done extensive remodeling and upgrading of their home; and Mike also has found time to take up golf again. Mike and Evelyn are active members of First Baptist Church in Jefferson City, Tennessee.

THE BIG PICTURE:
WHEN GOD REIGNS AS KING

Leadership is an area of intense interest in our world. Every area of life—from government to business, from education to the church—seems interested in finding, employing, and developing great leaders. You probably are familiar with the insight attributed to football coach Vince Lombardi, "Leaders are made, they are not born. They are made by hard effort, which is the price which all of us must pay to achieve any goal that is worthwhile."

That observation is rather characteristic of a democratic, Western worldview. Earlier generations and cultures, however, viewed leadership either in terms of hereditary entitlement or brute power. The doctrine of the divine right of kings claimed that God had sanctioned the hereditary office. Even when subsequent heirs of the throne were weak and ineffective, the system prevailed until conditions became so bad that another power arose and seized authority. Even those who seized power by anarchy and violence often established a family dynasty.

While all the nations around them were ruled by kings, Israel sought a true theocracy—a rule by God. Even a theocracy, however, required human leadership. Israel's leadership up until the time of the Exodus had been patriarchal and familial. With the Exodus, Moses arose as Israel's first leader. After guiding the nation in its escape from Egyptian bondage, delivering God's law to the people, and shepherding them through 40 years of wilderness wanderings, Moses handed off the leadership to Joshua. Joshua then led the nation in its conquest of Canaan and oversaw the division of the territory among the Israelite tribes. Until the anointing of Saul as Israel's first king several centuries later, Israel existed as a tribal confederation in Canaan with no central government or worship center. Military leaders called "judges" rallied them in times of crisis; but the tribes' primary bond was their faith in God, who was the titular head of the people. In essence, God was their king.

God as Israel's King

The first reference to kings in the Bible comes in Genesis 14:1. The kings listed were local leaders of city-states. These city-states soon began to join forces (14:3) to expand their control and to protect themselves against outside threats. The fact that Abraham and a contingent of 318 men could defeat invaders from the east (14:13-16) shows that these early kingdoms were not extremely powerful.

The first biblical example of a true national power emerges in the account of Joseph's arrival in Egypt. Pharaoh (the king of Egypt) is first referenced in Genesis 12:15 in relation to Sarai and Abram, but he plays a prominent role in Joseph's story, Genesis 39–50. Egypt was the first civilization to bind together widely separated areas into a nation under a central government. The Egyptians also gave divine status to their Pharaohs. The word of the king was law; and all land, properties, and people were under his absolute control.

Much of Israel's subsequent history was affected by the influence of Egypt directly and by Israel's location as a buffer between Egypt and powerful states like Assyria and Babylon that later would arise to Israel's north and east. While the notion that the king is a god is far different from the idea that God is the king, Israel may have been influenced in its understanding as it moved from a family with the patriarch as its leader to a confederation of tribes joined in divine covenant. Later they became a kingdom with a king chosen and anointed with God's blessing. In the stages between patriarch and king, the thing that bound people, tribes, and land together was God. God, who certainly was greater than any Pharaoh, ruled with absolute authority through the law and through appointed leaders.

The view that God was king of Israel is not addressed extensively in the Pentateuch. In those first five biblical books, we find only occasional glimpses as in Numbers 23:21: "The LORD their God is with them, acclaimed as a king among them." This passage indicates that the peoples around the Israelites recognized the unique role that God played in the governance and guidance of Israel. The few references in Israel's early traditions to God as king reflect the lack of a constructive model for kingship. The only concept the people had of a king came from the roles kings played in other societies. Attributing to God a title that in their experience reflected the characteristics of a Pharaoh or the warring and marauding leaders around them would not have been appealing. Later, when Israel had a king of its own, the attribution of kingship to God poured forth abundantly (Psalms 24; 47; 95; 145).

Samuel certainly represented an old conservative tradition when he opposed the appointment of a king. Even in God's instruction to Samuel to cede to the people's wishes and appoint a king, God said, "They have not rejected you [Samuel], but they have rejected me from being king over them" (1 Samuel 8:7). Samuel's strong opposition was based on his understanding that God alone was Israel's king. Even after Samuel explained all of the downsides of having a human king, the Israelites made their rejection absolute, "No! but we are determined to have a king over us, so that we also may be like other nations, and that our king may govern us and go out before us and fight our battles" (8:19-20). Interestingly, those who had known and experienced the Exodus might readily have noted, "Going before us and fighting our battles is exactly what God has done for us."

Ad Hoc Leadership

Leadership researchers Warren G. Bennis and Robert J. Thomas co-authored a book subtitled, *How Era, Values, and Defining Moments Shape Leaders*. In addition to listing numerous characteristics shared by leaders, they found that most significant leaders have had one intense, transformational experience in life.

The leaders of Israel between the patriarchs and Saul's anointing as king might generally be characterized as leaders shaped by such defining moments. Though their experiences vary widely, each had at least one intense, transformational experience that advanced them into the role as leader of Israel (Moses had the burning bush; others had angelic messengers or infillings of God's spirit). I have chosen to classify them as "ad hoc leaders" because they mostly were chosen by God for a specific task or cause. While some served for long periods of time (Moses over 40 years, and most until their deaths), their recorded tasks generally were focused on a particular threat or specific task. Only a few had influence beyond a tribe or two. When they passed from the scene, rarely was a specific successor chosen.

In our studies this quarter, Joshua will play the central role in the first unit. While he was the successor to Moses, he was chosen for his military skills in gathering intelligence and leading forces into battle. Joshua's task was to lead God's people in claiming the promises that God had made to Moses.

The second unit focuses on five of the leaders called "judges." These were leaders raised up by God to call the people back to faithfulness. This diverse group addressed situations in which foreign powers were allowed by God to chasten the people for their disobedience. The Book of Judges repeats a cycle of the Israelites being drawn away from God by practices of

354

other religions, suffering for their unfaithfulness when God withdraws protection, and calling out to God for deliverance. The judges became the rallying force that united the people, led them in victory over their oppressors, and called the people back to faithfulness and obedience.

Someone With a Face

You probably have heard the story about the little girl who, frightened by the darkness in the middle of the night, cried out for her mother. Her mother came to comfort her and reminded her that she did not need to be afraid, that God was with her. Thinking about that for a moment, the little girl replied, "But I want someone with a face."

The history of Israel shows that God's people also wanted someone with a face. Struggling with the shadowy concept of an "immortal, invisible, God only wise," they longed for concreteness to replace abstractions. They could follow a human leader like Moses; but when he disappeared for a while to commune with God, they lusted for an ever-present reality. They found it in a golden calf. In the Promised Land after the deaths of Moses and Joshua, God did not seem nearly as real and present as when they had been led by a pillar of cloud by day and a pillar of fire by night. Their neighbors had Baals, sacred poles called Asherah, and sanctuaries on high places for offering sacrifices. Israelites turned to these tangible embodiments of faith.

When God raised up judges to lead them in returning to faithfulness, they had a tangible leader for a while; but soon the judge was gone, and they had no face for God. They wanted something more permanent, and so they demanded a king. Of course, the kings also disappointed them and soon fell to foreign powers. Something more was still needed, and eventually God did provide a face, a Son, an incarnation, that summed up all of what God had been throughout the centuries. But now that face too has grown dim; modern-day people of God still seek substitutes in human leaders, edifices, ministries, and budgets. As we study these ancient believers, let us not look down on them too much lest we overlook our own attempts to find tangible substitutes that provide a face for God.

The Kingdom of God

While our studies this quarter focus on books in the Old Testament, we, as Christians, need to set these studies in the context of the full redemption story. When viewed in the scope of all the Scriptures, we should not be surprised to discover continuity between the Old and New Testaments and the extension of Old Testament themes into the New. Indeed, much of the New Testament testifies to the fulfillment of the themes and dreams that span the ages from the Garden of Eden to the New Jerusalem.

God as king is one of the clearest examples of this continuity. Most students of the New Testament recognize that "the kingdom of God" was the central theme of Jesus' message. The kingdom of God, however, was not a realm in Jesus' teaching. It was not a place, a country, or a location where God was king. Instead, the kingdom was declared by Jesus as the reign of God, the act of God ruling and reigning as sovereign in the hearts and lives of people. God's kingdom has no boundaries except between those who give God their allegiances and those who don't. Jesus declared that the kingdom of God was near, at hand, always accessible regardless of time, place, or circumstance.

Quite frankly, our problem is not with finding continuity between the Old Testament and New Testament on the theme of God as king. Our problem is finding continuity between biblical times and our own. We in Western democracies know little about kings and kingdoms as the idea was understood in Jesus' time. Since the Magna Carta, the concept of kingship has been democratized and civilized so that it bears little resemblance to the time of Jesus. Royalty in England (America's most ready example) and in other European countries is a pale example of the biblical concept. The closest example for us today is Saudi Arabia, but even there the king has been shaped by the constant observation of a world holding democratic principles. Maybe the Japanese emperor in pre–World War II—viewed as divine and all-powerful—would be a better example of how a king would have been viewed in biblical times.

Ancient kings could be benevolent, but many were not; and not much could be done if they weren't. They might have trusted advisors who assisted them, but it was "off with their heads" if these advisors provoked the king in any way. They held absolute power and authority, and they had the final word. They demanded reverence but would settle for fear. They demanded obedience but ensured compliance. Submission and humility were traits they valued most. To be their subject was to yield to the actions, power, control, and caprice of the king. Their word was law and was the primary governing authority. Absolute and unquestioned obedience was the primary expectation for citizens. Punishment, often of a severe nature, was the primary discipline. You became subject to the king by being born in his kingdom or by living in territory that he captured. Because power and might meant most in exercising authority, the king was viewed as a savior in victory but was worthless in defeat. The defeated generally lost both their territories and their lives at the hand of the victor.

With this kind of background, you might find it surprising that Jesus chose the kingdom of God as his central theme. Some recognizing this background have focused on the sovereignty of God as the central theme in the church's message, and much in Calvinism centers on a God who rules somewhat like an ancient king. Themes like total depravity, unconditional election, limited atonement, irresistible grace, and perseverance of the saints reflect the concepts of absolute authority and power that befit an ancient king. You will see some of this focus in the first two units this quarter. Joshua is a focus on obedience; and Judges is centered in the power to subdue, control, and extinguish all who oppose the Sovereign.

Ruth will provide somewhat of a departure from this focus. King David certainly is in the anticipatory background of the book, but Ruth was not a subject of God by birth, by coercion or, it appears, even by marriage. Naomi was ready to send Ruth back to her people and her god. Ruth, however, had a different plan; and in that plan we begin to see something of the "twist" that Jesus gave to the "God is king" theme.

Jesus taught that citizens of the kingdom become such by willing submission. They come to the kingdom by an invitation to follow One who shows that love casts out fear. Their sovereign king also is Abba, Father. Citizenship involves all God's subjects being adopted as children of the king—becoming princes and princesses, if you will. And the subjects are not chosen because of their sex, race, national origin, wealth, or any other criteria. They come like Ruth—a poor Moabite woman who has lost her husband, has no children, and has nothing to offer but the efforts of a laborer in the fields. But she came in faith to make the God of Naomi her God. She chose a new citizenship in a new land that brought her new opportunities in spite of great obstacles. And the God whom she chose somehow in the miracle of infinite love not only brought her into the family of faith but also sowed within her a seed of a line of descendants that would in the distant future bring forth a new King of kings, Lord of lords, and Prince of Peace.

CLOSE-UP: ISRAEL IN CANAAN

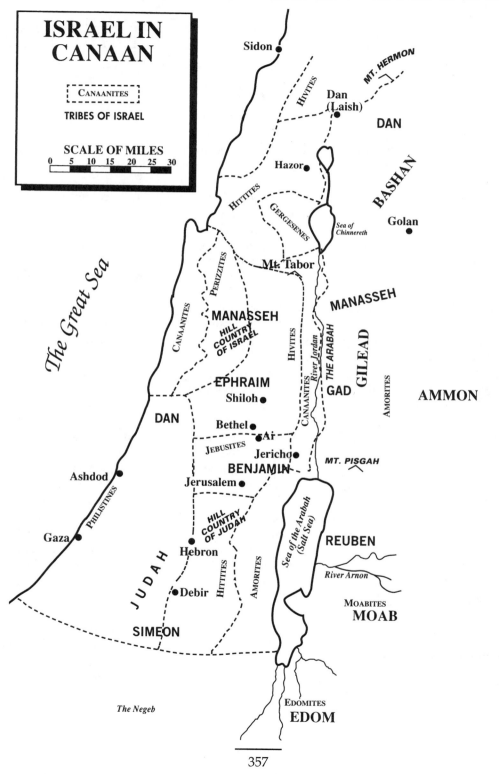

ISRAEL IN CANAAN

⌐ ¬ CANAANITES
└ ┘

TRIBES OF ISRAEL

SCALE OF MILES

0   5   10 15 20 25 30

Sidon

Dan
(Laish)

HIVITES

MT. HERMON

DAN

BASHAN

Hazor

Golan

HITTITES

GERGESENES

Sea of
Chinnereth

Mt. Tabor

The Great Sea

PERIZZITES

MANASSEH

MANASSEH

CANAANITES

HILL
COUNTRY
OF ISRAEL

HIVITES

River Jordan

THE ARABAH

GILEAD

AMORITES

AMMON

EPHRAIM

GAD

Shiloh

DAN

CANAANITES

Bethel

Ai

JEBUSITES

Jericho

BENJAMIN

MT. PISGAH

Ashdod

Jerusalem

PHILISTINES

HILL
COUNTRY
OF JUDAH

Sea of the
Arabah
(Salt Sea)

REUBEN

Gaza

J U D A H

Hebron

HITTITES

AMORITES

River Arnon

MOABITES

Debir

MOAB

SIMEON

The Negeb

EDOMITES

EDOM

357

Faith in Action:
Learning About God in the
Community of Faith

The focus of this quarter's sessions is on how God instructs the community of faith—and how the community responds. Although the Sunday school movement did not get underway until late in the eighteenth century, education has always been an important facet of the church's ministry. According to Acts 2:42, the first Christians "devoted themselves to the apostles' teaching."

What opportunities has your congregation provided for people to learn more about God? And what are the purposes of these activities? Knowing about God—having information—is one thing. Knowing God through a personal relationship with Jesus is quite another. Educational opportunities need to provide information, but their goal is transformation so that the students may become conformed to the image of Jesus.

All people need to have opportunities to know God through Christ better. Some of these opportunities will be informal—we observe other Christians in action and learn from them. Others will be structured, such as classes, workshops, and seminars.

Brainstorm with the class answers to these questions and write them on newsprint: **In addition to our class, what opportunities are available to the adults of our church to learn about God?**

Look at the list you have generated. It will probably include the names of specific on-going classes, perhaps some short-term studies, possibly a workshop offered by a guest leader, or even a field trip that was arranged with an educational purpose in mind. Your district, conference, or other judicatory may offer classes that include members from many churches. Maybe an ecumenical Bible study is held in your community. Add to this list by asking: **What else could our church be doing to help others learn about God?**

Brainstorm answers to another question on a separate sheet of newsprint: **What opportunities are available to us through the church to live out what we learn?** Whereas in the first list you were looking at opportunities to learn, this question prompts you to look at ways you can minister and serve as a faithful disciple. This list will include ideas such as: visiting the sick and homebound; supporting a missionary; providing food and shelter for those in need; welcoming strangers, perhaps as an usher or greeter; or collecting school supplies for children unable to afford them. Add to this list by asking: **What else do we have the time, talent, treasure, and vision to do as a congregation to show our love for one another and for those outside our walls?**

Conclude this activity by distributing paper and pencils. Ask the participants to tear the paper in half lengthwise. On one half they are to write ideas for topics they would like to study in order to draw closer to God. Collect these papers and tabulate responses after class. Pass this information on to the pastor. On the other half, the class members are to write actions they are willing to take as a result of their learning to demonstrate God's love. Challenge the adults to refer often to this list in order to begin (or continue) to take action.

God wants us To Jesus in every book of Bible (handwritten)

UNIT 1: GOD'S PEOPLE LEARN FROM PROSPERITY
GOD'S PROMISES FULFILLED

PREVIEWING THE LESSON

Lesson Scripture: Joshua 1:1-6; 11:16-19, 21-23
Background Scripture: Joshua 1:1-6; 11–12
Key Verse: Joshua 11:15

Focus of the Lesson:
People make promises in good faith, but they do not always fulfill them. Why is it so difficult to keep a promise? God makes promises that may seem to be unfilled; but in time, we can be confident that God stands behind the promises.

Goals for the Learners:
(1) to explore how the conquering of land is a fulfillment of God's promises.
(2) to assess their feelings and attitudes about keeping promises.
(3) to identify and act on ways they can participate on God's behalf in the world today.

Pronunciation Guide:
Achan (ay' kan)
Anab (ay' nab)
Anakim (an' uh kim)
Anakite (an' uh kite)
Hivite (hiv' ite)
Arabah (air' uh buh)
Ashdod (ash' dod)
Baal-gad (bay uhl gad' or bah uhl gad')
Debir (dee' buhr)
Gath (gath)
Gibeon (gib' ee uhn)
Goshen (goh' shuhn)

Halak (hay' lak)
Hazor (hay' zor)
Hermon (huhr' muhn)
Hittite (hit' tite)
Jabin (jay' bin)
Merom (mee' rom)
Moab (moh' ab)
Negeb (neg' eb)
Negev (neg' ev)
Pisgah (piz' guh)
Seir (see' uhr)
Sihon (si' hon)

Supplies:
Bibles, newsprint and marker, paper and pencils, hymnals, map of Canaan at the time of Joshua

---

READING THE SCRIPTURE

NRSV
Joshua 1:1-6
[1b]The LORD spoke to Joshua son of Nun, Moses' assistant, saying, [2]"My servant Moses

NIV
Joshua 1:1-6
[1b]The LORD said to Joshua son of Nun, Moses' aide: [2]"Moses my servant is dead.

is dead. Now proceed to cross the Jordan, you and all this people, into the land that I am giving to them, to the Israelites. ³Every place that the sole of your foot will tread upon I have given to you, as I promised to Moses. ⁴From the wilderness and the Lebanon as far as the great river, the river Euphrates, all the land of the Hittites, to the Great Sea in the west shall be your territory. ⁵No one shall be able to stand against you all the days of your life. As I was with Moses, so I will be with you; I will not fail you or forsake you. ⁶Be strong and courageous; for you shall put this people in possession of the land that I swore to their ancestors to give them.

Now then, you and all these people, get ready to cross the Jordan River into the land I am about to give to them—to the Israelites. ³I will give you every place where you set your foot, as I promised Moses. ⁴Your territory will extend from the desert to Lebanon, and from the great river, the Euphrates—all the Hittite country—to the Great Sea on the west. ⁵No one will be able to stand up against you all the days of your life. As I was with Moses, so I will be with you; I will never leave you nor forsake you.

⁶"Be strong and courageous, because you will lead these people to inherit the land I swore to their forefathers to give them.

Joshua 11:15-19, 21-23

¹⁵As the LORD had commanded his servant Moses, so Moses commanded Joshua, and so Joshua did; he left nothing undone of all that the LORD had commanded Moses.

¹⁶So Joshua took all that land: the hill country and all the Negeb and all the land of Goshen and the lowland and the Arabah and the hill country of Israel and its lowland, ¹⁷from Mount Halak, which rises toward Seir, as far as Baal-gad in the valley of Lebanon below Mount Hermon. He took all their kings, struck them down, and put them to death. ¹⁸Joshua made war a long time with all those kings. ¹⁹There was not a town that made peace with the Israelites, except the Hivites, the inhabitants of Gibeon; all were taken in battle. . . .

²¹At that time Joshua came and wiped out the Anakim from the hill country, from Hebron, from Debir, from Anab, and from all the hill country of Judah, and from all the hill country of Israel; Joshua utterly destroyed them with their towns. ²²None of the Anakim was left in the land of the Israelites; some remained only in Gaza, in Gath, and in Ashdod. ²³So Joshua took the whole land, according to all that the LORD had spoken to Moses; and Joshua gave it for an inheritance to Israel according to their tribal allotments. And the land had rest from war.

Joshua 11:15-19, 21-23

¹⁵As the LORD commanded his servant Moses, so Moses commanded Joshua, and Joshua did it; he left nothing undone of all that the LORD commanded Moses.

¹⁶So Joshua took this entire land: the hill country, all the Negev, the whole region of Goshen, the western foothills, the Arabah and the mountains of Israel with their foothills, ¹⁷from Mount Halak, which rises toward Seir, to Baal Gad in the Valley of Lebanon below Mount Hermon. He captured all their kings and struck them down, putting them to death. ¹⁸Joshua waged war against all these kings for a long time. ¹⁹Except for the Hivites living in Gibeon, not one city made a treaty of peace with the Israelites, who took them all in battle. . . .

²¹At that time Joshua went and destroyed the Anakites from the hill country: from Hebron, Debir and Anab, from all the hill country of Judah, and from all the hill country of Israel. Joshua totally destroyed them and their towns. ²²No Anakites were left in Israelite territory; only in Gaza, Gath and Ashdod did any survive. ²³So Joshua took the entire land, just as the LORD had directed Moses, and he gave it as an inheritance to Israel according to their tribal divisions.

Then the land had rest from war.

UNDERSTANDING THE SCRIPTURE

Joshua 1:1-6. "My servant Moses is dead" marks the break from the five books of law called the Pentateuch into the historical books of the Old Testament known as the Former Prophets. The simple, dramatic statement bears great weight. Moses, the man with whom God spoke "face to face— clearly, not in riddles" and who beheld "the form of the LORD" (Numbers 12:8) was dead. His death had to be announced because Moses had gone alone to the top of Mount Pisgah in Moab—where he died in view of, but short of, the Promised Land— and was buried in an unknown place (Deuteronomy 34:1-6). The foundational period that began with creation and spanned the centuries from the flood, to the call of Abraham, to the migration to Egypt in the days of Joseph, to long years of bondage in Egypt, to God's deliverance of the people from slavery and establishing a covenant with them, and then through forty years of wilderness wanderings finally had drawn to a close. A new day had dawned.

The mantle of leadership had passed to Moses' appointed successor, Joshua. Joshua, whose very name in Hebrew reminded the people that "God is salvation," had been a military leader (Exodus 17:8-16) who became Moses' "assistant" or "aide" (NIV). He was one of the two spies sent to survey Canaan who reported optimistically (Numbers 13:8; 14:6-8). God chose Joshua to be Moses' successor (Numbers 27:15-20).

Joshua was commissioned to lead the people across the Jordan River and to claim the land that God had promised to Moses. That land is described in rather imprecise terms. "Wilderness" (Joshua 1:4) can describe both the Negeb in the south and the Syrian Desert to the east. The "Great Sea" (Mediterranean) on the west and the river Euphrates on the northeast are more precise, but the boundaries of "the land of the Hittites" is uncertain and could reach as far north as Turkey.

Portions of modern Egypt, the Palestinian Territory, Lebanon, Syria, Israel, Jordan, and perhaps western Iraq might be included. Note, however, the limitations imposed by "every place that the sole of your foot will tread upon" (1:3) and "all the days of your life" (1:5). God promised success as long as Joshua was "strong and courageous" and acted in accordance with the law (1:6-7).

[handwritten margin note: will God's promise are conditional "If we do... He will do."]

Joshua 11:1-15. Joshua 2–3 describe a small spying expedition into Jericho and other preparations for crossing the Jordan (completed in chapter 3). A stone monument was set up to commemorate for future generations the crossing of the Jordan (chapter 4). In preparation for the conquest, the institution of the covenant symbol, circumcision, was revived (chapter 5). Its practice had lapsed during the 40 years in the wilderness.

Then, beginning with Jericho, the Israelites conducted a campaign in central Canaan (chapters 6–8). This was followed by successful campaigns in the south (chapter 10) before heading north (chapter 11).

Having "defeated the whole land, the hill country and the Negeb and the lowland and the slopes, and all their kings" (10:40), Joshua was recognized as a true threat by King Jabin of Hazor. Hazor, an important fortified city on the trade route that ran from Egypt toward the north and east, was located about ten miles north of the Sea of Galilee. It was the royal city of King Jabin and "the head of all those kingdoms" (11:10) in the north. Building a coalition with other Canaanite kings, Jabin gathered a formidable army "in number like the sand of the seashore, with very many horses and chariots" (11:4). They gathered at the waters of Merom to prepare for battle against the invading Israelites.

Encouraged by God in the face of this powerful foe, Joshua led a surprise attack on the coalition army and utterly defeated it. He then struck and destroyed each of the kingdoms that had joined the coalition until "there was no one left who breathed" (11:11). The recurring theme throughout the conquest period is summarized in 11:15: "As the LORD had commanded his servant Moses, so Moses commanded Joshua, and so Joshua did: he left nothing undone of all that the LORD had commanded Moses." By his own faithfulness, Joshua saw God's promises fulfilled.

Joshua 11:16–12:24. Joshua's feats were impressive. Although Joshua 11:18 notes that "Joshua made war a long time," a timetable is not given for his accomplishments. Joshua 11:16-23 describes the areas captured and gives geographical details about the extent of the territory taken by the Israelites and allotted to the tribes. Joshua 12 gives a detailed summary of the kings that the Israelites defeated on both sides of the Jordan—first under Moses' leadership in defeating the two major kings east of the Jordan, Sihon and Og, and then the 31 kings of city-states defeated by Joshua west of the Jordan. Embedded in the account, however, are hints that Israel's obedience was not quite as complete as the summary implies. Chapter 7 recounts the disregard shown by Achan toward the ban against taking possession of booty from the Canaanites that was supposed to be dedicated to the Lord. Chapter 9 records the deception through which the Gibeonites

made a treaty with Israel and gained protection from the command in Deuteronomy 20:16-18 to annihilate the inhabitants of Canaan (see also Joshua 11:19). Joshua 11:13 notes that, with the exception of Hazor, the Canaanite towns that stood on hills were not destroyed. This allows consistency with Moses' prophecy in Deuteronomy 6:10-11.

The purpose of God's command in Deuteronomy 20:16-18 was to cleanse Canaan of its corrupting influences that would draw the Israelites into sinning against God by doing all the abhorrent things that the Canaanites did for their gods. Israel's struggle in future generations against Baalism and other pagan practices can be traced back to the minor compromises made in the days of the conquest.

Joshua 11:23 draws this stage in Israel's history to a conclusion with the words, "And the land had rest from war." God's promises to Moses had been fulfilled. The Hebrew word for "rest" was used frequently in the Former Prophets to speak of periods of rest, peace, and quiet (see Joshua 14:15; Judges 3:11, 30; 5:31; 8:28). This rest foreshadows the hopes of generations of believers who long both for close relationship with God and harmonious relationships among all humanity.

INTERPRETING THE SCRIPTURE

Filling Big Shoes

Moses tops the list of the most significant people in the Old Testament. He is the central human character in the first five books in the Old Testament—beginning with his birth in Exodus 2 and ending with his death in Deuteronomy 34. Deuteronomy concludes, "Never since has there arisen a prophet in Israel like Moses, whom the LORD knew face to face" (34:10). He was "unequalled" in all the "signs and wonders" and "all the mighty

deeds and all the terrifying displays of power" he performed (34:11-12).

In spite of these credentials, Moses was not always successful in keeping the Israelites true to their God. Near the end of his life, Moses prayed, "Remember your servants, Abraham, Isaac, and Jacob; pay no attention to the stubbornness of this people, their wickedness and their sin" (9:27). In his valedictory address he enumerated the blessings that would come upon the people if they followed God faithfully and the curses if they abandoned God and God's law (chapters 27–28). From subsequent history we know that Moses' warnings often went unheeded.

If a person like Moses had such tentative success, can you imagine what Joshua must have felt when the mantle of leadership fell upon him? Yet under the leadership of Joshua, Israel was exceedingly successful in fulfilling God's call to take possession of the land God had promised Moses. Joshua rallied the people time and again in the face of imposing foes.

Most of us at some time will be called to fill big shoes. Maybe we will succeed a successful parent in running a family business or a popular predecessor in some job. Maybe a parent has gained notoriety in entertainment, sports, politics, or the church. Maybe we will become the spouse of a widow or widower, the stepparent of grieving children, or the sibling of a popular student leader, talented athlete, or outstanding scholar. Maybe we will even try to follow and emulate Jesus Christ—very big shoes indeed!

Strength and Courage

The Lord instructed Joshua to "be strong and courageous" (Joshua 1:6). The strength God urged upon Joshua was not mere physical prowess. No automatic relationship exists between physical attractiveness, prowess, or health and significant human achievement. You only have to think of someone like physicist Stephen Hawking to recognize that fact.

The Hebrew verb translated "be strong" in Joshua 1:6, 7, 9, 18 and 10:25 is translated in other contexts as "repair" (2 Kings 12:5-14; 2 Chronicles 24:5, 12; Ezra 9:9; Amos 9:11). Strength often involves taking something that is broken down and falling apart and making it strong and useful again. Strength is not dogged inflexibility; that kind of strength is brittle and can shatter under a test load. True strength is malleable and flexible. It is releasing ourselves into the hands of the Craftsman who can shape us

and make us strong. God's call to Joshua was a call to release himself into God's providence and power. Joshua's strength was not solely personal fortitude; it was deep devotion to, trust in, and reliance on God. God's promises were fulfilled because of Joshua's commitment to God.

The verb translated "be . . . courageous" also means to make firm, strengthen, or repair (2 Chronicles 24:12); but it adds boldness, alertness, and determination to the mix. Making yourself available to God must be complemented by a willingness to act in the face of obstacles. Only by such self-release can God's promises be fulfilled.

Expressions of faith have been compared to a thermometer and a thermostat. The former reflects its environment; the latter influences its environment. The strength and courage that God called Joshua to exhibit was a thermostat-kind of faith that did not shrink back from opponents, obstacles, or odds. With little regard for the mammoth task ahead, Joshua reflected a faith in the God who keeps promises.

Obedience

Far too many atrocities have been committed in the name of God to allow us to adopt Joshua's model too easily. That model could promote a view of God far different from the God who gave the Beloved Son as a way of showing love for the whole world. A general disregard for human life is reflected in phrases like: "devoted to destruction by the edge of the sword all in the city, both men and women" (Joshua 6:21); "utterly destroyed all the inhabitants" (8:26); "inflicting a very great slaughter on them, until they were wiped out" (10:20); "utterly destroyed every person" (10:28); "left no one remaining" (10:30); "leaving him no survivors" (10:33); "utterly destroyed all that breathed" (10:40); "might be utterly destroyed, and might receive no mercy, but be exterminated" (11:20). The matter is further complicated in that these people had done nothing to oppress or trouble Israel.

Generations of Christians have struggled with how these Old Testament events square with Jesus' command to "love your enemies" (Matthew 5:43-48). Some argue for a militant approach against all forces of evil. Some see pragmatic reality at work and argue that extreme situations call for extreme measures. Some contend that humanity's understanding of God has progressed through the generations and that the teachings of Christ surpass primitive Old Testament understandings.

Our desire to be obedient to God is complicated by which voice we obey. Are we listening to our own internal voices? Are we listening to the voice of the majority around us? Are we listening to prophetic voices that speak counter to our culture? Are we listening to the words of Scripture, to Jesus, or to the Holy Spirit? Each of us will struggle with how to hear, how to understand, and how to follow the true voice of God.

One further caution: An immediate victorious conclusion does not always mean that God's will prevailed. We must not forget that the cross and death preceded the victory of the resurrection, and we still look for a final victory whose shape is clouded in mystery.

Confronting Evil Influences

An underlying rationale for Joshua's commission from God was to protect Israel from the corrupting influences of pagan beliefs and practices. Believers face similar influences in our society, and many people long for a society where God is honored and all corrupting influences are banished.

Joshua was not successful in ridding Israel of Canaanite influences. Those influences troubled Israel for generations. A question remains, however: If Joshua had been successful in weeding out all of the Canaanite influences, would Israel thereby have banished all evil, corruption, hatred, unfaithfulness, and sin from its society? This side of Eden, the answer is surely no.

The reality is that evil is not just around us; it is in us. We cannot create a perfect society because we have no perfect people to inhabit such a society. Killing off the heinous evildoers around us will not kill the sin within us.

While sin always grows out of personal choice, external factors almost always play a role. James 1:12-15 expounds on temptation, its source, its enticements, and its results. We should not underestimate the powerful, corrupting influence of evil; and we certainly should work for laws and social structures that protect our society from personally and socially destructive influences.

True success will come when we recognized that evil is not defeated by being restrained. It is defeated when confronted by a greater power. First John 4:4 reminds us that "the one who is in you is greater than the one who is in the world." Maintaining a vital relationship with that One is our only hope in conquering evil personally and socially.

SHARING THE SCRIPTURE

Preparing Our Hearts

Explore this week's devotional reading, found in Acts 26:1-7. Brought before King Herod Agrippa II to defend himself against charges brought by other Jews (see Acts 25:7), in this fifth and final defense, Paul recounts his "hope in the promise made by God to our [Jewish] ancestors" (26:6). Paul is speaking here of Christ. How would you defend your faith if pressed to do so? What promises has God fulfilled in your life? Give thanks for what God has given you.

Pray that you and the adult learners will

be mindful of God's promises and grateful for their fulfillment.

Preparing Our Minds

Study the background Scripture from Joshua 1:1-6 and chapters 11 and 12. The lesson Scripture is from Joshua 1:1b-6; 11:16-19, 21-23. As you contemplate the Scripture, think about why it is so difficult to keep a promise, even if that promise is made in good faith.

Write on newsprint:
❑ the list of place names that appear in Joshua 11:16-19, 21-23 for "Explore How the Conquering of Land Is a Fulfillment of God's Promises."
❑ information for next week's lesson, found under "Continue the Journey."
❑ activities for further spiritual growth in "Continue the Journey."

Review the introduction to this quarter, "The Big Picture," "Close-up," and "Faith in Action." Consider how you will use this additional information for this session and throughout the quarter.

LEADING THE CLASS

(1) Gather to Learn

❖ Welcome the class members and introduce any guests.

❖ Pray that those who have come today will receive with joy the Word of the Lord.

❖ Brainstorm answers to this question: **What promises have you heard elected officials make?** List responses on newsprint. Go back over the list, placing a check mark by promises kept and an X by promises that are not yet fulfilled.

❖ Ask: **Why do promises made in good faith go unfulfilled?** (Be careful that this brief discussion does not focus on certain politicians or a political party. A political debate is not the purpose here.)

Read aloud today's focus statement: **People make promises in good faith, but**

they do not always fulfill them. Why is it so difficult to keep a promise? God makes promises that may seem to be unfilled, but in time, we can be confident that God stands behind the promises.

(2) Explore How the Conquering of Land Is a Fulfillment of God's Promises

❖ Choose a volunteer to read Joshua 1:1b-6.

❖ Read Genesis 12:1-3 and ask: **How do the events in Joshua 1 relate to God's promise to Abraham?**

❖ Display a map showing the land of Canaan at the time of Joshua. (See Close-up.) Invite the students to locate the places mentioned in Joshua 1:1-6. Read or retell Joshua 1:1-6 from Understanding the Scripture to help the adults recognize the scope of the territory God had promised.

❖ Read Joshua 11:16-19, 21-23, which is a summary of the land Joshua has conquered. (There are many names here that you will find in the Pronunciation Guide.)

❖ Refer to the list of names you have posted on newsprint and help the students locate these places on the map. Encourage them to compare the places that Joshua conquered so far with the land God had promised.

❖ Discuss these questions:
    (1) What have you learned about Joshua as a leader?
    (2) What have you learned about the land of Israel?
    (3) What have you learned about God?
    (4) What questions or surprises arise for you as you study this chapter in Israel's early history?

❖ **Option:** Provide time for those who want to raise questions about God's way of keeping an important promise to Abraham and his descendents—a way that led to war, death, and destruction. While some of the class will likely oppose war and question this means to an end, reading "Confronting Evil Influences" in Interpreting the Scripture may be helpful in explaining why the Israelites believed that holy war was God's will.

(3) Assess the Learners' Feelings and Attitudes About Keeping Promises

❖ Form small groups of three or four adults. Invite the learners to tell about a promise someone made to them—and then either reneged on or fulfilled. Encourage them to express their feelings about their responses to promises—those that are kept and those that are broken.

❖ Form small groups with different people. This time, ask the learners to talk about a promise they made. Did they keep this promise? If not, how did they feel about letting someone down?

(4) Identify and Act on Ways the Learners Can Participate on God's Behalf in the World Today

❖ Lead the class in a unison reading of today's key verse, Joshua 11:15.

❖ Encourage comments on the work Joshua did that enabled God to fulfill an important promise to the covenant people. Read "Strength and Courage" in Interpreting the Scripture to underscore Joshua's attributes as a military leader who was obedient to God.

❖ Ask these questions:
   (1) In what situations today are strength and courage among Christians necessary to fulfill God's will?
   (2) Who are the "Joshuas" of our day, the ones who are obedient to God and show strength and courage to carry out God's will?
   (3) In what ways can we as a class or church act as courageous leaders on behalf of God?

❖ Conclude this portion of the session by distributing paper and pencils. Invite the participants to write a sentence or two stating how they intend to act on behalf of God in the world during the coming week.

(5) Continue the Journey

❖ Pray that all who have made a commitment will faithfully carry out God's instructions so that God's will may be done.

❖ Read aloud this preparation for next week's lesson. You may also want to post it on newsprint for the students to copy.
   ■ **Title: God Has Expectations**
   ■ **Background Scripture: Joshua 1:7-16**
   ■ **Lesson Scripture: Joshua 1:7-16**
   ■ **Focus of the Lesson: People generally expect rules to be associated with all endeavors of life. Why does it seem that those who violate regulations prosper and are successful? The Bible teaches that prosperity and success are contingent on obeying God.**

❖ Challenge the students to complete one or more of these activities for further spiritual growth related to this week's session. Post this information on newsprint for the students to copy.
   (1) **Research the concept of "holy war" in ancient Israel. Why are such wars fought? What rules does God set forth? As a Christian, what is your position on war? Why?**
   (2) **Read about current tensions between Israelis and Palestinians. What role do land disputes play in these tensions? What relationship do you see between the Israelites' understanding of what God had promised to Abraham, Joshua's conquest of people who were on the land, and current problems?**
   (3) **Page through your Bible in search of God's promises. Do you perceive God to be a promise-keeper? Why or why not?**

❖ Sing or read aloud "Hymn of Promise."

❖ Conclude today's session by leading the class in this benediction: **May you go forth now in peace, surrounded by the love of God and by the love of this community of faith. Amen.**

UNIT 1: GOD'S PEOPLE LEARN FROM PROSPERITY
GOD HAS EXPECTATIONS

PREVIEWING THE LESSON

Lesson Scripture: Joshua 1:7-16
Background Scripture: Joshua 1:7-16
Key Verse: Joshua 1:7

Focus of the Lesson:
People generally expect rules to be associated with all endeavors of life. Why does it seem that those who violate regulations prosper and are successful? The Bible teaches that prosperity and success are contingent on obeying God.

Goals for the Learners:
(1) to examine what God's words meant when speaking to Joshua about being strong and courageous.
(2) to reflect on their obedience to God's commandments.
(3) to make a commitment to Bible reading that will enable them to learn the rules so as to live up to God's expectations.

Pronunciation Guide:
Gadite (gad' ite)   Reubenite (roo' bin nite)
Manasseh (muh nas' uh)

Supplies:
Bibles, newsprint and marker, paper and pencils, hymnals

READING THE SCRIPTURE

NRSV
Joshua 1:7-16

⁷Only be strong and very courageous, being careful to act in accordance with all the law that my servant Moses commanded you; do not turn from it to the right hand or to the left, so that you may be successful wherever you go. ⁸This book of the law shall not depart out of your mouth; you shall

NIV
Joshua 1:7-16

⁷Be strong and very courageous. Be careful to obey all the law my servant Moses gave you; do not turn from it to the right or to the left, that you may be successful wherever you go. ⁸Do not let this Book of the Law depart from your mouth; meditate on it day and night, so that you may be

meditate on it day and night, so that you may be careful to act in accordance with all that is written in it. For then you shall make your way prosperous, and then you shall be successful. ⁹I hereby command you: Be strong and courageous; do not be frightened or dismayed, for the LORD your God is with you wherever you go."

¹⁰Then Joshua commanded the officers of the people, ¹¹"Pass through the camp, and command the people: 'Prepare your provisions; for in three days you are to cross over the Jordan, to go in to take possession of the land that the LORD your God gives you to possess.'"

¹²To the Reubenites, the Gadites, and the half-tribe of Manasseh Joshua said, ¹³"Remember the word that Moses the servant of the LORD commanded you, saying, 'The LORD your God is providing you a place of rest, and will give you this land.' ¹⁴Your wives, your little ones, and your livestock shall remain in the land that Moses gave you beyond the Jordan. But all the warriors among you shall cross over armed before your kindred and shall help them, ¹⁵until the LORD gives rest to your kindred as well as to you, and they too take possession of the land that the LORD your God is giving them. Then you shall return to your own land and take possession of it, the land that Moses the servant of the LORD gave you beyond the Jordan to the east."

¹⁶They answered Joshua: "All that you have commanded us we will do, and wherever you send us we will go."

careful to do everything written in it. Then you will be prosperous and successful. ⁹Have I not commanded you? Be strong and courageous. Do not be terrified; do not be discouraged, for the LORD your God will be with you wherever you go."

¹⁰So Joshua ordered the officers of the people: ¹¹"Go through the camp and tell the people, 'Get your supplies ready. Three days from now you will cross the Jordan here to go in and take possession of the land the LORD your God is giving you for your own.'"

¹²But to the Reubenites, the Gadites and the half-tribe of Manasseh, Joshua said, ¹³"Remember the command that Moses the servant of the LORD gave you: 'The LORD your God is giving you rest and has granted you this land.' ¹⁴Your wives, your children and your livestock may stay in the land that Moses gave you east of the Jordan, but all your fighting men, fully armed, must cross over ahead of your brothers. You are to help your brothers ¹⁵until the LORD gives them rest, as he has done for you, and until they too have taken possession of the land that the LORD your God is giving them. After that, you may go back and occupy your own land, which Moses the servant of the LORD gave you east of the Jordan toward the sunrise."

¹⁶Then they answered Joshua, "Whatever you have commanded us we will do, and wherever you send us we will go."

UNDERSTANDING THE SCRIPTURE

Joshua 1:7-9. Verses 7 and 9 repeat God's admonition to Joshua that we examined in the last lesson, "Be strong and courageous" (Joshua 1:6). Each repetition has a different focus, however. The focus in verse 6 was on Joshua's role in taking possession of the land that God had promised to Moses and the ancestors of the people.

The admonition in verse 7 begins with a small Hebrew word that is omitted in the New International Version but is translated "only" in the New Revised Standard Version. The restrictive force of this word heightens the emphasis to "be only, altogether, and surely strong." The same heightened emphasis is placed on being "courageous" in verse 7 by the addition of another small word translated "very." This word focuses on abundance ("be abundantly or exceedingly courageous") and force ("be vehemently courageous").

The emphasis in this second admonition is to "act in accordance with all the law that my servant Moses commanded you." Joshua obviously understood this action in a broader sense than merely taking possession of the land God promised to Moses. Joshua revived the neglected practice of circumcision (5:1-9, which symbolized God's covenant with Israel), inscribed all the covenant law on stones, and read it to the whole assembly (8:30-35). Thereby Joshua demonstrated his understanding that success and prosperity would come more by cleaving to God and the covenant than by cleaving the enemy with swords. Cleaving to God would require more strength and courage than taking possession of the land. It necessitated both meditating on God's law day and night and acting in accord with its instruction (1:8; compare Psalm 1:2).

The third call to strength and courage was designed to build up the people's confidence in the face of the daunting foes that were before them. The writer used two words that describe the kind of response that would immobilize the people and ensure their defeat. The first word, "frightened," comes from the Hebrew verb for "tremble." It can denote either awe or terror. The second word, "dismayed," has its roots in the idea of being "shattered." We might paraphrase these to read, "Do not tremble and crumble in the face of your foes."

The antidote to such debilitating fear is the recognition that "the LORD your God is with you wherever you go" (1:9). Prosperity and success would come to them as long as the Lord accompanied them in their endeavors; but the Lord would be with them only so long as they walked in the paths of righteousness.

Joshua 1:10-11. In response to God's instruction, Joshua immediately began to prepare for crossing the Jordan River. He first commanded the "officers" to inform the people of the plans. The Hebrew word used here for "officers" first appears in Exodus 5:6-19 with reference to Israelite supervisors who oversaw work crews in Egypt. Numbers 11:16 uses the term to apply to the seventy elders and officers of Israel appointed by Moses to assist in judging the people. Deuteronomy 1:15 describes the selection and organization of these assistants. Moses put in place and Joshua continued an organizational structure likely adapted from Egyptian models, but Joshua began to shift it from an administrative/judicial function to a military one.

Joshua gave the people three days to prepare their provisions. Note that in his secular concern for provisioning the troops, he did not fail to encourage them with the assurance that they were taking possession of a land that God was in the process of giving them.

Joshua 1:12-15. According to verse 12, as first recorded in Deuteronomy 3:12-17, after Moses had conquered the nations east of the Jordan River, he assigned that land to the tribes of Reuben, Gad, and Manasseh (though part of the tribe of Manasseh would receive land west of the Jordan as well). To maintain the solidarity of the people, however, Moses insisted that these tribes for whom territory had been secured could not fully settle in until all of the tribes had claimed their lands. In fact, these tribes were to serve as the "vanguard" (3:18), leading the other tribes in the conquest of Canaan. Joshua reminds the people of Moses' command: Those who already had their land could not enjoy their "place of rest . . . until the Lord gives rest to your kindred" (Joshua 1:13-15).

Leaving "your wives, your little ones, and your livestock" behind (1:14) provided additional incentive to get the job done quickly. Since "all the warriors" among them were being called into service in Joshua's army, and since these tribes themselves had settled on captured land, leaving their families behind created a vulnerability to possible attacks from the people they had displaced. Protection would depend upon those too young or too old to join Joshua's forces. Numbers 32:1 also notes that "the Reubenites and the Gadites owned a very great number of cattle," so their economic security also was being left behind in the hands of the more vulnerable.

Once the other tribes had taken possession of the land that God was giving them, the tribes of Reuben, Gad, and half-tribe of Manasseh could return to their own land "and take possession of it" (1:15; compare 22:1-6). Joshua implied that, though the land east of the Jordan might be under control, it really couldn't become theirs until each tribe had the same opportunity.

Joshua 1:16. Moses and Joshua had prepared the people well for the task ahead. The way in which the tribes embraced the challenge without question or dispute is a testimony to the groundwork that had been laid to establish unity. The tribes were ready to submit to Joshua's command and to go wherever Joshua sent them. They could move ahead in the assurance that the Lord their God would be with them wherever they went (1:9)—evidence again that they were strong and courageous through their faith in God.

INTERPRETING THE SCRIPTURE

Strength and Courage Within

God's threefold call to strength and courage in Joshua 1:1-16 emphasizes the importance of these qualities in facing the challenges of life. We tend to view strength and courage as inward qualities embedded in the character of the individual. Though we know that early experiences in life can foster self-confidence or harm one's self-image, we all have seen determination develop in the abused—and sloth in the privileged. We have seen prodigals flee from the embrace of loving families, and we have seen elder siblings remain in that embrace while inwardly harboring resentment and anger. We have seen promise destroyed by alcohol, drug abuse, or destructive lifestyles. We have seen promise emerge from diseased, broken, and disfigured bodies. What causes such disparate expressions of strength and courage?

God's call to Joshua to be strong and courageous was an invitation for him to look within, and that is a place where each of us can begin. Self-examination that leads to self-understanding is a starting point in assessing our strength of character and will.

It will help us weigh our courage in the face of challenging situations or unexpected troubles. If we make an honest assessment, we likely will find some areas of strength and promise and other areas of weakness and disappointment. We also will likely find some persistent areas of weakness that we feel helpless to overcome.

God called Joshua to examine himself, to discover the areas of strength and courage already within him. Digging deep within would help Joshua to know his capabilities and his limitations. It also would drive him to seek other sources of strength and courage.

Strength and Courage Through Obedience

God's second call to Joshua to be strong and courageous is associated with "being careful to act in accordance with all the law that my servant Moses commanded you" (Joshua 1:7). We may not see how strength and courage relate to obedience, unless we see them as precursors to obedience. We need strength and courage to live moral lives.

Most of us experience the social pressures and discomforts of trying to maintain moral bearings in a basically amoral world. We frequently find ourselves in situations where doing the expedient thing overrides doing the right thing. We recognize that strength of character and some degree of courage often are required for believers to stand up against social pressures.

In Joshua, the call to strength and courage reverses this typical understanding. Strength and courage grow out of careful adherence to the law. Success in any and every endeavor comes by acting in accordance with the law, adhering fully to this central moral compass.

When a commitment to obey the law, to do the right thing, or to live by moral principles is made prior to confronting a particular moral choice, we lessen the tension in choosing how to act. Rather than deciding on the spur of the moment under the pressure of the immediate situation, we pre-decide. We set our moral compass and commit ourselves always to refrain from some types of behavior or always to act in certain ways. That commitment becomes a source of strength when we face moral dilemmas. By confronting the decision out from under the tension of a particular situation, we avoid the confusion, the compromises, the embarrassment, and the subsequent regret that often plague moral choices.

We must be careful here to avoid understanding the law as always restrictive—thou shalt not. Moral decision-making is not solely a matter of deciding that I will not engage in certain actions, activities, or practices. We make moral decisions daily when we decide to respond to situations in ways that demonstrate that we love God with all of our hearts, souls, minds, and strength and that we love our neighbors as ourselves. In following that compass, we will discover the strength of commitment and the courage for moral living to which God called Joshua and the people of Israel.

Strength and Courage Through Direction

Joshua 1:9 provides a third source of strength and courage, "I hereby command you: Be strong and courageous." Have you ever thought of strength and courage as being something that could be commanded?

Soldiers are trained to follow commands without hesitation, and a multitude of examples could be given of individual acts of heroism and valor that resulted from a single soldier bravely following the directives of a commanding officer. In team sports, each player is given an assignment, which if executed completely will result in victory for the team. Most of us on occasion have counseled a child, a relative, or a friend with a direct course of action to take in dealing with an overwhelming situation. Like the moral compass we examined earlier, the command of a trusted parent, boss, or leader can become the turning point in the life of another that invokes the courage and strength needed to get through a trying circumstance.

In human situations we may be too quick to offer directives to others. We may tell a grieving person to get over it before they have had time to work through their grief. Or we counsel a teenager in a course of action that suits us and our temperament but is contrary to theirs. When the command comes from God, however, we move to a new level of understanding. We are obeying a loving, compassionate, and omniscient Heavenly Parent whose command is always true, just, and appropriate for each of our circumstances.

God's command goes further, however. It is accompanied by a promise, "The LORD your God is with you wherever you go" (1:9). A similar promise was made in 1:5. God is not a general sitting in the comfort of headquarters giving commands to the soldier on the battlefield. God is not a counselor offering advice or direction for circumstances the counselor has never faced personally. God is not the friend who has never walked in your shoes telling you how to handle the problems you are facing. God is with us wherever we go. God! With us! Wherever we go! In the midst of the fiery furnaces in our lives, Another walks with us (Daniel 3:19-30). God does not fail us or forsake us. Strength and courage are ours because of the One who stands beside us in all the circumstances in life.

Strength and Courage Through Community

Moses had the wisdom to recognize that twelve tribes acting together would demonstrate a level of strength and courage that surpassed what any of them could demonstrate alone. Joshua implemented that vision by keeping the tribes settling east of the Jordan engaged in the entire campaign against Canaan.

We often say that there is strength in numbers. A greater truth is that strength is found in unity even when the numbers are small (Matthew 18:20). When the two-and-a-half tribes responded to Joshua, "All that you have commanded we will do, and wherever you send us we will go" (Joshua 1:16), they showed the kind of unity that gives communities power and commitment to succeed even in the face of great obstacles.

Too many people today are assuming their places of rest when their kindred still are unsettled. We fragment ourselves into splinter groups, power blocks, political parties, denominations, nationalities, and races, erecting a "dividing wall" that symbolizes "the hostility between us"—a dividing wall that Christ broke down (Ephesians 2:14). The people of God often lack strength and courage because of our fragmented existence and the self-centered interests that keep us divided.

Until we recover a spirit of community, until we join hands with our brothers and sisters in the faith, until we pledge ourselves to obey God and follow wherever God sends us, we will never have the strength or the courage to claim and fulfill the promises God has given us.

SHARING THE SCRIPTURE

Preparing Our Hearts

Explore this week's devotional reading, found in Deuteronomy 5:22-33. As the people were on the brink of entering the Promised Land, Moses recalled how God spoke to them directly and gave the Ten Commandments. Moreover, God wrote these commandments on stone and gave them to Moses. Clearly, God has given us rules for living so that we might know how to relate to God and to other people. Which rules set comfortable boundaries for you? Which rules challenge you? Why is it important to know God's rules? Ponder these questions and write responses in your spiritual journal.

Pray that you and the adult learners will be attuned to God's rules so that you can live as God intended.

Preparing Our Minds

Study the background Scripture and the lesson Scripture, both of which are from Joshua 1:7-16. Why do you think some people who seem to violate all the rules still come out on top—or do they?

Write on newsprint:
❑ Bible reading plans for "Make a Commitment to Bible Reading that Will Enable the Participants to Learn the Rules So as to Live Up to God's Expectations."

❏ information for next week's lesson, found under "Continue the Journey."

❏ activities for further spiritual growth in "Continue the Journey."

Find several plans for daily Bible reading. Print out a few samples for the students to see. Be sure to label the plans so the adults can find the ones they choose.

LEADING THE CLASS

(1) Gather to Learn

❖ Welcome the class members and introduce any guests.

❖ Pray that all who are present recognize that God has expectations for them.

❖ Prompt the students to identify nationally or internationally known figures who have broken rules or laws and apparently thrived for a time. List these names on newsprint. The list may include business figures (for example, Bernie Madoff), politicians (Richard Nixon), sports or entertainment celebrities (O. J. Simpson), or spiritual leaders (Ted Haggard).

❖ Ask these questions:

(1) **What do you think finally caused these once-respected leaders to fall?**

(2) **How might these falls have been prevented?**

❖ Read aloud today's focus statement: **People generally expect rules to be associated with all endeavors of life. Why does it seem that those who violate regulations prosper and are successful? The Bible teaches that prosperity and success are contingent on obeying God.**

(2) Examine What God's Words Meant When Speaking to Joshua About Being Strong and Courageous

❖ Choose someone to read Joshua 1:7-9.

❖ Use information from Joshua 1:7-9 in Understanding the Scripture to clarify the meaning of this passage.

❖ Continue by have a volunteer read Joshua 1:10-16.

❖ Identify reasons for expecting all the men to fight to secure the land, even though the tribes of Reuben, Gad, and half of Manasseh already had their land. Read or retell "Strength and Courage Through Direction" from Interpreting the Scripture to add ideas to the discussion.

❖ Discuss with the class how working together as a faith community enables them to accomplish God's purposes. Encourage them to give some examples of ways your congregation has worked together to build up God's kingdom. Some examples may include: *sending a mission team out to rebuild homes devastated by a natural disaster; sponsoring a tutoring program; working ecumenically to provide shelter for the homeless; constructing a building for Sunday school.* As you talk together, recall the importance of strength and courage in completing this project.

(3) Reflect on the Learners' Obedience to God's Commandments

❖ Distribute paper and pencils. Read these partial sentences, pausing at the appropriate places so that the adults may write their thoughts. Tell the group at the outset that they will not be asked to share their responses.

(1) **If Jesus were to rate me on a scale of 1-10, with 10 being "fantastic," in terms of obedience to God's commands, he would give me a rating of ___.** (pause)

(2) **I need to ___ in order to better know and follow God's commands.** (pause)

(3) **This week I will ___ in order to more faithfully obey God.** (pause)

❖ Provide a few moments of quiet time for the adults to reflect on their answers and ask God to lead them in being more obedient.

(4) Make a Commitment to Bible Reading that Will Enable the Participants to Learn the Rules So as to Live Up to God's Expectations

❖ Lead the class in reading again today's key verse, Joshua 1:7.

❖ Ask: **What relationship do you see here between strength, courage, obedience to God's law, and success?**

❖ Point out that although our key verse emphasizes the importance of acting in accordance with God's law, the only way we can do that is to be intimately familiar with the Bible. The fact that you are in Sunday school speaks of your desire to know and heed God's Word, but biblical illiteracy is rampant in the United States, even in churches.

❖ Discuss these questions:

(1) **Why do you think so many people, including Christians, are biblically illiterate?**

(2) **What do you think can be done to solve this problem?**

(3) **What difference would it make if we all became more biblically literate?**

❖ Post this information, which you have written prior to class, concerning types of Bible reading plans. Have samples of each type available for the students to choose from. Perhaps you can have copies made of the ones the individuals selected for distribution next week. If not, suggest that the students go online to find a plan that suits their desire to know the Word of God better. Here are just a few of the many possibilities:

■ **Chronological**
■ **Old Testament/New Testament**
■ **People of the Bible**
■ **Major events**
■ **The Psalms in a month**
■ **Topical**

❖ Conclude this part of the lesson by challenging the students to systematically read their Bibles so as to become better aware of God's expectations for them.

(5) Continue the Journey

❖ Pray that the participants will go forth committed to learning God's expectations and living by God's rules.

❖ Read aloud this preparation for next week's lesson. You may also want to post it on newsprint for the students to copy.

■ **Title: God Protects**
■ **Background Scripture: Joshua 2**
■ **Lesson Scripture: Joshua 2:3-9, 15-16, 22-24**
■ **Focus of the Lesson: Most people want to know they are or can be protected from harm. On whom can we depend for protection? God used Rahab to protect the spies from harm when she hid them from the soldiers the king of Jericho had sent to find them.**

❖ Challenge the students to complete one or more of these activities for further spiritual growth related to this week's session. Post this information on newsprint for the students to copy.

(1) **Check the Internet or other sources for a systematic Bible reading plan. Many are available from which to choose. Make a commitment to select and follow one in order to better understand God's expectations.**

(2) **Be alert for news of people who are "strong and courageous." What motivates people to act in ways that far exceed human expectations? How do you imagine God figures into their behavior?**

(3) **Be alert for media stories concerning actions that people have taken "in God's name." Evaluate their actions. Based on your beliefs, do you think they acted according to God's expectations? If not, what could they have done differently?**

❖ Sing or read aloud "Trust and Obey."

❖ Conclude today's session by leading the class in this benediction: **May you go forth now in peace, surrounded by the love of God and by the love of this community of faith. Amen.**

UNIT 1: GOD'S PEOPLE LEARN FROM PROSPERITY
GOD PROTECTS

PREVIEWING THE LESSON

Lesson Scripture: Joshua 2:3-9, 15-16, 22-24
Background Scripture: Joshua 2
Key Verse: Joshua 2:24

Focus of the Lesson:
Most people want to know they are or can be protected from harm. On whom can we depend for protection? God used Rahab to protect the spies from harm when she hid them from the soldiers the king of Jericho had sent to find them.

Goals for the Learners:
(1) to examine the relationship between Rahab and the two spies sent out by Joshua.
(2) to appreciate the challenge of deciding between "the lesser of two evils."
(3) to identify experiences of protection they have had and praise God for them.

Pronunciation Guide:
Amorite (am' uh rite)
Rahab (ray' hab)

Supplies:
Bibles, newsprint and marker, paper and pencils, hymnals

READING THE SCRIPTURE

NRSV
Joshua 2:3-9, 15-16, 22-24

3Then the king of Jericho sent orders to Rahab, "Bring out the men who have come to you, who entered your house, for they have come only to search out the whole land." 4But the woman took the two men and hid them. Then she said, "True, the men came to me, but I did not know where they came from. 5And when it was time to close

NIV
Joshua 2:3-9, 15-16, 22-24

3So the king of Jericho sent this message to Rahab: "Bring out the men who came to you and entered your house, because they have come to spy out the whole land."

4But the woman had taken the two men and hidden them. She said, "Yes, the men came to me, but I did not know where they had come from. 5At dusk, when it was time the gate at dark, the men went out. Where the men went I do not know. Pursue them quickly, for you can overtake them." [6]She had, however, brought them up to the roof and hidden them with the stalks of flax that she had laid out on the roof. [7]So the men pursued them on the way to the Jordan as far as the fords. As soon as the pursuers had gone out, the gate was shut.

[8]Before they went to sleep, she came up to them on the roof [9]and said to the men: "I know that the LORD has given you the land, and that dread of you has fallen on us, and that all the inhabitants of the land melt in fear before you.

[15]Then she let them down by a rope through the window, for her house was on the outer side of the city wall and she resided within the wall itself. [16]She said to them, "Go toward the hill country, so that the pursuers may not come upon you. Hide yourselves there three days, until the pursuers have returned; then afterward you may go your way."

[22]They departed and went into the hill country and stayed there three days, until the pursuers returned. The pursuers had searched all along the way and found nothing. [23]Then the two men came down again from the hill country. They crossed over, came to Joshua son of Nun, and told him all that had happened to .them. **[24]They said to Joshua, "Truly the LORD has given all the land into our hands; moreover all the inhabitants of the land melt in fear before us."**

to close the city gate, the men left. I don't know which way they went. Go after them quickly. You may catch up with them." [6](But she had taken them up to the roof and hidden them under the stalks of flax she had laid out on the roof.) [7]So the men set out in pursuit of the spies on the road that leads to the fords of the Jordan, and as soon as the pursuers had gone out, the gate was shut.

[8]Before the spies lay down for the night, she went up on the roof [9]and said to them, "I know that the LORD has given this land to you and that a great fear of you has fallen on us, so that all who live in this country are melting in fear because of you.

[15]So she let them down by a rope through the window, for the house she lived in was part of the city wall. [16]Now she had said to them, "Go to the hills so the pursuers will not find you. Hide yourselves there three days until they return, and then go on your way."

[22]When they left, they went into the hills and stayed there three days, until the pursuers had searched all along the road and returned without finding them. [23]Then the two men started back. They went down out of the hills, forded the river and came to Joshua son of Nun and told him everything that had happened to them. **[24]They said to Joshua, "The LORD has surely given the whole land into our hands; all the people are melting in fear because of us."**

UNDERSTANDING THE SCRIPTURE

Joshua 2:1-7. Jericho was located on one of the major east-west trade routes in the verdant Jordan River valley about 10 miles northwest of the river's entrance into the Dead Sea. It is one of the oldest continuously inhabited cities in the world. Archaeologists have unearthed at the site over 20 successive settlements dating back to 9000 B.C.

From the Israelite encampment in the Plains of Moab east of the Jordan River (the modern-day country of Jordan), Joshua sent two spies to scope out Canaan. The spies were sent especially to gather information about Jericho, the first major city the Israelites would encounter after crossing the Jordan (see Joshua 6). Rather than sleeping openly in the public square (see Genesis 19:2-3; Judges 19:15-21), the spies secured lodging in the house of Rahab. The Scriptures do not hesitate to call her "a prostitute" (Joshua 2:1; 6:17; Hebrews 11:31; James 2:25), though the New International Version footnotes an alternate translation of "an innkeeper." This reference likely stems from early rabbinic sources that describe Rahab as an innkeeper. When word reached the king of Jericho that two Israelites were staying at Rahab's house, orders were issued that Rahab should turn over the men to the king. The Scriptures provide no immediate explanation for why Rahab decided to protect the spies and cover up their presence by lying to the king. Hiding them on the roof amid stalks of flax, she misdirected those seeking them. The spies had indeed been there, she said; but they had left just before the gates were to be closed for the night. Claiming not to know where they were, she encouraged the king's men to pursue them quickly, since there was a good possibility that the men could be overtaken.

Joshua 2:8-11. With the king's men in hot pursuit of the phantom spies, Rahab went back to the roof to talk with the spies. She then explained her actions. First, the reputation of the Israelites had been circulating for over 40 years. The news of their escape from Egypt and the crossing of the dry bed of the Red Sea had become widely known. The utter defeat of the two powerful Amorite kings east of the Jordan had heightened the Canaanites' fear.

Two different Hebrew words translated "melt/melted" were used to describe the reaction of the Canaanites to the Israelites' successes. The first word, "all the inhabitants of the land melt in fear before you" (Joshua 2:9, compare 2:24), speaks of softening or dissolving into a helpless state of disorganization. The same word was used in 1 Samuel 14:16 of the melting away of the Philistine army in the face of an attack by Jonathan and his armor-bearer.

The second word, "our hearts melted" (Joshua 2:11), employs a word that is used of melting wax (Psalm 68:2) and dissolving manna (Exodus 16:21); but it is used most often to speak figuratively of a heart that is faint, fearful, or despairing.

Because dread of the Israelites had fallen upon the citizens of Jericho (Joshua 2:9) and no courage was left in any of them (2:11), Rahab concluded that "the LORD has given you the land" (2:9). More importantly, she recognized that "the LORD your God is indeed God in heaven above and on earth below" (2:11).

Joshua 2:12-21. Given the mood among her people and the portent in the visit of the spies, Rahab was savvy enough to recognize an opportunity to strike a deal. Having ingratiated herself to the spies by taking a risk in protecting them, Rahab asked for some reciprocation. She wanted them to take an oath in God's name and to provide "a sign of good faith" (2:12; "a sure sign" in NIV or "a true token" in KJV) that they would "deal kindly with" her family. References in verses 12 and 13 to her father, mother, brothers, and sisters imply that she was unmarried and may have provided for some of their upkeep as well. She had no way of knowing the utter destruction that would be visited on Jericho; but sensing the significant threat that the Israelites represented, she was confident that her best interests lay with them.

With the city gates closed, the spies were hidden but not yet safe. The oath, "our life for yours," was conditioned on Rahab's silence about the spies' business (2:14). In turn, the spies pledged to "deal kindly and faithfully" with Rahab (2:14). The "sign of good faith" perhaps was the crimson cord that Rahab was instructed to tie in her window. The cord served both as a signal to the Israelites that all of those in Rahab's house were to be preserved and a sign that Rahab herself trusted the spies to fulfill their part of the oath. The deal was sealed by Rahab: "According to your words, so be it" (2:21).

Rahab's house was "on the outer side of the city wall, and she resided within the wall itself" (2:15). This description fits that of a casement wall, which according to *The New Interpreter's Study Bible*, is "two parallel walls separated by about ten feet and connected intermittently by internal walls to divide the space into dwelling or storage areas." Rahab helped the spies escape by letting them down on a rope from her window opening outside the city wall. Then she counseled them on the best way to avoid detection by the men of Jericho who were pursuing them.

Joshua 2:22-24. Following Rahab's advice, the spies headed west into the hills, where they remained three days until their pursuers had given up their search and returned to Jericho. The spies crossed over the Jordan and brought their report to Joshua. Based on Rahab's assessment and even using her words, "all the inhabitants of the land melt in fear" (2:9, 24), they confidently reported, "the LORD has given all the land into our hands" (2:24).

Rahab's actions in protecting the spies and her confession of the God of Israel established a place for her among the Israelites that continued at least until the time the Book of Joshua was written (6:25). If the "Rahab" listed in Matthew 1:5 refers to her, she later married Salmon and became the mother of Boaz in the lineage of Jesus.

INTERPRETING THE SCRIPTURE

Hospitality, Sanctuary, and Protection

In January of 1993 I made a solo trip to Moscow to plan a conference. That trip helps me understand the journey to Canaan for the two Israelite spies. In a strange country with strange people, a strange language, and strange customs, you are dependent on the kindness, hospitality, and accommodation of others to make it from one day to the next. You feel vulnerable, anxious, and wary all at once. You do not want to stand out too much, and you also are reluctant to ask for or accept help in fear that you might be exploited or wind up penniless in some back alley.

Only a generation away from abusive Egyptian slavery and following 40 years of nomadic wanderings in the wilderness, the Israelite spies certainly felt vulnerable and uneasy. Lacking the conveniences of today's travel industry, the spies could sleep in Jericho's public square or could seek lodging with a hospitable citizen. The former was not a good choice for undercover work, and the latter was unlikely given the fear already brewing about the Israelite threat. The only other choice was to seek out a place where other travelers found lodging. In Jericho that was Rahab's house. We probably could compare Rahab's to the hotels and boarding houses of the old American West. Most of the travelers were men. Most of them were tired, dirty, hungry, and lonely. While the good citizens of Jericho probably didn't take too kindly to such an establishment, they tolerated it because it kept the traveling vagabonds out of sight and away from the public square. Upstanding citizens didn't have to dirty their hands taking care of the riff raff.

Rahab was like *Gunsmoke*'s Miss Kitty. She was a smart, congenial, competent businesswoman who knew how to keep customers happy while providing for herself and her family. She also had an eye on the future, and she was a better judge of what was ahead for Jericho than her fellow citizens. Rahab was just what the spies needed. She provided hospitality; but more than

Lesson 3 GOD PROTECTS

that, she provided sanctuary and protection at the risk of her own life. What she did was traitorous; but she was one of those whom God seems to put in the right place at the right time in our lives.

Truth and Consequences

The phrase "truth or consequences" well expresses the either-or orientation that people often take toward truth. In our purity of thought, we argue that truth is always right and falsehood deserves grave consequences. We swear to tell the truth, the whole truth, and nothing but the truth, so help us God.

In reality, the phrase ought to be "truth and consequences." Truth has consequences that can be good or bad. Weighing the consequences of the truth does not make for easy decisions. If we had been citizens of Jericho, what Rahab did would have been unforgiveable. She lied. She protected the enemy. She hindered the capture of the spies. She increased the vulnerability of all her fellow citizens. She ultimately was responsible for the slaughter of all her neighbors. She certainly didn't love them as she loved herself. Rahab not only lied, she also fabricated a story full of deceptions.

The issue of truth is further complicated by the too-frequent claim that lies for holy purposes are okay. We want to overlook Rahab's deceit because she was serving God's purposes. Too many people, however, cover up embarrassing situations or perpetuate falsehoods for the sake of the church or for God. Beneath the surface they are taking the route that most ensures self-preservation and self-interest. If God's purposes were always crystal clear, perhaps we could evaluate the consequences more easily. Since those purposes often are shrouded in mystery, we cannot always know when shading the truth is justified. Many Christian martyrs have clung to the truth in the face of torture and death.

Sometimes we withhold the truth to protect others, as for example, two people I know who have chosen to keep their bout with cancer a secret from their young children. Whenever we withhold the whole truth, we would do well to weigh the consequences carefully and make sure that it is for the benefit of others and not of ourselves.

Friend of Sinners

Christians often feel uneasy about sex. The Bible offers a lot of restraint on the expression of sexuality among the people of God, but it rarely shows the prudishness that sometimes characterizes Christian views of sexuality. Because sex is such an intimate experience and reaches so deeply into our very beings, we know that its misuse can have devastating consequences on people. Because it can be exploitative and manipulative, it can leave deep scars in psyches and relationships. Sex can be the ultimate expression of selfishness or of communion.

Because of our uneasiness, we often shun people whose sexual standards do not meet our expectations. We almost make sexual immorality the ultimate sin. We rarely associate with such folks, afraid that perhaps even being seen with such "sinners" will somehow besmirch our reputations. Somehow we hear clearly the words of James, "Adulterers! Do you not know that friendship with the world is enmity with God? Therefore whoever wishes to be a friend of the world becomes an enemy of God" (James 4:4).

What a contrast from the example of Jesus, who was known as a friend of sinners (Matthew 11:19; Luke 7:34). Luke's record of that sentiment is followed by Jesus' encounter with a woman who was a sinner. Jesus' conclusion in that encounter was, "Her sins, which were many, have been forgiven; hence she has shown great love. But the one to whom little is forgiven, loves little" (7:47). In reality we all are great sinners;

we just do not always acknowledge or confess the less obvious sins of the spirit. By withholding the acknowledgement of our own deep sin, we lift ourselves above the more blatant sinners and pride ourselves that we are not like them (18:11). In that we also miss the deep experience of grace.

If the truth about us were known, we would hardly want to be friends with ourselves. As we see how God can take Rahab, a woman traditionally thought to have been a prostitute, and graciously bring her into the people of God, perhaps we too can experience a grace for ourselves that will allow us to love much.

God Indeed

Would it not be wonderful if people looked at our churches and all that we do and concluded, "The LORD your God is indeed God in heaven above and on earth below" (Joshua 2:11). We often claim that the Lord is our God. We affirm that God is God of heaven and earth. But the world's

response to our confessions often lacks the one word of emphasis found in Rahab's confession—the word "indeed." That word, composed of the two words "in" and "deed," displays what often is lacking in our confessions. We fail to put our words into practice. The deeds are missing.

God demonstrated such great power in the lives of those Egyptian slaves who were molded into a great nation that their reputation preceded them. The evidence of God at work in and through them struck fear in the hearts of their enemies. It also brought Rahab to the realization that the God of Israel is not like the gods of Canaan. The powerless gods of wood and stone, the capricious gods of fertility and bounty, the diminutive gods of nearby mountains and hills were small indeed compared to the God of Israel.

Oh, if only our deeds would demonstrate the presence, the power, the greatness, and the love of our God, then perhaps others would follow Rahab in confessing the Lord our God is God indeed!

SHARING THE SCRIPTURE

Preparing Our Hearts

Explore this week's devotional reading, found in James 2:18-25. In making his case that "faith without works is dead," James uses two examples from Israel's early life: Abraham and Rahab. In both instances James argues that these two people were justified by their works, Abraham because he believed God and Rahab because she welcomed and protected Israelite spies. Many Christians understand works not as a means to salvation but as a fruit of it. People who know Christ do good deeds joyfully for others. What can you do this week to allow others to see your faith through your works?

Pray that you and the adult learners will help someone in need this week.

Preparing Our Minds

Study the background Scripture from Joshua 2 and the lesson Scripture from Joshua 2:3-9, 15-16, 22-24. Think about whom you can depend on if you need protection.

Write on newsprint:

❑ questions for "Identify Experiences of Protection the Learners Have Had and Praise God for Them."

❑ information for next week's lesson under "Continue the Journey."

❑ activities for further spiritual growth under "Continue the Journey."

LEADING THE CLASS

(1) Gather to Learn

❖ Welcome the class members and introduce any guests.

❖ Pray that all who have gathered today will be ready to receive the Word of God and act upon it.

❖ Brainstorm answers to this question and list them on newsprint: **Who (or what) needs protection in today's world?**

❖ Discuss together or in small groups (a) why these people (and things) need protection and (b) who may be looking out for them.

❖ Read aloud today's focus statement: **Most people want to know they are or can be protected from harm. On whom can we depend for protection? God used Rahab to protect the spies from harm when she hid them from the soldiers the king of Jericho had sent to find them.**

(2) Examine the Relationship Between Rahab and the Two Spies Sent Out by Joshua

❖ Choose a volunteer to read Joshua 2:3-9, 15-16, 22-24.

❖ Dig deeper into this Bible lesson by reading or retelling information from Understanding the Scripture, which covers all of Joshua 2.

❖ Discuss these questions:
  (1) **Why do you think the spies trusted Rahab?**
  (2) **Why do you think Rahab trusted the spies?**
  (3) **What motivated Rahab to betray her own people by helping the Israelites?** (Be sure to consider the role that fear of the Israelites might have played.)
  (4) **What words would you use to describe Rahab?** (See the last paragraph of "Hospitality, Sanctuary, and Protection" in Interpreting the Scripture.)

(3) Appreciate the Challenge of Deciding Between "the Lesser of Two Evils"

❖ Read: **Recall that Rahab faced a huge moral dilemma. She had offered hospitality to Israelite spies and had learned of their business. Based on what she knew of the Israelites, she expected them to be able to bring down Jericho—and with it her family and herself. When local authorities came to track down the spies, Rahab had to choose: Would she turn them in or act as a traitor to her own people?**

❖ Read this modern moral dilemma: **The father of a child suffering from a rare and deadly disease learns of a new drug that has shown great promise. He hears that he can get this drug from a nearby lab, but when he inquires he is told that it will be $25,000. The father scrapes together savings and borrows from friends but is still short. Knowing that his child will die without treatment, he begs to buy the drug for the $17,500 he has raised, but his offer is refused because the lab is in business to make money. Having tried to get the drug legally, the desperate father now considers a break-in to steal the drug. What would you do under these circumstances? Why?** (See www.haverford.edu/psych/ddavis/p109g/kohlberg.dilemmas.html for more dilemmas.)

❖ Talk with the class members about the choices they would have made had they been this father. What criteria did they use to decide? Was there a single value that drove their decision? (Recognize that not all class members may use the same criteria or draw the same conclusion.)

❖ Wrap up this portion by reading "Truth and Consequences" from Interpreting the Scripture. Note that often there are no "good" choices. Rather, we must decide between the lesser of two evils, just as Rahab did. The real challenge is in choosing which one is actually "the lesser."

(4) Identify Experiences of Protection the Learners Have Had and Praise God for Them

❖ Invite the students to talk in small groups about experiences they have had that required God's protection. Suggest that they look at the list brainstormed earlier during the Gather to Learn activity for ideas. (Be aware that some adults may be in the midst of a situation that they do not wish to disclose.)

❖ Guide the discussion by posting these questions:

(1) **What kind of situation were you in that cried out for God's protection?** (Possible responses include: *illness, job loss, family crisis, death of a loved one, natural disaster, a financial crisis.*)

(2) **How had you tried to address this situation on your own?**

(3) **What did you do to solicit God's help—and when did you do it?**

(4) **How did God respond?**

(5) **How did God's response affect your faith and your willingness to trust God even more?**

❖ Conclude by inviting volunteers to offer a word of praise for God's protection.

(5) Continue the Journey

❖ Pray that all who have come today will go forth trusting in God's protection and care.

❖ Read aloud this preparation for next week's lesson. You may also want to post it on newsprint for the students to copy.

■ **Title: God Is Victorious**
■ **Background Scripture: Joshua 5:13–6:27**
■ **Lesson Scripture: Joshua 6:2-3, 4, 12-20**
■ **Focus of the Lesson: People in general hope to obtain victory in all endeavors. Is destruction of land and people justified by achieving victory? The Bible teaches that God used destruction of Jericho for the benefit of God's people.**

❖ Challenge the students to complete one or more of these activities for further spiritual growth related to this week's session. Post this information on newsprint for the students to copy.

(1) **Give careful attention to planning a major project for church, community, or home, just as Joshua carefully considered an attack on Jericho.**

(2) **Look for opportunities to trust someone you hardly know, perhaps for something as simple as directions. Was your trust rewarded? If not, what went wrong?**

(3) **Examine your own life. Where, right now, do you need to trust God for protection? Turn the problem over to God in prayer.**

❖ Sing or read aloud "Give to the Winds Thy Fears."

❖ Conclude today's session by leading the class in this benediction: **May you go forth now in peace, surrounded by the love of God and by the love of this community of faith. Amen.**

UNIT 1: GOD'S PEOPLE LEARN FROM PROSPERITY
GOD IS VICTORIOUS

PREVIEWING THE LESSON

Lesson Scripture: Joshua 6:2-3, 4, 12-20
Background Scripture: Joshua 5:13–6:27
Key Verse: Joshua 6:16

Focus of the Lesson:

People in general hope to obtain victory in all endeavors. Is destruction of land and people justified by achieving victory? The Bible teaches that God used destruction of Jericho for the benefit of God's people.

Goals for the Learners:

(1) to look into the story of Jericho to see how and why victory was obtained.
(2) to explore their own feelings toward war and violence of any nature.
(3) to look at the walls of Jericho in society and find ways to cause them to tumble down.

Pronunciation Guide:

Adonai (ad oh' ni)   Sabaoth (sab' ay oth)
Rahab (ray' hab)

Supplies:

Bibles, newsprint and marker, paper and pencils, hymnals

READING THE SCRIPTURE

NRSV
Joshua 6:2-3, 4b, 12-20b

²The LORD said to Joshua, "See, I have handed Jericho over to you, along with its king and soldiers. ³You shall march around the city, all the warriors circling the city once. Thus you shall do for six days. . . . On the seventh day you shall march around the city seven times, the priests blowing the trumpets.

NIV
Joshua 6:2-3, 4b, 12-20b

²Then the LORD said to Joshua, "See, I have delivered Jericho into your hands, along with its king and its fighting men. ³March around the city once with all the armed men. Do this for six days. . . . On the seventh day, march around the city seven times, with the priests blowing the trumpets.

¹²Then Joshua rose early in the morning, and the priests took up the ark of the LORD. ¹³The seven priests carrying the seven trumpets of rams' horns before the ark of the LORD passed on, blowing the trumpets continually. The armed men went before them, and the rear guard came after the ark of the LORD, while the trumpets blew continually. ¹⁴On the second day they marched around the city once and then returned to the camp. They did this for six days.

¹⁵On the seventh day they rose early, at dawn, and marched around the city in the same manner seven times. It was only on that day that they marched around the city seven times. **¹⁶And at the seventh time, when the priests had blown the trumpets, Joshua said to the people, "Shout! For the LORD has given you the city.** ¹⁷The city and all that is in it shall be devoted to the LORD for destruction. Only Rahab the prostitute and all who are with her in her house shall live because she hid the messengers we sent. ¹⁸As for you, keep away from the things devoted to destruction, so as not to covet and take any of the devoted things and make the camp of Israel an object for destruction, bringing trouble upon it. ¹⁹But all silver and gold, and vessels of bronze and iron, are sacred to the LORD; they shall go into the treasury of the LORD." ²⁰So the people shouted, and the trumpets were blown. As soon as the people heard the sound of the trumpets, they raised a great shout, and the wall fell down flat.

¹²Joshua got up early the next morning and the priests took up the ark of the LORD. ¹³The seven priests carrying the seven trumpets went forward, marching before the ark of the LORD and blowing the trumpets. The armed men went ahead of them and the rear guard followed the ark of the LORD, while the trumpets kept sounding. ¹⁴So on the second day they marched around the city once and returned to the camp. They did this for six days.

¹⁵On the seventh day, they got up at daybreak and marched around the city seven times in the same manner, except that on that day they circled the city seven times. **¹⁶The seventh time around, when the priests sounded the trumpet blast, Joshua commanded the people, "Shout! For the LORD has given you the city!** ¹⁷The city and all that is in it are to be devoted to the LORD. Only Rahab the prostitute and all who are with her in her house shall be spared, because she hid the spies we sent. ¹⁸But keep away from the devoted things, so that you will not bring about your own destruction by taking any of them. Otherwise you will make the camp of Israel liable to destruction and bring trouble on it. ¹⁹All the silver and gold and the articles of bronze and iron are sacred to the LORD and must go into his treasury."

²⁰When the trumpets sounded, the people shouted, and at the sound of the trumpet, when the people gave a loud shout, the wall collapsed.

UNDERSTANDING THE SCRIPTURE

Joshua 5:13-15. The conquest of Jericho began with a deeply personal religious experience for Joshua. The exact time and circumstances of this experience are not given. The "once" (NRSV) or "now when" (NIV) that begins Joshua 5:13 is like "once upon a time," and Joshua's being "by" or "near" Jericho provides no specific context.

Joshua saw a man armed with a sword; and when he asked whether the man was friend or foe, the man answered that neither applied. He was the "commander of the army of the LORD" (5:14, 15)—a title that Joshua might rightly have thought belonged to himself.

Joshua recognized something special

about the man and bowed down before him in reverence. Joshua's address, "my lord," employs the Hebrew word *Adonai*. This word can be used either as a name of God or as an address for a person of rank. The NIV understands it in the former sense ("What message does my Lord have for his servant?") but footnotes the latter sense, and the NRSV follows the latter sense ("What do you command your servant, my lord?"). The man had neither a "command" (NRSV) nor a "message" (NIV), but rather staked a claim on a holy place. He repeated the words of God spoken to Moses from the burning bush (Exodus 3:5) and thereby implied that Jericho "and all that is in it shall be devoted to the LORD" (Joshua 6:17).

Divine messengers often prepare believers for tasks that are both demanding and challenging (Genesis 22:11; Exodus 3:2). God was about to commission a military attack that was imposing and unconventional. Joshua had to be prepared to listen and to obey.

Joshua 6:1-14. Jericho was shut up tight under the threat of the Israelite army. The city was well-fortified. Archaeologists have uncovered evidence of a stone retaining wall 12-15 feet tall supporting an embankment that led up to a mudbrick wall six feet thick and 20-26 feet high. Because the city had abundant water from numerous springs and had supplies from a recently gathered harvest (3:15), it was prepared for a long siege. In the face of such fortifications, the Lord declared to Joshua, "See, I have handed Jericho over to you" (6:2), and proceeded to give Joshua specific instructions on how the city would be captured.

Joshua meticulously followed God's instructions in executing the plan. A procession of the army, guarding the ark of the covenant both before and aft, circled the city of Jericho early in the morning. The ark was a chest, originally made at God's command by Moses to house the two stone tablets of the law (Deuteronomy 10:1-5). It served as a visible symbol of the presence of Yahweh among the chosen people and as a unifying institution for the twelve tribes. On occasions such as this, it seems to have been viewed as a safeguard that protected the nation.

Priests carried the ark and were preceded by seven priests who continuously blew trumpets made of ram's horn. A contingent of armed men marched ahead of the trumpeters, and a rearguard followed behind the ark. Joshua told the members of the procession to remain silent until instructed otherwise. For six consecutive days, the procession circled the city once early each morning. Only the sound of the trumpets was heard—the whole approach was the epitome of psychological warfare.

Joshua 6:15-21. On the seventh day, the routine was broken—an ominous sign for the citizens of Jericho. After the first rotation around the city, instead of returning to the camp as before, the army marched on. A second time, then a third, and on, until seven circuits had been made of the city. Apparently the trumpets then fell silent, and the voice of Joshua rose over the silence, "Shout! For the LORD has given you the city" (Joshua 6:16; compare 6:2). The trumpets then sounded, the people "raised a great shout," and the wall of the city "fell down flat" (6:20). Whether by natural means like an earthquake or some other providential act, the strong and seemingly impenetrable walls of the mighty city collapsed. Apparently the inner mudbrick walls fell outward (the Hebrew suggests it "fell beneath itself"), covering the retaining walls and providing a ramp-like access into the city.

The instructions Joshua gave the people in 6:17-19 seem to have been inserted between the command to shout in verse 16 and the people shouting in verse 20. Certainly Joshua would have spelled out earlier (perhaps as part of the preparation for the assault in verse 10) that the city and all in it were devoted to the Lord for destruction. The oath to protect Rahab and her household also would fit reasonably in that earlier context. The last moment seems an inappropriate time to spell out in detail how certain booty was devoted to destruction and other more precious booty was devoted to the treasury of the Lord, though a reminder would have been appropriate.

The army charged straight ahead into the city from all sides and captured it, devoting all they encountered "to destruction by the edge of the sword" (6:21).

Joshua 6:22-27. All the men and women in Jericho, young as well as old, along with all the oxen, sheep, and donkeys were killed. Only Rahab and all her kindred were spared (6:23). The two spies whom Rahab had protected went in and brought them out of the city. Since Rahab's house was in the city wall, this might have been a rescue mission aided by the crimson cord in the window. Excavations of Jericho by the German archaeologists in 1907-11, however, found an undamaged eight-foot-high portion of Jericho's north wall with houses built against it. Some later scholars think the Germans were more zealous to validate the Bible story than to do scientific study, and the dating of that wall to the time of Joshua is still disputed; but it does provide another possible explanation of how Rahab and her family were saved from the destruction.

INTERPRETING THE SCRIPTURE

Devotion to God

Though the term is not used, most interpreters would equate the armed "commander of the army of the LORD" (Joshua 6:14, 15) with an angel. The words for "angel" in both Hebrew and Greek originally meant "messenger" or "envoy." The term did not always signify a spiritual being, though the association with a spiritual being was closer in New Testament times. Yet, the Greek term was used of the forerunner of the Messiah (Matthew 11:10; Mark 1:2, Luke 7:27), the disciples of John (7:24) and Jesus (9:52), and even of Joshua's spies (James 2:25).

Joshua did not need a messenger per se from God. Although we do not know the exact means of communication, God already had been speaking directly and specifically to Joshua (Joshua 1:1-9; 3:7-8; 4:1-3, 15; 5:2, 9). God did, however, send a messenger. With sword drawn, the messenger declared himself to be "commander of the army of the LORD." The term "army" is the singular form of the familiar Sabaoth, which is sometimes left untranslated in the King James Version. It can be translated "armies," "hosts," or "almighty." The Lord Almighty has hosts of armies, but this messenger was commander-in-chief of them all.

The messenger called Joshua to a decisive moment of spiritual reflection. Such moments are imperative before undertaking a command from God that is both so challenging and so filled with ethical and moral consequences. Joshua had to prepare himself for absolute obedience. Conquering Jericho required discipline to follow the explicit directions for seven days of pomp and circumstance—and faith to think that a shout could bring down the citadel walls. In the face of moral ambiguities, it required unswerving obedience to devote to destruction all the men, women, and animals in the city.

Given issues our country has faced recently in dealing with just war, appropriate force, the treatment of prisoners, and interrogation techniques, we will struggle with the moral implications of Joshua's conquest. Before we enter into battle, we had best stand for a while on holy ground ensuring that we are serving God, not asking God to serve us. We win our battles when we are aligned with God, not when we ask God to align with us. Standing on holy ground, we too will ask, "What do you command your servant?" (5:14).

Your Will Be Done

One thing we must not overlook in the conflicting moral viewpoints raised by Joshua's example is a truth learned at the foot of the cross. Sometimes the most despicable acts, the most brutal force, and the most heinous deeds produce positive outcomes in God's redemptive plan.

In our sensitivities as followers of Jesus, we certainly should feel some discomfort in using Joshua's conquest as a source for biblical principles to be followed. So much of what Jesus taught conflicts with the attitudes and actions that seem to underlie Joshua's destruction of Jericho. Where is love of neighbor or of enemy evidenced in Joshua? Where is turning the other cheek, doing good to those who hate you, or going the second mile? Where is the God who sees the sparrow fall?

Many people prefer to leave moral ambiguity out of the picture. The end justifies the means in their view. If the goals are worthy and morally acceptable, then any method no matter how repulsive is justified to achieve those means. Unfortunately, too often our views of what is worthy, morally acceptable, and good are shaped by self-centered concerns devoid of sensitivity to God's voice and will. We certainly should feel uncomfortable when God is depicted using means that seem questionable to our beliefs to achieve worthy goals. We probably will feel less uncomfortable if we view God as bringing the best results out of humanity's reprehensible means.

Trusting God to know what is best and to bring constructive outcomes is part of the challenge we face when we pray, "Your kingdom come. Your will be done, on earth as it is in heaven" (Matthew 6:10). Just as

God can take broken, sinful individuals and redeem them, so God can bring good results from the despicable things done by broken, sinful humanity. We confidently see that in the cross. We may not see it so confidently in Jericho, Hiroshima, Bagdad, or Kabul.

Keeping Promises

In the midst of giving the final orders that would bring the walls of the city down, Joshua reminded the troops of the promise made to Rahab (6:17). After the walls had fallen and the city was under full attack, Joshua sent the two men whose lives Rahab had protected to bring her and her kindred out of the midst of the destruction (6:22).

Rahab had made the promise a sacred one, "Swear to me by the LORD" (2:12). She demonstrated her good faith by protecting the spies and then by guiding them in their escape. She kept the sign of their agreement, the crimson cord, in her window (2:18, 21). She kept their business secret. The only unfulfilled stipulation was to gather her kindred into her house where Rahab and her family would be protected. There the spies found that she had been fully faithful in their covenant.

The spies put their lives at risk when they pledged to keep their promise: "If a hand is laid upon any who are with you in the house, we shall bear the responsibility for their death" (2:19). If Rahab or any kin had died in the attack, their pledge, "Our life for yours" (2:14) would have been broken. The reverse, "Our death for yours," would have been justified.

Too many promises are broken today. "I'll pay you back." "You can count on me." "I'll make it good." " 'Til death do us part." Few people seem to care if their reputations are marred by broken promises. Personal integrity is not a high priority for many. Believers, however, bear a high accountability because God's reputation is at stake in our integrity. In the Sermon on the Mount, Jesus called his disciples to a personal integrity so complete that a mere yes or no from a believer is trustworthy and no oath is required (Matthew 5:33-37). A life of integrity is "the light of the world" that "cannot be hid" (5:14). It gives glory to God.

Facts and Faith

Jericho is one of the most excavated archaeological sites in the Middle East. Numerous archaeologists have explored the site, each generation using improved techniques and more sophisticated methods in gathering and evaluating data. The conclusions have varied widely. Some contend the data fully validate the biblical account. Others find no such validation.

Most archaeologists agree that Jericho was destroyed and burned; they disagree on the when. The Book of Joshua does not provide a date for the fall of Jericho. Some have attempted to assign a date based on evidence in the Bible alone. Scientific data tell us that the city was destroyed and burned about 1550 B.C.

If the Bible intentionally provided a detailed chronology, we would be concerned if scientific data contradicted that chronology. In reality, much of the dating of Old Testament times is based on extrapolation from a multitude of disjointed passages that in themselves were not attempting to provide a comprehensive chronology. Enough gaps exist to allow a considerable range of possible dates.

The fact is that Jericho and many other Canaanite sites were destroyed. When that happened is clearer now than in the early years of excavation, but how it happened is beyond our ability to establish scientifically. The facts do not "prove" the biblical account, but they provide sufficient support for us to affirm generally the biblical record.

SHARING THE SCRIPTURE

Preparing Our Hearts

Explore this week's devotional reading, found in Psalm 98:1-6. Notice how this psalm praises God for deeds of salvation. God is not only able to save but also committed to doing so. God is always victorious! For that reason people and all of nature are called to praise God. What reasons do you have to praise God today? Use a musical instrument or your voice to sing a new and joyful song to the Lord.

Pray that you and the adult learners will continually praise our saving God who does "marvelous things" (98:1).

Preparing Our Minds

Study the background Scripture from Joshua 5:13–6:27 and the lesson Scripture from Joshua 6:2-3, 4b, 12-20b. Explore your beliefs as to whether the destruction of land and people can be justified to achieve a victory.

Write on newsprint:
❑ information for next week's lesson, found under "Continue the Journey."
❑ activities for further spiritual growth in "Continue the Journey."

Locate the words to "Joshua Fit the Battle of Jericho." You can find them on many Internet websites. Enlist a singer in the group to sing the verses and have the class join on the chorus for your closing hymn.

Research the concept of "holy war." Plan to use this material as an option under "Explore the Learners' Feelings Toward War and Violence of Any Nature." *The New Interpreter's Study Bible* includes information on "holy war" on page 314.

LEADING THE CLASS

(1) Gather to Learn

❖ Welcome the class members and introduce any guests.

❖ Pray that all who have gathered for today's session will be open to hearing and responding to God's message for them.

❖ Prompt the students to name modern instances where one group of people attacked another to gain control of land. Likely, the victors also killed the residents of the land they were hoping to conquer. Talk with the class about their beliefs about whether or not killing and taking land are justifiable actions.

❖ Read aloud today's focus statement: **People in general hope to obtain victory in all endeavors. Is destruction of land and people justified by achieving victory? The Bible teaches that God used destruction of Jericho for the benefit of God's people.**

(2) Look Into the Story of Jericho to See How and Why Victory Was Obtained

❖ Call on a volunteer to read Joshua 6:2-3, 4b, 12-20.

❖ Discuss these questions with the class:

(1) **How did Joshua and the people conquer Jericho?**

(2) **God sets forth a battle plan in verses 1-5, which is executed in the remaining verses of the lessons. How were the Israelite people able to be victorious, even though they apparently had no weapons?**

(3) **Had you been an Israelite, how would you have felt about this victory, seeing the destruction and yet knowing that this was the land of promise?**

(4) **What does this story reveal to you about the nature of God?**

❖ Use information from Understanding the Scripture and "Facts and Faith" in Interpreting the Scripture to discuss the lay-out of the city, preparations for war made by both sides, and archeological evidence about the siege of Jericho.

(3) Explore the Learners' Feelings Toward War and Violence of Any Nature

❖ Read or retell "Your Will Be Done" from Interpreting the Scripture.

❖ Form groups of three and ask each group to respond to this question: **The story of the conquest of Jericho leads readers to the conclusion that God used the destruction of this city for the benefit of God's people. As a follower of Christ, what moral dilemmas does the story of Joshua's conquest of Jericho raise for you?**

❖ Bring the groups together and invite them to report on key points of their discussions.

❖ Post a sheet of newsprint with these words written at the top: *Whenever I hear of war or violence, my first response is. . . .* Invite the students to add a word or phrase to finish this sentence. Some responses may focus on feelings; others may want to seek information about the "why" of the conflict; others may indicate actions that support or undermine the war effort.

❖ **Option:** Present information about the Israelites' understanding of "holy war" that you have researched. Field comments from the students.

(4) Look at the Walls of Jericho in Society and Find Ways to Cause Them to Tumble Down

❖ Challenge the adults to consider "walls of Jericho" present in their community. Are there major barriers that need to be removed so that God's plans for the kingdom can move forward? List these barriers on newsprint. They may include situations such as: *few safe activities for teens; crime; environmental degradation; pockets of poverty; lack of affordable housing.*

❖ Distribute paper and pencils. Form groups of three or four. Ask each group to select one barrier and brainstorm ways that this class (or the entire congregation or a coalition of churches) can work together, under God's direction, to cause this barrier to tumble.

❖ Invite the groups to discuss their ideas. Poll the class to see if there is interest in "attacking" one of these barriers. If so, form a task force that will:

- more fully research the problem.
- learn how governmental, non-profit, or church groups in the community are working to address it.
- evaluate the brainstormed ideas for workable solutions.
- consider the resources available to the class (church or coalition) and suggest ways that this group can work to alleviate the problem.
- report back to the class in several weeks with their findings.

❖ Help the class to understand that they will likely not, for example, solve the problem of homelessness. But they may be able to provide shelter in the church building during winter months. Or they may be able to put together kits of toiletries, ready-to-eat food, and other useful items to distribute to homeless persons in the community. They may also be able to work with elected officials to bring about policy changes that will improve life for those who are currently homeless, such as more transitional housing.

❖ Conclude this portion by inviting all who are willing to march around this "Jericho wall" to help tear it down to clap their hands.

(5) Continue the Journey

❖ Pray that all who have come today will work together to obtain victories that God calls them to accomplish.

❖ Read aloud this preparation for next week's lesson. You may also want to post it on newsprint for the students to copy.

- **Title: God Reacts to Disobedience**
- **Background Scripture: Joshua 7:1–8:29**
- **Lesson Scripture: Joshua 7:1, 10-12, 22-26**
- **Focus of the Lesson: The fear of God means different things to different people. Are we punished for disobeying God? The Bible teaches that the consequence for disobeying God is severe punishment.**

❖ Challenge the students to complete one or more of these activities for further spiritual growth related to this week's session. Post this information on newsprint for the students to copy.

(1) **Examine archeological research related to Jericho. You will find conflicting reports. Which research seems most compelling to you?**

(2) **Think about a project in your own church where real teamwork is needed. What are you trying to accomplish? How are you pulling together with a team leader to get the job done? What obstacles are you facing? What do you need to overcome these obstacles?**

(3) **Consider this question: Is war ever justifiable? What reasons can you give to support your answer?**

❖ Sing or read aloud "Joshua Fit de Battle of Jericho." You can easily locate the words of this spiritual on the Internet. The tune will probably be familiar to at least some of the class members.

❖ Conclude today's session by leading the class in this benediction: **May you go forth now in peace, surrounded by the love of God and by the love of this community of faith. Amen.**

UNIT 1: GOD'S PEOPLE LEARN FROM PROSPERITY
GOD REACTS TO DISOBEDIENCE

PREVIEWING THE LESSON

Lesson Scripture: Joshua 7:1, 10-12, 22-26
Background Scripture: Joshua 7:1–8:29
Key Verse: Joshua 7:1

Focus of the Lesson:
The fear of God means different things to different people. Are we punished for disobeying God? The Bible teaches that the consequence for disobeying God is severe punishment.

Goals for the Learners:
(1) to explore how sin and punishment are seen in the story of Achan.
(2) to discern their feelings about punishment for wrongdoing and their thoughts about whether violence is the way God reacts.
(3) to identify actions within the church they deem as disobedience to God and take steps to correct the problem.

Pronunciation Guide:
Achan (ay' kan)   Carmi (kahr' mi)
Achor (ay' kohr)   Zabdi (zab' di)
Ai (eye)   Zerah (zihr' uh)

Supplies:
Bibles, newsprint and marker, paper and pencils, hymnals, map showing Ai

---

READING THE SCRIPTURE

NRSV
Joshua 7:1, 10-12, 22-26

¹But the Israelites broke faith in regard to the devoted things: Achan son of Carmi son of Zabdi son of Zerah, of the tribe of Judah, took some of the devoted things; and the anger of the LORD burned against the Israelites.

NIV
Joshua 7:1, 10-12, 22-26

¹But the Israelites acted unfaithfully in regard to the devoted things; Achan son of Carmi, the son of Zimri, the son of Zerah, of the tribe of Judah, took some of them. So the LORD's anger burned against Israel.

---

¹⁰The LORD said to Joshua, "Stand up! Why have you fallen upon your face? ¹¹Israel has sinned; they have transgressed my covenant that I imposed on them. They have taken some of the devoted things; they have stolen, they have acted deceitfully, and they have put them among their own belongings. ¹²Therefore the Israelites are unable to stand before their enemies; they turn their backs to their enemies, because they have become a thing devoted for destruction themselves. I will be with you no more, unless you destroy the devoted things from among you. ²²So Joshua sent messengers, and they ran to the tent; and there it was, hidden in his tent with the silver underneath. ²³They took them out of the tent and brought them to Joshua and all the Israelites; and they spread them out before the LORD. ²⁴Then Joshua and all Israel with him took Achan son of Zerah, with the silver, the mantle, and the bar of gold, with his sons and daughters, with his oxen, donkeys, and sheep, and his tent and all that he had; and they brought them up to the Valley of Achor. ²⁵Joshua said, "Why did you bring trouble on us? The LORD is bringing trouble on you today." And all Israel stoned him to death; they burned them with fire, cast stones on them, ²⁶and raised over him a great heap of stones that remains to this day. Then the LORD turned from his burning anger. Therefore that place to this day is called the Valley of Achor.

¹⁰The LORD said to Joshua, "Stand up! What are you doing down on your face? ¹¹Israel has sinned; they have violated my covenant, which I commanded them to keep. They have taken some of the devoted things; they have stolen, they have lied, they have put them with their own possessions. ¹²That is why the Israelites cannot stand against their enemies; they turn their backs and run because they have been made liable to destruction. I will not be with you anymore unless you destroy whatever among you is devoted to destruction. ²²So Joshua sent messengers, and they ran to the tent, and there it was, hidden in his tent, with the silver underneath. ²³They took the things from the tent, brought them to Joshua and all the Israelites and spread them out before the LORD. ²⁴Then Joshua, together with all Israel, took Achan son of Zerah, the silver, the robe, the gold wedge, his sons and daughters, his cattle, donkeys and sheep, his tent and all that he had, to the Valley of Achor. ²⁵Joshua said, "Why have you brought this trouble on us? The LORD will bring trouble on you today."

Then all Israel stoned him, and after they had stoned the rest, they burned them. ²⁶Over Achan they heaped up a large pile of rocks, which remains to this day. Then the LORD turned from his fierce anger. Therefore that place has been called the Valley of Achor ever since.

UNDERSTANDING THE SCRIPTURE

Joshua 7:1-15. After the successful campaign against Jericho, Joshua implemented a similar strategy against the city of Ai. Spies were sent to reconnoiter Ai, and the spies' assessment corresponds with that of contemporary scholars—the city did not amount to much. It was overshadowed by its nearby neighbor west of Jericho, Bethel, which dominated the central highlands area and is mentioned more in the Bible than any other city except Jerusalem. With the exception of Jeremiah 49:3 and references in Joshua 7–10, Ai is always referenced in association with its more prominent neighbor.

The spies concluded that Ai would be a slam-dunk. Only a few men were there, and a couple of thousand Israelite soldiers should make quick work of its capture.

Then the surprise—the meager forces of Ai routed the Israelites. The ones who had melted the hearts of those in Jericho learned what the experience was like: Their hearts "melted and turned to water" (7:5; compare 2:11 and 5:1).

Joshua and the elders of Israel were distraught. After their successes across the Jordan and in Jericho, they expected their enemies to fall easily before them. Now they saw defeat being snatched out of the jaws of victory. This defeat had the potential of rallying the Canaanites and would surely lead to Israel's being wiped out.

God revealed the problem to Joshua. Israel had sinned. Against God's command, someone among them had taken as their own possessions some of the devoted things from Jericho. This breach of the covenant resulted in the withdrawal of God's protection over the people. The only remedy was to consecrate themselves, remove the devoted things from among them, and destroy the one who broke the ban along with all that belonged to him.

Joshua 7:16-26. Following God's instructions, Joshua called the twelve tribes to come before the Lord. Lots were probably drawn, and the tribe of Judah was chosen. The clans of Judah were called forward, and the clan of Zerah was chosen by lots. Next the families in the clan came forward, and the family of Zabdi was chosen. Joshua then had Zabdi's family come forward man by man. The lot fell on Achan, Zabdi's grandson.

Joshua confronted Achan, and Achan confessed that he had sinned against the Lord. The plunder, which was to have been dedicated to destruction or consecrated to the Lord and held in the treasury, had appealed to Achan. He coveted what he saw and took a beautiful Babylonia robe, 200 silver shekels (about five pounds), and a wedge of gold weighing 50 shekels (about 1¼ pounds). Achan had hidden this plunder in the ground inside his tent.

Joshua sent messengers to Achan's tent.

They found the booty and brought it to Joshua, who spread it out before the Lord in view of all the Israelites. Then Joshua and the Israelites gathered up the booty, Achan, all of his children, all of his animals, and even his tent. They took all to the Valley of Achor ("achor" means "trouble" in Hebrew). This valley was located southwest of Jericho on what would later be the northern border of Judah. From the prophetic references of a hopeful future for the valley (Isaiah 65:10 and Hosea 2:15), it must have been isolated and barren.

With a word play on the name of the place (or the valley may have been named subsequently with reference to this event), Joshua asked, "Why did you bring trouble on us? The LORD is bringing trouble on you today" (Joshua 7:25). Then "all Israel" stoned Achan to death; burned him, his family, and possessions; and "raised over him a great heap of stones" (7:26). The writer of Joshua notes that the pile of stones was still serving as a marker of this event in his own time.

The burning of Achan turned aside the "burning anger" of the Lord.

Joshua 8:1-13. With the issue of broken "faith in regard to the devoted things" (7:1) resolved, the Lord assured Joshua that he had no further reason for fear. The Lord declared in advance that Ai, its king, people, city, and land had been handed over to Joshua. In this case, however, perhaps in recognition of the way the people had handled the previous ban against the sacred things, God declared that all the booty from Ai could be kept by the Israelites.

As with Jericho, the Lord also gave Joshua the strategy for taking the city. Recognizing that the citizens of Ai had been emboldened by their prior victory, the strategy involved hiding a large contingent of Israelite troops on the far side (south) of the city away from the main Israelite forces. The next day Joshua brought the main army to Ai, putting a small contingent on the west side (toward Bethel) and the main army on the north side of the city. There they spent the night.

Joshua 8:14-29. Early the next morning, the king of Ai hurriedly brought his confident troops out to engage the Israelites in battle. Once engaged, the Israelites feigned defeat and fled. The king summoned all the men of Ai and of their neighbor Bethel to join in the pursuit. In doing so, they left Ai open and unprotected.

With the city vulnerable, God told Joshua to give the signal—a sword raised toward the city—that would launch the attack of the forces waiting in ambush. These troops rushed unimpeded into the city; and following the instructions given them earlier (8:8), they immediately set the city on fire. The smoke of the burning city quickly caught the attention of the Canaanite forces and took the wind out of their sails. With the Canaanites confused and disoriented, the Israelites who had been pursued, turned and attacked. Caught between the attack from those they had been pursuing and an attack from those who had burned the city, none of the warriors from Ai survived or escaped.

The Israelites then turned back to the city and completed the devastation. Twelve thousand—all the people of Ai (8:25)—died at the hands of the Israelites. Only the king of Ai was taken alive (8:23). Later he was hanged and buried under a heap of stones at the city gate (8:29). That marker also continued to exist in the day of the writer of Joshua; and the name of the city itself—Ai, "the ruin"—remained attached to this "heap of ruins."

INTERPRETING THE SCRIPTURE

Obeying the Rules

Contrary to popular wisdom, rules are not made to be broken. Rules are designed to ensure fairness and equal opportunity. Those who choose to break the rules generally do so to gain some personal advantage. Most who break the rules fail to recognize that their advantage comes at the expense of those who abide by the rules.

Armies (like all kinds of societies) operate on the basis of rules and discipline. While some may view the rules as excessive and overbearing, in reality the rules establish levels of expectation that ensure a consistent performance under the pressure of combat conditions. Those who have witnessed the vandalism of urban riots understand what happens when each person is out for self. If every Israelite soldier had entered Jericho with the primary purpose of grabbing the most booty possible, the army would have become a mob and members would have turned on each other. Without a clear and equitable plan, anarchy would have prevailed. In the end, everyone would have done what was right in their own eyes.

The story of Achan is a story of broken rules. Of all the warriors in the Israelite army, only one chose to ignore the ban against taking booty. Some might dismiss this as a story about a capricious God who withholds booty on one hand and hands it out on another, who punishes an entire nation for one person's sin and destroys all the inhabitants of a city for no apparent reason, and who speaks directly to humanity on one hand while forcing the Israelites to cast lots to determine God's will on the other. Some see God as following the secularist's Golden Rule, that is, the one who has the gold makes the rules.

Army discipline is based on immediate obedience to every command. The assumption is that the commander knows more about the strategic situation than do the troops. Questioning a command or hesitating to follow one can result in chaos and defeat. Jesus reminded his followers that "the sabbath was made for humankind, and not humankind for the sabbath" (Mark 2:27); and the same can be said for all God's rules. Our divine Commander-in-Chief knows how best to guide us in finding fulfillment. All we must do is follow the rules.

Disobedience and Its Consequences

In the view of many today, sin is an outmoded concept. It speaks of unnatural repression, unwarranted restraint, and trumped-up guilt. It inhibits rather than frees. It limits rather than expands. It fosters introspective navel-gazing and quashes the "just-do-it" spirit of our time. It stifles natural drives, human experiences, and self-expression. It strips the joy out of life. Taking personal or corporate sin seriously in the face of such contemporary thinking is difficult.

While a few might think that success is a winning lottery ticket by chance, most people would acknowledge that success requires discipline. Focus, determination, passion, and hard work characterize most of those who succeed in any field. Too often, however, discipline is not enough; and too many individuals try to enhance their chances of success by breaking the rules to gain an advantage. Athletes take performance-enhancing drugs. Business executives cook the financial books. Public servants accept "contributions" in exchange for influencing legislation. Law enforcement officials receive "gifts" for looking the other way. Judges tilt the balance in favor of the wealthy and powerful. Sexual favors are exchanged for promotions. Friends pave the way for their buddies. Specifications are changed midstream so that a contract goes to a friend.

Often such behaviors are conducted out of the public view. The perpetrators think nothing of their indiscretions until someone takes notice and announces it. Though we may not see immediate benefits for the obedient, we certainly see the detriments that haunt the disobedient. Things done in secret

are shouted from the housetops (Luke 12:3). Promising careers are ruined. Marriages are shattered. The innocent suffer. Victims seek revenge. God turns away. "If I had only known" voices regretful grief.

Make a note that justice will ultimately prevail. The guilty will be punished. The righteous will be blessed. The God who knows all will judge graciously but righteously. The consequences will fall justly on the disobedient.

Justice and Its Application

Justice often is depicted as a blindfolded woman holding a set of scales in her hand. That symbol emerged in ancient Egypt, Greece, and Rome; but the depictions often included different symbols. In Egypt, Justice carried a sword (symbolizing justice) and wore an ostrich feather in her hair (symbolizing truth). In Rome, Justice often was portrayed wearing a blindfold and evenly balancing both scales and a sword. Sometimes she held the fasces (a bundle of rods around an ax symbolizing judicial authority). Each of those symbols represents an important dimension of justice: truth, fairness, impartiality, authority, and punishment.

While Hebrew society shunned graven images, we can see in the story of Ai the central elements of the Hebrew concept of justice. Fundamentally Israel's concept was founded in the law of God. The parameters of right and wrong were established by God, not legislated by human authorities. From the commandments given to Moses on Mount Sinai through the vast array of regulations incorporated in the rest of the Pentateuch, God's law stood supreme. When God spoke—whether by revelation, by edict, or by prophet—the people were bound by covenant to obey. At Ai, Joshua acted as the spokesman for God in establishing the ban on all the booty from the city.

Israel's concept of justice was strengthened by the clear statement of the law and the consequences of breaking it and by the equal application of the law to all. In the last lesson, we noted the somewhat awkward insertion of the ban between the command to shout (Joshua 6:16) and the actual shout (6:20). This last-minute reminder clearly stated the expectations of the ban. It noted the consequences that would fall on all the people if the ban were broken (6:18). It clearly applied to all and was accepted by all—except Achan.

Note the community's involvement in upholding justice. When sin affected the people, all Israel was brought together to seek justice. All the people were examined equally. When the lot fell on Achan, he was confronted before all the people. He was called to acknowledge God's justice by giving glory to God and making a confession.

Note the references to "all the Israelites" and "all Israel" in 7:23, 24, and 25. When the evidence of Achan's wrongdoing was retrieved, it was laid out before the whole congregation. Together they took Achan to the Valley of "Trouble," and together they executed the sentence by stoning Achan and burning him, his family, and all his possessions.

Some may think the kind of punishment inflicted on Achan was primitive and excessive, but the process by which justice was sought and rendered clearly upheld the values of truth, fairness, impartiality, authority, and punishment that we hold dear even today.

Justice is not easy in our day of confusing and conflicting regulations, sporadic and selective administration, inequitable treatment for those who cannot afford legal representation, and punishment often meted out away from public scrutiny. Confidence in our ideal of justice for all would be strengthened if we had clearer statements of the law, clearer warnings of the consequences of disobeying the law, equal application of the law to all, and greater community involvement in all aspects of our legal system—just as the Israelites did.

SHARING THE SCRIPTURE

Preparing Our Hearts

Explore this week's devotional reading, found in Romans 6:1-11. In contrast to today's lesson, which focuses on Achan's sin and punishment, Paul writes to the church at Rome that those who follow Christ are not to sin. We have been buried with Christ and have risen with him in our baptism. As a result, we are no longer "enslaved to sin" (6:6). Paul insists that, on one hand, we must consider ourselves "dead to sin" and on the other, "alive to God in Christ Jesus" (6:11). What evidence supports Paul's assertion that you are dead to sin and alive to God?

Pray that you and the adult learners will recognize your wrongdoings and do whatever possible to correct them.

Preparing Our Minds

Study the background Scripture from Joshua 7:1–8:29 and the lesson Scripture from Joshua 7:1, 10-12, 22-26. As you read think about whether you believe that we are punished for disobeying God.

Write on newsprint:
- ❑ information for next week's lesson, found under "Continue the Journey."
- ❑ activities for further spiritual growth in "Continue the Journey."

LEADING THE CLASS

(1) Gather to Learn

❖ Welcome the class members and introduce any guests.

❖ Pray that those in attendance will be sensitive to their impact on the community of faith that surrounds them.

❖ Read these quotations about "the fear of God."

- Sir Thomas Browne (1605–1682): **I fear God, yet am not afraid of him.**
- Oswald Chambers (1874–1917): **The remarkable thing about fearing God is that when you fear God, you fear nothing else, whereas if you do not fear God, you fear everything else.**
- Samuel Johnson (1709–1784): **Shame arises from the fear of men, conscience from the fear of God.**

❖ Engage the class in a conversation about what the term "the fear of God" means to them. List their ideas on newsprint.

❖ Read aloud today's focus statement: **The fear of God means different things to different people. Are we punished for disobeying God? The Bible teaches that the consequence for disobeying God is severe punishment.**

(2) Explore How Sin and Punishment Are Seen in the Story of Achan

❖ Choose a volunteer to read Joshua 7:1, 10-12, 22-26.

❖ Use the map on page 357 to locate Jericho, Bethel, and Ai.

❖ Fill in the blanks by summarizing points from Understanding the Scripture. This information covers all of the background Scripture, which will help the students better understand what happened at Ai and how Achan's hoarding of booty from Jericho disobeyed God. This disobedience had a terrible affect on the entire community of faith, as well as on Achan himself.

❖ Discuss these questions:

(1) **What does this story tell you about God's expectations for obedience?**

(2) **What does this story tell you about God's response to disobedience?**

(3) **Do you believe that one disobedient person within a faith community can bring as much hardship to the group as Achan did? Explain your answer.**

(4) **What do you learn about God's justice from this story?**

(3) Discern Feelings About Punishment for Wrongdoing and Thoughts About Whether Violence Is the Way God Reacts

❖ Read or retell "Justice and Its Application" from Interpreting the Scripture.

❖ Ask these questions:

(1) **How do you feel about the punishment inflicted upon Achan for his disobedience?**

(2) **How do you feel about the lethal punishment inflicted upon Achan's family for his disobedience?**

(3) **What are the risks and rewards in trying to keep an entire faith community obedient to God?**

(4) **The Bible clearly records God's reaction to Achan's disobedience and sin. Do you perceive God as acting the way the Book of Joshua describes? If not, why not? If so, what attributes of God prompt you to accept this description?**

❖ Form groups of three or four. Distribute paper and pencils. Invite each group to make a list of crimes and suggest a fair penalty for each one. Remind them to take into account how each crime has affected a larger group of people when they determine the punishment. For example, how would the penalty meted out to a businessman who has defrauded people out of millions of dollars be different from the one meted out to the pickpocket who stole a wallet containing $50?

❖ Call the class together to share these lists. Invite them to comment on any insights they have gained about justice, particularly as we humans understand that concept.

(4) Identify Actions Within the Church the Learners Deem as Disobedience to God and Take Steps to Correct the Problem

❖ Read or retell "Disobedience and Its Consequences" from Interpreting the Scripture.

❖ Post a sheet of newsprint. List ways the class thinks that the contemporary church is acting disobediently toward God. Include both actions and attitudes that could be seen as contrary to the will of God. (Recognize that not all class members may agree on each example of disobedience. Also, look at the church in general, rather than issues within your own congregation, which need to be addressed in another context.)

❖ Write a brief description of the consequences the students see for each type of disobedience next to the action or attitude listed.

❖ Discuss with the class (or in small groups) steps that the church can take to correct at least two of these problems.

(5) Continue the Journey

❖ Pray that today's participants will learn lessons from the Bible so that they may avoid the agony of defeat that Achan and the Israelites experienced.

❖ Read aloud this preparation for next week's lesson. You may also want to post it on newsprint for the students to copy.
- **Title: Listen to God's Judges**
- **Background Scripture: Judges 2; 21:25**
- **Lesson Scripture: Judges 2:11-19**

■ **Focus of the Lesson: When things are going well, people tend not to worry about spiritual things. When things are not going well, what spiritual resources will we need? In the period of the judges, the people ignored God when things were going well, but in times of trouble, they repented and cried out to God for help. God raised up a judge to provide the help they needed.**

❖ Challenge the students to complete one or more of these activities for further spiritual growth related to this week's session. Post this information on newsprint for the students to copy.

(1) **Read the story of Ananias and Sapphira, found in Acts 5:1-11. What similarities and differences do you note between the way these two dealt deceitfully with the church and the way Achan dealt with the Israelite faith community?**

(2) **Review the story of Achan in Joshua 7:10-26. Think about ways that you are violating God's directions. Confess those sins. Be ready to make amends as God leads you.**

(3) **Help someone who has experienced hardship as a result of the sin or disobedience of someone else.**

❖ Sing or read aloud "Jesus Calls Us."

❖ Conclude today's session by leading the class in this benediction: **May you go forth now in peace, surrounded by the love of God and by the love of this community of faith. Amen.**

UNIT 2: LISTENING FOR GOD IN CHANGING TIMES
LISTEN TO GOD'S JUDGES

PREVIEWING THE LESSON

Lesson Scripture: Judges 2:11-19
Background Scripture: Judges 2; 21:25
Key Verse: Judges 2:17

Focus of the Lesson:
When things are going well, people tend not to worry about spiritual things. When things are not going well, what spiritual resources will we need? In the period of the judges, the people ignored God when things were going well, but in times of trouble, they repented and cried out to God for help. God raised up a judge to provide the help they needed.

Goals for the Learners:
(1) to investigate the story of the judges that God raised up to help the Israelites.
(2) to appreciate the impact of obedience and disobedience on their relationship with God.
(3) to design a plan that will help them depend on God through good times and bad times.

Pronunciation Guide:
Ashtoreth (ash' tuh reth)   Baal (bay' uhl) or (bah ahl')
Astarte (as tahr' tee)

Supplies:
Bibles, newsprint and marker, paper and pencils, hymnals

READING THE SCRIPTURE

NRSV
Judges 2:11-19
   ¹¹Then the Israelites did what was evil in the sight of the LORD and worshiped the Baals; ¹²and they abandoned the LORD, the God of their ancestors, who had brought them out of the land of Egypt; they followed

NIV
Judges 2:11-19
   ¹¹Then the Israelites did evil in the eyes of the LORD and served the Baals. ¹²They forsook the LORD, the God of their fathers, who had brought them out of Egypt. They followed and worshiped various gods of the

other gods, from among the gods of the peoples who were all around them, and bowed down to them; and they provoked the LORD to anger. ¹³They abandoned the LORD, and worshiped Baal and the Astartes. ¹⁴So the anger of the LORD was kindled against Israel, and he gave them over to plunderers who plundered them, and he sold them into the power of their enemies all around, so that they could no longer withstand their enemies. ¹⁵Whenever they marched out, the hand of the LORD was against them to bring misfortune, as the LORD had warned them and sworn to them; and they were in great distress.

¹⁶Then the LORD raised up judges, who delivered them out of the power of those who plundered them. **¹⁷Yet they did not listen even to their judges; for they lusted after other gods and bowed down to them.** They soon turned aside from the way in which their ancestors had walked, who had obeyed the commandments of the Lord; they did not follow their example. ¹⁸Whenever the LORD raised up judges for them, the LORD was with the judge, and he delivered them from the hand of their enemies all the days of the judge; for the LORD would be moved to pity by their groaning because of those who persecuted and oppressed them. ¹⁹But whenever the judge died, they would relapse and behave worse than their ancestors, following other gods, worshiping them and bowing down to them. They would not drop any of their practices or their stubborn ways.

peoples around them. They provoked the LORD to anger ¹³because they forsook him and served Baal and the Ashtoreths. ¹⁴In his anger against Israel the LORD handed them over to raiders who plundered them. He sold them to their enemies all around, whom they were no longer able to resist. ¹⁵Whenever Israel went out to fight, the hand of the LORD was against them to defeat them, just as he had sworn to them. They were in great distress.

¹⁶Then the LORD raised up judges, who saved them out of the hands of these raiders. **¹⁷Yet they would not listen to their judges but prostituted themselves to other gods and worshiped them.** Unlike their fathers, they quickly turned from the way in which their fathers had walked, the way of obedience to the Lord's commands. ¹⁸Whenever the LORD raised up a judge for them, he was with the judge and saved them out of the hands of their enemies as long as the judge lived; for the LORD had compassion on them as they groaned under those who oppressed and afflicted them. ¹⁹But when the judge died, the people returned to ways even more corrupt than those of their fathers, following other gods and serving and worshiping them. They refused to give up their evil practices and stubborn ways.

UNDERSTANDING THE SCRIPTURE

Judges 21:25. Although Israel had "rest" during Joshua's last days (Joshua 21:43-44) and the tribes settling east of the Jordan had been released to return home (22:1-4), all of Canaan had not been subdued. Following the death of Joshua, some tribes of Israel acted independently to secure their territo-

ries (Judges 1:22) or joined with a neighboring tribe to do so (1:3). Against God's explicit command, however, most of the tribes allowed Canaanites to continue to live in their midst (1:27-33). This disobedience opened the door for pagan influences that drew the Israelites away from God. The result was a cycle of sin, suffering, restoration, and deliverance that became the theme of the Book of Judges.

Prior to the choice of Saul as Israel's first king, Israel was led by a series of leaders called "judges," from whom the Book of Judges derived its name. The Hebrew word for "judge" could mean a law-giver, an official who settled controversies, or a governing authority who executed judgments. The term is applied specifically in the Book of Judges, however, to a military leader specially empowered by God in a time of oppression to deliver and lead God's people. Their role was situational and focused on restoring the integrity of God's people as keepers of the law and the covenant.

Judges 21:25 serves both as a conclusion to the Book of Judges and as a summary of the consequences when God's people fail to heed God's voice, follow God's law, and keep God's covenant.

Judges 2:1-10. The covenant that God made with Israel involved a promise that God would deliver the nation from Egyptian bondage and guide the people to a new land. Israel's part of the covenant was to secure the land, avoid entanglements with the inhabitants of the land, and rid the land of pagan influence. As long as they remained obedient, God would aid them in driving out their enemies.

The Israelites broke the covenant by allowing Canaanites to continue to live in their midst. God confronted the nation by sending an "angel" (Judges 2:1, "messenger of God" in Hebrew), who indicted their disobedience and highlighted the consequences. The Canaanites would be constant "adversaries" (2:3). The term translated "adversaries" is literally "sides" and probably recalls God's warning to Moses about "thorns in your sides" (Numbers 33:55). Their gods would become a "snare" for God's people (Judges 2:3).

The response to this indictment was immediate. The Israelites wept and offered sacrifices to God. They returned to their apportioned lands to take possession of them. As long as Joshua and the "elders" who had served with Joshua lived to remind them of what great things God had done for Israel, the people remained faithful to God; but they still failed to purge the Canaanite influence from their midst. After Joshua's generation passed, "another generation grew up after them, who did not know the LORD or the work that he had done for Israel" (2:10).

Judges 2:11-15. The new generation, which had little personal experience with God and few memories of God's interaction with the nation, soon fell under the influence of the Canaanite gods. The "Baals" (2:11) were associated with fertility among the Canaanites. Baal meant "master" and signified ownership. The name generally was joined to a locality or particular sphere of influence under the god's control (see Deuteronomy 4:3). As the Israelites settled in the Promised Land, locality became more important. As they turned their occupations toward agriculture, fertility gained import.

The "Astartes" (2:13 NRSV) is actually a Greek form of a Hebrew word "Ashtoreths" (NIV), which itself is an intentional mispronunciation of Athtarath or Ashtarath. Late Hebrew scribes added the vowels from the Hebrew word for "shame" to the Canaanite name to produce Ashtoreth.)

The Astartes' association with the Baals is strong, and they likely were goddesses of love and fertility who were reverenced as givers of life.

The Israelites abandoned their devotion to God and followed, bowed down to, and worshiped the gods of the people around them. "They provoked the LORD to anger" (Judges 2:12). In response to their unfaithfulness, God withdrew protection from the people. The Israelites could no longer withstand their enemies; they suffered misfortune at every turn; and they were plundered by the enemies all around them.

Judges 2:16-23. Though the Israelites had abandoned God, God did not abandon them. The first reference to "judges" in the book at verse 16 reflects the initiative of God to address the distress into which the people had fallen. Before the book gets into accounts about particular judges, the writer gives an overview of the cycle in which the people found themselves throughout this period in their history.

The account stresses these aspects of God's role in the stories to follow: God's compassion for Israel when the people suffered from oppression (2:18); God's initiative in raising up judges (2:16, 18); God's presence with the judge in the deliverance of the people (2:18); God's anger at Israel's stubbornness when they fell back into old ways (2:20); and God's unwillingness to restrain adversaries when Israel continued in sin (2:21).

On the other hand, the account underscores these aspects of Israel's role in the stories: the people's failure to follow the example of their ancestors (2:17); their lusting after other gods and worshiping them (2:17); their refusal to listen to the judges provided by God (2:17); the constant relapse into deeper sins by each generation (2:19); and the stubbornness of the people in holding on to their sinful ways (2:19).

Verse 22 affirms the absolute sovereignty of God in all that was happening to Israel. Israel's failure to drive out its adversaries actually was the result of God's plan. God did not hand these adversaries over to Joshua but instead left them in place to test Israel, to see whether "they would take care to walk in the way of the Lord as their ancestors did" (2:22; compare 3:4). Thus, the issue was not so much Israel's failure to destroy the adversaries as it was Israel's willingness to make covenants with these people (2:2) and accommodate their evil influences.

INTERPRETING THE SCRIPTURE

Passing on Faith

Often in the secular media people refer to the strong influence on their lives of a parent, grandparent, or another person of faith and spiritual strength. Too often the life of the person claiming the influence demonstrates little of that faith and spirituality. The values of many admirers depart significantly from the values exhibited by their role models.

Joshua and the elders of Israel were people of faith. They had traveled the hard road from Egyptian bondage through wilderness wanderings to warfare in the Promised Land. They weren't perfect, and they made mistakes along the way; but when they perceived that they had departed from God's course, they changed directions and sincerely sought to follow God's way. They somewhat compare to "the Great Generation" in our day—the men and women who suffered the Great Depression, overcame the tyranny of two world wars, and built strong institutions of church, education, and industry.

Joshua and his contemporaries discovered that great achievements made through faith do not ensure that the faith will be preserved in or appreciated by the next generation. Faith can be communicated but not transferred, embraced but not inherited. It can be believed deeply, lived exemplarily, and communicated passionately; but nothing ensures that it will be accepted, cherished, or even acknowledged by those who follow.

"Inherited" faith often is expressed with less passion, less conviction, and less devotion. The foundations laid by one generation only partially meet the needs of the next. Each new generation must discover its own foundations and have fresh experiences with God.

The School of Hard Knocks

The Book of Judges reminds us that good times often breed complacency. Prosperity can create presumption that we earned and deserve all that we enjoy. Happiness often is tied to how much we have, own, control, or consume; and many go to great lengths (and into deep debt) to ensure that such shallow happiness continues. Comfort often causes us to be less than sympathetic toward those who were not born into our favorable circumstances or who "have not worked as hard as we worked."

Individuals, families, communities, and nations often have to experience the lessons of hard times. Too often God's blessings already have departed before we even begin to acknowledge that God might make a difference after all. Sometime we have to be deprived before we recognize the lust for Mammon (Matthew 6:24; NRSV "wealth" or NIV "Money") that was controlling our lives.

The gods of our day are not called Baal or Astarte, but we have our own pantheon. We cannot relegate our God to some temple closet while we worship other gods and assume that we are exempt from the judgment of God and the school of hard knocks that is God's discipline.

The American generation that struggled through the Great Depression certainly did not wish for economic hardships; but during those difficult times, the values of faith, discipline, community, and simplicity were rediscovered. Sometimes great reversals are necessary to focus our attention on the path that we should have been taking all along.

Withdrawing, Destroying, or Permeating

"Their gods shall be a snare to you" (Judges 2:3) highlights the dangers of living in a pagan culture. Sin's enticements regularly ensnare many who find themselves in the wrong places or with the wrong people.

The natural reaction to danger is to shrink in fear and raise walls of protection. These two reactions are well-evidenced in our society. Some fearing the corrupting influence of a secular society withdraw into protected environments. They build tight communities based on common faith and practice. They home-school their children; they restrict what is read, heard, and watched. They think that what is endangered must be protected by a wall of separation. By withdrawing they often lose opportunities to foster change in their communities and weaken their influence on society.

By contrast, zealots seize the initiative and seek to destroy the threat. They wage war against the doctrines, the people, and the institutions that reflect values different from their own. They ban, banish, and sometimes bomb those who hold different points of view. They go for the jugular and seek to win regardless of the cost. Often the very values they espouse are denied by their attitudes and actions.

A third approach is reflected in several biblical analogies: "You are the salt of the earth; . . . you are the light of the world" (Matthew 5:13-14); "A little yeast leavens the whole batch of dough" (Galatians 5:9); and "Overcome evil with good" (Romans 12:21). Rather than withdrawing or destroying, God's people seek to permeate the world with good. Their good slowly but surely leavens the whole, transforms societies, and overcomes evil in the process.

Rather than being a leavening influence that transforms society from the inside, we can easily be overwhelmed by the influences around us. Too often our lights are not bright; our salt has lost its taste; and our good is undermined by self-centeredness (Luke 12:19; 1 Corinthians 15:32).

We cannot avoid being in the world, but we must guard against being of the world. Perhaps that is why so many of Jesus' last teachings to his disciples emphasized the need to be awake, aware, prepared, and ready to welcome his powerful presence that will overcome evil with good.

Temptation and Testing

After making a case for Israel's failures in maintaining fidelity to God, the writer of Judges drops a theological bombshell. All of the circumstances that led to Israel's failures were really part of a test God set up to see "whether or not Israel would take care to walk in the way of the LORD as their ancestors did" (Joshua 2:22). Israel's failure to follow God's direction and keep the covenant to drive out all of the Canaanites was part of God's plan. God had "left those nations, not driving them out at once, and had not handed them over to Joshua" (2:23).

The tension between such expressions of God's sovereignty and human accountability has been a divisive factor in Christendom that manifests itself in theological divisions among and within Christian denominations. The sovereignty versus free will controversy created a divide during the Protestant Reformation, and its roots go back much earlier. While we cannot resolve that issue here, we can gain some perspective from this study.

In both Hebrew and Greek, the words translated "tempt" also mean "test, try, or prove." The same word was used for "test" Israel (2:22) and for Gideon's "trial" or test of God with the fleece (6:39). Rather than viewing temptation as enticement to evil, temptation is testing to discover genuineness—like an assayer testing to discover if metal is genuine gold.

James equated enduring temptation with standing the test (James 1:12). He asserted that just as God is not tempted by evil, God does not tempt anyone (1:13). Rather, temptation involves one's own desires, which lure, entice, and finally conceive the embryo that gives birth to sin (1:14-15). Recall the example of Achan's sin (Joshua 7:20-21).

God's test of Israel revealed that their desires had lured them into the sinful practices of Canaanite religion. If God had created a wall of protection around Israel or had removed all of the Canaanite influence, Israel's faith and fidelity would have been untested and uncertain, not tried and true.

SHARING THE SCRIPTURE

Preparing Our Hearts

Explore this week's devotional reading, found in Psalm 78:1-8. The psalmist writes here of teaching our children about God's deeds and commandments so that they will not become "a stubborn and rebellious generation" (78:8). In today's Scripture lesson we will encounter a generation that did not follow God's ways and consequently were enmeshed in a cycle of unfaithfulness requiring God's deliverance. What are you and your congregation teaching children by words and by actions? What do they seem to be learning from these lessons and examples? What other help do they need?

Pray that you and the adult learners will be mindful of children so that they might learn and practice the ways of the Lord.

Preparing Our Minds

Study the background Scripture from Judges 2 and 21:25. The lesson Scripture is from Judges 2:11-19. Think about the kinds of spiritual resources people need when things are not going well.

Write on newsprint:

❑ information for next week's lesson, found under "Continue the Journey."

❑ activities for further spiritual growth in "Continue the Journey."

LEADING THE CLASS

(1) Gather to Learn

❖ Welcome the class members and introduce any guests.

❖ Pray that all who have gathered will listen for the message that God has for them today.

❖ Read this information: **According to information from the well-known Barna Research Group, after the 9/11 attacks in the United States, "church attendance spiked for several weeks, rising to about half of the adult public attending religious services during a typical week. That attendance boon proved to be short-lived, though, as levels were back to normal by November [2001]."**

❖ Ask: **Why does it seem that people reach for God when there is a crisis but revert to former ways when the immediate problem has passed?**

❖ Read aloud today's focus statement: **When things are going well, people tend not to worry about spiritual things. When things are not going well, what spiritual resources will we need? In the period of the judges, the people ignored God when things were going well, but in times of trouble, they repented and cried out to God for help. God raised up a judge to provide the help they needed.**

(2) Investigate the Story of the Judges that God Raised Up to Help the Israelites

❖ Set the stage for today's lesson by reading or retelling information for Judges 2:1-10 from Understanding the Scripture.

❖ Choose a volunteer to read Judges 2:11-19.

❖ Work with the students to identify the cycle that recurs among the Israelites throughout Judges: *prosperity, turning away from God, punishment by being oppressed by their enemies, repentance by the Israelites, God's raising up of a judge (military leader) who delivers the Israelites.* List this pattern on newsprint or illustrate it as a circle with spokes on a wheel.

❖ Discuss these questions:

(1) **Why do you suppose that when the Israelites experienced prosperity, a cycle of apostasy followed?** (Add to the discussion by reading the first paragraph of "The School of Hard Knocks" in Interpreting the Scripture.)

(2) **Why do you suppose that God both punished the people and then raised up someone who God empowered to deliver them?**

(3) **What similarities, if any, do you see between the Israelites and members of today's church?**

(3) Appreciate the Impact of Obedience and Disobedience on the Learners' Relationship With God

❖ Post newsprint and challenge the class to brainstorm answers to this question: **The Baals of the days of the judges caused the people to disobey and abandon God. Who are the gods of our age that beckon us Christians to follow them?**

❖ Form small groups to review the list and discern why people who have accepted Christ are so strongly pulled toward other gods. (Ideas may include: *society values what the gods of power and status have to offer; the materialism of our age runs counter to Christ's command to take up our cross daily and follow him; we want rewards in this life that cannot be obtained by making the choices and sacrifices necessary to be Christ's disciples.*)

❖ Bring the groups together to discuss their ideas.

❖ Invite the class members to tell brief stories of times when obedience to God truly strengthened their relationship, or times when disobedience threatened to rupture their relationship with God. Ask: **What lessons were learned from these two different approaches to one's relationship with God?**

❖ Conclude this portion of the lesson by providing a few moments of silence for the adults to reflect on this question: **If God is most important in my life, what steps can I take to be more faithful to God by steering clear of the idols that cause me to disobey?** Break the silence as the adults seem ready.

(4) Design a Plan that Will Help the Learners Depend on God Through Good Times and Bad Times

❖ Distribute paper and pencils. Ask the students to list as many situations as they can in 60 seconds where one needs to depend upon God.

❖ Form several small groups and encourage the groups to compare notes. Suggest that each group select one "good time" from their lists and one "bad time." Examples of "good times" when we really need to depend upon God may include: *welcoming a new family member, moving to a new community, starting a new job, getting married.* Examples of "bad times" may include: *serious illness, death of a loved one, financial crisis, unwanted life changes.*

❖ Create a plan or strategy for dealing with the selected "good time" and also the named "bad time." Remind the class that people often forget God in times of prosperity when things are going well. Often, it is harder to recognize our dependence on God during such good times.

❖ Invite each group to share one of their plans with the class. Other students may want to comment. It will be interesting to see the approach that two or more groups take to the same situation.

(5) Continue the Journey

❖ Pray that the learners will listen and obey God in all circumstances.

❖ Read aloud this preparation for next week's lesson. You may also want to post it on newsprint for the students to copy.

- ■ **Title: Use God's Strength**
- ■ **Background Scripture: Judges 3:7-31: 21:25**
- ■ **Lesson Scripture: Judges 3:15-25, 29-30**
- ■ **Focus of the Lesson: When the community is troubled and needs change, they may call for help and receive it. To whom should the people look for help? When the people cried to God for help, God answered by raising Ehud to save them from their oppressors.**

❖ Challenge the students to complete one or more of these activities for further spiritual growth related to this week's session. Post this information on newsprint for the students to copy.

(1) **Investigate the judges, the military leaders, whose stories are told in the Book of Judges. What impact do their periods of leadership have on the Israelites?**

(2) **Help someone who has turned away from God to turn back and be restored to God.**

(3) **Think about your congregation. Have they as a group turned from God in any way? If so, what needs to happen to return them to God? Pray for your church. Do whatever you can to be a helpful leader.**

❖ Sing or read aloud "Stand by Me."

❖ Conclude today's session by leading the class in this benediction: **May you go forth now in peace, surrounded by the love of God and by the love of this community of faith. Amen.**

UNIT 2: LISTENING FOR GOD IN CHANGING TIMES
USE GOD'S STRENGTH

PREVIEWING THE LESSON

Lesson Scripture: Judges 3:15-25, 29-30
Background Scripture: Judges 3:7-31; 21:25
Key Verse: Judges 3:15

Focus of the Lesson:

When the community is troubled and needs change, they may call for help and receive it. To whom should the people look for help? When the people cried to God for help, God answered by raising Ehud to save them from their oppressors.

Goals for the Learners:

(1) to explore the story of Ehud's saving the Israelites from King Eglon of Moab.
(2) to recognize that pleas for help can be answered with help from God.
(3) to ask for help in solving a current problem.

Pronunciation Guide:

amphictyony (am fik' tee uh nee)

Aram-naharaim
 (eh rahm'–nah' eh rah' yeem)

Asherahs (ah sher' rahs)

Astartes (as tahr' teez)

Cushan-rishathaim
 (koo' shahn–rihsh' ah thah' yeem)

Eglon (eg' lon)

Ehud (ee' huhd)

Gera (gee' ruh)

Gilgal (gil' gal)

Moab (moh' ab)

Othniel (oth' nee uhl)

Supplies:

Bibles, newsprint and marker, paper and pencils, hymnals

READING THE SCRIPTURE

NRSV
Judges 3:15-25, 29-30

15But when the Israelites cried out to the LORD, the LORD raised up for them a deliverer, Ehud son of Gera, the Benjaminite, a left-handed man. The Israelites sent tribute by him to King Eglon of Moab. 16Ehud made

NIV
Judges 3:15-25, 29-30

15Again the Israelites cried out to the LORD, and he gave them a deliverer—Ehud, a left-handed man, the son of Gera the Benjamite. The Israelites sent him with tribute to Eglon king of Moab. 16Now Ehud had for himself a sword with two edges, a cubit in length; and he fastened it on his right thigh under his clothes. [17]Then he presented the tribute to King Eglon of Moab. Now Eglon was a very fat man. [18]When Ehud had finished presenting the tribute, he sent the people who carried the tribute on their way. [19]But he himself turned back at the sculptured stones near Gilgal, and said, "I have a secret message for you, O king." So the king said, "Silence!" and all his attendants went out from his presence. [20]Ehud came to him, while he was sitting alone in his cool roof chamber, and said, "I have a message from God for you." So he rose from his seat. [21]Then Ehud reached with his left hand, took the sword from his right thigh, and thrust it into Eglon's belly; [22]the hilt also went in after the blade, and the fat closed over the blade, for he did not draw the sword out of his belly; and the dirt came out. [23]Then Ehud went out into the vestibule, and closed the doors of the roof chamber on him, and locked them.

[24]After he had gone, the servants came. When they saw that the doors of the roof chamber were locked, they thought, "He must be relieving himself in the cool chamber." [25]So they waited until they were embarrassed. When he still did not open the doors of the roof chamber, they took the key and opened them. There was their lord lying dead on the floor.

[29]At that time they killed about ten thousand of the Moabites, all strong, able-bodied men; no one escaped. [30]So Moab was subdued that day under the hand of Israel. And the land had rest eighty years.

made a double-edged sword about a foot and a half long, which he strapped to his right thigh under his clothing. [17]He presented the tribute to Eglon king of Moab, who was a very fat man. [18]After Ehud had presented the tribute, he sent on their way the men who had carried it. [19]At the idols near Gilgal he himself turned back and said, "I have a secret message for you, O king."

The king said, "Quiet!" And all his attendants left him.

[20]Ehud then approached him while he was sitting alone in the upper room of his summer palace and said, "I have a message from God for you." As the king rose from his seat, [21]Ehud reached with his left hand, drew the sword from his right thigh and plunged it into the king's belly. [22]Even the handle sank in after the blade, which came out his back. Ehud did not pull the sword out, and the fat closed in over it. [23]Then Ehud went out to the porch; he shut the doors of the upper room behind him and locked them.

[24]After he had gone, the servants came and found the doors of the upper room locked. They said, "He must be relieving himself in the inner room of the house." [25]They waited to the point of embarrassment, but when he did not open the doors of the room, they took a key and unlocked them. There they saw their lord fallen to the floor, dead.

[29]At that time they struck down about ten thousand Moabites, all vigorous and strong; not a man escaped. [30]That day Moab was made subject to Israel, and the land had peace for eighty years.

UNDERSTANDING THE SCRIPTURE

Judges 21:25. During the period when Israel had neither a king nor a central government, a loose confederation existed among the twelve tribes. Though the term is not used in the Bible, some have described this confederation as an "amphictyony." Derived from a Greek term meaning "dwellers around," amphictyony describes a league organized around a temple to protect and maintain it. Israel did not have a formal temple until the time of Solomon; but the "tent of meeting" at Shiloh (Joshua 18:1; 1 Samuel 2:22) is called a "house" (Judges 18:31; 1 Samuel 1:7) and a "temple" (1 Samuel 1:9 and 3:3).

The tent of meeting housed the ark of the covenant. Although the ark played an important role in the first eight chapters of Joshua, it is only mentioned once between Joshua 8:33 and the end of the Book of Judges. On that occasion the ark was in Bethel (Judges 20:26-27). After drawing lots at Shiloh to divide the conquered territory among the tribes (Joshua 18:1-6), neither Shiloh, the tent of meeting, nor the ark of the covenant seems to have played a very significant role for the tribes. Even the stories of the judges indicate that most had influence only in a tribe or two.

Amphictyony implies more agreement, structure, and relationship than seems to have existed following the time of Joshua. In actuality, not only "all the people" but also each of the tribes "did what was right in their own eyes."

Judges 3:7-11. Intermarriage between the Israelites and the Canaanites (Judges 3:5-6) led to an erosion of fidelity to God and the breaking of at least the first two of the Ten Commandments (Exodus 20:2-6). Attracted to the beliefs of their Canaanite spouses, the Israelites forgot the Lord and began worshiping the Baals and the Asherahs.

The Asherahs differ from the goddesses called Astartes (Judges 2:13, or Ashtoreths in NIV). The Old Testament does not clearly distinguish between the goddess Asherah and the objects that represented her and were part of her worship. Exodus 34:13 and other passages reference "Asherah poles" (NIV), which the New Revised Standard Version translates "sacred poles." "Asherah" was translated "wood" or "grove" in early Greek and Latin translations, and this precedent was followed in the King James Version.

In ancient mythology Asherah was a mother goddess who gave birth to 70 gods, including Baal. In depictions she was represented by poles, staffs, trees, and other wooden images. Those objects were called Asherahs. They stood upright on hills and in groves (1 Kings 14:23) and were associated with pagan practices (2 Kings 23:7). Her worship was supported later by Queen Jezebel (1 Kings 18:19).

This infidelity led God to subject the Israelites for eight years to King Cushan-rishathaim of Aram-naharaim, the area better known as Mesopotamia, from whence Abraham originally came. When the Israelites cried out to the Lord, God raised up Othniel, a nephew of Caleb, as "deliverer." That title is used in Judges only in chapter 3 for Othniel and Ehud. The title carries the idea of rescuer and savior. It shares the same Hebrew root from which the names Joshua and Jesus derived.

The Lord's spirit came upon Othniel, who judged Israel and led in a war of liberation of the people. Othniel judged Israel for 40 years, and the nation enjoyed "rest" during his time (Judges 3:11).

Judges 3:12-15. The cycle then repeated itself. Israel again did what was evil in the Lord's sight. God strengthened King Eglon of Moab. Eglon formed an alliance with the Ammonites and the Amalekites to attack Israel. The alliance defeated Israel, took possession of Jericho ("the city of palms"), and subjugated Israel for 18 years.

The Moabites and the Ammonites both descended from Lot through different daughters (Genesis 19:37-38). The Amalekites descended from Esau through his son and a concubine (36:12). Moab and Ammon had been protected territory during the Conquest (Deuteronomy 2:9, 37), although a king of Moab later fought against Israel (Joshua 24:9). The Amalekites had long provoked Israel, and God instructed Moses to "blot out the remembrance of Amalek from under heaven" (Deuteronomy 25:17-19).

Suffering again under foreign domination, the Israelites once again "cried out to the LORD" (Judges 3:15). Several Hebrew words are used for "cry out" in the Old Testament. One term found in Judges 15:18 is a general call. Another in Judges 14:17 and 21:3 refers to actual weeping. Two parallel terms, however, occur repeatedly beginning in Joshua 24:7 and continuing into Judges. They stress the anxious cry for help that grows out of alarm, distress, and need. One is used in Judges 3:9, 15, the other term in 4:3.

In response to their cry, God raised up another "deliverer," Ehud, from the tribe of Benjamin. Ehud was sent to Eglon with the required tribute, but he had another objective in mind.

Judges 3:16-25. Ehud was left-handed in a time of hand-to-hand combat predominantly fought right-handed. Ehud's left-handedness gave him an opportunity to conceal a sword under his clothes on the right side. A search for weapons would have focused on the left side from which a right-handed person would draw a sword.

"Eglon was a very fat man" (3:17). He could not move quickly to escape an up-close attack, and he certainly was no contest for a nimble fighter. More importantly, however, Eglon was over-confident. Ehud had just humbled himself before Eglon and had presented tribute from the subservient Israel. Eglon saw as a threat neither the Israelites in general nor one of them who recently had shown obeisance.

Ehud conspired to gain a one-on-one meeting with Eglon to deliver a "secret . . . message from God" (3:19-20). When he had Eglon alone in a chamber on the palace roof, Ehud drew his sword and killed Eglon. Quickly exiting the chamber, Ehud locked the chamber door and made his escape while the king's servants hesitated to knock at the door, afraid that they might interrupt the king's toilet. When they finally opened the door, they found the king lying dead on the floor.

Judges 3:26-31. Ehud quickly gathered an army in Ephraim, and the army followed Ehud into battle with the Moabites. They seized the fords across the Jordan so that the Moabites could not flee. Stripped of their leader, the Moabites were completely vanquished. Israel once again had rest, this time for 80 years.

Verse 31 briefly chronicles the achievements of another judge, Shamgar, who killed 600 Philistines and delivered Israel from a similar threat in the southwest.

INTERPRETING THE SCRIPTURE

The Consequences of Disobedience

Many people see little correlation between fidelity to God and what happens to individuals, families, churches, or nations. The idea that God intervenes directly or even indirectly in human affairs seems foreign to them. Stories like those about the judges seem like fairy tales to such folks.

Even believers struggle with such concepts because no direct correlation can be made between sin and punishment. Some times the most notorious sinners enjoy the greatest success, prominence, and wealth. They die with no remorse and little evidence of justice being rendered. Some of the most pious believers suffer failures, chronic diseases, and poverty. Their examples seem unnoticed.

Unable to reconcile such inequities, many hope for justice beyond the grave; but we can anticipate such justice only in faith. This lesson is about justice in this life. It deals with divine intervention both in the situations of believers and non-believers. It addresses the ups and downs that come from fidelity and infidelity to God.

To see God's hand at work in our world requires both eyes of faith and sensitivity to our own personal standing with God. When we are insensitive to God's presence, will, and ways in our lives, we likely will be equally insensitive in recognizing God's correction, discipline, and judgment. We will call it bad luck, bad karma, hard times, or momentary setbacks. When we evaluate success by worldly standards of dollars, possessions, health, and friends, we will overlook the consequences of disobedience and sin to the human spirit. Purpose, happiness, fulfillment, satisfaction, and achievement are hard to measure if the standards are not spiritual.

Maybe we can find God's hand judging and rewarding in statistical analyses (the righteous live longer, for example) or in the broad sweep of history (God and good win out in the end), but more likely we will find it personally when led by a "judge." That judge may be your conscience, a friend, a spiritual leader, the message of the Bible, the example of Christ, the Holy Spirit, or some other standard of spiritual valuation that discloses the emptiness of life without God and the prospect of abundant life with God. The problem is that we cannot move through the cycle from disobedience to forgiveness until we acknowledge our sin, repent, and return to faith and obedience. The alternative is alienation from God and spiritual bondage.

Calls for Help

We humans are better at calling for help than we are at identifying why we are in trouble in the first place. The financial crises that struck the world markets in the summer of 2007 illustrate that well. For five years the stock market roared upward, housing prices advanced dramatically, personal consumption of fluff took off into the stratosphere, mountains of debt were accumulated to support lavish lifestyles, and many apparently thought it would last forever.

When the foundations of the illusion began to crack, people looked for someone else to blame. They demanded protection from the consequences of their actions. They wanted scapegoats punished. They wanted to be bailed out by governmental saviors. There was enough blame to go around for almost everyone touched by the matter. I found myself wishing that people were more willing to own up to their bad judgments, irresponsible behaviors, and deceptive practices. No matter how loudly someone cries for help, if they do not acknowledge the need to change behaviors and practices, I wonder how seriously we can take their calls for help.

Fortunately God is more gracious than I am. Look through Judges 3 for some signs of repentance on the part of the Israelites. Can you find it? And the more the cycle of sin, oppression, deliverance, and restoration occurs in the book, the fewer and fewer reasons I can find for God to deal compassionately with a people who seem obstinate in their sins and inclined to repeat the same mistakes again and again.

One good thing is that under the judges' leadership, the Israelites came back to keeping God's law and holding on to the covenant—at least for a while. Maybe obedience is more important to God than we thought. Why else would God take those who repeatedly failed God's test and deliver them again and again under the guidance of judges like Othniel, Ehud, and Shamgar? Grace can be the only reason.

Sometimes we think that asking often, asking loudly, or asking persistently will make a difference. I am drawn by the example of the thief on the cross. In one last gasp of breath, that thief simply asked, "Jesus, remember me when you come into your kingdom" (Luke 23:42). Somehow the grace of God, unmerited but true, touched a life with loving forgiveness when he cried out for help. God requires nothing more complicated than that. If only we would stop demanding remorse, ritual cleansing, reformed lives, and 100 percent fidelity, perhaps we too would find that grace greater than our sins is only a call away.

Gifts for the Task at Hand

His introduction is intriguing: "The LORD raised up for them a deliverer, Ehud son of Gera, the Benjaminite, a left-handed man" (Judges 3:15). After labeling him "a deliverer," the writer first associated Ehud with his family, which was of the tribe of Benjamin. Although four people named "Gera" are mentioned in the Old Testament—two from the sixteenth century B.C. and one from the tenth century B.C.—Ehud's father is the Gera who lived during the twelfth century B.C.

Hidden from our English translation is a play on words. The name "Benjamin" means "son of the right hand." Ehud is a left-handed man in a tribe named for Jacob's youngest and cherished son, Benjamin, who after Joseph's disappearance was Jacob's "right-hand man."

If Ehud's day was like ours, the 7-10 percent of those who are left-handed experienced a number of obstacles. Society is so geared to the handedness of the majority that we have institutionalized our preferences. We shake with our right hands to show the good will of unarmed trust.

Grooms stand with the bride on the left, freeing their right hands to fend off other suitors. Even Jesus is placed at the right hand of God, symbolizing a place of dignity and honor. In many languages like Latin where *sinister* is the word for "left," even etymology shows preference for the right.

Sometimes being left-handed has advantages. In some sports left-handedness offers advantages. Left-handed pitchers, batters, and first basemen are highly prized in baseball. In earlier times, Roman phalanxes were formed by soldiers carrying swords in their dominant right hands and shields in their left. This tactic was successful until opponents discovered that when attacked from the shield side, the phalanx tended to rotate counter-clockwise as soldiers tried to bring their swords into action. When the phalanx rotated far enough, it was vulnerable from the rear. Putting left-handed soldiers on the left side of the phalanx solved that problem.

God took Ehud's left-handedness, which might be considered a hindrance, and used it for achieving God's purposes. We are likely very troubled by Ehud's deceitfulness, murder of King Eglon, and the subsequent death of ten thousand Moabites. Yet through this bloodshed the tribe of Benjamin was liberated from the oppression that they had endured under King Eglon for 18 years by Ehud, the deliverer chosen, gifted, and strengthened by God.

SHARING THE SCRIPTURE

Preparing Our Hearts

Explore this week's devotional reading, found in Psalm 27:7-14. In these verses we hear the cries of the psalmist as he asks God to pay attention to him and guide him. Are you seeking God? Why do you need God to focus attention on you right now? What guidance do you need to live your life more faithfully?

Pray that you and the adult learners will be confident in God's willingness to care for you.

Preparing Our Minds

Study the background Scripture from Judges 3:7-31; 21:25 and the lesson Scripture from Judges 3:15-25, 29-30. Contemplate who a community should look to when it needs help.

Write on newsprint:

❑ information for next week's lesson, found under "Continue the Journey."

❑ activities for further spiritual growth in "Continue the Journey."

Prepare the suggested lecture for "Explore the Story of Ehud's Saving the Israelites from King Eglon of Moab."

LEADING THE CLASS

(1) Gather to Learn

❖ Welcome the class members and introduce any guests.

❖ Pray that those who are present will become aware of where they can look for help.

❖ Encourage the class to think of times when a community has needed help and list those situations on newsprint. They may recall a specific incident. The event might have been a natural disaster such as a wildfire, flood, or hurricane. It might have been a community tragedy, such as school shooting, or a sniper who paralyzed an area, or a national upheaval such as 9/11.

❖ Invite the adults to talk about the kind of help the communities would need in each situation and where they might expect to find such help.

❖ Read aloud today's focus statement: **When the community is troubled and needs change, they may call for help and receive it. To whom should the people look for help? When the people cried to God for help, God answered by raising Ehud to save them from their oppressors.**

(2) Explore the Story of Ehud's Saving the Israelites From King Eglon of Moab

❖ Give a brief lecture based on Judges 3:7-11, 12-15 in Understanding the Scripture. Your presentation will set the stage for the rest of the lesson.

❖ Choose a volunteer to read Judges 3:15-25, 29-30.

❖ Discuss these questions, adding any information from Understanding the Scripture that may clarify the discussion.

(1) Why did the Israelites cry to the Lord?

(2) How did the Lord respond?

(3) What do you learn about Ehud? (Use "Gifts for the Task at Hand" in Interpreting the Scripture to fill in gaps.)

(4) Where do you see humor in this story?

(5) What questions might this story raise for you about God and the way God deals with people? (Recognize that the adults may have concerns about Ehud's deceitfulness, the immorality of an assassination plot, and God's role in Ehud's actions. This story does present difficult issues for Christians, so allow time for the students who choose to raise their concerns.)

(3) Recognize that Pleas for Help Can Be Answered With Help From God

❖ Read "Calls for Help" from Interpreting the Scripture.

❖ Post again the ideas brainstormed during the Gather to Learn segment. Suggest that the students review the list and recall the Bible lesson.

❖ Invite the students to tell brief stories of such situations and how they perceive that God was instrumental in solving them by asking: **What examples can you give of God helping people, including yourself, who cry out in need?** (Be aware that some class members may want to share stories of times when they feel they did not receive the help they needed, even from God. Be supportive of their concerns as well.)

❖ Form small groups and challenge them to think of instances in the Bible where an individual or group called upon God for help. In what ways did God respond? If time permits, invite the groups to report to the entire class.

(4) Ask for Help in Solving a Current Problem

❖ Distribute paper and pencils. Provide quiet time for the adults to reflect on a current problem that they are facing as individuals, as a church, or as a community. Encourage them to write a prayer asking for God's help.

❖ Invite volunteers to read aloud what they have written, as the class is in an attitude of prayer. After each reading, lead this unison response: **Lord, in your mercy, hear our prayer.**

❖ **Option:** Pull together those concerns raised about a church or community issue. As time permits, try to identify the cause of the problem, resources available for solving it, and any steps that the class might take to assist in this situation. Word of caution: Steer clear of "personality issues," which likely should not be discussed publicly. Instead, look for issues that require a concrete solution. Here's an example: The church is not attracting young families, though the neighborhood is teeming with children. The class is able to identify the lack of a nursery and inability to attract teachers to keep a children's Sunday school operating. Talk about how class members could help the Sunday school and how they might have a "toy shower" and do some painting to create a nice room where parents would feel comfortable leaving their precious infants and toddlers. Conclude this activity by asking for a show of hands of those who are willing to help be part of the solution to this problem.

(5) Continue the Journey

❖ Pray that today's participants will recognize that God's help comes to us in many ways, often through unexpected sources.

❖ Read aloud this preparation for next week's lesson. You may also want to post it on newsprint for the students to copy.

■ **Title: Let God Rule**
■ **Background Scripture: Judges 6–8; 21:25**
■ **Lesson Scripture: Judges 7:2-4, 13-15; 8:22-25**
■ **Focus of the Lesson: When leadership of a community is in transition, the people may abandon wise practices. To whom should the people look for wise leadership? The people should follow leaders who follow God.**

❖ Challenge the students to complete one or more of these activities for further spiritual growth related to this week's session. Post this information on newsprint for the students to copy.

(1) **Page through the Book of Judges. Make a list of the names of the judges. Research several to learn what you can about them. Why do you think each judge was chosen by God to lead and deliver the Israelites?**

(2) **Recall that Ehud took action against King Eglon of Moab, who imposed a huge tax burden on the Israelites. Use a concordance or other reference to find additional examples in the Bible where burdensome taxes pushed people into action.**

(3) **Listen for cries of oppressed people around the world. Who are these people? What are their circumstances? What can you do? Take whatever action you can.**

❖ Sing or read aloud "Out of the Depths I Cry to You."

❖ Conclude today's session by leading the class in this benediction: **May you go forth now in peace, surrounded by the love of God and by the love of this community of faith. Amen.**

UNIT 2: LISTENING FOR GOD IN CHANGING TIMES
LET GOD RULE

PREVIEWING THE LESSON

Lesson Scripture: Judges 7:2-4, 13-15; 8:22-25
Background Scripture: Judges 6–8; 21:25
Key Verse: Judges 7:15

Focus of the Lesson:

When leadership of a community is in transition, the people may abandon wise practices. To whom should the people look for wise leadership? The people should follow leaders who follow God.

Goals for the Learners:

(1) to investigate Gideon's attempts and mistakes in following God.
(2) to appreciate God's ability to rule, even when the learners and their leaders make mistakes.
(3) to examine whose rule they are following and adjust in order to follow God.

Pronunciation Guide:

Amalekite (uh mal' uh kite)   Joash (joh' ash)
ephod (ee' fod)   Keturah (ki tyoor' uh)
Ishmaelite (ish' may uh lite)   Manasseh (muh nas' uh)
Jerubbaal (ji ruhb bay' uhl)   Midian (mid' ee uhn)
Jezreel (jez' ree uhl)   teraphim (tehr' ah fihm)

Supplies:

Bibles, newsprint and marker, paper and pencils, hymnals

READING THE SCRIPTURE

NRSV
Judges 7:2-4, 13-15

²The LORD said to Gideon, "The troops with you are too many for me to give the Midianites into their hand. Israel would only take the credit away from me, saying,

NIV
Judges 7:2-4, 13-15

²The LORD said to Gideon, "You have too many men for me to deliver Midian into their hands. In order that Israel may not boast against me that her own strength has

'My own hand has delivered me.' [3]Now therefore proclaim this in the hearing of the troops, 'Whoever is fearful and trembling, let him return home.'" Thus Gideon sifted them out; twenty-two thousand returned, and ten thousand remained.

[4]Then the LORD said to Gideon, "The troops are still too many; take them down to the water and I will sift them out for you there. When I say, 'This one shall go with you,' he shall go with you; and when I say, 'This one shall not go with you,' he shall not go."

[13]When Gideon arrived, there was a man telling a dream to his comrade; and he said, "I had a dream, and in it a cake of barley bread tumbled into the camp of Midian, and came to the tent, and struck it so that it fell; it turned upside down, and the tent collapsed." [14]And his comrade answered, "This is no other than the sword of Gideon son of Joash, a man of Israel; into his hand God has given Midian and all the army."

[15]**When Gideon heard the telling of the dream and its interpretation, he worshiped; and he returned to the camp of Israel, and said, "Get up; for the LORD has given the army of Midian into your hand."**

Judges 8:22-25

[22]Then the Israelites said to Gideon, "Rule over us, you and your son and your grandson also; for you have delivered us out of the hand of Midian." [23]Gideon said to them, "I will not rule over you, and my son will not rule over you; the LORD will rule over you." [24]Then Gideon said to them, "Let me make a request of you; each of you give me an earring he has taken as booty." (For the enemy had golden earrings, because they were Ishmaelites.) [25]"We will willingly give them," they answered. So they spread a garment, and each threw into it an earring he had taken as booty.

saved her, [3]announce now to the people, 'Anyone who trembles with fear may turn back and leave Mount Gilead.'" So twenty-two thousand men left, while ten thousand remained.

[4]But the LORD said to Gideon, "There are still too many men. Take them down to the water, and I will sift them for you there. If I say, 'This one shall go with you,' he shall go; but if I say, 'This one shall not go with you,' he shall not go."

[13]Gideon arrived just as a man was telling a friend his dream. "I had a dream," he was saying. "A round loaf of barley bread came tumbling into the Midianite camp. It struck the tent with such force that the tent overturned and collapsed."

[14]His friend responded, "This can be nothing other than the sword of Gideon son of Joash, the Israelite. God has given the Midianites and the whole camp into his hands."

[15]**When Gideon heard the dream and its interpretation, he worshiped God. He returned to the camp of Israel and called out, "Get up! The LORD has given the Midianite camp into your hands."**

Judges 8:22-25

[22]The Israelites said to Gideon, "Rule over us—you, your son and your grandson—because you have saved us out of the hand of Midian."

[23]But Gideon told them, "I will not rule over you, nor will my son rule over you. The LORD will rule over you." [24]And he said, "I do have one request, that each of you give me an earring from your share of the plunder." (It was the custom of the Ishmaelites to wear gold earrings.)

[25]They answered, "We'll be glad to give them." So they spread out a garment, and each man threw a ring from his plunder onto it.

UNDERSTANDING THE SCRIPTURE

Judges 21:25. The conclusion that "in those days there was no king in Israel" is a recurring theme in Judges (17:6; 18:1; 19:1) and appears to indicate a time when the writer knew that a king ruled in Israel (compare Genesis 36:31). Deuteronomy 17:14-20 indicates that Moses knew that the Israelites in time would want a king like other nations (see also 28:36), and he warned of potential dangers. Some passages like Numbers 23:21 and 24:7 imply that the ideal was for God to rule as Israel's king, and the prophet Samuel appears to have held this view fervently. He only relented to the people's demands when God instructed him to anoint Saul as king (1 Samuel 8:4–9:17).

Prior to the time of Samuel and Saul, Israel sought to establish a dynastic kingship involving Gideon and his descendents.

Judges 6:1-32. Israel's cycle of sin began again with the people doing evil in the sight of the Lord. This time God gave the nation into the hand of the Midianites for seven years (6:1). The Midianites were descendents of Midian, a son of Abraham born to Keturah, Abraham's concubine and third wife. Midian and the other children of Keturah were given gifts and sent away so that Isaac could be established as Abraham's sole heir (Genesis 25:2-6). The Midianites became a nomadic people who roamed the desert regions east and south of Canaan.

The Midianites (with the Amalekites and other tribes from the east) regularly raided Israel, taking agricultural produce and livestock and leaving the Israelites with "no sustenance" (Judges 6:4) and "greatly impoverished" (6:6). Once again the people cried out to the Lord for help.

This time God chose Gideon as the judge to deliver God's people from oppression. Gideon was not the logical choice. He had deep doubts about God's intention to deliver Israel. He came from the weakest clan in the tribe of Manasseh and viewed himself as the least in his family. Yet God commissioned Gideon and assured him both that God would be with him and that Gideon was the one who would deliver Israel from the control of Midian. Still unconvinced, Gideon insisted on a sign from God. When the meal Gideon had prepared for the angel of the Lord was consumed by fire, Gideon was persuaded and cried out for the Lord's help.

God next instructed Gideon to pull down his father's altar to Baal and cut down the Asherah pole beside it. In their place he was to build an altar to God and sacrifice one of his father's bulls on the altar. Afraid of what his family and neighbors would think, Gideon did this at night. The next morning when the townspeople discovered what had been done and learned that Gideon was the culprit, they wanted to kill him for desecrating Baal's altar. His father, Joash, intervened, insisting that, if Baal were indeed a true god and was concerned about the destruction of his altar, Baal could contend for himself. This first act of purging the influence of Baalism earned Gideon the title "Jerubbaal," which means, "Let Baal contend against him."

Judges 6:33–7:14. Next Gideon turned his attention to Israel's oppressors. When the Midianites and their fellow invaders crossed the Jordan and set up a base in the Valley of Jezreel (a fertile valley that separates the regions later known as Galilee and Samaria and provided an east-west trade route from the Mediterranean to the Jordan Valley), "the spirit of the Lord took possession of Gideon" (6:34). Calling out members of his own clan first, Gideon sent messengers to neighboring tribes in the north. Thirty-two thousand men responded from four tribes, but Gideon showed lingering uncertainty about whether he was indeed the one to deliver Israel. He proposed a test for God. First Gideon laid out a fleece of wool overnight and asked God to give him a sign. If the fleece was wet but the ground around it dry the next morning, then Gideon claimed he would know that God was working through him. When that test confirmed his call, Gideon repeated the test asking for the opposite results as a sign— dry fleece and dew-covered ground.

With Gideon's call ascertained, God reversed the situation and put Gideon to the test. Sure that Israel would claim victory based on their own efforts, God insisted that Gideon pare the number of warriors. When those who were afraid were allowed to go home, the number of volunteers dropped to 10,000 (7:3). God then proposed another test. The men were led down to the river and were allowed to drink. God instructed Gideon to choose only those who lapped the water with their tongues, as a dog laps. Only 300 remained after this test. Gideon only retained jars and trumpets of those sent home.

That night God told Gideon to attack; but in recognition of Gideon's inclination to be afraid, God offered one more comforting sign. Gideon and his servant were to sneak down into the opponents' camp and listen to their conversations. When they overheard one guard telling of his dream and his comrade answering, "This is no other than the sword of Gideon . . .; into his hand God has given Midian and all the army" (7:14), Gideon received his last dose of inspiration.

Judges 7:15–8:21. Dividing the 300 into three groups and equipping each fighter with a trumpet and a jar with a torch inside, Gideon surrounded the enemy's camp. On signal from Gideon, each blew his trumpet, broke his jar unveiling the torch, and shouted, "A sword for the LORD and for Gideon" (7:20). Awakened from sleep the enemy panicked. They turned on one another in the darkness and confusion and fled back toward the Jordan with the Israelites in pursuit. Gideon then called the tribes who had contributed warriors to join the pursuit, along with others from Ephraim.

Crossing the Jordan in pursuit of the kings of Midian, Gideon sought supplies for his troops from inhabitants of two towns in the tribal territory of Gad. Later he punished those cities severely for their refusal to provide aid. Once Gideon had captured the kings of Midian, he confronted them with their earlier killing of his brothers. He then put them to death.

Judges 8:22-35. Following Gideon's triumph over the Midianites, the Israelites asked him to rule over them and to establish a hereditary succession. Gideon refused, holding to the tradition that only God will rule over the chosen people. Judges 9 records the tragic results for Gideon's family when one of his sons later tried to claim the office of king.

That was not the only tragic result of Gideon's victory. From the booty that Gideon and the rest of the Israelites took from the Midianites, Gideon made a gold ephod that weighed over 40 pounds. Most frequently "ephod" means a priestly garment (Exodus 28; 39; 1 Samuel 22:18), but two other references in Judges tie ephods to household idols called "teraphim" and the shrines in which they were housed (Judges 17:5; 18:14-20). Judges 8:27 implies that the ephod resulted in unfaithfulness to God in Gideon's family, as well as "all Israel."

Though Israel enjoyed 40 years of rest as long as Gideon lived, following his death Israel relapsed into their worship of the Baals. The cycle began again.

INTERPRETING THE SCRIPTURE

God Rules!

With the strong emphasis in the Old Testament on the monarchy that began with Saul, David, and Solomon, we, like Israel, sometimes forget that the underlying premise of the Old Testament is that God rules. The king was to be the visible symbol and the agent of the true king, God.

We also frequently fail to connect this Old Testament theme with the core of Jesus' message: the kingdom of God. In reality the foundational principle of both Testaments is that God is King who rules over the subjects of the kingdom.

Like the people of Old Testament times, we too are prone to want some visible symbol of God's rule. We incorrectly interpret God's kingdom as a realm where place, people, and power are evident. So we want buildings and organizations, popes and bishops, systems and controls that represent God's rule but too easily displace it.

When the writer of Judges repeatedly stated that "in those days there was no king in Israel" (21:25, for example), he omitted one very import phrase, "except God." The problem was that the people had rejected God's sovereignty in their lives and in their communities. But God was still King and remained so even when Saul, David, Herod, or Caesar sat on a throne.

When Jesus calls us back to God's rule, he doesn't call us to a place—to buildings, properties, realms, or countries. He doesn't call us to visible leaders who substitute for God, become exclusive channels for God's voice, or exercise authority and control over God's people and affairs. He doesn't call us to submit to human authorities and powers that dictate truth, define justice, or demand conformity. Jesus calls us to live under the guidance and protection of God, the King.

Of course, we cannot live without buildings, communities, leaders, and rules; but none of those must ever displace God from the throne of our hearts, our lives, and our churches.

Blessed Assurance

Most of us are very much like Gideon. We need a lot of assurance from God before we act on our commissions for God. We know that God loves us. We know that Christ died

for us. We know that we have been called to be part of a community of faith. We know that we have been sent into the world as ambassadors for Christ and witnesses to his life, death, and resurrection. We know that the Holy Spirit is with us guiding us each day. But translating all of that head knowledge into life experiences where we really do something for God is another matter.

Like Gideon, we wish for some angelic messenger who would just tell us what to do; but even when the messages come, we want some confirmations. *Surely not me! I'm just a nobody*, we think. Even when the messages, the invitations, and the calls are repeatedly confirmed, we draw back in fear. When God encourages us to be bold and assures us with peace, we still would rather build an altar to worship God than to get at the task to which God called us.

When the calls are explicit, confirmed, and certain, we test God by putting out the fleeces of alternatives, contingencies, and extenuations. When we do act, we act timidly like Gideon, preferring to be out of the spotlight even with our family and neighbors.

What should we do with our doubts and fears? First, we should admit them. We will make no progress in our discipleship if we fail to admit that we have doubts and fears. Second, we should acknowledge them to others. The ominous aspects of doubt and fear shrink when shared with others, primarily because we learn that we are not alone in experiencing them. We will make much better progress in dealing with doubt and fear when we confront them together rather than alone. Finally, we should be open in asking God to assuage our doubts and fears. We can expect God to be as patient and gracious with us as God was with Gideon. We also can pray that the spirit of the Lord will take possession of us as it did with Gideon (Judges 6:34).

Who's in Charge and Who Gets the Credit?

The best leaders and workers generally are those who do not care who gets credit for successes. They know that corporate success is never the result of one individual's efforts. Yet, many people make getting credit their primary goal even when they have contributed little to the actual effort involved. The desire for attention, affirmation, and status is strong and deep in all of us. Sometimes the competition for credit undermines teamwork and prevents the best results from being achieved.

God had Gideon pare the number of warriors in the battle against the Midianites for the express purpose of preventing the boasting that so often accompanies victories. The writer carefully records all of the Lord's interactions in the defeat of the Midianites. When the victory is assured, however, the late-arriving Ephraimites want to join in so they can take some credit for the victory. When the final celebration is under way, the Israelites want to name Gideon king, displacing the King who had been the primary force in the victory. Somehow they thought that breaking jars, blowing trumpets, and shouting in the night won the victory. They gave Gideon (and themselves) the credit.

When the story is finally concluded, however, the Israelites not only have cast aside the Lord "who had rescued them from the hand of all their enemies on every side" (Judges 8:34), but they also had withdrawn their loyalty from the family of Gideon, forgetting his contributions to Israel (8:35). The God who was such a necessary help in hard times suddenly finds no place at the head table when times are good.

Sometimes we fail our leaders by compromising our loyalty, our obedience, and our commitment. When the leader is God, such compromises are disastrous for individuals, families, churches, communities, and nations. When spiritual leadership is at stake, sometimes our false idols are our own take-charge egos. Maybe the time has come to snap to attention and respond with a resounding, "Aye, Aye, Sir!" We need to let God rule!

SHARING THE SCRIPTURE

Preparing Our Hearts

Explore this week's devotional reading, found in 1 Samuel 2:1-10. This passage, referred to as Hannah's prayer, gives thanks to God who delivered the people from oppression. Hannah, as you will recall, is the mother of Samuel, the prophet who God sends to anoint both Saul and David as king. What do you learn about God from this prayer?

Pray that you and the adult learners will seek and support leaders who are wise in the ways of the Lord.

Preparing Our Minds

Study the background Scripture from chapters 6, 7, 8, and 21:25 of Judges. Focus on the lesson Scripture from Judges 7:2-4, 13-15 and 8:22-25. Think about who you look to for wise leadership.

Write on newsprint:
- ❑ information for next week's lesson, found under "Continue the Journey."
- ❑ activities for further spiritual growth in "Continue the Journey."

Read Understanding the Scripture carefully, as Gideon's story includes much background that you need to mention.

LEADING THE CLASS

(1) Gather to Learn

❖ Welcome the class members and introduce any guests.

❖ Pray that those who have come today will seek God in all situations.

❖ Read this information about the Branch Davidians: **Most Americans are familiar with the horrific events in Waco, Texas at the compound of the Branch Davidians, "Ranch Apocalypse," in 1993. This group was rooted in a faction that broke away from the Seventh Day Adventist Church (SDA) in 1942 under the leadership of Victor Houteff. The group shared many beliefs with most Christians, though added some additional tenets. It also followed many practices of the SDA and looked forward to the imminent return of Christ. Leadership changed hands several times. Although many group members left after the prophesied end of time did not occur on April 22, 1959, the group continued. Ultimately Vernon Howell, later known as David Koresh, assumed leadership, and was at the helm on that fateful day when what seemed to be Armageddon occurred.**

❖ Ask: **Why do you think a group of 130 people from different racial, ethnic, and national backgrounds would follow a leader such as Koresh?**

❖ Read aloud today's focus statement: **When leadership of a community is in transition, the people may abandon wise practices. To whom should the people look for wise leadership? The people should follow leaders who follow God.**

(2) Investigate Gideon's Attempts and Mistakes in Following God

❖ Read or retell background information concerning Judges 6 from Understanding the Scripture. Be sure to emphasize that the people had fallen back to evil ways and again needed to be rescued.

❖ Select three volunteers to read Judges 7:2-4, 13-15 and 8:22-25. You may choose to fill in additional background, unless most of the students read the background Scripture and prepare at home.

❖ Focus on God as the ruler by taking these steps:

(1) Talk about how a smaller contingent of troops would demonstrate that God is the leader. Look at Judges 7:2-7 to see how God commanded Gideon to pare the original 32,000 volunteers down to the 300 God actually needed.

(2) Look at the dream in Judges 7:13-15. Consider how this dream would have been a sign and confidence-builder for Gideon. Explain, as *The New Interpreter's Study Bible* notes, that the "cake of barley bread" symbolized settled farmers, whereas the tent would have been associated with the nomadic Midianites. Remind the class that whatever they currently believe about dreams, in Gideon's day this dream would have been viewed as a means of divine communication. (You may wish to read "Blessed Assurance" from Interpreting the Scriptures in conjunction with these verses.)

(3) Examine Judges 8:22-25, in which the people call on Gideon, who has defeated Midianites, to establish a hereditary monarchy. Note Gideon's response. (You may wish to read "God Rules!" from Interpreting the Scripture.)

(3) Contemplate Problems that May Arise When the Learners Fail to Follow God's Rule

❖ Invite the adults to consider how ridiculous, from our perspective, it would be to turn away 22,000 volunteers (Judges 7:3) and then dismiss all but 300 of the 10,000 who remained, based on how they drank water from a spring (7:1, 4-7).

❖ Discuss these questions:

(1) **What does this story tell you about the way God leads?**

(2) **What do you think would happen in the contemporary church if church leaders turned away so many volunteers, based on an understanding that this was God's will? How would those who were turned away respond? How would those who were left respond?**

(3) **What kinds of problems arise for the church as a corporate body and for us as individuals when we fail to acknowledge that God is in charge and then act as if we truly believe that?** List ideas on newsprint.

❖ Form small groups. Invite each group to think of one problem facing the church at large and discuss how they think the problem is being made worse by people who refuse to listen to God. Ask the groups to consider how they believe God would want to solve this problem. Provide time, if possible, for the groups to report to the class.

(4) Examine Whose Rule the Learners Are Following and Adjust in Order to Follow God

❖ Distribute paper and pencils. Read the following statements, pausing after each one so that the students may write their ideas.

- **I believe the two or three most important commandments God gives are . . .** (pause)
- **I honestly believe that I follow . . .** (words to indicate which commandments). (pause)
- **Here's an example of when I (or our congregation) fell on hard times because we refused to follow God's rule . . .** (pause)
- **I plan to make the following adjustments to follow God more faithfully . . .** (pause)

❖ End this activity by inviting volunteers to share with the group any new insights they gleaned.

(5) Continue the Journey

❖ Pray that today's participants will recognize that God is still in charge and adjust their activities accordingly.

❖ Read aloud this preparation for next week's lesson. You may also want to post it on newsprint for the students to copy.

- ■ **Title: Return to Obedience**
- ■ **Background Scripture: Judges 10:6-11:33; 21:25**
- ■ **Lesson Scripture: Judges 10:10-18**
- ■ **Focus of the Lesson: When the community standards of behavior are low, the community will suffer. What must the community do to improve conditions of living? The people must turn to God, realize their misdeeds, and repent in order to have any hope of rescue.**

❖ Challenge the students to complete one or more of these activities for further spiritual growth related to this week's session. Post this information on newsprint for the students to copy.

(1) **Record your dreams for several nights. Do you see evidence that God is speaking to you through your dreams? If so, how will you respond?**

(2) **Rethink the number of people who may be needed for a particular church project. Gideon's story shows that God can give the victory to a well-chosen group of brave souls who meet God's criteria for service.**

(3) **Be aware of news about churches that have experienced difficulties because their leader(s) did not follow God's will. Pray that God will raise up leaders who have the wisdom to let God be in charge.**

❖ Sing or read aloud "Lead On, O King Eternal."

❖ Conclude today's session by leading the class in this benediction: **May you go forth now in peace, surrounded by the love of God and by the love of this community of faith. Amen.**

UNIT 2: LISTENING FOR GOD IN CHANGING TIMES
RETURN TO OBEDIENCE

PREVIEWING THE LESSON

Lesson Scripture: Judges 10:10-18
Background Scripture: Judges 10:6–11:33; 21:25
Key Verse: Judges 10:16

Focus of the Lesson:
When the community standards of behavior are low, the community will suffer. What must the community do to improve conditions of living? The people must turn to God, realize their misdeeds, and repent in order to have any hope of rescue.

Goals for the Learners:
(1) to discover God's abandonment of the Israelites when they turned to other gods.
(2) to appreciate that sometimes God allows us to suffer the consequence of our choices.
(3) to repent of their bad choices and follow the true God.

Pronunciation Guide:
Amalakite (uh mal' uh kite)
Ammonite (am' uh nite)
Amorite (am' uh rite)
Chemosh (key' mahsh)
Gilead (gil' ee uhd)

Jephthah (jef' thuh)
Maonite (may' uh nite)
Mizpah (miz' puh)
Sidonian (si doh' nee uhn)

Supplies:
Bibles, newsprint and marker, paper and pencils, hymnals

READING THE SCRIPTURE

NRSV

Judges 10:10-18

[10]So the Israelites cried to the LORD, saying, "We have sinned against you, because we have abandoned our God and have worshiped the Baals." [11]And the LORD said to the Israelites, "Did I not deliver you from the

NIV

Judges 10:10-18

[10]Then the Israelites cried out to the LORD, "We have sinned against you, forsaking our God and serving the Baals." [11]The LORD replied, "When the Egyptians, the Amorites, the Ammonites, the

Egyptians and from the Amorites, from the Ammonites and from the Philistines? ¹²The Sidonians also, and the Amalekites, and the Maonites, oppressed you; and you cried to me, and I delivered you out of their hand. ¹³Yet you have abandoned me and worshiped other gods; therefore I will deliver you no more. ¹⁴Go and cry to the gods whom you have chosen; let them deliver you in the time of your distress." ¹⁵And the Israelites said to the LORD, "We have sinned; do to us whatever seems good to you; but deliver us this day!" ¹⁶So they put away the foreign gods from among them and worshiped the LORD; and he could no longer bear to see Israel suffer.

¹⁷Then the Ammonites were called to arms, and they encamped in Gilead; and the Israelites came together, and they encamped at Mizpah. ¹⁸The commanders of the people of Gilead said to one another, "Who will begin the fight against the Ammonites? He shall be head over all the inhabitants of Gilead."

Philistines, ¹²the Sidonians, the Amalekites and the Maonites oppressed you and you cried to me for help, did I not save you from their hands? ¹³But you have forsaken me and served other gods, so I will no longer save you. ¹⁴Go and cry out to the gods you have chosen. Let them save you when you are in trouble!"

¹⁵But the Israelites said to the LORD, "We have sinned. Do with us whatever you think best, but please rescue us now." ¹⁶Then they got rid of the foreign gods among them and served the LORD. And he could bear Israel's misery no longer.

¹⁷When the Ammonites were called to arms and camped in Gilead, the Israelites assembled and camped at Mizpah. ¹⁸The leaders of the people of Gilead said to each other, "Whoever will launch the attack against the Ammonites will be the head of all those living in Gilead."

UNDERSTANDING THE SCRIPTURE

Judges 21:25. Israel was founded in the covenant relationship that God established with the Israelites at Mount Sinai. Having delivered Israel from bondage in Egypt, God spoke: "If you obey my voice and keep my covenant, you shall be my treasured possession out of all the peoples. Indeed, the whole earth is mine, but you shall be for me a priestly kingdom and a holy nation" (Exodus 19:5-6). The "voice" and the "covenant" were embodied in the Law (Exodus 20).

When, as Judges 21:25 reports, "all the people did what was right in their own eyes," what is right became the subjective judgment of each individual. Every person claimed the right to be an absolute autocrat—to follow whatever desire, whim, or course he or she pleased. Thus, there really

was "no king in Israel," for no earthy king had yet been crowned and the Heavenly King had been dethroned. When God reigns as King, only one definition of "right" counts—God's! By forsaking the voice, the covenant, and the law, Israel forsook God as King. By forsaking God as King, Israel also forsook the guiding voice, the covenantal relationship, and the moral law.

Judges 10:10-18. Israel sinned again, doing evil in God's sight and worshiping foreign gods (Judges 10:6). For 18 years the Israelite tribes beyond the Jordan in the land of the Amorites were severely oppressed (10:8). The area especially affected was called "Gilead," the hilly region near the Jabbok River that was named after the grandson of Manasseh.

Beginning with the Egyptians, verses 11-12 list seven nations from whom the Lord already had delivered the Israelites. The Amorites, Philistines, and Sidonians were inhabitants of Canaan prior to Israel's conquest. The Amalekites and Ammonites ("sons of Ammon"), descendents of Esau and Lot respectively, were distant relatives who had settled in the desert regions south and east of Canaan. The Maonites are only mentioned in this passage and could be the inhabitants of a city in Judah named after Maon, a descendent of Caleb (1 Chronicles 2:45).

Now that the Israelites had forsaken God again and were serving other gods, the Lord was fed up with them. "I will deliver you no more," God declared (Judges 10:13). If the people were so attracted to the foreign gods, let those gods deliver them.

The Israelites' recognition of their sin is decidedly absent from both Joshua and Judges. Of the 239 times the primary Hebrew word for "sin" occurs in the Old Testament, it is found only three times in Joshua—once in God's accusation against Israel (Joshua 7:11), once in Achan's confession (7:20), and once in Joshua's final warning to Israel (24:19). Judges 10:10, 15 are the first two of three occurrences in Judges and the only ones that involve confession. The cycle of sin and deliverance finally had reached a point where confession played a part. Though the primary focus still was on "deliver us this day" (10:15), the Israelites demonstrated fruits of their repentance by putting away the foreign gods and serving the Lord. God's compassion was stirred once again, and the people looked expectantly for the next deliverer.

Judges 11:1-11. The deliverer who emerged was an unlikely candidate. Jephthah was a son of Gilead by a prostitute. Gilead's legitimate sons drove Jephthah away from home so that he would receive no inheritance from their father. He settled in the land of Tob, on the northern border between Gilead and Syria near the headwaters of the Yarmuk River. He gathered a band of outlaws around him and developed the reputation of a mighty warrior.

Jephthah's selection as deliverer was made by the elders of Gilead (ironically the very people who had driven him away) and not by God. First they asked him to be the commander of their army. When Jephthah rebuffed their appeal, they were so desperate that they offered to make Jephthah the "head" over them and all the inhabitants of Gilead. They swore before God that if Jephthah could deliver them, he would become their leader. Jephthah agreed and the deal was sealed before the Lord at Mizpah, the name given by Jacob to the pillar of stone that had been erected as a "witness" to the covenant between Jacob and Laban (Genesis 31:43-54). It now witnessed the covenant between Jephthah and the leaders of Gilead.

Judges 11:12-28. Before engaging in outright battle, Jephthah sent messengers to the king of the Ammonites to seek reasons for his war against Gilead. The king responded that he wanted the land restored to him that had been seized by the Israelites during their conquest. Jephthah then recounted for him the history of the conquest, noting that Israel had sought permission to pass through the lands of the Edomites and the Moabites and had skirted their territories when permission was withheld. When Israel sought similar permission from Sihon, the king of the Amorites, Sihon chose to attack Israel. Jephthah credited the Lord with the subsequent victory over the Amorites and said that Israel's claim to the land grew out of the victory that Israel's God had won over Chemosh, the god of the Amorites.

Jephthah concluded that the Ammonites should be content with what Chemosh had provided for them, and Israel should possess what the Lord had provided for them. For the Ammonites to claim now what they had not claimed for 300 years was an indication that they were sinning against Israel in making war. As the one who had won the victory, the Lord should judge who should possess the land.

Judges 11:29-33. The Ammonites rejected Jephthah's argument, and war ensued. Only at this point did Gilead's choice of Jephthah find confirmation from the Lord. God's spirit came upon Jephthah, and the inspired leader passed through Gilead, Manasseh, and Mizpah gathering support for the battle against the Ammonites.

Jephthah made an unfortunate pledge to God. If God would give him victory, he would offer up to God as a burnt offering whatever came out of the doors of his house when he returned home in victory. The Hebrew of 11:31 does not specify that this would be a human sacrifice, although such sacrifices were practiced by some (Leviticus 20:2; Deuteronomy 12:29-31). As Judges 11:34-40 reports, Jephthah's daughter, his only child, was the one who was sacrificed to fulfill this vow.

Jephthah led his army into a decisive defeat of the Ammonites and subdued them. He served as a judge for a mere six years (Judges 12:7).

INTERPRETING THE SCRIPTURE

Abandoning God

The announcement, "The King is in the house," often preceded an appearance by Elvis Presley. The announcement stirred a sense of anticipation for the pending performance. When Elvis died, however, many of his fans felt abandoned and forsaken. "The King" had left the stage, the building, and their lives.

Many times we feel that same sense of abandonment in our relationship with God. Life throws us lots of curve balls, and we seem always to be striking out. Hard times come. Sickness, death of a loved one, loss of job, divorce, or some other calamity makes us feel that God has left the house and has abandoned us.

If you look up the word "abandoned" in the dictionary, you will find contrasting definitions. One defines "abandoned" as given up, forsaken, and deserted. That's how we often feel. Another definition is "shamefully wicked, immoral." Oops! Too often that is the real problem. Israel frequently felt abandoned in the time of the judges, but God would say that the feeling was mutual. In reality the Israelites were the ones who had abandoned God. They had ceased to worship the Lord and instead adopted the base standards of the pagan society around them. They valued the things they could see, feel, handle, and manipulate. They nurtured the secular passions and vices of their neighbors. "Shamefully wicked and immoral" pretty well sums up their abandonment.

Every problem we face as individuals is not a result of our abandoning God. Even the righteous suffer. Corporately, however, many of the problems we face in our society can be traced back to our abandoning God. What we don't practice personally, we tolerate in others and call it "pluralism." God is shuttled aside in the drive for beauty, power, money, influence, sex, entertainment, escape, and untroubled sleep. We have ceased to merely fall short of the mark (the standard definition of "sin"). We have picked a whole new target that is focused on and centered in the self. We have forgotten that the first commandment is to love God with heart, soul, mind, and strength. By loving "other gods," we have abandoned God.

Repentance and Confession

In our media-driven world, hardly a day goes by that some scandalous word or action by a public figure is not disclosed. We have become accustomed to their "public apologies," which usually come across as, "I'm sorry if my words or actions have caused discomfort for some people." Subtly they shift the blame to those whose sensibilities were offended. Little blame or shame is expressed by them.

The Bible uses a number of words that reflect the idea of repentance. The words connote a range of meanings from feelings of regret or remorse to changing one's mind to turning away from sin and back to God. While repentance certainly involves each aspect of those meanings, too much of the repentance we see, feel, and express falls short of being a transforming experience.

Feelings of regret and remorse can be genuine; but if the offending behavior doesn't change, the remorseful feelings seem to go away rather quickly. Repentance becomes a temporary purging of bad feelings. The regret is quick, brief, and lacks consequence.

Changing one's mind often ends there—in the mind. This kind of repentance involves significant peril. We believe that because we think differently about something and do not repeat the mistake, our repentance must be sincere. Here the purging is of offending behavior, but the result can be a vacuum. Not breaking a law is not the same as intentionally living or abiding by the law.

Sin is more than feelings and actions, and repentance is more than regret and confessing faults. Sin is relational. It is turning away from a loving, beneficent God. It is the creature rejecting the Creator, the beloved rejecting the Lover, the chosen rejecting the Chooser, the saved rejecting the Savior. Repentance is turning away from that rejection and back toward God. It is restoring faith, relationship, commitment, and devotion. It renews worship, fosters spiritual disciplines, revives relationships, and reinvigorates service.

Repentance is not a once-in-a-lifetime experience. Israel's example demonstrates that God's people too easily slipped back into the old ways, the old sins. Turning toward God must be a conscious effort, a persistent practice, and a daily experience if we are to maintain a vital relationship with God.

The Right Orientation

The Hebrew word translated "right" (Judges 21:25) literally mean "to be straight or even." When put into action it means "to go straight," but going straight always depends on the initial orientation. When the Scriptures speak of the "upright" or the "righteous," they generally are speaking of those who are going straight according to an orientation established by God in the law.

I remember playing in a church league basketball game during high school in which I became disoriented after just entering the game. I grabbed a loose ball, dribbled all the way to the other end of the court, and scored a basket for the other team. In consequence that may not compare with "Wrong Way" Riegels, who gained his nickname from the 1929 Rose Bowl. He picked up a Georgia Tech fumble and ran about 70 yards to his team's one-yard line before being stopped by a California teammate. Going straight or being a straight-shooter does not make much difference if you are aiming in the wrong direction.

The Epistle of James is well-known for its practical expression of what faith involves. James wrote, "Anyone, then, who knows the right thing to do and fails to do it, commits sin" (James 4:17). James recognized that knowledge is important. While ignorance may have a certain innocence about it, it can only be an excuse one time. Knowing "the right thing" implies recognition of right and wrong, something we gain from the guidance of the law and the gospel.

James's word "right" is often translated "good" (see Matthew 5:16; 26:10). Right and wrong involve clear obedience or disobedience; but doing "good" involves value judgments, motives, and outcomes based on moral sensitivities. Doing good reflects love of neighbor and doing unto others as you would have them do unto you. James's point is that failure to act in obedience or to strive for the good is sin. Not doing the right or the good thing is as sinful as doing wrong or evil. God's law guides us in the right; and the life and teachings of Jesus guide us in the good. Together they provide the right orientation for living faithfully.

Even God Can Use a Thug

Jephthah is too much like the kind of politicians that we seem to choose these days. His success had been demonstrated in the school of hard knocks. Rejected and ostracized by the "good" folk, he turned lemons into lemonade. He gathered a crafty group of cohorts, went to a district where he could operate with little oversight, and built his reputation as a hard-nosed, successful, get-it-done-by-any-means kind of guy.

When the situation became critical, the leaders back home wanted someone with the strength, courage, and mettle to deal with desperate times. Jephthah suddenly was their kind of guy.

God did not get hold of Jephthah until late in the process; but when the spirit of the Lord came upon him, Jephthah proved to be more than a thug. He was God's kind of guy—a deliverer. Somehow I feel like Jephthah would have fit right in with the tough fishermen, despised tax collectors, political radicals, prostitutes, and other hoi polloi that made up Jesus' followers.

We should never underestimate what God can do when the Spirit gets hold of someone like you and me.

SHARING THE SCRIPTURE

Preparing Our Hearts

Explore this week's devotional reading, found in 2 Corinthians 7:5-11. Here Paul writes to the church at Corinth that he is pleased by their repentance, which he says was brought about by a "godly grief." Paul further writes that their repentance leads to salvation. Are you experiencing any "godly grief" that is leading you toward repentance? If so, offer your repentance to God. What changes do you experience as a result of this repentance?

Pray that you and the adult learners will obey God and return to God whenever you stray.

Preparing Our Minds

Study the background Scripture from Judges 10:6–11:33 and 21:25 and the lesson Scripture from Judges 10:10-18. Consider what a community must do to improve when it is faced with low standards of behavior.

Write on newsprint:
❑ information for next week's lesson, found under "Continue the Journey."
❑ activities for further spiritual growth in "Continue the Journey."

LEADING THE CLASS

(1) Gather to Learn

❖ Welcome the class members and introduce any guests.

❖ Pray that all who have come today will recognize the importance of listening for and worshiping God.

❖ Read the following from a November 9, 2009, *Business Week* online article: **Alfredo Flores grew up in the Segundo Barrio in El Paso, Texas. Raised by a mother who was** addicted to heroin, Alfredo himself abused alcohol and marijuana and participated in the gang activities of his community. He spent a year on the streets. Now at age 32, the proprietor of his own business has been married for twelve years. Alfredo wants his sons to have a different role model. At age 24 he turned to God. His pastor, Paul Stephens reports: "Because of the powerful conversion in [Alfredo's] life and the radical change that took place, he really has become a new man in Christ."

❖ Discuss these questions:

(1) How did the community standards where Alfredo grew up influence him?

(2) What impact did Alfredo's conversion to Christ have on his life?

(3) What impact might this "new man in Christ" have on his community?

❖ Read aloud today's focus statement: **When the community standards of behavior are low, the community will suffer. What must the community do to improve conditions of living? The people must turn to God, realize their misdeeds, and repent in order to have any hope of rescue.**

(2) Discover God's Abandonment of the Israelites When They Turned to Other Gods

❖ Set the stage by reading the first two paragraphs under Judges 10:10-18 in Understanding the Scripture.

❖ Choose a volunteer to read Judges 10:10-18.

❖ Return to Understanding the Scripture to read the last two paragraphs under Judges 10:10-18.

❖ Ask these questions:

(1) What does this passage tell you about God's nature and how God relates to humanity?

(2) In what ways, if any, do you perceive that the church has abandoned God?

(3) Note that Judges 10:6 lists gods the Israel turned to and then later "put away" so as to return to the Lord. What gods does the current church need to "put away" so as to repent and return to the Lord?

(4) Look at Judges 10:15-16. What do these verses tell you about God's intentions for Israel—and the church?

(3) Appreciate that Sometimes God Allows Us to Suffer the Consequence of Our Choices

❖ Brainstorm with the class some choices that may have a significant negative impact on peoples' lives. Here are some examples: *being unfaithful to one's spouse; eating the wrong kinds of foods; using tobacco, alcohol, street drugs, or other addictive substances; committing an act that you know to be morally or ethically wrong.*

❖ Review the list. Encourage the students to give examples of the negative impact that such behaviors have not only on the individual who chooses them but also on family, friends, co-workers, and the church.

❖ Point out that sometimes people who make poor choices look to someone to "bail them out." At times, that "someone" is God, who may respond by letting the person suffer the consequences of a poor choice. Think together about what such consequences might be. Here's a brief example: *An unfaithful spouses contracts and passes a sexually transmitted disease to his or her partner. The children of this couple experience psychological problems, especially when used by parents as pawns in a messy divorce.*

❖ End this segment by asking:

(1) What has our discussion suggested to you about the consequences of ungodly behavior on the individual and on the community?

(2) What implications does your conclusion have for how we are to conduct ourselves as followers of Christ?

(4) Repent of Bad Choices and Follow the True God

❖ Read "The Right Orientation" from Interpreting the Scripture.

❖ Distribute paper and pencils. Invite the students to consider "the right orientation" in their own lives by identifying where they have gone astray. Encourage them to think about acts they have committed or attitudes they hold that are not pleasing to God. Suggest that they write a paragraph or so in which they repent of their poor choices and pledge to obediently follow God. As you begin this activity, let the group know that they will not be asked to share what they have written.

(5) Continue the Journey

❖ Pray that all who have come today will adhere to high moral and ethical standards so as to be beacons for God in their community.

❖ Read aloud this preparation for next week's lesson. You may also want to post it on newsprint for the students to copy.

- ◼ **Title: Walk in God's Path**
- ◼ **Background Scripture: Judges 13; 21:25**
- ◼ **Lesson Scripture: Judges 13:1-8, 24-25**
- ◼ **Focus of the Lesson: When poor leadership results in community**

troubles, new leadership must be prepared. How is someone to be prepared for assuming leadership? God instructed Manoah and his wife how to raise their child to become a wise leader.

❖ Challenge the students to complete one or more of these activities for further spiritual growth related to this week's session. Post this information on newsprint for the students to copy.

(1) Scan the local news for instances of community standards that would displease God. What might you as an individual or together with the church be able to do to improve these standards?

(2) Volunteer with a group, such as a Boys or Girls Club, where you could help to raise community standards by being a positive role model.

(3) Consider ways that you may have abandoned God. Repent of your actions and do all that you can to obey God's will for your life.

❖ Sing or read aloud "Just As I Am, Without One Plea."

❖ Conclude today's session by leading the class in this benediction: **May you go forth now in peace, surrounded by the love of God and by the love of this community of faith. Amen.**

UNIT 2: LISTENING FOR GOD IN CHANGING TIMES
WALK IN GOD'S PATH

PREVIEWING THE LESSON

Lesson Scripture: Judges 13:1-8, 24-25
Background Scripture: Judges 13; 21:25
Key Verses: Judges 13:24-25

Focus of the Lesson:
When poor leadership results in community troubles, new leadership must be prepared. How is someone to be prepared for assuming leadership? God instructed Manoah and his wife how to raise their child to become a wise leader.

Goals for the Learners:
(1) to learn how God prepared Manoah and his wife to give birth to Samson and raise him for God's purposes.
(2) to realize that God has a purpose for them.
(3) to identify and support emerging leaders in their church.

Pronunciation Guide:
Danite (dan' ite)
Eshtaol (esh' tay uhl)
Mahaneh-dan (may hun uh dan')
Manoah (muh noh' uh)

nazarite (naz' uh rite)
Timnah (tim' nuh)
Zorah (zor' uh)

Supplies:
Bibles, newsprint and marker, paper and pencils, hymnals

READING THE SCRIPTURE

NRSV
Judges 13:1-8, 24-25

¹The Israelites again did what was evil in the sight of the LORD, and the LORD gave them into the hand of the Philistines forty years.

²There was a certain man of Zorah, of the tribe of the Danites, whose name was

NIV
Judges 13:1-8, 24-25

¹Again the Israelites did evil in the eyes of the LORD, so the LORD delivered them into the hands of the Philistines for forty years.

²A certain man of Zorah, named Manoah, from the clan of the Danites, had a wife who

Manoah. His wife was barren, having borne no children. ³And the angel of the LORD appeared to the woman and said to her, "Although you are barren, having borne no children, you shall conceive and bear a son. ⁴Now be careful not to drink wine or strong drink, or to eat anything unclean, ⁵for you shall conceive and bear a son. No razor is to come on his head, for the boy shall be a nazirite to God from birth. It is he who shall begin to deliver Israel from the hand of the Philistines." ⁶Then the woman came and told her husband, "A man of God came to me, and his appearance was like that of an angel of God, most awe-inspiring; I did not ask him where he came from, and he did not tell me his name; ⁷but he said to me, 'You shall conceive and bear a son. So then drink no wine or strong drink, and eat nothing unclean, for the boy shall be a nazirite to God from birth to the day of his death.'"

⁸Then Manoah entreated the LORD, and said, "O LORD, I pray, let the man of God whom you sent come to us again and teach us what we are to do concerning the boy who will be born."

²⁴The woman bore a son, and named him Samson. The boy grew, and the LORD blessed him. ²⁵The spirit of the LORD began to stir him in Mahaneh-dan, between Zorah and Eshtaol.

was sterile and remained childless. ³The angel of the LORD appeared to her and said, "You are sterile and childless, but you are going to conceive and have a son. ⁴Now see to it that you drink no wine or other fermented drink and that you do not eat anything unclean, ⁵because you will conceive and give birth to a son. No razor may be used on his head, because the boy is to be a Nazirite, set apart to God from birth, and he will begin the deliverance of Israel from the hands of the Philistines."

⁶Then the woman went to her husband and told him, "A man of God came to me. He looked like an angel of God, very awesome. I didn't ask him where he came from, and he didn't tell me his name. ⁷But he said to me, 'You will conceive and give birth to a son. Now then, drink no wine or other fermented drink and do not eat anything unclean, because the boy will be a Nazirite of God from birth until the day of his death.'"

⁸Then Manoah prayed to the LORD: "O Lord, I beg you, let the man of God you sent to us come again to teach us how to bring up the boy who is to be born."

²⁴The woman gave birth to a boy and named him Samson. He grew and the LORD blessed him, ²⁵and the Spirit of the LORD began to stir him while he was in Mahaneh Dan, between Zorah and Eshtaol.

UNDERSTANDING THE SCRIPTURE

Judges 13:1; 21:25. The writer of Judges for the seventh time recounts that "the Israelites did what was evil in the sight of the LORD" (Judges 2:11; 3:7, 12; 4:1; 6:1; 10:6; 13:1). The "sight of the LORD" contrasts with "all the people did what was right in their own eyes" (21:25). The eyes of the people lacked the insight into what truly was right in the spiritual view of the Lord. Their repetitive return to evil resulted in their periodic falling, this time under the hand of the Philistines for forty years.

The Philistines were from a seafaring people who in the Late Bronze Age began attacking coastal regions of the eastern Mediterranean. A strong contingent of them settled along the fertile coast of Palestine, and they fortified five strong cities there. They were primarily warrior overlords who dominated the local Canaanite population but gradually were assimilated into the Canaanite language and culture. They were part of the territory that was not subdued under Joshua (Joshua 13:2-3) and were part of the nations that the Lord left to test Israel (Judges 3:1-3; see 3:31; 10:6-11).

Judges 13:2-5. God again would raise up a judge to deliver Israel, but that outcome required a period of preparation. The preparation began among a family in the tribe of Dan that was so obscure that the name of the wife is unrecorded. The husband, Manoah, lived in a town called Zorah, which itself has a confusing history. Joshua 15:33 lists Zorah and its neighbor Eshtaol as towns in the lowland assigned to the tribe of Judah. Joshua 19:41 lists these towns as part of the territory of the tribe of Dan. Judges 18:2 implies that Danites who lived in Zorah had not yet received their allotment of land.

Like many Old Testament narratives that deal with a birth to a barren woman (Genesis 18:1-15; 25:21; 30:1-2, 22-24; 1 Samuel 1:2), Manoah's wife had borne no children. "A man of God" (Judges 13:6, identified to readers as an "angel," that is a messenger "of the LORD" in 13:3), appeared to the woman and told her that she was going to conceive and give birth to a son. The messenger said that her son was to be consecrated as a nazirite. In accordance with the instructions concerning the nazirite vow (Numbers 6:1-21), the angel instructed her to drink no wine or strong drink, to eat no unclean foods, and to leave her son's hair uncut. While a nazirite vow generally was a temporary consecration to God, Samson's vow began with the abstinence of his mother. The angel revealed that her son would help deliver Israel from the oppression of the Philistines.

Judges 13:6-10. The woman told her husband of the encounter with the man of God. She described his appearance as "very awesome" (13:6 NIV) and "like that of an angel," but she confessed that she had not inquired about his name or origin. In her recounting the experience, she also extended Samson's nazirite vow "from birth to the day of his death" (13:7).

Whether out of skepticism or from a sincere desire for instruction in "what we are to do concerning the boy" (13:8), Manoah prayed that God would send the man of God again. God answered the prayer, and the angel once again appeared to the woman. She ran quickly to her husband and beckoned him to follow her to meet the visitor.

Judges 13:11-18. Manoah questioned the angel, "What is to be the boy's rule of life; what is he to do?" (13:12). The Hebrew word translated "rule" is a word most frequently translated "judgment" referring to the act of a judge deciding a case. In this case, however, Manoah seems to be asking, "What manner of boy will he be?" Similar uses of that meaning are found in Judges 18:7 ("the manner of the Sidonians") and 2 Kings 1:7 ("What sort of man was he?").

Manoah's concern for what he and his wife "are to do concerning the boy" (Judges 13:8) elicits no more information from the angel than what had been previously disclosed to Manoah's wife (13:13-14). Indeed, as previously disclosed by the angel, the focus remained on what the woman was not to eat or drink. The only extension stated relates to not eating "anything that comes from the vine," but that was already explicitly prohibited in Numbers 6:4 for nazirites.

Manoah offered hospitality to the angel, asking him to linger while a meal was prepared. The angel said that he would not eat food prepared for him but suggested that instead a burnt offering be prepared for the Lord. The writer notes that Manoah still did not know that the messenger was an angel of the Lord. When he inquired about the messenger's name, promising to honor him when his words came true (perhaps by naming the child after him), the angel stated that his name was "too wonderful" for a human to understand (13:18). Another occurrence of that Hebrew term is found in Psalm 139:6, "Such knowledge is too wonderful for me; it is so high that I cannot attain it."

Judges 13:19-25. Manoah took a young goat and some grain and offered them upon a rock in sacrifice to the LORD. The NRSV and the NIV interpret the next phrase differently. The NRSV understands the phrase to be an extension of "the LORD," describing God as one who "works wonders." The NIV follows the literal Hebrew ("and working wonders, while Manoah and his wife looked on") a little more closely, beginning a new sentence with "And the LORD did an amazing thing while Manoah and his wife watched." The amazing wonder was that the angel of the Lord went up in the flame as the sacrifice was ignited and smoke ascended toward heaven.

Suddenly the impact of it all—the angel, the message from God, and the acceptance of the sacrifice—struck Manoah and his wife. They prostrated themselves in the fear of having seen God. Manoah feared that God would strike them for viewing the Supreme Holiness. His wife astutely observed that, if God were offended by all that had transpired, God would not have accepted the sacrifice, revealing self and announcing such plans to them.

The woman bore a son, Samson. The Lord was with him and blessed him until the time approached when God began to stir in Samson how the promise to deliver Israel would be fulfilled through him.

INTERPRETING THE SCRIPTURE

Hidden Influences on Leaders

To raise up a judge who would lead the Israelites in throwing off the oppression of the Philistines, God began with a yet-to-be-born child of an undistinguished family from a minor tribe living in an inauspicious place. The prospects here were even less than with Mary and Joseph from the prominent tribe of Judah (Luke 2:4) or Zechariah and Elizabeth from the priestly clans of Abijah and Aaron (1:5). Women thought to be barren who later bore children earned high recognition in the biblical accounts of Sarah, Rachel, Hannah, and Elizabeth; but Manoah's wife, who was Samson's mother, remains nameless.

Behind every person who makes some significant contribution to society you usually will find a host of "nameless" supporters. Mothers, fathers, grandparents, spouses, teachers, coaches, and Sunday school teachers are among those you frequently will hear the achievers thank for their behind-the-scenes influence, direction, and encouragement. Such supporters are able to tap something within their charges that shape their perspectives, skills, and confidence and foster their success.

That shaping usually begins in the immediate family with a focus on parenting. In recent years, however, interest in a child's future has been pushed back into prenatal concerns. Our modern understanding of genetics has made us aware that the genes we receive from our parents establish a number of propensities. We also are gaining understandings about how genes themselves can be altered by environmental factors. The use of legal and illegal drugs, the consumption of alcohol, and the exposure to natural and industrial chemicals have the potential for altering both genes and their influences on human development.

When Manoah's wife adopted the nazirite vow as instructed by the angel of God, she was acting solely in faith. With our knowledge, her vow seems more reasonable and prudent; but all of us are dealing with unseen realities that we can only partially understand. While exercising caution in areas of uncertainty, we should seize aggressively the opportunities we have to influence young lives. Stable homes, affirming relationships, sound direction, and unconditional love do much to launch children on the path of success and leadership. Broken homes, self-focused relationships, autocratic control, and constant criticism do much to undermine opportunities for success.

Train Up a Child

What parent doesn't start out with Manoah's inherent question, "What should I do in rearing this child?" Manoah was searching for the "rule of life" or manner of child that his son would become (Judges 13:12) and what his role might be in helping his son to fulfill God's plan. His objective certainly was in sight when the writer of Judges stated, "The boy grew, and the LORD blessed him" (13:24). Those words certainly resonate with the experience of another child of whom it was said: "The child grew and became strong, filled with wisdom; and the favor of God was upon him" (Luke 2:40).

The wisdom of the Old Testament finds expression in a familiar passage related to parenting: "Train a child in the way he should go, and when he is old he will not turn from it" (Proverbs 22:6 NIV). The key to this instruction is found in the word "train," a word that occurs only five times in the Old Testament and is translated "train" only in this passage. The word provides the root for the word "Hanukkah," the Jewish Feast of Dedication that celebrates the rededication of the Jerusalem Temple in 164 B.C. The idea of dedication is included in all other Old Testament usages of the word. Fundamentally, the training of a child is dedicating the child to God and to God's purposes. It is entrusting the child to God to bring devotion and dedication out of our parenting.

Training is not squeezing a child into a preset mold, demanding strict adherence to external regulations, or repetitiously repeating routines until a child gets it right. Rather, training invokes the heart, appeals to the will, and invites commitment. We do not bring about moral development in the life of another. Rather we work as agents with God for communicating God's truth.

Dedicating a child to a "way" involves some standards of conduct, "in the way he should go." But also notice the "he." The way is not the parents' way, the teacher's way, the pastor's way, or the way I think the child should go; it is the child's way. We must recognize that each child has unique needs, interests, and abilities. We dedicate the child in accordance with that uniqueness, not imposing some fixed expression of social conformity on the child.

Proverbs 22:6 also involves a promise, "When he is old he will not turn from it." The promise comes only as we dedicate and entrust the child to God, nurture the child's unique gifts and abilities, and guide the child in discovering and following the way to which God has called.

We cannot do much about influencing a child's physical growth—the child will grow. Our goal rather is to help the child find the blessing of God. Manoah and his wife saw both of those things accomplished in the life of Samson.

Stirred by the Spirit

Leadership researchers Warren G. Bennis and Robert J. Thomas co-authored a book, *Geeks and Geezers*, subtitled, *How Era, Values, and Defining Moments Shape Leaders*. In addition to listing numerous characteristics shared by leaders, they also found that leaders have had one intense, transformational experience in life.

We can see each of these factors at work in the life of Samson. The era in which he lived was a time when leadership often emerged from unexpected places. The values held by Samson explain both his strengths and his weaknesses, his victories over the Philistines and his vulnerabilities to Philistine seductresses. He also had some defining moments that propelled him on his mission.

Judges 13:25 records that "the spirit of the LORD began to stir" Samson in a place called Mahaneh-dan. That is all we know about this initial experience, but from that point on the spirit of the Lord moves decisively in Samson's life. A few verses later the writer notes that "the Spirit of the LORD came upon him mightily" at the vineyards of Timnah (14:6, *New American Standard Bible,* 1995 Update). The same phrase occurs in 14:19 and 15:14. Each manifestation of the spirit in his life seems to propel Samson to greater feats of strength. From the slaying of

the lion at Timnah, Samson was empowered by the spirit in throwing off the oppression of the Philistines.

Followers of Christ also have defining moments when the Spirit of God moves in their lives. Some moments come early in life, many during the adolescent years, some in early adulthood, and a few even at the final moments of life. Some bring dramatic changes of direction in life. Some provide clear direction for living as a disciple. Some confirm inward stirrings and fan the flame of passionate commitment. In many ways that one intense, transforming experience gives us a sense of possibility and a willingness to take risks as we walk in the steps of Christ.

SHARING THE SCRIPTURE

Preparing Our Hearts

Explore this week's devotional reading, found in Romans 2:1-8. Paul writes about God's judgment of us, while warning us to refrain from judging others. We in our self-righteousness may sometimes be guilty of judging others. Be alert for thoughts and words that indicate you are judging someone else. If you find yourself slipping into this pattern, repent and ask God to forgive you.

Pray that you and the adult learners will be sensitive to how your words and actions lift up others or put them down.

Preparing Our Minds

Study the background Scripture from Judges 13 and 21:25 and the lesson Scripture from Judges 13:1-8, 24-25. Think about how someone prepares to assume leadership.

Write on newsprint:
❑ list shown under "Gather to Learn."

❑ information for next week's lesson, found under "Continue the Journey."
❑ activities for further spiritual growth in "Continue the Journey."

LEADING THE CLASS

(1) Gather to Learn

❖ Welcome the class members and introduce any guests.

❖ Pray that those in attendance today will seek to walk in God's path and follow leaders who will help them on the journey.

❖ Post this list of leadership traits, which you have written on newsprint prior to class:

Gives credit to others
Expects excellence
Makes all decisions
Confronts problems
Avoids work
Delegates whole jobs
Talks a lot
Listens carefully
Uses mistakes to learn

Responds to problems
Orders people around
Motivates others
Expects poor work
Uses mistakes to punish

❖ Work with the class to separate the traits of a good leader (using a +) from those of a poor leader (using a -). Then discuss the kind of impact good and poor leadership has on a group, be it in the workplace, government, a civic organization, or the church.

❖ Read aloud today's focus statement: **When poor leadership results in community troubles, new leadership must be prepared. How is someone to be prepared for assuming leadership? God instructed Manoah and his wife how to raise their child to become a wise leader.**

(2) Learn How God Prepared Manoah and His Wife to Give Birth to Samson and Raise Him for God's Purposes

❖ Read information for Judges 13:1; 21:25 from Understanding the Scripture to put this week's lesson in context.

❖ Select volunteers to read the parts of a narrator, Manoah, his wife, and the angel of the Lord. Give them a few moments to review their parts in Judges 13:1-8. Read verses 24-25 yourself, using the Pronunciation Guide to help you if needed.

❖ Flesh out this story by reading or retelling Judges 3:6-10, 11-18, 19-25 from Understanding the Scripture.

❖ Invite the students to turn to Numbers 6:1-8 (9-21), which gives instructions for how one is to live under a Nazirite vow. Point out that usually someone was a Nazirite for a specified period, though Samson's mother tells her husband that the child is to be a Nazirite from his birth until his death (Judges 13:7).

❖ Discuss these questions:
  (1) **Had you been Manoah or his wife, what would your reaction have been to a messenger from God announcing that you would**
  have a child and being told how you were to prepare for him?
  (2) **How would you have planned to train this child?** (Read or retell "Train Up a Child" from Interpreting the Scripture to add ideas to the discussion.)
  (3) **What would your expectations have been for this child?**

(3) Realize that God Has a Purpose for the Learners

❖ Read the first paragraph of "Stirred by the Spirit" from Interpreting the Scripture. Encourage the students to comment on the observation that "leaders have had one intense, transformational experience in life." Perhaps some of the adults will be able to briefly tell about such a transformational experience in their own lives. Others may recall stories of famous leaders who have had such experiences.

❖ Point out that although today's lesson focuses on the parents of Samson, whose child would grow to be a leader of God's people, God also needs those who are followers. Every person has a purpose in God's household.

❖ Distribute paper and pencils. Challenge the learners to identify at least one purpose that they believe God has for them. Note that few of us are called to throw off the yoke of an oppressor as Samson was, but we all have a purpose in life. These words from Frederick Buechner's book, *Wishful Thinking: A Seeker's ABC*, may be helpful in defining our purpose or, as Buechner has it, our "vocation": **By and large a good rule for finding out is this: The kind of work God usually calls you to is the kind of work (a) that you most need to do and (b) that the world most needs to have done."** Add that this "vocation" is not necessarily how we earn our living.

❖ Invite volunteers to read at least one of their purposes.

❖ Affirm that everyone does have a purpose, a vocation, to which God calls them.

(4) Identify and Support Emerging Leaders in the Church

❖ Read or retell "Hidden Influences on Leaders" from Interpreting the Scripture.

❖ Talk about how your congregation intentionally—and perhaps without realizing it—trains young people and new Christians of any age to be leaders within the church. Do you offer classes? Do you have mentors who support those who are apprenticing? Do you think the church either assumes people know how to be leaders, or just expects them to do "what we've always done"?

❖ Ask: **If we are not intentionally training our leaders, what steps do we, as a congregation, need to take to change?**

❖ Encourage the group to identify children, youth, and adults in the congregation who seem to have gifts for leadership. Write their names on newsprint.

❖ Challenge each class member to make a commitment (a) to pray for at least one person on the list and (b) to do whatever they can to support and mentor this fledgling leader, including letting this person know that the class thinks he or she has leadership potential for the kingdom of God.

(5) Continue the Journey

❖ Pray that all who have come today will develop their own leadership skills, even as they help others prepare to be leaders in the community of faith.

❖ Read aloud this preparation for next week's lesson. You may also want to post it on newsprint for the students to copy.
- ■ **Title: Choosing a Community**
- ■ **Background Scripture: Ruth 1:8-18**
- ■ **Lesson Scripture: Ruth 1:8-18**
- ■ **Focus of the Lesson: Everyone lives in more than one community. How do we choose or identify our communities? Ruth chose to make her community with Naomi as an expression of her faith in the God of Israel.**

❖ Challenge the students to complete one or more of these activities for further spiritual growth related to this week's session. Post this information on newsprint for the students to copy.

   (1) Encourage people who are testing their leadership skills in the church (or elsewhere) to hone their abilities so as to be effective leaders.

   (2) Support parents who have a young family. Do what you can to help them raise their children as God's sons or daughters.

   (3) Pray for those in leadership positions in the church, businesses, and at all levels of government.

❖ Sing or read aloud "Take Time to Be Holy."

❖ Conclude today's session by leading the class in this benediction: **May you go forth now in peace, surrounded by the love of God and by the love of this community of faith. Amen.**

UNIT 3: A CASE STUDY IN COMMUNITY
CHOOSING A COMMUNITY

PREVIEWING THE LESSON

Lesson Scripture: Ruth 1:8-18
Background Scripture: Ruth 1:8-18
Key Verse: Ruth 1:16

Focus of the Lesson:

Everyone lives in more than one community. How do we choose or identify our communities? Ruth chose to make her community with Naomi as an expression of her faith in the God of Israel.

Goals for the Learners:

(1) to examine the story of Ruth, a Moabite who, because of faith, chose to move into Naomi's community.
(2) to name and appreciate the multiple communities they are part of, such as family, friends, town, work, and church.
(3) to make a commitment to a community that will love and nurture them in their faith.

Pronunciation Guide:

Elimelech (i lim' uh lek)   Orpah (or' puh)

Supplies:

Bibles, newsprint and marker, paper and pencils, hymnals

READING THE SCRIPTURE

NRSV
Ruth 1:8-18

⁸But Naomi said to her two daughters-in-law, "Go back each of you to your mother's house. May the LORD deal kindly with you, as you have dealt with the dead and with me. ⁹The LORD grant that you may find security, each of you in the house of your husband." Then she kissed them, and they wept

NIV
Ruth 1:8-18

⁸Then Naomi said to her two daughters-in-law, "Go back, each of you, to your mother's home. May the LORD show kindness to you, as you have shown to your dead and to me. ⁹May the LORD grant that each of you will find rest in the home of another husband."

aloud. [10]They said to her, "No, we will return with you to your people." [11]But Naomi said, "Turn back, my daughters, why will you go with me? Do I still have sons in my womb that they may become your husbands? [12]Turn back, my daughters, go your way, for I am too old to have a husband. Even if I thought there was hope for me, even if I should have a husband tonight and bear sons, [13]would you then wait until they were grown? Would you then refrain from marrying? No, my daughters, it has been far more bitter for me than for you, because the hand of the LORD has turned against me." [14]Then they wept aloud again. Orpah kissed her mother-in-law, but Ruth clung to her.

[15]So she said, "See, your sister-in-law has gone back to her people and to her gods; return after your sister-in-law." [16]But Ruth said,

"Do not press me to leave you
    or to turn back from following you!
Where you go, I will go;
    where you lodge, I will lodge;
your people shall be my people,
    and your God my God.
[17] Where you die, I will die—
    there will I be buried.
May the LORD do thus and so to me,
    and more as well,
if even death parts me from you!"

[18]When Naomi saw that she was determined to go with her, she said no more to her.

Then she kissed them and they wept aloud [10]and said to her, "We will go back with you to your people."

[11]But Naomi said, "Return home, my daughters. Why would you come with me? Am I going to have any more sons, who could become your husbands? [12]Return home, my daughters; I am too old to have another husband. Even if I thought there was still hope for me—even if I had a husband tonight and then gave birth to sons— [13]would you wait until they grew up? Would you remain unmarried for them? No, my daughters. It is more bitter for me than for you, because the LORD's hand has gone out against me!"

[14]At this they wept again. Then Orpah kissed her mother-in-law good-by, but Ruth clung to her.

[15]"Look," said Naomi, "your sister-in-law is going back to her people and her gods. Go back with her."

[16]But Ruth replied, "Don't urge me to leave you or to turn back from you. **Where you go I will go, and where you stay I will stay. Your people will be my people and your God my God.** [17]Where you die I will die, and there I will be buried. May the LORD deal with me, be it ever so severely, if anything but death separates you and me." [18]When Naomi realized that Ruth was determined to go with her, she stopped urging her.

UNDERSTANDING THE SCRIPTURE

Ruth 1:8-9. The story about Ruth and her mother-in-law, Naomi, is set in both historical and immediate contexts. The broad historical context is subtly raised by reference to "Bethlehem in Judah" (Ruth 1:1)— a pointer toward the book's conclusion (4:17-21), where we discover that the book is providing genealogical background about the ancestors of King David.

The immediate setting was a time of famine during "the days when the judges ruled" (1:1). To flee the famine a man named Elimelech (whose name means "my God is King"), his wife, Naomi, and their two sons crossed the Jordan River and resettled in the country of Moab east of the Dead Sea. Elimelech almost immediately departed the scene when he died and left his wife and sons in this foreign land. During the next ten years both of the sons took Moabite wives and then died leaving Naomi and her two daughter-in-laws as childless widows. The deaths may all be consequences of an extended famine.

When Naomi heard that the Lord was blessing the people in Israel with food, she decided to return with her daughters-in-law to her family's hometown in Judah. On the way to Judah, however, Naomi reconsidered the situation with her two daughters-in-law. Rather than having them depend on her and her uncertain future for their security, she deemed that they would have greater security if they returned to their own families. Interestingly, she urged each of them to return to "your mother's house" (1:8). This certainly indicates that, rather than returning them to their fathers as dependents, she hoped they would find new husbands among the Moabites who would provide them with security. By emphasizing that they had dealt kindly with her and with her deceased sons, Naomi assured them that no personal animosity influenced her decision. Giving them a parting kiss, Naomi was joined by her daughters-in-law in shedding tears of sorrow.

Ruth 1:10-13. So sincere was their grief in breaking ties with Naomi, Orpah and Ruth decided that they would stick with Naomi and return with her to her people. Naomi, however, was insistent. What could these two young women hope to gain by accompanying her?

Naomi's own future was in doubt. In her culture, a woman without a male provider (a husband, father, or kinsman) faced enormous hardships. Her father certainly was deceased. Her husband had died. Her immediate kin represented by her sons also were gone. Perhaps she would find refuge in the care of some distant kinsman, but would that kinsman also welcome two additional widows—and ones of foreign origin at that?

In the same vein, Naomi's hope for her daughters-in-law rested in their finding a male provider. She knew that she could not provide other sons by any imaginable means. Probably aware of the animosity against Moabites in her own country, she saw little hope of their finding welcome among her people. Once she died, what would become of them? The only practical solution was for them to return to their families. Like so many people held in the grip of grief, Naomi experienced bitter feelings of abandonment. She thought that the hand of the Lord had certainly turned against her. Her resources and hopes were depleted. "Turn back, my daughters, go your way" (1:12), was her best advice. She would face her grief alone and free them for a better future.

Ruth 1:14-15. Orpah relented and kissed her mother-in-law goodbye. Ruth, however, clung to Naomi. The Hebrew word translated "clung" in the NRSV means to abide or remain with or close to someone. While retaining the idea of physical proximity, it also connotes figuratively such ideas as loyalty, affection, and bonding (see 1 Kings 11:2, "clung"; Deuteronomy 11:22; 30:20, "holding fast"; 2 Samuel 20:2, "followed steadfastly").

Ruth obviously had a special relationship with Naomi. We also can surmise that she had a genuine concern for Naomi's fate if she were left by her daughters-in-law to make it on her own. The prospect of an elderly woman traveling alone and returning to an uncertain situation in Judah surely gave Ruth pause.

Ruth 1:16-18. Verses 16-17 are the most often quoted from the Book of Ruth. Some have questioned their contemporary citation in wedding vows. Ruth's "clinging to" Naomi recalls another use of that term in Genesis 2:24: "Therefore a man leaves his father and his mother and clings to his wife, and they become one flesh." This implies that Ruth saw the bond of marriage as encompassing her husband's family and even extending beyond his death. Her clinging to Naomi represented a full embrace of the new family and community of which she had become a part in her marriage. Her plea and pledge are filled with the kinds of commitments that easily flow out of a marriage covenant.

The first sentence in verse 16 is Ruth's plea. In honor of her elder, she could not persist without Naomi's consent. "Press" or "urge" (NIV) invokes the image of an encounter that involves an entreaty. "Leave" involves ideas of forsaking, abandoning, deserting, or neglecting. "Turn back" also can mean turn away and has some intimations of backsliding. These are strong words that recast Naomi's request. For Ruth, going back to her people would be abandonment and desertion of Naomi and turning away from her marriage covenant. Ruth pled that Naomi not force her to act in such an irresponsible manner.

The remainder of verses 16-17 contains Ruth's pledge. That pledge certainly extends the commitment she made in her marriage beyond the primary husband-wife relationship. Ruth seems to understand that becoming one flesh in marriage (Genesis 2:24) involves the uniting of generations of progenitors. Ruth not only loved Naomi as her mother-in-law but she also felt responsible for fulfilling the obligations of her deceased husband to care for his mother.

The extent of Ruth's commitment to Naomi is spelled out in the pledge to go with her, to live with her, and to embrace her people and her God. Her commitment was a commitment for life, and she called upon the Lord to witness her vow. In the face of such determination, Naomi ceased her protest, probably with some sense of relief and comfort.

INTERPRETING THE SCRIPTURE

The Individual and the Community

Because of our Western heritage, we have a deep sense of ourselves as individuals. In recent generations, the mobility of our society has broken many of the bonds of the extended family and the community. The nuclear family has become the primary context in which most of us live. With the strains of divorce and dysfunction, even those nuclear families have become fragile.

If we read the Book of Ruth from our individualistic perspective, we may misunderstand many of the dynamics that underlie the story. While Ruth certainly acted and made decisions about her life as an individual, she chose between the patriarchal societies of Israel and Moab. When she made that choice, the issues of going, lodging, people, and God would follow. Hers is the story of how an ancient society dealt with fundamental issues like family, bereavement, widowhood, inheritance, marriage, and faith.

While we cannot and would not want to lose our sense of self, we can learn something from the Hebrew mindset about community and the interrelatedness in families, neighborhoods, and faith groups. As today's key verse makes clear, Ruth symbolized her bond with Naomi by sharing in the journey ("where you go"), sharing in daily life ("where you lodge"), sharing in community ("your people shall my people"), and sharing in faith ("your God my God"). When we truly walk together, live together, meet together, and worship together, we will be willing to set aside our individual pettiness for the good of the whole community. When we recognize how our mutual good enhances individual good, we will find bonds of love, strength, support, and oneness in our families, churches, communities, nations, and world.

Ruth recognized that failing to take the initiative in cleaving to Naomi would have been irresponsible, callous, and self-defeating. Her commitment unto death even in the face of Naomi's resistance is a high example of how to build community.

The Individual in the Community

The differing locations of the Book of Ruth in the Hebrew and the Christian Bibles explain some of the varying significance of the book in the two faiths. In the Hebrew Bible, Ruth is located in the third division called the "Writings." It falls between the Song of Songs ("Song of Solomon") and Lamentations. It is part of five books, each of which was read during one of the five annual Jewish festivals. Ruth was read during the Feast of Weeks celebrating the close of the grain harvest. It also was connected with the giving of the law to Moses. Christians are familiar with the Feast of Weeks under another name, "Pentecost." Many interpreters think that Ruth was preserved in the Hebrew Scriptures because it records King David's ancestry.

The location of the Book of Ruth in English Bibles follows the pattern set when the Old Testament was translated into Greek. The Greek Old Testament (called "the Septuagint") arranged the Old Testament in a more historical order. With Ruth's setting in the period of the judges, the Septuagint placed Ruth among the historical books like Joshua, Judges, and Samuel. This location resulted in an important shift in our understanding of the message of Ruth. In the midst of books that focus on the Canaanites, Ammonites, Midianites, Moabites, and Philistines as enemies whom God commanded the Israelites to destroy, Ruth emerges as a remarkable exception. Not only is a Moabitess the central figure in the story but she also adopts the God of Israel as her God, marries a prominent Israelite leader, and becomes the great-grandmother of King David. The significance of this example is on the same level as Peter's breakthrough in sharing the gospel with the Gentile Cornelius in Acts 10.

While we think of conversion as an individual confession of faith and association with a church, Ruth exemplifies a more significant change of direction. It began with her marriage to an Israelite, but the real reorientation came after her husband's death when she transferred to a new way, a new location, a new people, and a new God. Ruth did not just profess faith; she redirected her identity, allegiances, relationships, and faith.

Our churches need to be more than just welcoming places where people can come to us. Jesus taught that we are to go out onto the highways and byways and offer invitations of community and fellowship. Our mission is not merely to people like ourselves; we are sent to the poor, the sick, the broken, the sinful, the hungry, and the disenfranchised. If Ruth had remained solely as a festal book, it would not have offered a vision of what can happen in the midst of warring, suffering, sinful people when God beckons them to become part of a new community of faith.

Gripped by Grief/Lifted by Love

Naomi was a sorrowful woman gripped by grief and overwhelmed by a sense of being abandoned even by her God. She was in a foreign land, had lost her husband, and then, when the prospects were looking up in the marriages of her two sons, they too died leaving a decimated family of three widows. Add to this the economic hardships of a time of famine, and her only glimmer of hope was a rumor that the famine had lifted in Judah.

Robert Frost wrote, "Home is the place where, when you have to go there, They have to take you in." That is not a very happy definition. "Having to go there" (rather than wanting to be among the people you love and who love you) makes it seem as if home is a refuge of last resort.

"Having to take you in" implies a burdensome obligation that they have to fulfill, no matter how much they might wish otherwise.

Because Elimelech and Naomi had left Judah in hard times, their loved ones likely resented their accepting immigrant status in Moab over toughing out the famine with their family at home. Going back empty-handed and impoverished would be humbling and difficult, but Naomi may have felt like home in Bethlehem was a refuge of last resort. At least in Israel concern was expressed for desperate widows with no means of support. In Moab, who would care for a foreigner and her desperate plight?

As the surviving matriarch of her family, Naomi felt some obligation for Orpah and Ruth; but what prospects did she have for supporting them? How would her relatives in Bethlehem react to three additional mouths to feed when the economy was just recovering? Though she loved them desperately, she saw no way that she could help them except by sending them back to their Moabite families. She hoped that the families would welcome them and some neighbors might even consider marrying them

and giving them a better life. As depressed people often do when they can see no hope, Naomi sought to cut off her daughters-in-law so that she could mope back home for help.

The Book of Ruth is the story of how the love of Ruth lifted Naomi out of this slough of despondency. A grieving widow herself, Ruth knew that she was still young and strong. She was willing to work hard. She knew that her old, tired, depressed mother-in-law might not even make it to Bethlehem on her own. She decided to switch roles with Naomi, not removing her from being the honored matriarch, but instead shouldering the obligation to make sure Naomi was protected, cared for, and sustained. With a spirit not unlike the waiting father in the parable of the prodigal son, Ruth took Naomi under her care and led her back home.

All of us need people like Ruth around us, people who will lift us by their love in times of trouble. What might our churches accomplish if we became havens of rest and support for people who are hurting and longing for love?

SHARING THE SCRIPTURE

Preparing Our Hearts

Explore this week's devotional reading, found in Romans 10:5-13. In this passage, in which Paul emphasizes that Jesus came to offer salvation to all people, we read these words in verse 12: "There is no distinction between Jew and Greek." As we will see in today's text from Ruth, people of all backgrounds have been choosing to be part of God's community of faith for millennia. Why did you choose the church you currently attend? What drew you there? What prompts you to invite others to join you there?

Pray that you and the adult learners will choose carefully all communities or groups in which you participate.

Preparing Our Minds

Study the background Scripture and the lesson Scripture, both of which are from Ruth 1:8-18. Consider how people go about choosing or identifying their communities.

Write on newsprint:

❏ information for next week's lesson, found under "Continue the Journey."

❑ activities for further spiritual growth in "Continue the Journey."

LEADING THE CLASS

(1) Gather to Learn

❖ Welcome the class members and introduce any guests.

❖ Pray that all who have come today will be receptive to hearing God's word through the story of Naomi and Ruth.

❖ Post a sheet of newsprint, oriented sideways. Draw a horizontal line across the paper. Add lines above and below, off to an angle, to create a "fishbone" look. Invite the students to call out types of groups or communities to which they belong, such as: *family, church, workplace, civic organization, fraternal organization, sports team, and so on.* Write those groups on the angled lines.

❖ Talk with the class about how each type of group is important in their lives. (Note that all are connected to the center line, which in this case represents the individual class member.) Also point out that most people belong to more than one group.

❖ Read aloud today's focus statement: **Everyone lives in more than one community. How do we choose or identify our communities? Ruth chose to make her community with Naomi as an expression of her faith in the God of Israel.**

(2) Examine the Story of Ruth, a Moabite Who, Because of Faith, Chose to Move Into Naomi's Community

❖ Read or retell Ruth 1:8-9 from Understanding the Scripture to set today's story in its context.

❖ Choose volunteers to play the parts of Naomi, narrator, and Ruth from Ruth 1:1-18. You may wish to read the narrator's portion yourself. Consult the Pronunciation Guide for help.

❖ Choose six volunteers for a panel discussion—two to speak for Naomi, two for Ruth, and two on behalf of Orpah. (Note that these volunteers may be men or women.) Ask each panel member to discuss how "she" felt about the decisions the other two had made.

❖ Examine the relationship between Naomi and her daughters-in-law by discussing these questions:

(1) **What signs do you see that Naomi had a healthy relationship with her daughters-in-law?**

(2) **How does it appear that Naomi relates to these younger women who grew up with a very different belief system than her own?**

(3) **How do these Moabite young women relate to Naomi?**

(4) **Do you believe that our society has lost the depth of care and fidelity to family that Ruth exhibits toward Naomi? Explain your answer.**

❖ Read "Gripped by Grief/Lifted by Love" from Interpreting the Scripture to further consider the predicament of Naomi and her daughters-in-law.

❖ **Option:** If time allows, encourage those who have family members from other religious traditions to talk about the challenges they face and the common ground they found.

(3) Name and Appreciate the Multiple Communities of Which the Learners Are Part

❖ Recall that in the Gather to Learn portion we identified types of groups or communities to which class members belong. Again post this newsprint where it can be seen by all.

❖ Distribute paper and pencils. Encourage the students to make a similar diagram, this time naming specific groups, such as Christ Community Church, or the Rotary Club, or Hoops basketball team, to which they personally belong. Some may be subgroups. For example, off of the "family" line, they may add nuclear family, birth family, extended family. Or, off of the "sports" line, they may list several teams to which they are connected.

❖ Form small groups and suggest that the adults discuss:
- why they belong to certain groups.
- how these groups enhance their lives.
- how their lives might be different if they were not part of a particular group.

❖ Call the class back together. Invite volunteers to talk about any new discoveries they have made about the importance of a particular group or community in their lives.

(4) Make a Commitment to a Community that Will Love and Nurture the Learners in Their Faith

❖ Form small groups and invite the adults to talk about why they chose this particular church or this particular class. Suggest that they answer questions such as:

(1) What drew you into this community of the faithful?

(2) What keeps you coming?

(3) What would you miss if you were not part of this church or class?

❖ Invite the adults to stand, if possible, and form a circle. Go around the circle, allowing time for each person to make a commitment to the group by completing this sentence: **I intend to remain committed to this class because. . . .** Some members may have the same reason, so repetition is certainly acceptable. If there are visitors in the group today, thank them for coming and invite them back. Encourage them to stand in the circle, but they may choose to say "pass."

❖ Conclude by thanking the students for their commitment to this group.

(5) Continue the Journey

❖ Remain in the circle. Pray that today's participants will make a wise commitment to a community that helps them to grow in their faith.

❖ Read aloud this preparation for next week's lesson. You may also want to post it on newsprint for the students to copy.
- ■ **Title: Empowering the Needy**
- ■ **Background Scripture: Ruth 2–3; Leviticus 19:9-10**
- ■ **Lesson Scripture: Ruth 2:8-18**
- ■ **Focus of the Lesson: Many people believe in the concept of sharing, but they often run into obstacles in carrying out their best intentions for helping others. Why is it so hard to be generous with those in need? The Bible illustrates the principle of sharing with the poor through the practice of gleaning.**

❖ Challenge the students to complete one or more of these activities for further spiritual growth related to this week's session. Post this information on newsprint for the students to copy.

(1) Offer to help someone who is grieving. Often a "listening ear," perhaps over lunch, can be healing.

(2) Use a Bible dictionary or other resource to learn more about the plight of widows in the ancient world.

(3) Do something special for an in-law, if you have one. A phone call, visit, or a "just because" gift would be an appropriate way to say "I love you."

❖ Sing or read aloud "Draw Us in the Spirit's Tether."

❖ Conclude today's session by leading the class in this benediction: **May you go forth now in peace, surrounded by the love of God and by the love of this community of faith. Amen.**

UNIT 3: A CASE STUDY IN COMMUNITY
EMPOWERING THE NEEDY

PREVIEWING THE LESSON

Lesson Scripture: Ruth 2:8-18
Background Scripture: Ruth 2–3; Leviticus 19:9-10
Key Verse: Ruth 2:12

Focus of the Lesson:

Many people believe in the concept of sharing, but they often run into obstacles in carrying out their best intentions for helping others. Why is it so hard to be generous with those in need? The Bible illustrates the principle of sharing with the poor through the practice of gleaning.

Goals for the Learners:

(1) to understand the practice of gleaning and how it affects the actions of Boaz.
(3) to explore their feelings about being generous to those in need.
(3) to commit to ministries that empower the poor.

Pronunciation Guide:

Boaz (boh' az)   *levir* (le´ver)
ephah (ee' fuh)

Supplies:

Bibles, newsprint and marker, paper and pencils, hymnals

READING THE SCRIPTURE

NRSV
Ruth 2:8-18

⁸Then Boaz said to Ruth, "Now listen, my daughter, do not go to glean in another field or leave this one, but keep close to my young women. ⁹Keep your eyes on the field that is being reaped, and follow behind them. I have ordered the young men not to bother you. If you get thirsty, go to the vessels and

NIV
Ruth 2:8-18

⁸So Boaz said to Ruth, "My daughter, listen to me. Don't go and glean in another field and don't go away from here. Stay here with my servant girls. ⁹Watch the field where the men are harvesting, and follow along after the girls. I have told the men not to touch you. And whenever you are thirsty,

drink from what the young men have drawn." [10]Then she fell prostrate, with her face to the ground, and said to him, "Why have I found favor in your sight, that you should take notice of me, when I am a foreigner?" [11]But Boaz answered her, "All that you have done for your mother-in-law since the death of your husband has been fully told me, and how you left your father and mother and your native land and came to a people that you did not know before. **[12]May the LORD reward you for your deeds, and may you have a full reward from the LORD, the God of Israel, under whose wings you have come for refuge!"** [13]Then she said, "May I continue to find favor in your sight, my lord, for you have comforted me and spoken kindly to your servant, even though I am not one of your servants."

[14]At mealtime Boaz said to her, "Come here, and eat some of this bread, and dip your morsel in the sour wine." So she sat beside the reapers, and he heaped up for her some parched grain. She ate until she was satisfied, and she had some left over. [15]When she got up to glean, Boaz instructed his young men, "Let her glean even among the standing sheaves, and do not reproach her. [16]You must also pull out some handfuls for her from the bundles, and leave them for her to glean, and do not rebuke her."

[17]So she gleaned in the field until evening. Then she beat out what she had gleaned, and it was about an ephah of barley. [18]She picked it up and came into the town, and her mother-in-law saw how much she had gleaned. Then she took out and gave her what was left over after she herself had been satisfied.

go and get a drink from the water jars the men have filled."

[10]At this, she bowed down with her face to the ground. She exclaimed, "Why have I found such favor in your eyes that you notice me—a foreigner?"

[11]Boaz replied, "I've been told all about what you have done for your mother-in-law since the death of your husband—how you left your father and mother and your homeland and came to live with a people you did not know before. **[12]May the LORD repay you for what you have done. May you be richly rewarded by the LORD, the God of Israel, under whose wings you have come to take refuge."**

[13]"May I continue to find favor in your eyes, my lord," she said. "You have given me comfort and have spoken kindly to your servant—though I do not have the standing of one of your servant girls."

[14]At mealtime Boaz said to her, "Come over here. Have some bread and dip it in the wine vinegar."

When she sat down with the harvesters, he offered her some roasted grain. She ate all she wanted and had some left over. [15]As she got up to glean, Boaz gave orders to his men, "Even if she gathers among the sheaves, don't embarrass her. [16]Rather, pull out some stalks for her from the bundles and leave them for her to pick up, and don't rebuke her."

[17]So Ruth gleaned in the field until evening. Then she threshed the barley she had gathered, and it amounted to about an ephah. [18]She carried it back to town, and her mother-in-law saw how much she had gathered. Ruth also brought out and gave her what she had left over after she had eaten enough.

UNDERSTANDING THE SCRIPTURE

Leviticus 19:9-10. Leaving Moab together, Naomi and Ruth arrived in Bethlehem (whose name meant "house of bread") at a propitious time. The barley harvest was just beginning (Ruth 1:22), and the wheat harvest would soon follow (2:23).

As representatives of the poor and the alien, the impoverished Naomi and Ruth were eligible to benefit from a provision in the law found in Leviticus 19:9-10. This law instructed farmers to leave the edges of their fields ungleaned and to leave behind the kernels that fell to the ground so that the poor and the alien could gather food for themselves. This was a kind of passive charity, not a substitute for giving alms to those unable to work. It required work and diligence that offered the poor a sense of independence and achievement.

This law is from "the Holiness Code," a name given to Leviticus 17–26 because the chapters outline how God's people should reflect God's holiness in the way they live. Frequently the imperative from God is prefaced or followed by "I am the LORD your God" (18:2-6, 30; 19:2-4, 10), a reminder of the origin, the character, and the significance of the law. In this same context we find, "You shall love your neighbor as yourself: I am the Lord" (19:18).

Ruth 2:1-16. Although the Book of Ruth does not reference Leviticus 19:9-10, the practice is assumed. According to verses 6-7, Ruth asked permission from the field boss, and he allowed her to glean behind the reapers without question. He also was impressed by her diligence.

While chapter 2 began by introducing Boaz as a rich kinsman of Naomi, Ruth just happened to be in the part of the field that belonged to Boaz when he arrived on the scene. She may have been gleaning earlier in neighboring fields. Boaz inquired about who she was (2:5), certainly indicating that he also had not engineered a meeting. Once her identity was discovered, however, Boaz realized who she was. He had heard of all that she had done for Naomi and the sacrifice she had made in leaving her family and native country to accompany Naomi back to Bethlehem.

In addition to praying the Lord's blessings upon her, Boaz became an instrument of the Lord in rewarding her for her faith-fulness. He made generous provisions for ensuring that Ruth would be successful in her gleaning. Not only did he openly offer her access to his fields but he also allied her with the young women who assisted in the harvest. He ensured her safety by ordering the young men not to bother her. He offered her the same refreshments provided for the field hands and provided such a bounteous lunch that Ruth had leftovers to take home to Naomi. He instructed the field hands to allow her to glean among the standing sheaves and to leave behind handfuls from their bundles for her to gather.

Ruth 2:17–3:4. Ruth gleaned in the field until evening, but her work was not yet completed. The grain still needed to be threshed to separate the grain from its husks. The output of her day's labor was an ephah of barley, about half of a bushel. By modern standards, this seems a modest amount for the amount of labor involved; but Naomi was greatly impressed not only with the amount Ruth harvested but also with the leftovers from Ruth's lunch. Naomi recognized that some patron had gone beyond the expectations of the law by showing such generosity to Ruth.

When Ruth revealed that her patron was Boaz, Naomi finally identified him to Ruth as one of Naomi's "nearest kin." The Book of Ruth actually used three Hebrew terms to describe Boaz's kinship. In Ruth 2:1 and 3:2 two different nouns derived from the verb "to know" (intimately, compare Genesis 4:1) identify Boaz as close kin ("kinsman"). The word used in Ruth 2:20 (and in seven verses in Ruth 3 and 4) is derived from a verb that means "to redeem, to act as a kinsman, or to do the duty of the next of kin." Leviticus 25:25, 47-49; Number 5:8, 35:12; and passages in the Book of Ruth itself spell out the role of a kinsman to redeem property, receive inheritance, and avenge the death of a relative. Naomi encouraged Ruth to accept Boaz's protection and follow his suggestion to glean in his fields in the company of his young women.

By the time the barley and wheat harvests had ended, Naomi had conceived another idea. Always concerned about Ruth's future security, Naomi decided to appeal to Boaz to act as her kinsman-redeemer. This appeal was not based on viewing Ruth as "property" to be redeemed, but the appeal was to take Ruth as a wife based on an extension of the concept of levirate marriage (Deuteronomy 25:5-10). Perhaps Naomi viewed the protective attitude Boaz had shown toward Ruth as subtle attraction to her.

Naomi's plan was risky and somewhat risqué. She had Ruth bathe, anoint herself, and put on her best clothes. She sent her at the end of the day to the threshing floor where Boaz had been winnowing, anticipating that after working all day, he would fall asleep after eating and drinking. She instructed Ruth to go to him where he slept, uncover his feet, and lie down. Some commentators interpret "feet" as a reference to sex organs, and the Hebrew verb for "lie down" is frequently used to speak of sexual relations. Naomi expected Boaz to respond honorably.

Ruth 3:5-18. Ruth agreed to carry out her mother-in-law's plan and did exactly as she had suggested. When Boaz awoke in the middle of the night with a woman lying with him, Ruth revealed who she was and spoke words that certainly had been rehearsed, "I am Ruth, your servant; spread your cloak over your servant, for you are next-of-kin." She not only asked him to fulfill his role as kinsman-redeemer, but she also asked him to marry her. In essence she asked him to become a *levir*, a brother of her deceased husband, who would raise up descendants on her husband's behalf as required by levirate marriage.

Boaz interpreted Ruth's overtures as honorable. Her pursuit to maintain the name and inheritance of her husband's family was a better expression of loyalty than her initial marriage. Boaz also recognized that she could have sought marriage with one of the young men. By seeking marriage with a kinsman she demonstrated that she was a worthy woman.

One problem remained—that of a closer kinsman—but Boaz sent Ruth back to Naomi with six measures of barley as a sign that he indeed would act honorably. He then went into the city to settle the matter.

INTERPRETING THE SCRIPTURE

Opening Our Eyes

The Old Testament focused frequently on three classes of people who were especially vulnerable: the fatherless, the widows, and the aliens. Each faced personal circumstances and life situations that created hardships in sustaining life. The lack of easy access to basic essentials drained them of strength, opportunity, and hope.

In a society dominated by males, the lack of a husband or father removed the widows and fatherless from the economic, social, and political powers that ensured their well-being. If extended family structures were strong, many were cared for but often at a lesser level than if a husband/father were present. Aliens (as in our day) often worked as laborers and were dependent on host citizens for their employment.

Although our society is quite different, some of the same problems persist. A welfare system that is strained, underfunded, and lacking adequate human resources often lets children fall through the cracks. Broken families weaken our support structures. Immigrant workers often become objects of resentment. Perhaps most significantly, social welfare programs remove the desperate from the sight, awareness, and responsibility of individual citizens as a let-the-government-do-it mentality prevails. Yet, amazingly, even the neediest in our society are wealthy by global standards.

How do we in the church get a handle on helping those who are facing hard times and difficult life situations? We can begin by opening our eyes to the poor. Most of us even with modest means are insulated from the desperate poor around us. Because we do not have contact with them and are not aware of their pressing daily needs, we place little emphasis on ministering to the fatherless, widows, and aliens. We assume that government programs, funded through our taxes, are dealing with these problems in our stead. In many ways we are like the rich man in Jesus' parable about Lazarus, a poor man covered with sores who lay at the rich man's gate and daily longed for the crumbs that fell from the rich man's table (Luke 16:19-31). The poor are near but outside. We pass them by without taking notice. We feast on our plenty and often treat our pets with greater compassion than we do these "invisible" poor. We need the eyes of Jesus who, when he saw the multitudes, was moved with compassion (Matthew 9:36).

Sharing Our Resources

"How much is enough?" has become a frequently asked question in our day. The Internet contains hundreds of websites that address that question. I find the question generally is being asked by two groups: (1) those seeking to amass enough wealth to support themselves until they die, and (2) those concerned with the rapid depletion of natural resources who are seeking to reduce their consumption while maintaining a healthy and happy lifestyle. The first focuses on security; the second, on stewardship.

If Abraham Maslow was right, we can naturally expect all people to desire a basic level of security that meets their physiological needs. Any deficiency in the steady satisfaction of these needs will prevent our focusing on much else. The need for safety and security introduces interaction with others, but the focus tends to be on self and the meeting of our needs even to the neglect of others. When these people ask, "How much is enough?" they are anxious, striving, and self-focused.

Once we move beyond our physiological and safety needs, we can begin to relate to others based on our perceptions of their needs. "How much is enough?" becomes a comparative question where we strive to keep up with the Joneses or we share with those whose needs are greater than our own. When our eyes are opened to the needs of others, we can begin to share generously.

If, by the grace of God, we get past the keeping-up-with-the-Joneses stage, "How much is enough?" can be asked in a different fashion. Giving can become sacrificial, and its focus can be on more than merely giving money. We have resources of time, energy, attention, love, and faith that can be shared with those whose needs are great, deep, and extensive.

Where would you place Boaz in addressing "How much is enough?" Where would you place Ruth or Naomi? Where would you place Jesus? Finally, as a follower of Jesus Christ, where would you place yourself? How much is enough for you?

Empowering the Poor

Almsgiving was one of the pillars of Jewish piety in the biblical world. Though Jesus criticized its ostentatious practice, he stayed firmly in the line of the Old Testament prophets who saw the poor as a special focus of God's concern. One of the things we have not done well in our welfare programs is to distinguish between almsgiving and other means of addressing the needs of the poor. Almsgiving focused on helping those who were unable to meet their own needs.

I serve on the benevolence committee at my church. One of the things I have come to appreciate is the breadth of assistance available to needy people through government-funded programs. While I know these programs often are criticized and sometimes abused, I see people week after week who could not survive if they had to depend upon local resources to help them. As I write these lessons, we are nine-and-a-half months into our budget year, and all of our church's budgeted funds and most of the designated funds have been distributed to people who by and large are desperately needy.

Another thing I have learned is the difference between a handout and a hand-up. You can see the difference in those who come for assistance. Handouts really are alms. Hand-up are investments in the future prospects for those who still have the desire to improve their situations. Ruth's story features a hand-up kind of assistance that our society would do well to apply appropriately. While Ruth was given generous opportunities by Boaz, she maintained her dignity through hard work, dedication, and pride in her ability to do something for herself and Naomi. Naomi probably was too old to glean; but I expect if Ruth had not been with her, Naomi also would have been in the fields gleaning what she could.

When I first visited Russia, I was impressed, not by the adequacy of the assistance given the elderly, but by the dedication of multitudes of babushkas (grandmothers, older women) who, brooms in hand, kept the city streets clean. Everyone should give back to the community whatever they are able to contribute. No one who is able should receive a handout without returning something that benefits the community.

Ruth is an example of the poor being empowered to live with dignity by assuming some responsibility that matches their abilities. We too should look for ways to empower the poor, not to get a bigger handout, but to make a contribution through what strength, ability, and dedication they can muster.

SHARING THE SCRIPTURE

Preparing Our Hearts

Explore this week's devotional reading, found in Romans 10:5-13. We looked at this reading last week, but again encounter it, this time from the perspective of God's generosity to "all who call on him" (10:12). Think about your community. Who needs to experience God's gracious generosity through you? What time, talents, and treasures do you have that you could share with those who need them? Do whatever you can with whatever you have.

Pray that you and the adult learners will be aware of those in need and willing to be the instrument through whom God's generosity flows.

Preparing Our Minds

Study the background Scripture from chapters 2 and 3 of Ruth and Leviticus 19:9-10. The lesson Scripture is from Ruth 2:8-18. Think about why some people, even some believers, find it hard to be generous with those in need.

Write on newsprint:

❑ information for next week's lesson, found under "Continue the Journey."

❑ activities for further spiritual growth in "Continue the Journey."

Option: Locate information on Abraham Maslow's "Hierarchy of Needs." You may want to discuss these needs very briefly in conjunction with "Sharing Our Resources" under Gather to Learn.

LEADING THE CLASS

(1) Gather to Learn

❖ Welcome the class members and introduce any guests.

❖ Pray that those in attendance will hear God's call to them through today's Scripture lesson and respond obediently.

❖ Read all but the final paragraph of "Sharing Our Resources" from Interpreting the Scripture.

❖ **Option:** Add information about Maslow's "Hierarchy of Needs," if you chose to research that information.

❖ Draw a line down the center of a sheet of newsprint. On the left side, write answers to this question: **Why do some folks freely share their resources with those who need help?** On the right side, write answers to this question: **Why do some people find it difficult to be generous with those in need?**

❖ Read aloud today's focus statement: **Many people believe in the concept of sharing, but they often run into obstacles in carrying out their best intentions for helping others. Why is it so hard to be generous with those in need? The Bible illustrates the principle of sharing with the poor through the practice of gleaning.**

(2) Understand the Practice of Gleaning and How It Affects the Actions of Boaz

❖ Set the stage for today's session by reading the information from Understanding the Scripture for Leviticus 19:9-10. This information will help the students become familiar with the concept of gleaning and understand its role within Jewish law.

❖ Retell the events of Ruth 2:1-7 as background to the conversation they will overhear in today's story.

❖ Select three volunteers to read the parts of a narrator, Ruth, and Boaz in Ruth 2:8-18.

❖ Discuss these questions:
  (1) What do you learn about Boaz from this story?
  (2) How do you see Boaz as a man who lives according to God's Word?
  (3) What does this story tell you about Ruth?
  (4) How do you see God at work in this story?

❖ **Option:** Finish the portion of today's background readings by retelling Ruth 2:17–3:4 and 3:5-18 from Understanding the Scripture. Since the Book of Ruth is a story, rather than a series of teachings, this information will help the group to put the story together so as to be ready to study Ruth 4 next week.

(3) Explore the Learners' Feelings About Being Generous to Those in Need

❖ Generate a list of non-profit and church-related groups that work to alleviate the difficulties faced by the poor, particularly hunger, homelessness, and lack of health insurance. Write the group's ideas on newsprint. Here are some examples: *Habitat for Humanity, Feeding the Hungry (formerly America's Second Harvest), Bread for the World, and Heifer International.*

❖ Invite class members who have first-hand experiences with one or more of these organizations to tell stories of how these groups operate, who they help, and how the class member has been involved.

❖ Distribute paper and pencils. Read the following statements aloud and ask the students to rate them 1-4, with 1 being "completely disagree," 2 being "somewhat disagree," 3 being "somewhat agree," and 4 being "completely agree."
  (1) Most people who seek help truly need it.
  (2) I feel that I am acting as Christ calls me to act when I share with those in need.

(3) **When I share, I believe that I am offering to another person part of what God has given me.**

(4) **When I see someone in need, I consider that an opportunity to allow God's love and grace to work through me.**

(5) **I do not expect thanks from anyone I help.**

❖ Talk with the class members about the feelings and attitudes expressed by their ratings. Point out that all that we have and all that we are is a gracious gift from God and so when we share, we are being good stewards of what God has entrusted to us.

(4) Commit to Ministries that Empower the Poor

❖ Read or retell "Empowering the Poor" from Interpreting the Scripture. Note the example of the grandmothers in Russia being cared for in a way that allows them to live with dignity. Invite the students to comment on similar examples in your community.

❖ Ask the class to think about these three groups of people who are often vulnerable but do not always get the assistance they need: veterans, poor children, and people with psychiatric problems. Discuss resources in the community that are available to these groups.

❖ Talk about ways the class could help one or more of these groups. Here are some ideas: *serving as a "foster grandparent" by volunteering at a school; working with a trained pet to do animal-assisted therapy with a psychiatric population; visiting wounded soldiers in a hospital or rehabilitation facility.* You may want to write ideas on newsprint.

❖ Distribute paper and pencils if needed. Invite the students to write one action they will take to help someone who needs to be empowered and recognize how valued they are.

(5) Continue the Journey

❖ Pray that all who have participated in today's session will recognize that some people must depend on the community for assistance and that God calls all of us to care for one another, particularly those who are most vulnerable.

❖ Read aloud this preparation for next week's lesson. You may also want to post it on newsprint for the students to copy.

- ■ **Title: Respecting Community Standards**
- ■ **Background Scripture: Ruth 4**
- ■ **Lesson Scripture: Ruth 4:1-10**
- ■ **Focus of the Lesson: Publicly following the community's standards leads to understanding, acceptance, and trust. How can one best function in society? Boaz conducted his business according to the law and in front of the ruling elders so that he would have the support of the community.**

❖ Challenge the students to complete one or more of these activities for further spiritual growth related to this week's session. Post this information on newsprint for the students to copy.

(1) **Learn more about groups, such as Society of Saint Andrew (www.endhunger.org), that glean to feed hungry people. Provide financial support or labor in the field to support such an organization.**

(2) **Research hunger in your community or state. What is the extent of the problem? Who is involved? What action can you and your congregation take to alleviate this problem?**

(3) **Donate non-perishable food to your church's food pantry or to another organization that provides food for those in need.**

❖ Sing or read aloud "Cuando El Pobre (When the Poor Ones)."

❖ Conclude today's session by leading the class in this benediction: **May you go forth now in peace, surrounded by the love of God and by the love of this community of faith. Amen.**

UNIT 3: A CASE STUDY IN COMMUNITY

RESPECTING COMMUNITY STANDARDS

PREVIEWING THE LESSON

Lesson Scripture: Ruth 4:1-10
Background Scripture: Ruth 4
Key Verse: Ruth 4:5

Focus of the Lesson:
Publicly following the community's standards leads to understanding, acceptance, and trust. How can one best function in society? Boaz conducted his business according to the law and in front of the ruling elders so that he would have the support of the community.

Goals for the Learners:
(1) to recount the story of Boaz's actions before the elders in taking possession of the assets of Elimelech according to community tradition and law.
(2) to value the importance of following ethical community practices in making important transactions that affect the whole community.
(3) to assess what they can do to have a positive effect on their faith community.

Pronunciation Guide:
Chilion (kil' ee uhn)   *levir* (le´ver)
Elimelech(i lim' uh lek)   Mahlon (mah' lon)
Kilion (kil' ee uhn)   Moabite (moh' uh bite)

Supplies:
Bibles, newsprint and marker, paper and pencils, hymnals

READING THE SCRIPTURE

NRSV
Ruth 4:1-10
¹No sooner had Boaz gone up to the gate and sat down there than the next-of-kin, of

NIV
Ruth 4:1-10
¹Meanwhile Boaz went up to the town gate and sat there. When the kinsman-redeemer

whom Boaz had spoken, came passing by. So Boaz said, "Come over, friend; sit down here." And he went over and sat down. [2]Then Boaz took ten men of the elders of the city, and said, "Sit down here"; so they sat down. [3]He then said to the next-of-kin, "Naomi, who has come back from the country of Moab, is selling the parcel of land that belonged to our kinsman Elimelech. [4]So I thought I would tell you of it, and say: Buy it in the presence of those sitting here, and in the presence of the elders of my people. If you will redeem it, redeem it; but if you will not, tell me, so that I may know; for there is no one prior to you to redeem it, and I come after you." So he said, "I will redeem it." [5]Then Boaz said, **"The day you acquire the field from the hand of Naomi, you are also acquiring Ruth the Moabite, the widow of the dead man, to maintain the dead man's name on his inheritance."** [6]At this, the next-of-kin said, "I cannot redeem it for myself without damaging my own inheritance. Take my right of redemption yourself, for I cannot redeem it."

[7]Now this was the custom in former times in Israel concerning redeeming and exchanging: to confirm a transaction, the one took off a sandal and gave it to the other; this was the manner of attesting in Israel. [8]So when the next-of-kin said to Boaz, "Acquire it for yourself," he took off his sandal. [9]Then Boaz said to the elders and all the people, "Today you are witnesses that I have acquired from the hand of Naomi all that belonged to Elimelech and all that belonged to Chilion and Mahlon. [10]I have also acquired Ruth the Moabite, the wife of Mahlon, to be my wife, to maintain the dead man's name on his inheritance, in order that the name of the dead may not be cut off from his kindred and from the gate of his native place; today you are witnesses."

he had mentioned came along, Boaz said, "Come over here, my friend, and sit down." So he went over and sat down.

[2]Boaz took ten of the elders of the town and said, "Sit here," and they did so. [3]Then he said to the kinsman-redeemer, "Naomi, who has come back from Moab, is selling the piece of land that belonged to our brother Elimelech. [4]I thought I should bring the matter to your attention and suggest that you buy it in the presence of these seated here and in the presence of the elders of my people. If you will redeem it, do so. But if you will not, tell me, so I will know. For no one has the right to do it except you, and I am next in line."

"I will redeem it," he said.

[5]Then Boaz said, **"On the day you buy the land from Naomi and from Ruth the Moabitess, you acquire the dead man's widow, in order to maintain the name of the dead with his property."**

[6]At this, the kinsman-redeemer said, "Then I cannot redeem it because I might endanger my own estate. You redeem it yourself. I cannot do it."

[7](Now in earlier times in Israel, for the redemption and transfer of property to become final, one party took off his sandal and gave it to the other. This was the method of legalizing transactions in Israel.)

[8]So the kinsman-redeemer said to Boaz, "Buy it yourself." And he removed his sandal.

[9]Then Boaz announced to the elders and all the people, "Today you are witnesses that I have bought from Naomi all the property of Elimelech, Kilion and Mahlon. [10]I have also acquired Ruth the Moabitess, Mahlon's widow, as my wife, in order to maintain the name of the dead with his property, so that his name will not disappear from among his family or from the town records. Today you are witnesses!"

UNDERSTANDING THE SCRIPTURE

Introduction. Today the transfer of property is a routine matter. In ancient Israel, property was viewed differently. Property had a theological and a legal significance. From the time that God allotted land to each of the tribes and that allotment was distributed to the tribal clans, the land was viewed as an inheritance from God to be claimed, maintained, and protected (Joshua 1:6; 13:6-8; 23:4). Everything possible was done to keep land within the family, even to the point of returning to the original owner every fiftieth year (the Year of Jubilee, Leviticus 25:8-17) land that had been sold to others. In this agricultural society, "sold" land was in essence leased, with the harvests going to the new "owner" until the Year of Jubilee.

Inheritance laws favored the eldest son, but laws and cases established precedents for passing inheritances on to others (Numbers 27:1-11). In the male-oriented society, however, childless widows could not inherit their deceased husband's property. Their only protection came through the practice of levirate marriage (Deuteronomy 25:5-10), which provided for a brother of the husband to father offspring with the widow on behalf of her deceased husband. These offspring would inherit the property in the name of the deceased.

The land of Elimelech passed to his sons at his death; but with the subsequent death of both sons, ownership was unsettled. Since neither Naomi nor Ruth could inherit the property, a kinsman-redeemer was required to keep the inheritance in the family. Naomi's plan (Ruth 3:1-4) surfaced this need for a kinsman-redeemer.

Ruth 4:1-2. Since Boaz ranked behind one other family member as the nearest relative, he had to deal with Ruth's request that he marry her. To act as next-of-kin, he had to meet the community's standards and expectations. The other kinsman had to be offered the opportunity to become kinsman-redeemer first. That offer had to be made openly, and witnesses had to testify to any agreements reached.

The gate of the city was where business was transacted, disputes were settled, and community judgments rendered. When Boaz sat down at the gate, he signaled that something important was on his mind. His invitation to the closest kin to sit with him was an invitation to negotiate. The gathering of ten elders as witnesses and guardians of the community's standards indicated that the matter at hand involved community concerns. Interestingly, later Jewish tradition maintained this same quorum of at least ten adult males for carrying out synagogue worship.

Ruth 4:3-6. Boaz began the deliberations as a representative and spokesperson for Naomi. He told of Naomi's return from Moab and of her desire to sell the land that belonged to her deceased husband, Elimelech. The Hebrew word translated "sell" means to hand over something in exchange for something else. A form of the word in Aramaic means "to marry" (that is, "to buy a wife"). What Naomi hoped to gain in exchange was not specified, but her closest kinsman probably thought she wanted to be cared for in her old age—something he evidently was willing to do.

Boaz pressed the kinsman for a decision, saying that if he would not buy the property as the closest kinsman, Boaz was next in line. Already a wealthy man, Boaz implied that he wanted the property if the closest kinsman turned it down. The kinsman immediately jumped at the opportunity, thinking he would snatch something valuable out from under the nose of Boaz.

Only after the kinsman had committed to buy the property did Boaz reveal that marrying the Moabitess Ruth was part of the deal. The kinsman was not just buying the property; he was becoming a *levir* ("a husband's brother") to raise up children to preserve Elimelech's family and name. The fact that the kinsman had jumped so quickly to seal the deal became an advantage for Boaz. Backing out would be a source of embarrassment that he would try to remedy quickly. The kinsman had let his greed surpass his concern for the family's well-being.

We cannot be certain what specifically concerned the next-of-kin that his own inheritance would be damaged (NRSV) or his estate would be endangered (NIV). The Hebrew word translated "damaged" or "endangered" carries a hint of corruption, perversion, or spoiling. If he were not already married, he may have been concerned that all of his inheritance would be subsumed into Elimelech's lineage rather than his own. If already married, he may have been concerned about his family's reaction to his taking another wife. Taking a Moabitess as a wife might have been viewed as corrupting the family line. Whatever the reason, the next-of-kin immediately reversed his "I will redeem it" (4:4) to "I cannot redeem it" (4:6).

Ruth 4:7-12. Verse 7 explains a practice that evidently had ceased by the time the Book of Ruth was written. Confirming a transaction and attesting to its validity was sealed by removing a sandal and giving it to the other party. Still focused on the property, the next-of-kin took off his sandal and told Boaz to acquire the property himself. Boaz then called the assembled elders and people to serve as witnesses to the next-of-kin's renouncement of his claim. Boaz announced his accepting from Naomi all that belonged to Elimelech, Chilion, and Mahlon; and he further announced his taking Ruth as his wife so that this inheritance would be maintained in the name of Mahlon, Ruth's deceased husband.

All the people at the gate along with the elders witnessed this agreement and pronounced a blessing on Ruth that she might build up the house of Israel and the clan of Perez in the house of Judah.

Ruth 4:13-21. For later readers of this book, the blessing of Ruth was perfectly fulfilled. Boaz took Ruth as his wife. She conceived and bore a son, but the child was welcomed as a son of Naomi. The book concludes with Boaz being praised for acting as the kinsman-redeemer. Ruth is praised for her love of Naomi and birthing the child. But once the name of Obed is mentioned, the writer immediately jumps to his lineage. He was the father of Jesse, who was the father of David, the king of Israel and the pride of Judah.

INTERPRETING THE SCRIPTURE

Living in the Light

Social structures in biblical times were much less complex than ours. The community was valued more, and one's standing in the community was a more significant concern. To maintain the integrity of the community, important decisions, agreements, and judgments were made in public. Records were kept in the "mind" of the community by publicly attesting to agreements before the elders of the community. All disputes could be handled by the community because the negotiations and agreements had been witnessed openly.

Boaz followed the community standards in negotiating the disposition of Naomi's request. He used the forum wisely, showing that the closest kinsman was more interested in gaining property than in protecting the well-being of the family. Boaz embraced both the explicit requirement of the law and its intended objective. Naomi's confidence that Boaz would act with integrity was sustained in the open resolution of her petition.

The Scriptures often contrast living

openly in the light with hiding from public scrutiny by living in darkness. Jesus established the principle, "Nothing is hidden that will not be disclosed, nor is anything secret that will not become known and come to light" (Luke 8:17). Jesus also said, "Nothing is covered up that will not be uncovered, and nothing secret that will not become known. Therefore whatever you have said in the dark will be heard in the light, and what you have whispered behind closed doors will be proclaimed from the housetops" (12:2-3).

Most of the attitudes and actions that cause us trouble could be remedied if we remembered and practiced the wisdom behind Jesus' teachings. The roots of all sorts of misdeeds are sown in the assumption that people will never know what we have said or done in private. Today the media often digs up "dirt" about public and private citizens, and we recognize that hypocrisy is not solely a sin of the religious.

"Sunshine laws" have been implemented to ensure that public affairs are conducted in the light of public scrutiny. Some complain that these laws hinder the negotiation of compromises, but too often compromises merely balance self-interests rather than seek the greatest public good.

If we are to be people of integrity, we must live in the light with authenticity and openness. We may not be able to rid our society of all corruption, but we know that full disclosure will come at a final judgment when all secrets will be revealed.

Viewing Life as a Gift

Of all the stages in life, infancy is most reflective of life as a gift. Infants do not birth themselves, feed themselves, clothe themselves, or house themselves. While they certainly have some innate gifts and capabilities, most of what they learn, do, and say comes by imitating others. Yet, you do not have to be around children long before you hear disputes arising over what is "mine."

Even when something comes as a gift, children assert their claim of personal possession, right, or privilege.

Unfortunately that self-centered view of life intensifies as we age. By adulthood we view most all we have and hold not only as something that is "mine" but also something I earned or deserve. The sense of receiving gifts fades with our identity as self-sufficient and self-made individuals.

The Israelites received their land as a gift of the Creator God, who gave it to them as a perpetual inheritance. While this concept raises many theological questions, we clearly see the implication of this understanding in the laws, in the pronouncements of prophets, and in Hebrew life in the Old Testament. The affirmation that all belongs to God and comes as God's gift underlies our concepts of stewardship and ecology.

Our society is quite self-centered. You probably have seen the bumper sticker, "I am spending my children's inheritance." Those who receive bequests often think, "It's mine by right, and I deserve it!" Sometimes family members are driven apart by disputes over their inheritances.

On one occasion a man asked Jesus to intervene in such a dispute. Jesus refused to be judge or arbitrator. Instead he said, "Be on your guard against all kinds of greed; for one's life does not consist in the abundance of possessions" (Luke 12:15). Then Jesus told a parable about a rich fool who tore down his barns to build bigger ones; but just as he prepared to enjoy his success, he died. Jesus concluded with a warning, "So it is with those who store up treasures for themselves but are not rich toward God" (Luke 12:16-21).

How do we become rich toward God? We see examples in Ruth's commitment to care for Naomi and in Boaz's generosity toward a poor widow of foreign origins. We see it in Ruth's hard work in the fields to support herself and Naomi. We see it when Boaz shows concern for his family's welfare. We also hear it in Jesus' words, "Do not keep striving for what you are to eat and what you are to drink, and do not keep worrying. . . . Your Father knows that you need them. Instead strive for [God's] kingdom, and these things will be given to you as well. . . . Sell your possessions, and give alms. Make purses for yourselves that do not wear out, an unfailing treasure in heaven. . . . For where your treasure is, there your heart will be also" (Luke 12:29-34).

Jesus calls us to be childlike in our trust and mature in our understanding that all that really counts comes to us as a gift from God.

The Legacy of Providence

Although my grandfather had five sons and four grandsons, with three daughters I am the last male descendent of my grandfather to bear the family name. This has led me to reflect on my family's legacy. I have three grandsons and a granddaughter who will carry on the family legacy but not the family name.

This study of Ruth calls us to reflect on legacies and especially on the last five verses of the book—the very verses that likely caused the story of Ruth to be preserved. While generations had passed since the one from whom the tribe of Judah took its name, few are remembered as people of note. David, of course, is the name that first made the headlines and has continued to be referenced in diverse contexts for almost three millennia. But what was the legacy that David received?

We learned a good bit from Naomi, Ruth, and Boaz in these lessons. We've seen their character, their strength, and their faith in good times and bad. We know of Boaz's wealth and also of Ruth's foreign origin. We learned of Naomi's cleverness and of Ruth's devoted love. Their stories give a strong foundation to the successful rise of David. But what of Obed and Jesse, the two generations between Boaz and David?

Searching for information about Obed will disappoint you. He is never mentioned outside a genealogy (Ruth 4:17-22; 1 Chronicles 2:12; Matthew 1:5; Luke 3:32). In fact, others who share his name (like Obed-Edom) have far more prominence in the Old Testament. Jesse rises to prominence in 1 Samuel 16–17, but he is mentioned most frequently in references to David as the "son of Jesse." Saul frequently used that phrase as a way to avoid speaking of David directly (see 1 Samuel 20–22), but other biblical writers used it along with the "root of David" positively, sometimes in messianic contexts.

In retrospect we can see the providence of God at work in the lives of these men and women—great and small—that eventually led to a "Son of David," without whom even the greatest king of Israel would have been relegated to dusty volumes of history. What a legacy!

SHARING THE SCRIPTURE

Preparing Our Hearts

Explore this week's devotional reading, found in Philippians 1:3-11. Here Paul gives thanks for the community at Philippi that has supported him with love and prayer, even as he is imprisoned. The church has cared for Paul just as he has cared for them. How do you offer God's loving care to the community of faith? In what ways have you experienced the love of the church when you needed care? Give thanks for the care shown to you, and do whatever you can to assist others who need care right now.

Pray that you and the adult learners will always be ready to extend a helping hand to others.

Preparing Our Minds

Study the background Scripture from Ruth 4 and the lesson Scripture from Ruth 4:1-10. Consider how one can best function in a society according to community standards.

Write on newsprint:

❑ information for next week's lesson, found under "Continue the Journey."

❑ activities for further spiritual growth in "Continue the Journey."

Prepare a lecture for "Recount the Story of Boaz's Actions Before the Elders in Taking Possession of the Assets of Elimelech According to Community Tradition and Law."

LEADING THE CLASS

(1) Gather to Learn

❖ Welcome the class members and introduce any guests.

❖ Pray that as you study together the students will be alert to God's ways of caring for those in need.

❖ Read these headlines based on actual criminal cases:

■ **DC Metro area sniper John Allen Mohammed executed**

■ **Phillip Garrido accused of kidnapping and raping Jaycee Dugard**

■ **Leonidas Vargas, notorious Columbian drug lord, shot dead in his Madrid hospital bed**

■ **Psychiatrist Nidal Malik Hasan goes on shooting spree at Fort Hood**

■ **Coatsville, Pennsylvania, plagued by arsonist**

❖ Remark that most people are shocked and outraged by such behavior, but a small group of people do engage in such destructive, anti-social behavior. Ask: **Why to you think people who perpetrate heinous crimes are willing to challenge the moral and ethical standards of their communities?**

❖ Read aloud today's focus statement: **Publicly following the community's stan-**

dards leads to understanding, acceptance, and trust. How can one best function in society? Boaz conducted his business according to the law and in front of the ruling elders so that he would have the support of the community.

(2) Recount the Story of Boaz's Actions Before the Elders in Taking Possession of the Assets of Elimelech According to Community Tradition and Law

❖ Present a lecture from Introduction, Ruth 4:1-2, 3-6, and 7-12 from Understanding the Scripture. Your purpose is to help the class better understand property transfers and levirate marriage in ancient Israel.

❖ Select volunteers to read the parts of the narrator, Boaz, and the other kinsman from Ruth 4:1-10.

❖ Use this passage to explore facets of Boaz's personality. Discuss these questions:

(1) **What do you learn about Boaz's skills as a business person?**

(2) **How do you see Boaz's relationship with God coming to the forefront?**

(3) **In what ways is Boaz a responsible family man?**

(4) **How do you see Boaz as a citizen who respects his community's standards?**

❖ Read "Living in the Light" from Interpreting the Scripture. Invite the class to draw any connections they see between Boaz and a respected member of your own community.

(3) Value the Importance of Following Ethical Community Practices in Making Important Transactions that Affect the Whole Community

❖ Invite the students to identify practices that adversely impact the morals and ethics of their community. List them on newsprint. Here are some examples: *a politician who accepts bribes or other illicit gifts;*

businesses that knowingly cheat people; citizens who do not pay their full share of taxes; schemers who buy property, fix it poorly, and then try to resell it quickly at a greatly inflated price; drivers who break traffic laws.

❖ Ask: **What harm do you see in such practices?**

❖ Turn the discussion to a more positive note by asking: **What moral and ethical traits have a positive impact on our community?** Here are some possibilities: *the community shows compassion to the poor and others in need; people are honest in their business dealings; gossip and other weapons of character assassination are not tolerated; adults watch out for other people's children to be sure all are safe; all people, regardless of their ethnic, racial, or religious heritage, are welcomed.*

❖ Ask: **How do such practices build up our community and make it a place where we want to live—and God is pleased to dwell?**

(4) Assess What the Learners Can Do to Have a Positive Effect on Their Faith Community

❖ Distribute paper and pencils. Invite the students to list three steps they can take that will have a positive impact on the church. In turn, it is hoped that these steps will have a positive impact on the community at large. Here are some simple suggestions: *pray for the church that it might be a beacon of God's love to the entire community; participate in a church-sponsored program or event that will show compassion and care for those in the community; provide opportunities for unchurched people to interact with church members.*

❖ Enlist volunteers to read what they have written. See if several people are thinking along the same line and could work together to develop their ideas outside of class.

❖ End by reminding the class that as a result of Boaz doing the right thing, both in the eyes of his community and in the eyes of God, the child of Ruth's that he fathered, Obed, became the grandfather of King David, Israel's greatest king and the ancestor of Jesus.

(5) Continue the Journey

❖ Pray that today's participants will go forth to care for one another while respecting the norms and boundaries of their Christian community.

❖ Read aloud this preparation for next week's lesson. You may also want to post it on newsprint for the students to copy.

■ **Title: Righteousness and Wisdom**
■ **Background Scripture: Proverbs 3:1-35**
■ **Lesson Scripture: Proverbs 3:1-12**
■ **Focus of the Lesson: People want their lives to have purpose and meaning. Is there a way of living that really works toward that end? Proverbs is rooted in a tradition of instruction that encourages godly living.**

❖ Challenge the students to complete one or more of these activities for further spiritual growth related to this week's session. Post this information on newsprint for the students to copy.

(1) **Make or update your own last will as a means of ensuring that your property and possessions will be transferred to those who you want to receive it.**

(2) **Take care of a relative or someone else who needs assistance. Consider running errands, cooking a meal, or providing transportation to an appointment.**

(3) **Serve as a buddy or mentor to someone who is new to your congregation or Sunday school class. Help this person to feel included and at home.**

❖ Sing or read aloud "O God of Every Nation."

❖ Conclude today's session by leading the class in this benediction: **May you go forth now in peace, surrounded by the love of God and by the love of this community of faith. Amen.**